National Geographic Guide to the

National
Parks

of the United States

National Geographic Guide to the

National
Parks
of the United States

Prepared by
The Book Division
National Geographic Society
Washington, D.C.

Published by
The National
Geographic Society

John M. Fahey, Jr.
*President and Chief
Executive Officer*

Gilbert M. Grosvenor
Chairman of the Board

Nina D. Hoffman
Senior Vice President

William R. Gray
*Vice President and
Director, Book Division*

Prepared by
the Book Division

Guidebook Staff

Elizabeth L. Newhouse
*Editor and Director of Travel
Books*

Linda B. Meyerriecks
Illustrations Editor

David M. Seager
Art Director

Carl Mehler
Director of Maps

Melanie Ann Patt-Corner
Research Editor

Thomas B. Allen
Carole Douglis
Writer-Editors

John L. Culliney
Kim Heacox
Catherine Herbert Howell
Gary Krist
Mark Miller
Jeremy Schmidt
Gene S. Stuart
John M. Thompson
Scott Thybony
Writers

Paulette L. Claus
Mary Grady
Mary Jennings
Lise Swinson Sajewski
Anne E. Withers
Editorial Researchers

Mary Grady
Map Editor

Lise Swinson Sajewski
Style

T. Destry Jarvis
Chief Consultant

Staff for 2001 Edition

Keith R. Moore
Project Manager

Kim Kostyal
Text Editor

Cinda Rose
Art Director

Gillian Carol Dean
Designer

Joseph F. Ochlak
Gregory Ugiansky
GeoSystems Global Corp.
XNR Productions
*Map Edit, Research and
Production*

Caroline Hickey
Charles Kogod
Barbara A. Noe
Jane Sunderland
Louisa Caroline Wagley
Contributors

R. Gary Colbert
Production Director

Richard S. Wain
Production Project

Cover: Snake River and Teton Range, Grand Teton NP
Preceding pages: Hikers surveying falling water and granite cliffs, two
of Yosemite's main attractions

Contents

Green River canyon in Canyonlands National Park

The Gift of the Parks

One of the things that distinguishes this guidebook is its conscience—its attention to the welfare of the parks it describes. As you read, you will find the travel information interspersed with news of some threat to a park, or the history of a threat that lost out. National parks have been battle-grounds of the conservation movement, and the battles continue.

But even the battles can offer inspiration and instruction, and both the parks and the ideals by which we manage them evolve continually. Indeed, it has been said that the establishment of a park is only the beginning; that if we do it right, we never stop establishing that park, because we never stop learning about it, and about ourselves.

There was a time when Congress set up national parks to protect a few specific things: the wildlife here, the gey-sers there, the scenery over there. Other parts of the park got less attention, or were even mistreated. Well into the 1930s managers killed predators in some parks to protect the "good" animals. In the early days of Yosemite National Park, woodpeckers were shot if their tapping disturbed the sleep of hotel guests. Yellowstone allowed commercial fishing until well after 1900.

Only as the science of ecology matured, and we began to realize that everything in the park was interrelated, did our view change. Slowly, we realized that what we had was not best measured in acres of meadow and that a park is not a zoo.

Instead, we seek to save the whole thing, the whole creeping, flying, grazing, preying, photosynthe-sizing, eroding, raining, erupting, evolving scene. Call it wildness, or nat-

uralness, or an ecosystem, or whatever you like, it is this entangled collection of processes that we must save.

That means many things, some of which haven't been easy to hear. It means that people like me, who love to fish, have to leave enough trout in the streams to feed the otters, pelicans, bears, and other wild fishermen. It means we don't pick flowers, or collect rocks, removing them from their place in the natural system. It means we stop feeding wildlife, and let the animals find their own way, in balance with their environment.

In short, it means a revolution in the way we appreciate nature. We as a nation have decided that here, in these precious, rare places, we shall give nature a little more room to make its choices. If that means we must be prepared to watch a bear half a mile away through binoculars rather than watch it eating aluminum foil right outside the car window, so be it; everybody knew all along which was best for the bear. If that means we must respect the role naturally caused fire has played in regenerating forests for thousands of years, so be it.

Anyone who reads the papers knows that this doesn't always work smoothly. Nature isn't much for respecting our rules. Bears have a way of reminding us we're not always in charge. And, as Yellowstone showed us in 1988, fires can get a lot bigger than anybody expected. Nobody said this was going to be easy. But the more we try, the more we learn.

And so these great parks, which enchant us with their beauty and restore us with their peace, have yet another gift to give. They are laboratories of ideas, offering profound lessons in the natural way of things, and in what that way can mean to the human soul. The lessons don't always come easily, but they're always worth the trip.

Paul Schullery
Yellowstone National Park

Sightseers at Geyser Hill, Yellowstone

Using the Guide

Each of the 55 scenic parks offers you fun, adventure, and—usually—enthralling splendor. What you experience will depend on where you go and what you do. But exploring an unknown land is best done with a guide, a companion who has tested the trail and learned the lore. Our coverage of each park begins with a portrait of its natural wonders, ecological setting, history, and, often, its struggles against pollution, erosion, development, and other environmental threats. You'll see why a single step off a trail can harm fragile plants, and why visitors are detoured from certain areas that shelter wildlife. The parks are not just for people; they conserve ecosystems that sustain plants and animals. Eleven parks have been designated United Nations World Heritage sites for their outstanding scenic wonders; twenty-two have International Biosphere Reserve

status, signaling the distinctive qualities of their natural environments.

Before starting off on your park exploration, use the *Guide* to preview the parks you may want to visit. You'll notice that each park introduction is followed by the following three how-and-when sections:

How to Get There

You may be able to include more than one park in your trip. The maps at the beginning of each regional section show the connecting highways. Base your itinerary not so much on mileage as on time, remembering that parks do not lie alongside interstates; park roads are usually rugged—and, in summer, crowded.

When to Go

Instead of going to a popular park in midsummer, avoid peak crowds by scheduling the trip for June or late August and timing your arrival early on a weekday. In many parks, fall is glorious, and autumn vistas coincide with a relative scarcity of visitors. Spring brings wildflowers to many parks and with winter comes snow-swept beauty, summoning skiers, snowshoe hikers, and ice skaters. Although parks are generally open year-round, off-season visitor facilities may be limited. Consult this heading in each park chapter.

How to Visit

Don't rush through a park. Give yourself time to savor the beauty. Incredibly, the average time the typical visitor spends in a park is half a day. Often, that blur of time flashes past a windshield. No matter how long you decide to stay, spend at least part of that time in the park, not in your car. Each park's **How to Visit** section recommends a plan for visits of ½, 1, 2, or more days. *Guide* writers devised the plans and trekked every tour, but don't be afraid to explore on your own. And don't neglect the **Excursions** at the end of most park chapters; they take you to other natural areas nearby.

Other features of the *Guide:*

Maps

The park maps and regional maps were prepared as an aid in planning your trip. For more detail on hiking trails and other facilities inside a park, contact the Park Service or the park itself. Always use a road map when traveling.

The maps note specially designated areas within park borders: *Wilderness Areas* are managed to retain their primeval quality. Roads, buildings, and vehicles are not allowed in them. *National Preserves* may allow hunting.

The following abbreviations are used for federal lands:

NP   *National Park*
NRA   *National Recreation Area*
NF   *National Forest*
NM   *National Monument*
NWR   *National Wildlife Refuge*

Information & Activities

This section, which follows each park chapter, offers detailed visitor information. Call, write, or visit the park's website for further details. Brochures are usually available free of charge from the parks. For a small fee you can buy a copy of the National Park System Map and Guide by writing

Hikers, young and old, in Waterton Lakes

Exploring Big Bend's backcountry

to the Consumer Information Center, P.O. Box 100, Pueblo, Colo. 81002-0100, or phoning (719) 948-3334. Visit the Park Service website at: http:// www.nps.gov.

Entrance Fees. In 1996 Congress approved a trial program to allow national parks to increase their fees (or charge fees for the first time) in order to raise funds for improving public land. The entrance fees listed in this book for the most part reflect these increases. In addition to daily or weekly fees, most parks also offer a yearly fee, with unlimited entries.

For $50 you can buy a Golden Eagle Passport, which is good for a year and admits all occupants of a private vehicle to all national parks and other federal sites. People over 62 can obtain a lifetime Golden Age Passport for $10, and disabled people are entitled to a lifetime Golden Access Passport for free, both of which admit all occupants of a private vehicle to all national parks and other federal sites. These documents are available at any Park Service facility that charges entrance fees.

Pets. Generally they're not allowed on trails, in buildings, or in the backcountry. Elsewhere, they must be leashed. Specific rules are noted.

Facilities for Disabled. This section of the *Guide* explains which parts of each park, including visitor centers and trails, are accessible to visitors with disabilities.

Special Advisories. ● Don't take chances. People are killed or badly injured every year in national parks. Most casualties are caused by recklessness or inattention to clearly posted warnings.

● Stay away from wild animals. Don't feed them. Don't try to touch them. Not even raccoons or chipmunks (which can transmit diseases). Try not to surprise a bear and don't let one approach you. If one does, scare it off by yelling, clapping your hands, or banging pots. Store all your food; keep it out of sight in your vehicle, with windows closed and doors locked. Or suspend it at least 15 feet above ground, and 10 feet out from a post or tree trunk.

● Guard your health. If you are not fit, don't overtax your body. Boil water that doesn't come from a park's drinking-water tap. Chemical treatment of water will not kill *Giardia*, a protozoan that causes severe diarrhea and lurks even in crystal clear streams. Heed park warnings about

hypothermia and Lyme disease, which is carried by ticks.

• Expect RV detours. Check road regulations as you enter a park. Along some stretches of many roads you will not be able to maneuver a large vehicle, especially a trailer.

Campgrounds. Most park campgrounds admit people first come, first served, with limits on length of stay and number of persons. National Parks Reservation System (NPRS) handles advance reservations for campgrounds at the following parks: Acadia, Channel Islands, Death Valley, Everglades, Grand Canyon, Great Smoky Mountains, Joshua Tree, Katmai, Mammoth Cave, Mount Rainier, Rocky Mountain, Sequoia & Kings Canyon, Shenandoah, Waterton-

Glacier, Yosemite and Zion. For a single campsite, reserve up to 5 months in advance by calling 800-365-CAMP (365-2267), or visiting the NPRS website at www.reservations.nps.gov. Pay by credit card over the phone or Internet, or by check or money order within 21 days. Or, write to NPRS, 3 Commerce Drive, Cumberland, Maryland 21502.

Hotels, Motels, & Inns. The *Guide* lists accommodations as a service to its readers. The lists are by no means comprehensive, and listing does not imply endorsement by the National Geographic Society. The information can change without notice. Many parks keep full lists of accommodations in their areas, which they will send you on request.

Maps of:
Alaska, pages 392-3
American Samoa, page 217
Hawaii, page 214
Virgin Islands, page 17

Preceding pages: Along the Blue Ridge Parkway

The East

Not until well into the 20th century, long after the idea of preserving the West's grand vistas had taken hold, did park planners turn their attention to the more subtle beauties of eastern scenery. The threats to nature from expanding cities and, after World War I, the surge in automobile travel and highway building boosted the movement to create eastern parks. Between 1919 and 1926, Congress authorized the first three in the crumpled belt of the Appalachian Mountains. Today these parks—Acadia, Great Smoky Mountains,

0 100 200 km
0 100 200 mi

CANADA

St. Lawrence

MAINE

MOOSEHORN NWR

PETIT MANAN NWR

Acadia NP

VT.

Portland

N.H.

RACHEL CARSON NWR

Lake Ontario

NEW YORK

MASS.

Boston

CONN. R.I.

Lake Erie

Ohio

PENNSYLVANIA

New York

NEW JERSEY

Philadelphia

OHIO

MD.

DEL.

ATLANTIC OCEAN

Washington, D.C.

MASON NECK NWR

GEORGE WASHINGTON NF

Shenandoah NP

GEORGE WASHINGTON NF

Charlottesville

WEST VIRGINIA

VIRGINIA

JEFFERSON NF

JEFFERSON NF

Blue Ridge Parkway

N.C.

JEFFERSON NF

This map plots all the U.S. national parks, plus the Excursions sites featured in this book.

and Shenandoah—rank among the most visited in the nation.

Acadia protects the plants and animals that inhabit the mountains, islands, sea, and tide pools along a stretch of wild New England coast. The hardwood forests and flowering meadows of Shenandoah, on land that had been logged, farmed, and grazed for 250 years, are studies in nature's power of recuperation. Great Smoky preserves large stands of virgin forest on 6,000-foot slopes and shelters more than a hundred species of trees.

Since the 1920s, Congress has moved to safeguard other distinctive eastern biomes. Inside Mammoth Cave lies the world's largest known

cave network, with more than 330 miles of mapped passages. Isle Royale on the US-Canada border

Americans' love for the automobile led to the demand for highways to drive and helped spur the creation of national parks in the East. In 1935 the Blue Ridge Parkway was begun as a public works project; it became part of the Park Service the following year. The nation's most traveled federal parkway, the Blue Ridge links Shenandoah's Skyline Drive to Great Smoky Mountains National Park. Together, the drives create a spectacular 574-mile stretch of ridgetop road punctuated by wayside exhibits and trails.

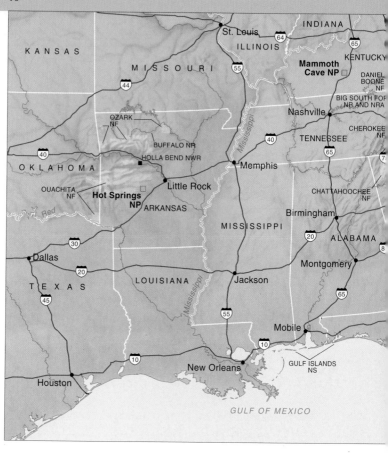

encompasses an entire island ecosystem. In and around its lakes, thick forest, and fjordlike coast live wolves and moose, their prey.

Not far away, scores of lakes and streams lace the forests of Voyageurs National Park, named for the French-Canadian fur traders who for 100 years paddled these waters.

Other kinds of waters—those flowing from hot springs—inspired the creation of diminutive Hot Springs National Park. Most of the 47 hot springs lead into the plumbing of this former resort town's bathhouses.

Underwater wilderness awaits visitors to Florida's Biscayne National Park, home of the northernmost living coral reef in the continental us. West of Biscayne lies Everglades National Park, established in 1947 less to preserve scenery than to safeguard the unique ecosystem created by a slow-moving river, inches deep and 50 miles wide. Itself endangered by

the diversion of water to the towns and agribusinesses of south Florida, Everglades provides habitat for an enormous variety of wildlife.

Offshore, on a 7-mile-long archipelago rich with birds and marine creatures, Dry Tortugas National Park maintains an abandoned 19th-century fort. And far to the southeast, the Virgin Islands National Park protects much of St. John, where hillsides thick with bay, mango, and trumpet trees slope to crescent beaches rimmed by coral reefs.

In the 1960s the National Park Service set a goal to create a park as a "vignette of primitive America" in every major natural community in the country. The newer parks of the East—Virgin Islands, Biscayne, Voyageurs, and Dry Tortugas— expanded the already considerable diversity of the region's parks.

Sunrise on Acadia's pink granite coast

Acadia

Maine

Established February 26, 1919

47,633 acres

Sea and mountain meet at Acadia, where, as one presumably ambidextrous visitor wrote, "you can fish with one hand and sample blueberries from a wind-stunted bush with the other."

Most of Acadia is on Mt. Desert Island, a patchwork of parkland, private property, and seaside villages that seasonally fill with what residents call "the summer people." Other bits of the park are scattered on smaller islands and a peninsula.

Mt. Desert Island once was continental mainland, a mountainous granite ridge on the edge of the ocean. Some 20,000 years ago, towering glacial ice sheets—sometimes a mile thick— flowed over the mountains, rounding their tops, cutting passes, gouging out

lake beds, and widening valleys. As the glaciers melted, the sea rose, flooding valleys and drowning the coast. The pre-glacier ridge was transformed into today's lake-studded, mountainous island, which thrusts from the Atlantic like a lobster's claw.

Samuel de Champlain, who explored the coast in 1604, named the island L'Isle des Monts Déserts, sometimes translated as "the island of barren mountains." From his ship he probably could not see the mountains' forested slopes. The summer people rediscovered Mt. Desert in the mid-19th century, built mansions they called "cottages," anchored their yachts in rock-girt harbors, and cherished the wild. To preserve it, they donated the nucleus land for the park, the first east of the Mississippi. The original name, Lafayette National Park, was changed in 1929.

When to Go

All-year park, but main visitor center is open from about May 1 to November 1. Expect heavy traffic in July and August. Spectacular foliage also attracts crowds around the end of September. Snow and ice close most park roads from December through April, but parts of the park are open for cross-country skiing.

How to Visit

Allow at least a day for **Mt. Desert Island,** with a drive on the 20-mile **Park Loop Road** and the road to the summit of **Cadillac Mountain.** If fog comes, enjoy its gift: a softening of sights and sounds. On a second day, enjoy an uncrowded view of the rocky coast of Maine by visiting the **Schoodic Peninsula.** If you have more time, take your pick of one of the trails or smaller islands.

Dependent on donated land since its inception, the park took what it could get, skirting around private property and growing piece by piece. Acadia's real estate was so patchy that not until 1986 did Congress set its official boundaries.

The fifth smallest national park, Acadia is one of the ten most visited— by almost three million people a year. Heavy traffic can produce a phenomenon unknown to Mt. Desert's first summer people: gridlock. The recently introduced Island Explorer Shuttle Bus has helped alleviate the problem.

How to Get There

From Ellsworth (about 18 miles north), take Maine 3 to Mt. Desert Island, where most of the park is located; the visitor center is about 3 miles north of Bar Harbor. Another section lies southeast of Ellsworth, on the Schoodic Peninsula, a 1-hour drive from Bar Harbor. To get to the park's islands, see **The Islands** p. 23. Airports: Bangor and Bar Harbor.

Mt. Desert Island

60 miles; at least a full day

To get the most from a tour of Mt. Desert Island on the Park Loop Road in summer, get up very early. (On clear days, traffic is heaviest between 10 a.m. and 3 p.m.) The day before, check the time of sunrise in a local newspaper or at the visitor center. About 30 minutes before dawn, take coffee and a blanket and drive from the visitor center to 1,530-foot Cadillac Mountain. The 3½-mile mountain road switchbacks up to a parking area.

Autumn on Cadillac Mountain

Bass Harbor Head lighthouse at dusk

From there walk to the **Summit Trail,** find an east-facing niche in the rocks, and settle in on the highest east coast mountain north of Brazil. Here is one of the places where dawn first touches the continental United States. After enjoying the dawn, hunt for blueberries along the trails radiating from the summit. The blueberry season runs from mid-July through August.

On the way down, stop at one of the eastern overlooks for a view of **Frenchman Bay,** a vast, island-dotted seascape; its name takes note of the area's early French settlers. (Another way to see the bay is on a 2-hour sea cruise; check schedules at the Municipal Pier in Bar Harbor.)

Return to the loop road and turn right. Less than a half mile farther on, bear right again (here the road becomes one-way), and continue south toward the ocean. Pass up **Sand Beach** for now. You may want to return to the beach later for sunbathing or a very brisk swim (the summer water temperature remains between 50° and 55°F).

Not quite a mile farther, a sign marks **Thunder Hole.** Park on the right and walk down the concrete steps to the cleft in the rocks, named for the roars produced when air, trapped and squeezed by incoming surf, explodes out of a cavern. A stop here may disappoint you, for you'll probably hear the thunder only at half tide with a rising sea, or during a storm. Other times, you may hear only gurgles and sloshes.

Continue to the 110-foot **Otter Cliffs.** Park, cross the road, and walk the shore path to **Otter Point.** Numerous brightly colored lobster buoys bob offshore. Linger here to savor the essence of the Maine coast: rocks, gulls, the tang of salt air. At **Hunters Head** the loop road turns away from the sea and soon becomes two-way as you head back to where you started. You'll pass **Jordan Pond,** one of many glacier-carved ponds on the island.

Your drive has taken you around the eastern side of the island. To explore the western side, you must drive out of park property and back in again. Continue north on the loop road, cross the

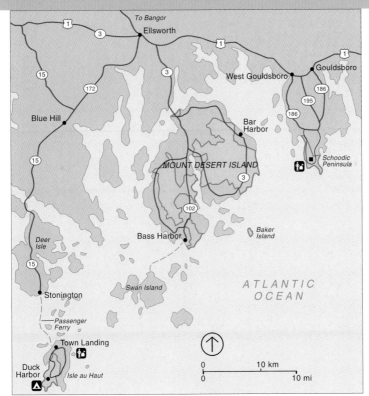

bridge, and bear right to get on Maine 233. Head west on 233 to Maine 198, then head south on Maine 102 toward Southwest Harbor. Continue south. On your left though obscured is **Somes Sound,** the only fjord on the US Atlantic coast. On your right is Echo Lake, a swimming spot with a small beach.

Maine 102 passes through Southwest Harbor. Just beyond, near Manset, bear left on Maine 102A, which takes you into a large patch of park property. You can picnic at **Seawall** and then stretch your legs on the nearby 1¼-mile **Ship Harbor Nature Trail,** which gives you a lesson in how a forest shore is knit to the tidal sea.

A short detour off Maine 102A takes you to **Bass Harbor Head,** site of a 19th-century lighthouse. Take 102A through **Bass Harbor** and bear left on Maine 102 toward Tremont. Continue north for 7 miles to a tract of park called **Pretty Marsh,** a beautiful picnic spot. A short worn path leads to the rock-strewn shore. Continue on 102 and retrace your route from Somesville to the visitor center.

Schoodic Peninsula

100 miles; a full day

To drive the 45 miles from Bar Harbor to the park's outpost, the **Schoodic Peninsula,** take Maine 3 to US 1, south of Ellsworth, and head east to West Gouldsboro. Go south via Maine 186 to Winter Harbor, then follow signs to the park entrance.

From there, take the 6-mile one-way drive to **Schoodic Point.** The massive granite rocks here are laced by black diabase dikes, the product of magma that welled up into cracks. Schoodic's displays of thundering surf usually top those of Mt. Desert Island. And the audiences are much smaller; the peninsula does not draw crowds the way Mt. Desert does.

Continue on the drive and park opposite **Little Moose Island.** At low tide, take the short walk through the intertidal puddles and muck to the island. A meandering path leads you seaward for a panoramic view of the Atlantic. Stay on the path to avoid damaging the fragile plants.

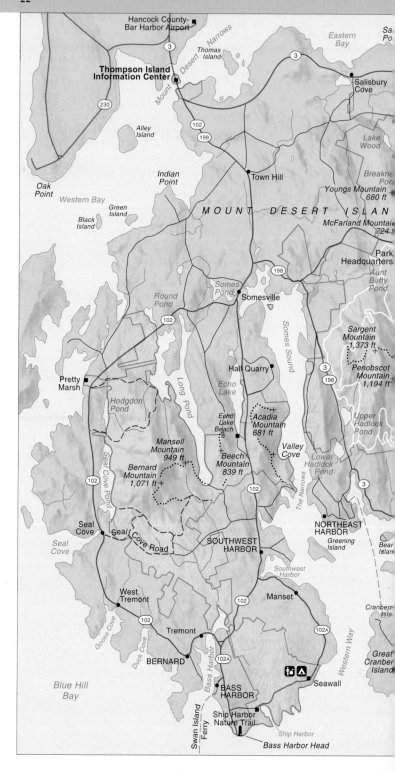

Hancock County-
Bar Harbor Airport

Eastern
Bay

Thomas
Narrows
Island

Sa
Po

Thompson Island
Information Center

Salisbury
Cove

230

Alley
Island

Lake
Wood

Oak
Point

Indian
Point

Town Hill

Youngs Mountain
680 ft

Breakne
Por

Western Bay

MOUNT DESERT ISLAN

McFarland Mountai
724

Green
Island

Black
Island

Park
Headquarters

Aunt
Betty
Pond

Round
Pond

Somes
Pond

Somesville

198

Sargent
Mountain
1,373 ft

Somes
Sound

102

Pretty
Marsh

Hall Quarry

Echo
Lake

Penobscot
Mountain
1,194 ft

198

Hodgdon
Pond

Long
Pond

Echo
Lake
Beach

Acadia
Mountain
681 ft

Upper
Hadlock
Pond

Mansell
Mountain
949 ft

Beech
Mountain
839 ft

Valley
Cove

Lower
Hadlock
Pond

Bernard
Mountain
1,071 ft

102

3

Seal
Cove
Pond

NORTHEAST
HARBOR

Seal
Cove

Seal Cove Road

SOUTHWEST
HARBOR

Greening
Island

Bear
Islan

Seal
Cove

Southwest
Harbor

West
Tremont

102

Manset

Cranber
Isle

Goose Cove

Tremont

102A

Western Way

Duck Cove

102

Blue Hill
Bay

BERNARD

102A

Bass Harbor

Great
Cranber
Island

BASS
HARBOR

Seawall

Swan Island
Ferry

Ship Harbor
Nature Trail

Ship Harbor

Bass Harbor Head

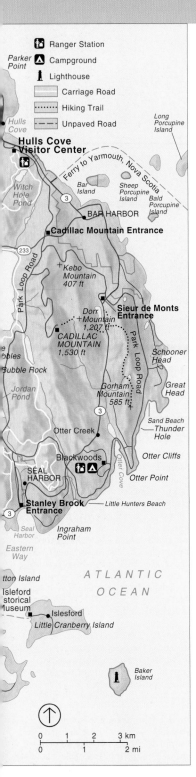

Ranger Station

Parker Point ▲ Campground

🛈 Lighthouse

Carriage Road

Hiking Trail

Unpaved Road

Hulls Cove

Hulls Cove Visitor Center

Ferry to Yarmouth, Nova Scotia

Witch Hole Pond

Long Porcupine Island

Bar Island

Sheep Porcupine Island

Bald Porcupine Island

3

BAR HARBOR

Cadillac Mountain Entrance

233

Park Loop Road

+Kebo Mountain 407 ft

Dorr +Mountain 1,207 ft

Sieur de Monts Entrance

CADILLAC MOUNTAIN 1,530 ft

Schooner Head

bbles

Bubble Rock

Jordan Pond

Gorham Mountain 585 ft

Great Head

3

Sand Beach Thunder Hole

Otter Creek

Blackwoods

Otter Cliffs

SEAL HARBOR

Otter Point

Otter Cove

Stanley Brook Entrance

Little Hunters Beach

3

Seal Harbor

Ingraham Point

Eastern Way

tton Island

ATLANTIC OCEAN

Isleford storical Museum

Islesford

Little Cranberry Island

Baker Island

↑

0   1   2   3 km

0   1   2 mi

The Islands

a full day each

Fragments of Acadia are on islands. Two worth visiting are **Isle au Haut,** about half of which is park property, and **Baker Island,** which is almost entirely park owned. Isle au Haut is served all year by mail boats, Baker Island in summer only by tour boats. Get boat schedules from the visitor center or from the boat operators.

The trip to Isle au Haut, or "high island," named by Samuel de Champlain, begins at Stonington, at the tip of **Deer Isle,** about 40 miles from Ellsworth. To make the boat on time from Mt. Desert Island, allot at least 2 hours for the drive and for finding a rare legal parking place near the harbor. Bring lunch. The mail boat takes passengers on a first-come, first-served basis. The 45-minute voyage ends at the Town Landing. In summer the boat also stops at **Duck Harbor,** a park campsite and trailhead.

Great blue heron

Blue mussels and a dog whelk with eggs

Grove of white birch, sunrise

For a fine hike, get off at the town landing and turn right. A short distance down the road is a ranger station. Here begins the 4-mile **Duck Harbor Trail,** which takes you through upland forest, along the shore, and past blueberry brambles (picking and eating allowed) to Duck Harbor. Spend the day here wandering the area's trails, enjoying woods-and-water scenery, and watching for ospreys and bald eagles. Get the late-afternoon boat back.

For Baker Island, round-trip tour boats leave daily in summer, weather permitting, from Northeast Harbor, a town at the tip of Mt. Desert Island. During the 45-minute trip, a park naturalist points out ospreys and seals and tells the story of the Gilley family, 19th-century inhabitants of Baker Island. The enterprising and self-sufficient pioneer family, which eventually included 12 children, lived on fish, duck, home-raised sheep, cattle, potatoes, and lobsters plucked from shallow waters.

When the boat reaches the island, you transfer to a launch or skiff and land on a rocky beach. With the naturalist, you tour the island, seeing a white brick lighthouse built in 1855, a beach piled high with boulders, and the island graveyard filled with Gilleys.

Son John is not buried there. On a fall day in 1896, his boat capsized in heavy seas; his body was never found.

Carriage Roads & Hikes

In 1917 John D. Rockefeller, Jr., a summer resident of Mt. Desert Island, launched the building of a 57-mile network of broken stone roads for horse-drawn carriages. Convinced that the newfangled automobile would destroy the tranquillity of the island, he banned it from the carriage roads. The roads were graced by 17 hand-built granite bridges, each a unique work of art. Rockefeller later donated most of the road network, along with 11,000 acres of his land, to the park. The carriage roads, still not open to cars, are a treasure prized by hikers, bikers, horseback riders, cross-country skiers, and anyone seeking a respite from the incessant hum of the internal combustion engine.

To introduce yourself to the carriage roads, try the 3 9/10-mile **Hadlock Brook Loop.** Park at the Maine 198 (Parkman Mountain) parking area just north of **Upper Hadlock Pond** and walk to the trailhead. Take the left fork east toward **Hemlock Bridge,** a

View of the Porcupines in Frenchman Bay, from Cadillac Mountain

Herring gull in Schoodic fog

gem of hand-hewn stone. Follow the rising road to another handsome span, **Waterfall Bridge,** site of a 40-foot cascade. (You can turn around here, cutting your hike to about two miles round-trip.) Cross the bridge and walk south for a mile to one of the network's well-marked intersections. Turn right at intersection 19 and right again at intersection 18 and continue along the pond. Watch for loons—and listen for their haunting call. The road crosses **Hadlock**

Brook Bridge and loops back to the trailhead.

The park also has 120 miles of hiking trails, which range from easy strolls along the ocean or around ponds to steep climbs up Cadillac and other mountains. For a jaunt into history try the **Gorge Path,** which, like several other trails, has stone steps to ease your way up slopes. The steps, flat stones imbedded in rising ground, were built by turn-of-the-century summer people who wanted to rough it, but not too much. The path begins at a parking spot on the Park Loop Road, near 407-foot **Kebo Mountain,** and leads to a wood trail. Cairns mark the trail when it follows a rocky, brook-washed ravine. About a mile into the woods is an intersection. Depending upon your time and stamina, you can turn and retrace your steps or push on to Cadillac or **Dorr Mountain,** each a steep hike of more than 1½ miles.

Information & Activities

Headquarters
P.O. Box 177, Bar Harbor, Maine 04609. Phone (207) 288-3338. www.nps.gov/acad

Seasons & Accessibility
Park open all year. In winter visitor facilities close and much of the Park Loop Road is unplowed. For recorded weather information call (207) 667-8910. For boats to Isle au Haut call (207) 367-5193; for Baker Island call (207) 276-3717.

Visitor & Information Centers
Visitor center on Maine 3 just south of Hulls Cove, open daily May through October. Thompson Island Information Center on Maine 3, just before crossing onto Mt. Desert Island. Off season, information available at headquarters 2½ miles west of Bar Harbor on Maine 233.

Entrance Fee
May–Oct. only: $10 per vehicle for 7-day pass.

Pets
Permitted on leashes except on swimming beaches, in public buildings, on a few hiking trails, and at Isle au Haut campsite.

Facilities for Disabled
Visitor center, some rest rooms, and carriage roads are wheelchair accessible. Free guidebook available.

Things to Do
Free ranger-led activities: nature walks, photography workshops, star-gazing, films, slide shows. Also available, bus tours—call (207) 288-3327), bay and island cruises, carriage rides, auto tape tour, hiking, bicycling, swimming, fishing, cross-country skiing, snowshoeing, ice-skating and ice fishing, and snowmobiling.

Special Advisories
● Be careful on ledges and rocks along shore; algae are slippery.
● In spring and fall, watch out for strong storm waves.

Overnight Backpacking
Not allowed.

Campgrounds
Two campgrounds, 14-day limits. Blackwoods open all year. Reserve through National Parks Reservation Service (see page 11)—recommended June 15 to Sept. 15; other times first come, first served. **Seawall** open late May to Sept. 30. First come, first served. Fees $12-$18 per night. Showers outside park. Tent and RV sites; no hookups. Food services in park.

Hotels, Motels, & Inns
(unless otherwise noted, rates are for 2 persons in a double room, high season)
In Bar Harbor, Maine 04609: ·
Bar Harbor Inn (on Newport Dr.) P.O. Box 7. (207) 288-3351 or (800) 248-3351. 153 units. $169-$459. Pool, rest. **Bar Harbor Regency Holiday Inn** 123 Eden St. (207) 288-9723 or (800) 234-6835. 221 units. $145-$265. AC, pool, rest. Mid-May to mid-Oct. The **Bayview** 111 Eden St. (207) 288-5861 or (800) 356-3585. 38 units. $140-$440. Pool, rest. Late May to late Oct. **Best Western Inn** (on Maine 3) Route 3, Box 1127. (800) 528-1234 or (207) 288-5823. 70 units. $105-$125. AC, pool, rest. May to late Oct. **Cleftstone Manor** 92 Eden St. (207) 288-4951. 16 units. $100-$195. Mid-April to Nov. **Cromwell Harbor Motel** 359 Main St. (207) 288-3201. 24 units. $85-$96. **Wonder View Motor Lodge** (Eden Street) P.O. Box 25. (888) 439-8439 or (207) 288-3358. 79 units. $98-$142. Pool, rest. May to October.
In Northeast Harbor, Maine 04662:
Asticou Inn (on Maine 3). (800) 258-3373 or (207) 276-3344. 47 units. $235-$325, 2 meals. Pool, rest. Mid-May to mid-October. **Kimball Terrace Inn** Huntington Road. (800) 454-6225 or (207) 276-3383. 70 units. $118-$145. Pool, rest.
In Southwest Harbor, Maine 04679:
Moorings Inn (on Shore Road, Manset) P.O. Box 744. (800) 596-5523 or (207) 244-5523. 22 units, some kitchens; 4 cottages. $75-$135. Rest. May to October.

For additional accommodations, call the Chambers of Commerce of Bar Harbor (207) 288-5103, Northeast Harbor (207) 276-5040, or Southwest Harbor (207) 244-9264.

Excursions

Moosehorn National Wildlife Refuge

Calais, Maine

At dawn and dusk in spring, the male woodcock soars into the air to begin his mating ritual. The refuge's two units protect the essential habitat of the American woodcock as well as other waterfowl and forest wildlife species. Contains two wilderness areas. 24,409 acres. Facilities: hiking, boating, bicycling, fishing, hunting, winter sports. Open all year, dawn to dusk. Headquarters at the Baring Unit, off US 1, about 75 miles from Acadia NP. (207) 454-7161.

Petit Manan National Wildlife Refuge

Steuben, Maine

Migrating waterfowl and shorebirds take rest on Petit Manan Peninsula and more than 25 offshore islands here. The peninsula's 2 hiking trails lead visitors through spruce-fir forests, blueberry barrens, and along the rugged rocky coastline. Petit Manan Island features one of the largest seabird nesting colonies in Maine and a 123-foot lighthouse; contact refuge manager before attempting a visit. 7,000 acres. Hiking trails. Peninsula open all year, dawn to dusk. Accessible from US 1 in Steuben, about 35 miles from Schoodic Unit of Acadia NP. (207) 546-2124.

Rachel Carson National Wildlife Refuge

Wells, Maine

Stretching along Maine's southern coast from Kittery to Cape Elizabeth, this refuge's ten units offer closeup looks at the fragile and dynamic world of the tidal estuary. The unit at Wells contains the 1-mile-long self-guided Carson Trail. Breeding and migrating shorebirds, wading birds, waterfowl, and raptors also featured. 5,000 acres. Facilities include hiking, canoeing, hunting, picnic areas, scenic drives, cross-country skiing, handicapped access. Open all year, dawn to dusk. Headquarters at Wells, on Maine 9, off US 1, about 160 miles from Acadia NP. (207) 646-9226.

School of blue-striped grunts in the underwater splendor of Biscayne Bay

Biscayne

Florida

Established June 28, 1980

172,924 acres

Biscayne, a seascape in watercolor, offers vistas ashore and beneath the sea. Standing on the park's narrow shore, you look out upon a bay that is tranquil on the surface and teeming with life below. Aboard a glass-bottom boat, you look down and see some of that life—dazzlingly colored fish, fantastically shaped corals, gently waving fronds of sea grass.

Biscayne is an underwater wilderness. Only five percent of the park is land—about 40 small barrier islands and a mangrove shoreline, the longest such undeveloped shore on the East Coast. Park wildlife musters under water in the form of minuscule, unusual, or rarely seen animals. The most extensive life-form is a community known as the coral reef—colonies of tiny polyps that secrete limestone and live within ever growing rocky crannies. The coral reefs at Biscayne are part of the only living ones in the continental United States.

The park reprieved a living system condemned to die under the pressure of progress. The threat came in the 1960s, when developers were making plans to build resorts and subdivisions on Florida's northern keys, from Key Biscayne to Key Largo. Conservationists campaigned to preserve Biscayne Bay; it became a national monument in 1968. When Biscayne National Park was established, boundaries were expanded to encompass several more of the bay's keys and reefs.

Biscayne embraces a complex ecosystem that extends from the

When to Go

All-year park. The best time to visit the park's islands is from mid-December to mid-April, subtropical Florida's dry season. In summer, you face the perils of mosquitoes and fast-moving thunderstorms, but seas are generally the calmest—making it ideal for snorkeling and diving. Hurricanes are occasional.

How to Visit

Unless you have your own boat, plan to see Biscayne on a concessioner-run cruise. You can look underwater on a **reef cruise** aboard a glass-bottom boat or swim the shallow waters on a snorkeling cruise. There are also scuba cruises to the outer reef for qualified divers. You should make reservations in advance. Cruises may be canceled if there are too few passengers or the weather is inclement. Although this is a water park, a walk around the mangrove shore will give you a chance to examine the coastal edges of the bay's ecosystem. The Dante Fascell Visitor Center offers a museum, audiovisual programs, and ranger talks.

Reef Cruise

a half day

Sign up for a cruise well ahead (see **Information & Activities** for details). Schedules vary by season. At **Convoy Point,** the glass-bottom boat's home port and site of park headquarters, you can get an orientation to the bay's unique flora and

mangrove shoreline to the Gulf Stream. Besides the mangrove coast and living reef, the ecosystem includes two other biological realms found on the small islands and the shallow bay's marine nursery. The realms are interwoven, and each sustains still other webs of life.

Guarding all this are the northernmost Florida Keys, barrier islands that keep ocean waves from battering the bay. Thus shielded, the bay offers sanctuary to the life within it and beauty to those who come to look beneath the surface.

How to Get There

From Miami, take Florida's Turnpike (Fla. 821) south to Speedway Boulevard, and turn left (south). Continue 4 miles on Speedway Blvd. to North Canal Dr. and turn left (east). Follow Canal Dr. to the park entrance. From Homestead (about 9 miles), take SW 328th St. (North Canal Drive) to the park entrance at Convoy Point. Airport: Miami.

Diver and sea fans near Elliott Key

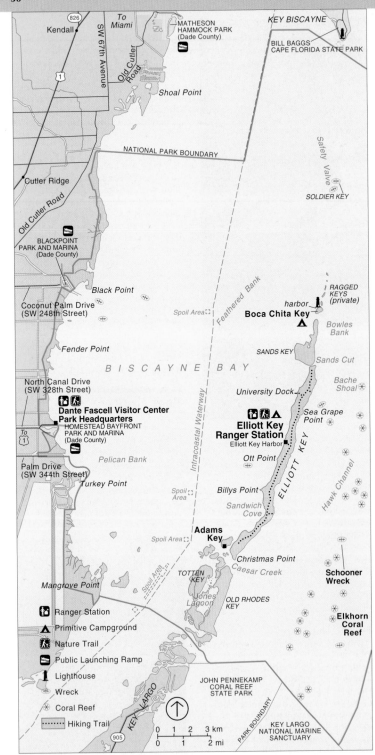

826
Kendall
SW 67th Avenue
To Miami
MATHESON HAMMOCK PARK
(Dade County)
KEY BISCAYNE
BILL BAGGS CAPE FLORIDA STATE PARK
Old Cutler Road
1
Shoal Point
NATIONAL PARK BOUNDARY
Safety Valve
Cutler Ridge
Old Cutler Road
SOLDIER KEY
BLACKPOINT PARK AND MARINA (Dade County)
Coconut Palm Drive (SW 248th Street)
Black Point
Spoil Area
Feathered Bank
RAGGED KEYS (private)
harbor
Boca Chita Key
Bowles Bank
Fender Point
SANDS KEY
Sands Cut
Bache Shoal
B I S C A Y N E   B A Y
University Dock
Sea Grape Point
North Canal Drive (SW 328th Street)
Dante Fascell Visitor Center Park Headquarters
HOMESTEAD BAYFRONT PARK AND MARINA (Dade County)
Elliott Key Ranger Station
Elliott Key Harbor
Intracoastal Waterway
ELLIOTT KEY
Hawk Channel
To 1
Pelican Bank
Ott Point
Palm Drive (SW 344th Street)
Turkey Point
Spoil Area
Billys Point
Sandwich Cove
Adams Key
Spoil Area
Christmas Point
Caesar Creek
Schooner Wreck
Mangrove Point
Spoil Area
TOTTEN KEY
Jones Lagoon
OLD RHODES KEY
Elkhorn Coral Reef

Ranger Station
Primitive Campground
Nature Trail
Public Launching Ramp
Lighthouse
Wreck
Coral Reef
Hiking Trail

KEY LARGO
JOHN PENNEKAMP CORAL REEF STATE PARK
PARK BOUNDARY
KEY LARGO NATIONAL MARINE SANCTUARY
905
0 1 2 3 km
0 1 2 mi

Tropical hardwood edging Elliott Key's shoreline

fauna before setting out. A cruise takes about three hours. Cruises for snorkel and scuba divers last longer and cost more.

The center of the boat's deck is a rectangular viewing chamber. Its floor is made up of rows of broad, angled windows. Passengers line rails around the chamber and peer down at the constantly changing, green-tinted scene.

As the boat crosses the bay, a park ranger prepares the audience by passing out pieces of hard coral and previewing the sights that will be seen in the reefs. A ruffled seabed and waving strands of turtle grass pass under the windows. Vast beds of turtle grass and water only 4 to 10 feet deep make Biscayne Bay a nursery for a host of young marine animals, including shrimp, spiny lobsters, sponges, and crabs. You can see some of these animals through the windows. More than 200 types of fish swim in park waters. You may also see large, graceful sea turtles.

If you walk to the outer edge of the deck, you can watch boats skimming the bay and brown pelicans flapping by. When they spot fish, they dive

Nursing manatee with mother

headfirst into the sea to scoop them up in their huge bills. Among the many other birds you will see are cormorants and herons; together, their calls can be deafening.

Through the bay runs the Intracoastal Waterway, marked by posts whose signs bear numbers keyed to navigational charts. In one short, shallow stretch near the waterway are natural grass beds rising near the surface and visible at low tide. Bonefish, prized by sportfishermen for their speed and strength, inhabit the grass beds.

Spiny lobsters in the sea grass of Biscayne Bay

The boat slips through the keys toward the reefs beyond. Once it arrives at its destination, the boat lingers for the floor show: the multicolored flash of a passing parrotfish, the sinuous glide of an angelfish, the little jungles of coral. Slowly the boat moves to another vantage point, and a new seabed show begins to roll by. Giant brain coral and mountainous star coral dominate the reefs, many so high that the glass bottom of the boat seems close enough to graze them. Sea fans and other soft corals ripple in the calm, clear water. The ranger helps viewers identify the vibrantly colored fish flitting around the massive coral formations. Before reaching the outer reefs the boat turns for home.

The cruise passes through **Caesar Creek,** named for Black Caesar, a legendary pirate said to have lurked here in the 1600s. More than 50 shipwrecks have been cataloged within park boundaries. Federal law protects them from salvagers or souvenir collectors. Visitors who have made the trip in their own boats can also dock at Adams Key for a picnic and walk on a nature trail.

Elliott Key has primitive campsites, rest rooms, a nature trail, a swimming area, a ranger station, and what conservationists label a "road scar"—a bulldozer's legacy and a reminder of how close devastation came to these keys. To the north is **Boca Chita Key,** which has a boat dock, primitive campsites, and rest rooms, but no drinking water. The lighthouse is only ornamental.

Mangrove Shore

¼ mile; at least an hour

If you have little time, no boat, and some curiosity, walk the shore around Convoy Point, a fine place for a picnic. If you have more time, inquire about renting a canoe to explore mangrove tidal creeks.

The mangroves are critical to this marine environment. They stabilize the shore, trapping their own fallen leaves and other organic material in the tangles of their stilt-like roots. The trees attract many birds—including, on rare occasions, the peregrine falcon and bald eagle, 2 of the 13 endangered animal species monitored by park scientists. Barnacles, fish, and other sea creatures cluster at the trees' half-submerged roots. The decaying mangrove leaves, rich in protein, provide food to the tiny animals at the bottom of a food chain that ends with the fisherman who eats the gray snapper he caught in the bay.

The beneficial mangroves also filter damaging pollutants from the freshwater runoff into the bay. Whether you walk or paddle a boat, watch carefully for the bay animals that find food and refuge in the mangrove waterways. On a winter's day the creatures may include the gentle manatee, a huge, grass-chewing "cow of the sea." The scene keeps changing as each outgoing tide carries its bounty of nutrients out to sea and each incoming tide brings in new inhabitants for the sheltering mangroves.

Life on the Coral Reef

Tunneling through a school of fish

Queen angelfish

Filefish on soft coral

Porcupinefish

Nassau grouper

Information & Activities

Headquarters
9700 SW 328th St., Homestead, Florida
33033. Phone (305) 230-1144.
www.nps.gov/bisc

Seasons & Accessibility
Open year-round. Keys (islands)
can be reached by boat only. Private
concessioners operate daily, though
underbooked cruises may be canceled
in the off-season. Private boats
allowed; boat docks available ($15
docking fee) on Elliott, Adams, and
Boca Chita Keys.

Visitor & Boat Information
Dante Fascell Visitor Center open
daily all year. For park information,
call (305) 230-7275.

For information and reservations
for concessioner-run glass-bottom
boat, snorkeling, scuba diving, island
and canoe trips, write Biscayne
National Underwater Park, Inc., 9700
SW 328th St., Homestead, Fla. 33033,
or call (305) 230-1100. Rentals available. Tours leave from Convoy Point.

Entrance Fees
None. $15 docking fee for private
boats. Fees charged by concessioner
for boat trips.

Pets
Allowed on leashes (6-ft. maximum
length) in the developed areas of Convoy Point and Elliott Key. Not permitted on boat tours.

Facilities for Disabled
Dante Fascell Visitor Center is fully
accessible, as are restrooms at Elliott
Key and Boca Chita Key. Concessioner
boat tours accessible with assistance.

Things to Do
Ranger-led activities: glass-bottom
boat tours, canoe trips, island nature
tours, interpretive exhibits. Also
available, swimming, snorkeling,
scuba diving, water skiing, boating,
canoe rentals, fishing, lobstering,
hiking, birding.

Special Advisories
• Do not touch coral or other living
things on the reef. They are easily damaged; they can also inflict deep cuts
and cause serious infections.

• Mosquitoes and other insects can be
a problem on the islands, particularly
from April to December; carry plenty
of repellent.

Campgrounds
Two boat-in campgrounds, both with
14-day limit. **Elliott Key** and **Boca
Chita Key** open all year first come, first
served. Water at **Elliott Key** only. Tent
sites only. Group Campground at
Elliott Key.

Hotels, Motels, & Inns
*(unless otherwise noted, rates are for 2
persons in a double room, high season)*
In Florida City, Florida 33034:
Coral Roc Motel 1100 N. Krome Ave.
(800) 692-6725 or (305) 247-4010. 16
units, 4 with kitchenettes. $51. AC,
pool. **Comfort Inn** 333 SE First Ave./
US Hwy. 1. (800) 352-2489 or (305)
248-4009. 82 units. $79.50-$99.50. AC,
pool. **Knights Inn** 1223 NE First Ave./
US Hwy. 1. (305) 247-6621. 49 units,
6 with kitchenettes. $79-$89. AC, pool.
In Homestead, Florida 33030:
Days Inn 51 S. Homestead Blvd. (305)
245-1260. 100 units. $99-$179. AC,
pool, restaurant. **Everglades Motel** 605
S. Krome Ave. (305) 247-4117. 14
units. $68. AC, pool.

*For other area accommodations,
write or call the Homestead/Florida
City Chamber of Commerce, 160 US
Hwy. 1, Florida City, Florida 33034.
(305) 247-2332.*

Excursions

John Pennekamp Coral Reef State Park
Key Largo, Florida

In the world's first undersea park, a living coral reef may be viewed through a diver's mask or a glass-bottom boat. 56,097 acres. Facilities: visitor center, 47 campsites, trails, boating, boat ramps, fishing, picnic areas, water sports, handicapped access. Open all year during daylight. Off US 1 in Key Largo, about 40 miles from Biscayne NP and 35 from Everglades NP. (305) 451-1202.

National Key Deer Refuge
Big Pine Key, Florida

The Key deer—a diminutive subspecies of the white-tailed deer—struggle to survive in this mangrove and pine-palm habitat. It's illegal to feed them. 8,542 acres. Hiking and wildlife observation. Open year-round, dawn to dusk. Off US 1 on Big Pine Key, about 150 miles south of Biscayne NP. (305) 872-2239.

Great White Heron National Wildlife Refuge
Big Pine Key, Florida

Dedicated to the protection of the great white heron, this site partly overlaps the National Key Deer Refuge. These mangrove islands also shelter ibis, white-crowned pigeon, and the roseate spoonbill. 192,493 acres. No facilities. Access by boat only. Open all year, dawn to dusk. Information at National Key Deer Refuge; see above.

Key West National Wildlife Refuge
Big Pine Key, Florida

Encompassing nearly all the islands west of Key West, this refuge offers protection to terns, frigatebirds, ospreys, herons, and pelicans. 6,686 acres. No camping or other facilities. Access by boat only. No pets allowed island. Open year-round, dawn to dusk. Information at National Key Deer Refuge; see above.

Bird's-eye view of Fort Jefferson

Dry Tortugas

Florida

Established October 26, 1992

64,701 acres

In the Gulf of Mexico, about 70 miles west of Key West, Florida, a 7-mile-long archipelago of seven low-lying islands forms the centerpiece of Dry Tortugas National Park, a bird and marine life sanctuary with some of the healthiest coral reefs remaining off North American shores. Towering incongruously in the midst of this subtropical Eden is Fort Jefferson, a relic of 19th-century military strategy. The largest American coastal fort built in that century, it sprawls over 16-acre Garden Key

Barely 85 acres of the park's 100 square miles are above water. Three easterly keys are little more than spits of white coral sand. A stone's throw from park headquarters in Fort Jeffer-

son, Bush Key is home to a tangle of bay cedar, seagrape, mangrove, sea oats, and prickly-pear cactus that reflect the original "desert island" character of the islands. The chain ends about 3 miles west with 30-acre Loggerhead Key, where a lighthouse completed in 1858 still flashes a beacon to mariners.

Spanish explorer Juan Ponce de León, the first European to describe the Florida peninsula, dropped anchor here in 1513, found pellucid waters teeming with green, hawksbill, leatherback, and loggerhead turtles, and so named the islands *las tortugas*. For the next three centuries, pirates relied on the turtles for meat and eggs; they also raided the sandy nests of roosting sooty and noddy terns, over 100,000 of which descend on Bush Key every year between March and September. By 1825, when the

disrupt shipping lanes in the Gulf of Mexico. As a result, they decided to build a 450-gun, 2,000-man fort on Garden Key. The intimidating bulk of the 50-foot-high, three-level hexagon, whose 2,000 arches run half a mile around, spared it from ever having to fire a shot in anger. A Union prison for Civil War deserters, it also held physician Samuel Mudd, who was convicted of conspiracy in Abraham Lincoln's murder after he (unknowingly, he claimed) set the broken leg of fugitive assassin John Wilkes Booth. He served four years before being released.

Unfinished after nearly 30 years of intermittent construction, the "Gibraltar of the Gulf" succumbed in 1874 to several factors: yellow fever, hurricane damage, and the new rifled cannon, which rendered its 8-foot-thick walls obsolete. Revived in 1898 as a Navy coaling station—the battleship *Maine* steamed from here to its infamous destiny in Havana Harbor 90 miles south—the fort was permanently abandoned in 1907.

How to Get There

Access to Dry Tortugas is by boat or seaplane. Yankee Fleet and Sunny Days run regular boat service. For Yankee Fleet, call (800) 634-0939 or (305) 294-7009; for Sunny Days, call (305) 292-6100. For names of authorized air taxis and charter boats, call park headquarters. Boat passage from Key West takes about 3 hours; by air, 40 minutes. Private boaters should refer to NOAA Chart #11434 ("Sombrero Key To Dry Tortugas") and Chart #11438 ("Dry Tortugas").

islands' first lighthouse began to alert sailors of surrounding reefs and shoals—a grave for more than 200 ships wrecked here since the 1600s— nautical charts warned that the Tortugas were "dry."

In 1846, US Army strategists were concerned that hostile nations could

Divers surveying the rich marine life off Garden Key

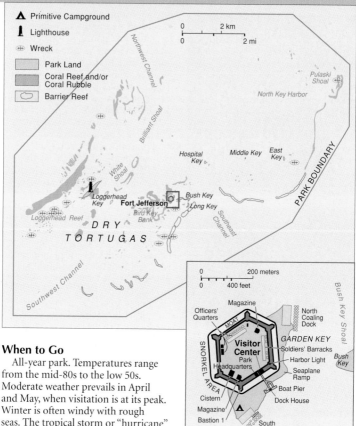

▲ Primitive Campground

⚓ Lighthouse

⊕ Wreck

Park Land

Coral Reef and/or Coral Rubble

Barrier Reef

FORT JEFFERSON

When to Go

All-year park. Temperatures range from the mid-80s to the low 50s. Moderate weather prevails in April and May, when visitation is at its peak. Winter is often windy with rough seas. The tropical storm or "hurricane" season lasts from June through November, when temperatures and humidity are highest.

How to Visit

A day trip by boat or floatplane permits an unhurried visit to **Garden Key** including a self-guided walking tour of **Fort Jefferson**, a stroll around the fort's marine life-rich seawall, swimming, and snorkeling. If **Bush Key** is open to visitors and you can spare an hour, consider swimming the narrow channel to experience a true "desert island" environment.

Garden Key and Fort Jefferson

70 miles from Key West; a full day

When you arrive, check dockside announcement boards for ranger-led activities. The **Visitor Center** is just inside the fort entrance. A Florida National Parks and Monuments Association bookstore opens upon

request. View the self-operated video orientation program, then take a self-guided tour of Fort Jefferson's massive architecture and parklike parade ground. Granite spiral staircases lead to open-air gun emplacements atop the fort, where visitors will find splendid 360-degree views— excellent vantage points for binocular-aided birdwatching. (Early on, the Tortugas' population of terns, cormorants, gulls, boobies, plovers, pelicans, peregrine falcons, and twin-tailed frigate birds caught the attention of naturalists like John James Audubon, who sailed here from Key West in 1832 to study them.) Visit the Garden Key harbor light, and stroll the grassy parapet, where huge coastal guns are on display.

Read the "Walking the Seawall" brochure, which will add considerable interest to a stroll along the fort's 0.6-

mile-long **Seawall** and moat, a sheltered habitat favored by queen conch, yellow stingray, gray snapper, and other creatures. Outside the wall, a superb snorkeling area—chest deep and decorated with sea fans, brain coral, and turtle grass—teems with many of the 442 species of fish identified here. (The visitor center has a limited number of goggles, snorkels, and flippers available for loan.) If you can enlist a companion for mutual safety, consider swimming from the campground's bathing beach along the wall, where fish tend to congregate. Watch for barracuda,

Sunlit archways of Fort Jefferson

which though seldom aggressive are territorial and should be given wide berth.

Information & Activities

Headquarters
Dry Tortugas NP headquarters is located at Everglades NP, 40001 State Road 9336, Homestead, Fla. 33034. Phone (305) 242-7700. There is no Key West office for Dry Tortugas; however, inquiries may be sent to P.O. Box 6208, Key West, Fla. 33041. www.nps.gov/drto

Seasons & Accessibility
Park open year-round. Visitation peaks in spring, when advance boat or plane reservations are advised. Only Garden Key offers overnight stays (in campgrounds). Loggerhead and Bush Keys available for day use only. Bush Key is closed from March to September during nesting season.

Visitor & Information Centers
Visitor center open daily all year.

Entrance Fee
None for day visit. Overnight camping fee is $3 per person per day.

Pets
Permitted only in the campground and must be leashed at all times.

Facilities for Disabled
Dock, visitor center, ground level, and Fort Jefferson campground accessible.

Things to Do
Occasional ranger-led activities. Self-guided walking tours of Fort Jefferson. Also, swimming, snorkeling, wreck diving, underwater photography, bird-watching, sport fishing, camping, star-gazing.

Special Advisories
● Plan to bring all water, food, fuel, and supplies. There is no fresh water available for campers, and no showers for rinsing after swimming.
● Private boats must anchor offshore in designated areas. There are no public boat moorings or slips.
● No public telephone service to the Tortugas.

Campgrounds
Camping is permitted only on Garden Key, which has 10 primitive sites available. First come, first served. 14-day limit. Fees are $3 per person per night. Groups of ten or more must obtain a special permit in advance from park headquarters.

Hotels, Motels, & Inns
(unless otherwise noted, rates are for 2 persons in a double room, high season)
In Key West, Florida 33040:
Best Western Key Ambassador Resort Inn 3755 S. Roosevelt Blvd. (800) 432-4315 or (305) 296-3500. 101 units. $89-$189. AC, pool. **Duval House** 815 Duval St. (305) 294-1666. 28 units, 3 kitchenettes. $145-$265. AC, pool. **The Marquesa Hotel** 600 Fleming St. (305) 292-1919. 27 units. $245-$380. AC, pool, rest. **Westwinds** 914 Eaton St. (800) 788-4150 or (305) 296-4440. 22 units, 4 kitchenettes. $105. AC, pool, continental breakfast included.

For other area accommodations, contact the Key West Chamber of Commerce, 402 Wall St., Fla. 33040. (800) 527-8539 or (305) 294-2587.

Sunrise over the mangroves in Florida Bay

Everglades

Florida

Established December 6, 1947

1,508,570 acres

A short parade of visitors follows a ranger on an Everglades nature walk. For more than an hour she has shown them the living wonders around them—butterflies and snails, alligators and fish, and bird after bird. Near the end of the walk, she gathers the visitors around her. She points to a string of nine white ibis coursing a cloudless sky.

"Imagine seeing ibis in the 1930s," she says. "That would have been a flight of about 90 birds. We are seeing only about 10 percent of the wading birds that were here then. When you get home, write your congressmen and tell them we have to save Everglades." In this threatened national park, lobbying happens on nature walks and appears in official literature.

The park is at the southern tip of the Everglades, a hundred-mile-long subtropical wilderness of saw-grass prairie, junglelike hammock, and mangrove swamp, running from Lake Okeechobee to Florida Bay. Water, essential to the survival of this ecosystem, once flowed south from the lake unhindered. But as the buildup of southern Florida has intensified, canals, levees, and dikes have increasingly diverted the water to land developments and agribusinesses. Vast irrigated farmlands have spread to the park's gates. The waning of the ibis carries a warning: Watery habitats in the park are shrinking because not enough water is getting to Everglades.

The park's special mission inspires the crusade to save it. Unlike early parks established to protect scenery,

When humans change it, they put Everglades life at risk.

How to Get There

South from Miami, take US 1 to Florida City, then west on Fla. 9336 (Palm Drive) to the Main Visitor Center, about 50 miles from Miami. West from Miami, take US 41 (the Tamiami Trail) to Shark Valley Visitor Center. From Naples, head east on US 41 to Fla. 29, then south to Everglades City. Airports: Miami and Naples.

When to Go

Everglades has two seasons: dry (mid-December through mid-April) and wet (the rest of the year). The park schedules most of its activities in the dry season; hot, humid weather and clouds of mosquitoes make park visitors extremely uncomfortable during the wet season.

How to Visit

If you can stay only a day for a drive-in visit, get out of your car and learn about Everglades ecology by taking self-guided walks at road turnoffs on the drive from the **Ernest F. Coe Visitor Center** to Flamingo. For a longer stay, pick either **Flamingo** or **Everglades City** as your base and time your travels to the schedules of concession boat tours. In wet or dry season, only a boat or canoe gives you access to the backcountry. Because of mosquitoes, the dry season is best for canoeing. (Near park entrances you'll see signs advertising airboat rides; airboats, which disturb wildlife and tear up saw grass, are banned in the park.)

Everglades was created to preserve a portion of this vast ecosystem as a wildlife habitat. The park's unique mix of tropical and temperate plants and animals—including more than 700 plant and 300 bird species, as well as the endangered manatee, crocodile, and Florida panther—has earned it International Biosphere Reserve and United Nations World Heritage site designations.

Everglades crusaders urge the purchase of privately owned wetlands east and north of the park. This would further protect the ecosystem and give the park a larger claim to the water that Everglades shares with its thirsty neighbors.

The diverse life of Everglades National Park, from algae to alligators, depends upon a rhythm of abundance and drought. In the wet season, a river inches deep and miles wide flows, almost invisibly, to the Gulf of Mexico. In the dry season, the park rests, awaiting the water's return. The plants and animals are a part of this rhythm.

Royal Palm to Flamingo

76 miles round-trip; a full day

The main **park road** connects the main entrance, southwest of Florida City, with **Flamingo** on **Florida Bay**. Make the drive an exploration, not a 55-mph dash. Stops at the sites suggested can be made on the way to or from Flamingo, depending upon when you want to board a concession tour boat there. Check on that day's cruises by calling the concessioner (see **Information & Activities** p. 48).

At the **Ernest F. Coe Visitor Center,** get oriented to this complex park. A short film stresses environmental

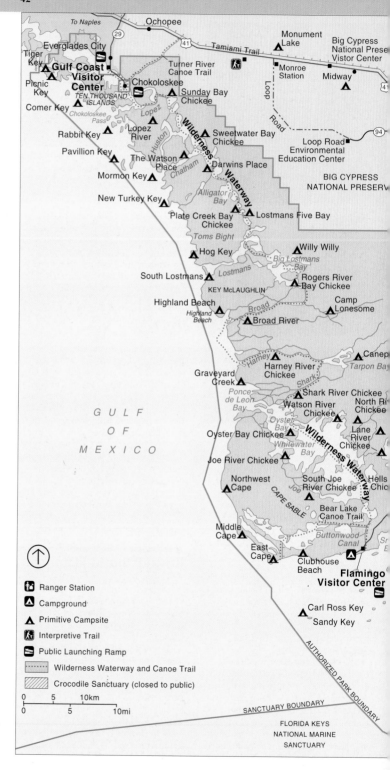

To Naples
Ochopee
Tiger Key
Everglades City
29
41
Tamiami Trail
Monument Lake
Big Cypress National Prese Vistor Center
Gulf Coast Visitor Center
Picnic Key
Turner River Canoe Trail
Monroe Station
Midway
TEN THOUSAND ISLANDS
Chokoloskee
Comer Key
Sunday Bay Chickee
Chokoloskee Pass
Lopez
Rabbit Key
Lopez River
Sweetwater Bay Chickee
Loop Road Environmental Education Center
94
Pavillion Key
Huston
The Watson Place
Wilderness
Darwins Place
BIG CYPRESS NATIONAL PRESERV
Mormon Key
Chatham
New Turkey Key
Waterway
Alligator Bay
Plate Creek Bay Chickee
Lostmans Five Bay
Toms Bight
Hog Key
Willy Willy
Big Lostmans Bay
South Lostmans
Lostmans
Rogers River Bay Chickee
KEY McLAUGHLIN
Camp Lonesome
Highland Beach
Highland Beach
Broad
Broad River
Harney
Canep
Harney River Chickee
Tarpon Bay
Graveyard Creek
Ponce de Leon Bay
Shark
Shark River Chickee
Watson River Chickee
North Ri Chickee
Oyster Bay
Oyster Bay Chickee
Lane River Chickee
Whitewater Bay
Joe River Chickee
Wilderness Waterway
GULF
OF
MEXICO
Northwest Cape
South Joe River Chickee
Hells Chic
CAPE SABLE
Joe
Bear Lake Canoe Trail
Middle Cape
Buttonwood Canal
Sr
East Cape
Clubhouse Beach
Flamingo Visitor Center

Carl Ross Key
Sandy Key

Ranger Station
Campground
Primitive Campsite
Interpretive Trail
Public Launching Ramp
Wilderness Waterway and Canoe Trail
Crocodile Sanctuary (closed to public)

0   5   10km
0   5   10mi

AUTHORIZED PARK BOUNDARY

SANCTUARY BOUNDARY

FLORIDA KEYS
NATIONAL MARINE
SANCTUARY

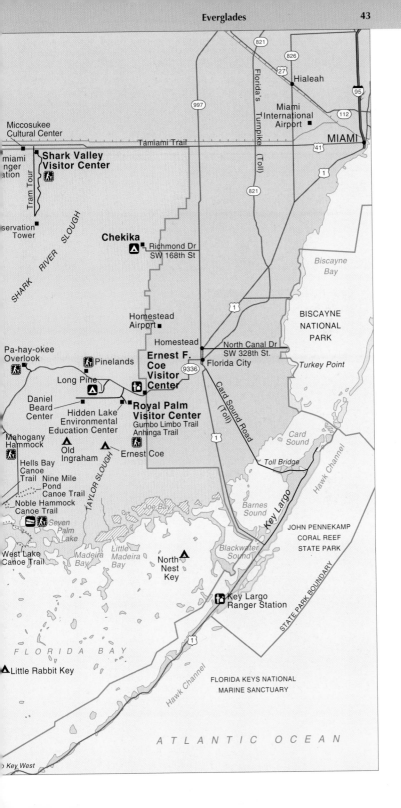

Miccosukee
Cultural Center

miami
nger
ation

**Shark Valley
Visitor Center**

Tram Tour

servation
Tower

SHARK RIVER SLOUGH

Chekika
Richmond Dr
SW 168th St

Homestead
Airport

Homestead

**Ernest F.
Coe
Visitor
Center**

Florida City

Pa-hay-okee
Overlook

Pinelands

Long Pine

Daniel
Beard
Center

Hidden Lake
Environmental
Education Center

**Royal Palm
Visitor Center**
Gumbo Limbo Trail
Anhinga Trail

Mahogany
Hammock

Old
Ingraham

Ernest Coe

TAYLOR SLOUGH

Hells Bay
Canoe
Trail   Nine Mile
Pond
Canoe Trail

Noble Hammock
Canoe Trail

Seven
Palm
Lake

West Lake
Canoe Trail

Madeira
Bay

Little
Madeira
Bay

Joe Bay

North
Nest
Key

Blackwater
Sound

Barnes
Sound

FLORIDA   BAY

Little Rabbit Key

Key Largo
Ranger Station

North Canal Dr
SW 328th St.

Card Sound Road
(Toll)

Biscayne
Bay

BISCAYNE
NATIONAL
PARK

Turkey Point

Card
Sound

Toll Bridge

Hawk Channel

Key Largo

JOHN PENNEKAMP
CORAL REEF
STATE PARK

STATE PARK BOUNDARY

Hawk Channel

FLORIDA KEYS NATIONAL
MARINE SANCTUARY

A T L A N T I C   O C E A N

Key West

MIAMI

Miami
International
Airport

Hialeah

Tamiami Trail

Florida's Turnpike (Toll)

821
826
27
95
112
997
821
41
1
9336
1
1
1

Paddling on a channel into Florida Bay

Snail kite in search of food

American alligator

threats to the park and alerts you to the subtle, imperiled beauty you will be seeing. Check the center's posted daily schedule for ranger-led walks and talks at the **Royal Palm Visitor Center,** just ahead, and for that day's cruises at Flamingo, 38 miles away. Time your road travel each way by adjusting to the day's schedules.

Egrets, herons, and other species dot the saw grass and roadside trees. On the road, use a passenger as a bird spotter; simultaneous driving and birdwatching can be dangerous. At 4 miles, turn off to **Royal Palm.** If you have time while waiting for a ranger-led walk on the **Anhinga Trail,** take your own plunge into the canopied shadows of the ½-mile **Gumbo Limbo Trail,** named for a tree whose peeling red bark gives it another name: tourist tree.

The trail takes you to a hammock, an elevated island of tropical hardwood—including gumbo limbos and some magnificent examples of strangler figs—in a sea of saw grass. The slight elevation keeps the ground drier, permitting the hardwoods to flourish and creating a shaded habitat for many creatures, from snakes to deer, foxes, and raccoon.

Watch for "solution holes," limestone depressions that hold moisture and become miniature ecosystems in the dry season. Filled with organic material and seeded by winds or bird droppings, some solution holes evolve into hammocks.

Watching the alligators at Shark Valley

You can also walk the ½-mile Anhinga Trail on your own. But you have a better chance of spotting wildlife if a ranger is available to guide you. The boardwalk trail skirts a shallow, freshwater slough (pronounced slew). You almost certainly will see alligators and some fascinating birds, including the long-necked, long-beaked fish-spearer for which the trail is named.

The ranger adds lore to what you see: That beautiful zebra butterfly tastes terrible; a predatory bird never tries for second helpings. Those white egg sacs on that branch will hatch apple snails, the prime food of the endangered snail kite. That slim, long-snouted fish gliding through the clear water is a gar; in the dry season it can survive in a mudhole because a primitive lung allows it to breathe air. That alligator loosens the muck in water-filled solution holes and sweeps it away with its tail; in the dry season the gator-made oasis keeps fish, frogs, snails, and birds alive—as long as they are wary of the major resident. In Everglades, unusual adaptations and delicate balances sustain the park's astonishing variety of animals and plants.

Back on the road, visit the roadside exhibits. Stop-and-walk lessons begin on the ¾-mile **Pineland Trail,** 7 miles along the road. Slash pines grow on high ground, so pinelands were wiped out to develop Miami and other towns. What you see here are remnants of the pines that once covered southeastern Florida.

Driving toward Flamingo, you can stop and take a short boardwalk stroll that leads you to **Pinnacle Rock,** a sample of the porous limestone that is south Florida's bedrock. At 12 miles, stop again to see dwarf cypress, trees stunted by shallow soil.

Half a mile farther is a overlook called **Pa-hay-okee,** or "grassy waters," the Indian name for the Everglades. A boardwalk takes you to a shaded observation stage where you can look out on a seemingly endless prairie of grassy waters. At 19½ miles is **Mahogany Hammock,** where a boardwalk leads to the largest living mahogany tree in the United States.

If you want to picnic, there are fine spots at **Paurotis Pond** (at 24½ miles), **Nine Mile Pond** (at 26½ miles), and **West Lake** (at 30½ miles).

At Flamingo, sign up for a boat tour in the marina ticket office near the visitor center. While you are waiting, take the self-guided, ½-mile walk around the waterfront to see Florida Bay, a marine nursery protected by the park. The 2-hour backcountry cruise begins in the marina and enters **Buttonwood Canal,** built in 1957. Among the spidery roots of the three species of mangrove you will see along the waterway, watch for shy crocodiles, sometimes seen sunning on the banks of the canal. The cruise crosses Coot Bay and enters **Whitewater Bay,** where backcountry canoeists camp on chickees, tent-size platforms raised on poles. Don't expect to see flamingos; they rarely appear at their namesake town.

White ibis, herons, pelicans, and spoonbills on mangrove islands

Raccoon hiding in mangrove roots

Shark Valley to Everglades City

49 miles one way; a full day

The **Tamiami Trail** (US 41) forms part of the park's northeastern border. Near the eastern park entrance, stop at the **Shark Valley Visitor Center.** Here is a 15-mile loop road accessible only on foot, on bike, or, year-round, on a 2-hour, narrated tour aboard an open-sided concessioner tram.

You will not see sharks. The valley gets its name from the **Shark River;** sharks gather at its mouth in the Gulf of Mexico. But you will see alligator trails leading to hammocks in the saw grass—and you will almost certainly see alligators and wading birds. The trail leads to a 65-foot tower looking down on the vista that became a name: glades that seem to go on forever.

Return to US 41, which veers northward into the 2,400-square-mile Big Cypress National Preserve, part of the Everglades ecosystem. Most of the water flowing into the park comes through four floodgates that you can see north of the highway along the park boundary.

Slash pines and saw-palmettos, remnants of Florida's flatwoods

Bull thistle in Shark Valley

At Fla. 29, turn south for Everglades City. Follow the highway through the town to the waterfront. Sign up for one of the regularly scheduled, round-trip, narrated concessioner boat tours.

The Ten Thousand Island trip explores mangrove islands along the Gulf of Mexico. On the way to and from the islands, protected sea mammals—sleek bottlenose dolphins and lumbering manatees—often pop up to look at the boat. You can usually see ospreys, pelicans, and cormorants. From a distance, the islands look like a solid stretch of low-lying green land. Close up, you see a labyrinth of thousands of waterways.

There are far fewer than 10,000 islands, but the number is unknown and ever changing. Islands form from the buildup of leaves and other organic material among the stilt-rooted mangroves. As an island grows, storms and tidal forces may break it into fragments, which continue to grow and spread. The islands, ranging in size from a couple of trees to several hundred acres, provide shelter and food for many creatures in the gulf web of life.

The boat crosses **Chokoloskee Bay,** which shares its name with an island of shells, 15 feet high and 147 acres, built by Native Americans long before the first white men appeared here. The bay is the northern end of the 99-mile Everglades City-to-Flamingo **Wilderness Waterway,** a system of backcountry canoe trails through the estuarine fringes of the park.

Information & Activities

Headquarters
40001 State Park Rd., Homestead, Florida 33034. Phone (305) 242-7700. www.nps.gov/ever

Seasons & Accessibility
Park open daily, year-round; some facilities and services limited or unavailable during off-season, May 1 to mid-December.

Visitor & Information Centers
Ernest F. Coe Visitor Center on Fla. 9336 at park entrance. Royal Palm Visitor Center off main park road a few miles inside park entrance. Flamingo Visitor Center on main park road at Florida Bay. Shark Valley Visitor Center at north end of park on US 41. Gulf Coast Visitor Center at Everglades City on Fla. 29 at northwest entrance. Flamingo Visitor Center may close temporarily in off-season.

Entrance Fees
$10 per car per week at main entrance; $4 at Shark Valley and Chekika.

Pets
Pets must be on leashes and are allowed in the campgrounds only.

Facilities for Disabled
All visitor centers, campgrounds, restrooms, and tram tours are accessible. Several trails are at least partly accessible. In the backcountry, Pear Bay Chickee is accessible.

Things to Do
Free naturalist-led activities: nature walks and talks, hikes, exhibits, evening programs. Also, day and evening tram tours; sight-seeing boats; canoe, houseboat, motorboat, and bicycle rentals; fishing (need license); crabbing; shrimping (ask about regulations). In winter and on holidays, call to reserve space on guided tours and activities. Rentals and boat tours in Flamingo: (941) 695-3101. Tram tour at Shark Valley: (305) 221-8455. Boat tours and rentals at Everglades City: (941) 695-2591, or (800) 445-7724 in Fla.

Special Advisories
• You'll need insect repellent year-round, but especially April to Dec.
• Swimming not advised; alligators and snakes live in ponds, sharks and barracuda in saltwater areas.

Wilderness Camping
Permits required; they are obtainable in person, no more than 24 hours before trip, at Flamingo and Everglades City. Fees collected mid-Nov. through April only. No reservations; first come, first served; limits on number of people and length of stay.

Campgrounds
Three campgrounds, 14-day limit Nov. to May; otherwise 30-day limit. $14/night per site collected Nov.-May only. **Flamingo, Long Pine Key,** and **Chekika** open all year. The first two require reservations from mid-Dec. to April; reserve through National Parks Reservation Service (see page 11). Rest of year, first come, first served. Cold showers at **Flamingo.** Tent and RV sites; no hookups. Three group campgrounds; reservations required; contact headquarters April–Nov.; other times, contact the National Parks Reservation Service. Food services in park.

Hotels, Motels, & Inns
(unless otherwise noted, rates are for 2 persons in a double room, high season)
INSIDE THE PARK:
Flamingo Lodge (end of main park road) 1 Flamingo Lodge Hwy. (800) 600-3813 or (941) 695-3101. 127 units. Lodge rooms $95; cottages with kitchens $135. AC, pool, restaurant.
OUTSIDE THE PARK:
In Florida City, Florida 33034:
Coral Roc Motel 1100 N. Krome Ave. (305) 247-4010. 16 units, 4 kitchenettes. $51. AC, pool. **Knights Inn** 1223 NE First Ave./US Hwy. 1. (305) 247-6621. 49 units, 6 kitchenettes. $79-$89. AC, pool. **Comfort Inn** 333 SE First Ave./US Hwy. 1. (800) 352-2489 or (305) 248-4009. 82 units. $39-$200. AC, pool.
In Homestead, Florida 33030:
Days Inn 51 S. Homestead Blvd. (305) 245-1260. 100 units. $99-$179. AC, pool, restaurant. **Everglades Motel** 605 S. Krome Ave. (305) 247-4117. 14 units. $68. AC, pool.

For other lodgings, contact the Homestead/Florida City Chamber of Commerce, 43 N. Krome Ave., Homestead, Fla. 33030. (305) 247-2332.

Excursions

Big Cypress National Preserve

Ochopee, Florida

Dispensing life-giving fresh water to the Everglades and coastal estuaries, this preserve contains marshes, wet and dry prairies, hardwood hammocks, pinelands, and mangrove forests, along with wading birds and alligators. The endangered Florida panther roams the area. 728,000 acres. Five primitive campgrounds, hiking, fishing, hunting, canoeing, off-road vehicles, picnic areas, scenic drives. On US 41 (Tamiami Trail); adjoins Everglades NP. (941) 695-4111.

Corkscrew Swamp Sanctuary

Naples, Florida

A 2½-mile-long boardwalk takes visitors on a self-guided tour through this Audubon Society site featuring the country's largest stand of virgin cypress forest and varied wildlife, including alligators. 10,560 acres. Hiking and picnic areas. Open year-round. Off Fla. 846, about 50 miles northwest of Everglades NP. (941) 657-3771.

J. N. "Ding" Darling National Wildlife Refuge

Sanibel, Florida

Migratory songbirds and a large population of roseate spoonbills feature among the 291 bird species on this island refuge named for Pulitzer Prize-winning political cartoonist and refuge system pioneer Jay Norwood Darling. 6,300 acres. Facilities: hiking, boating, bicycling, fishing, scenic drive. Open all year, dawn to dusk (closed on Fridays). Visitor center off Fla. 80, about 100 miles northwest of Everglades NP. (941) 472-1100.

Mist-shrouded autumn view from Clingmans Dome

Great Smoky Mountains

North Carolina and Tennessee

Established June 15, 1934

521,621 acres

The fact invariably stated about Great Smoky is this: It is the nation's busiest park, drawing some ten million visitors a year, more than twice the number of any other national park. Most of the millions see the park from a mountain-skimming scenic highway that, on a typical weekend day during the summer, draws 60,000 people, bumper-to-bumper.

Luckily, there is plenty of park, thinly laced by 384 miles of mountain roads. And you can pull off the road, park the car, and stroll one of Great Smoky's many Quiet Walkways, ¼-mile paths into what the signs call a "little bit of the world as it once was." Eight hundred miles of hiking trails, from ½ mile to 70 miles long, also give you that

world. Relatively few visitors walk the trails, for most people prefer to stay in their cars.

The park, which covers 800 square miles of mountainous terrain, preserves the world's best examples of deciduous forest and a matchless variety of plants and animals. Because it contains so many types of eastern forest vegetation—much of it old-growth—the park has been designated an International Biosphere Reserve.

The Smoky Mountains are among the oldest on earth. Ice Age glaciers stopped their southward journey just short of these mountains, which became a junction of southern and northern flora. Rhododendron and mountain laurel thrust from the weathered rocks. Amid the woodland and craggy peaks bloom more than 1,500 species of flowering plants, some

How to Get There

From Knoxville, Tenn. (about 25 miles away), take I-40 to Tenn. 66, then US 441 to Gatlinburg entrance. From Asheville, N.C. (about 40 miles away), take I-40 west to US 19, then US 441, to park's southern entrance near Cherokee, N.C. For a scenic, low-speed approach, take the 469-mile Blue Ridge Parkway that connects Virginia's Shenandoah National Park with Great Smoky. Airports: Knoxville and Asheville.

When to Go

All-year park. In summer and in fall (when spectacular foliage draws huge crowds), time your visit to midweek, and arrive early. Visitor centers open year-round.

How to Visit

On a 1-day visit, take the **Newfound Gap Road** to **Clingmans Dome** and get the best overview of the park by seeing it from the highest point. The best second-day activity is the **Cades Cove Loop Road,** a chance to drive or cycle through pioneer history. For a longer stay, focus on the self-guided nature trails and drives, which get you away from the crowds and show you the flora and fauna.

found only here. Shrubs take over in places, creating tree-free zones called heath balds, laurel slicks (because of the shiny leaves), or just plain hells (because they are so hard to get through).

The tangle of brush and trees forms a close-packed array of air-breathing leaves. The water and hydrocarbons exuded by the leaves produce the filmy "smoke" that gives the mountains their name. Air pollution in recent years has added microscopic sulfate particles to the haze, cutting visibility back about 60 percent since the 1950s. The pollution has also affected the park's red spruce stand—the southern Appalachians' largest. And insects are destroying the Fraser fir, the spruce's high-altitude companion.

The park also preserves the humble churches, cabins, farmhouses, and barns of the mountain people who began settling here in the late 1700s. When the park was founded, most people left. But some chose to stay and live out their lives here.

Newfound Gap Road to Clingmans Dome

40-45 miles; a half to full day

Newfound Gap Road, which begins at 2,000 feet and ascends to 5,048 feet, connects the park's major visitor centers, **Sugarlands** and **Oconaluftee.** The road, passing from lowland hard-wood timber to high-altitude spruce-fir forests, gives you a vertical trip that is ecologically equivalent to a journey from Georgia to Canada. Be prepared for rain on almost any day. A clear day below can be a day of mist and fog on high. From Sugarlands (for an Oconaluftee start, reverse the order below), stop after 5 miles at **Chimneys,** a fine picnic spot. Stretch your legs on the ¾-mile self-guided

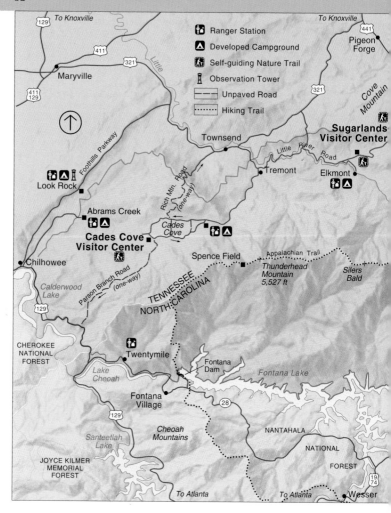

To Knoxville
129
411
321
Maryville
411
129
Little

Ranger Station
Developed Campground
Self-guiding Nature Trail
Observation Tower
Unpaved Road
Hiking Trail

To Knoxville
441
Pigeon
Forge

Townsend
321
Cove
Mountain

Sugarlands
Visitor Center

Look Rock

Little River Road

Tremont
Elkmont

Rich Mtn. Road (one-way)

Abrams Creek

Cades Cove
Visitor Center

Cades
Cove

Spence Field

Appalachian Trail

Thunderhead
Mountain
5,527 ft

Silers
Bald

Chilhowee

Calderwood
Lake

129

Parson Branch Road (one-way)

TENNESSEE
NORTH CAROLINA

Twentymile

Fontana
Dam

Fontana Lake

Lake
Cheoah

Fontana
Village

28

129

Cheoah
Mountains

NANTAHALA

Santeetlah
Lake

JOYCE KILMER
MEMORIAL
FOREST

CHEROKEE
NATIONAL
FOREST

NATIONAL

FOREST

19
74

To Atlanta
To Atlanta
Wesser

Cove Hardwood Nature Trail. Then return to the car for a short drive to the **Chimney Tops Overlooks,** which offer views of the double summits the Cherokee called Duniskwal-guni ("forked antlers").

Here you can extend your stop with a hike on the steep **Chimney Tops Trail** (4-mile round-trip) through an old-growth forest and up 1,335 feet to the sheer cliffs named the Chimneys. Depending on your time and stamina, you can also get out of the car and hike at the next overlook, where a trailhead leads to a steep climb to **Alum Cave Bluffs,** site of a 19th-century commercial alum mine and reputedly a source of saltpeter for Civil War gunpowder. The trail begins with an easy 2½-mile trail along a tree-bordered creek to **Arch Rock,** a tunnel made by eons of erosion. The trees include towering 200-year-old eastern hemlocks. This is a magnificent spot for a spring wildflower hike graced by the songs of nesting warblers. You can return to your car or continue on a steep ¾-mile ascent to the bluffs.

Back in the car continue on to **Newfound Gap** (5,048 feet), through which runs the Tennessee-North Carolina state line and a long leg of the Appalachian Trail. From the overlook here, on a clear day, you can see **Mt. LeConte** (6,593 feet) and your next stop, **Clingmans Dome.** The 7-mile **Clingmans Dome Road** veers sharply off here and winds through a spruce-fir forest to a parking lot.

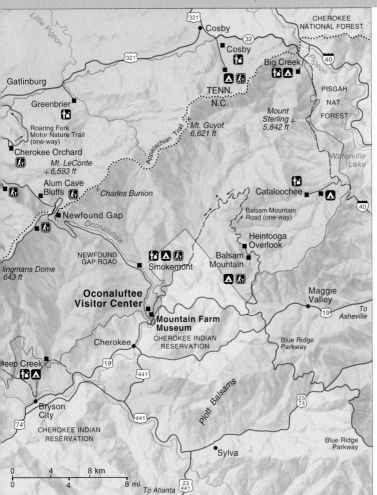

Little Pigeon

321
Cosby
32
Cosby

CHEROKEE
NATIONAL FOREST

321
Gatlinburg

Greenbrier

Big Creek

Pigeon

40

PISGAH

Mount
Sterling +
5,842 ft

NAT.

FOREST

Roaring Fork
Motor Nature Trail
(one-way)
Cherokee Orchard

TENN.
N.C.

Mt. Guyot
6,621 ft

Appalachian Trail

Waterville
Lake

Mt. LeConte
+ 6,593 ft

Alum Cave
Bluffs

Charles Bunion

Cataloochee

40

Newfound Gap

Oconaluftee

Balsam Mountain
Road (one-way)

Heintooga
Overlook

NEWFOUND
GAP ROAD
Smokemont

Balsam
Mountain

lingmans Dome
643 ft

**Oconaluftee
Visitor Center**

Maggie
Valley

19

To
Asheville

**Mountain Farm
Museum**

Cherokee

CHEROKEE INDIAN
RESERVATION

Blue Ridge
Parkway

eep Creek

19

Bryson
City

74

CHEROKEE INDIAN
RESERVATION

441

441

Plott Balsams

23
74

Blue Ridge
Parkway

Sylva

0   4   8 km

0   4   8 mi

To Atlanta

23
441

Carter Shields Cabin in Cades Cove

Summer sunlight on a Smokies creek

There begins a steep ½-mile trail ending at a spiral ramp. It leads to a lookout tower at the top of the 6,643-foot dome, the highest point in the park, where you get either a panoramic view or a sense of floating on a sea of churning clouds. From here retrace the route to Sugarlands or, depending on time and destination, continue on to Oconaluftee Visitor Center. The **Mountain Farm Museum,** a cluster of farm buildings gathered from their original locations within the park, stands adjacent to the visitor center. Pioneer-costumed park employees, playing farmstead roles, give demonstrations spring through October. (Between May and October, at **Mingus Mill,** a miller produces cornmeal and flour on an ingenious water-run turbine.)

Cades Cove Loop Road

11 miles; at least a half day

Follow **Little River** and **Laurel**

Creek Roads from Sugarlands Visitor Center to the **Cades Cove** loop road. Cades Cove traces its history to 1819, when, under a treaty with the Cherokee Indians, settlers cleared the broad, high valley. By 1850 more than 680 people were living there. They left behind structures that evolved into an open-air museum whose galleries are sites along the paved, 11-mile one-way loop road. Official sites are well marked. But you may find yourself making unofficial stops to admire the quietude, to watch white-tailed deer bounding across the valley, or to spot curious woodchucks popping out of their burrows along the road.

The first stop is **John Oliver Place,** site 3. The cabin was built with hand-hewn logs. Stand on the porch and look down the long, green-carpeted valley that drew the family to this place, the edge of the American world in 1826. **Primitive Baptist Church,** site 4, is skipped by some visitors because it lies on a two-way dirt road off the loop road. Don't miss it. The plain church guards a small graveyard. Time has made many stones nameless, but the past still can be read on them. The church shut down during the Civil War because, a letter says, "we was Union people and the Rebels was too strong here in Cades Cove." **Methodist Church,** site 5, had a door for men and another for women and children. During services, the separation was enforced in the pews by a barrier.

Just past the church is **Hyatt Lane,** an old road out of Cades Cove and today a shortcut that slices off a big piece of the tour. Stay on the loop road and continue to **Missionary Baptist Church,** site 7, formed in 1839 by expelled members of the Primitive Baptist Church. Because the congregation split between Union and Confederacy sympathizers, this church also closed during the Civil War.

Continue on the road, past **Rich Mountain Road,** site 8. Save this for another day. The gravel road, laid over an Indian trail, goes up **Rich Mountain** and provides a spectacular backward glance at Cades Cove before exiting the park. Also skip **Cooper Road Trail,** site 9, a onetime wagon road that is now a 13-mile hiking trail ending outside the park. Ahead on the right is a short, two-way road to the next stops, **Abrams Falls,** site 10, and **Elijah Oliver Place,** site 11.

If you take the offshoot road, you come to a parking lot and a choice: a 2-hour, 2½-mile hike up to stunning Abrams Falls, or a ½-mile hike to another farmstead. Or continue your drive along the loop road to the next offshoot, which leads to **Cable Mill,** site 12. At the **Cades Cove Visitor Center** artifacts and pictures depict life in Cades Cove which helps visitors connect intellectually and emotionally with the people who called this serene valley their home. Now leave the center and wander about, reliving the life that centered on the old mill.

Other buildings—a blacksmith shop, a large cantilever barn, a smokehouse—were imported from elsewhere in the park. Check at the visitor center for schedules of farm-life demonstrations; they include the making of sorghum molasses: a horse-powered mill squeezes juice from the stalks, which is then boiled down in an open-air vat. Just beyond the Cable Mill area is **Parson Branch Road,** which can take you out of the park—and the 20th century. The narrow winding one-way dirt road (sometimes closed by weather) was carved out of wilderness about 1838. The

Rhododendron along Clingmans Dome

Raccoon in a yellow poplar

8-mile trip to US 129 can take an hour. If prudence keeps you on the loop road, your next stop will be **Tipton Place,** site 17. Built by Hamp Tipton shortly after the Civil War, it later became the home of a blacksmith, who put up his shop nearby.

Drive on to the last stop, **Carter Shields Cabin,** site 18. Log cabins like this would be succeeded by board houses, which arrived with lumbering in the early 1900s.

Hikes & Drives

Self-guided nature trails begin with an honor system document rack. You drop in a quarter and pluck out a leaflet keyed to numbered stops. **Balsam Mountain Trail** is the easiest climbing trail in the park, a 1½-mile loop from Balsam Mountain Campground. The trail gives you a short lesson in the identification of trees and, especially in spring, wildflowers. **Laurel Falls Trail** is paved. The 2½-mile round-trip trail, which starts on Little River Road near Elkmont, winds through thickets of mountain-laurel and rhododendron to one of the park's many waterfalls.

For a longer stay in the park, try some of the more rugged trails. The

Two of at least 400 black bears living in the park

White-tailed buck, often seen at dawn and dusk

Slimy salamander, one of park's 23 kinds

most rewarding hike is to Mt. LeConte, at 6,593 feet the park's third highest peak. The shortest (though steepest) way up is via **Alum Cave Trail,** which starts at Newfound Gap Road (see Newfound Gap Road tour). Here begins a steep 5-mile climb to the summit of LeConte. At one point the trail skirts a cliff face so sheer that hikers must grasp a cable to make their way up. For the motorist, there are also self-guided nature trails using roads. The **Roaring Fork Motor Nature Trail,** 4 miles from Gatlinburg off **Cherokee Orchard Road,** is a 5-mile curvy, one-way road with a well-warranted 10 mph speed limit. About a mile before the trail begins, you will see the **Noah "Bud" Ogle Place** on your right. A ¾-mile path takes you around the remains of a farm—a mill, a barn, and the historic Ogle family house.

At the Roaring Fork trail, avail yourself of the self-guiding booklet that suggests scenic stops. The road climbs a hill that provides, on clear days, a splendid view of **Sugarland** and **Cove Mountains.** Along the roadside is an old-growth hemlock forest. Here and there are moldering chestnut logs, poignant reminders of the blight that struck down the one-time forest king.

Information & Activities

Headquarters
Gatlinburg, Tennessee 37738. Phone (865) 436-1200. www.nps.gov/grsm

Seasons & Accessibility
Park open year-round. The road to Clingmans Dome and some unpaved roads closed in winter.

Visitor & Information Centers
Open daily all year: Sugarlands, on US 441 south of Gatlinburg, Tenn., entrance; Oconaluftee, on US 441 north of Cherokee, N.C., entrance; Cades Cove Visitor Center, near Townsend, Tenn., entrance; enter off US 321, east of Townsed. Call park headquarters for information.

Facilities for Disabled
Visitor centers and rest rooms are wheelchair accessible. The Sugarlands Valley Nature Trail ($\frac{1}{4}$ mile south of the Sugarlands Visitor Center) was custom built for visitors with visual or mobility impairments. Clingmans Dome and Laurel Falls Trails are paved but steep; negotiable with assistance only. Free brochure.

Things to Do
Free naturalist-led activities: nature walks (day and evening), children's and campfire programs, pioneer exhibits and demonstrations, slide talks. Also, annual festivals, auto tape tour, hiking, bicycling, fishing (permit needed), horseback riding (several stables in park).

Overnight Backpacking
Permit required; available free from visitor centers and ranger stations. You can reserve rationed sites and shelters up to 30 days in advance; write Backcountry Permit, c/o park, or call (865) 436-1231.

Campgrounds
Ten campgrounds, most with a 7-day limit. **Cades Cove, Elkmont,** and **Smokemont** open all year ; 7-day limit mid-May to Oct. 31; other times 14-day limit; reservations required for Cades Cove, Smokemont and Elkmont May 15 to Oct. 31; available through the National Parks Reservation Service (see page 11). Other campgrounds open mid-March to Oct. 31, first come, first served. Fees $12-$17 per night. No showers. Tent and RV sites; no hookups. Seven group campgrounds; reservations recommended; contact park headquarters.

Hotels, Motels, & Inns
(unless otherwise noted, rates are for 2 persons in a double room, high season)
INSIDE THE PARK:
LeConte Lodge (atop Mt. LeConte; access by hiking trail) 250 Apple Valley Rd., Sevierville, Tenn. 37862. (865) 429-5704. 10 cabins, no electricity, shared bathrooms. $77, includes 2 meals. Open late March to late Nov.
OUTSIDE THE PARK:
In Bryson City, N.C. 28713:
Hemlock Inn (on Galbraith Creek Rd., off US 19) P.O. Drawer EE. (828) 488-2885. 22 units: rooms $137-$186, cottages $132-$173, includes 2 meals. Rest. Open mid-April through Oct.
In Cherokee, N.C. 28719:
Best Western Great Smokies Inn (US 441 and Acquoni Rd.) P.O. Box 1809. (800) 528-1234 or (828) 497-2020. 152 units. $89. AC, pool, rest.
Holiday Inn Cherokee (US 19 West) P.O. Box 1929. (828) 497-9181. 154 units. $99-$130. AC, pool, rest.
In Fontana Dam, N.C. 28733:
Fontana Village Resort (N.C. 28) P.O. Box 68. (800) 849-2258 or (828) 498-2211. 90 rooms, $79; 120 cottages with kitchens, $59-$209. AC, pool, rest.
In Gatlinburg, Tenn. 37738:
Buckhorn Inn 2140 Tudor Mountain Rd. (865) 436-4668. 6 rooms, 4 cottages, 2 guest houses. $115-$250. Includes breakfast. AC, rest. **Gillette Motel** (172 Airport Rd.) P.O. Box 231. (800) 437-0815 or (865) 436-5601. 80 units. $75-$95. AC, pool. **Holiday Inn of Gatlinburg** (520 Airport Rd.) P.O. Box 1130. (800) 435-9201 in Tenn. or (865) 436-9201. 400 units. $119-$129. AC, pool, rest. **Park Vista Hotel** (Airport Rd.) P.O. Box 30. (800) 421-7275 or (865) 436-9211. 312 units. $109-$149. AC, pool, rest.

For other accommodations in Gatlinburg, call the Chamber of Commerce at (800) 822-1998 or (865) 436-4178.

Excursions

Pisgah National Forest
Asheville, North Carolina

The Blue Ridge Parkway traverses this mountainous forest with slopes of mixed hardwoods, azaleas, and rhododendrons, rocky gorges, and delicate waterfalls. Outstanding in spring and fall. Contains three wilderness areas and Mt. Mitchell, the highest peak east of the Mississippi. 495,712 acres. Facilities include 448 campsites, hiking, fishing, horseback riding, hunting, picnic areas, scenic drives, swimming. Open all year; most campsites open spring to late fall. Visitor center on US 276, about 50 miles from Great Smoky Mountains NP. (828) 257-4200.

Nantahala National Forest
Asheville, North Carolina

The hardwood-covered mountains here contain deep, narrow valleys, canyons, and waterfalls. Noted for azaleas, rhododendrons. Contains three wilderness areas. 528,782 acres. Facilities include 175 campsites, hiking, boating, boat ramps, fishing, horseback riding, hunting, picnic areas, scenic drives, handicapped access. Open all year; most campsites open spring to late fall. Adjoins Great Smoky Mountains NP on the south. (828) 257-4200.

Breaks Interstate Park
Breaks, Virginia

Russell Fork cuts through the Pine Mountains here, creating Breaks Canyon, the "Grand Canyon of the South." Features class VI white water. Two rhododendron species provide long blooming season, mid-May through June; fall leaves peak mid-October. Gospel music festival Labor Day weekend. 4,600 acres. Facilities include 138 campsites, cottages and motel units, visitor center, food service, hiking, boating, boat ramp, fishing, picnic areas, scenic drives, swimming, handicapped access. Open all year; most facilities available April to mid-December. On Va. 80, about 190 miles from Great Smoky Mountains NP. (540) 865-4413.

Big South Fork National River & Recreation Area

Oneida, Tennessee

The Big South Fork of the Cumberland River bisects the Cumberland Plateau, yielding white water as well as calm stretches, sandstone cliffs, waterfalls, and natural arches. 116,000 acres, part in Ky. Facilities: 235 campsites, hiking, horseback riding, boating, boat ramp, fishing, swimming, hunting, picnic areas. Open all year. Off US 27, about 100 miles northwest of Great Smoky Mountains NP. (423) 879-4890.

Cherokee National Forest

Cleveland, Tennessee

This rugged mountain backcountry is densely wooded with mixed pines and hardwoods, azaleas, mountain laurels. 635,000 acres. 29 campgrounds, hiking, boating, boat ramp, fishing, hunting, 30 picnic sites, scenic drives, swimming. Open all year; most campgrounds open May-October. Adjoins Great Smoky Mountains NP on northeast and southwest. (423) 476-9700.

Chattahoochee National Forest

Gainesville, Georgia

This hardwood forest encompasses a mix of terrain—lakes, streams, valleys, mountains, and piedmont plateau. Contains ten wilderness areas and a stretch of the Chattooga Wild and Scenic River with Tallullah Gorge. Also, Brasstown Bald, the state's highest mountain at 4,784 feet. 750,000 acres. Facilities include over 25 campgrounds, food service, hiking, sailing, boat ramp, fishing, hunting, picnic areas, scenic drives, swimming, handicapped access. Open year-round; campsites open May-September. On US 441, about 65 miles from Great Smoky Mountains NP. (770) 297-3000.

View west from Hot Springs Mountain Tower

Hot Springs

Arkansas

Established March 4, 1921

5,549 acres

Most national parks cover hundreds of thousands of acres, are far from city streets, and keep natural resources away from commercial users…
But not Hot Springs. This smallest of national parks is centered in a city that has made an industry out of tapping and dispensing the park's major resource: mineral-rich waters of hot springs.

The heart of this peculiar park is Central Avenue, the main street of Hot Springs, Arkansas. Rising above Central Avenue is Hot Springs Mountain, from which the waters flow. The mountain's lower western side once was coated with tufa, a milky-colored, porous rock formed of minerals

deposited from the hot springs' constant cascade.

When Hot Springs prospered as a health spa in the mid-19th century, promoters covered, piped, and diverted the springs into Central Avenue bathhouses. They also prettified the slope by covering it with tons of dirt and planting grass and shrubs. "Ever since then," a longtime Hot Springs resident says, "it's been afflicted by eastern landscape architects who can't stand the sight of rocks."

The park calls itself the "oldest area in the national park system" because in 1832, 40 years before Yellowstone became the first national park, President Andrew Jackson set aside the hot springs as a special reservation. The federal land became a national park in 1921. By then Hot Springs had long been famous as a spa where people "took the

duce spectacular foliage. Winter is usually short and mild; four-petaled bluets, the first of many wildflowers, appear in February.

How to Visit
Walk **Central Avenue's Bathhouse Row,** then continue north to explore Hot Springs on the genteel trails of an urban hillside. To see a more rugged side of the park, hike the woodland trails of **Gulpha Gorge.**

Bathhouse Row
4 city blocks; 2 hours

In the early years of this century, elegant buildings lined a stretch of **Central Avenue** dubbed **Bathhouse Row.** In later years, as medical science's faith in hot springs faded, so did the bathhouses. But you can still enjoy the mystique of taking the waters. First visit the **Hot Springs National Park Visitor Center** (in the former Fordyce Bathhouse), a restored "temple of health and beauty" adorned with stained-glass windows and statuary. In rooms full of gleaming plumbing and luxurious tubs, you walk through a museum of the ritual, which in its full form involved three weeks of daily baths and massage. The Buckstaff is the Row's only bathhouse still offering a traditional bath. (Some hotels also have baths; ask for information at the visitor center.)

waters," seeking relief from bunions, rheumatism, and other afflictions.

The park preserves the springs' "recharge zone," slopes where rain and snow soak into the ground, and the "discharge zone," which contains 47 springs belonging to the park. Each day about 850,000 gallons of water—at 143°F—flow from the springs into a complex piping and reservoir system. This supplies water to commercial baths and to park-maintained "jug fountains," where people flock daily to fill containers with the odorless, fresh-tasting, chemical-free water.

How to Get There
From Little Rock, about 55 miles west on US 70 to Ark. 7; from the south, Ark. 7; from the west, US 70 or US 270. Airport: Little Rock.

When to Go
All-year park. Summers are hot and July is crowded. Try the late fall, when mountains around Hot Springs pro-

Springs flowing over Tufa Terrace

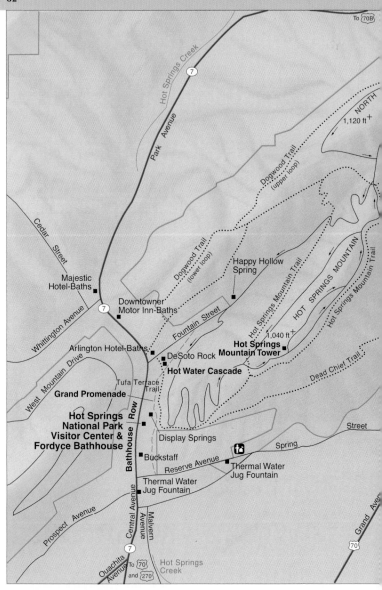

Hot Springs

a half mile; 2 hours

At the foot of the mountain (the corner of Central Avenue and Fountain Street) look for **DeSoto Rock,** a huge boulder that commemorates both the Indians who named this "place of the hot waters" and the explorer Hernando De Soto. He and his party are supposed to have bathed in the waters in 1541, beginning a tourist tradition. Head up the trail to **The Hot Water Cascade,** created in 1982 when decades of turf were cleared away so that a hot spring could again be seen. The water flowing here began its journey as long as 4,000 years ago when it fell as rain and seeped through fractures. Heated deep in the earth, the water returns through the faults in the rock of the mountain in a year or two, hardly enough time to cool off.

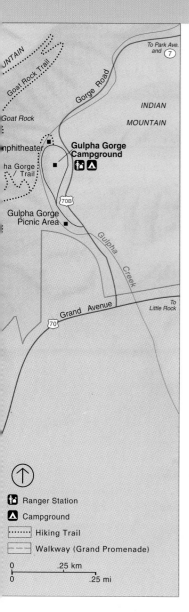

Tiled tub in Fordyce Bathhouse

a landscaped brick walkway that runs behind the bathhouses.

The springs are sealed off—and thus kept sterile—by locked green bunkers that jut out of the lawns carpeting the slope. When some of the hillside springs were open, men and women discreetly took turns soaking their feet at one of them; at another, people cooked eggs. To see more of the famous hot water bubbling out of the earth, follow the trail to **Open Springs** behind the **Maurice Bathhouse.** The two springs flow into a collecting pool, where you can safely touch the water.

Go up the stairs and finish your trek on the Grand Promenade. The walkway, which took 30 years to build and landscape, serves as a pleasant transition between the formal architecture of the bathhouses and the trails of the wooded hillside.

Gulpha Gorge

1 ⅗ miles round-trip; 2 hours

To find the more traditional terrain of a national park, leave **Hot Springs** on Ark. 7 heading north and turn right onto US 70B for Gulpha Gorge Campground, about 3 miles from downtown Hot Springs. Near the amphitheater pick up the **Gulpha Gorge Trail,** which crosses **Gulpha Creek** on stepping-stones and courses a woodland rich in dogwood and redbud; in spring and early summer wildflowers flank the trail. In less than a mile the trail intersects with another up to **Goat Rock,** a fine overlook for viewing the mountains around the city. In nearby quarries, Indians once mined novaculite for making arrowheads and spearpoints; under the name Arkansas Stone it is used today as a whetstone.

Map legend:

- ▥ Ranger Station
- ◭ Campground
- ┄┄┄ Hiking Trail
- ╌╌╌ Walkway (Grand Promenade)

0   .25 km
0   .25 mi

The tufa created by the cascade's splashing waters is building up at the rate of ⅛ inch a year. The brilliant blue-green algae is the only plant species that can survive in the hot waters. So can ostracods, a crustacean about the size of a sand grain found in some of the other springs.

Near The Hot Water Cascade is the **Tufa Terrace Trail,** which takes you by many concealed springs. To get there, cross the **Grand Promenade,**

Information & Activities

Headquarters
P.O. Box 1860, Hot Springs, Arkansas 71902. Phone (501) 624-3383. www.nps.gov/hosp

Seasons & Accessibility
Park open year-round. Bathing facilities open generally Monday through Saturday all year.

Visitor & Information Centers
Hot Springs National Park Visitor Center, in the middle of Bathhouse Row. Open daily except Thanksgiving, Christmas, and New Year's Day. For information call (501) 624-3383.

Entrance Fee
None, but fees charged for the concessioner-operated thermal baths.

Pets
Not allowed in buildings; otherwise permitted on leashes.

Facilities for Disabled
Visitor center is fully accessible to wheelchairs; the Thermal Feature and the Bathhouse Row Tours are partially accessible.

Things to Do
Free naturalist-led activities: hikes and bathhouse tours, campfire programs at Gulpha Gorge Campground. Also available, audiovisual and interpretive exhibits, hiking, horseback riding; six bathing facilities offering thermal baths, whirlpools, steam cabinets, hot packs, massages.

Special Advisory
● Bathing in thermal waters not recommended for people with certain ailments; consult your doctor if in doubt.

Overnight Backpacking
Permitted in campground only; see below.

Campground
One campground, **Gulpha Gorge,** with 14-day limit. Open all year on first-come, first-served basis. Fees $10 per night. No showers. Tent and RV sites; no hookups.

Hotels, Motels, & Inns
(unless otherwise noted, rates are for 2 persons in a double room, high season)
Arlington Resort Hotel & Spa 239 Central Ave., Hot Springs, Arkansas 71901. (800) 643-1502 or (501) 623-7771. 484 units. $58-$295. AC, 2 pools, 3 restaurants.
Budget Inn 1871 E. Grand Ave., Hot Springs, Ark. 71901. (800) 238-4891 or (501) 624-4436. 50 units. $55-$89. AC, pool, restaurant.
Buena Vista Resort (off Ark. 7) 201 Aberina St., Hot Springs, Ark. 71913. (800) 255-9030 or (501) 525-1321. 50 units with kitchenettes. $106. AC, pool. Open year-round.
Austin Hotel 305 Malvern Ave., Hot Springs, Ark. 71901. (800) 445-8667 or (501) 623-6600. 200 units. $79-$89. AC, pool, restaurant.
Lake Hamilton Resort 2803 Albert Pike, Hot Springs, Ark. 71914. (800) 426-3184 or (501) 767-5511. 104 units. $104-$119. AC, pool, restaurant.
SunBay Resort 4810 Central Ave., Hot Springs, Ark. 71913. (800) 468-0055 or (501) 525-4691. 109 condos. $175. AC, pool, restaurant.
Williams House Bed & Breakfast Inn 420 Quapaw Ave., Hot Springs, Ark. 71901. (800) 756-4635 or (501) 624-4275. 5 units. $70-$90, includes breakfast. AC.

For additional accommodations, write or call the Hot Springs Convention and Visitors Bureau, P.O. Box K, Hot Springs, Ark. 71902. (800) 543-2284 or (501) 321-2277.

Excursions

Ouachita National Forest

Hot Springs, Arkansas

Pine-hardwood forest blankets the Ouachita Mountains, and water abounds in lakes, springs, waterfalls, and the Ouachita River. Contains six wilderness areas. 1,762,947 acres, part in Oklahoma. Facilities: 657 campsites, hiking, boating, boat ramp, fishing, horseback riding, hunting, picnic areas, water sports, handicapped access. Open all year, including many campsites. Entrance on US 270, about 5 miles west of Hot Springs NP. (501) 321-5202.

Holla Bend National Wildlife Refuge

Dardanelle, Arkansas

Wintering bald eagles and immense flocks of migratory waterfowl share this site along the Arkansas River. 7,055 acres. Facilities include hiking, boating, boat ramp, fishing, hunting, scenic drives. Open year-round, dawn to dusk. Off Arkansas Hwy. 7, about 60 miles from Hot Springs NP. (501) 229-4300.

Ozark National Forest

Russellville, Arkansas

Oak, hickory, and pine cover the high Ozark mountain bluffs. Many streams and lakes offer excellent fishing. Features Blanchard Springs Caverns and five wilderness areas. 1.2 million acres. Facilities: 335 campsites, 8 cabins, hiking, boating, boat ramp, fishing, hunting, horseback riding, picnic areas, scenic drives, water sports, handicapped access. Open year-round, including some of the campsites. Information in Russellville on US 64, about 80 miles from Hot Springs NP. (501) 968-2354.

Buffalo National River

Harrison, Arkansas

This park preserves 135 miles of the wild Buffalo River and adjacent lands. White water on upper river, more benign stretches on lower. 95,700 acres. 14 campgrounds, food services, boating, fishing, hunting, picnic areas, swimming. Open all year, including most campsites. Headquarters at Harrison on Ark. 7, about 110 miles from Hot Springs NP. (870) 741-5443.

Kayaker on Five Finger Bay

Isle Royale

Michigan

Authorized March 3, 1931

571,790 acres

Out of the vastness of Lake Superior rises an island known more for its immigrant wolves and moose than for its splendors as a park. But the people who discover Isle Royale treat this isolated realm like no other park: Isle Royale visitors typically stay there 3½ days, while the average visit to a national park is about 4 hours.

Most people get to the 45-mile-long island aboard a commercial or Park Service boat. As soon as they touch land in this wilderness park, they are on their own. They must pack in what they need and carry out their refuse.

This is rough, untamed country. Trails may be fogbound and muddy. Blackflies and mosquitoes may descend upon hikers in swarms. And, because campsites cannot be reserved, a backpacker is never certain where the day's trek may end.

"It's not like deciding to drive into Yellowstone, see Old Faithful, and drive out," a ranger says. In an entire year Isle Royale gets fewer people than Yellowstone sees in a day.

Everyone who lands on Isle Royale—even day-trippers—must stop near dockside to hear a ranger talk about low-impact hiking and camping. For example, water must be boiled for 2 minutes or filtered; chemical purifiers will not wipe out tapeworm cysts.

Human hikers share trails with wolves and moose, the island's most famous inhabitants. They are descendants of the mainlanders that made Isle Royale an unexpected ark—moose presumably by swimming to it in the

Royale is 56 miles from the Michigan mainland, 18 miles from Minnesota's shore, 22 miles from Grand Portage. Airports: Houghton, Michigan; Duluth, Minnesota.

When to Go

Late June to September; park closes from November 1 to mid-April. Mosquitoes, blackflies, and gnats are most pesky in June and July. Summer can be cool (40°F at night). Blueberries ripen in late July and Aug.

How to Visit

Although 1-day visits are feasible at **Rock Harbor** or **Windigo,** you need a longer stay to appreciate the wild beauty of **Isle Royale.** A 1-day visitor must sandwich a couple of hours of sightseeing between boat arrival and departure. Voyages take 2 to 6½ hours, depending on the starting point. The best way to see the park is to backpack to campgrounds strung along the park's 165 miles of trails. Noncampers who plan well ahead can reserve lodgings at Rock Harbor and explore on tour boats and on foot.

Windigo

a full day

Take the *Wenonah,* a concessioner passenger boat that makes the trip from Grand Portage, Minn., in 3 hours, the shortest from any port serving Isle Royale. On the way into fjordlike **Washington Harbor,** watch for the buoy marking the resting place

early 1900s; wolves likely by walking across the ice in 1949. Scientists have been studying the interplay of predator and prey since 1958.

On the trails, all you can expect to see are the animals' tracks and droppings, although quietly grazing moose do surprise hikers, particularly in lush meadows. On beaver ponds you may spot the rippling Vs of the ponds' creators. In campgrounds watch for fox looking for a hand-out. Remember: Feeding the animals is illegal. It is not healthy for them and increases the likelihood that they will scavenge for people's food and equipment.

How to Get There

Make reservations well in advance for passenger boats from Houghton or Copper Harbor, Mich., or Grand Portage, Minn. The port you pick will determine the length of your visit. Interpretive programs are held aboard the *Ranger III* between Houghton and Isle Royale. For information about boats and charter seaplane service, see **Information & Activities** p. 71. Isle

Backpacking along Greenstone Ridge Trail

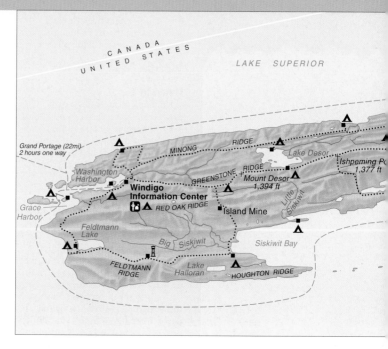

of the *America*, a 183-foot lake steamer that went down in 1928; the wreck rests at a sharp angle, its ghostly bow about 2 feet below the surface. Scuba divers, with permits, frequently prowl this and the other nine major wrecks around Isle Royale.

As soon as you land, check at the ranger station for the next **Windigo Nature Walk,** a 1-hour ramble around this western entrance to the park explores many of the area's natural and cultural resources.

If you miss the ranger-guided walk, try the **Windigo Nature Trail,** a 1¼-mile loop that shows the power that Lake Superior exerts on an island molded by fire and ice. You'll learn how the island was born: As glacial ice retreated some 10,000 years ago, Isle Royale rose above what would become Lake Superior. Gouges in the barren rocks became lakes. Early migrants—lichens, mosses, birdborne seeds—drifted into cracks and crannies, beginning the long work of building soil. Animals also found their way onto Isle Royale, and an ecosystem emerged. It still evolves, with some animals appearing, as did the wolves and moose, and some animals disappearing, as did caribou and coyotes. Be sure to take the short side trip to the fenced-in **Moose Exclosure,** which shows how differently a forest grows when moose don't munch on it. Your stay—about 2½ hours—will depend on your boat's schedule. So you may have time to stroll westward a while along **Feldtmann Lake Trail.** This shoreline stretch gives you a view of **Beaver Island** and the harbor's forested northern shore.

Rock Harbor

1 or more days

A 1-day visit to **Rock Harbor,** the park's eastern gateway, can be tight. The voyage aboard *Isle Royale Queen III* from Copper Harbor takes about 4½ hours. You get a quick glimpse of the Rock Harbor area while looking over your shoulder to make sure the *Queen* is still at dock.

If you can stay longer and aren't a backpacker, Rock Harbor offers many relatively easy sojourns. But make advance reservations at the Rock Harbor Lodge (see **Information & Activities** p. 71). From there you can set out for a choice of adventures.

Begin with a walk along **Stoll Trail,** a 4-mile loop that starts at Rock Harbor

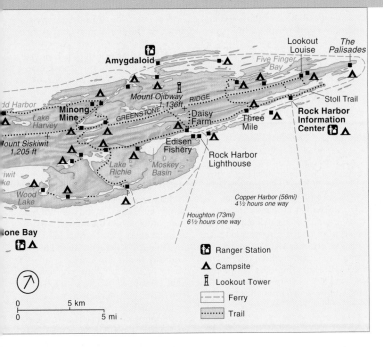

Bull moose feeding on water plants

Lodge and winds through forest and plank-pathed bog. After about ½ mile you'll come to an area where Indians once chipped away, stone on stone, at shallow mining pits to extract outcrops of copper. Unmarked, these pits are hard to detect. Mining here began around 2500 BC and continued for at least 1,500 years. The copper, traded along the upper Mississippi Valley, was formed into fishhooks, knives, and awls. More than a thousand mining pits have been found on Isle Royale.

Continue another 1½ miles, mostly along a rocky shore, to craggy **Scoville Point,** a fine spot for viewing some of the roughly 200 rocky islets that form the Isle Royale archipelago. On the way back you can switch to a branch trail that clings to the forested shore of **Tobin Harbor.** As the trail nears the lodge, you can see traces of **Smithwick Mine,** one of many relics of 19th-century mining ventures.

For a small round-trip fee you can take a shuttle boat from Rock Harbor across ½ mile of usually calm water to **Raspberry Island,** where a 1-mile trail introduces you to a boreal forest—white spruce, balsam fir, paper birch, aspen—and a bog. You'll also see a pit dug in 1848 in a vain search for copper. Bring a picnic.

For another fee a boat takes you on a ½-day, guided tour into history. The first stop is **Edisen Fishery,** which belonged to the late Pete Edisen, one of the last commercial fishermen on the island. The Park Service has restored his jumble of moss-chinked log cabins and shacks made of odds and ends. Here park employees demonstrate mid-20th-century fishing techniques for visitors, and their catch makes it to Rock Harbor Lodge. A short trail leads to the **Rock Harbor Lighthouse,** which contains a maritime exhibit. Erected in 1855 to guide ore ships, the lighthouse closed in 1859 when the mines shut down and reopened from 1874-79 during a second mining venture.

Into the Backcountry

3 to 5 days

To savor Isle Royale's isolated grandeur you must venture into the island's great beyond. Plan your 3- or 5-day stay around passenger boat arrivals and departures.

A sample 5-day itinerary: Arrive at Rock Harbor on Monday aboard the *Isle Royale Queen III* and hike southwest along the **Rock Harbor Trail** that courses forest, bog, and slanted rocks and roots. At not quite 2 miles, look for a sign to **Suzy's Cave,** about 80 yards up a side trail. The cave is an unusual, water-carved arch. At 3 miles is Three Mile Campground. Stay here and head out next morning on the 4½-mile shore trail to **Daisy Farm;** in this spot daisies have flourished where vegetables never would.

You can camp here for 3 days and start back early Friday to meet the returning *Queen.* Or you can split the hike into 2 days by spending Thursday night at Three Mile Campground.

While at Daisy Farm, climb **Mount Ojibway Trail,** a moderate 1¾-mile ascent up the 1,136-foot mountain, which is topped by a lookout tower. You're welcome to climb as far as the cabin, which houses a solar-powered, air-monitoring station. The Park Service runs a network of such monitors to check on air quality in 65 national park areas. From the tower take the **Greenstone Ridge Trail,** which runs about 40 miles along the backbone of the island. About 1½ miles west of the tower look for the wooden post marking the **Daisy Farm Trail,** which winds back to the campground.

The Wolves of Isle Royale

Visitors to Isle Royale probably will never see a gray wolf. Wolves avoid people, but live in packs as social animals. Only the dominant male and female—the alpha pair—mate and produce young. Others help protect and feed the pups born each spring.

Hundreds of thousands of wolves once roamed North America. But early settlers killed or drove away most of them. Today North America has only about 60,000 gray wolves, principally in Canada and Alaska.

When Isle Royale's first wolves crossed frozen Lake Superior in 1949, they found a growing moose herd with no natural predators. The wolves hunted the old, the young, and the sickly, preventing overpopulation. Both species prospered, the wolves increasing to 50 in 4 packs.

By 1980 a smaller moose herd provided few easy targets, and the wolf population began to fall. As moose

Gray wolf

numbers rose, the wolves' decline mysteriously continued. The wolf population had dropped to 14 by 1998, but had increased to 25 two years later and to 29 by March 2000, in spite of being highly inbred.

Information & Activities

Headquarters
800 East Lakeshore Dr., Houghton, MI 49931. Phone (906) 482-0984. www.nps.gov/isro

Seasons & Accessibility
Park open mid-April to October 31; can be reached by boat or seaplane only; full services available mid-June to Aug. 31. $4 per day fee. Weather and rough waters may delay departures; allow extra time. Mainland headquarters open year-round.

Boat & Seaplane Information
Reservations required (one to two months in advance suggested).

Write or call headquarters for boat schedule from Houghton to Rock Harbor. (The Park Service's boat, *Ranger III*, will transport boats 20 feet and under between those points.)

For boats from Copper Harbor to Rock Harbor, write to The Royale Line, Box 24, Copper Harbor, Mich. 49918, or call (906) 289-4437. For boats from Grand Portage to Windigo and Rock Harbor write to GPIR Transport Lines, 1507 N. First St., Superior, Wis. 54880, or call (715) 392-2100. For seaplane information, write to Isle Royale Seaplane Serv., Box 371, Houghton, MI 49931, or call (906) 482-8850 in summer.

Visitor & Information Centers
Windigo Information Center at west end of island, Rock Harbor Information Center at east end. Both open daily all season. Phone park headquarters for information.

Pets
Not allowed on boats or within park boundaries, which extend $4\frac{1}{2}$ miles into Lake Superior.

Facilities for Disabled
Park headquarters at Houghton, Rock Harbor Lodge, both information centers, and a campsite at Daisy Farm are wheelchair accessible. Boats to island require assistance.

Things to Do
Free naturalist-led nature walks and evening programs. Canoe tour; lighthouse, copper mine, and Edisen Fishery tours; and films. Also, boating (motorized crafts permitted on Lake Superior only), canoeing (rentals at Windigo and Rock Harbor; permit required), hiking, scuba diving, fishing (license required for Lake Superior only), boat cruises to the outer islands.

Special Advisories
● Expect sudden squalls and rough seas on Lake Superior; do not attempt to take boats under 20 feet across it. See above.
● No public phone service in the park.

Camping
Thirty-six backcountry camping areas; 1-day to 5-day limit. Camping allowed from mid-April through October. First come, first served. No fees. Permit required; available at ranger stations. Seventeen of the areas permit group camping; contact park headquarters for information.

Hotels, Motels, & Inns
(unless otherwise noted, rates are for 2 persons in a double room, high season)
INSIDE THE PARK:
Rock Harbor Lodge P.O. Box 605, Houghton, Mich. 49931. (906) 337-4993. From Oct. to April write c/o Mammoth Cave, Ky. 42259. (502) 773-2191. 80 units. $228 with meals. Cottages with kitchenettes $146. Rest. Open mid-June to mid-Sept.
OUTSIDE THE PARK:
In Copper Harbor, Mich. 49918:
Bella Vista Motel P.O. Box 26. (906) 289-4213. 30 units. $45-$55. Open May–Sept. **Keweenaw Mountain Lodge** US 41. (906) 289-4403. 42 units. $67. Cottages $82. Rest. Open May to mid-Oct. **Lake Fanny Hooe Resort & Campground** (off US 41) 505 2nd St. (800) 426-4451. 17 units. $63-$68.
In Grand Portage, Minn. 55605:
Grand Portage Lodge & Casino US 61 and Marina Rd. (800) 543-1384 or (218) 475-2401. 100 rooms. $64. Pool, rest.
In Houghton, Mich. 49931:
Best Western King's Inn 215 Shelden Ave. (800) 528-1234 or (906) 482-5000. 69 units. $69. AC, pool.
Best Western-Franklin Square Inn 820 Shelden Ave. (888) 487-1700 or (906) 487-1700. 104 units. $99. AC, pool, restaurant.

Excursions

Grand Portage National Monument
Grand Portage, Minnesota

In the 18th and 19th centuries, fur traders called voyageurs converged at this central supply depot of the North West Company. Visitors can tour the reconstructed stockade, great hall, kitchen, and canoe warehouse. Open mid-May to mid-October. The Grand Portage Trail, open all year, follows the route used by voyageurs who portaged their furs almost 9 miles to avoid the rapids and falls of the Pigeon River. 710 acres. Facilities: hiking, cross-country skiing, historic exhibits, handicapped access. On US 61, about 22 miles from Isle Royale NP by boat to Grand Portage. (218) 387-2788.

Chequamegon National Forest
Park Falls, Wisconsin

Wisconsin's largest national forest, Chequamegon (*sho-wah-ma-gon*) means "place of shallow water." Laced with many lakes, streams, and a river, the forest is a lush medley of spruce, maple, aspen, balsam, and pine. 850,000 acres. Facilities: campgrounds, boating, picnic areas, scenic drives, hunting, snowshoeing, nature study, birdwatching, photography. Headquarters on Wisc. 13, about 220 miles from Isle Royale NP (via Michigan-side ferry). Open year-round. (715) 762-2461.

Hiawatha National Forest
Escanaba, Michigan

In two units, this mixed evergreen-and-hardwood forest dotted with lakes descends to the shores of Lake Superior, Lake Michigan, and Lake Huron. Contains six wilderness areas and a section of the North Country National Scenic Trail. 860,000 acres. Facilities include 709 campsites, boating, fishing, horseback riding, hunting, scenic drives, winter sports, water sports, handicapped access. Open all year; most campsites open May 15-October. Info. at Rapid River, Manistique, Munising, and other locations. More than 300 miles from Isle Royale NP (via Michigan-side ferry). (906) 786-4062.

Apostle Islands National Lakeshore
Bayfield, Wisconsin

This national lakeshore encompasses 21 of the 22 remote, densely forested Apostle Islands and 12 miles of Lake Superior shoreline. Access to islands by boat; commercial and charter boats, charter fishing trips available. 42,140 acres. Facilities: 63 campsites (permits required). Activities include hiking, boating, fishing, picnic areas, winter sports, water sports, handicapped access. Open year-round, including campsites. Visitor center in Bayfield near Wisc. 13, about 250 miles from Isle Royale National Park (Michigan-side ferry). (715) 779-3397.

Pictured Rocks National Lakeshore
Munising, Michigan

Sandstone cliffs sculptured by nature into formations resembling castles and palisades give this first national lakeshore (1966) its name. The site also features extensive dunes and banks, sand beaches, forests, inland lakes, streams, and waterfalls. 71,400 acres. Facilities: 66 campsites, picnic areas, handicapped access. Activities include hiking, boating, backpacking, fishing, hunting, winter sports, water sports. Open year-round; campsites open mid-May to October. Visitor center at Munising on Mich. 28, about 335 miles from Isle Royale NP (via Michigan-side ferry). (906) 387-3700 or 2607.

Ottawa National Forest
Ironwood, Michigan

Lakes, streams, rivers, and waterfalls abound in this isolated ski-country forest. Also features three wilderness areas, Black River Harbor Recreation Area, and the North Country National Scenic Trail. 983,012 acres. Facilities include more than 485 campsites, hiking, canoeing and kayaking, boat ramp, fishing, hunting, picnic areas, winter sports, handicapped access. Open all year, campsites included. Visitor center in Watersmeet on US 2, about 140 miles from Isle Royale NP (via Michigan-side ferry). (906) 932-1330.

Torch tossing—no longer done—to demonstrate 19th-century way of lighting caves

Mammoth Cave

Kentucky

Established July 1, 1941

52,830 acres

Under a swath of Kentucky hills and hollows is a limestone labyrinth that became the heartland of a national park. The surface of Mammoth Cave National Park encompasses about 80 square miles. No one knows how big the underside is. More than 350 miles of the five-level cave system have been mapped, and new caves are continually being discovered. Two layers of stone underlie Mammoth's hilly woodlands. A sandstone and shale cap, as thick as 50 feet in places, acts as an umbrella over limestone ridges. The umbrella leaks at places called sinkholes, from which surface water makes its way underground, eroding the limestone into a honeycomb of caverns.

Mammoth, the world's largest known cave system, a United Nations World Heritage site and the core area of an International Biosphere Reserve, still is as "grand, gloomy, and peculiar" as it was when Stephen Bishop, a young slave and early guide, described it. By a flickering lard-oil lamp he found and mapped some of Mammoth's passages. Bishop died in 1857. His grave, like his life, is part of Mammoth; it lies in the Old Guide's Cemetery near the entrance.

Most visitors see the eerie beauty of the caverns on some of the 12 miles of passages available for tours. Rangers dispense geological lore and tell tales about real and imagined happenings 200 or 300 feet down. The tours are hikes inside the Earth; uphill stretches can be hard going for some visitors. Few seem frightened; people terrified

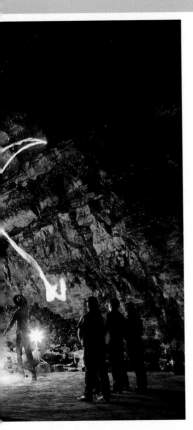

70 to the park. Don't be misled by signs proclaiming commercial "mammoth" caves. Airports: Nashville and Louisville.

When to Go

All-year park. Underground, all days are about the same; temperatures in interior passages fluctuate from the mid-50s to the low 60s. Summer brings the most people, and frequent tours are offered. Though there are fewer tours the rest of the year, they are less crowded.

How to Visit

The tours vary greatly; pick ones to fit your time and stamina. All require you to buy a ticket. Reservations are strongly advised in summer, on holidays, and on spring and fall weekends. For a 1/2-day visit, you might take the **Historic Tour,** which combines geology with Mammoth's rich history, or the **Introduction to Caving Tour.** If you plan to stay longer, consider the fairly strenuous **Grand Avenue Tour** (there are three steep hills, each nearly 90 feet high). To enjoy the caves safely and comfortably, wear shoes with nonskid soles and take a jacket. Top off your underground trips with a river trip or a walk on the **River Styx Spring Trail.**

The least arduous cave tour (¼ mile, 75 minutes) is the **Travertine Tour.** A modified version of the **Frozen Niagara Tour,** it has only 18 steps each way (plus an optional 49) and is designed for visitors who want a short and easy trip. The toughest challenge is the 5-mile, 6-hour, belly-crawling **Wild Cave Tour,** offered daily in summer and weekends year-round. By reservation.

Historic Tour

2 miles; 2 hours

You leave daylight and walk into dimly lit gloom at the **Historic Entrance,** discovered by pioneers in the 1790s and by Indians thousands of years before. Near the entrance, at the **Rotunda,** 140 feet down, are relics of the cave's use as a nitrate mine. Slaves hauled in logs, built leaching vats, and filled them with cave dirt. Water, poured into the vats, trickled into a trough as brine. Two pipelines of hollowed-out logs carried water in and

by darkness or tight spots naturally avoid caves. Rangers say they rarely have problems guiding the 500,000 men, women, and children who venture below yearly.

Mammoth does not glamorize the underworld with garish lighting. You never forget that you are deep in the Earth. And nowhere else can you get a better lesson in the totality of darkness and the miracle of light. Sometimes on a tour a ranger gathers everyone and, after a warning, switches off the lights. The darkness is sudden, absolute. Then the ranger lights a match and the tiny dot of light magically spreads, illuminating a circle of astonished faces.

How to Get There

Mammoth Cave, 9 miles northwest of I-65, is nearly equidistant (about 85 miles) between Louisville, Kentucky, and Nashville, Tennessee. From the south, take the exit at Park City and head northwest on Ky. 255 to the park; from the north, take the exit at Cave City and head northwest on Ky.

brine out. The residue, nitrate crystals, was used to make gunpowder, some of which was used in the War of 1812.

Broadway, an underground avenue, leads to a spot called **Methodist Church,** where services may have been conducted in the 1800s. Farther on, **Booth's Amphitheater** recalls the visit of actor Edwin Booth. Here, Edwin, brother of assassin John Wilkes Booth, recited Hamlet's famous Soliloquy.

The **Bottomless Pit** looked that way to early visitors; it's 105 feet deep; looking up, you see its dome 38 feet above. (The top of a shaft is a dome, the bottom a pit.) On your way back toward the entrance you pass through **Fat Man's Misery,** a passage polished smooth by generations of squirming spelunkers. You emerge into **Great Relief Hall,** a large chamber where you are able to stand upright. Then back on the trail for the final spectacles: **Mammoth Dome**—192 feet from floor to ceiling—carved by water dripping through a sinkhole, and the **Ruins of Karnak,** a cluster of gleaming limestone pillars that look like an Egyptian temple.

Introduction to Caving

1 mile; about 3 hours

Cave exploring, otherwise known as "spelunking," can be fun and challenging. Led by park rangers, the "Introduction to Caving" tour gives visitors 10 and up some first-hand experience in underground exploration. Offered daily in summer and on weekends in spring and fall, this trip involves hand-and-knees crawling, climbing, stooping, and even canyon-walking, with feet on different ledges and nothing but air in between. Straying from traditional walking paths, you will visit the twisting, convoluted canyons and crawls of **Fox Avenue,** emerging at **Frozen Niagara.** Along the way rangers will explain the geologic processes that result in the varied subterranean spaces. You will also learn the basic rules of safe caving, including what to do if you get lost.

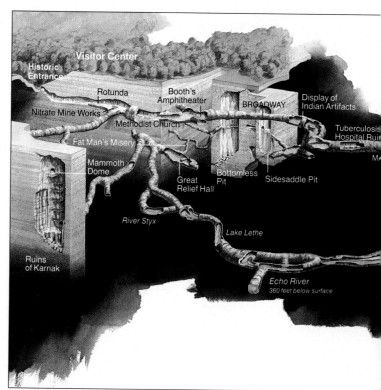

Crawling through a stretch of the Wild Cave Tour

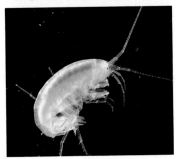

Eyeless, colorless cave shrimp

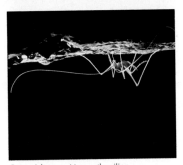

Cave cricket on a Mammoth ceiling

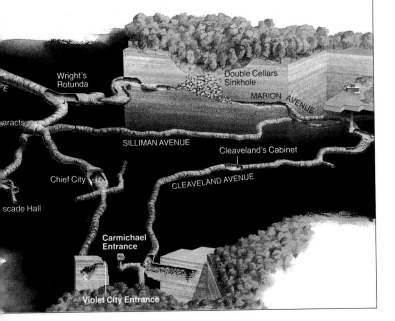

Wright's Rotunda

Double Cellars Sinkhole

MARION AVENUE

aracts

SILLIMAN AVENUE

Cleaveland's Cabinet

Chief City

CLEAVELAND AVENUE

scade Hall

Carmichael Entrance

Violet City Entrance

Crystal Lake beneath Moonlight Dome

Grand Avenue Tour

4 miles; 4½ hours

The tour (likely to be very crowded in summer) begins with a 2-mile bus ride from the visitor center to the **Carmichael Entrance,** a concrete bunker and stairway that leads down to **Cleaveland Avenue,** a long tubular chamber tunneled out by a river. Its walls sparkle with flowery patches of gypsum. The white mineral crystallizes below the surface of the limestone from seeping moisture, then bursts out in blossom-like designs.

About a mile beyond is the **Snowball Room,** where the tour stops for lunch. Food service here is limited to sandwiches, candy, and drinks. The snowball-like features on the roof, once a dull gray, have been cleaned of much of the black fungus that grows on cave formations, which is caused by the residue of phosphates found in the lint from visitors' clothing. Environmentalists have long been lobbying for the restaurant's removal.

Another river canyon, **Boone Avenue,** takes you 300 feet into the Earth along a passage so narrow you can touch both walls. The tour ends at **Frozen Niagara,** a massive cascade of flowstone—the legacy of mineral-laden water that seeped here, vanished, and left behind the shimmering stalactites and stalagmites. Such formations build up at

Helmets and lights are provided. Participants should bring knee pads (no rollerblade type or hard plastic knee pads allowed). Long pants and boots required and gloves recommended. Rest rooms not available. Youths 10 to 15 must be accompanied by an adult.

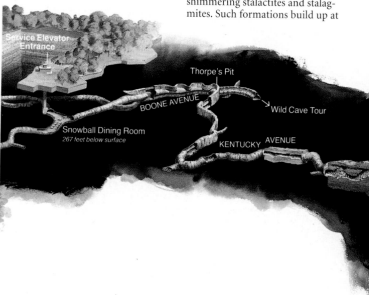

Service Elevator Entrance

Thorpe's Pit

BOONE AVENUE

Wild Cave Tour

Snowball Dining Room
267 feet below surface

KENTUCKY AVENUE

Scenic boat cruise on Green River

the rate of about a cubic inch every 200 years.

Boat Trips & Hikes

To explore the **Green River,** which winds through the park, you can buy tickets at the visitor center for a sedate, 1-hour scenic boat cruise aboard the *Miss Green River II.* Or you can walk the **River Styx Spring Trail,** which leads to the river. The trail, which begins near the Historic Entrance to Mammoth, shows you the interplay between surface features and the cave's underworld. At **River Styx Spring** you can see water emerging from the cave and flowing into the Green River. Farther along the shore, you see **Cave Island,**

formed of waterborne logs, silt, and other materials.

Most of the park's 70 miles of trails are in the backcountry across the Green River. Within the park, there are no bridges over the river. You can drive onto the Green River Ferry at a crossing southwest of the visitor center, or Houchins Ferry at the western edge of the park; ferries have carried people and their vehicles across the river since the 1800s. Head north on **Mammoth Cave Ferry Road** to Maple Spring Group Campground. A gravel road there leads to **Good Spring Church,** founded in 1842. From here you can walk 10 miles on a trail that winds through forests slowly reclaiming land once cleared by farming and logging.

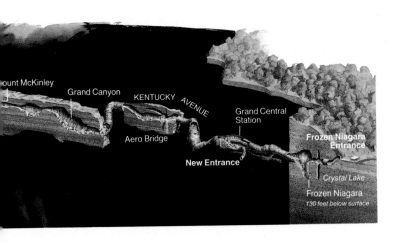

Information & Activities

Headquarters
Mammoth Cave, Kentucky 42259.
Phone (270) 758-2328.
www.nps.gov/maca

Seasons & Accessibility
Park open year-round. Visitors must join a tour to view the caves; tours offered every day but Christmas.

Visitor & Information Centers
Visitor Center open daily all year except Christmas. If space is available, you can buy tickets there on the day, or 1 day in advance, for all tours except Wild Cave, for which advance reservations are essential. But tours sell out quickly—especially in summer, on holidays, and on spring and fall weekends—so if at all possible, buy tickets in advance through National Parks Reservation Service (see page 11).

For more information on ranger-led activities, call (270) 758-2328.

Entrance Fees
None. Fees required for tours, $3-$18 for adults and youths; free for children under 6. Higher fees for special tours; the Wild Cave Tour is $35 per person. Prices subject to change.

Pets
Permitted on leashes except in caves and Visitor Center. Kennel facilities through the Mammoth Cave Hotel.

Facilities for Disabled
Visitor Center, some sites at Headquarters Campground, and rest rooms are accessible. Also, cave tour available for persons in wheelchairs; ½-mile Heritage Trail on surface is fully accessible.

Things to Do
Naturalist-led activities: cave tours, (12 in summer, 5 the rest of the year), children's exploration program, nature walks, evening programs. Nature trails, fishing (no license required), horseback riding, Green River boat trip, bicycling, occasional special events.

Special Advisory
• Cave tours are strenuous; talk with a ranger before selecting one if you have difficulty walking or trouble with your heart or lungs. Wear sturdy shoes and bring a jacket.

Overnight Backpacking
Permits required. They are free and available from ticket office at the Visitor Center.

Campgrounds
Three campgrounds, all with a 14-day limit. Fees: None to $14 per night. Showers near **Headquarters** for a fee. Tent and RV sites at **Headquarters** and **Houchins Ferry;** no hookups. Use National Parks Reservation Service (see page 11) to reserve at Headquarters and Maple Springs. Tent sites only at Dennison Ferry. Open all year; first come, first served. Water unavailable at **Dennison Ferry.** Reservations required at **Maple Spring Group Campgrounds;** contact headquarters. Food services in park.

Hotels, Motels, & Inns
(unless otherwise noted, rates are for 2 persons in a double room, high season)
INSIDE THE PARK:
Mammoth Cave Hotel Mammoth Cave, Ky. 42259. (270) 758-2225. 92 units. Hotel $68; motor lodge $72; cottages $52. AC, restaurant.
OUTSIDE THE PARK:
In Cave City, Kentucky 42127:
Best Western Kentucky Inn 1009 Doyle Ave. (800) 528-1234 or (270) 773-3161. 51 units. $69-$79. AC, pool. **Days Inn Cave City** 822 Mammoth Cave St. (800) 329-7466 or (270) 773-2151. 110 units. $66. AC, pool, restaurant. **Holiday Inn Express** (Ky. 90/I-65) P.O. Box 675. (800) HOLIDAY or (270) 773-3101. 105 units. $70. AC, pool. **Quality Inn** (I-65 and Mammoth Cave Rd.) P.O. Box 427. (800) 228-5757 or (270) 773-2181. 100 units. $80. AC, pool, restaurant.
In Park City, Kentucky 42160:
Park Mammoth Resort (I-65 & US 31 W) P.O. Box 307. (270) 749-4101. 92 units. $60. AC, pool, restaurant.
In Bowling Green, Kentucky 42104:
Bowling Green Bed & Breakfast 3313 Savannah Dr. (502) 781-3861. 3 rooms. $44-$55, includes breakfast. AC. **New's Inn** 3160 Scottsville Rd. (270) 781-3460. 51 units. $44-$65. AC, pool.

For additional accommodations, call the Chambers of Commerce of Cave City (270) 773-3131 and Bowling Green (270) 782-0800.

Excursions

Daniel Boone National Forest

Winchester, Kentucky

Impressed with eastern Kentucky's vegetative bounty, Daniel Boone called this land Eden. The region's geologic wonders also attracted the 18th-century pioneer: more than 80 natural sandstone arches in the Red River Gorge Geological Area, left by 70 million years of wind and water. One of these arches, Sky Bridge, offers a panoramic view of the gorge. The Sheltowee Trace National Recreation Trail, linking many of the forest's recreation sites, memorializes Boone's Indian name, Sheltowee, or "Big Turtle." Also contains two wilderness areas. 690,000 acres. 900 campsites, hiking, boating, boat ramps, marinas, fishing, hunting, off-road-vehicle routes, picnic areas, scenic drives, water sports, cross-country skiing, handicapped access. Open all year; most campsites open April-Nov. Info. at London off I-75, about 125 miles from Mammoth Cave NP. (859) 745-3100.

Cumberland Gap National Historical Park

Middlesboro, Kentucky

Following the path trod by bison and deer, Indian hunters breached the great wall of the Appalachians long before westering pioneers "discovered" the gap in the mid-18th century. In 1775 Daniel Boone and his band of axmen forged the Wilderness Trail into Kentucky, opening the West to its first wave of expansion. Some 50 miles of hiking trails lead visitors to the Pinnacle Overlook, White Rocks, Sand Cave, and to the Hensley Settlement atop Brush Mountain—an early 20th-century effort at self-sufficient living. 20,281 acres, part in Virginia and Tennessee. Facilities include 160 campsites, hiking, picnic areas, scenic drives, handicapped access. Open all year, including campsites. Visitor center at Middlesboro on US 25E, about 190 miles from Mammoth Cave NP. (606) 248-2817.

October morning at Buck Hollow Overlook

Shenandoah

Virginia

Established December 26, 1935

196,295 acres

The Skyline Drive, which runs for 105 miles along the crest of the Blue Ridge mountains, is flanked by a rumpled panorama of forests and mountains. To many who travel the drive, the highway itself is a park, complete with numerous deer-sitings along the way. But the cars are passing the real Shenandoah. Nearly 500 miles of trails crisscross Skyline Drive, and the Appalachian Trail roughly parallels it for its entire length.

The long, narrow park flows outward, upward, and downward from the highway that splits it. The drive, following ridge trails walked by Indians and early settlers, transports visitors to a park built on a frontier that lingered into modern times.

Unlike most national parks, Shenandoah is a place where settlers lived for over a century. To create the park, Virginia state officials acquired 3,850 privately owned tracts and donated the land to the nation. Never before had a large, populated expanse of private land been converted into a national park. And never before had planners made a park of land so used by humans.

In the decade before the park opened, some 465 families moved or were moved from their cabins and resettled outside the proposed park boundaries. A few mountaineers, though, lived out their lives in the park and were buried in the secluded graveyards of Shenandoah's vanished settlements.

Much of Shenandoah consisted of farmland and second- or third-growth forests logged since the early 1700s.

in October to see the foliage. To avoid fall traffic jams, arrive early (preferably on a weekday), park at an overlook, and walk a trail. Snowstorms sometimes close the Skyline Drive, the park's north-south highway. Facilities close in winter. Campgrounds fill on summer weekends, but day trippers still have plenty of park. Wildflowers bloom from early spring to late fall.

How to Visit

On a day's drive-in visit, whatever entrance you use, get out and walk a trail. Even if you venture only a few hundred feet from an overlook, you will be in the real park and not on a scenic highway. For a longer stay, make a base at one place, such as **Big Meadows** or **Skyland,** and explore from there.

Skyline Drive from Front Royal to Big Meadows

51 miles; a full day

Not quite 5 miles south of the **Front Royal Entrance Station** is the **Dickey Ridge Visitor Center,** where exhibits introduce you to the park and its facilities along **Skyline Drive.** To walk a path of mountain life, cross the drive at the visitor center and start the self-guided, $1\frac{1}{3}$-mile **Fox Hollow Trail,** named for the family that first settled this hollow, as tenant farmers, in 1837. Their houses have disappeared, but you can see relics of their toil: large, well-stacked piles of rock cleared from farmland. Other stones—rough and dimly lettered—jut from the family graveyard.

Along the drive, stop at overlooks for views of the **Shenandoah Valley** and the peaks looming above it. The views are magnificent (except when pollution levels or fog mar visibility). At many overlooks there are signposts for well-marked trails. Daubs of paint on trees identify the trails: white, the **Appalachian Trail;** blue, a park hiking trail; yellow, a horse trail (hiking also allowed).

At Mathews Arm Campground, 22 miles from Front Royal, the easily accessible $1\frac{3}{4}$-mile **Traces Trail** takes you back through an oak forest to the time of the earliest white settlers. The traces are faint: an old road,

Today the marks of lumbering, grazing, and farming are disappearing as forests make a slow, steady comeback.

Spring arrives first in the park valleys and then moves upward. Walking a valley trail, a visitor can follow spring's path and see, in a single day, a variety of flowers that bloom elsewhere over a span of weeks.

How to Get There

From Washington, D.C. (about 70 miles away), take I-66 west to US 340, then head south to the park's Front Royal (North) Entrance. From Charlottesville, take I-64 to the Rockfish Gap (South) Entrance. From the west, take US 211 through Luray to the Thornton Gap Entrance or head east on US 33 to the Swift Run Gap Entrance. Airports: Dulles International, near Washington, and Charlottesville.

When to Go

Of the nearly 2,000,000 people who visit the park each year, 400,000 go

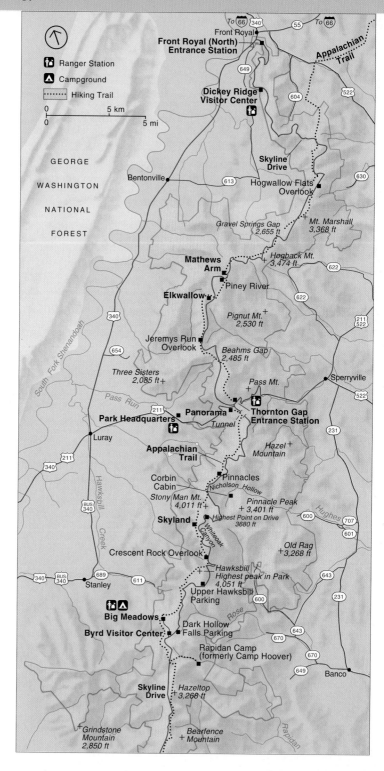

Ranger Station
Campground
Hiking Trail

0   5 km
0   5 mi

GEORGE

WASHINGTON

NATIONAL

FOREST

To 66 340   55   *To* 66
Front Royal
**Front Royal (North)
Entrance Station**

Appalachian
Trail

649

**Dickey Ridge
Visitor Center**   604

522

**Skyline
Drive**   630

Bentonville   613   Hogwallow Flats
Overlook

*Gravel Springs Gap
2,655 ft*   + *Mt. Marshall
3,368 ft*

*Hogback Mt.
3,474 ft*

**Mathews
Arm**   622

Piney River

Elkwallow   622

*Pignut Mt.
2,530 ft*   211
522

340

Jeremys Run
Overlook   *Beahms Gap
2,485 ft*

654

*Three Sisters
2,085 ft* +   *Pass Mt.*   Sperryville

Pass Run   522

Panorama   **Thornton Gap
Entrance Station**

Park Headquarters   *Tunnel*   231

Luray   *Hazel
Mountain*

**Appalachian
Trail**

Corbin
Cabin   **Pinnacles**

Nicholson Hollow

*Stony Man Mt.
4,011 ft* +   *Pinnacle Peak
+ 3,401 ft*

Skyland   *Highest Point on Drive
3680 ft*   600   707

Whiteoak Canyon   601

*Old Rag
+3,268 ft*

Crescent Rock Overlook

340   BUS
340   689   611   *Hawksbill
Highest peak in Park
4,051 ft*   643

Stanley   Upper Hawksbill
Parking   600   231

Big Meadows   *Rose*

Byrd Visitor Center   Dark Hollow
Falls Parking   670   643

Rapidan Camp
(formerly Camp Hoover)   670

Banco   649

**Skyline
Drive**   *Hazeltop
3,268 ft*

*Grindstone
Mountain
2,850 ft* +   *Bearfence
+ Mountain*   *Rapidan*

South Fork Shenandoah

Hawksbill Creek

Hughes

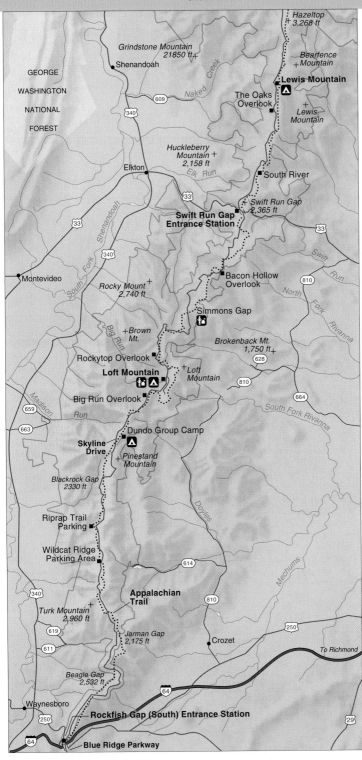

Hazeltop
+ 3,268 ft

Grindstone Mountain
21850 ft +

Shenandoah

Bearfence
+ Mountain

GEORGE

Lewis Mountain

WASHINGTON

The Oaks
Overlook

NATIONAL

Lewis
Mountain

FOREST

Huckleberry
Mountain +
2,158 ft

Elk Run

Elkton

South River

Swift Run Gap
+ 2,365 ft

Swift Run Gap
Entrance Station

Montevideo

Bacon Hollow
Overlook

Rocky Mount +
2,740 ft

Simmons Gap

+ Brown
Mt.

Brokenback Mt.
1,750 ft +

Rockytop Overlook

Loft Mountain

+ Loft
Mountain

Big Run Overlook

South Fork Rivanna

Dundo Group Camp

Skyline
Drive

+ Pinestand
Mountain

Blackrock Gap
2330 ft

Riprap Trail
Parking

Wildcat Ridge
Parking Area

Appalachian
Trail

Turk Mountain +
2,960 ft

Jarman Gap
2,175 ft

Crozet

Beagle Gap
2,532 ft

To Richmond

Waynesboro

Rockfish Gap (South) Entrance Station

Blue Ridge Parkway

Ferns on forest floor near Swift Run Gap

trees, tumbling stone walls. For a more rugged hike into the past, stop at the parking area past milepost 37 and take the **Corbin Cabin Cutoff Trail.** The steep trip (1½ miles each way) ends at **Corbin Cabin,** a typical mountain residence. In 1909 George Corbin cut and hewed logs, and, with the help of neighbors, built this cabin. The Corbin family, like many others, lived on what they grew or made, including brandy from peaches and apples. The Potomac Appalachian Trail Club maintains the cabin for rent to members and the public, along with five other rustic cabins scattered through the park's backcountry.

Skyland (near milepost 42) dates from the 1890s. The resort, which includes guest rooms, dining room, and cabins, is open from April through November. The 1½-mile **Stony Man Trail** begins near the parking area and, climbing about 340 feet, reaches the cliffs of **Stony Man's** summit (4,011 feet, second highest point in the park). From an outcrop on the cliffs you get a sweeping view. The trail loops back around to the start.

The **Limberlost Trail** (near milepost 43), a gently winding walkway of crushed green stone, passes though old-growth hemlocks before crossing over

Whiteoak Canyon Run on a wooden bridge. The 1⅓-mile trail is wheelchair accessible with numerous benches located at intervals for hikers to rest and contemplate their surroundings.

Stop at **Crescent Rock Overlook** (near milepost 44) for a look at **Hawksbill Mountain** (4,051 feet, highest point in park). Then, 6 miles farther, stop at the parking area for **Dark Hollow Falls Trail,** a 1½-mile round-trip to waterfalls, the shortest route to any falls in the park. The steep trail takes you past clusters of ferns, mosses, and liverworts. Split-log benches offer a rest en route.

Big Meadows (milepost 51) has trails, a campground, a lodge, facilities for visitors, and the **Byrd Visitor Center,** where changing exhibits tell the stories of the park.

Today the defoliated trees you see attest to the presence of a natural phenomenon—the gypsy moth. But, unlike the chestnut blight early in the 20th Century, the moths will not wipe out an entire species. Healthy trees will renew the forest in future decades.

You can end your day at Big Meadows with a wildflower walk through the gently undulating meadowlands that give the area its name. On the way, you may startle a deer or two.

Corbin Cabin, relic of a mountaineer past

Scarlet tanager in summer plumage

Rapidan Camp to Rockfish Gap

54 miles; a full day

Park at the west side of the Skyline Drive at **Milam Gap** (mile 52.8). Cross the drive to a trail marker to begin the 4-mile round-trip to **Rapidan Camp** (formerly Camp Hoover). You walk a short distance on the Appalachian Trail, then turn left onto the **Mill Prong Trail**, which passes through a wooded tract, descends to a small waterfall, crosses three streams, and meets a road. Turn right and continue toward the cabins of **Rapidan Camp**, a National Historic Landmark. The camp satisfied President Herbert Hoover's three requirements for a hideaway: It had to be within 100 miles of Washington, have a trout stream, and be high enough to discourage mosquitoes. The President and First Lady used the camp as a summer White House in 1931.

You can walk around and look at the outside of the cabins that are currently being restored to their 1931 condition, slated to be completed in 2002. President Hoover's cabin can be visited during the summer and fall on tours from Byrd Visitor Center.

A ⅘-mile, 1½-hour hike to **Bearfence Mountain** starts at mile 56.4 before the Lewis Mountain Campground. It demands some scrambling over rocks but finally rewards you with a spectacular, 360-degree view. The 2-mile round trip hike to the **Pocosin Mission**, which starts past milepost 59, takes you to the ruins of a missionary church and graveyard.

The **Swift Run Gap Entrance** (near milepost 65) is an old Blue Ridge crossing now paved by US 33. In May, wildflower seekers climb the nearby **Hightop Summit Trail** (3 miles round-trip) to see wildflowers.

Loft Mountain (near milepost 79), with campground and information center, is a southern base for exploring the park. Near a service complex along Skyline Drive, look for the trailhead to the **Frazier Discovery Trail**, a 1½-mile loop hike that demonstrates how pasture is evolving back into forest. After the demise of the chestnut trees, other trees and shrubs began repopulating the land. You can see it happening here, and from a rocky vantage point on the trail you can also see it happening on a grand scale throughout the park.

At **Rockfish Gap**, near the **Rockfish Entrance Station**, a bison path evolved into a colonial road, and later a modern highway. Here, at the southern end of the park, begins the **Blue Ridge Parkway**, a National Park Service highway that connects Shenandoah and Great Smoky Mountains National Parks.

Information & Activities

Headquarters
3655 US 211 E Luray, Virginia 22835.
Phone (540) 999-3500.
www.nps.gov/shen

Seasons & Accessibility
Park open year-round. For recorded
information call (540) 999-3500.
Skyline Drive may close temporarily
during heavy snow or hazardous ice
conditions. For weather and road
information, call (540) 999-3500.

Visitor & Information Centers
Dickey Ridge Visitor Center, near
North Entrance, open daily late March
through November. Byrd Visitor Center at Big Meadows, near center of
park, open daily late March through
November. Opening and closing dates
vary each year.

Entrance Fee
$10 per car allows 7-day access.

Pets
Must be kept on leash; not allowed
on posted trails or in park buildings.

Facilities for Disabled
Visitor centers, amphitheaters, picnic
areas, and campgrounds are accessible
to wheelchairs. Rest rooms, lodges,
and restaurants are also accessible.
Free brochure.

Things to Do
Free ranger-led activities: interpretive
walks, talks, evening programs
(summer-fall only). Also available,
fishing, horseback riding, hiking on
some 500 miles of trails.

Special Advisories
• Rocks around waterfalls are very
slippery and dangerous.
• Pull off the road completely when
stopping for a view.

Overnight Backpacking
Permits required and available free of
charge from headquarters, visitor centers, and entrance stations.

Campgrounds
Four campgrounds, all with 14-day
limit. **Mathews Arm, Lewis Mountain**
and **Loft Mountain** open mid-May
through October, first come, first
served. **Big Meadows** open late
March through November; reservations recommended from Memorial
Day weekend through October;
available through National Parks
Reservation Service (see page 11);
other times, first come, first served.
Fees $14-$17 per night. Showers and
laundry facilities (except at Mathews
Arm). Tent and RV sites; no hookups.
Camp stores and restaurants near
the campground.

Hotels, Motels, & Inns
*(unless otherwise noted, rates are for 2
persons in a double room, high season)*
INSIDE THE PARK:
P.O. Box 727, Luray, Va. 22835. (800)
999-4714 or (540) 743-5108.
www.visitshenandoah.com
Big Meadows Lodge (milepost 51.3)
Lodge rooms $68-$129; cabins $75-
$87; suites $105-$142. Restaurant.
Late April through October.
Lewis Mountain (mile 57.6) Ten cabins with outdoor grills. $62-$94. Mid-
May through October.
Skyland Lodge (miles 41.7 & 42.5)
177 units. Lodge units $82-$120; suites
$116-$170; cabins $53-$103. Restau-
rant. Early April through November.
OUTSIDE THE PARK:
In Front Royal, Virginia 22630:
Woodward House on Manor Grade
413 S. Royal Ave. (800) 635-7011 or
(540) 635-7010. 8 units. $90-$120,
includes breakfast. AC.
Quality Inn 10 Commerce Ave. (800)
821-4488 or (540) 635-3161. 107 units.
$75. AC, pool, restaurant.
In Sperryville, Virginia 22740:
The Conyers House Inn and Stable
3131 Slate Mills Road. (540) 987-8025.
7 units. $150-$300, includes breakfast.
AC, restaurant.
In Stanley, Virginia 22851:
Jordan Hollow Farm Inn 326 Hawksbill Park Rd. (888) 418-7000 or (540)
778-2285. 21 rooms. $110-$154. AC,
restaurant.
In Waynesboro, Virginia 22980:
The Inn at Afton I-64 at US 250. (800)
860-8559 or (540) 942-5201. 118 units.
$83-$91. AC, pool, restaurant.

Excursions

George Washington National Forest

Harrisonburg, Virginia

This mountain forest flanks the Shenandoah Valley, rich in Civil War history. Excellent fishing and fall color. Contains four wilderness areas and 57 miles of Appalachian Trail. 1,064,487 acres in three sections, part in W.Va. 807 campsites, food services, boating, boat ramp, fishing, hiking, horseback riding, hunting, picnic areas, water sports, winter sports, handicapped access. Open all year, including many campsites. Visitor center at Massanutten on US 211, about 8 miles from Shenandoah NP. (540) 564-8300.

Jefferson National Forest

Roanoke, Virginia

Some 300 miles of the Appalachian Trail traverse mountains blanketed in hardwood, pine, and rhododendron. Streams and waterfalls abound. Contains 11 wilderness areas and Mount Rogers National Recreation Area. More than 700,000 acres, part in W.Va. and Ky. Facilities include 670 campsites, hiking, boating, boat ramp, fishing, horseback riding, hunting, picnic areas, water sports, handicapped access. Open all year, including some campsites. Information at USFS Roanoke headquarters, about 120 miles south of Shenandoah NP. (540) 265-5100.

Mason Neck National Wildlife Refuge

Lorton, Virginia

The nation's first refuge dedicated to the protection of the bald eagle lies on a peninsula in the Potomac River, near Washington, D.C. Hardwood forest and marsh combine to form ideal habitat or the eagles and for numerous other wildlife species such as great blue herons, wood ducks, bluebirds, beavers, and deer. 2,277 acres. Facilities include hiking and birdwatching. Open year-round during daylight hours. On Va. 242, about 75 miles from Shenandoah NP. (703) 490-4979.

Trunk Bay, renowned for its beauty

Virgin Islands

United States Virgin Islands

Established August 2, 1956

12,909 acres

High green hills dropping down to enchanting turquoise bays, white powdery beaches, coral reefs, and ruins that evoke an era of sugar and a tragic period of slavery all find protection on St. John, one of about a hundred specks of Caribbean land known as the Virgin Islands.

Despite its small size—19 square miles—St. John's wide range of rainfall and exposure give it surprising variety. More than 800 subtropical plant species grow in areas from moist, high-elevation forests to desertlike terrain to mangrove swamps, among them mangoes, soursops, turpentine trees, wild tamarind, century plants, and seagrapes. Around the island live the fringing coral reefs—beautiful, complex, and exceedingly fragile communities of plants and animals, which St. John's famous beaches depend upon.

In 1493 Columbus sighted the large assemblage of islands and cays and named it after St. Ursula's legendary 11,000 virgins. Since then, Spain, France, Holland, England, Denmark, and the United States have controlled various islands at different times. The Danes began colonization in the 17th century, and in 1717 planters arrived on St. John. By mid-century 88 plantations had been established there; slaves stripped the steep hillsides of virgin growth and cultivated the cane. By the time the Danes abolished slavery in 1848, the sugar industry was doomed. A fallow, century-long period known as the "subsistence era" followed.

Fearful that the Germans might capture the islands during World War I, the United States bought St. John, St. Croix, St. Thomas, and about 50 smaller islands from Denmark for $25,000,000. In 1956 conservationist Laurance S. Rockefeller donated more than 5,000 acres for a national park on St. John; in 1962 the park acquired 5,650 undersea acres off the northern and southern coasts. Today, though its boundary includes three-quarters of St. John, the park owns only slightly more than half the island. Of increasing concern is the escalating pace of development on private inholdings inside its borders. It also feels pressure from the many cruise ships that disgorge large numbers of visitors at once, badly straining park resources. Some of the park's trails may be closed for maintenance work; ask at the visitor center.

When to Go

All-year park. High season is mid-December to mid-April.

How to Get There

By plane to Charlotte Amalie, St. Thomas, then taxi or bus to Red Hook, then ferry across Pillsbury Sound to Cruz Bay, a 20-minute ride. Or, try to catch one of the less frequently scheduled ferries from Charlotte Amalie—the boat takes 45 minutes, but the dock is much nearer the airport.

How to Visit

If you have only 1 day, drive the **North Shore Road** as far as the **Annaberg Sugar Mill Ruins,** taking time to stretch your legs along some seaside trails—and perhaps do a little snorkeling. Return via **Centerline Road,** stopping at the ruins of **Catherineberg Sugar Mill.** On a second day, consider hiking the **Reef Bay Trail,** explore the island's **East End,** visit **Saltpond Bay,** and walk to **Ram Head.** With more time, sign up for some of the excellent ranger-led tours and activities.

If you're driving yourself, be prepared for steep, often potholed roads with blind curves, and *stay on the left.* The speed limit is 20 mph. An alternative is to hire a taxi and guide.

North Shore Road-Centerline Road Loop

15 miles; 3 hours to a full day

Begin your visit with a stop at the park visitor center in **Cruz Bay** to pick up a map and a trail brochure, and to find out what ranger-led activities are scheduled. Head north out of town along the **North Shore Road** (Route 20). This road is in good condition but very steep in places. Near the top of the hill, pull off at the overlook for a bird's-eye view of the picturesque town and harbor, the many small adjacent islands, and the big island of **St. Thomas** across the sound. For an even better view of **St. John's West End,** climb **Caneel Hill;** the ⅖-mile, moderately strenuous trail begins a short distance ahead on the right, across the road from the Park Service sign. (Or save this hike for sunset, when it's cooler and the view from the hilltop spectacular.)

Stop at the next overlook ½ mile farther along the road for a view of **Caneel Bay** and, to the northeast, the big island of **Jost van Dyke,** one of the British Virgins. Since the 1930s the site

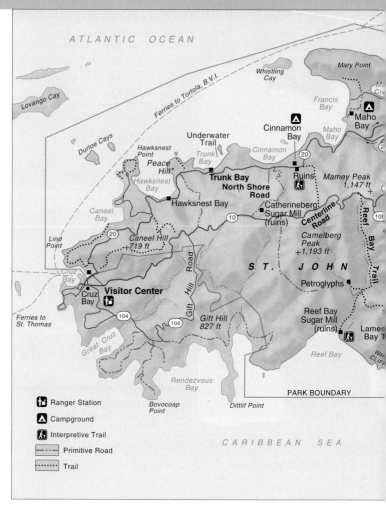

ATLANTIC OCEAN

Lovango Cay

Durloe Cays

Hawksnest Point

Peace Hill

Hawksnest Bay

Caneel Bay

Lind Point

Cruz Bay

Cruz Bay

Visitor Center

Ferries to St. Thomas

Great Cruz Bay

Ferries to Tortola, B.V.I.

Whistling Cay

Mary Point

Maho Point

Francis Bay

Maho Bay

Cinnamon Bay

Cinnamon Bay

Underwater Trail

Trunk Bay

Trunk Bay
North Shore
Road

Ruins

Mamey Peak
1,147 ft

Catherineberg
Sugar Mill
(ruins)

Centerline Road

Reef Bay Trail

Camelberg Peak
+1,193 ft

Caneel Hill
+719 ft

Gift Hill Road

S T.   J O H N

Petroglyphs

Gift Hill
827 ft

Reef Bay
Sugar Mill
(ruins)

Lames Bay T

Reef Bay

Rendezvous Bay

Bovocoap Point

Dittlif Point

PARK BOUNDARY

C A R I B B E A N   S E A

Ranger Station

Campground

Interpretive Trail

Primitive Road

Trail

of a famous resort, Caneel Bay was a sugar plantation for most of the 18th and 19th centuries. Its name, both Dutch and Danish for "cinnamon," comes from the cinnamony leaves of the bay tree, a member of the myrtle family. (From the 1860s to the 1930s, oil from the leaves was used to make St. John Bay Rum cologne.)

The entrance to the Caneel Bay resort is down the hill on the left, past road marker 1.5. The land belongs to the park but is leased to the resort, owned until recently by the Rockefellers. To get a look at its lovely beaches and bays—and palm-studded grounds flowered with bougainvillea and pink oleander—walk the mostly level **Turtle Point Trail** around **Hawksnest Point,** which takes about an

hour. The resort management asks only that you register as a day guest at the front desk; ask there for directions to the trailhead.

From Caneel Bay the road climbs steeply and descends to **Hawksnest Beach,** where you can swim, snorkel, and picnic. Visitors tend to bypass this beach, but locals flock here on weekends. Exhibits describe the damage being done to the island's fragile reefs by pollutants, swimmers, snorkelers, and the anchors of careless boaters— and strongly urge you not to touch, stand, or sit on the coral.

One of the Caribbean's premier vistas awaits you a mile farther up the road. From the overlook, **Trunk Bay** with its lush palm-fringed crescent beach and dozens of bobbing

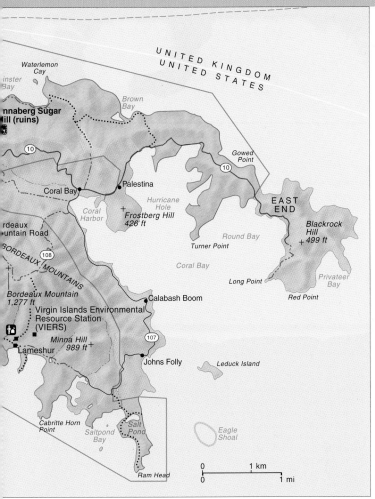

UNITED KINGDOM
UNITED STATES

Waterlemon
Cay

inster
Bay

Annaberg Sugar
ill (ruins)

Brown
Bay

Gowed
Point

10

10

Coral Bay   Palestina

Coral
Harbor

Hurricane
Hole
Frostberg Hill
426 ft

EAST
END

Blackrock
Hill
499 ft

rdeaux
untain Road

108

BORDEAUX MOUNTAINS

Round Bay

Turner Point

Coral Bay

Bordeaux Mountain
1,277 ft

Virgin Islands Environmental
Resource Station
(VIERS)

Minna Hill
989 ft

Lameshur

Calabash Boom

107

Johns Folly

Long Point

Red Point

Privateer
Bay

Leduck Island

Cabritte Horn
Point

Salt
Pond

Saltpond
Bay

Eagle
Shoal

Ram Head

0   1 km
0   1 mi

Partly restored Annaberg Sugar Mill, built in the 18th century

Snorkelers bobbing toward a coral reef off Caneel Bay resort

sailboats lies before you. Off a point in the middle distance is **Whistling Cay,** where in the 19th century a customs shed stopped boats plying the passage between the Danish and British Virgins. Trunk Bay's beauty draws many visitors, especially on days when cruise ships are in. The park has set up an underwater nature trail for snorkelers here; some 16 plaques identify the reef's plants and animals. If you're a serious snorkeler, however, you might want to skip this reef for a less traveled one farther along.

Beyond Trunk Bay's entrance be prepared for the road to sharply steepen. Near the top of the hill is the multimillion-dollar development at **Peter Bay,** a private inholding that has been a model for preventing the sediment runoff that other developments have allowed. Park officials and environmentalists say that runoff damages the reefs and sea grass beds.

At **Cinnamon Bay** (road marker 4.5) are a campground and, across the road, the ruins of the Danish (first Dutch) Cinnamon Bay sugar factory, one of the island's oldest. Plaques along the 1-mile trail tell you its history and point out native trees such as bay, lime, teyer palm, and calabash, which produces a gourd-like fruit

that's carved into bowls. If you're lucky enough to be there for a tour led by one of the Virgin Islanders on the park staff, you'll learn some colorful local lore as well.

Continue down the road ½ mile to yet another stunning, sweeping view—**Maho Bay, Francis Bay,** where sea turtles come to feed, and **Mary Point.** You'll see diving pelicans and frigatebirds, which, to avoid water-logging their own enormous wings, harass other seabirds for food. The red roofs visible in the trees belong to a house built in 1952 by an American eccentric named Ethel McCully, who swam ashore from a boat and stayed. Since no paved roads or automobiles existed on St. John then, donkeys hauled the materials from Cruz Bay—a 4-hour trip.

Down the hill, the road flattens, passing a stretch of beach on the left. Continue on for a mile to the road's end and then turn right toward **Annaberg.** On the right, you'll see a thick mangrove swamp, one of many on the island. Its large, tangled roots help protect the shoreline and provide a breeding ground for fish.

On the left, about 100 yards from the turnoff, look for the marker identifying one of the toxic manchineel trees common to the

Sea horse, a seldom seen Caribbean creature

Caribbean; Columbus called their green fruit "death apples." Do not stand under this tree in the rain: Runoff can raise painful blisters on your skin.

Just ahead is **Mary Creek** with a view of **Mary Point.** An important marine community inhabits the shallow reefs and sea grass beds of the creek, site of a weekly naturalist-led seashore walk. If you wade out (be sure to wear something on your feet), you can find brilliantly colored conchs, spiny black sea urchins, and brittle stars that regenerate their tentacles. Coral rocks host many tiny animals. Pick up and examine the rocks, but put them back as you found them.

From here consider an easy walk along the $\frac{2}{5}$-mile **Leinster Bay Trail,** which follows the seashore east to **Waterlemon Bay** and some of the best snorkeling in the park.

You can swim and snorkel off the sandy beach at the trail's end. Better yet if you have the stamina, walk out to the point and swim across the narrow channel to snorkel around little **Waterlemon Cay.**

Back at the Leinster Bay trailhead, park in the small lot and walk up the hill to the partially restored ruins of the **Annaberg Sugar Mill.** A $\frac{1}{4}$-mile self-guided walk introduces you to the

workers' quarters, windmill, horse mill, oven, cistern, and factory that for much of two centuries produced raw sugar, molasses, and rum for Denmark. Native stone, ballast brick, and coral went into building the thick walls.

From the overlook you can see a number of other Virgin Islands across the narrows, including **Tortola,** largest of the British Virgins, and the dinosaur shape of Britain's **Great Thatch** on the left. In winter, humpback whales sometimes cruise by. Annaberg slaves reportedly tried to swim to Great Thatch after the British freed their slaves in 1833, 15 years ahead of the Danes. Before leaving the overlook, treat yourself to the scent of a frangipani blossom from the nearby tree.

To return to Cruz Bay, drive the more level **Centerline Road** (Route 10), watching out for blind curves. Slow speeds should pose no hardship, however: The views of the island's **East End** are truly spectacular. If you have time, look for the **Catherineberg Road** on the right after driving about 3 miles. A short way up this road are the ruins of the area's 18th-century **Catherineberg Sugar Mill.** The outer shell of the windmill has been restored, and there are 4-foot stone walls, handsome archways, a massive stone pillar, and some original beams to see.

East End: Coral Bay & Saltpond Bay

26 miles round-trip; at least a half day

Take Centerline Road (Route 10) out of Cruz Bay, stopping after nearly 3 miles at the Catherineberg Sugar Mill (see above), if you haven't already been there. About ½ mile farther is the **Konge Vey Overlook,** where a wayside exhibit points out Jost van Dyke, Great Thatch, and other islands and bays to the north.

The popular **Reef Bay Trail** begins after another 1¼ miles. It descends into a steep V-shaped valley through moist, subtropical forest to dry forest to acacia scrub near the coast. Ruins of sugar estates can be seen along its 2½ miles and nearby are some mysterious petroglyphs. Walk this trail at least partway to experience the lush forest, or even better, save it for the ranger-led trip ($15), when a boat meets you at the coast and spares you the hike back up.

Back in your car, continue on to the overlook near **Mamey Peak** for a lovely view of **Coral Bay** and the island's East End. The name of the bay comes not from the island's abundant coral but from an 18th-century Dutch corral *(kraal)* here. The Danes established their first plantations at this end of the island, among them the vast Estate Carolina, once the property of the king. They built a fort—called **Fort Frederik**—on **Fortsberg Hill** on the bay's eastern shore. In 1733 a bloody slave uprising began here, reputedly the first in the New World. It would have succeeded— 1,087 of the island's 1,295 inhabitants were slaves—had the French not sailed in to quell it.

Continue on Route 10 as it winds eastward outside the park to the village of **Coral Bay,** about 2 miles away. You may well see a mongoose scuttering across the road. Introduced a century ago to kill rats, the mongoose has multiplied explosively, to the detriment of some native island fauna. At Coral Bay, stop to see the handsome pink-roofed **Emmaus Church,** built by Moravian missionaries in the 1780s. If you continued on, you'd be rewarded with magnificent views of **Hurricane Hole, Round Bay,** and the British Virgins. But for now backtrack a short distance and turn left at the intersection of Route 108. Drive 4 miles along the coast to the trailhead for **Saltpond Bay** and a wilder part of the island.

About ⅕ mile beyond the parking area, the horseshoe bay is fringed by a wide, sandy beach, gently lapped by transparent waters. Continue around the beach and onto the rocky ⁹⁄₁₀-mile **Ram Head Trail** that winds up a promontory and down the other side. There a blue pebbly beach and an arid environment await you. Plants include several kinds of cactuses and the century plant, which takes 15 to 20 years to bloom, then dies.

Continue to the crest of the hill for a grand Caribbean view. Watch your footing and hold onto any children you've brought on this windswept point 200 feet above the sea. Here at **Ram Head** you'll be standing on rock that emerged some 108 million years ago, the oldest land on St. John.

Information & Activities

Headquarters
P.O. Box 710, St. John, US Virgin Islands 00831. Phone (340) 776-6201. www.nps.gov/viis

Seasons & Accessibility
Park open year-round. Access by boat. Climate does not vary much during the year, though summers can be hot. Hurricane season here runs typically from June through November.

Visitor & Information Centers
Cruz Bay Visitor Center, at west end of St. John, open daily all year. Call (340) 776-6201.

Entrance Fee
There is no entrance fee for the park. However, there is a user fee to enter Trunk Bay and Annaberg Mill ruins: $4 for adults; children 16 and under admitted free.

Pets
Not allowed on public beaches, in picnic areas, or in campgrounds. Permitted elsewhere on leashes.

Facilities for Disabled
Some ferries to St. John are accessible to wheelchairs, with assistance. The visitor center, several Cinnamon Bay campsites, and rest rooms there and at Trunk Bay and Hawksnest Bay are also accessible.

Things to Do
Free naturalist-led activities: interpretive talks and exhibits, nature and history walks, hikes, snorkel tours, cultural demonstrations, evening programs. Also available, self-guided nature and underwater trails, swimming, snorkeling, boating, fishing (no license needed), occasional historic bus tours.

Overnight Backpacking
Not allowed in park.

Campgrounds
One park campground, **Cinnamon Bay;** 14-day limit Dec. to mid-May; other times 21-day limit. Open all year. Reservations recommended; contact Cinnamon Bay Campground, P.O. Box 720, Cruz Bay, St. John, USVI 00831, (800) 539-9998 or (340) 776-6330. Nightly for 2 persons: $17 for bare sites; $75 for tents; $95 for cottages. Cold showers. Groups contact Cinnamon Bay Campground, (800) 539-9998. Food services.

Also, **Maho Bay;** Maho Bay Camp, 17-A East 73rd St., New York, N.Y. 10021. (800) 392-9004 or (212) 472-9453. 114 equipped tent-cottages, central baths. $95 per night December through April; $60 per night May through November Reserve early for December to May.

Hotels, Motels, & Inns
(unless otherwise noted, rates are for 2 persons in a double room, high season)
On St. John, USVI 00831:
Caneel Bay P.O. Box 720, Cruz Bay. (800) 928-8889 or (340) 776-6111. 166 units. $400-$950. Pool, restaurant.
St. John Inn P.O. Box 566. (800) 666-7688 or (340) 693-8688. 13 units, some kitchens. $120-$175.
Gallows Point Suite Resort P.O. Box 58. (800) 323-7229 or (340) 776-6434. 52 units, kitchens. $295-$410. Pool, restaurant.
Westin Resort St. John P.O. Box 8310. (340) 693-8000. 285 units. $539-$709. AC, pool, restaurant.

Excursion

Buck Island Reef National Monument
St. Croix, US Virgin Islands

A coral reef nearly encircles this small island, one mile north of St. Croix. Two marked underwater trails guide snorkelers or passengers of glass-bottom boats through the exquisite reef ecosystem. Breathtaking views of St. Croix and the reef can be had from the top of Buck Island's hiking trail. 176 land acres; 704 undersea acres. Facilities include trails, picnic areas, water sports. Open year-round. Access by charter boat from Christiansted, St. Croix (charter operators supply snorkeling equipment). (340) 773-1460.

Forested islands of Rainy Lake; Canada in the background

Voyageurs

Minnesota

Established April 8, 1975

218,054 acres

From the air, the forest areas of Voyageurs look like green pieces of a jigsaw puzzle scattered on a huge mirror. A north woods realm of more than 30 lakes and more than 900 islands, Voyageurs spans a watery stretch of the US-Canada border.

A third of the park's area is water, most of it in four large lakes—Rainy, Kabetogama, Namakan, and Sand Point—linked by narrow waterways. Smaller lakes gleam in the forests and bogs of Voyageurs' terra firma, which consists of small islands, a strip of mainland shore, and the Kabetogama Peninsula, a long, bay-fringed landmass.

The splendors of this 55-mile-long park can be reached primarily by water. Motorboats (banned in the adjacent Boundary Waters Canoe Area Wilderness) churn the lakes. Canoes glide the narrow waterways. Fishermen sit at the rails of houseboats, hoping to hook walleye, smallmouth bass, and northern pike. Nearly every lake is haunted by the cry of the loon. And probably in no other national park in the lower 48 states is there a better chance to see bald eagles on the nest and on the wing or hear wolves howl at night.

The park is named for the voyageurs, French Canadians who paddled birch-bark canoes for fur trading companies in the late 18th and early 19th centuries. The voyageurs were famous for stamina—paddling up to 16 hours a day—and roisterous songs. Their canoe route between Canada's northwest and Montreal is cited as part of the US-Canada

County Roads 23 and 24. For Ash River, stay on US 53 for 25 more miles, turn right at the Ash River Trail sign, and continue for 10 miles. For Kabetogama Lake Visitor Center, stay on US 53 for 3 more miles, turn right onto County Road 122, and drive to the lakeshore. For Rainy Lake, stay on US 53 to International Falls, then head east for 12 miles on Minn. 11 to Island View and turn right to the visitor center. Airports: Duluth, International Falls, and Fort Frances, Ontario.

When to Go

All-year park, but most accessible from spring through early fall. Water travel is curtailed by freeze-up in late fall and ice break-up in early spring. Winter opens the park to cross-country skiing, snowshoeing, snow-mobiling, and ice fishing. And the 7-mile ice road at Rainy Lake provides a unique entry into the park: You drive your car on the ice to places that in other seasons you can reach only by boat or floatplane.

How to Visit

The only way to the heart of this park is by water. **Kabetogama Lake, International Falls, Crane Lake,** and **Ash River** are resort communities, which, though not within the park, serve as entrances. Begin your trip planning by choosing an entrance; each of them is widely spaced and offers a different experience. You can make motel or lodge reservations at one of the area's resorts on a park list (see **Information & Activities** p. 104), or stay in a car campground, and use the resort as a base for park activities, including fishing and wildlife watching. Or you can rent a houseboat or camp out by boat. Guides, canoes, houseboats,

border in the treaty that ended the American Revolution.

In a boat in the labyrinth of waterways and islands, you can unwittingly cross this border. Be sure to take along a high-quality map that includes navigational markers to tell you where you are.

How to Get There

From Duluth, drive north about 110 miles on US 53. For Crane Lake, turn east at Orr and drive 28 miles on

Modern voyageurs on Kabetogama Lake

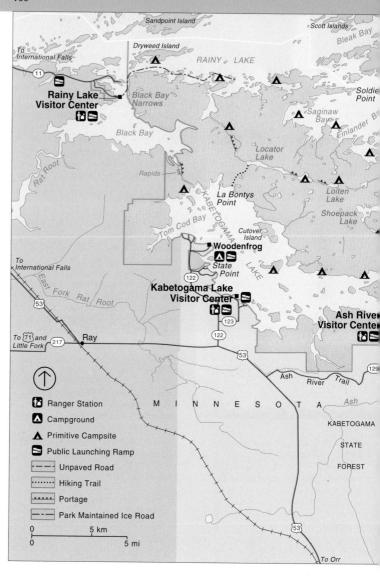

and motorboats are for hire. Or, if you feel sufficiently experienced, you can tow in your own craft.

Concessioner-run boats, with park naturalists aboard, also operate out of visitor centers. Even if you have your own boat, you may want to take a commercial cruise and rely on experienced navigators; the lakes are broad with submerged rocks in shallow areas, and they're sometimes brushed by stiff winds.

If your time is limited, Kabetogama Lake is a good place for exploring and understanding the park.

Kabetogama Lake
at least a full day

At the **Kabetogama Lake Visitor Center** reserve a naturalist-led Sunset Wildlife Cruise, Kettle Falls Cruise, a guided canoe trip, or a children's program. Or, borrow one of the park's cached canoes at Locator Lake by reserving it and picking up the key at the visitor center. If you do this, you must get to the Locator Lake trailhead on your own, with a guide, or in a rented boat. You leave the boat at the

ONTARIO

RAINY LAKE

Cormorant Bay

Pat River Bay

CANADA
UNITED STATES

Pound Net Bay

Mackenzie Point

Stokes Bay

Duff Creek

Oakpoint Island

Brown Lake

Beast Lake

Mica Bay

Kettle Falls

Cruiser Lake

Weir Lake

Dam

Voyageur Narrows

Moose Island

Blackstone Island

NAMAKAN LAKE

Namakan

Namakan Island

Namakan Narrows

Moose Bay

Hoist Bay

Sheen Point

Randolph Bay

Sivan Bay

Ash River

Moose

Tooth Lake

Sand Point Lake

Little Johnson Lake

Johnson Lake

SUPERIOR

Harrison Narrows

Mukooda Lake

Canada Customs

NATIONAL

King Williams Narrows

FOREST

CRANE LAKE

Crane Lake

Dovre Lake

U.S. Customs
To Orr and 53

Vermilion

Autumn forest and cattails on Rainy Lake

Showy lady's slipper

American white pelican

trailhead for a 2-mile hike along a spruce bog and past a beaver pond, dam, and lodge. Watch for the rippling V that marks a swimming beaver. The trail climbs to a ridge and drops to the lakeshore. There you launch your reserved cached canoe and paddle around the lake, watching for muskrat, bald eagles, ospreys, common loons, blue-winged teal, and great blue herons. Another exciting way to explore the park is on an all-day guided cruise to **Kettle Falls.** For details, see **Crane Lake & Ash River** below.

Rainy Lake
at least a half day

Although this lake is large—60 miles long, 12 miles wide—you can safely explore it in your own or a rented motorboat, houseboat, or canoe. At the **Rainy Lake Visitor Center** get weather and navigation information and take a self-guided waterborne excursion. About $1\frac{1}{2}$ miles northwest is **Little American Island,** where the discovery of gold set off a short-lived gold rush a hundred years ago. A short interpretive trail on the island gives a view to the past. About 2 miles east is **Bushyhead Island,** where you can see a mine shaft carved into the rock and a pile of tailings.

Lacking your own boat, you can still explore. The park offers free trips aboard a 26-foot replica of a voyageurs canoe, guided trips aboard contemporary canoes, and programs for children.

Crane Lake & Ash River
at least 1 to 2 days each

Near the Ash River resort area is a visitor center where you can launch your boat, get information about camping, set off on hikes (see below), and obtain charts for navigating the lakes. If you're new to the lakes, *don't fail to use charts.*

If you want a good exploratory voyage, go to Kettle Falls, a waterways hub used by Native Americans, voyageurs, loggers, fishermen, and, during Prohibition, bootleggers smuggling liquor from Canada.

From Crane Lake you travel north through **King Williams**

Sphagnum moss on a pine forest floor

Narrows, across **Sand Point Lake** and through **Namakan Narrows,** then west across **Namakan Lake** along the US-Canada border, which veers northward here.

From Ash River you go the length of **Sullivan Bay** to the mouth of the river, then weave through a string of islands into **Moose Bay.** For a scenic trip, pass through the channel on the south side of **Williams Island** (site of a primitive campsite) into **Hoist Bay,** named for the hoisting of logs that were loaded onto a train. You can see pilings that supported a train track, which ran from the middle of the bay to a white-pine sawmill on the mainland. Head north toward **Namakan Island,** site of other campsites, and go around the western side of the island.

Both courses take you to the southern end of **Squaw Narrows.** Pass through the narrows, then head east along the border through **Squirrel Narrows** to Kettle Falls. Near the dock is a dam that serves a regional system regulating water flow for electric power. At the dock is a gravel road, a portage trail. Walk the road for about ¼ mile to a red-roofed, white clapboard building with a long front porch—the **Kettle Falls Hotel.** Built in 1910, the hotel welcomed lumberjacks and their money, which they left in the bar and in little rooms upstairs. Today the hotel welcomes more genteel patrons: park visitors who make reservations well ahead.

Another way to get to Kettle Falls: Take a cruise boat. Trips are run several times a week out of visitor centers at both Rainy Lake and Kabetogama Lake. The all-day trip is timed for you to eat lunch at the hotel before the return voyage.

Trails near Ash River Visitor Center: Three short trails—the Voyageurs Forest, Beaver Pond, and Kabetogama Lake Overlook—leave from pull-offs on the road to the center. The 2-mile Blind Ash Bay Trail, from the visitor center to the mouth of Blind Ash Bay, wends along rock cliffs through pine forest.

Information & Activities

Headquarters
3131 Hwy. 53 South, International Falls, Minnesota 56649. Phone (218) 283-9821. www.nps.gov/voya

Seasons & Accessibility
Park open year-round. Travel within it is by boat, floatplane, and foot in summer; snowmobile, snowshoes, cross-country skis, and ski-plane in winter. Limited access during lake freeze-up (mid-November to mid-December) and thaw-out (April). In winter, weather permitting, an ice road on Rainy Lake connects the visitor center to Cranberry Bay, 7 miles into the park.

Visitor & Information Centers
Rainy Lake on Minn. 11 at northwest edge of park open daily May 1 to September 30, reduced hours from October 1 to April 30. Call (218) 286-5258. Kabetogama Lake on County Road 122 at southwest edge of lake open daily mid-May to September 30. Call (218) 875-2111. Ash River on southeast edge of Kabetogama Lake open mid-May through September. Call (214) 374-3221.

Entrance Fee
None.

Pets
Permitted on leashes in developed areas and on major lakes. Not allowed on park trails, in backcountry, or on interior lakes.

Facilities for Disabled
Kabetogama Lake, Rainy Lake, and Ash River Visitor Centers are wheelchair accessible, as is Kettle Falls Hotel, guided boat trips, and a campsite. Call Kabetogama Lake for reservations. Fact sheet available.

Things to Do
Free naturalist-led activities: nature walks, canoe trips (reserve at visitor centers), children's and campfire programs, films, exhibits, winter programs. Also, hiking, park canoes and rowboats (free of charge), boat tours, rental boats, fishing and ice fishing (guides available, ask park for list; license required), swimming, waterskiing, snowmobiling, cross-country skiing, and snowshoeing.

Special Advisory
● Practice safe boating: Use navigational maps; be aware of weather conditions; make sure your boat is well equipped; do not overload it.

Camping
All park sites reached by water. 214 backcountry boat-in campsites, 14-day limit. Open all year (though mostly inaccessible during fall freeze-up and spring thaw); first come, first served. No permit needed. No fees. No showers. Tent sites only. Two small campgrounds. In winter, access mainly by snowmobile, cross-country skiing, or snowshoeing. Private campgrounds with tent and RV sites near park.

Hotels, Motels, & Inns
(unless otherwise noted, rates are for 2 persons in a double room, high season)
INSIDE THE PARK:
Kettle Falls Hotel (17 miles by water from the Ash River Trail) 10502 Gamma Road, Ray, Minn. 56669. (888) 534-6835. 12 hotel rooms, shared baths, $65 double; lodge and suites nearby, some with kitchens, $140-$170.
OUTSIDE THE PARK:
In International Falls, Minn. 56649:
Holiday Inn 1500 US Hwy. 71. (800) 331-4443 or (218) 283-8000. 126 units. $80-$130. AC, pool, rest. **Island View Lodge** (on Rainy Lake) 1817 Minn. 11 East. (800) 777-7856 or (218) 286-3511. 9 rooms $69-$89; 12 cabins with kitchens, $140-$325. AC, rest.
In Ray, Minn. 56669 (on Kabetogama Lake):
Rocky Point Resort 12953 Ness Road (218) 875-2411. 8 cabins with kitchens, $300-$1000 per week; 2 lodge rooms, $25 per person. Restaurant. **Voyageur Park Lodge** 10436 Waltz Road (800) 331-5694 or (218) 875-2131) 11 cabins with kitchens (summer only), $560-$1,365 per week; 2 rooms, $65-$135 per night.

For a full listing of accommodations, call:
Kabetogama Tourism Bureau (800) 524-9085; Crane Lake Convention & Visitors Bureau (800) 362-7405; International Falls Area Convention & Visitors Bureau (800) 325-5766; Ash River Commercial Club (800) 950-2061.

Excursions

Superior National Forest

Duluth, Minnesota

Here the northern lights preside over stands of pine, spruce, fir, alder, and birch, and loons bob on the more than 1,000 portage-linked lakes of the Boundary Waters Canoe Area Wilderness. Reservations required for this popular site. 2.2 million acres. Campsites, food services, hiking, boating, boat ramp, fishing, hunting, picnic areas, winter sports, water sports, scenic drives. Open all year; campsites open May-Oct. La Croix Visitor Center west of Cook on US 53 about 15 miles from Orr, Minn., the southern gateway to Voyageurs NP. (218) 666-5251.

Chippewa National Forest

Cass Lake, Minnesota

This lake-country forest boasts one of the largest breeding bald eagle populations outside Alaska and offers a variety of water-based recreation, including the chance to explore the Mississippi's headwaters by canoe. 661,161 acres. Facilities: 23 campgrounds, hiking, boating, boat ramps, fishing, hunting, picnic areas, scenic drives, historic sites with summer interpretive programs, winter sports, handicapped access. Open all year; campsites generally open mid-May to mid-Sept. Information at Cass Lake on US 2, about 85 miles from Voyageurs NP. (218) 335-8600.

Agassiz National Wildlife Refuge

Middle River, Minnesota

More than 265 species of migratory and upland game birds utilize the many resources of this wetlands refuge on the Mississippi flyway. They share the site with some 250 moose and a resident pack of eastern gray wolves—one of the few such packs in any national refuge outside Alaska. 61,500 acres. Facilities include hiking, hunting, scenic drives. Open May 1-October 31, dawn to dusk. Headquarters on Route 7, 11 miles east of Holt, about 185 miles from Voyageurs NP. (218) 449-4115.

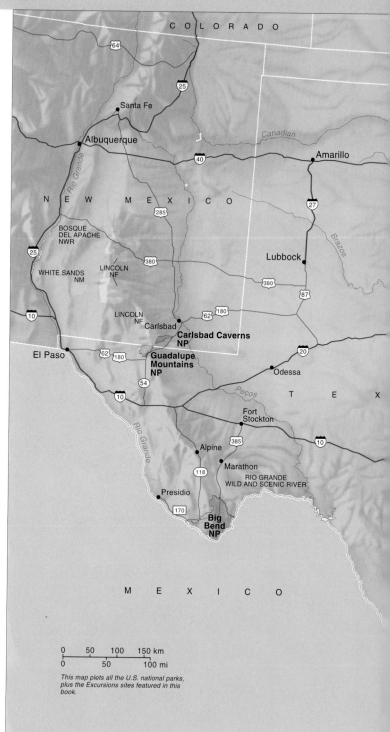

This map plots all the U.S. national parks, plus the Excursions sites featured in this book.

Preceding pages: Dunes, Guadalupe Mountains

The Southwest

The national parks of the Southwest, all set in the Chihuahuan Desert, offer scenery ranging from underground caves to high and rugged mountain peaks. Sparse vegetation opens the spectacular vistas up to visitors without their having to go above tree line.

Water sculptured these landscapes. A reef from an ancient sea forms the 50-mile-long Guadalupe mountain chain. The seeping of water over millions of years created the cool, dark world of Carlsbad Caverns. Rivers etched out the dramatic canyons of Big Bend, and flash floods still tumble boulders from the steep Chisos mountaintops, continuing to rearrange the scenery.

The vagaries of yearly precipitation also determine whether the visitor beholds a land of blossoms—Texas bluebonnets, brilliant red and orange cactus flowers, heavy stalks of white yucca blooms—or, more often, a parched terrain dominated by creosote bush, prickly pear, and dagger-sharp lechuguilla. Where water flows year-round, oases produce gardens that resonate with birdsong.

Visitors to the Southwest parks have a chance to view wildlife as diverse as multicolored lizards and snakes, the elusive mountain lion, deer, hundreds of species of birds, and, in Big Bend, pig look-alikes called javelinas. Paleontologists have found fossils of many other creatures, including giant crocodiles and the Big Bend pterosaur, the largest animal ever to fly.

Hikers may take their own trip back in time by climbing up to the pine-fir forests that cloak the cooler, moister mountaintops in the Guadalupes and Big Bend. This type of forest probably covered the region at the end of the last Ice Age, when early peoples hunted camels, mammoths, and four-horned antelope.

Carlsbad Caverns and Guadalupe Mountains National Parks are linked by the Lincoln National Forest; proposals would unite the three areas into one large park encompassing the Guadalupe range. Base yourself at Carlsbad or, even closer, in Whites City to visit these areas. Allow a day to drive the 250 miles from Guadalupe to Big Bend.

Agave on the South Rim, with Elephant Tusk peak in the distance

Big Bend

Texas

Established June 12, 1944

801,163 acres

As the Rio Grande winds south along the Texas-Mexico border, it suddenly veers northward in a great horseshoe curve before continuing its journey. Inside the horseshoe lies the region of Texas known as the Big Bend; Big Bend National Park flanks the river at the southerly tip of the curve. A wild and surprising land, the park remains remote enough that only the dedicated reach it.

Chihuahuan Desert vegetation—bunchgrasses, creosote bushes, cactuses, lechuguillas, yuccas, and sotols—covers most of the terrain. But the Rio Grande and its lush floodplains and steep, narrow canyons almost form a park of their own. So do the Chisos Mountains; up to 20 degrees cooler than the desert floor, they harbor pine, juniper, and oak, as well as deer, mountain lions, bears, and other wildlife. A heavy rain transforms the very desert: Normally dry creek beds roar with water, and seeds long dormant burst into fields of wildflowers.

The rocks of Big Bend are a complex lot. Two seas, one after another, flowed and subsided in the region hundreds of millions of years ago, leaving thick deposits of limestone and shale. The present mountains, except the Chisos, uplifted along with the Rockies, roughly 75 million years ago. Around the same time, a 40-mile-wide trough—most of the present-day park—sank along fault lines, leaving the cliffs of Santa Elena Canyon to the west and the Sierra del Carmen to the east rising 1,500 feet above the desert floor. In the center, volcanic activity

spewed layer upon layer of ash into the air and squeezed molten rock up through the ground to form the Chisos Mountains some 35 million years ago. Molten rock also cooled and hardened underground later to be exposed by erosion.

Big Bend's topographic variety supports a remarkable diversity of life, including a thousand plant species—some found nowhere else in the world. More species of birds—over 400—have been counted here than in any other US national park.

People have passed through this terrain for at least 10,000 years. The human pageant in historical times has included Apache, Spanish conquistadores, Comanche, US soldiers, miners, ranchers and farmers, Mexican revolutionaries, and international outlaws and bandits.

How to Get There

US 385 leads from Marathon to the north entrance to the park; Texas 118 from Alpine leads to the west entrance; Ranch Road 170, from Presidio, joins Texas 118 shortly before the west entrance. Nearest airports: El Paso (325 miles) and Midland-Odessa (230 miles).

When to Go

All-year park, though fall and winter may be the best seasons. Deciduous leaves turn color in the mountains in autumn; winters are mild. Summer temperatures in the desert can exceed 110°F; the Chisos Mountains remain cooler. If enough rain falls, the desert blooms stunningly in March through May, and again in August and September. Birdwatching is good all year, but especially in March, April, and May.

How to Visit

Allow several days, especially if you plan to hike. Explore the Chisos Mountains Basin and the Ross Maxwell Scenic Drive, engineered to take you past many of the park's geological and scenic highlights. Ideally, devote the better part of a day to each area. With extra time on the second afternoon, or on a third day, drive out to Rio Grande Village and the Boquillas Canyon Overlook to experience the river environment and enjoy views of the Sierra del Carmen, particularly spectacular at sunset. On your way in or out, view the landscape and exhibits along US 385 between Panther Junction and Persimmon Gap. For an extended visit, try more of the many rewarding hikes, drive some dirt roads, and consider a leisurely float trip along the Rio Grande through one of the park's three major canyons.

Rocks at entrance to Santa Elena Canyon

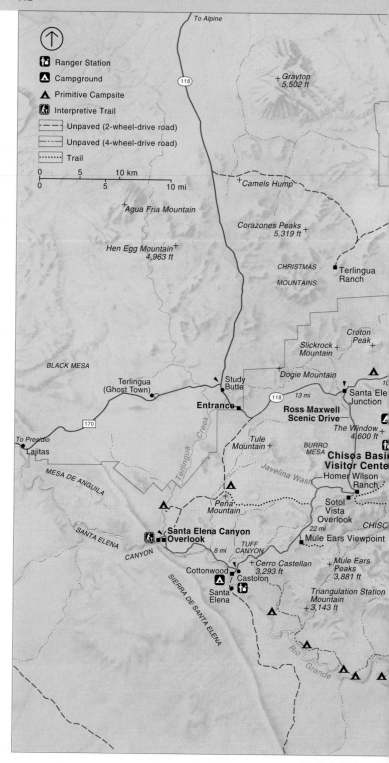

Legend

↑

🏠 Ranger Station

▲ Campground

▲ Primitive Campsite

🚶 Interpretive Trail

– – – Unpaved (2-wheel-drive road)

–·–·– Unpaved (4-wheel-drive road)

········· Trail

| 0 | 5 | 10 km |
| 0 | 5 | 10 mi |

To Alpine

118

+ Graytop
5,502 ft

+ Camels Hump

+ Agua Fria Mountain

Corazones Peaks +
5,319 ft

Hen Egg Mountain +
4,963 ft

CHRISTMAS
MOUNTAINS

■ Terlingua
Ranch

Croton
Peak +

Slickrock +
Mountain

BLACK MESA

Terlingua
(Ghost Town)

Study
Butte

Dogie Mountain

118   13 mi

■ Santa Ele
Junction

Entrance ■

**Ross Maxwell
Scenic Drive**

The Window +
4,600 ft

170

To Presidio
Lajitas

Tule
Mountain +

BURRO
MESA

**Chisos Basi
Visitor Cente**

Javelina Wash

Homer Wilson
Ranch ■

Terlingua Creek

MESA DE ANGUILA

▲

Peña
Mountain

Sotol
Vista
Overlook

CHISO

SANTA ELENA

**Santa Elena Canyon
Overlook**

22 mi

■ Mule Ears Viewpoint

CANYON

TUFF
CANYON

8 mi

+ Cerro Castellan
3,293 ft

+ Mule Ears
Peaks
3,881 ft

Cottonwood ●

SIERRA DE SANTA ELENA

▲ Castolon

🏠

Santa
Elena

Triangulation Station
Mountain
+ 3,143 ft

▲

Rio Grande

▲ ▲ ▲

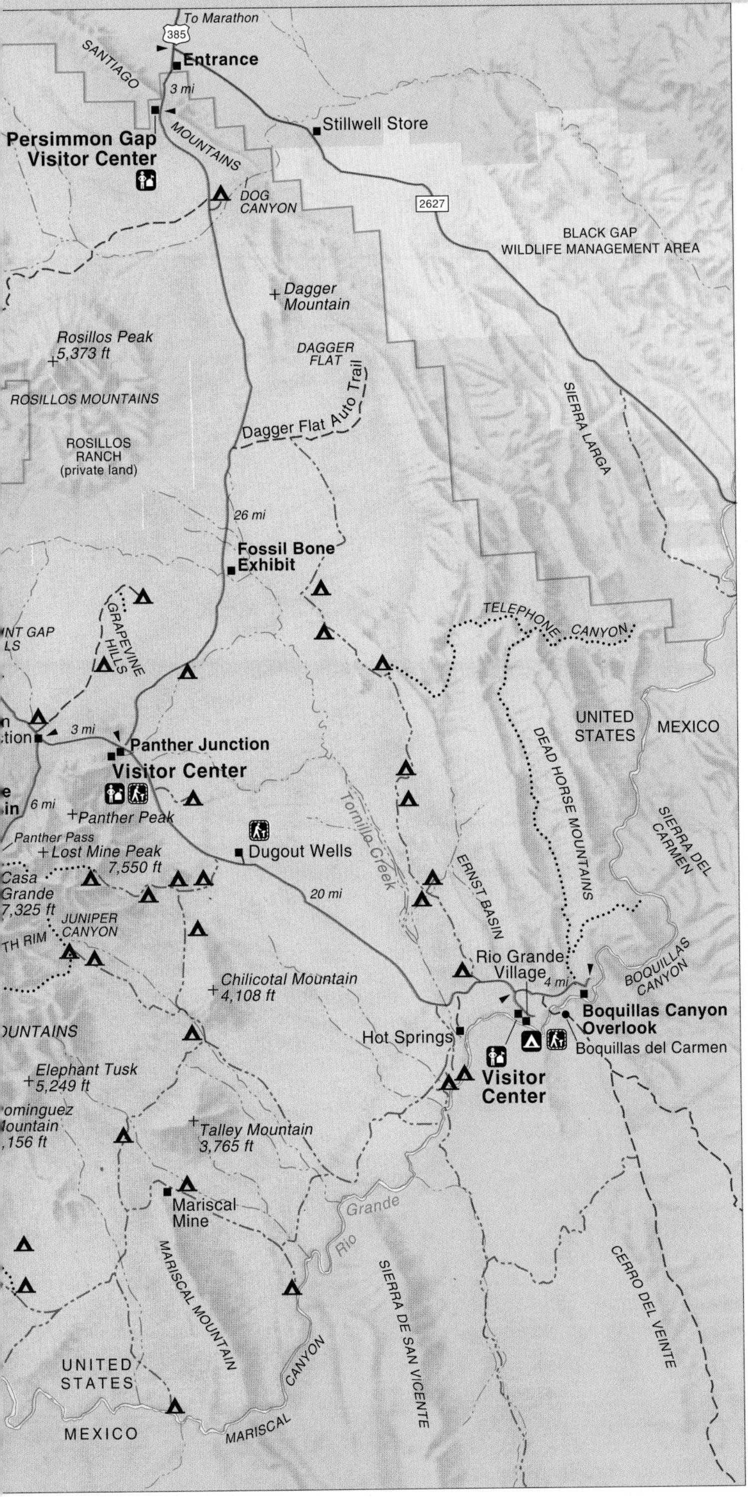

To Marathon

385

Entrance

3 mi

SANTIAGO

Stillwell Store

Persimmon Gap
Visitor Center

MOUNTAINS

DOG
CANYON

2627

BLACK GAP
WILDLIFE MANAGEMENT AREA

Dagger
Mountain

Rosillos Peak
5,373 ft

DAGGER
FLAT

ROSILLOS MOUNTAINS

SIERRA LARGA

ROSILLOS
RANCH
(private land)

Dagger Flat Auto Trail

26 mi

Fossil Bone
Exhibit

GRAPEVINE
HILLS

NT GAP
LS

TELEPHONE CANYON

UNITED
STATES

MEXICO

tion

3 mi

Panther Junction
Visitor Center

DEAD HORSE MOUNTAINS

in

6 mi

Panther Peak

Panther Pass

Lost Mine Peak
7,550 ft

Dugout Wells

Casa
Grande
7,325 ft

JUNIPER
CANYON

20 mi

Tornillo Creek

ERNST BASIN

SIERRA DEL
CARMEN

TH RIM

Rio Grande
Village

4 mi

BOQUILLAS
CANYON

Chilicotal Mountain
4,108 ft

UNTAINS

Hot Springs

Boquillas Canyon
Overlook

Boquillas del Carmen

Visitor
Center

Elephant Tusk
5,249 ft

ominguez
Mountain
,156 ft

Talley Mountain
3,765 ft

Grande

Mariscal
Mine

Río

MARISCAL MOUNTAIN

SIERRA DE SAN VICENTE

CANYON

CERRO DEL VEINTE

UNITED
STATES

MEXICO

MARISCAL

Sunset on the Maverick Badlands

Panther Junction to the Chisos Basin

10 miles one way; at least a half day

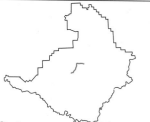

Start your tour at the visitor center at **Panther Junction.** Collect maps, information on hiking, and safety tips on avoiding encounters with rattlesnakes, mountain lions, and flash floods. Don't miss **Panther Path**—the 50-yard nature trail near the visitor center entrance whose self-guiding pamphlet provides an excellent introduction to the plants you'll see on much of your trip. Behind the visitor center lie the **Chisos Mountains,** the

southernmost range in the continental United States, and your destination. When ready, return to your car and turn left out of the visitor center, then left at **Basin Junction** in 3 miles. Ahead on the right looms **Pulliam Bluff.** Look closely and you might see in the mountain the profile of a man's face, reclining. Legend relates that the man is Alsate, an important Apache chief whose ghost lives on in the high Chisos Mountains, and whose campfire can occasionally be seen at night. At 2½ miles, the jagged summit to your left is **Lost Mine Peak.** Spanish explorers, it is told, discovered a rich silver mine near the summit and enslaved Indians to work it. The miners rebelled, killed their overlords, and sealed the entrance to the mine so that it might remain lost forever. As you drive on, the castle-like summit of **Casa Grande**—"big house"—will be straight ahead, a landmark for much of the park.

The road climbs higher into the mountains through a canyon called

Riding the slopes of the Chisos Basin

Green Gulch: Watch the vegetation change from desert shrub to sotol grasslands, then to pinyon pine, juniper, and oak woodland. The Chisos form a cooler, moister island in the surrounding desert. Some 10,000 years ago, pinyon-juniper forests extended down to the desert floor, but the trees withdrew to higher altitudes as the climate gradually warmed at the end of the Ice Age. In about 5 miles the road hits its highest point at **Panther Pass** (5,770 feet), named for the mountain lions that still roam these hills. Only the lucky few ever see one. If you have time, park at the nearby trailhead for the **Lost Mine Trail,** a self-guided nature trail with an informative booklet. The panorama from the top, one of the grandest in the park, makes the moderately strenuous 4⅘-mile round-trip well worth the trek. But if you're short of time, just hike the 2-mile round-trip to the **Juniper Canyon Overlook,** for good vistas of wooded **Juniper Canyon** to the south and Pulliam Bluff to the northwest.

After Panther Pass, the road descends in hairpin curves to the basin, a 3-mile-wide depression in the mountains, chiseled by wind and water. Many of the park's choice hikes start from the basin trailhead, west of the ranger station. At the least, make sure to stroll the easy ³⁄₁₀-mile round-trip **Window View Trail.** Particularly photogenic at sunset, the **Window** is a V-shaped opening, or pour off, in the mountains, through which all rain and meltwater from the

Claret cup cactus abloom in the high Chisos

basin drains. A more challenging trail descends through desert and shady canyon to the Window itself, offering classic afternoon views of Casa Grande framed by oaks and pines. In summer, take this and other lower elevation hikes in early morning or late afternoon.

The literal high point of many visitors' trips to the park is a hike to the **South Rim** (7,400 feet), a moderately steep 13-mile round-trip that provides unforgettable vistas of much of the park. At **Boot Canyon,** 4½ miles up the trail to the South Rim, lives an oasis of bigtooth maple, Douglas-fir, and Arizona pine. The gray-and-yellow Colima warbler nests on the canyon floor, its only home in the United States.

Before you hike, check at the **Chisos Basin Visitor Center** for maps and hiking tips, and make sure you carry plenty of water. At the visitor center, ask also about the presence of peregrine falcons. Several of these endangered birds nest in the Chisos.

Rafting the Rio Grande through Santa Elena Canyon

Ross Maxwell Scenic Drive: Santa Elena Junction to Santa Elena Canyon

30 miles one way; a half to full day

Heading south from **Santa Elena Junction, Burro Mesa**—named for the burros that once grazed the top—will be to your right, and the Chisos to your left. After 2 miles, stop at the exhibit on the left for a fine view of the Window framing Casa Grande. Drive on a little over a mile, then park at the old **Sam Nail Ranch** and stroll

the short path to the remains of windmills and a ranch house. The shade of the pecan and willow trees the Nails planted makes a fine resting and birdwatching spot. Walk back to your car and motor on. In about a mile, long walls of rock traverse the landscape. They are dikes, created by molten rock that squeezed up into underground cracks before hardening. The softer rock layers above them eventually eroded away, leaving the erosion-resistant dikes.

Stop next at the **Blue Creek Ranch (Homer Wilson Ranch) Overlook.** A century ago most of Big Bend was cloaked in grasses. But ranchers grazed thousands of cattle, sheep, and goats, destroying the grass and exposing the topsoil to erosion. Creosote, mesquite, allthorn, and other spiny shrubs moved into the damaged areas. Here, and elsewhere in the park, grasses are slowly returning.

Go back to the road and take a quick left onto the **Sotol Vista** spur road, named for the ridge's rich growth of sotol, the bright green plant with sawlike teeth on the edges of the leaves. Indians roasted and ate the heart of the sotol and fermented it to yield an alcoholic drink. The parking lot at the top provides vistas of the surrounding mountains, and a plaque at the end of the loop identifies what's what.

Return to the main road; an exhibit on the left in about 6½ miles describes how volcanism shaped this striking landscape. Take the next spur road on the left, for an excellent view of the peaks known as **Mule Ears,** a name explained at a glance. During the 1930s, Army Air Corps pilots drilled by flying planes between the twin peaks. Stop again after 4½ miles to see **Tuff Canyon,** carved by **Blue Creek** through layers of lava flows, boulders, and compressed volcanic ash called tuff. Stroll the short trail to the right to view the canyon. The trail at the left of the parking lot provides a moderately steep hike down into the canyon, a ¾-mile round-trip.

Back in your car, you'll be approaching **Cerro Castellan,** another important landmark, rising 1,000 feet above its surroundings. Turn left into **Castolon** to stroll around the old Army post that protected residents from bandits during the 1914-18 border troubles with Mexico. The main building, originally the barracks, was converted to a frontier trading post around 1920. Today you can buy cold drinks and picnic there.

After leaving Castolon, the road parallels the **Rio Grande,** passing the scattered remains of adobe houses dating back to the turn of the 20th century. The occupants once grew food crops and cotton in the Rio Grande's fertile floodplain.

Be sure to stop about 8 miles from Castolon, at the parking area for the **Santa Elena Canyon Overlook.** Laden with abrasive silt and gravel, the Rio Grande sculptured the canyon 1,500 feet deep, through the cliffs that tower above the geological trough that forms the bulk of the park.

Drive on to the end of the road, put on some old shoes, and, if the water is low, wade across **Terlingua Creek** to reach the **Santa Elena Canyon Trail.** The moderate 1⁷⁄₁₀-mile round-trip trail leads into the canyon mouth, amply rewarding the hiker with striking views.

Mule Ears Peaks and prickly pear cactus

Cerro Castellan looming over an old Army post

Panther Junction to Rio Grande Village & Boquillas Canyon Overlook

24 miles one way; a half to full day

Before starting this tour, check at the visitor center for the condition of the Hot Springs road. The main road, heading southeast, descends nearly 2,000 feet through desert shrub, terminating near the willows and cottonwoods on the banks of the Rio Grande. After about 6½ miles, turn left onto the unpaved road to see the spring at **Dugout Wells,** formerly the site of a ranch and schoolhouse, and now a fine place to picnic and look for wildlife. Return to the main road. As you continue, the peak aptly named **Elephant Tusk** will be on your right in the distance, and **Chilicotal Mountain** closer to the road. Far ahead looms the **Sierra del Carmen** in Mexico. Its striated rock formations are the same

Greater roadrunner speeding across the desert

limestone and shale as in the cliffs at **Santa Elena Canyon.**

If you're up to a somewhat rough ride, be sure to take the turnoff to **Hot Springs,** whose mineral waters were valued for centuries. Look for Indian pictographs on the cliffs along the trail to the springs, just beyond the old motel. After returning to the main road, pull over at the **Rio Grande Overlook** just past the tunnel on the right, and stroll a 50-yard trail for superb views of the Sierra del Carmen, the river floodplain, and part of **Boquillas del Carmen** village in Mexico. Big Bend bluebonnets bloom profusely here during a well-watered springtime. Back on the road, continue straight for ½ mile, then turn left and continue another 3 miles to the paved spur road to **Boquillas Canyon Overlook.** Then double back; if you wish to see a Mexican village, take the dirt road on your left in about a mile. At the riverbank, a ferryman should be waiting to row you across the Rio Grande for a small fee. The middle of the river forms the international border. Then pay for a donkey ride or walk the ¾ mile into Boquillas del Carmen. When you're back, turn left onto the main road, then left again to visit **Rio Grande Village,** an excellent place to watch birds. Don't miss the nature trail starting across from site No. 18 in the campground. This easy ¾-mile loop leads through jungle-like floodplain vegetation before climbing onto a ridge that provides terrific views of the river and the Sierra del Carmen.

Javelina, a cactus-loving omnivore

Panther Junction to Persimmon Gap

26 miles one way; 2 hours

This road follows an ancient trail used by the Comanches on their annual raiding forays into Mexico, and by Army expeditions, settlers, and miners of silver and lead. For an excellent self-guided auto tour, pick up a pamphlet at either end of the road and, if traveling in springtime, ask whether the giant dagger yuccas are in bloom. (If so, be sure to take the unpaved Dagger Flat Auto Trail to see stalkfuls of white blooms weighing up to 70 pounds; if not, skip the detour.) Much of the road traverses Tornillo Flat, one of the most overgrazed and poorly recovered areas of the park. Highlights of the drive include a view of Dog Canyon, through which camels once lumbered in a 19th-century US Army experiment, and the exhibit of fossil mammal bones found in the park.

Information & Activities

Headquarters
1 Panther Junction, Big Bend National Park, Texas 79834. Phone (915) 477-2251. www.nps.gov/bibe

Seasons & Accessibility
Open all year. Check current conditions before driving dirt roads.

Visitor & Information Centers
Panther Junction and Chisos Basin Visitor Centers open daily all year. Rio Grande Village Visitor Center open Nov. through April. Visitor center also at Persimmon Gap. Call headquarters for visitor information.

Entrance Fee
$10 per car per week.

Facilities for Disabled
Visitor center facilities and two nature trails are wheelchair accessible. Free brochure.

Things to Do
Free naturalist-led activities: nature walks, workshops, evening programs. Also, hiking, fishing, river-running (permits required), bicycling, nature seminars.

Overnight Backpacking
Free permits required. Obtain in person at visitor centers or ranger stations within 24 hours of trip.

Campgrounds
Four campgrounds with 14-day limit. Open all year, first come, first served. Fees $8-$15 per night. Tent and RV sites. At **Rio Grande Village Trailer Park,** full hookups only available. Three group campgrounds; reservations through headquarters.

Hotels, Motels, & Inns
(unless otherwise noted, rates are for 2 persons in a double room, high season)
Chisos Mountains Lodge National Park Concessions, Inc., Basin Rural Station, Big Bend NP, Texas 79834. (915) 477-2291. 72 rooms, $80; 6 cottages, $90. AC, rest. **Big Bend Motor Inn** (Junct. of Tex. 118 and Rte. 170) P.O. Box 336, Terlingua, Texas 79852. (800) 848-2363 or (915) 371-2218. 86 rooms, 10 with kitchenettes, $69; 4 duplexes with kitchens, $105-$124. AC, pool, rest. **Gage Hotel** (Junct. of US 90 and US 385) P.O. Box 46, Marathon, Texas 79842. (800) 884-4243 or (915) 386-4205. 37 units. $65-$175. AC, rest. **Lajitas on the Rio Grande** (on Texas 170) Star Rte. 70, Box 400, Terlingua, Texas 79852. (877) 525-4827 or (915) 424-3471. 218 rooms; 12 condos, kitchenettes. $81-$195. AC, pool, restaurant.

Excursion

Rio Grande Wild and Scenic River
Big Bend National Park, Texas

Floating the Rio Grande is an experience not to be missed. Big Bend NP administers both the section along its border and the Wild and Scenic stretches downstream. Easy floats include the Mariscal and Boquillas Canyons; Santa Elena and the Lower Canyons are more difficult. Boating permits required. Main access point to Lower Canyons in Mexico; most take-out points fall on private land in Texas (permission required). 196 Wild and Scenic miles. Facilities also include primitive camping, hiking, fishing; inner-tubing and swimming not recommended. Info. about outfitters offering half-day to 1-week trips at Panther Junction. (915) 477-2251.

Hall of Giants in the Big Room

Carlsbad Caverns

New Mexico

Established May 14, 1930

46,766 acres

The Chihuahuan Desert, studded with spiky plants and lizards, offers little hint that what Will Rogers called the "Grand Canyon with a roof on it" waits underground. Yet, at the northern reaches of this great desert, underneath a mountain range called the Guadalupes, lies one of the deepest, largest, and most ornate caverns ever found.

Water molded this underworld 4 to 6 million years ago. Some 250 million years ago, the region lay underneath the inland arm of an ancient sea. Near the shore grew a limestone reef. By the time the sea withdrew, the reef stood hundreds of feet high, later to be buried under thousands of feet of soil. Some 15 to 20 million years ago, the

ground uplifted. Slightly acidic groundwater seeped into cracks in the limestone, gradually enlarging them to form a honeycomb of chambers. Millions of more years passed before the cave decoration began. Then, drop by drop, limestone-laden moisture built an extraordinary variety of glistening formations. Some of these are six stories tall; others tiny, delicate confections.

Cave scientists have explored more than 30 miles of passageways of the main cavern of Carlsbad, and investigation continues. Visitors may tour 3 of these miles on a paved trail. The Slaughter Canyon Cave provides the hardy an opportunity to play spelunker, albeit with a guide. The park has more than 90 other caves open primarily to specialists.

Some visitors think the park's most spectacular sight is the one seen at the

When to Go

All-year park. The weather underground remains a constant 56°F. The main cavern gets crowded, especially in summer and on major holiday weekends. Either spring or fall, when the desert's in bloom, is an excellent time to go. You'll see the bats fly from April or early May through October, sometimes later.

How to Visit

One full day allows you time to tour the main cavern and take a nature walk or a drive before watching the bats fly at sunset. For a second day's activity, reserve space on a tour of "unimproved" **Slaughter Canyon Cave,** if you're ready for a more rugged caving experience.

At the visitor center, select either the Natural Entrance Tour or the Big Room Tour (both are 1-mile walks). Try the first unless you have walking, breathing, or heart problems. It starts at the natural entrance and is mostly downhill or level, except for one stretch where you climb 83 feet; an elevator whisks you back to ground level. The Main Corridor is more intimate and may be less crowded than the Big Room. Another option, the Palace Tour (see **Other Trails & Sights** p. 125) visits the stunning formations in the Scenic Rooms.

The Big Room Tour begins with an elevator ride directly to the Big Room, in which you can see most of the types of formations visible in the other sections. If after this tour you want to see more caves, take the elevator back up to ground level and proceed with the first half of the Natural Entrance Tour.

cave's mouth. More than a half million Mexican free-tailed bats summer in a section of the cave, and around sunset they spiral up from the entrance to hunt for insects. The nightly exodus led to the discovery of the cave in modern times. Around the turn of the century, miners began to excavate bat guano—a potent fertilizer—for shipment to the citrus groves of southern California. One of the guano miners, James Larkin White, became the first to explore and publicize the caverns beyond the Bat Cave.

How to Get There

The park is off US 62/180, 20 miles southwest of Carlsbad and 164 miles east of El Paso, Texas. For the visitor center, turn west at Whites City and drive 7 miles. For Slaughter Canyon, turn west on County Rd. 418, 5 miles south of Whites City; drive another 11 miles, some unpaved, to the parking lot. Airports: Carlsbad and El Paso, Texas.

Natural Entrance Tour

1 mile; about 1 hour

The visitor center rents a CD player for an audio tour, if you wish. Exit to the right, following the path to the cavern's natural entrance. The opening formed when part of the cave's ceiling collapsed thousands of years ago. Once in the mouth of the cave, glance right to spot 1,000-year-old red and black pictographs high on the wall. Indians knew of the cavern and used the entrance for shelter. But without dependable lighting they could not have gone very far past the small sunlit area. You are descending the **Main**

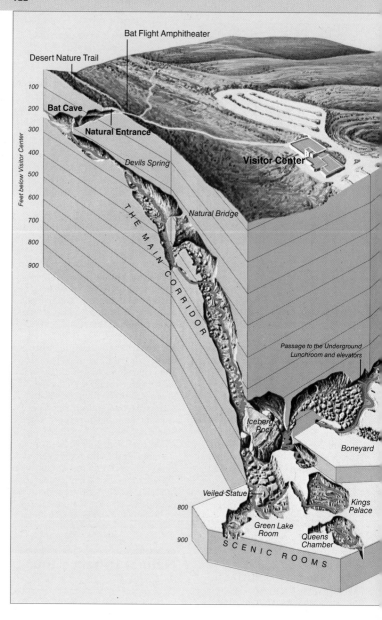

Bat Flight Amphitheater

Desert Nature Trail

100
200
300
400
500
600
700
800
900

Feet below Visitor Center

Bat Cave

Natural Entrance

Devils Spring

Visitor Center

THE MAIN CORRIDOR

Natural Bridge

Passage to the Underground
Lunchroom and elevators

Iceberg Rock

Boneyard

Veiled Statue

Kings Palace

800

Green Lake Room

Queens Chamber

900

SCENIC ROOMS

Corridor, which, if you keep looking around and up, conveys some of the cavern's enormity: The ceiling at times rises more than 200 feet above the path.

The trail soon passes **Devils Spring.** Here cave decoration continues. As water from rain and snow percolates through the ancient reef, it picks up calcite crystals from the limestone. The water then releases the crystals with each drop, splattering them onto the floor as the water drips—producing a stalagmite—or leaving them on the ceiling as the water discharges carbon dioxide into the cave air—creating a stalactite. (Park rangers like to repeat the mnemonic that stalactites "hang tight" to the ceiling, while stalagmites "might grow off your head.") You would have heard a lot more dripping 10,000 years ago,

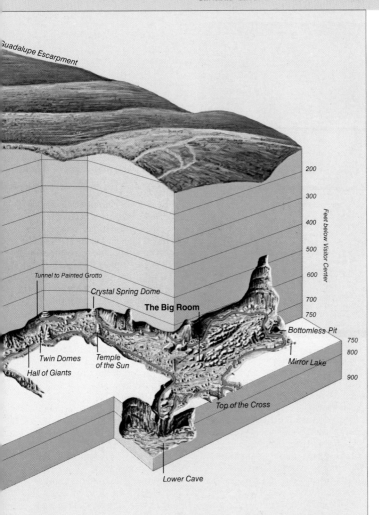

Guadalupe Escarpment

Feet below Visitor Center

200
300
400
500
600
700
750

Tunnel to Painted Grotto

Crystal Spring Dome

The Big Room

Bottomless Pit

750
800

900

Twin Domes

Temple of the Sun

Mirror Lake

Hall of Giants

Top of the Cross

Lower Cave

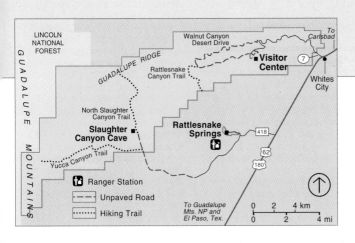

LINCOLN NATIONAL FOREST

To Carlsbad

Walnut Canyon Desert Drive

GUADALUPE RIDGE

Rattlesnake Canyon Trail

Visitor Center

7

Whites City

North Slaughter Canyon Trail

Slaughter Canyon Cave

Rattlesnake Springs

418

GUADALUPE MOUNTAINS

Yucca Canyon Trail

62

180

Ranger Station

Unpaved Road

Hiking Trail

To Guadalupe Mts. NP and El Paso, Tex.

0   2   4 km
0   2   4 mi

Twin Domes in the Hall of Giants

when the climate was wetter. Now the Guadalupes receive only about 14 to 19 inches of precipitation a year, and most of the formations are no longer growing.

The trail soon skirts **Iceberg Rock,** a 200,000-ton boulder that crashed down from the ceiling thousands of years ago. After climbing **Appetite Hill,** stroll on past the **Boneyard,** which probably resembles the cavern of 4–6 million years ago, when water filled the chambers. Follow the signs to the Underground Lunchroom to have a meal, if you like. To reach ground level, take the nearby elevator up to the visitor center.

Big Room Tour

1 mile; 1 hour

After a minute's elevator ride, you'll be 755 feet, or about 75 stories, underground. (Compare your entrance to that of visitors of the early 1920s: They entered by "bucket elevator," as a pulley lowered them into the Bat Cave in a guano bucket.) Follow the signs for the Big Room: For the next hour or so, you'll be circling one gigantic chamber.

The **Big Room** is the largest single room most visitors will ever see

(unless they go to Borneo, where there is a cave with a larger, undecorated chamber), 1,800 feet long at its longest point, and 1,100 feet at its widest. It encompasses 8.2 acres.

To best enjoy the tour, linger, look, listen, and above all let loose your imagination. What do the various formations look like to you? Layer cakes? Chinese friezes? Fossilized bonsai? In recent years the Park Service removed labels from many of the formations, so now you can name the fantasyscape yourself.

Near the beginning of the walk, the **Hall of Giants** sports some of the largest formations in the cave, many of them about six stories tall. Look for **Giant Dome,** a 62-foot-high stalagmite, flanked by two 42-foot-high deputies. Appearances are deceptive here because of the immensity of the chamber. The trail continues along the periphery of the room (resist the call of the shortcut) and leads past a view of the **Lower Cave,** one of the many explored passages inaccessible to the public. Farther along, at **Top of the Cross,** rangers sometimes give talks at an amphitheater. Glance up: The ceiling here soars to 255 feet, its highest point above the trail.

The footpath continues through a less ornate area that was once a bat roost. The so-called **Bottomless Pit** has been measured at about 140 feet in depth; it does not lead to other passages. As you proceed, take a good look at sparkling **Crystal Spring Dome,** the cave's largest active stalagmite: Each drop of water adds crystals that make it infinitesimally bigger. Iron carried in the water delicately stains the formations of the Painted Grotto. Just a few minutes past the grotto, you'll reach the elevator and ascend to daylight.

In the visitor center, don't miss the exhibits on cave restoration or the historical photographs of guano mining and early tourism. Then climb the stairs to the **Observation Tower.** Standing above the ancient reef, you see a striking vista of the reef's seaward side (the slope past the parking lot) and the ancient seabed, called the Delaware Basin. On clear days, the panorama before you extends 100 miles into Texas.

Mexican free-tailed bats emerging from their cave

Other Trails & Sights

The easy ½-mile loop **Desert Nature Trail** makes an interesting diversion before the evening bat flight program. The trail's interpretive plaques describe how Indians made use of virtually every plant in sight. The trail starts to the right of the cave's natural entrance.

Walnut Canyon Desert Drive is an alternative introduction to the area's natural history. A booklet available at the start guides you along this 9½-mile gravel loop off the main park road, just before the visitor center.

Kings Palace Tour: Led by park rangers, this 1½-hour tour visits four highly decorative rooms, including the Kings Palace, which may be one of the most ornate cave rooms in the world. Tour participants descend 830 feet to the deepest part of the cave allowed to the public. Look for the giant draperies, formed when water trickles down a slanted ceiling. Visitors will also find soda-straw stalactites, columns, and other interesting speleothems. Tours are offered several times a day throughout the year. Make reservations at the visitor center.

Bat Flight: Don't miss the evening cyclone of bats; at its peak, more than 5,000 bats per minute speed out of the

Immature bats in Bat Cave

cave on their way to consume some three tons of insects. From the visitor center, walk to the amphitheater, at the natural entrance, or drive there by turning right onto the main road, then right again.

Slaughter Canyon Cave: Be prepared to slip and slide as you explore an "unimproved" cave for 2 hours by flashlight. Accompanied by rangers, you'll see several types of formations not found in the main cave, after a steep ½-mile climb up to the cave's entrance from the parking lot in Slaughter Canyon. The cave is open daily in summer; weekends only in winter. Reservations are recommended; you can make them at the visitor center or by calling the park reservation number, (800) 967-2283.

Information & Activities

Headquarters
3225 National Parks Highway, Carlsbad, New Mexico 88220. Phone (505) 785-2232. Off-trail trip reservations (800) 967-2283. www.nps.gov/cave

Seasons & Accessibility
Park open year-round, except Christmas Day.

Visitor & Information Centers
The visitor center is 7 miles from Whites City; open daily all year, except Christmas. Call headquarters for information.

Entrance Fees
No entrance fee for park. Fees to enter cavern and tour Natural Entrance route and Big Room: adults $6; children ages 6-15, $3; children under 6 free. To tour Kings Palace, additional $8 for adults, children under age 16, $4, children under 6 free, under 4 not permitted. To tour Slaughter Canyon Cave, additional $15 for adults, $7.50 for children under age 16; children under 6 not permitted. For off-trail caving tour, additional $12 for adults, $6 for children under age 16; children under 6 not permitted. No charge for bat flight program.

Pets
Not allowed in caves or backcountry. Kennel at the visitor center.

Facilities for Disabled
The visitor center and Bat Flight Amphitheater are wheelchair accessible, as is a portion of the cave tour. Picnic area and rest rooms accessible at Rattlesnake Springs.

Things to Do
Ranger-led activities: tours of the main cavern (call park for details), cavern talks, dusk bat flight programs, flashlight trip into Slaughter Canyon Cave (see page 125; reservations required). Also available, self-guided Desert Nature Trail, self-guided Walnut Canyon Desert Drive, backcountry trails.

Special Advisories
● Wear low-heeled, non-skid shoes in the caverns, and bring a jacket.
● Intense summer thunderstorms may cause floods in low-lying areas, lightning strikes in higher areas.
● Watch out for rattlesnakes when hiking the backcountry trails.
● Cactuses and other spiny desert plants can inflict painful injuries.

Overnight Backpacking
Permits required. Available free at the visitor center.

Campgrounds
None; backcountry camping only. Food services in park.

Hotels, Motels, & Inns
(unless otherwise noted, rates are for 2 persons in a double room, high season)
In Whites City, N. Mex. 88268:
Best Western Cavern Inn (17 Carlsbad Cavern Hwy.) P.O. Box 128. (800) 228-3767 or (505) 785-2291. 42 units. $85. AC, pool, restaurant.
In Carlsbad, N. Mex. 88220:
Best Western Motel Stevens (1829 S. Canal St.) P.O. Box 580. (800) 730-2851 or (505) 887-2851. 204 units, 18 with kitchenettes. $59. AC, pool, restaurant.
Carlsbad Super 8 3817 National Parks Hwy. (800) 800-8000 or (505) 887-8888. 60 units. $59, includes breakfast. AC, pool.
Continental Inn 3820 National Parks Hwy. (505) 887-0341. 60 units. $39.95. AC, pool.
Quality Inn 3706 National Parks Hwy. (800) 321-2861 or (505) 887-2861. 124 units. $65-$75. AC, pool, restaurant.
Great Western Inn & Suites 3804 National Parks Hwy. (800) 987-5535 or (505) 887-5535. 87 units, 25 with kitchenettes. $69-$90. AC, pool.

Contact the Carlsbad Chamber of Commerce for a full list of accommodations: P.O. Box 910, Dept. bm, Carlsbad, New Mexico 88221. (505) 887-6516.

Excursions

Lincoln National Forest
Alamogordo, New Mexico

In 1950, a game warden here rescued a black bear cub from a forest fire and named him Smokey Bear—he became a famous symbol of fire prevention. Lincoln contains life zones from desert to subalpine forest and limestone caves. 1,103,441 acres. 370 campsites, hiking, fishing, horseback riding, hunting, picnicking, winter sports. Open all year; most campsites open seasonally. Adjoins Carlsbad Caverns NP on west. Info. at Carlsbad on US 285, about 20 miles from park. (505) 885-4181.

White Sands National Monument
Alamogordo, New Mexico

Waves of gypsum sand, some 50 feet high, offer an ever changing vista here in the Tularosa Basin. Weathered rock from surrounding highlands settles in Lake Lucero and adjacent alkali flats; scouring southwest winds create the dunes. Features 16-mile-long Dunes Drive. 144,420 acres. Primitive camping, food services, hiking, picnic areas. Open daily except Christmas. Visitor center on US 70, about 190 miles from Carlsbad Caverns NP. (505) 479-6124.

Bosque del Apache National Wildlife Refuge
Socorro, New Mexico

The Rio Grande bisects this refuge, where carefully maintained ponds and marshes shelter wintering snow geese and other waterfowl, as well as sandhill cranes and endangered whooping cranes, bald eagles, and peregrine falcons. 57,191 acres. Facilities include hiking, fishing (in summer), biking, hunting, scenic drives. Open year-round, from 1 hour before sunrise to 1 hour after sunset. Visitor center on New Mexico 1, off I-25, about 270 miles from Carlsbad Caverns NP. (505) 835-1828.

Sunset on El Capitan, beacon of the Guadalupes

Guadalupe Mountains

Texas

Established September 30, 1972

86,416 acres

In west Texas, only about 40 miles southwest of Carlsbad Caverns, lies a gem of a park that few people outside the state have ever heard of, let alone visited. Guadalupe Mountains National Park contains the southernmost, highest part of the 50-mile-long Guadalupe range. From the highway, the mountains resemble a nearly monolithic wall through the desert. But drive into one of the park entrances, take even a short stroll, and surprises crop up: dramatically contoured canyons, shady glades surrounded by desert scrub, a profusion of wildlife and birds.

Some 80 miles of trails can lead the more energetic hiker to Guadalupe Peak, the highest point in Texas (8,749 feet), and to mountaintops with scattered but thick conifer forests typical of the Rockies hundreds of miles to the north. The range's origins may be surprising too: The Guadalupe Mountains were once a reef growing beneath the waters of an ancient inland sea. That same vanished sea spawned the honeycomb of the Carlsbad Caverns.

Pottery, baskets, and spear tips found in the mountains suggest that people first visited the Guadalupes about 12,000 years ago, hunting the camels, mammoths, and other animals that flourished in the wetter climate of the waning Ice Age. When the Spaniards arrived in the Southwest in the mid-16th century, Mescalero Apache were periodically camping near the springs at the base of the mountains and climbing to the highlands to hunt and forage.

main visitor center, then continue 4 miles to the parking lot. For Dog Canyon, either hike 12 miles from Pine Springs Campground or drive north on US 62/180, then west on Cty. Rd. 408, and south on N. Mex. 137, about 105 miles total from Pine Springs. Airports: Carlsbad and El Paso.ˆ

When to Go

All-year park, but spring and fall are best. In spring, the foliage is fresh and, with enough rain, the blossoms abundant. In late October to mid-November, changing leaves provide splashes of red, yellow, burgundy.

How to Visit

On a day trip, head to the visitor center and **Pine Springs;** take at least a short hike. On a second day, visit **McKittrick Canyon** for a stroll through a hidden oasis. To visit a wilder, more isolated area, where trails take you quickly into the high country, drive about 3 hours to reenter the park at **Dog Canyon** in the north.

Pine Springs-Frijole Area
a half to full day

Pick up maps and trail information at the **Headquarters Visitor Center,** where you can also enjoy audiovisual programs on the park's ecology, geology, and history. Fill your water bottles before leaving. Then stroll to **The Pinery** or drive back to the highway, turn left in about 1/10 mile, and park. The stone walls remain from the 1858 Pinery Station of the Butterfield Overland Mail Line—forerunner of the Pony Express. Buy a self-guiding leaflet, if you wish, to learn about the colorful local history. Return to your car, and go back to the highway and turn left. Go left again in about a mile onto a dirt road. Park at the end near the **Frijole Ranch,** the 1870s ranch house that now preserves artifacts and exhibits the park's cultural history.

Be sure to walk the easy 2 3/10-mile loop trail to **Smith** and **Manzanita Springs,** an excellent introduction to the striking contrasts the Chihuahuan Desert presents. Bear right at the trailhead. The thorny plants may seem forbidding, but the Mescalero Apache

Both the Apache and Europeans spun legends of fabulous caches of gold in these mountains.

As American prospectors, settlers, and cavalry pushed west, the Apache made the mountainous areas their bases and fought to ward off encroachers. By the late 1880s, however, virtually all the Indians had been killed or forced onto a reservation. Donations of ranchlands eventually gave impetus to the park.

In 1998 the park acquired 10,000 acres adjacent to its then western boundary, including some 2,000 acres of white gypsum sand dunes and dunes of brick red quartzose, both deposits left by the ancient sea.

How to Get There

The main visitor center and most visitor activities are located in the Pine Springs-Frijole area, off US 62/180, 55 miles southwest of Carlsbad and 110 miles east of El Paso. For McKittrick Canyon, turn off US 62/180 about 7 miles northeast of the

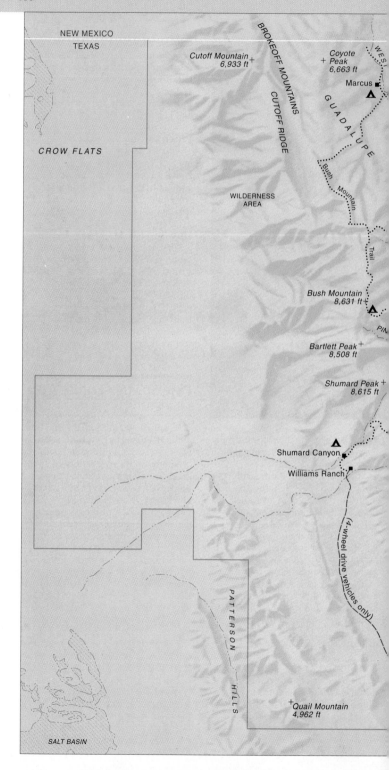

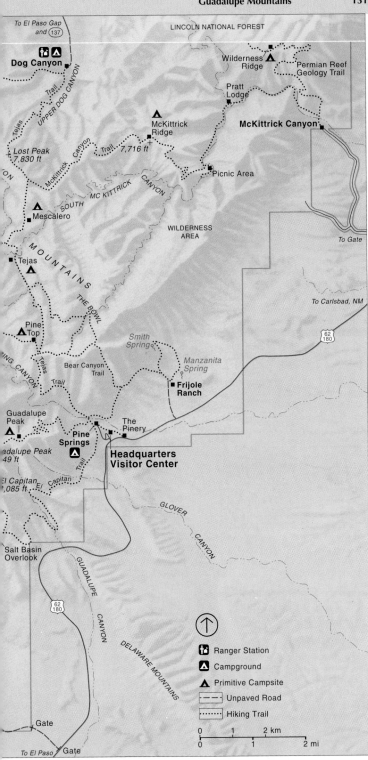

To El Paso Gap and (137)

LINCOLN NATIONAL FOREST

Dog Canyon

Trail

UPPER DOG CANYON

Tejas

Wilderness Ridge

Permian Reef Geology Trail

Pratt Lodge

McKittrick Ridge

7,716 ft

McKittrick Canyon

Lost Peak 7,830 ft

McKittrick   Canyon   Trail

MC KITTRICK   CANYON

Picnic Area

SOUTH

Mescalero

WILDERNESS AREA

To Gate

M O U N T A I N S

Tejas

To Carlsbad, NM

THE BOWL

62 180

Pine Top

Smith Spring

Tejas

Bear Canyon Trail

Manzanita Spring

Trail

Frijole Ranch

ING CANYON

Guadalupe Peak

The Pinery

Pine Springs

Headquarters Visitor Center

adalupe Peak 49 ft

El Capitan ,085 ft

El   Capitan

Capitan   Trail

GLOVER   CANYON

Salt Basin Overlook

GUADALUPE   CANYON

62 180

DELAWARE   MOUNTAINS

Gate

Gate

To El Paso   Gate

Ranger Station

Campground

Primitive Campsite

Unpaved Road

Hiking Trail

0   1   2 km
0   1   2 mi

Hiker's Staircase, in Pine Spring Canyon

used a great majority of the plants in sight for food or fiber. Their diet consisted largely of mescal—the heart of the agave plant, one of the succulents with spikes at the tips of the leaves—hence the culture's name. You'll soon approach **Manzanita Spring,** a place to spot wildlife.

Continue on to Smith Spring, a veritable garden of maidenhair ferns, Texas madrone trees (the ones shedding layers of paper-thin bark), alligator juniper (named for its distinctively textured bark), oak, and maple. As you loop back to your car, bear left at the fork.

Return to the highway and drive west-southwest about 2 miles, or at least as far as the first pullover, for a superb view of **El Capitan** (8,085 feet), the southernmost bluff of the Guadalupes. Late afternoon light shows off this imposing symbol of the region, once the beacon for conquistador, stagecoach driver, and homesteader.

McKittrick Canyon
foot tour; a half to full day

The walls of **McKittrick Canyon** shelter the only year-round stream in the park; the water creates a 3-mile-long oasis of oak and juniper, madrone and maple. The canyon itself is nearly 5 miles long. Pick up a self-guiding booklet on the area's human and natural history at the **McKittrick Canyon Contact Station** near the trailheads. For an easy hike (although the trail is

rocky and best negotiated in hiking boots), walk the $2\frac{3}{10}$ miles to the **Pratt Lodge.** If you have time, continue another mile through the woods that border the intermittent stream to the **Grotto** picnic area. Because the canyon plants are fragile, be sure to stay on the trail.

McKittrick Canyon exposes millions of years of geological events. During the Permian era, about 250 million years ago, an inland sea covered parts of west Texas and southeast New Mexico. Along the shore of the sea grew a reef of lime-secreting algae, sponges, other marine organisms, and calcium carbonate precipitated from the water. After millions of years, the climate changed and the ocean dried up; the Capitan Reef loomed hundreds of feet high in a horseshoe 400 miles long. Sediments and mineral salts buried both basin and reef over the next eons. Later, the region began to rise, and erosion slowly reexposed the seabed with part of the fossil reef—today's Guadalupe range—towering above.

As you walk into McKittrick Canyon, you are entering the Capitan Reef from the seaward side. To best observe the reef's varied formation and fossils, try the **Permian Reef Geology Trail.** You'll see layers of the ancient reef exposed by centuries of cutting by McKittrick Creek. The trail—$4\frac{1}{2}$ miles one way—climbs the 2,000-foot ridge to a ponderosa forest on the top.

Dog Canyon
a half to full day

Accessibility to the forested high country and its spectacular scenery make **Dog Canyon** well worth the drive. Ask a ranger to point out Apache mescal-roasting pits, still visible among the hip-high grasses, creosote bushes, and succulents. Then picnic and hike; the trails begin past the stables. Popular hikes include the **Bush Mountain Trail,** which, in about 3 miles, leads through open pinyon-juniper woodland to splendid views of the Guadalupes and the **Cornudas Mountains,** 55 miles to the west. The **Tejas Trail** offers similar views and in about 4 miles climbs into a temperate woodland of Gambel oak, Douglas-fir, and limber and ponderosa pine. This forest is a relict of the plant communities that cloaked the region in the last Ice Age. It still survives because of the particular, unusual combination of temperature and humidity at this high-altitude site.

Other Hikes

Hikers may find the following three treks rewarding. They all begin from Pine Springs Campground; ask a ranger for information:

Guadalupe Peak, 8⅓ miles round-trip. Because lightning storms can quickly gather on hot summer afternoons, it's best to begin your ascent by 8 a.m. and your descent by 1 p.m. *Watch the weather. If you see a storm coming, start down immediately.*
The Bowl, a lush area of relict ice age conifer forest. The 9½-mile loop is comprised of the Tejas, **Bowl,** and **Bear Canyon Trails.**
Devils Hall, a steep, narrow canyon; 4½ miles round-trip, mostly level.

Information & Activities

Headquarters
HC 60, Box 400, Salt Flat, Texas 79847. Phone (915) 828-3251. www.nps.gov/gumo

Seasons & Accessibility
Open year-round but may be inaccessible for brief periods in winter due to snowstorms. Best to phone park.

Visitor & Information Centers
Headquarters Visitor Center, ⅒ mile off US 62/180 at Guadalupe Pass, open all year except Christmas. McKittrick Canyon Visitor Center, off US 62/180 on eastern edge of park and Dog Canyon Ranger Station in the north open intermittently. Call park for details.

Entrance Fee
None.

Pets
Not permitted on trails or in buildings; elsewhere must be leashed.

Facilities for Disabled
The visitor centers, rest rooms, and Pine Springs Campground and amphitheater are wheelchair accessible.

Things to Do
Free ranger-led activities (summer only): hikes, horseback trail rides (no rentals), evening and children's programs. Also, hiking.

Special Advisories
● Rattlesnakes and other potentially harmful desert animals live here; watch out!
● Bring maps with you if planning to

hike; park is managed as wilderness, so trail signs are minimal.

Overnight Backpacking
Allowed at designated sites only; permits required; they are free and may be obtained at visitor centers. Backcountry use permits required to bring a horse into the park, available from main visitor center or Dog Canyon. Horses are not allowed in the backcountry overnight; they can be stabled in Frijole Ranch and Dog Canyon corrals, reserve space by calling (915) 828-3251.

Campgrounds
Two campgrounds, both with 14-day limit. Open all year, first come, first served. $8 per night at **Dog Canyon** and **Pine Springs.** No showers. Tent and RV sites; no hookups. Two group campgrounds; reservations required through headquarters.

Hotels, Motels, & Inns
(unless otherwise noted, rates are for 2 persons in a double room, high season)
In Whites City, New Mexico 88268:
Best Western Cavern Inn (12 Carlsbad Cavern Hwy.) P.O. Box 128. (800) 228-3767 or (505) 785-2291. 132 units. $85. AC, pool, restaurant.
In Van Horn, Texas 79855:
Best Western American Inn 1309 W. Broadway, Box 626. (800) 621-2478 or (915) 283-2030. 33 units. $50-$55. AC, pool.
Howard Johnson (200 Golf Course Drive) P.O. Box 1568 (915) 283-2780. 98 units. $35. AC, pool.

See also Carlsbad Caverns NP listings.

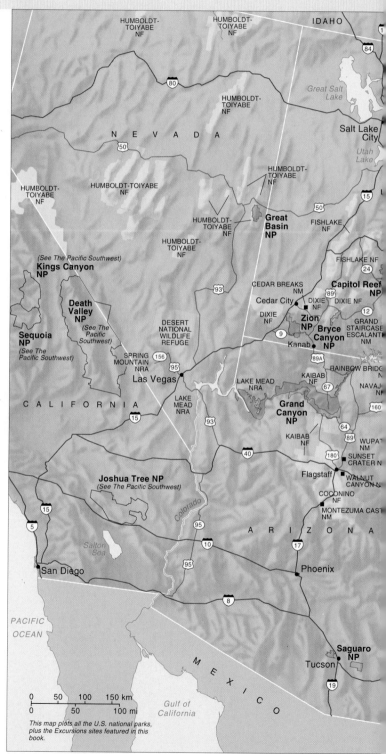

This map plots all the U.S. national parks, plus the Excursions sites featured in this book.

Preceding pages: Grand Canyon

The Colorado Plateau

Theodore Roosevelt called the Grand Canyon "the one great sight...every American should see." Although the Grand Canyon remains the most famous sight on the Colorado Plateau, this high desert drained by the Colorado River and its tributaries teems with scenic treasures. Numerous gorges slice the colorfully layered rock; stairstep terraces, buttes, and spires embellish it. The region contains the nation's largest concentration of national parks.

The striated cliffs of the canyon parks collectively encompass nearly two billion years of earth's history, divulging tales of ancient seas and volcanoes, deserts and dinosaurs. The rush of rivers sculptured the colossal gorges and side canyons of Grand Canyon, Zion, and Canyonlands. Grit-bearing winds and the freeze and thaw of water droplets chiseled multihued rock into the hoodoos, arches, and pinnacles visible in Arches and Bryce Canyon.

Although one of the most sparsely populated regions of the United States today, the plateau features some of the country's richest remains of early Indian civilizations. Archaeological highlights range from petroglyphs in Canyonlands, Capitol Reef, and Saguaro to pueblos and solstice markers in Petrified Forest to spectacular cliff dwellings in Mesa Verde.

Thanks to abrupt changes in elevation, the canyon parks shelter a wide diversity of plants and animals. Desert or semidesert at canyon bottom gives way to pinyon-juniper woodland and then ponderosa pine and spruce-fir forests. Lizards and deer, cottontails, and bighorn sheep can coexist in the same park. The desert park, Saguaro, protects North America's largest cactus, as well as the many other plants and animals of the vast Sonoran Desert.

Flagstaff, Arizona, makes a convenient base for the South Rim of the Grand Canyon and for Petrified Forest. From Kanab, Utah, you can visit Grand Canyon's North Rim, Bryce, Capitol Reef, and Zion. Just west of the plateau, a 5-hour drive from Kanab, lies Great Basin. For Arches and Canyonlands, Moab, Utah, is the place to stop, and to visit Saguaro, head for Tucson, Arizona.

Red rock of Delicate Arch ablaze at sunset

Arches

Utah

Established November 12, 1971

76,519 acres

This park contains more than 2,000 natural arches—the greatest concentration in the world. But numbers have no significance beside the grandeur of the landscape—the arches, the giant balanced rocks, spires, pinnacles, and slickrock domes against the enormous sky.

Perched high above the Colorado River, the park is part of southern Utah's extended area of canyon country, carved and shaped by eons of weathering and erosion. Most of the formations at Arches are made of soft red sandstone deposited 150 million years ago in a vast desert. As underlying salt deposits dissolved, the sandstone collapsed and weathered into a maze of vertical rock slabs called "fins." Sections of these slender walls eventually wore through, creating the spectacular rock sculptures you see today.

The land has a timeless, indestructible look that is misleading. Almost a million visitors each year threaten the fragile high desert ecosystem. One concern is a dark crust called cryptobiotic soil composed of algae, fungi, and lichens that grow in sandy areas in the park. Footprints tracked across this living community may remain visible for years. In fact, the aridity helps preserve traces of past activity for centuries.

Well-preserved petroglyphs carved into a low cliff near a pioneer cabin offer evidence that Indians roamed this land. Pictures of riders on horseback date the carvings to historic times, after the Spaniards introduced horses to the Southwest.

Arches Scenic Drive
18 miles one way; a half to full day

The scenic drive climbs from the floor of **Moab Canyon** to **Devils Garden,** passing through the heart of the park with spur roads leading to **The Windows Section, Wolfe Ranch,** and **Delicate Arch** area. Numerous pull-offs allow leisurely viewing of the park's major features.

From the visitor center the road winds up the canyon wall. Pull off after 2 miles at the **Park Avenue Viewpoint and Trailhead** for a view down an open canyon flanked by sandstone skyscrapers. If you have a willing driver—or don't mind the 320-foot return climb—walk the easy 1-mile path to the **Courthouse Towers** parking area, where you can be picked up. Here signs describe nearby rock formations that show the birth and death of an arch.

Continue your drive to the beautiful slickrock expanse known as the **Petrified Dunes.** Here you skirt knolls— ancient dunes turned to stone—as the **La Sal Mountains** rise nearly 13,000 feet in the far distance. Farther along, stop at the **Balanced Rock** pull-off where a ⅖-mile trail loops past this classic hoodoo, a strangely eroded rock spire 128 feet high. Edward Abbey wrote his classic *Desert Solitaire* after living in a trailer here as a park ranger. Just beyond, turn onto the paved road leading to The Windows.

The road passes a cluster of pinnacles and monoliths called **Garden of Eden** and ends at a parking area fronted by a sandstone wall perforated by several arches. Short trails lead to closeup views of these colossal gateways. The ³⁄₁₀-mile walk to **South Window,** 105 feet wide, also gives you good views of **North Window** and **Turret Arch.** If time allows walk the ½-mile trail for a dramatic closeup look at **Double Arch.**

Retrace your route back to the main road. A road leaves the scenic drive and leads 1½ miles to historic **Wolfe Ranch,** where a Civil War veteran raised cattle around the turn of the century, and the **Delicate Arch Viewpoint,** 1 mile farther. The distant view of **Delicate Arch** is disappointing, so if you have the stamina and at least 2 extra hours return to Wolfe Ranch and hike to the foot of

How to Get There
From Moab, take US 191 north 5 miles to the park entrance. From I-70, exit at Crescent Junction and follow US 191 south for 25 miles to the entrance. Airport 15 miles north of Moab and at Grand Junction, Colo., about 120 miles away.

When to Go
All-year park, but spring and fall are best; moderate temperatures are ideal for hiking in the high desert. Summers are hot and winters mild. Wildflowers peak in April and May.

How to Visit
Take the **Arches Scenic Drive** at least as far as **The Windows Section.** Allow time for hiking one of the park's spectacular trails. If it's spring, summer, or fall (and you're not bothered by heights), consider joining a naturalist-led 3-hour hike through **Fiery Furnace** (fee). It's strenuous, but you'll appreciate the shade in summer's heat. Contact the visitor center for reservations and tickets.

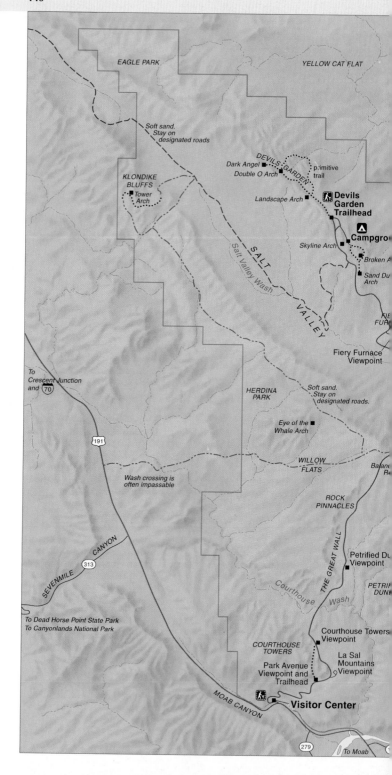

EAGLE PARK

YELLOW CAT FLAT

Soft sand.
Stay on
designated roads

DEVILS GARDEN

Dark Angel ■
Double O Arch ■

primitive
trail

KLONDIKE
BLUFFS
■ Tower
Arch

Landscape Arch ■

Devils
Garden
Trailhead

Campgro

Skyline Arch ■

Broken A

S A L T

Sand Du
Arch

Salt Valley Wash

V A L L E Y

FIE
FUR

Fiery Furnace
Viewpoint

To
Crescent Junction
and 70

HERDINA
PARK

Soft sand.
Stay on
designated roads.

Eye of the ■
Whale Arch

191

WILLOW
FLATS

Bala
R

Wash crossing is
often impassable

ROCK
PINNACLES

THE GREAT WALL

Petrified Du
Viewpoint

313

SEVENMILE

CANYON

Courthouse
Wash

PETRIF
DUN

To Dead Horse Point State Park
To Canyonlands National Park

Courthouse Towers
Viewpoint

COURTHOUSE
TOWERS

La Sal
Mountains
Viewpoint

Park Avenue
Viewpoint and
Trailhead

Visitor Center

MOAB CANYON

279   To Moab

the arch. The magnificent views make this one of the most rewarding hikes in canyon country, but you're better off saving it for a second day if you plan to take the full drive and other walks.

The trail to Delicate Arch gains 500 feet in elevation as it traverses 1½ miles across slickrock as smooth and cambered as the back of a whale. Near the trail, juniper trees grow from cracks so small the trunks seem to emerge from solid rock. Keep your eye out for the rock cairns that mark the trail; they're easy to miss. The arch perches on the edge of a bowl, framing white-capped mountains; the suddenness of your encounter with it at trail's end adds to its drama.

Return to the main road. Skip the **Salt Valley Overlook** but pull off at **Fiery Furnace,** a dense array of red fins that appear to ignite when the sun is low in the west. Here you see a world standing on end—hoodoos, spires, and slabs 200 feet high. It's easy to get lost in the maze of deeply grooved slots and dead-end passageways. Note that visitors who are not part of a guided walk will need a permit to explore Fiery Furnace.

Continue your drive. Take the short ⅕-mile walk to the cool shade of **Sand Dune Arch,** tucked between two fins, but save **Broken Arch** for another time. Farther down the road **Skyline Arch** comes into view. In 1940 a great rock mass broke from the arch, doubling the size of the opening to 45 by 69 feet.

The road ends at the Devils Garden campground and trailhead beyond. The 2¼-mile (one-way) **Devils Garden Trail** meanders to seven major arches, each with its own character. The trail takes about 2 to 3 hours to hike round-trip. Be sure to save enough time to walk at least as far as **Landscape Arch,** ⅘ of a mile. Here a narrow ribbon of stone

Landscape Arch framing pinyon pines

306 feet long appears to defy gravity as it floats in a graceful span above a steep dune. It's one of the world's longest free-standing natural arches. From here, take the curving, primitive trail that leads to **Double O Arch.**

If you walk the trail early in the morning, watch for the white flowers of the evening primrose. As the sun-light grows stronger, the flowers wilt, turning the petals pink. Though also primitive beyond Landscape Arch, the trail continues on another mile to Double O Arch, where a 160-foot-wide circular arch hangs above a smaller bore. From here you can walk about ½ mile to the rock spire known as the **Dark Angel.**

Information & Activities

Headquarters
P.O. Box 907, Moab, Utah 84532. Phone (435) 719-2299. www.nps.gov/arch

Seasons & Accessibility
Park open year-round. Some unpaved roads may become temporarily impassable after heavy rains. Call head-quarters for current weather and road information.

Visitor & Information Centers
Visitor center, on US 191 at park entrance, open daily all year except Christmas. Call headquarters number for visitor information.

Entrance Fees
$10 per car per week allows multiple entries. Yearly fee of $25 is also good at Canyonlands NP, and Natural Bridges and Hovenweep National Monuments.

Pets
Prohibited on all hiking trails and in the backcountry.

Facilities for Disabled
Visitor center and one of its rest rooms are wheelchair accessible. Rest room and one campsite accessible in Devils Garden Campground. Park Avenue and Delicate Arch Viewpoints are accessible to wheelchairs.

Things to Do
Naturalist-led activities: nature hikes and talks, evening programs. Also available, geological and historical exhibits, self-guided auto tour, hiking, jeep tours, sight-seeing flights. Contact park headquarters for list of concession-ers offering rental and guide services.

Special Advisories
● Always carry water on hikes—at least a gallon a day per person is recom-mended in summer.
● Stay on trails to protect fragile desert soils and plant life.
● Sandstone slickrock crumbles easily and can make climbing dangerous. Consult a ranger before going out.

Overnight Backpacking
Permits required (free, obtained at visi-tor center).

Campgrounds
One campground, **Devils Garden,** with a 7-day limit. Open all year. First-come, first-served. Fees $10 per night. No showers. Tent and RV sites; no hookups. Reservations required for **Devils Garden Group Campgrounds;** tent sites only. Central Reservations Office (801) 259-4351.

Hotels, Motels, & Inns
(unless otherwise noted, rates for 2 persons, double room, high season) In Moab, Utah 84532:
Best Western Green Well Motel 105 S. Main Street. (800) 528-1234 or (435) 259-6151. 72 units. $79-$130. AC, pool, rest. **Cedar Breaks Condos** Cen-ter and Fourth East. (435) 259-7830. Six 2-bedroom units with full kitchens. $88-$118. AC. **Big Horn Travelodge** 550 S. Main Street. (800) 325-6171 or (435) 259-6171. 58 units. $85. AC, pool, rest. **Pack Creek Ranch** (15 mi. SE of Moab, off LaSal Moun-tain Loop Rd.) P.O. Box 1270. (435) 259-5505. Cabins, houses, bunk-houses. $135-$300. Includes trail rides. AC, Pool. **Ramada Inn—Moab** 182 S. Main Street. (435) 259-7141. 82 units. $85-$109. AC, pool, rest.

For other accommodations in the area, contact Utah's Canyonlands Region, 805 N. Main St., Moab, Utah 84532. (800) 233-8824 or (435) 259-7814.

Excursions

Manti-LaSal National Forest
Moab, Utah

Mountains, densely wooded with aspen, pine, fir, and spruce and rugged grassland-covered plateaus, provide cool contrast here in red-rock country. Contains Dark Canyon Wilderness Area. 1,265,254 acres, part in Colorado. 136 campsites, hiking, boating, boat ramp, climbing, bicycling, fishing, horseback riding, hunting, picnic areas, winter sports, water sports. Open year-round; campsites open late May-Oct. Info. at Moab on US 191, about 5 miles southeast of Arches NP. (435) 259-7155 or (435) 637-2817.

Colorado National Monument
Fruita, Colorado

The 23-mile-long Rim Rock Drive and well-maintained trails with gentle switchbacks provide easy access to this monument's small, sheer-walled canyons and sandstone monoliths. Shelters mule deer, bighorn sheep, and mountain lions. 20,453 acres. 80 campsites, hiking, climbing, bicycling, horseback riding, picnic areas, scenic drives, winter sports, handicapped access. Open year-round. Located on Colo. 340, about 100 miles from Arches NP. (970) 858-3617.

Bryce Amphitheater, seen from Bryce Point

Bryce Canyon

Utah

Established September 15, 1928

35,835 acres

Perhaps nowhere are the forces of natural erosion more tangible than at Bryce Canyon. Its wilderness of phantom-like rock spires, or hoodoos, attracts more than a million visitors a year. Many descend on trails that give hikers and horseback riders a close look at the fluted walls and sculptured pinnacles.

The park follows the edge of the Paunsaugunt Plateau. On the west are heavily forested tablelands more than 9,000 feet high; on the east are the intricately carved breaks where the country drops 2,000 feet to the Paria Valley. Many ephemeral streams have eaten into the plateau, forming horseshoe-shaped amphitheaters. The largest and most striking is Bryce Amphitheater. Encompassing

6 square miles, it is the scenic heart of the park.

Water has been helping carve Bryce's rugged landscape for millions of years and is still at work. Water may split rock as it freezes and expands in cracks—a cyclic process that occurs some 200 times a year. In summer, runoff from violent cloudbursts etches into the softer limestones and sluices through the deep runnels. In about half a century the present rim will be cut back into the plateau another foot. But there is more here than spectacular erosion.

In the early morning you can stand for long moments on the rim, held by the amphitheater's mysterious blend of rock and color. Warm yellows and oranges radiate from the deeply pigmented walls as scatterings of light illuminate the pale rock spires.

There is a sense of place here that goes beyond rocks. Some local Paiute Indians explained it with a legend. Once there lived animal-like creatures that changed themselves into people. But they were bad, so Coyote turned them into rocks of various configurations. The spellbound creatures still huddle together here with faces painted just as they were before being turned to stone.

How to Get There

From Zion National Park (about 80 miles west), follow Utah 9 east, turn north onto Utah 89, then continue east on Utah 12 to Utah 63, which is the park entrance road. From Capitol Reef National Park (about 65 miles away), follow Utah 12 southward to Utah 63. Airport: Cedar City, 86 miles away.

When to Go

All-year park. Wildflowers are at their peak in spring and early summer; the greatest variety of the park's 170

bird species appears between May and October. Winter lasts from November through March; snow highlights the brilliantly colored cliffs and provides fine cross-country skiing.

How to Visit

On a 1-day visit, tour the **Bryce Amphitheater,** beginning, if possible, with sunrise at **Bryce Point.** If limited time requires choosing between the scenic drive or a walk beneath the rim, take the walk. On a longer stay, drive to **Rainbow Point;** consider a moonlight stroll among the hoodoos.

Bryce Amphitheater

8 miles; 2 hours to a full day

Watch sunrise from **Bryce Point,** one of the highest overlooks along the rim of the amphitheater. Drive about 4 miles south of the visitor center, then walk a short distance from the parking lot to the viewpoint.

Colors begin to glow even before the sun breaks over the **Aquarius Plateau,** at over 10,000 feet the highest plateau in North America. First light catches the rim of the amphitheater, then drops into the basin, igniting the crowded pillars of rock. From this vantage point you see shallow caves along the rim called the **Grottoes.** Look for the **Alligator,** a sharply incised butte that appears reptilian from above, and the **Sinking Ship,** which resembles a vanishing prow.

Drive back to **Inspiration Point,** bypassing the **Paria View** turnoff. From the parking lot walk up a short but steep trail to upper Inspiration Point. If the trail looks too ambitious, stay below at the lower viewpoint. Both look over the head of the amphitheater and place you close to the rock formations. No matter what time of day, they provide excellent all-around views.

In the valley below is the small town of **Tropic.** Scottish emigrant Ebenezer Bryce and his wife, Mary, homesteaded nearby in 1875. They grazed cattle in **Bryce Canyon** but moved away 5 years later, leaving behind little more than their name.

Continue on to **Sunset Point.** The name is misleading since the viewpoint faces east, limiting sundown views. But the mix of shadows and deep-hued colors makes this an excellent view-

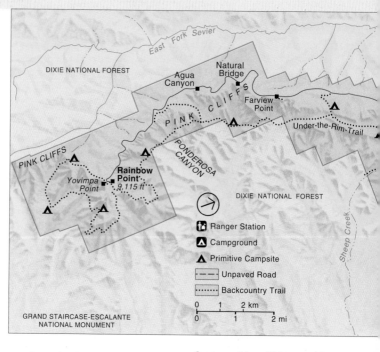

DIXIE NATIONAL FOREST

East Fork Sevier

Agua Canyon

Natural Bridge

PINK CLIFFS

Farview Point

Under-the-Rim-Trail

PINK CLIFFS

PONDEROSA CANYON

Rainbow Point 9,115 ft

Yovimpa Point

DIXIE NATIONAL FOREST

Sheep Creek

Ranger Station
Campground
Primitive Campsite
— — Unpaved Road
········ Backcountry Trail

0   1   2 km
0   1   2 mi

GRAND STAIRCASE-ESCALANTE
NATIONAL MONUMENT

Thor's Hammer at sunrise

point in the low-angled light of later afternoon. To the left is **Thor's Hammer;** to the right is the **Silent City**—a gridwork of deep ravines that divide turreted walls suggesting the ruins of an ancient metropolis.

Those with time and stamina can follow the **Navajo Loop Trail,** a fairly strenuous 1½-mile loop into the canyon. The trail drops steeply in a series of tight switchbacks before entering a narrow, steep-walled gorge called **Wall Street.** Several Douglas-

firs, two of them 700 years old, grow between the towering cliffs.

Continue down the trail to the junction with Queen's Garden Trail, the least strenuous trail below the rim. It winds along the bottom of the amphitheater to **Queen's Garden,** then climbs to the rim at **Sunrise Point,** passing weird rock formations and occasional bristlecone pines. From Sunrise Point follow the **Rim Trail** ½ mile back to your car at Sunset Point.

The Drive to Rainbow Point

17 miles; 3 hours to a half day

Following the edge of the gently tilted plateau, a scenic drive ascends over 1,000 feet to **Rainbow Point,** the plateau's southernmost reach. Before beginning the drive, be sure to see **Fairyland Point.**

Just after you enter the park boundaries, but before the entrance station, is a mile-long spur road leading to the Fairyland overlook. The temptation is to leave this for later, but here you see one of the finest vistas in the park. In colorful array, spires and monoliths rise close at hand. Some stand isolated like chess

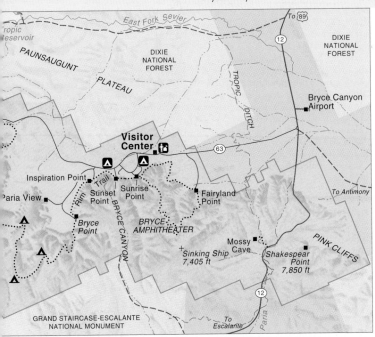

Exploring Bryce Canyon on horseback

pieces; others group together like a Greek chorus. A short hike down the trail takes you right among them—a quick immersion course in the effects of erosion.

When you return to your car, drive past the Sunset Point turnoff (trailers are not allowed beyond here) and on past the Bryce Point turnoff. You leave the ponderosa pine forest behind and quickly find yourself among the high-elevation Douglas-fir and blue spruce.

Pull in at **Farview Point** for a panoramic view of **Table Cliffs** and a series of broad platforms stairstepping southeast to the **Kaibab Plateau** at the North Rim of the **Grand Canyon.**

Continue south to **Natural Bridge** pull-off. Here you have a closeup view of a natural arch 85 feet long and 125 feet high. Its bright rusty red contrasts with the deep green of the trees below and the deep blue of the sky above.

The next pull-off is **Agua Canyon,** one of the finest vistas in the park.

Massive hoodoos stand close to the rim; farther off are the vividly colored **Pink Cliffs;** and on the far horizon is the domed profile of **Navajo Mountain,** over 10,000 feet high.

Continue to the end of the road at **Rainbow Point.** Stop here for a picnic among the thick stands of fir on the park's highest elevation, 9,115 feet. A pleasant mile walk follows the **Bristlecone Loop Trail** to expansive views. A spur trail leads to more views at **Yovimpa Point;** the cliffs that descend from there in stairsteps are named for their rock colors—pink, gray, white, vermilion, and chocolate. A stand of ancient bristlecone pines grows on the exposed edge of the plateau; the oldest in the park has been alive for more than 1,500 years.

Acoustic studies have found that the natural silence here equals the quality of a sound studio. Park air is superb, too. But rangers worry that this purity will be threatened by possible development on adjacent lands.

Information & Activities

Headquarters
Bryce Canyon, Utah 84717. Phone (435) 834-5322. www.nps.gov/brca

Seasons & Accessibility
Park open year-round. Roads may be closed for short periods due to snowstorms. Some spur roads closed in winter for cross-country skiing. Phone headquarters for information.

Visitor & Information Centers
Visitor center on main road, 1 mile inside park boundary, open all year except Thanksgiving, Christmas and New Years Day. Call headquarters for visitor information.

Entrance Fees
$20 per car per week. From mid-May through Sept., visitors may pay $15 and leave their cars near the entrance. From there, a new shuttle system will transport visitors to points throughout the park.

Facilities for Disabled
Visitor center partially accessible to wheelchairs; all viewpoints and a ½-mile stretch of trail between Sunset and Sunrise Points also accessible.

Things to Do
Free naturalist-led activities (summer): prairie dog and other nature walks, history and geology talks, evening programs, night sky programs, moonlight walks. Also, hiking, guided trail rides (inquire at Bryce Lodge or call 435-679-8665), cross-country skiing, snowshoeing.

Overnight Backpacking
Allowed only on the Under-the-Rim Trail near Bryce Point. Purchase permits for $5 at visitor center or, in summer, at nature center

Campgrounds
Two campgrounds; 14-day limit. Part of North open all year. Sunset open May to Sept. 30. Both first come, first served. Fees $10 per night. Showers nearby. Tent and RV sites; no hookups. Sunset Group Campground; reservations required; contact park. Food services in park.

Hotels, Motels, & Inns
(unless otherwise noted, rates for 2 persons, double room, high season)
INSIDE THE PARK:
Bryce Canyon Lodge (south of Utah 12 on Utah 63), AmFac Parks & Resorts, Bryce Canyon NP, Utah 84717. (435) 834-5361. Cabins, rooms, suites. $88. Rest. Open April–Oct.
OUTSIDE THE PARK:
In Bryce, Utah 84764:
Best Western Ruby's Inn (on Utah 63). (800) 528-1234 or (435) 834-5341. 368 units. $90-$125. AC, pool, rest. **Bryce Canyon Pines Motel** (on Utah 12) P.O. Box 43. (435) 834-5441. 45 rooms; 7 cabins, 2 kitchenettes. $75. Pool, rest. **Bryce Canyon Resorts** (on Utah 12) P.O. Box 6. (435) 834-5303. 5 cabins; 54 rooms. $85-$95. AC, pool, rest.
In Panguitch, Utah 84759:
Best Western New Western Motel (180 East Center St.) P.O. Box 73. (800) 528-1234 or (435) 676-8876. 55 units. $75. AC, pool. **Color Country Motel** (526 N. Main St.) P.O. Box 163. (435) 676-2386. 26 units. $52. AC, pool. All year. **Adobe Sands Motel** (390 N. Main St.) P.O. Box 593. (435) 676-8874. 33 units. AC, pool. Open May–Oct.

Excursions

Dixie National Forest
Cedar City, Utah

Four sections of this canyon-country forest fan out across southwestern Utah, featuring unusual rock formations, "stands" of petrified forest, and sections of the historic Spanish Trail. 1,967,129 acres. 27 campgrounds, hiking, boating, boat ramp, fishing, horseback riding, hunting, picnic areas, scenic drives, winter sports, water sports. Open year-round; most campsites open May-Oct. Info. at Cedar City on I-15, about 70 miles from Bryce Canyon NP. (435) 865-3700.

Cedar Breaks National Monument
Cedar City, Utah

Erosion carved an immense amphitheater in a 10,000-foot southern Utah plateau; in it are extraordinary rock shapes colored by iron and manganese. 6,155 acres. 30 campsites, hiking, picnic areas, scenic drives, winter sports, handicapped access. Services, roads, closed late fall and winter. Visitor center on Utah 148, about 60 miles from Bryce Canyon NP. (435) 586-9451.

Fishlake National Forest
Richfield, Utah

Fish Lake, hopping with splake and trout (including 35-pound Mackinaw), is only one attraction of this region of dense forests, mountains, and plateaus. The Skyline Trail winds through its 12,000-foot peaks and the largest known village of the prehistoric Fremont people lies within its boundaries. 1.5 million acres. Facilities include 40 campsites, hiking, boating, boat ramp, bicycling, fishing, horseback riding, hunting, scenic drives, winter sports, handicapped access. Open year-round; most campsites open May-October. Information at Richfield, off US 89, about 80 miles from Bryce Canyon NP. (435) 896-9233.

Monument Basin from Grand View Point, Island in the Sky

Canyonlands

Utah

Established September 12, 1964

337,598 acres

From the rim you glimpse only segments of the Green River and the Colorado River, which flow together at the heart of Canyonlands. But everywhere you see the water's work: canyon mazes, unbroken scarps, sandstone pillars.

The paths of the merging rivers divide the park into three districts. The high mesa known as the Island in the Sky rises as a headland 2,000 feet above the confluence. South of the Island and east of the confluence is The Needles, where red and white banded pinnacles tower 400 feet over grassy parks and sheer-walled valleys. A fine confusion of clefts and spires across the river to the west marks The Maze, a remote region of pristine soli-

tude. On every side the ground drops in great stairsteps. Flat benchlands end abruptly in rock walls on one side and sheer drops on the other. It is a right-angled country of standing rock, and only a few paved roads probe the edges of the park's 527 square miles.

Sandstone layers of varying hardness comprise Canyonland's visible rock. But the character of the land is largely shaped by underlying salt deposits, which, under tremendous pressure from the rock above, push upward, forming domes that fracture the surface.

Yearly rainfall averages 8 inches but varies greatly from year to year. Trees that grow here have to be tough and resilient. In drought years, junipers survive by limiting growth to a few branches, letting the others die. Gnarled juniper and pinyon pine take root in the rimlands wherever soil

How to Visit

The park's isolation and preponderance of backcountry make visiting a spectacular experience, but not for everyone; there are few visitor facilities and paved roads. A four-wheel-drive vehicle will let you explore. If you have only 1 day, visit the **Island in the Sky** for an overview. On another day, go to **The Needles** for a chance to explore classic canyon country. With more time, focus on the hiking trails and four-wheel-drive routes to **The Maze** and other remote areas.

Island in the Sky

40 miles; a half to full day

The road enters the park just before you cross **The Neck,** a rock span not much wider than the road that connects the mesa to the rimlands.

For a sweeping view of the park's narrow, interlocked canyons and its wide skies, drive right to the end of the road at **Grand View Point Overlook** (6,080 feet). Directly below in **Monument Basin,** stone columns rise more than 300 feet from the canyon floor.

Hidden in deep gorges to the south,

collects, including slickrock cracks and potholes.

How to Get There

Island in the Sky District. From Moab (35 miles away), take US 191 north to Utah 313 to The Neck entrance road.

Needles District. From Moab (75 miles away), follow US 191 south to Utah 211 and then west for 34 miles to park entrance.

Maze District. From Green River, take I-70 west to Utah 24, then south to a well-marked dirt road leading 46 miles to Hans Flat Ranger Station.

Ground shuttles are available from Salt Lake City and Grand Junction, Colo. Air shuttles fly between Canyonlands Airport and Salt Lake City. The airport at Grand Junction is about 115 miles from The Neck.

When to Go

Spring and fall are ideal for exploring by foot or vehicle. Summer is hot, but humidity low. Snow and cold can make it hard to get around in winter.

Snakeweed tussocks along the Colorado

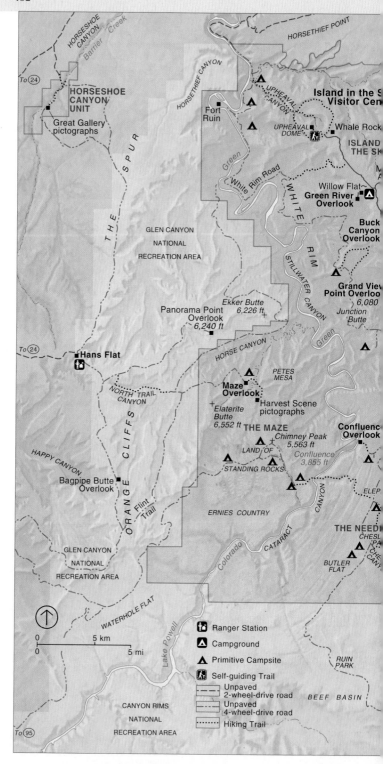

HORSESHOE CANYON

Barrier Creek

HORSETHIEF POINT

HORSETHIEF CANYON

To (24)

HORSESHOE CANYON UNIT

Great Gallery pictographs

Fort Ruin

UPHEAVAL CANYON

Island in the S Visitor Cen

UPHEAVAL DOME

Whale Rock

ISLAND THE SK

Green

White Rim Road

WHITE

Willow Flat
Green River Overlook

GLEN CANYON

NATIONAL

RECREATION AREA

THE SPUR

RIM

STILLWATER CANYON

Buck Canyon Overlook

Green

Ekker Butte 6,226 ft

Panorama Point Overlook
6,240 ft

Grand Vie Point Overloo
6,080

Junction Butte

To (24) ■**Hans Flat**

HORSE CANYON

NORTH TRAIL CANYON

PETES MESA

Maze Overlook

Harvest Scene pictographs

+*Elaterite Butte 6,552 ft*

THE MAZE

Chimney Peak *5,563 ft*

LAND OF

Confluenc Overlook

Confluence 3,855 ft

HAPPY CANYON

STANDING ROCKS

Bagpipe Butte Overlook

Flint Trail

ERNIES COUNTRY

CANYON

ELEP

THE NEEDL

ORANGE CLIFFS

GLEN CANYON

NATIONAL

RECREATION AREA

Colorado

CATARACT

BUTLER FLAT

CHESL PA

CAN

↑

0 ___ 5 km
0 ___ 5 mi

WATERHOLE FLAT

Lake Powell

RUIN PARK

CANYON RIMS

NATIONAL

RECREATION AREA

To (95)

BEEF BASIN

🏠 Ranger Station

🔺 Campground

▲ Primitive Campsite

🚶 Self-guiding Trail

— · — Unpaved 2-wheel-drive road

— — — Unpaved 4-wheel-drive road

· · · · · Hiking Trail

the **Green River** joins the **Colorado River.** During his exploration of the Colorado in 1869, John Wesley Powell scaled the canyon walls at the confluence and discovered a strangely carved landscape. "Wherever we looked," he wrote, "there was a wilderness of rocks."

Drive back the way you came, bypassing **Buck Canyon** and **Murphy Point Overlooks.** Turn onto the road leading to **Upheaval Dome,** then follow the graded spur road past Willow Flat Campground to **Green River Overlook.** Here you view a wide expanse of canyon country: Below, a quiet stretch of the Green River runs through **Stillwater Canyon,** with **The Maze** beyond and the **Henry Mountains** topping the distant horizon.

Continue on to Upheaval Dome, where the road ends at a good picnic spot shaded by junipers and pinyon pines. Stretch your legs on the ½-mile trail to the lip of this unusual geological feature. Here the surface drops into a mile-wide crater enclosed by rock strata upturned in concentric circles, with a rock spire at the center. Some geologists believe that a meteorite collided with earth here. Return to the main road.

Be sure to pull off at the **Mesa Arch Trailhead.** An easy ½-mile loop takes you through a pinyon-juniper woodland to a small natural arch carved from the rim. The curve of the arch frames a magnificent view of the **Washer Woman Arch** and the **La Sal Mountains,** snowy in winter.

Just before leaving the park, stop at the **Shafer Canyon Overlook.** The short trail leads along a promontory above canyons gouged from miles of layered stone. In late afternoon, the rocks seem to ignite in the low angle of the setting sun.

La Sal Mountains through Mesa Arch

The Needles, weathered spires of sandstone

The Needles

18 miles; most of a day

Unless you have decided to camp, you'll probably be driving from Moab, 1½ hours away, or Monticello, an hour away. **The Needles** area covers a lattice of canyons, flat-bottomed valleys called grabens, arches, and spectacular sandstone walls notched by rocky spires and columns. To the north, **Island in the Sky** and **Junction Butte** stand silhouetted against the horizon.

Utah 211 will take you directly to the Needles Visitor Center where a dirt road heads north to the **Colorado River Overlook.** This road makes for rough going; don't take it unless you have a four-wheel-drive vehicle.

Continue on the paved road to the **Roadside Ruin** pull-off. Stretch your legs on a ¼-mile self-guided nature trail that leads to a small but well-preserved granary used by Indians to store corn more than 700 years ago. These ancient farmers were related to the ancestral Puebloans of Mesa Verde and Chaco Canyon. Pick up an interpretive booklet at the trail-head to learn how they used the trail-side plants.

Your next stop will be **Pothole Point** where a ½-mile trail leads past

Unusual pictograph called the All-American Man

Pothole Point, in The Needles

depressions in the sandstone that fill with water after a rain. Although the water looks as still as the rock, they often teem with life. Snails, fairy shrimp, and horsehair worms lay eggs that survive the heat of summer encased in dried mud. When the rains come, they hatch in days.

The road ends at **Big Spring Canyon Overlook,** where squat columns of sandstone rise from barren bedrock. Here the 5½-mile **Confluence Overlook Trail** climbs the far side of the canyon by a ladder and ends at a point 930 feet above the junction of the rivers. This is a popular trail with most park visitors but less scenic than the 2½-mile **Slickrock Trail,** which begins just before the road ends at the overlook. If time allows, stop here on your return drive for a moderate hike across slickrock balds of Cedar Mesa sandstone.

The Needles' "Molar Rock" and Angel Arch

Turn on the **Elephant Hill** spur, a graded dirt road that leads to the base of a notorious climb for four-wheel drivers. Along the road are great views of The Needles. You see tall fingers of rock arrayed along the skyline, their red and white bands created by the interlayering of ancient river deposits with sand dunes. A shaded area at the end of the graded road makes a good place to picnic.

The Chocolate Drops, shale and sandstone formations in The Maze

Hikes & Four-Wheel-Drive Routes

To really explore Canyonlands—85 percent of which is backcountry—you must leave your car and proceed on foot, mountain bike, or four-wheel-drive vehicle.

In The Needles, **Chesler Park Trail** leads 2 9/10 miles to a grassland sunk in a wide rock pocket rimmed by colorful spires. **Druid Arch Trail** branches off at **Elephant Canyon** and leads another 2 2/5 miles with a short ladder climb to the great arch that resembles a megalithic ceremonial site.

Elephant Hill Trail, a route only for rugged four-wheel-drive vehicles, runs 9 miles to the **Confluence Overlook.** It begins by climbing Elephant Hill's jaw-clenching switchbacks and 40 percent grade and ends with a 1/2-mile walk to the overlook.

White Rim Road in Island in the Sky is one of the park's most popular jeep roads. Near the entrance, the **Shafer Trail** will take you to it. It follows a broad bench, lunar white along the edge where the red talus has been stripped to bedrock. For more than 80 miles it stays above the inner gorge, 1,200 feet below the Island, as it meanders through prime desert

bighorn sheep country.

Northwest of The Maze lies a detached section of the park, the **Horseshoe Canyon Unit,** entered by way of a 3 1/2-mile trail. You follow an old road into the canyon, then walk up **Barrier Creek** past some of the continent's finest prehistoric rock art. At the **Great Gallery,** ghostly figures painted in red ocher stare through eerie hollow eyes as the centuries pass. Archaeologists believe these life-size pictographs may be more than 3,000, perhaps as much as 6,000, years old.

The **Maze Overlook** can be reached by a 14-mile hike beginning at **North Trail Canyon,** 3 1/2 rough miles past **Hans Flat Ranger Station.** Reaching the trailhead can be an adventure, but the views from the rim of this isolated wedge of canyon country make it worth the effort. And the quiet is as expansive as the vistas. The trail passes north of **Elaterite Butte** for a tantalizing view into the twists and blind alleys of The Maze.

With a high-clearance four-wheel-drive vehicle you can drive the 34 miles from **Hans Flat** to the overlook. This is one of the park's classic jeep routes. Negotiating steep switchbacks allows the driver little chance to sightsee, and with winter snows the route becomes impassable.

Information & Activities

Headquarters
2282 SW Resource Blvd., Moab, Utah 84532. Phone (435) 719-2313. www.nps.gov/cany

Seasons & Accessibility
Park open year-round. Flash floods from July through Sept. can temporarily close dirt and gravel roads.

Visitor & Information Centers
Moab boasts a large multi-agency visitor center. Visitor centers by entrances to Island in the Sky and The Needles, and at Hans Flat Ranger Station, just outside park near The Maze, open all year. Headquarters is 3 miles south of Moab.

Entrance Fees
$10 per vehicle good for 7 days, multiple entries. Annual permit $25, also good at Arches National Park, and Natural Bridges and Hovenweep National Monuments.

Pets
Must be leashed at all times. Not allowed on hiking trails, in river corridors, or on backcountry roads.

Facilities for Disabled
The visitor centers and Moab headquarters are wheelchair accessible.

Things to Do
Free naturalist-led activities: nature walks, interpretive exhibits. Hiking, boating, rafting (permit needed), bicycling, fishing (license required). Contact park for list of concessioners offering four-wheel-drive (some areas require permit), mountain biking, hiking, and river-running trips.

Special Advisories
● Always carry water when hiking—at least a gallon per person per day. Water available near Squaw Flat Campground and at visitor centers.
● Use care near cliff edges and on slickrock surfaces; falls often fatal.
● Do not walk on cryptobiotic crust; it is a fragile, crunchy, black soil that is composed of living plants.

Overnight Backpacking
Permits and reservations fee required for backpacking and 4-wheel-drive trips. May be obtained at visitor centers, ranger stations, and park headquarters. For information on reservations, call (435) 259-4351. Campsites along the White Rim Trail, in Island in the Sky, are available to mountain bikers and campers in four-wheel-drive high-clearance vehicles.

Campgrounds
Two campgrounds, **Squaw Flat** and **Willow Flat,** both with 14-day limit. Open all year, first come, first served; March to Oct. filled by midmorning. Fees: $5-$10 per night. No showers. Tent and RV sites; no hookups. Three group campsites in The Needles; reservations required; contact park headquarters. No food services inside park.

Hotels, Motels, & Inns
(unless otherwise noted, rates are for 2 persons in a double room, high season)
In Moab, Utah 84532:
Best Western Green Well Motel 105 S. Main Street. (800) 528-1234 or (435) 259-6151. 72 units. $130. AC, pool, rest.
Cedar Breaks Condos Center and Fourth East. (435) 259-7830. 62 units, all with full kitchens. $88. AC.
Travelodge 550 S. Main Street. (800) 325-6171. 58 units. $70-$82. AC, pool, restaurant.
Pack Creek Ranch (15 mi. SE of Moab, off LaSal Mountain Loop Rd.) P.O. Box 1270. (435) 259-5505. Cabins, houses, bunkhouses. $135-$300. Includes breakfast, trail rides. AC, pool.
Ramada Inn—Moab 182 S. Main Street. (435) 259-7141. 82 units. $85-$109. AC, pool, restaurant.
In Monticello, Utah 84535:
Best Western Wayside Inn 197 East Central Highway 666. (800) 633-9700 or (435) 587-2261. 35 units. $64-$69. AC, pool.
Triangle H Motel 164 East Central Highway 666. (800) 657-6622 or (435) 587-2274. 26 units. $42-$59. AC, restaurant.

For other area accommodations, contact Utah's Canyonlands Region, P.O. Box 550-R9, Moab, Utah 84532. (800) 635-MOAB or (435) 259-8825.

Excursions

Westwater Canyon
Moab, Utah

The names of the rapids on this 17-mile section of the Colorado River tell all: Funnel Falls, Skull, Sock-it-to-Me, Last Chance. Only experienced boaters should attempt them; permits and reservations required. Sights: natural arches, mining ruins, a desperadoes' hideout, and many bird species. Primitive camping, hiking, boating, boat ramp, fishing, picnic areas, swimming. Open all year. Info. (April–Oct.) at Westwater, about 80 miles NE of Canyonlands NP. (435) 259-2196.

Henry Mountains Buffalo Herd
Hanksville, Utah

The 400 or so bison of this herd roam to 11,000 feet in summer. 150,000 acres. 3 campgrounds, primitive campsites, hiking, climbing, rockhounding, hunting, picnicking, horseback riding, scenic drives. Open all year. Info. at Hanksville BLM, jct. of Utah 24 & 95, about 110 miles west of Canyonlands NP. (435) 542-3461.

Natural Bridges National Monument
Lake Powell, Utah

Three natural bridges here represent different states of development: youth, maturity, and old age. First discovered by white men in 1883, the three bridges bear Hopi names: Sipapu, Kachina, and Owachomo. Site also features ancestral Puebloan ruins and what was once the world's largest photovoltaic power system. 7,779 acres. Facilities: 1 campground, primitive campsites, picnic area, scenic drive. Trails closed in winter; campsites open all year. Visitor center on Utah 275, 4 miles off US 95, about 95 miles from Canyonlands NP. (435) 692-1234.

Excursions

Glen Canyon National Recreation Area

Page, Arizona

The centerpiece of Glen Canyon NRA is Lake Powell, 186 miles of the Colorado River backed up behind one of the world's highest dams. The lake and the desert and canyons around it offer memorable experiences for boaters, anglers, hikers, and campers. Fishing for bass, black crappie, catfish, walleye available; trout thrive below the dam. Free dam tours. 1,245,855 acres, most in Utah. Tent and RV campsites, 6 marinas, lodging, food services, boating (rentals available), boat ramp, fishing, hunting, picnic areas, water sports, handicapped access. Area and campsites open all year. Adjoins Canyonlands NP to the north. (520) 608-6404.

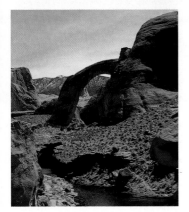

Rainbow Bridge National Monument

Page, Arizona

To the Navajo this 290-foot-high pink sandstone bridge is a sacred "rainbow of stone." Rough foot- or horsetrails lead to it through the Navajo reservation (permits required)—a vigorous trip for the fit only. Most visitors to the world's largest natural bridge boat in from Lake Powell in Glen Canyon NRA (see above), via Halls Crossing, Bullfrog, or Wahweap Marinas. 160 acres. Facilities: boat dock, rest rooms. No water. About 135 miles from Canyonlands NP. (520) 608-6404.

Layers of rock uplifted and exposed on the west face of Waterpocket Fold

Capitol Reef

Utah

Established December 18, 1971

241,904 acres

The unifying geographic feature of Capitol Reef is the Waterpocket Fold. For a hundred miles its parallel ridges rise from the desert like the swell of giant waves rolling toward shore. Exposed edges of the uplift have eroded into a slickrock wilderness of massive domes, cliffs, and a maze of twisting canyons.

Geologists know the fold as one of the largest and best exposed monoclines on the North American continent. Travelers know it as a place of dramatic beauty and serenity so remote that the nearest traffic light is 78 miles away. And even though its 378 square miles are off the beaten track, the park still attracts nearly 750,000 visitors each year.

Capitol Reef is named for a particularly colorful section of the fold near the Fremont River where sheer cliffs formed a barrier to travel for early pioneers. It reminded them of an ocean reef. Although a highway now crosses the "reef," travel is still challenging for those wishing to see the park's more remote regions.

The southern end of the fold offers fine wilderness backpacking in Lower Muley Twist Canyon and Halls Creek Narrows. Along the park's northern border lies Cathedral Valley, a repository of quiet solitude where jagged monoliths rise hundreds of feet.

The middle region is best known. Here the raw beauty of the towering cliffs contrasts with the green oasis that 19th-century Mormon pioneers created along the Fremont River, establishing the village of Fruita. Their irrigation ditches still water fruit trees

in fields abandoned by Fremont Indians 700 years ago. Mule deer now graze on orchard grasses and alfalfa, and park visitors harvest the apples, peaches, and apricots.

The most striking reminder of the Fremont culture is the fine rock art it produced. Figures resembling bighorn sheep crowd many petroglyph panels. The last sighting in the park of a native desert bighorn, a subspecies, occurred in 1948. Their disappearance is attributed to overhunting and various diseases caught from domestic sheep. The Park Service reintroduced desert bighorn sheep in 1984, 1996, and 1997. These herds have survived.

How to Get There

From Green River (about 85 miles away), take I-70 to Utah 24, which leads to the east entrance. For a scenic approach, start at Bryce Canyon National Park. Follow Utah 12 over Boulder Mountain to Utah 24, just outside the park's west entrance. Airport: Salt Lake City.

When to Go

All-year park. Spring and fall are mild and ideal for hiking. Winter is cold but brief. Back roads can become impassable during spring thaw, summer rains, and winter snows at higher elevations.

How to Visit

On a 1-day visit, take Utah 24 along the **Fremont River** and then the **Scenic Drive** through the heart of the park. This section offers fine hiking on nearly 40 miles of developed trails. The best second-day activity is a drive along portions of the **Burr Trail Loop** with a walk to **Strike Valley Overlook.** For a longer stay, drive the **Cathedral Valley Loop** or hike in one of the more remote canyons of the **Waterpocket Fold.**

Fremont River & Scenic Drive

35 miles; a half to full day

Drive east on Utah 24 as you enter the park from the west. Ahead of you rises the eroded west face of the **Waterpocket Fold,** a massive line of cliffs running north and south. After the first few miles, the highway follows the course cut through the rock wilderness by the swift **Fremont River,** named for frontier explorer John C. Frémont.

Take the unpaved spur road to the **Goosenecks Overlook.** From the parking area an easy $\frac{1}{10}$-mile trail ends above the deeply entrenched meanders

Imposing Chimney Rock

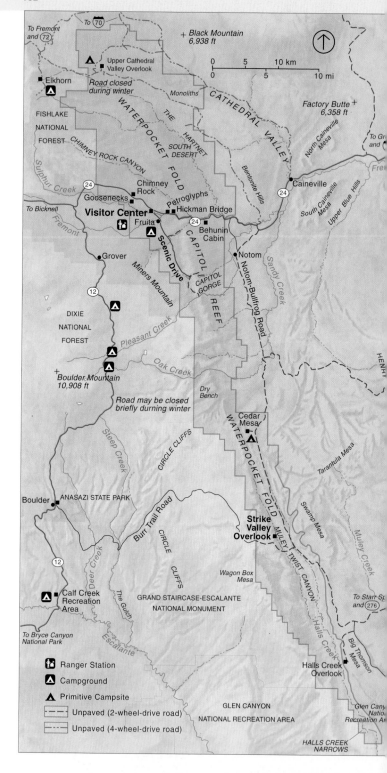

To Fremont and (72)

To (70)

+ Black Mountain
6,938 ft

Upper Cathedral Valley Overlook

Elkhorn

Road closed during winter

Monoliths

CATHEDRAL VALLEY

Factory Butte +
6,358 ft

FISHLAKE NATIONAL FOREST

WATERPOCKET FOLD

THE HARTNET

SOUTH DESERT

North Caineville Mesa

To Gr and

CHIMNEY ROCK CANYON

Sulphur Creek

Bentonite Hills

(24) Caineville

Fre

Chimney Rock

Goosenecks

Petroglyphs

Hickman Bridge

South Caineville Mesa

Upper Blue Hills

To Bicknell

Visitor Center

Fremont

Fruita

(24)

Behunin Cabin

CAPITOL

Notom

Sandy Creek

Grover

Miners Mountain

Scenic Drive

CAPITOL GORGE

Notom-Bullfrog Road

(12)

REEF

DIXIE

NATIONAL

FOREST

Pleasant Creek

Oak Creek

HENRY

Boulder Mountain
10,908 ft +

Road may be closed briefly durring winter

Dry Bench

WATERPOCKET FOLD

Cedar Mesa

Tarantula Mesa

Steep Creek

CIRCLE CLIFFS

Swamp Mesa

Muley Creek

Boulder

ANASAZI STATE PARK

Deer Creek

Burr Trail Road

CIRCLE

Strike Valley Overlook

MULEY TWIST CANYON

(12)

CLIFFS

Wagon Box Mesa

To Starr Sp and (276)

Calf Creek Recreation Area

The Gulch

GRAND STAIRCASE-ESCALANTE
NATIONAL MONUMENT

Halls Creek

Muley Mesa

To Bryce Canyon National Park

Escalante

Big Thomson Mesa

Halls Creek Overlook

Ranger Station

Campground

Primitive Campsite

- - - Unpaved (2-wheel-drive road)

GLEN CANYON
NATIONAL RECREATION AREA

Glen Cany Natio Recreation Ar

Unpaved (4-wheel-drive road)

HALLS CREEK
NARROWS

0 5 10 km
0 5 10 mi

of **Sulphur Creek.** Another short walk takes you to **Sunset Point** for a sweeping view of the **Capitol Reef** section of the Waterpocket Fold.

Bypass the **Chimney Rock** turnoff unless you plan to walk the 3½-mile Chimney Rock loop trail or the more ambitious 9-mile **Spring Canyon** route. This follows a deep gorge cutting through fine exposures of Wingate and Navajo sandstones and ends with a ford at the Fremont River to rejoin Utah 24. (Check on river levels and trail conditions before setting out.)

Stop at the visitor center on the edge of **Fruita,** the remnants of the Mormon frontier community settled in the 1880s and now part of the national park. Be sure to see the 10-minute slide show—the view of the red sandstone cliffs from the theater window is itself worth the stop.

Take the 25-mile round-trip **Scenic Drive** along the rugged face of Capitol Reef. This paved road follows a century-old wagonway known as the Blue Dugway. The old road was used by Indians, outlaws, gypsies, and once even the devil himself, according to an early pioneer who chased him off by brandishing the *Book of Mormon.* Take the short spur road into **Grand Wash.** Look high on the cliff rim for **Cassidy Arch** named for outlaw Butch Cassidy, who reportedly used the canyon as a hideout. A 2¼-mile trail from the parking area leads down Grand Wash through spectacular narrows to the Fremont River. Another trail climbs 1¾ miles to Cassidy Arch. The Scenic Drive ends with a winding 2-mile spur road into **Capitol Gorge.** This was the main road through the reef before 1962. It now ends at a parking area where an easy 1-mile trail continues down into the canyon to historic inscriptions and a series of natural waterpockets, popular among desert denizens.

Return by the same road to Fruita, then go east on Utah 24, passing well-maintained orchards. Turn in at the **Petroglyphs** pull-off. Here Fremont Indians pecked into the cliff large human figures in headdresses. Since you can view this cliff art only at a distance, binoculars come in handy.

The origin of these Indian farmers about AD 600 and their disappearance six centuries later are still mysteries.

Fruita orchards along the Fremont River

Desert bighorn sheep

Early settlers found what appeared to be remnants of their irrigation ditches, granaries, and pit-houses. One unusual discovery was a brick of tule sugar, grass seeds, and pulverized grasshoppers—thought to have been emergency food.

Continue down the highway a short distance to the **Hickman Bridge** parking area. Stretch your legs with a 1-mile hike up a self-guided nature trail that leads under the natural bridge, 125 feet above. For a longer and more arduous hike, take the 2¼-mile **Rim Overlook Trail** along the cliff tops. It ends at a 1,000-foot drop to the Fremont River, providing a good vantage point to view the green pocket of Fruita enclosed in a landscape of tilted rock.

Farther along the road, pull off at the **Behunin Cabin.** This one-room stone cabin was once home to a family of ten. The parents and two youngest children slept inside, the girls in a wagon box outside, and the boys in a nearby rock alcove.

Temple of the Sun, a butte

Claret cup cactus

Burr Trail Loop

125 miles; at least a full day

The drive begins at the visitor center. Go east on Utah 24 to the **Notom-Bullfrog Road.** Paved for the first five miles of its southbound route, the road becomes dirt, skirting the uplift where rock has pushed skyward at 70-degree angles. It crosses several washes that turn into slot canyons where they cut into the east flank of the Waterpocket Fold.

At the junction with the **Burr Trail Road,** you must decide whether to return to the visitor center (½-day trip) or take a full day to complete the loop. If you decide to continue, turn west and climb a series of spectacular switchbacks to the high rim of the fold. Views of the **Henry Mountains** to the east, and **Burr Canyon** straight below, are dramatic.

One of the finest vistas in the park is the **Strike Valley Overlook** in **Upper Muley Twist Canyon.** Many visitors walk the 2½ miles from the hikers' parking area to the overlook trailhead through a beautiful canyon with double arches and a large rock window on the rim. Four-wheel-drive vehicles can follow the canyon floor to a parking area near the overlook. From the parking area the trail continues up canyon another 6½ miles, passing several large arches.

Those looking for solitude can backpack into **Lower Muley Twist Canyon** and its miles of fine slickrock wilderness. Bends in the canyon are so tight, early teamsters said, a mule had to twist itself to get through.

Burr Trail Road becomes paved as it leaves Capitol Reef and continues west to the town of Boulder. Turn north on paved Utah 12, which winds up and over **Boulder Mountain** through a high alpine forest. Here you join Utah 24 about 10 miles west of the visitor center.

Cathedral Valley Loop

70 miles; a half to full day

A high-clearance or four-wheel-drive vehicle is recommended for this scenic trip; check unpaved road conditions before setting out. Follow Utah 24 for 11 miles east of the visitor center. At a marked crossing, turn off Utah 24 and ford the Fremont River. If the river is too high for your vehicle, use the Caineville access to reach the Cathedral Valley.

As the road heads north, it passes through the colorful badlands of the **Bentonite Hills** and follows a mesa called **The Hartnet** to the edge of a 400-foot escarpment overlooking **South Desert.** On the opposite side of the mesa is a spectacular view into **Upper Cathedral Valley.** In this vast open space, keep a lookout for soaring golden eagles.

Eroded spires and monoliths of Entrada sandstone jut 500 feet from the valley floor like enormous weathered teeth. The road loops to the south and drops among the unusual formations, following the valley past such landmarks as the **Walls of Jericho,** the **Gypsum Sinkhole,** and the **Temples of the Sun** and **Moon.** The drive ends at Utah 24, near Caineville.

Information & Activities

Headquarters
HC 70 Box 15, Torrey, Utah 84775.
Phone (435) 425-3791.
www.nps.gov/care

Seasons & Accessibility
Park open year-round. Many roads are unpaved. The Scenic Drive may close briefly during rainy weather and in winter. Driving dirt roads, including Cathedral Valley Loop, may require high-clearance or four-wheel-drive vehicles. Call headquarters or ask at visitor center for latest weather and road conditions.

Visitor & Information Centers
The visitor center on Utah 24 at the north end of park is open all year except Thanksgiving and Christmas. Phone headquarters for information.

Entrance Fee
$4 per car per week.

Pets
Permitted on leashes, except on trails and in backcountry.

Facilities for Disabled
The visitor center, rest rooms, and the Petroglyphs Trail are accessible to wheelchairs.

Things to Do
Free ranger-led activities: nature walks, evening programs. Also available, interpretive exhibits, auto tour, hiking, fruit picking, birdwatching. For information on horseback trips, jeep tours, and other recreational activities, contact the Wayne County Travel Council (800) 858-7951.

Special Advisories
● Always carry water, even on short hikes. Except for tap water, most water in park is not drinkable.
● Watch out for flash floods between July and September.
● Let someone know your itinerary.

Overnight Backpacking
Permits required. They are free and can be obtained at the visitor center or from any park ranger.

Campgrounds
Three campgrounds, all with 14-day limit. Open year-round on a first-come, first-served basis. Fees: None to $8 per night. No showers. Tent sites at **Cathedral Valley** and **Cedar Mesa.** Tent and RV sites at **Fruita;** no hookups.

Hotels, Motels, & Inns
(unless otherwise noted, rates are for 2 persons in a double room, high season)
In Bicknell, Utah 84715:
Aquarius Inn 240 West Main St. (435) 425-3835. 28 units, 6 with kitchenettes. $40. AC, RV park, restaurant.
Sunglow Motel (63 East Main St.) P.O. Box 158. (435) 425-3821. 15 units, half with AC. $38. Restaurant.
In Torrey, Utah 84775:
Capitol Reef Inn (360 West Main St.) P.O. Box 100. (435) 425-3271. 10 units. $44. Restaurant. Open Easter through October.
Wonderland Inn Junction of Utah 12 and Utah 24. (800) 458-0216 or (435) 425-3775. 50 units. $64. AC, pool, restaurant.

For a more complete list of accommodations near the park, write or call park headquarters.

Isis Temple from Hopi Point on the West Rim

Grand Canyon

Arizona

Established February 26, 1919

1,218,376 acres

The road to the Grand Canyon from the south crosses a gently rising plateau that gives no hint at what is about to unfold. You wonder if you have made a wrong turn. All at once an immense gorge a mile deep and up to 18 miles wide opens up. The scale so vast that even from the best vantage point only a fraction of the canyon's 277 miles can be seen.

Nearly five million people travel here each year; 90 percent first see the canyon from the South Rim with its dramatic views into the deep inner gorge of the Colorado River. So many feet have stepped cautiously to the edge of major overlooks that in places the rock has been polished smooth. But most of the park's 1,904 square miles are maintained as wilderness. You can avoid crowds by hiking the park's many trails or driving to the cool evergreen forests of the North Rim where people are fewer and viewing more leisurely.

Canyon views are not always clear, though you can see 100 miles on a good day. Increasingly, air pollution blurs vistas that had once been sharp and rich hued. Hazy days have become more common, with visibility dropping as low as 20 miles. Haze from forest fires and pollen has always been present, but the recent increase is traced to sources outside the park, like copper smelters and urban areas in Arizona, southern California, and even Mexico.

It's hard to look at the canyon and not be curious about geology. Some of the oldest exposed rock in the world, dating back 1.8 billion years,

ber–Mid-May. Hikers and mule riders to the inner canyon, where temperatures reach 118°F, prefer spring and fall; the prime river season is April through October. During summer months on the South Rim, time your visit to midweek, arriving early to avoid the crowds.

How to Visit

On a 1-day visit to the South Rim take the **Hermit Road** (West Rim Drive) for classic views of the main canyon. The drive is closed to automobiles, but buses take you to the overlooks. The best second-day activity is the **Desert View Drive** (East Rim Drive) tour for great views of the **Colorado River** and eastern canyon. On a longer stay take the **North Rim's Cape Royal Road** for broad panoramic vistas. You may also enjoy a hike on a backcountry trail; a mule ride down the **Bright Angel Trail;** a week-long raft trip through the canyon on the Colorado River; and a scenic flight for a bird's-eye view of the canyon. The mule and raft trips and backcountry hikes require reservations far in advance.

South Rim: Hermit Road

8 miles; at least a half day - closed to vehicles March—Nov.

Begin at the new Canyon View Information Center near Mather Point for a classic panoramic view into the heart of the Grand Canyon. Great solitary buttes rise from narrow ridges reaching out from the distant **North Rim.** Far below, a green cluster of Fremont cottonwood trees marks **Phantom Ranch,** a lodge and campground reached only by mule or foot. The observation station at Yavapai Point explores the canyon's geological history and identifies major landmarks. If bad weather threatens, duck into its glass-enclosed observation room and watch as storm clouds roll in.

Board the Hermit Road Loop bus. The free shuttle buses operate March–November. They can be crowded during peak times of day. The loop, which skirts the rim for 8 miles, ends at a limestone curio shop called **Hermits Rest.** Along the way are superb views of the **Colorado River** and the labyrinth of side canyons and broad platforms below the rim. The

lies at the bottom. Exactly how the river formed the canyon is still unclear, but geologists generally agree that most of the cutting occurred within the last five million years.

How to Get There

South Rim: From Flagstaff, Ariz. (about 90 miles away), take US 180 skirting the San Francisco Peaks to South Rim entrance, or take US 89 to Cameron, then Ariz. 64 with views of the Little Colorado River Gorge to Desert View entrance.

North Rim: Take Ariz. 67 from Jacob Lake through the Kaibab National Forest to North Rim entrance. The two rims are 10 air miles apart but 215 miles by car, a 5-hour drive. Airports: Grand Canyon near South Rim; Flagstaff; Las Vegas; Phoenix.

When to Go

South Rim is open all year; North Rim facilities are closed from mid-October to mid-May. Ariz. 67 usually closed due to deep snows late-Novem-

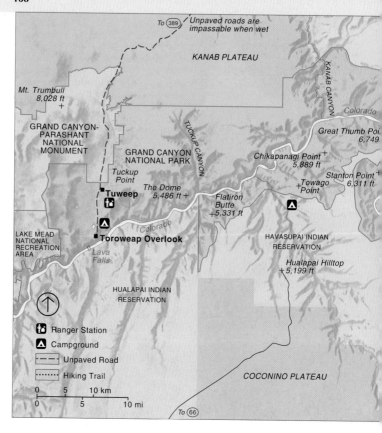

To (389) Unpaved roads are impassable when wet

KANAB PLATEAU

Mt. Trumbull
8,028 ft

GRAND CANYON-
PARASHANT
NATIONAL
MONUMENT

GRAND CANYON
NATIONAL PARK

Tuckup
Point

The Dome
5,486 ft

Tuweep

LAKE MEAD
NATIONAL
RECREATION
AREA

Toroweap Overlook

Lava
Falls

Colorado

KANAB CANYON

TUCKUP CANYON

Great Thumb Poi
6,749

Chikapanagi Point
5,889 ft

Stanton Point
6,311 ft
Towago
Point

Flatiron
Butte
5,331 ft

HAVASUPAI INDIAN
RESERVATION

Hualapai Hilltop
5,199 ft

HUALAPAI INDIAN
RESERVATION

COCONINO PLATEAU

Ranger Station

Campground

Unpaved Road

Hiking Trail

0   5   10 km
0   5   10 mi

To (66)

first stop is the **Trailview Overlook.**

Here you get a hint of the canyon's size. To the southwest, the historic **El Tovar Hotel** and Bright Angel Lodge look small and insignificant perched on the brink of the great precipice. Mule strings and hikers file along the **Bright Angel Trail** as it zigzags 8 miles and 4,460 feet down to the river.

The **Rim Trail,** generally level except for a steep stretch between the village and Trailview, hugs the canyon's edge for about 9 miles from **Mather Point** to Hermits Rest, roughly paralleling Hermit Road. The section between Yavapai Point and **Maricopa Point** is paved; the rest is a dirt path. Short hikes can be combined with rides by catching the shuttle bus at any of the main overlooks. Bypass Maricopa Point and the **Powell Memorial** for now.

Don't miss **Hopi Point**, a promontory jutting deep into the gorge. Magnificent views 45 miles eastward and 45 miles westward make this an ideal

spot for watching sunset or sunrise. To avoid crowds, leave the main overlook and walk along the rim trail to find your own observation point. Across the river rise the intricately carved walls of **Isis Temple** and tree-topped **Shiva Temple,** described as "the grandest of all buttes."

Continue west passing **Mohave Point** and skirting breathtakingly close to **The Abyss,** where a sheer cliff plunges 3,000 feet to a plateau below. From here the road follows the sweep of the rim out to **Pima Point,** where you see the Colorado River threading through the deep gorge. On a still day you can hear the distant rumble of **Granite Rapids** almost a mile below. What looks like a stream from above is a river 300 feet wide that, with its tributaries, drains $\frac{1}{12}$ of the continental United States.

The road ends at Hermits Rest, a stone building that looks as if Hobbits built it on the canyon's rim. Those with time and stamina can hike partway down the steep **Hermit Trail**

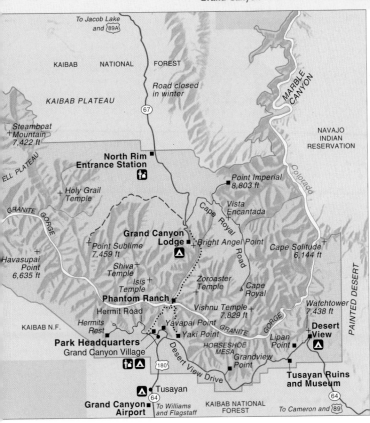

To Jacob Lake
and 89A

KAIBAB   NATIONAL   FOREST

KAIBAB PLATEAU

Road closed
in winter

MARBLE CANYON

NAVAJO
INDIAN
RESERVATION

Steamboat
Mountain
7,422 ft

ELL PLATEAU

67

North Rim
Entrance Station

Holy Grail
Temple

GRANITE GORGE

Point Imperial
8,803 ft

Vista
Encantada

Colorado

Grand Canyon
Lodge

Point Sublime
7,459 ft

Bright Angel Point

Cape Royal Road

Cape Solitude
6,144 ft

Havasupai
Point
6,635 ft

Shiva
Temple

Isis
Temple

Zoroaster
Temple

Cape
Royal

PAINTED DESERT

Phantom Ranch

Hermit Road

Vishnu Temple
7,829 ft

Watchtower
7,438 ft

KAIBAB N.F.

Hermits
Rest

Yavapai Point

Yaki Point

GRANITE

GORGE

Lipan
Point

Desert
View

Park Headquarters
Grand Canyon Village

HORSESHOE
MESA

Grandview
Point

Desert View Drive

180

Tusayan Ruins
and Museum

Tusayan

64

Grand Canyon
Airport

To Williams
and Flagstaff

KAIBAB NATIONAL
FOREST

To Cameron and 89

64

White-water rafting down the Colorado River

Abert's squirrel

to **Dripping Springs,** 7 miles and 6 to 9 hours round-trip. Here the hermit Louis Boucher raised goldfish in a watering trough at the turn of the century. It's a good place to see some of the canyon's 315 species of birds. Permits are not needed for day hikes, but first ask a park ranger for conditions and advisories. On the return, buses stop only at Mohave and Hopi Points.

South Rim: Desert View Drive

23 miles; a half to full day

The **Desert View Drive** (Ariz. 64) begins just south of Mather Point. The drive skirts the rim for 23 miles to **Desert View,** providing numerous pull-offs for long views of the main canyon. In summer, parking at the major overlooks can be a problem, so between March and November only the park shuttle is allowed on the Yaki Point/South Kaibab road. (Board at the Canyon View Information Center.) Along the roadside are shaggy-barked Utah juniper and low clumps of Gambel oak.

Yaki Point provides a fine view of the darkly shining **Granite Gorge,** the innermost canyon. The imposing pyramid-shaped profile of **Vishnu Temple,** 7,829 feet high, dominates the eastern skyline. The practice of naming major park landforms after world deities began with Clarence Dutton, who published a classic report on the geology of the Grand Canyon in 1882.

On the way back to the main road

you can leave the shuttle and hike the **South Kaibab Trail,** which switchbacks down the west side of Yaki Point. Allot a third of your time for going down and two-thirds for hiking back up. The trail eventually reaches the Colorado River at the bottom of the canyon, but a strenuous 3-mile, 2½-hour round-trip takes you only part-way down to **Cedar Ridge.** Even though you drop 1,460 vertical feet, none of the major landforms of the canyon look any closer. Fossil ferns lie exposed in the bedrock on the west side of Cedar Ridge.

Return to your car and follow the main road as it climbs into a tall ponderosa forest. Take the turnoff to **Grandview Point,** one of the finest vistas on the **South Rim.** From the overlook, **Grandview Trail** drops a rugged 3 miles to **Horseshoe Mesa,** where miners once worked copper ore from the Last Chance Mine. John Hance, a prospector known for his tall tales and quick wit, led the first sightseeing parties into the canyon near here in the 1880s. On one trip a woman with a knowledge of botany described to him how trees breathe. "You know," Hance said, "that explains something that has puzzled me a long time; I used to make camp under a big mesquite tree, and night after night that thing would keep me awake with its snoring."

Drive farther east to **Moran Point** for the best view of one of the Colorado's major rapids. Here you look directly down on **Hance Rapids;** its rocky 30-foot drop is considered by river guides to be among the most difficult to run. Continue on down the road, and if you need a change of pace, stop at the small **Tusayan Museum.** It displays well-designed exhibits of Indian cultures, and the nearby ruins offer a self-guided tour of an excavated ancestral Puebloan village from AD 1185.

Take your time when you reach **Lipan Point,** the finest view of the eastern canyon. Here the Colorado River makes a great bend to the west, where it has carved through the **Kaibab Plateau** to form the deepest portion of the Grand Canyon. Below, the river makes an S-curve around **Unkar Delta,** which prehistoric people extensively farmed.

Bypass **Navajo Point** and continue on to Desert View, where you migh stop at the snack bar and curio shop.

North Rim aspen in fall foliage

While here, climb the stairs to the top of the 70-foot **Watchtower,** built in 1932. On the tower's walls Indian artist Fred Kabotie painted murals depicting Hopi legends.

North Rim: Cape Royal Road

23 miles; a half to full day

Averaging 1,000 feet higher than the South Rim, the North Rim's alpine vegetation and more varied vistas appeal to many travelers. Still, you won't find the South Rim crowds here. The focus is the historic **Grand Canyon Lodge** built in the 1920s on the lip of the canyon and rebuilt after a disastrous fire in 1932. From its Sun Room you'll get an excellent view of **Bright Angel Canyon** incised 11 miles into the plateau and overshadowed by **Deva, Brahma,** and **Zoroaster Temples.**

Pick up a self-guiding pamphlet from the box by the log shelter near the parking lot. Follow one of the paved trails to **Bright Angel Point,** which divides a side canyon called **The Transept** from **Roaring Springs Canyon.** Listen for the sound of the springs cascading from a cave 3,000 feet below the rim. This is a fine spot for watching sunrise or sunset. Those needing to stretch their legs can take the **Transept Trail,** 1½ miles along the nearly level canyon rim, or a short hike on the **North Kaibab Trail** (1 mile down takes you 650 feet beneath the rim—and that mile back up feels like 3).

From the lodge, drive north 3 miles to the **Cape Royal Road,** one of the most scenic drives in the park. It passes through forests of spruce, fir, locust, and ponderosa pine mixed with stands of quaking aspen, and through lovely meadows of blue lupine and scarlet bugler. Long-eared mule deer often bound across the road, and you might glimpse the reclusive white-tailed Kaibab squirrel found only in the North Rim forests on the Kaibab Plateau.

Those looking for a dramatic sunrise perch can turn off onto the 3-mile road to **Point Imperial,** at 8,803 feet the highest viewpoint on either rim. Here amid tall evergreens you look across the canyon to the high plateau of the Navajo Indian Reservation. Return to the main road and continue on, passing through the forested **Walhalla Plateau.** Stop at **Vista Encantadora** for superb views of the northeastern canyon and the carved pinnacles of **Brady** and **Tritle Peaks.**

The road ends at a parking lot on **Cape Royal.** A paved ½-mile nature trail leads along a narrow peninsula past **Angel's Window,** an opening eroded through the rock spur that frames the river below. Watch your children. From the overlook **Wotans Throne** and Vishnu Temple dominate the foreground. Across the canyon rise the **Palisades of the Desert.** The unusually broad vista here provides a fine vantage point to watch the sun set and to absorb what naturalist John Burroughs described as Grand Canyon's "strange new beauty."

Mule trip on the North Kaibab Trail

Mule, River, & Air Trips

If the extremely challenging hike to the canyon floor (8 miles down the Bright Angel Trail and 6½ miles on the steeper South Kaibab Trail) is not for you, consider going by muleback. (Though mule trips are not for everyone either—acrophobes especially!) Mules leave the South Rim for day trips and overnights at **Phantom Ranch**, which accommodates guests in rustic cabins and dormitories. The ranch lies in a deep gorge of the inner canyon near the confluence of **Bright Angel Creek** and the Colorado River. The creek's clear waters are known for their excellent trout fishing. The lodge is the only place within the canyon where you can spend the night without camping, and it serves as a good base for hikes up Bright Angel Canyon. Advance reservations—as much as 6 months ahead for mule trips—are necessary.

Many regard a raft trip through the Grand Canyon as the experience of a lifetime. Long, quiet stretches through the scenic heart of the canyon are broken by more than 150 major rapids, two of which are consistently rated 10 on a scale of 10. Most trips stop for day hikes at waterfalls, Indian ruins, and interesting side canyons. A number of river companies offer the raft trips, which generally take 1 to 2 weeks; some companies offer partial trips. Write the park for a list of the companies and reserve well in advance.

Companies giving helicopter and airplane tours are based at Grand Canyon Airport. Flights are no longer allowed below the rim, and because of safety and noise concerns, use of the canyon's airspace is being regulated.

Carving Grand Canyon

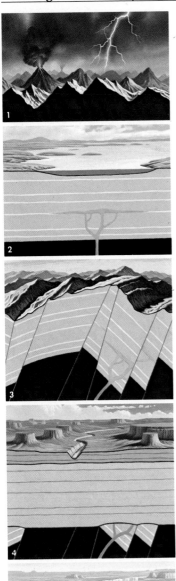

What looks timeless is constantly changing: The Grand Canyon's variegated layers encode two billion years of earth's history.

Some of the earth's oldest rock lies at the canyon's bottom. Thousands of feet thick, the rock formed from sediments. About 1.8 billion years ago, cataclysmic geological forces crumpled and uplifted this rock to create a range of mountains that towered probably 5 to 6 miles high. (1)

The tremendous heat and pressure recrystallized the rock to schist; molten material from deep inside the earth oozed up, forcing itself into the rock and hardening into veins of pink granite. Over eons, wind and water gnawed the mountain range into a plain, and a primordial sea submerged it. Again, sediments wafted to the sea bottom, solidifying into rock; magma continued to well up from inside the earth. (2)

About a billion years ago, the earth shuddered again, cracking its crust into giant fault blocks that tilted upward to form a second range of mountains. (3) The rains, frosts, and winds of millions of years wore away these mountains also.

Much of the Grand Canyon rock visible today (blue layers, 4) accumulated over the schist in the last 600 million years. During some ages the region sank beneath advancing seas; primitive shellfish fossilized in sea bottoms that hardened to shale. During other periods the restless region rose. Topping the Grand Canyon today—some 8,000 feet above sea level—is a 300-foot layer of cream-colored limestone, formed from the remains of countless corals, sponges, and other marine animals.

In recent geological time (about six million years ago) the young, southward-flowing Colorado River—perhaps later captured by the ancestral Hualapi River encroaching from the west—began to slice into the upper layers of the canyon. Gouging inch by inch over the centuries, the river eventually reached the schist 4,000 feet below the rim and continued to cut. (5) Wind and water still wear away at the massive gorge, ever widening and ever deepening the canyon's floor and walls.

Information & Activities

Headquarters
P.O. Box 129, Grand Canyon, Arizona 86023. Phone (520) 638-7888.

Seasons & Accessibility
South Rim open year-round. North Rim roads often closed due to snow mid-Nov. to mid-May. For weather and road information, call (520) 638-7888.

Visitor & Information Centers
Canyon View Information Plaza near Grand Canyon Village open all year. Call (520) 638-7888. North Rim Visitor Station open mid-Nov. through mid-May. Call (520) 638-7864.

Entrance Fee
$20 per car for 7 days; $10 per person arriving on foot, bike, or motorcycle.

Pets
Allowed, leashed, on rim trails, but not below the rim. Kennels available; phone (520) 638-0534.

Facilities for Disabled
Visitor center and shuttle buses are wheelchair accessible. Free brochures available. Hermit Drive open to vehicles carrying disabled persons, with permit.

Things to Do
Free ranger-led activities: day and evening nature walks, slide shows, talks, cultural demonstrations, and campfire programs. Also, horse and mule trips into canyon, hiking, bicycling, fishing, river rafting, air tours, cross-country skiing. For activities, call (520) 638-7888. Write headquarters for list of concessioners offering wide variety of tours.

Special Advisory
● Be very careful near the rim; protective barriers are intermittent.

Overnight Backpacking
Permits required; $10 fee plus $5 per person per night. Backcountry Information Center, P.O. Box 129, Grand Canyon, Ariz. 86023. (520) 638-7875.

Campgrounds
Four campgrounds, 7-day limit, 3 in South Rim, 1 in North Rim. **Mather** open all year; recommend reservations March to December; reserve through National Parks Reservation Service (see page 11); other times, first come, first served. **Desert View** (first come, first served) and **North Rim** (recommend reservations through National Parks Reservation) mid-May to mid-Oct. **Trailer Village** open all year; recommend reservations. Contact AmFac Parks & Resorts, (303) 297-2757. Fee $20 per night. Showers at **North Rim** and near **Mather** campground. Tent and RV sites at all campgrounds; hookups only at Trailer Village. Two group campgrounds; must reserve. Food services in park.

Hotels, Motels, & Inns
(unless otherwise noted, rates are for 2 persons in a double room, high season)
The first 9 hotels and lodges listed below are operated by AmFac Parks & Resorts (303) 297-2757; www.amfac.com; Recommend reservations 6 to 9 months in advance. For same-day reservations, try (520) 638-2631.
INSIDE THE PARK (On South Rim):
Bright Angel Lodge & Cabins 89 units, some share baths. Cabins $73-$234; rooms $46-$63. Rest. **El Tovar Hotel** 78 units. $116-$284. AC, rest. **Kachina Lodge** 49 units. $114-$124. AC. **Maswik Lodge** 288 units. Cabins $63 (June-Aug.); rooms $73-$118. Rest. **Phantom Ranch** (reached by hiking, mule, or raft trips) Dormitories $22 per person. AC, rest., shared showers. Mule trips from $250 per night, per person, w/meals. Reserve early. **Thunderbird Lodge** 55 units. $114-$124. AC. **Yavapai Lodge** 358 rooms. $88-$102. Rest. March to Nov.
(On North Rim): **Grand Canyon Lodge** (303) 297-2757. 200 units. $60-$97. Rest. Mid-May to mid-Oct.
OUTSIDE THE PARK:
In Kaibab National Forest:
Moqui Lodge (303) 297-2757. 136 units. $94. Rest. Mid-Feb.–Nov.
In Grand Canyon, Ariz. 86023:
Quality Inn (on Ariz. 64) P.O. Box 520. (800) 228-5151 or (520) 638-2673. 176 units. $118-$168. AC, pool, rest. **Seven Mile Lodge** (on Ariz. 64) P.O. Box 56. (520) 638-2291. 20 units. $75-$82. No reservations; first come, first served. AC. Closed January.

Excursions

Lake Mead National Recreation Area

Boulder City, Nevada

Lake Mead, water impounded from the Colorado River by Hoover Dam, is the center of this NRA, the nation's first (established in 1936). More than 2,000 bighorn sheep roam the desert canyons and plateaus surrounding the reservoir. 1,501,216 acres, part in Arizona. 1,021 campsites, 191 rooms, food services, boating, fishing, horseback riding, picnic areas, naturalist programs, water sports, handicapped access. Open all year. Adjoins Grand Canyon NP on west. Visitor center at US 93 & Nevada 166, about 280 mi. from park's South Rim entrance. (702) 293-8906.

Wupatki National Monument

Flagstaff, Arizona

Eight hundred years ago, people moved to the Wupatki area to farm the volcanic soil. Little more than a century later they left behind extensive accomplishments, including a 100-room pueblo, amphitheater, ball court, and pottery. 35,253 acres. Enjoy hiking, picnics, scenic drives. Open all year. Off US 89, about 65 mi. southeast of Grand Canyon NP. (520) 679-2365.

Canyon de Chelly National Monument

Chinle, Arizona

These spectacular red-rock canyons, spires, and mesas rival any natural site in the Southwest. The same is true of their cultural legacy: ancient Basketmaker pithouses, the remains of ancestral Puebloan dwellings on 1,000-foot cliffs, and the many reminders of the Navajo past and present. Navajo guides offer tours into the canyons; only the White House ruin may be visited without a guide. North and South Rim drives have many scenic overlooks. 83,840 acres. Facilities include 95 campsites, food services, hiking, horseback riding, jeep tour, scenic drives, handicapped access. Open all year. Off US 191, about 230 miles east of Grand Canyon NP. (520) 674-5500.

Fall morning on Wheeler Peak

Great Basin

Nevada

Established October 27, 1986

77,180 acres

An Ice Age landscape of glacier-carved peaks rises more than a mile from the desert floor. The park takes its name from the vast region that extends east from California's Sierra Neavada Range to Utah's Wasatch Range, and from southern Oregon to southern Nevada, encompassing most of Nevada and western Utah. Called Great Basin by explorer John C. Frémont in the mid-1800s, the region actually comprises not one but at least 90 basins, or valleys, and its rivers all flow inland—not to any ocean.

The park road winds up Wheeler Peak, the second highest mountain in the state of Nevada. When the road ends at 10,000 feet, trails lead to the 13,063-foot summit and to the region's only glacier, near a stand of bristlecone pines. Great Basin is a young park compared to the likes of a Yellowstone or Yosemite, yet within its confines are some of the world's oldest trees.

The bristlecones form the rear guard of a Pleistocene forest that once covered much of the region. Now surviving in scattered stands, some trees are 3,000 years old—alive when Tutankhamun ruled Egypt.

In the flank of the mountain, at an altitude of 6,800 feet, lies Lehman Caves with 1½ miles of underground passages. These formed when higher water tables during the Ice Age made pockets in the limestone. Park rangers guide visitors past flowstone, stalactites, and delicate white crystals that grow in darkness.

The number of visitors has reached more than 85,000 since 1986, when the cave and neighboring mountains

derstorms that can catch them on exposed ridges anytime of year.

Candlelight tours of Lehman Caves are offered only in the summer. The best time to view Wheeler Peak is in early morning. In winter, visitors enjoy excellent cross-country skiing.

How to Visit

On a one-day visit, take the **Wheeler Peak Scenic Drive** for dramatic views of high alpine landscapes. On your way back, stop at **Lehman Caves** for a chance to walk underground through intriguing passages.

Wheeler Peak Scenic Drive

12 miles; 1½ hours to most of a day

A paved road climbs steeply from the visitor center to the Wheeler Peak Campground at 10,000 feet. Those not used to mountain driving may find both the view and the drive breathtaking. The road passes from the tough, drought-resistant pinyon-juniper woodland into the high-elevation forest of Engelmann spruce, limber pine, and aspen.

Begin the scenic drive near the visitor center. A short trail at the first pull-off takes you to the historic **Osceola Ditch** built in the late 1880s to carry water for hydraulic gold mining. Save this for your next trip, if pressed for time.

Skip the **Mather Overlook,** but notice the old stand of mountain mahogany. These usually grow as

became a national park. But the park has 65 miles of trails, offering access to the hills and a chance to see glacial moraines, alpine lakes, and spectacular sweeping views of the surrounding basin and range country.

How to Get There

From Las Vegas (about 300 miles away), take I-15 to US 93, then US 50 to Nev. 487. At Baker, take Nev. 488 to the park entrance. From Salt Lake City, Utah (about 250 miles away), take I-15 to US 50, then Nev. 487 to Baker and Nev. 488 to the park entrance. Airport: Ely (about 67 miles away).

When to Go

Great Basin is open year-round, but the Wheeler Peak Scenic Drive is closed from November to May, or as long as heavy snows makes it impassable. In summer, the most popular season for people to visit, temperatures are generally mild. September and October bring cool weather and fewer crowds. Hikers must beware of sudden thun-

Ancient bristlecone pine on Mount Washington

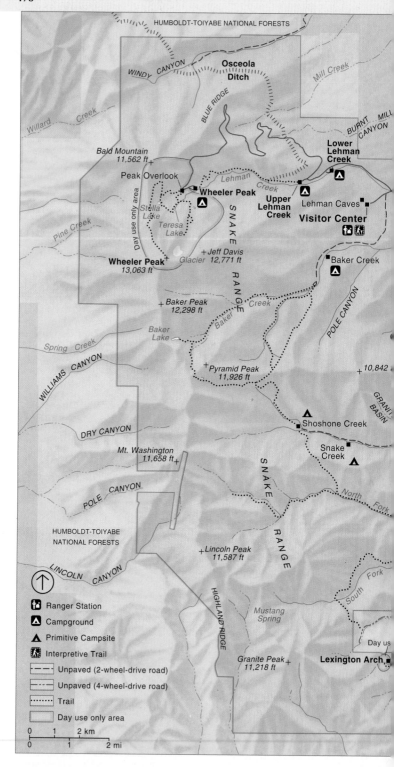

HUMBOLDT-TOIYABE NATIONAL FORESTS

Osceola
Ditch

WINDY CANYON

BLUE RIDGE

Mill Creek

Willard Creek

BURNT MILL CANYON

Bald Mountain
11,562 ft

Lower
Lehman
Creek

Peak Overlook

Lehman Creek

Wheeler Peak

Upper
Lehman
Creek

Lehman Caves

Day use only area

Stella
Lake

Visitor Center

Teresa
Lake

Pine Creek

SNAKE

Baker Creek

Wheeler Peak
13,063 ft

Jeff Davis
Glacier 12,771 ft

RANGE

Baker Peak
12,298 ft

Baker Creek

POLE CANYON

Baker
Lake

Spring Creek

WILLIAMS CANYON

Pyramid Peak
11,926 ft

10,842

GRANITE BASIN

DRY CANYON

Shoshone Creek

Mt. Washington
11,658 ft

Snake
Creek

POLE CANYON

SNAKE

HUMBOLDT-TOIYABE
NATIONAL FORESTS

North Fork

RANGE

LINCOLN CANYON

Lincoln Peak
11,587 ft

South Fork

HIGHLAND RIDGE

Mustang
Spring

Day us

Ranger Station

Campground

Primitive Campsite

Interpretive Trail

Granite Peak
11,218 ft

Lexington Arch

- - - Unpaved (2-wheel-drive road)

-·-·- Unpaved (4-wheel-drive road)

······ Trail

Day use only area

0   1   2 km

0   1   2 mi

Parry's primrose near alpine Stella Lake

Desert prickly pear cactus

Blue columbine on Baker Lake Trail

a shrub but here reach tree height. Pull off at **Peak Overlook** for spectacular views of **Wheeler Peak** on the right and **Jeff Davis Peak** on the left. The north face of Wheeler drops 1,800 feet to a glacier below. Snow often dusts the jagged walls of gray quartzite.

The road ends at Wheeler Peak Campground where you have your choice of several fine walks. One of the most popular follows the 3-mile **Alpine Lakes Loop Trail** past **Stella** and **Teresa**

Bristlecone pines worn smooth by centuries of wind, sand, and ice

New-growth bristlecones and needles

Climbing the northwest face of Mount Washington

Lakes. This leads you to a dramatic alpine setting with a barren, sawtooth ridge rising above the smooth surface of the lake.

If time and stamina allow, follow the **Wheeler Summit Trail** to the ridge above the lakes for an overview of the park and sweeping views of Great Basin's seemingly endless succession of mountain ranges. The trail leaves the Alpine Lakes Loop Trail near Stella Lake and climbs another 3,000 feet to the summit. Once above tree line, watch for sturdy alpine flowers like primrose and phlox. And be prepared for harsh weather. A terse entry in the summit register reads, "Wind took no prisoners."

Just as spectacular is the 3-mile **Bristlecone/Glacier Trail.** This leaves from Teresa Lake and takes you to **Wheeler Cirque,** a glacier-hollowed valley enclosed by sheer cliffs. At the far end lies the glacier, the Great Basin's only permanent one and one of the southernmost in the country.

Before reaching the glacier be sure to take the **Bristlecone Forest Loop.** This self-guided nature trail passes ancient trees with twisted trunks carved and polished by wind-driven snow and ice. Nearby a tree called Prometheus lived for almost 5,000 years until it was cut down in 1964.

Even after most of its trunk and branches die, a bristlecone pine can continue to survive, sustained by very little moisture. The tree holds onto its needles for 20 to 30 years, assuring stable photosynthesis regardless of

Stalactites and stalagmites in the Gothic Palace, Lehman Caves

environmental stress.

Lehman Caves

⁶/₁₀ mile; 1 ½ hours

Rangers lead groups through underground chambers filled with intricate formations. Guided cave tours began in 1885 with Absalom Lehman, a miner turned rancher. Over the years dozens of legends have grown around his discovery of the cave.

One claims he was racing along on horseback when he suddenly dropped through the entrance. He lassoed a tree and managed to hold on until rescued 4 days later. The hard part was keeping his legs wrapped around the horse to prevent it from falling.

After purchasing tickets, meet your guide behind the visitor center near the cave entrance.

The attraction of **Lehman Caves** does not lie in massive rooms and big drops, but in the beauty of its formations, well represented in the first room you visit, the **Gothic Palace.** The cave is so filled with columns, draperies, and stalactites that the first explorers used sledgehammers to break through them. Because of the cave's manageable scale, you get closeup views of bizarre helictites and delicate aragonite crystals.

The walkway takes you past fine examples of rare cave shields. These large disks grow from cracks in the ceiling where seeping water deposits minerals in flat, circular forms.

Continuing deeper, you reach two of the cave's most beautiful rooms. Rimstone pools and soda straws decorate the **Lake Room;** shields, massive columns, and bacon-rind draperies fill the **Grand Palace.**

A small variety of cave life makes its home here, including pack rats, cave crickets, and the rare pseudoscorpion—an arachnid with scorpion-like pinchers. Bats, however, stay away, finding the cave's vertical entrance too hard to negotiate.

Information & Activities

Headquarters
100 Great Basin National Park Baker, Nevada 89311. Phone (775) 234-7331. www.nps.gov/grba

Seasons & Accessibility
Park open year-round. Snow may close high-elevation trails until late June or July. Some park roads require four-wheel-drive vehicles. Call headquarters about current trail and road conditions.

Visitor & Information Centers
Visitor center and Lehman Caves, located on Nev. 488 at northeast end of park, open daily all year, except Thanksgiving, Christmas, and New Year's days. Phone park headquarters number for visitor information.

Entrance Fees
None for park. Fee for cave tours.

Pets
Permitted on leashes except in Visitor center, caves, backcountry, and on trails.

Facilities for Disabled
Visitor center and the first room in Lehman Caves are wheelchair accessible, as are some campsites.

Things to Do
Free ranger-led activities: nature walks and talks, exhibits, movie, campfire programs. Also available: cave tours, Wheeler Peak scenic drive, hiking, fishing (license required), climbing, and cross-country skiing.

Special Advisories
• Park's high elevation can cause altitude sickness. People who have heart or respiratory problems should take it slowly.
• Don't expect to find water sources along the trails; always carry drinking water when hiking.
• Watch out for rattlesnakes along hiking trails.
• Summer thunderstorms are common; check weather conditions with park before setting off on a hike.

Overnight Backpacking
Those heading out to the backcountry should stop at the park's visitor center and complete the free permit registration form. In addition to helping to ensure visitor safety, permits allow the park to monitor how its resources are being used.

Campgrounds
Four campgrounds, all with 14-day limit, all first come, first served. **Baker Creek** and **Upper Lehman Creek** open mid-May through October. **Wheeler Peak** open June 15 to October 1. **Lower Lehman Creek** open all year. Snowstorms may close campgrounds occasionally. Fees subject to change; call the park. No showers. Tent and RV sites; no hookups. Food services in the park. Potable water available at visitor center in summer.

Hotels, Motels & Inns
(unless otherwise noted, rates are for 2 persons in a double room, high season)
In Baker, Nevada 89311:
The Border Inn (on US 50) P.O. Box 30. (775) 234-7300. 28 units. $29-$37. AC, restaurant.
Silver Jack Motel (on Main Street) P.O. Box 166. (775) 234-7323. 9 units. $37-$65.
In Ely, Nevada 89301:
Bristlecone Motel 700 Avenue I. (800) 497-7404 or (775) 289-8838. 31 units. $42-$44. AC.
Ramada Copper Queen Hotel and Casino 701 Avenue I. (800) 851-9526 or (775) 289-4884. 65 units. $60-$69. AC, pool, restaurant.
Hotel Nevada 501 Aultman Street. (775) 289-6665. 58 units. $25-$85. AC, restaurant.
Jailhouse Motel and Casino 5th and High Streets. (800) 841-5430 or (775) 289-3033. 61 units. $45-$58. AC, rest.
Petrelli's Fireside Inn (2 miles N of Ely) SR 1, Box 2. (800) 732-0288 or (775) 289-3765. 14 units. $45. AC, rest.

Excursions

Humboldt-Toiyabe National Forests

Elko, Nevada

This immense national forest is the largest in the continental US. Contains glacier-carved Lamoille Canyon, historic mining towns, and Jarbridge Wilderness, in Nevada, one of the country's least used wilderness areas. About 6,500,000 acres. Enjoy 1,000 campsites, hiking, boating, boat ramp, fishing, horseback riding, hunting, picnic areas, scenic drives, winter sports, water sports, handicapped access. Open year-round; most campsites open late May-October. The forest's Snake Division surrounds Great Basin NP. (775) 355-5340.

Desert National Wildlife Range

Las Vegas, Nevada

Wildlife is the focus of this Mojave Desert refuge, just a long roll of the dice from Las Vegas. Bighorn sheep, mule deer, coyotes, and some 260 species of birds are found in the refuge, the largest in the lower 48. 1,600,000 acres. Primitive camping, hiking, hunting, scenic drives (high-clear-vehicle required). Open year-round. Interpretive kiosk at Corn Creek Field Station entrance, off US 95, about 250 miles from Great Basin NP. (702) 646-3401.

Spring Mountain National Recreation Area

Las Vegas, Nevada

Many people are surprised to find a forest so close to Las Vegas: The Spring Mountains rise to almost 12,000 feet from the harsh desert of southern Nevada. The cool mountain forests are home to a wilderness of ponderosa pine, sheer limestone cliffs, and assorted wildlife. About 316,000 acres. Enjoy camping, picnic areas, scenic drives, hiking, and wildlife viewing. Take US 95 to the Kyle Canyon turnoff (Nev. 157). About 250 miles from Great Basin NP. (702) 873-8800.

Winter at Cliff Palace, a 13th-century ancestral Puebloan site

Mesa Verde

Colorado

Established June 29, 1906

52,074 acres

At Mesa Verde, Spanish for "Green table," ancient multistoried dwellings fill the cliff-rock alcoves that rise 2,000 feet above Montezuma Valley. Unique for their number and remarkable preservation, the cliff dwellings cluster in sandstone canyons that slice the mesa into narrow tablelands fingering southward. Here, and on the mesa top, archaeologists have located more than 500 prehistoric sites dating from about AD 550 to 1300.

The sites, from mesa-top pithouses and multistoried dwellings to cliffside villages, document the dramatic changes in the lives of a prehistoric people that archaeologists once dubbed the Anasazi. They are now more accurately called the ancestral Puebloans, and 24 Native American tribes in the southwest today consider themselves descendants of these ancestral people. Some 40 pueblos and cliff dwellings are visible from park roads and overlooks; many of these are open to the public.

Beginning in about AD 750, the ancestral Puebloans grouped their dwellings in mesa-top pueblos, or villages. Around 1200 they moved down into recesses in the cliffs. Massive overhanging rock has so sheltered these later villages that they seem to stand outside of time, aloof to the present.

In 1888 two cowboys tracking stray cattle through snow stopped on the edge of a steep-walled canyon. Through the drifting flakes they could make out traces of walls and towers of a great cliff dwelling across the

allowed their populations to grow perhaps as high as 5,000. Gradually woodlands were cut, wild game hunted out, and soils depleted. Years of drought and poor crops may have been aggravated by village squabbles. By the end of the 13th century the ancestral Puebloans had left the plateau, never to return.

How to Get There

From Cortez, take US 160 east for 8 miles to the park entrance, then follow the winding park road 15 miles to Far View Visitor Center and 5½ miles farther to park headquarters area, which includes the museum and main cliff dwellings. Trailers are not allowed past Morefield Village. Airports: Cortez and Durango.

When to Go

All-year park. Wetherill Mesa, Far View Visitor Center, Cliff Palace Loop, Balcony House, and many services are closed in winter. Wildflowers bloom from April through September. In winter, cross-country skiing is allowed on parts of Mesa Top Road when conditions permit.

How to Visit

On a one-day visit, begin early and stop first at the **Chapin Mesa Museum** for an overview; then visit nearby **Spruce Tree House.** From there take the **Cliff Palace Loop** of **Mesa Top Road.** In the afternoon, follow the other loop. Wear sturdy shoes and be prepared for some strenuous climbing if you plan to visit the cliff dwellings. Binoculars are useful for enhancing your views from across the canyon. With extra time, visit less crowded **Wetherill Mesa.**

canyon. Novelist Willa Cather, a later visitor, described the scene: "The falling snowflakes sprinkling the piñons, gave it a special kind of solemnity. It was more like sculpture than anything else...preserved...like a fly in amber."

Climbing down a makeshift ladder to the deserted city, the excited cowboys explored the honeycombed network of rooms that they named Cliff Palace. Inside, they found stone tools and pottery and other artifacts. Later investigators learned that these rooms had been uninhabited for some seven centuries.

Why the Mesa Verde people eventually left their homes may never be known. Indeed, they lived in the cliffside dwellings for only about the last 75 to 100 years of their occupation of Mesa Verde. Early observers guessed warfare, but the evidence for this never turned up in later excavations. Archaeologists now think they may have been victims of their own success. Their productive dry farming

Chapin Mesa Museum & Spruce Tree House

2 hours to a half day

Before descending to the sites, go through the **Chapin Mesa Museum** located at the **Spruce Tree House Trailhead** and park headquarters area. Here you pick up self-guiding booklets to the major sites and see excellent dioramas that bring to life the changing world of the Mesa Verde people. Also displayed are some of the Southwest's finest artifacts and Indian arts and crafts.

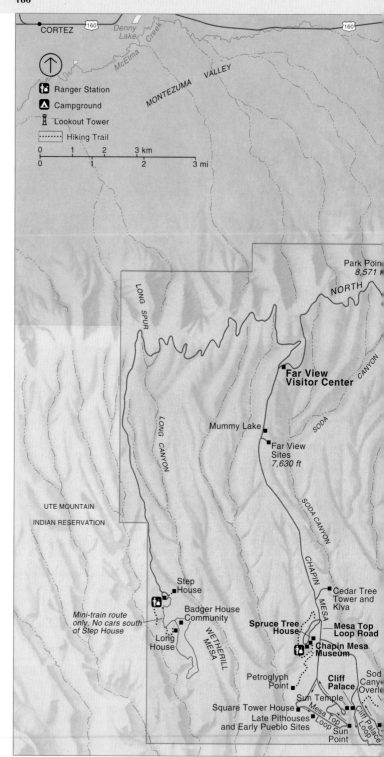

CORTEZ 160

Denny Lake
McElma Creek

↑

🏚 Ranger Station
🔺 Campground
🗼 Lookout Tower
····· Hiking Trail

0   1   2   3 km
0   1   2   3 mi

MONTEZUMA VALLEY

NORTH

Park Point
8,571

LONG SPUR

LONG CANYON

**Far View
Visitor Center**

CANYON

Mummy Lake

SODA

Far View
Sites
7,630 ft

SODA CANYON

UTE MOUNTAIN
INDIAN RESERVATION

CHAPIN MESA

Step
House

Cedar Tree
Tower and
Kiva

Badger House
Community

**Spruce Tree
House**

**Mesa Top
Loop Road**

*Mini-train route
only. No cars south
of Step House*

Long
House

WETHERILL MESA

**Chapin Mesa
Museum**

Petroglyph
Point

**Cliff
Palace**

Sod
Cany
Overl

Sun Temple

Square Tower House

Late Pithouses
and Early Pueblo Sites

Mesa Top
Loop Road

Cliff
Palace
Loop

Sun
Point

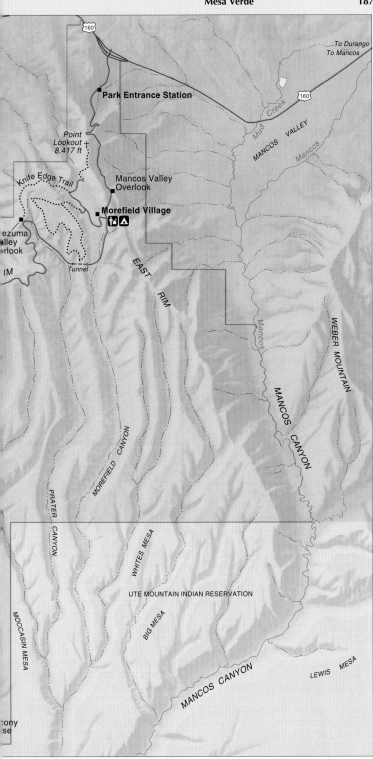

Narrow passageway in Balcony House

Pottery in Spruce Tree House

View the collection of **Mesa Verde pottery.** Decorated with black geometric designs against a white background, the pots represent the highest artistic expression of the ancestral Puebloans.

The park naturally focuses on the dramatic cliff dwellings, but they represent only the final scene in a long story. The genius of the earlier culture was best expressed not in building but in weaving. Watch for outstanding examples in the museum, including a long sash of braided dog hair still as strong and pliable as it was when worn 1,500 years ago.

During summer, pick up a self-guiding booklet to **Spruce Tree House** and walk the paved ¼-mile trail to the park's best preserved site. Here you will see the skillful building techniques and stone work of the ancestral Puebloans; 90 percent of the stonework is original. Rangers will be on duty to answer questions. (From mid-October to late April, when the park is less crowded, the rangers lead guided tours.) The trail crosses the canyon bottom, thick with Gambel oak, whose acorns were eaten by the Indians. The site got its name from a tall Douglas-fir that, it is said, early explorers climbed down to reach the site—they thought it was a spruce.

The cliff dwelling, built in an alcove more than 200 feet wide, housed 100-125 people. Three of its eight kivas—underground ceremonial rooms—have reconstructed roofs. At one of them, you may climb down the ladder through the smoke hole into the dark chamber below.

Either now or later—if time and stamina allow—take the 2⅘-mile **Petroglyph Point Trail,** a self-guided nature walk that branches off the Spruce Tree House Trail. Register and pick up a guidebook at the trailhead. The trail offers a good place to stretch your legs, familiarize yourself with plants and their prehistoric uses, and see one of the park's largest petroglyphs, a panel 12 feet across.

Mesa Top Loop Road

12 miles; a half day

Dotted with wayside interpretive exhibits, two 6-mile one-way loops wind through **Chapin Mesa's** thick pinyon-juniper woodland. Begin your tour by turning onto the **Cliff Palace Loop** and driving to the parking area at **Cliff Palace.** A short trail takes you to a striking view of the largest cliff dwelling in North America. The ¼-mile trail continues down to the 150-room site that once housed more than 100 Indians.

The ancestral Puebloans built their dwellings in natural shelters formed by water percolating down through the sandstone. Where it reaches the denser shale layer, it seeps horizontally through the canyon wall, forming springs. These weaken the overlying rock, eroding the cliff face into eye-shaped alcoves.

Continue driving to the **Balcony House** parking area. This 40-room dwelling is one of the highlights of the park. But it is not for everyone. *Acrophobes and claustrophobes, beware!* Rangers guide adventurous groups up a 32-foot ladder to an easily defended ledge site and a panoramic view of **Soda Canyon.** To leave Balcony House, you must crawl through a tunnel on your hands and knees. Balcony House is closed in winter; you can view it then from a promontory at the end of the ¾-mile **Soda Canyon Overlook Trail.**

Keep going along the road until the junction with the **Mesa Top Loop,** where you turn left. Stop at the first pull-off to pick up a guide booklet and continue on to the **Square Tower House** overlook. A 500-foot trail leads to a dramatic viewpoint above the park's tallest site, the four-story remnant of a more extensive, multi-tiered structure. The site itself is not open to the public.

Return to your car and continue a short distance to the **Late Pithouse and Early Pueblo Ruins** pull-off. The squarish, sunken pithouses, earliest of Mesa Verde's permanent dwellings, were forerunners of the kivas. Farther along the trail are the excavated remains of three villages built on the same site between AD 900 and 1075. They show the evolution in architectural style, from post-and-adobe construction to stone masonry.

Drive to **Sun Point Overlook,** saving **Sun Point Pueblo** for your next trip. Here at the junction of **Fewkes Canyon** and **Cliff Canyon** you see a dozen cliff dwellings—among them, distant views of Cliff Palace to the northeast; **Sunset House** perched on a high rock ledge to the east; and **Mummy House,** directly across the canyon. The house was named for he naturally desiccated mummy of a child discovered there.

Continue past **Oak Tree House** and **Fire Temple** pull-offs to **Sun Temple.** Built by skilled masons—the stones were molded and their surfaces "dimpled"—this long, D-shaped structure with doorless chambers presents an enigma to archaeologists. Never inhabited, it may have been a ceremonial center; or perhaps it was used to record the annual movements of the sun, an attempt to counter the changeable weather. The canyon edge next to the parking area offers a superb view of Cliff Palace.

Sunset on Point Lookout, above Mancos Valley

Wetherill Mesa

13 miles; a half day or more

Accessible only in summer, the **Wetherill Mesa Road** starts on the west side of **Far View Visitor Center.** The steep road takes you to sites opened to the public in 1972 after an extensive archaeological study. Under sponsorship of the National Geographic Society and National Park Service, several major cliff dwellings and mesa-top sites were excavated.

Drive to the kiosk area and park. From here take the ½-mile, self-guided walk to **Step House,** named for its prehistoric stairway. The site is unusual, for pithouses have been uncovered next to a multistoried pueblo built in the same alcove.

Return to the kiosk area and take the mini-train to the head of **Long House Trail.** Rangers lead groups down the ¼-mile trail to the park's second largest cliff dwelling—150 rooms with 21 kivas, an unusually high number. Gustaf Nordenskiöld, a Swedish scientist, excavated portions of **Long House** and other sites in 1891, publishing the first scientific report on Mesa Verde.

You can extend your visit by taking the mini-train to the ½-mile, self-guided trail that threads through the ruins of **Badger House Community.** These excavated pithouses and pueblos show the contrast between life on the mesa top and that in the canyon alcoves below. The mini-train will return you to the kiosk area.

Information & Activities

Headquarters
Mesa Verde National Park, Colorado 81330. Phone (970) 529-4465. www.nps.gov/meve

Seasons & Accessibility
Park open year-round, but most visitor facilities and services available mid-May to mid-October only. Spruce Tree House open all year; Cliff Palace open mid-April to mid-October; Balcony House open late May to late September; Wetherill Mesa open summer only. In winter, snow or ice may close Mesa Top Road. For weather and road conditions, call (970) 529-4461 or (970) 529-4465.

Visitor & Information Centers
Far View Visitor Center at northwest section of park open daily mid-May to mid-October. Chapin Mesa Museum at southern end of park, located 21 miles from entrance, open daily year-round. Phone (970) 529-4465 for visitor information.

Entrance Fee
$10 per car per week. Tours of Cliff Palace, Balcony House, and Long House require tickets; purchase for small fee at Far View Visitor Center.

Pets
Permitted on leashes. Not allowed in buildings, in sites, or on trails.

Facilities for Disabled
Visitor center, museum, $\frac{1}{2}$-mile trail at Wetherill Mesa, some campsites, and most rest rooms are wheelchair accessible. Site tours are not accessible, but most major cliff dwellings can be viewed from the mesa-top roads and overlooks. Free brochure.

Things to Do
Ranger-led activities: archaeological walks, tours of Balcony House (spring to fall), Spruce Tree House (fall to spring), and Long House (summer only); evening campfire programs. Also available, wayside exhibits, archaeological museum, self-guided tours; also, limited hiking (registration required for two trails), cross-country skiing, snowshoeing.

Special Advisories
● Visits to the cliff dwellings are strenuous. Wear sturdy shoes and use caution, especially if you have heart or respiratory problems.
● Hold onto your children on cliff trails and canyon rims.

Overnight Backpacking
Not permitted in park.

Campgrounds
One campground, **Morefield,** with a 14-day limit. Open mid-April to mid-October. First come, first served. Fees $7-$14 per night. Showers within 1 mile of campground. Tent and RV sites; 14 hookups. **Morefield Group Campgrounds** available first come, first served. Food services in park (mid-April to mid-October).

Hotels, Motels, & Inns
(unless otherwise noted, rates are for 2 persons in a double room, high season)
INSIDE THE PARK:
Far View Lodge Mesa Verde Co., P.O. Box 277, Mancos, Colo. 81328. (800) 449-2288. 150 units. $88-$99. Restaurant. Open mid-April through mid-October.
OUTSIDE THE PARK:
In Cortez, Colorado 81321:
Anasazi Motor Inn 640 S. Broadway. (800) 972-6232 or (970) 565-3773. 85 units. $65-$71. AC, pool, restaurant.
Best Western Sands 1120 E. Main St. (800) 528-1234 or (970) 565-3761. 81 units. $89. AC, pool, restaurant.
Best Western Turquoise Inn and Suites 535 E. Main St. (800) 547-3376 or (970) 565-3778. 77 units. $80-$129. AC, pool, restaurant.
In Durango, Colorado 81301:
Strater Hotel (699 Main Ave.) P.O. Drawer E. (800) 247-4431 or (970) 247-4431. 93 units. $169-$205. AC, restaurant.
In Mancos, Colorado 81328:
Mesa Verde Motel (191 Railroad Ave.) P.O. Box 552. (800) 825-6372 or (970) 533-7741. 16 units. $59. AC.

Excursions

San Juan National Forest
Durango, Colorado

The vegetation ranges from high alpine forest to sage-and-pinyon desert in this rugged San Juan Mountains area. Contains lakes, rivers, wilderness areas, and many archaeological sites. Two million acres. Facilities include 900 campsites, hiking, boating, boat ramps, climbing, bicycling, fishing, horseback riding, llama trekking, hunting, winter sports, water sports, handicapped access. Open all year; most campsites open May-November. Information at Durango on US 550, about 50 miles east of Mesa Verde NP. (970) 247-4874.

Aztec Ruins National Monument
Aztec, New Mexico

Misnamed by early Anglo settlers, this masonry-and-timber pueblo shows the influence of two ancestral Puebloan groups. It features the Southwest's only restored great kiva. 319 acres. Exhibits, picnic areas. Open all year. Off US 516, about 60 mi. SE of Mesa Verde NP. (505) 334-6174.

Hovenweep National Monument
Cortez, Colorado

Hovenweep—a Ute term meaning "deserted valley"—consists of six ancestral Puebloan sites: two in Utah and four in Colorado. They feature stone pueblos and square, circular, and D-shaped towers. Square Tower Group—located in Utah midway between Cortez and Blanding, Utah—is best preserved and most accessible. 785 acres. Open all year. Facilities: interpretive exhibits, hiking, picnic areas. 30 campsites (but not always available, so call ahead). Headquarters at Square Tower Group off Utah 262, about 55 miles from Mesa Verde NP. (970) 562-4282.

Fossilized logs, remnants of ancient conifers in Blue Mesa

Petrified Forest

Arizona

Established December 9, 1962

93,533 acres

A sun-swept corner of the Painted Desert draws over 900,000 visitors each year. While most come to see one of the world's largest concentrations of brilliantly colored petrified wood, many leave having glimpsed something more. The 147 square miles of Petrified Forest open a window on an environment more than 200 million years old, one radically different from today's high desert.

Where you now see ravens soaring over a stark landscape, leathery-winged pterosaurs once glided over rivers teeming with armor-scaled fish and giant, spatula-headed amphibians. Nearby ran herds of some of the earliest dinosaurs. Scientists have identified several hundred species of fossil plants and animals in Petrified Forest.

The park consists of two main sections. Located in the south are the major concentrations of the famous petrified wood; in the north rise the colorful banded badlands of the Painted Desert. Giant fossilized logs, many of them fractured into cordwood-size segments, lie scattered throughout, like headstones bearing a deceased's likeness.

Much of the quartz rock that replaced the wood tissue 200 million years ago is tinted in rainbow hues. Many visitors cannot resist taking rocks, despite strict regulations and stiff fines against removing any material.To see how fast the rock was disappearing, rangers placed a number of invisibly marked pieces next to a well-used trail. Within two weeks 20 percent of them were gone.

When to Go

All-year park. Summer's dramatic clouds and thunderstorms enhance the beauty of the landscape. Fall, with its milder weather, also attracts many visitors. Winter in the high desert can be cold with brief snowstorms, but moderate afternoon temperatures are not uncommon. The desert blooms colorfully in spring; winds can be high.

How to Visit

Many of the features at Petrified Forest are on a scale best appreciated by leaving the car. Plan enough time to walk among the fossil logs and **Painted Desert** badlands. For a ½-day visit, follow the **park road** from the **Rainbow Forest Museum** to **Pintado Point.** If you can stay longer, include a walk to **Agate House,** take the trail into the **Blue Mesa** badlands, and consider a hike in the **Painted Desert Wilderness.**

The Park Road

28 miles; a half to full day

A scenic drive connecting the south and north entrances passes through high desert grasslands broken by unexpected escarpments and bare hills banded in pastels. Begin at the south entrance with a stop at the **Rainbow Forest Museum.** (Or, from the north, begin at the **Painted Desert Visitor Center** and reverse this tour.) Be sure to see the dioramas of ancient environments and the display of pre-Columbian Indian artifacts made from petrified wood.

The museum sits in the **Rainbow Forest,** one of four major concentrations of petrified logs called "forests." Behind it winds the ½-mile **Giant Logs Trail** (closes 15 mins. before park); the largest fossil log is **Old Faithful** with a 9½-foot diameter. Continue on to **Long Logs** (closes ½ hour before park). From the parking lot there, a ⅗-mile loop trail, taking about 20 minutes by foot, leads you to the largest concentration of petrified wood in the park. Here you see logs up to 120 feet long—many crisscrossed in logjams.

The majority of the park's petrified wood comes from tall conifers called *Araucarioxylon.* These ancient trees grew 200 million years ago in

The problem is not new. Military survey parties passing through the region in 1851 filled their saddlebags with the petrified wood. As word of these remarkable deposits spread, fossil logs were hauled off by the wagonload for tabletops, lamps, and mantels. In the 1890s gem collectors began dynamiting logs searching for amethyst and quartz crystals. To prevent further destruction of it's unique bounty, the area was designated a national monument in 1906 and a national park more than a half century later.

How to Get There

If you are traveling west on I-40, exit south into park. When leaving the south end of the park, the road joins US 180. Follow US 180 for 19 miles to Holbrook and back to I-40. If you are traveling east on I-40, take the US 180 exit. The south entrance is 19 miles from Holbrook. After driving through park, leave via I-40. Airports: Flagstaff and Winslow.

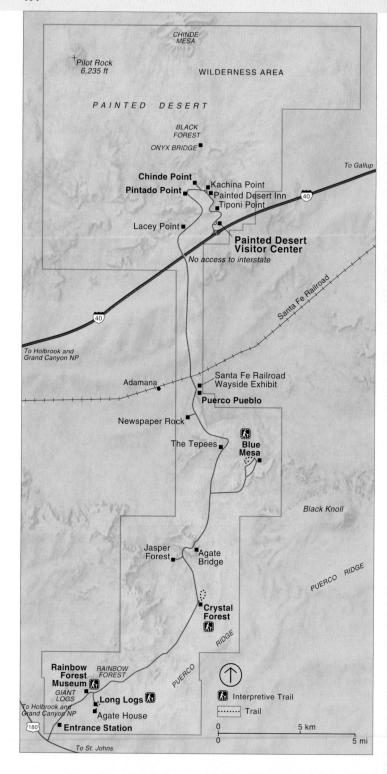

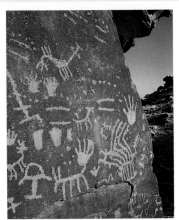
Petroglyphs on Newspaper Rock

distant highlands, where floods or perhaps mudflows uprooted them. Tumbled and abraded, the fallen trees washed into logjams and were quickly buried by silt and ash. Silica-laden water percolated through the wood, replacing organic tissue with multicolored quartz.

Next, if you have time, strike out on the paved, ½-mile trail to **Agate House,** which closes ½ hour before the park. During the 1930s crews restored one of the rooms in this eight-room dwelling built by ancestral Puebloans more than 800 years ago. The prehistoric structure was of wood and adobe; the reconstruction uses concrete to stabilize the walls.

Continue your drive north, bypassing three turnoffs—**Crystal Forest, Jasper Forest,** and **Agate Bridge,** unless you have plenty of time. Take the 3-mile spur road that climbs **Blue Mesa.** You loop through strange badlands layered in blue, purple, and cream colors that change with weather and time of day.

The **Blue Mesa Trail** winds along a 1-mile, 45-minute route through the badlands. The trail is paved and nearly level except for one very steep section. Even if you can't take the full hike, park your car and walk 100 feet to where the trail begins to descend. Here are good views of the intricately eroded mesa.

Return to the main road and drive north through **The Teepees,** bare, conical hills whose reddish hues are produced by iron and other minerals.

The trail to the **Newspaper Rock** petroglyphs has been closed, making them difficult to see from the overlook above. Skip this and continue driving a short distance to the **Puerco Pueblo,** one of the largest prehistoric sites in the park. Here you see the partially excavated remains of an ancestral Puebloan village abandoned around 1380 as well as many fine petroglyphs of animals and geometric designs pecked into the outcropping rock.

Scientists believe a chiseled circle here was used by the Indians as a solar calendar. The week preceding and following the advent of the summer solstice, the sun interacts with this petroglyph. Early in the morning on the day of the summer solstice, rangers guide observers to the place where a shaft of sunlight pierces and fills the very center of the ancient symbol.

The road crosses the intermittent **Puerco River** that divides the park in two. No permanent streams flow in Petrified Forest, and less than nine inches of precipitation fall each year, half in summer thunderstorms.

After crossing I-40, the drive reaches the edge of a volcanic escarpment overlooking a particularly colorful section of the **Painted Desert.**

Pull off at **Lacey Point,** the first of eight overlooks. Here the bare Chinle slopes are tinted in the chalky shades of a Navajo rug. The colors are especially vivid when the sun shines on sediment still wet from a thunderstorm.

Continue on to the sweeping panoramic vista at **Pintado Point**—the highest along the Painted Desert rim. Below lies **Lithodendron Wash,** braiding through the red badlands of the **Black Forest.** In the distance stands the dark profile of **Pilot Rock,** at 6,235 feet the park's highest point.

For a longer hike, walk through the rugged beauty of the **Painted Desert Wilderness.** The trail begins at **Kachina Point** behind the old **Painted Desert Inn,** originally built as a roadside inn, now open daily as a historical site. Once in the flats below the rim, the trail disappears, requiring you to do your own route-finding. Look for the Black Forest, an area of dark fossilized wood, and **Onyx Bridge.** Finding the bridge can be an adventure since there are no landmarks to guide you.

The scenic drive ends at the Painted Desert Visitor Center, which is the park headquarters located at the north entrance.

Information & Activities

Headquarters
P.O. Box 2217, Arizona 86028. Phone (520) 524-6228. www.nps.gov/pefo

Seasons & Accessibility
Open all year, except Christmas; extended hours May through August. Snow or icy roads may close park temporarily in winter.

Visitor & Information Centers
Painted Desert Visitor Center at north entrance, just off I-40, and Rainbow Forest Museum near south entrance, just off US 180. Painted Desert Inn National Historic Landmark, two miles from the north entrance, also has archaeological displays and historic information.

Entrance Fee
$10 per car, good for 7 days.

Pets & Horses
Pets permitted on leashes except in public buildings, wilderness areas, and on Giant Logs Trail. Horses permitted throughout park in groups of six or less when accompanied by riders, but grazing is prohibited. No water available.

Facilities for Disabled
Visitor centers, museum, and rest rooms are wheelchair accessible.

Things to Do
Free ranger-led activities: nature talks, wildlife viewing, and birdwatching. Also available, a film, interpretive exhibits, self-guided auto tours, hiking, horseback riding (no rentals in area).

Special Advisories
● Stay on trails to prevent damage to the fragile desert environment and personal injury from sharp edges of petrified logs.
● Take nothing from the park but memories, not even a tiny piece of petrified wood; pieces quickly add up to tons.
● Carry water when you hike; none is available outside developed areas.
● Do not approach any wildlife; as cute as they are, park animals may carry bubonic plague, Hantavirus, and rabies.

Overnight Backpacking
Allowed in the Painted Desert Wilderness. Permit required; available free at visitor center or museum up to one hour before park closing.

Campgrounds
None inside the park, but food service available.

Hotels, Motels, & Inns
(unless otherwise noted, rates are for 2 persons in a double room, high season) In Holbrook, Arizona 86025:
Best Western Adobe Inn 615 W. Hopi Drive. (520) 524-3948. 54 units. $50-$54. AC, pool.
Best Western Arizonian Inn 2508 E. Navajo Blvd. (800) 528-1234 or (520) 524-2611. 70 units. $79. AC, pool, restaurant.
Holbrook Comfort Inn 2602 E. Navajo Blvd. (800) 228-5150 or (520) 524-6131. 63 units. $54-$64. AC, pool.
Best Inn 2211 E. Navajo Blvd. (800) 551-1923 or (520) 524-2654. 40 units. $45. AC.

Contact the Holbrook Chamber of Commerce for additional accommodations: 100 E. Arizona Street, Holbrook, Arizona 86025. (520) 524-6558.

Excursions

El Morro National Monument

Ramah, New Mexico

Here in 1605 Spaniard Juan de Oñate scratched his name at the base of a sandstone cliff. Others added inscriptions to the carvings of pre-Columbian Indians. Two ancestral Puebloan ruins sit on the cliff-top mesa. 1,279 acres. 9 campsites (open April to mid-Oct.), hiking, picnic areas, handicapped access. Open year-round. Campground open April to mid-Oct. On N. Mex. 53, off I-40, about 125 miles from Petrified Forest NP. (505) 783-4226.

El Malpais National Monument and National Conservation Area

Grants, New Mexico

El Malpais—"the badlands"—is located in the lava beds of western New Mexico. Featuring spatter cones, a 17-mile-long lava-tube system, and ice caves, the site also contains ancestral Puebloan ruins, a freestanding natural arch, and two wilderness areas. 376,000 acres. Primitive camping, hiking, bicycling, horseback riding, scenic drives. Open all year. Information at center at N. Mex. 53 (23 miles south of Grants). About 140 miles east of Petrified Forest NP. (505) 783-4774.

Walnut Canyon National Monument

Flagstaff, Arizona

More than 800 years ago, Indians now known as the Sinagua lived in caves in cliff dwellings here at the edge of Flagstaff. The Sinagua's name (Spanish for "without water") is a tribute to their remarkable ability to survive in a dry region. The cliff dwellings are accessible by trail. 3,541 acres. Facilities include a visitor center and picnic areas. Open daily (except Christmas). Located off I-40, just east of Flagstaff. About 107 miles west of the I-40 exit at Petrified Forest NP. (520) 526-3367.

Mighty saguaro, outlined at dusk

Saguaro

Arizona

Established October 14, 1994

91,443 acres

Symbol of the American Southwest and North America's largest cactus, the saguaro's imposing stature and uplifted arms give it a regal presence. Perhaps that's why this burly giant, whose only bits of exuberance are seasonal blossoms and figlike fruits at the tip of its limbs, has been dubbed the "desert monarch."

Carnegiea gigantea is the trademark of the Sonoran Desert, whose basins and ranges rumple 120,000 square miles of northwestern Mexico, southern Arizona, and southeastern California. Saguaro National Park is composed of two sections. The westerly Tucson Mountain District embraces about 24,000 acres of the hotter, drier, less-vegetated "low"

Sonoran ecosystem, which occurs below 3,000 feet. Thirty miles east, on the other side of Tucson's urban sprawl, is the 67,000-acre Rincon Mountain District, which occupies loftier ground and has a cooler, slightly wetter "high desert" environment. Most of it is inaccessible save by foot or on horseback. Here the terrain inclines from saguaro forests into nearly pristine woodlands of oak and pine. Hikers pressing on to higher elevations find Douglas-fir, ponderosa pine, and solitude.

The Sonoran Desert's extreme temperatures, perennial drought, frequent lightning, banshee winds, and voracious predators keep the saguaro forever at the limit of its endurance. Odds against survival rival a lottery: Though the cactus annually produces tens of thousands of pinhead-size seeds—some 40 million

How to Visit

On a 1-day visit, begin early and view the **Arizona-Sonora Desert Museum** before heading to **Saguaro West;** then pause at the **Red Hills Visitor Center** for an overview. Take the **Bajada Scenic Loop Drive,** stopping en route to walk the **Desert Discovery Nature Trail.** Return to Tucson, continuing east to Saguaro's **Rincon Mountain District.** Take the **Cactus Forest Drive** and walk the **Desert Ecology Trail.** For a scenic rest stop along the drive, visit **Mica View Picnic Area.**

Saguaro West: Tucson Mountain District

About 25 miles; a half day

The drive west through **Tucson Mountain County Park** takes you past the excellent, zoolike **Arizona-Sonora Desert Museum,** whose 12 acres include every Sonoran Desert life zone and most of its animals and plants. It's worth a stop.

Continue on Kinney Road to the **Red Hills Visitor Center,** where an orientation slide show and desert life exhibits will enhance your understanding of what you'll encounter here and in Saguaro East. Walk the center's **Cactus Garden Trail,** a paved path through an unruly crowd of cactuses: hedgehog, barrel, fishhook, chainfruit cholla, and prickly pear.

Saguaros thrive in the coarse, absorbent soil of *bajadas,* long desert mountain slopes of eroded rock, gravel, sand, and clay, where a mature plant's shallow, wide-ranging roots can absorb up to 200 gallons from one rainstorm, enough to last a year. The 9-mile **Bajada Loop Drive** beginning at the visitor center explores one of these life zones. En route, about 1 mile west, look left for the **Desert Discovery Nature Trail,** a half-mile-long path across a bajada at the base of the Tucson Mountains.

Hook right onto **Hohokam Road.** (Part of the loop is one-way; enter here to drive it all in one direction.) About 1½ miles from the turn-off, **Valley View Overlook Trail** winds up a mile to panoramas of rugged, cactus-studded landscapes. Unpaved **Golden Gate Road** turns off about a mile farther on and passes a pleasant picnic area near the head of **Sendero Esperanza Trail,** a moderately strenuous,

over a life that may last two centuries—few ever even sprout. Even fewer seedlings achieve the grandeur of towering 50 feet and weighing up to 16,000 pounds.

How to Get There

Saguaro West: From Tucson take Speedway Boulevard west to Gates Pass Road, turning right on Kinney Road. (Buses, RVs, and towed vehicles are not recommended on Gates Pass; instead take Ariz. 86 west from Tucson to Kinney.) **Saguaro East:** Take Broadway Boulevard east from central Tucson to Old Spanish Trail.

When to Go

All-year park. From October through April, temperatures reach the upper 60s–mid-70s and can drop below freezing overnight. From May through September, highs routinely exceed 100°F. July through September is characterized by brief but fierce thunderstorms. Saguaros bloom nightly from late April into June.

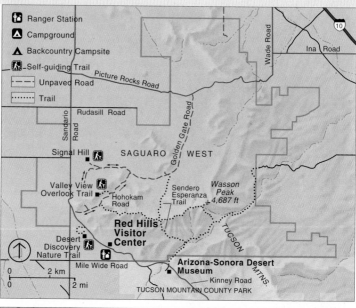

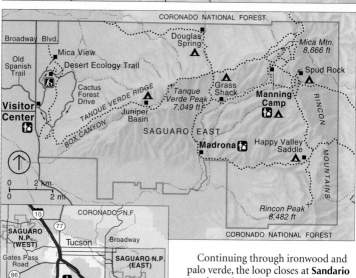

Continuing through ironwood and palo verde, the loop closes at **Sandario Road,** an alternative route back to Tucson via Picture Rocks, Wade, and Ina Roads to I-10.

popular half-day hike into the mountainous backcountry.

Backtrack on Golden Gate Road past Hohokam Road to **Signal Hill Picnic Area,** where rocks are etched with centuries-old Hohokam petroglyphs. Archaeologists believe the symbols, chipped through a brown patina of iron-manganese oxide called "desert varnish," signify territorial claims, clan migrations, personal accounts, visions, and pure artistic whimsy.

Saguaro East: Rincon Mountain District

About 25 miles; a half day

Higher elevations here create Sonoran Desert environments markedly different from Saguaro West's lowland desert zone. A steady, east-trending incline slants up into the roadless Rincon Mountain wilderness area, which is dotted with forests of oak, pine, and fir accessible only by foot or on horseback.

Make your first stop the **Saguaro East Visitor Center** at park headquarters. If you plan to hike into backcountry, this is the place to acquire trail guides, maps, and permits. If time is limited, pick up a guide to the **Cactus Forest Drive** and take the 8-mile loop, where many of the saguaros are over 150 years old.

About 2 miles along the route, look left for a gravel road leading to scenic overlooks at **Mica View Picnic Area,** a pleasant place to stop. About a mile farther, the ¼-mile paved **Desert Ecology Trail** is designed to illustrate the crucial role of water in desert

Elf owl amid cactus blossoms

ecosystems. What you are more likely to remember from this 20-minute amble, however, is the desert's perfect stillness.

Information & Activities

Headquarters
3693 S. Old Spanish Trail, Tucson, AZ 85730. For information call (520) 733-5158 (Saguaro West) or (520) 733-5153 (Saguaro East). www.nps.gov/sagu

Seasons & Accessibility
Park open year-round. Visitor centers, nature trails, and roadside picnic areas are wheelchair accessible.

Visitor & Information Centers
Saguaro West Red Hills Visitor Center off Kinney Road. Saguaro East Visitor Center (park headquarters) on Old Spanish Trail. Daily except Christmas.

Entrance Fee
Saguaro West: None. Saguaro East: $6 per vehicle.

Pets
Not permitted on trails, in backcountry, or in public buildings; elsewhere allowed on leashes.

Things to Do
Ranger-led hikes and night walks, scenic drives, trail walks, bird- and wildlife watching, picnicking, bicycling, backcountry hiking. Horsebacking riding is permitted on some trails; ask park for details.

Special Advisories
● Avoid open and low-lying areas during thunderstorms, when lightning and flash floods pose a danger.

● Stay on trails. Abandoned mine shafts in Saguaro West make off-trail hiking and riding hazardous.
● Carry a flashlight at night to avoid encounters with rattlesnakes, scorpions, and Gila monsters.
● There is no water at picnic areas or along most trails. If hiking, carry at least one gallon of water per day.

Overnight Backpacking
Allowed only at designated backcountry sites. Use permits must be obtained at visitor centers in advance of trip.

Campgrounds
Four backcountry campsites in Saguaro East, accessible by trail. Campground in Tucson Mountain County Park, next to Saguaro West.

Hotels, Motels, & Inns
(unless otherwise noted, rates for 2 persons, double room, high season) In Tucson, Arizona:
Arizona Inn 2200 E. Elm St., 85711. (800) 933-1093 or (520) 325-1541. 86 units. $180-$215. AC, pool, rest. **Tucson East Hilton** 7600 E. Broadway, 85710. (800) 445-8667 or (520) 721-5600. 233 units. $145-$200. AC, pool, rest. **Best Western** 1015 N. Stone Ave., 85705. (800) 528-1234 or (520) 622-8871. 79 units. $89-$139. AC, pool, rest.

For more lodgings, contact Tucson Chamber of Commerce. (520) 792-1212.

Sunset gilding Mt. Kinesava and The West Temple

Zion

Utah

Established November 19, 1919

147,551 acres

Rising in Utah's high plateau country, the Virgin River carves its way to the desert below through a gorge so deep and narrow that sunlight rarely penetrates to the bottom. As the canyon widens, the river runs a gauntlet of great palisade walls rimmed with slick-rock peaks and hanging valleys.

The scale is immense—sheer cliffs dropping 3,000 feet, massive buttresses, deep alcoves. Nineteenth-century Mormon pioneers saw these sculptured rocks as the "natural temples of God." They called the canyon Little Zion after the celestial city.

A million years of flowing water has cut through the red and white beds of Navajo sandstone that form the sheer walls of Zion. The geologic heart of the canyon began as a vast desert millions of years ago; almost incessant winds blew one dune on top of another until the sands reached a depth of 2,000 feet. You can still see the track of these ancient winds in the graceful crossbedded strata of Zion's mighty cliffs.

Unlike the Grand Canyon where you stand on the rim and look out, Zion Canyon is usually viewed from the bottom looking up. The vertical topography confines most of Zion's 2.5 million yearly visitors between canyon walls.

Streamside on the canyon floor grow thick stands of Fremont cottonwood, boxelder, willow, and, a short distance away, cactus and Utah Juniper. Vegetation changes rapidly as the terrain rises almost a mile in elevation. The high plateaus support Douglas-fir and ponderosa pine.

hiking. Summer rains can bring spectacular clouds and numerous waterfalls. Rock colors are heightened by contrast with winter snows, green summer foliage, deep blue fall skies.

How to Visit

On a 1-day visit, take the **Zion-Mt. Carmel Highway** and the **Zion Canyon Scenic Drive** for the best overview of the park. For longer stays, begin with one of the classic walks in **Zion Canyon,** then take a road tour of the **Kolob Canyons** in late afternoon.

Zion-Mt. Carmel Highway & Zion Canyon Scenic Drive

18 miles; a half to full day

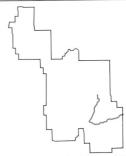

Within the park's 229 square miles lies a landscape of remote terraces and narrow gorges. A number of these canyons are so well hidden that early surveyors overlooked some that are 20 miles long. More than 100 miles of wilderness trails crisscross the backcountry, while 23 miles of paved trails encourage casual visits.

How to Get There

From Cedar City to the Kolob Canyons Entrance, take I-15 about 18 miles south. To Zion Canyon, take I-15 to Utah 17 then Utah 9 to the South Entrance (about 60 miles). From Kanab, take US 89 to Utah 9 (at Mt. Carmel junction) to the East Entrance. From Las Vegas and St. George, take I-15 and Utah 9 to the South Entrance. Airports: Cedar City and St. George.

When to Go

Open all year, but main season is March through October. Mild spring and fall temperatures are ideal for

Zion-Mt. Carmel Highway (Utah 9) descends almost 2,000 feet from the high mesa country at the **East Entrance** to the **South Entrance** desert. Begin the drive on the east to see the park in the most dramatic possible way—from a

Pinyon pine near Checkerboard Mesa

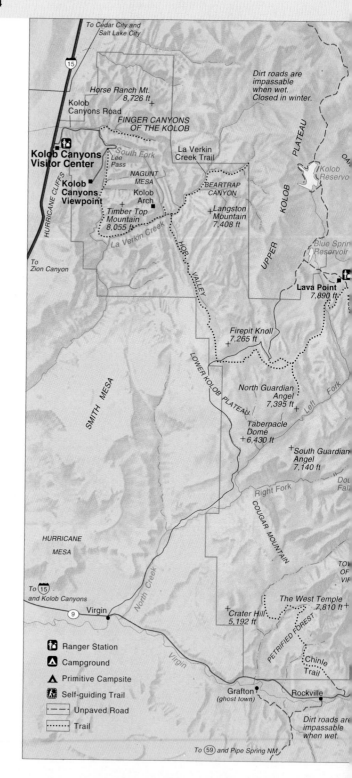

To Cedar City and
Salt Lake City

15

Horse Ranch Mt.
8,726 ft

Kolob
Canyons Road

Dirt roads are
impassable
when wet.
Closed in winter.

*FINGER CANYONS
OF THE KOLOB*

La Verkin
Creek Trail

**Kolob Canyons
Visitor Center**

*South Fork
Lee
Pass*

*NAGUNT
MESA*

*BEARTRAP
CANYON*

Kolob
Reservo

**Kolob
Canyons
Viewpoint**

Kolob
Arch

Langston
Mountain
7,408 ft

*Blue Sprin
Reservoir*

Timber Top
Mountain
8,055 ft

UPPER KOLOB PLATEAU

HURRICANE CLIFFS

La Verkin Creek

Lava Point
7,890 ft

To
Zion Canyon

HOB VALLEY

Firepit Knoll
7,265 ft

LOWER KOLOB PLATEAU

North Guardian
Angel
7,395 ft

Left Fork

SMITH MESA

Tabernacle
Dome
6,430 ft

South Guardian
Angel
7,140 ft

Right Fork

*Dou
Fal*

COUGAR MOUNTAIN

*HURRICANE
MESA*

*TO
OF
VIR*

To 15
and Kolob Canyons

9 Virgin

North Creek

The West Temple
7,810 ft

Crater Hill
5,192 ft

PETRIFIED FOREST

Chinle
Trail

Ranger Station

Campground

Primitive Campsite

Self-guiding Trail

– – – **Unpaved Road**

······· **Trail**

Virgin

Grafton
(ghost town)

Rockville

Dirt roads are
impassable
when wet.

To 59 and Pipe Spring NM

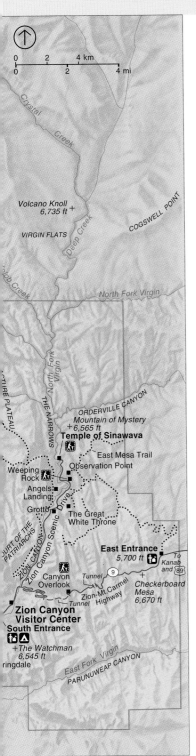

Volcano Knoll
6,735 ft

VIRGIN FLATS

COGSWELL POINT

North Fork Virgin

ORDERVILLE CANYON
Mountain of Mystery
6,565 ft
Temple of Sinawava

East Mesa Trail

Weeping
Rock

Observation Point

Angels
Landing

Grotto

The Great
White Throne

East Entrance
5,700 ft

To
Kanab
and 89

Zion
Canyon
Overlook

Tunnel 9

Zion-Mt.Carmel

Checkerboard
Mesa
6,670 ft

Tunnel   Highway

**Zion Canyon
Visitor Center**
South Entrance

The Watchman
6,545 ft

ringdale

East Fork Virgin

PARUNUWEAP CANYON

tunnel on the wall of the canyon, 800 feet above the floor.

Shortly after passing through the East Entrance, stop at the **Checkerboard Mesa** pull-off. Here is a classic view of weathered sandstone beds crosshatched with vertical joints. Continue driving as the road winds along the normally dry creek bed. For the full impact of the approaching canyon, turn off at the **Canyon Overlook** parking area. If you are ready for a stop, this is a good place to stretch your legs along a 1-mile round-trip trail. You walk above the winding narrows of **Pine Creek** to an impressive view of **The West Temple** and the **Towers of the Virgin.**

The road disappears into the canyon wall at the narrow **Zion-Mt. Carmel Tunnel,** breaking into the blue sky again $1\frac{1}{10}$ miles farther. The tunnel was completed in 1930 at a cost of a half million dollars and the lives of two men. The road switchbacks down the side of **Pine Creek Canyon,** passing close to **The Great Arch,** which is 400 feet high. Geologists call it a blind arch because it is recessed into the cliff.

You next enter **Zion Canyon,** where Pine Creek meets the **North Fork Virgin River.** The canyon has an average width of $\frac{1}{2}$ mile, with walls 2,000 to 3,000 feet high. At Zion Canyon Visitor Center, catch a free shuttle for the $6\frac{3}{5}$-mile **Zion Canyon Scenic Drive** that follows the winding Virgin River. Get out at the **Court of the Patriarchs.** A short trail leads up the slope to a view of the **Three Patriarchs,** sheer

Isaac, one of the Three Patriarchs, in winter

Waterfall at Emerald Pools

Canyon treefrog

Indian paintbrush

faces carved by wind and water from Navajo sandstone.

Back on the shuttle, the road continues past the **Emerald Pools** area. This is the trailhead for a popular stroll on a paved walkway to natural rock basins fed by small streams. The lowest pool on the climbing path is a tiny oasis tucked into the side of the cliff and sheltered by bigtooth maple trees.

After a sojourn at the pools, the shuttle continues past **Zion Lodge** to the Grotto picnic area, a good place to take a break. Here is the trailhead for **Angels Landing** and **West Rim Trail.**

A short distance farther, the shuttle reaches **Weeping Rock.** Here, the trailhead of a self-guided nature walk (½-mile round-trip) leads behind a curtain of water showering from the ceiling of an alcove. Water percolates through the sandstone until it hits shale and then seeps through to the surface of Weeping Rock—1,000–4,000 years after falling as rain on the high plateau above. The strenuous **East Rim Trail** and a branch trail that climbs to **Hidden Canyon** start here.

Just past Weeping Rock, a stop offers superb views of **The Great White Throne** rising some 2,500 feet above the river. The scenic drive ends where the canyon narrows at the **Temple of Sinawava,** named for the coyote-spirit of the Paiute Indians.

Here and elsewhere in the park, keep watch for the tiny creatures of Sinawava's realm—canyon tree-frogs, pocket gophers, eastern fence lizards. There are also more than 270 species of birds, including roadrunners, Gambel's quail, and the water-skimming American dipper.

Kolob Canyons Road

5½ miles; 1 hour to a half day or more

One of the most spectacular and most accessible regions of the park is also one of the least visited. The **Hurricane Cliffs,** forming the western boundary of the park, screen the great towers of the Kolob from I-15. Follow the **Kolob Canyons Road** past the **Kolob Canyons Visitor Center** as it winds into **Taylor Creek Canyon.** Here you get a hint of what's to come when the jagged face of **Tucupit Point** appears.

The Great White Throne from the Temple of Sinawava

The Narrows

Continue up the road, skirting the beautiful **South Fork** of **Taylor Creek.** Each vista becomes more striking as you cross **Lee Pass,** the trailhead for routes into the hidden canyons of **La Verkin Creek.** If time and stamina allow, you can backpack (usually done as an overnight) the 14-mile round-trip to **Kolob Arch,** one of the world's largest freestanding natural arches, 310 feet long.

Drive to the parking area at the end of the road for a dramatic view of the **Finger Canyons.** Sheer cliffs of pale red sandstone lift more than 2,000 feet into the blue sky. Narrow canyons work deep into the sides of **Timber Top Mountain,** connecting **Shuntavi Butte** with **Nagunt Mesa.**

Other Hikes

The full impact of Zion's great carved landscape is best experienced from a high vantage point above the river. The park's extensive trail system gives you a wide range of choices, from walks of ½ hour to backpacking trips lasting for days.

The park's most popular trail is the **Riverside Walk,** an easy, 2-mile round-trip amble. This paved path can be

Virgin River Valley from Observation Point

Mountain lion in western Zion

negotiated by strollers and assisted wheelchairs. Beginning where the Zion Canyon Scenic Drive ends at the Temple of Sinawava, the trail leads past hanging gardens of maidenhair fern and golden columbine and stands of shady cottonwood and ash. It ends where the North Fork rushes from a defile so narrow the only way to look is up.

Flash floods here are a real danger; deeper in **The Narrows** the walls are 2,000 feet high but in places only 18 feet apart. In the 1960s, a sudden flood caught 26 hikers, drowning 5.

Perched midway between the river and the rim of the canyon, the high and open spire of rock called **Angels**

Landing provides one of Zion's best overall views. The strenuous trail climbs 2½ miles, at times cutting into a knife-edge ridge that joins the landing to the western wall. Sheer 1,500-foot drops surround the promontory on three sides and allow excellent cross-canyon views of The Great White Throne and down the deep cut of Zion Canyon. *Not recommended for those with a fear of heights.*

Observation Point Trail, 8 miles round-trip, is not recommended for acrophobes either. One of the best routes to reach the very top of the canyon, the strenuous trail passes through a beautiful narrows and winds into the slickrock country. As it swings back to the main canyon, the trail cuts into the very edge of the cliff and opens to dramatic views. After a thunderstorm, clouds steaming up from the white sandstone of the western wall look as if the rock itself is evaporating.

Once on top, the route crosses a sandy mesa through stands of pinyon pine and juniper to **Observation Point,** with fine views of the main canyon. Stand here and listen to what Frederick Dellenbaugh called "the whisper of the wind that comes and goes, breathing with the sound of centuries."

Information & Activities

Headquarters
Springdale, Utah 84767. Phone (435) 772-3256. www.nps.gov/zion

Seasons & Accessibility
Park open year-round. Kolob Canyons Road and main roads in Zion Canyon are plowed in winter. Dirt roads are impassable when wet. Lava Point inaccessible in winter and early spring due to snow. Call headquarters for weather conditions.

Shuttle service on Zion Canyon Scenic Drive. Pick up free shuttle at Springdale or the Zion Canyon Visitor Center.

Visitor & Information Centers
Zion Canyon Visitor Center, near the South Entrance on Utah 9, and Kolob Canyons Visitor Center, in the northwest corner of the park off I-15, are both open daily all year.

Entrance Fee
$20 per car per week, multiple entries. Also, $10 charge for escorting oversize vehicles through the mile-long tunnel on East Entrance road.

Pets
Not permitted in backcountry, on shuttles, in public buildings, or on trails; elsewhere allowed on leashes.

Facilities for Disabled
Visitor centers and shuttles are wheelchair accessible, as are some rest rooms and trails. Handicapped sites available in campgrounds.

Things to Do
Free ranger-led activities: nature walks and talks, evening programs, children's programs. Also, hiking, horseback trail rides—inquire at Zion Lodge or call—(435) 772-3810—climbing, bicycling (bicyclists must transport their bikes through the long tunnel—check at entrance or visitor center), limited cross-country skiing.

Special Advisories
● Summer temperatures in park can exceed 105°F. Always carry bottled or treated water when hiking—at least a gallon a day per person in summer.

Overnight Backpacking
Permits required, $5; available at visitor centers.

Campgrounds
Three campgrounds, 14-day limit. **Watchman** open all year; **South** open May through Sept.; **Lava Point** open May through Oct., depending on weather. Reservations for **Watchman** through National Park Reservation Service (see p. 11). Others, first come, first served. Fees $14 per night. Showers nearby but outside park. Tent and RV sites; no hookups.

Hotels, Motels, & Inns
(unless otherwise noted, rates are for 2 persons in a double room, high season)
INSIDE THE PARK:
Zion Lodge (off Utah 9)AmFac Parks & Resorts, Cedar City, Utah 84720. (303) 297-2757. 75 rooms, with AC; 40 cabins. $74-$109. Restaurant.
OUTSIDE THE PARK:
In Springdale, Utah 84767:
Best Western Driftwood Lodge (1515 Zion Park Blvd.) P.O. Box 98, Utah Hwy. 9. (800) 528-1234 or (435) 772-3262. 47 units. $72-$102. AC, pool, hot tub. **Bumbleberry Inn** (97 Bumbleberry Lane) P.O. Box 346. (800) 828-1534 or (435) 772-3224. 47 units. $67-$77. AC, pool, rest. **Canyon Ranch Motel** (668 Zion Park Blvd.) P.O. Box 175. (435) 772-3357. 22 units, 4 with kitchenettes. $68-$88. AC, pool. **Cliffrose Lodge & Gardens** (281 Zion Park Blvd.) P.O. Box 510. (800) 243-8824 or (435) 772-3234. 36 units. $119. AC, pool. **Flanigan's Inn** (428 Zion Park Blvd.) Zion Canyon, P.O. Box 100. (800) 765-7787 or (435) 772-3244. 36 units. $79. AC, pool, rest. **O'Toole's Under the Eaves Guest House** 980 Zion Park Blvd. (435) 772-3457. 6 rooms, 4 private baths. $69-$125. AC. In Kanab, Utah 84741:
Parry Lodge 89 E. Center St. (800) 748-4104 or (435) 644-2601. 89 units. $67. AC, pool, rest. **Shilo Inn** 296 West 100 North. (800) 222-2244 or (435) 644-2562. 118 units. $115. AC, pool.

For additional accommodations near Zion NP, call Kane County Travel at (435) 644-5033.

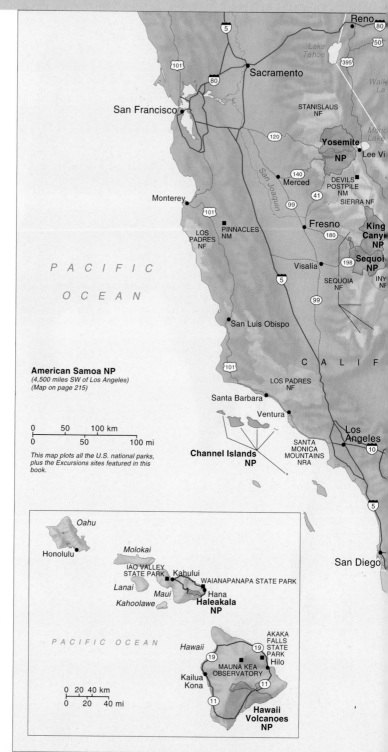

American Samoa NP
(4,500 miles SW of Los Angeles)
(Map on page 215)

0   50   100 km
0   50   100 mi

This map plots all the U.S. national parks, plus the Excursions sites featured in this book.

PACIFIC

OCEAN

Reno

Lake Tahoe

Sacramento

San Francisco

STANISLAUS NF

Yosemite NP

Lee Vi

Merced

DEVILS POSTPILE NM

SIERRA NF

Monterey

San Joaquin

Fresno

King Cany NP

PINNACLES NM

LOS PADRES NF

Visalia

Sequoi NP

SEQUOIA NF

INY NF

San Luis Obispo

C A L I F

LOS PADRES NF

Santa Barbara

Ventura

Los Angeles

SANTA MONICA MOUNTAINS NRA

Channel Islands NP

San Diego

Oahu

Honolulu

Molokai

IAO VALLEY STATE PARK

Kahului

WAIANAPANAPA STATE PARK

Lanai

Maui

Hana

Kahoolawe

Haleakala NP

PACIFIC OCEAN

Hawaii

AKAKA FALLS STATE PARK

Hilo

MAUNA KEA OBSERVATORY

Kailua Kona

Hawaii Volcanoes NP

0 20 40 km
0 20 40 mi

Preceding pages: El Capitan, Yosemite

The Pacific Southwest

Visitors to the national parks of the Pacific Southwest can bask on a tropical isle or climb a snow-clad peak. They can watch the vegetation change from tropical to subalpine in a single Hawaii drive, observe plants and animals that make their home in only one place in the world, and see the earth build itself.

The island parks, all of them on volcanoes except Channel Islands, are microcosms of evolution and laboratories of the effects of humans on the land. In Hawaii Volcanoes and Haleakala, preservation efforts seek to stem the damage done over centuries to the native plants, about 90 percent of which are endemic—found nowhere else. Some 2,300 miles south of Hawaii, American Samoa National Park shelters fragments of tropical rain forest and coral reef as well as an endangered 3,000-year-old human culture. Off the coast of California, the Channel Islands safeguard numerous threatened seals, sea lions, and seabirds. They also harbor some 70 endemic plants.

On the mainland, Sequoia & Kings Canyon and Yosemite National Parks provide haven for a multitude of plant and animal communities in what John Muir called "the range of light"—the Sierra Nevada. Chaparral and wild oats robe the foothills; cathedral-like groves of conifers embellish slopes; wildflowers overrun alpine meadows. Marmots and pikas scurry the glacier-carved heights, some of which soar 12,000 feet.

To the south, Joshua Tree National Park preserves the unique high Mojave Desert habitat of the giant branching yucca, while the 120-mile-long, erosion-sculptured basin that is Death Valley National Park—the continent's hottest spot—shelters more than 900 plant varieties, as well as bobcats and desert bighorn sheep.

Yosemite and Sequoia & Kings Canyon lie about 4 hours apart by car. From Sequoia, 6 road hours will get you to Death Valley, with 3½ more to Joshua Tree. A drive from there to the Channel Islands takes 3 hours, plus a 90-minute boat ride. To reach Hawaii from California, count on at least a 5½-hour flight, and to American Samoa, expect an 11-hour plane trip, see p. 215, plus a Honolulu layover.

Fisherman casting his net off Tutuila's rocky coast

American Samoa

American Samoa

Authorized October 31, 1988

About 10,000 acres

For some 3,000 years, the people of Polynesia's oldest culture have been keenly attuned to their island environment, holding it to be precious and managing it communally. The name they gave their land reflects their attitude: Samoa means "sacred earth."

Located about 2,300 miles southwest of Hawaii, American Samoa, a US territory, comprises five volcanic islands and two coral atolls. In 1988 Samoan tribal chiefs agreed to lease a portion of their lands for a national park. In 1993 a 50-year lease was signed that enables the National Park Service to manage an area of rain forest, beach, and coral reef on three islands. Samoans help manage the park, and their villages offer a few guest facilities.

The park protects hundreds of plant species in five distinct rain forest communities: lowland, montane, coast, ridge, and cloud. It is the only such rain forest on American soil, similar to forests in Africa and Asia. Among the fauna visitors can see are myriad tropical birds and the endangered flying fox—a fruit bat with the wingspan of an eagle.

On Tutuila, American Samoa's largest island, lofty volcanic ridges overlook the deep blue waters of Pago Pago Harbor. Except for a few settlements, and the scenic drive that skirts the harbor and the dramatic southern coastline, there is little level land. Atop this crumbled terrain and plunging steeply toward the sea on the island's northern side lies the park area—about 2,500 acres of land and some 1,200 acres of ocean. Parkland on Ta'u, the easternmost island,

ern coast. Small and remote, **Ofu Island** includes what many call American Samoa's loveliest beach. Its main attraction, though, is the 350-acre coral reef, one of the best examples of healthy coral reef in the Pacific.

How to Get There

There are flights to Pago Pago from Honolulu twice a week that take 5½ hours. Time from California is about 14 hours, including a 3- or 4-hour Honolulu layover. From the airport, taxi or rent a car to the Rainmaker Hotel, Pago Airport Inn, or Tessarea Vaitogi Inn. You can reach the park by bus or car, or by walking about 25 minutes. Accommodations are also available on Ta'u, Ofu, and Olosega. To get to Ta'u and Ofu requires about a ½-hour flight each from Pago Pago. Ofu's park begins at the edge of the airport; parkland on Ta'u is about a ½-hour walk from the airport, or hitch a ride.

When to Go

Any time. The islands are 14° south of the Equator, giving them a hot and rainy climate year-round. The heat abates slightly from June through September.

How to Visit

Contact the park headquarters before you visit. For information, write National Park of American Samoa, Pago Pago, American Samoa 96799. Phone (011) (684) 633-7082. www.nps.gov/npsa

encompasses about 5,400 acres—including Lata Mountain, American Samoa's highest peak—and 1,000 acres offshore. Unforgettable is the panoramic view from the cloud forest toward the rugged cliffs of the south-

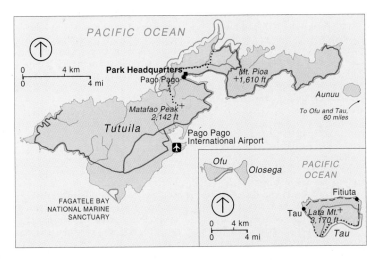

Sunrise over Anacapa Island

Channel Islands

California

Established March 5, 1980

249,354 acres

Strung along a stretch of California coast are five separate pieces of land surrounded by 1,252 square nautical miles of sea. Channel Islands National Park and Channel Islands National Marine Sanctuary protect these islands, the sea around them, and a dazzling array of wildlife.

Two of the islands in this unusual park, Anacapa and Santa Barbara, were earlier designated a national monument, a refuge for nesting seabirds, seals, sea lions, and other long-threatened marine animals. When those islands and three others were joined in a national park, the mission of refuge continued.

Today the park manages a long-term ecological research program that may

be the best in the park system. The marine sanctuary, also established in 1980, extends for 6 nautical miles around each island. Among the resources it protects is a giant kelp forest with nearly a thousand kinds of fish and marine plants. The park and sanctuary also guard the area from encroachment by another kind of island—the seagoing oil rigs of the Santa Barbara Channel.

About 70 different species of plants grow only on the Channel Islands, and some plants exist on but one of them. The islands shelter the only breeding colony of northern fur seals south of Alaska. To help native animals, park managers have gotten rid of such non-native species as burros, rabbits, and house cats gone feral. Efforts to eradicate black rats—descendants of ancestors that jumped ship—have been less successful.

A permanent ranger resides on each island. Reservations are needed for camping. Fishing and diving are strictly regulated and airplanes are asked to keep their distance.

Chumash Indians lived on the Channel Islands until the early 19th century. They traveled from island to island in plank canoes caulked with tar from oil seeps. The tar from such seeps still appears on mainland beaches, reminding strollers of the reason for the oil rigs on the horizon.

How to Get There

Take US 101 to Ventura. North-bound, exit at Victoria Avenue; south-bound, at Seaward Avenue. Follow park signs to the harbor and then to the visitor center on Spinnaker Drive. Get oriented here and then go to the nearby Island Packers office and inquire about boat and plane schedules to the islands. Airports: Camarillo, Oxnard, Santa Barbara, and Los Angeles International.

When to Go

All-year park. Boat schedules peak in spring and summer, but you should be able to book a trip in any month. Best whale-watching time: late December-March and June-Sept.

How to Visit

Your exploration of this unique park depends on your time and resources. Even a short stop at the mainland visitor center will give you an understanding and appreciation of the park. Displays include a tide pool alive with creatures. For a 1-day visit, see the closest island, **Anacapa.** Take all necessities, especially food and water, and dress warmly. Trips to the other islands require substantial advance planning. (See **Information & Activities** p. 220.) The park cautions people from doing more than treading lightly on the islands, which are maintained for the well-being of the residents, both flora and fauna.

Anacapa Island

14 miles from Ventura; a full day

As the Island Packers boat plies through **Santa Barbara Channel,** flyingfish skip through the waves and pelicans skim over them. Oil rigs stand on dark stilts. Gray whales may glide by during winter trips. Seals appear and disappear in the channel waters year-round.

Approaching the landing cove, the boat passes Anacapa's **Arch Rock** and sails close enough to the rocky coast for you to see resident California sea lions. At the end of the 90-minute voyage (which can be rough), a dinghy transports you to the landing platform. Then you climb 154 steps up a metal-and-concrete stairway to the top of the cliff-girt island.

There you can walk the 1½-mile nature trail on your own or fall in behind a ranger who dispenses island lore: That plain gray plant (giant coreopsis) is a tree sunflower; in late winter and spring it bursts into glorious gold. Those finely ground shells you are walking on are remnants of a Chumash midden. The Indians hunted on the island and used it as a stopover on trips to the mainland. The trail skirts the edge of a cliff 150 feet above the sea. Stand well back from the unstable cliff edges.

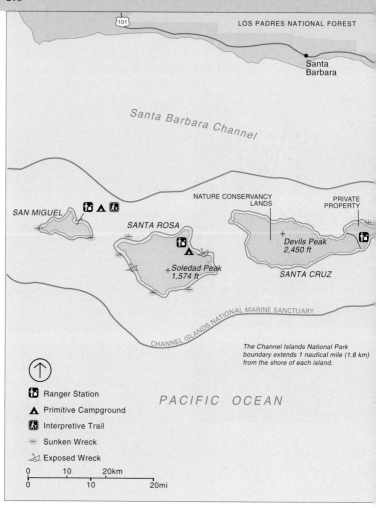

LOS PADRES NATIONAL FOREST

Santa Barbara

Santa Barbara Channel

NATURE CONSERVANCY LANDS

PRIVATE PROPERTY

SAN MIGUEL

SANTA ROSA

Devils Peak 2,450 ft

+Soledad Peak 1,574 ft

SANTA CRUZ

CHANNEL ISLANDS NATIONAL MARINE SANCTUARY

The Channel Islands National Park boundary extends 1 nautical mile (1.8 km) from the shore of each island.

PACIFIC OCEAN

Ranger Station

Primitive Campground

Interpretive Trail

Sunken Wreck

Exposed Wreck

0	10	20km
0	10	20mi

You are ominously warned: *Don't risk your life for a view.*

A building that looks like a Spanish mission church is not what it seems. The structure protects two large water tanks. Vandals who in years past took potshots at the wooden tanks refrain from sniping at a "church." The few buildings date from days when the island lighthouse, now automated, had a crew. Your day ends with a descent to the boat, which picks up the passengers about 3 or 4 hours after arrival; the time depends on tide and sea conditions.

Anacapa consists of three islets. You visit only **East Anacapa.** Scuba divers, subject to strict conservation laws, plunge off **Middle Anacapa** to see the kelp forests or the remains of

the S.S. *Winfield Scott*, which sank here in 1853 with no loss of life. Divers can take only photographs. **West Anacapa** is closed to the public to protect the largest nesting brown pelican population on the Pacific coast of the United States.

The Other Islands

If you decide to go to the other islands, your visits will be controlled by weather, regulations, and boat and plane schedules.

Santa Cruz (21 miles from Ventura; 60,000 acres) is the largest of the Channel Islands. The Nature Conservancy runs the western portion of the island and strictly limits visitors. The

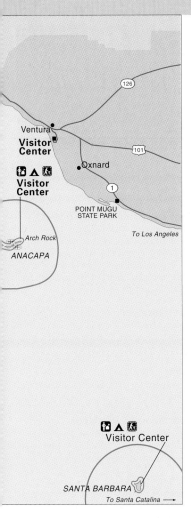

park owns the east end, the point where Island Packers stops. Among Santa Cruz's distinctive species are the island oak, the cat-size island fox, and the scrub jay.

Santa Rosa (45 miles from Ventura; 53,000 acres) has more than 160 archaeological sites; people may have lived there as long as 10,000 years ago. Ranchers raised cattle on the island's grasslands from the middle of the 19th century until 1998. A freshwater marsh sustains waterfowl. There are more than 195 bird species on the island.

San Miguel (63 miles from Ventura; 9,325 acres), the westernmost island, is also rich in archaeological sites. Six seal species gather here; as many as 35,000 haul out at times. A bizarre caliche "forest" spikes a plateau. Caliche—a kind of limey sand—encrusted vegetation that died and decayed, leaving only the hollow, calcified sand castings.

Once used as a bombing range and missile test site, the island is owned by the United States Navy and administered by the National Park Service, which limits visitors to the beach unless they are accompanied by one of the park's rangers.

Santa Barbara (52 miles from Ventura; 640 acres), once a sheep pasturage, has 5½ miles of nature trails. In springtime, burrows on the island's steep hillsides house the world's largest known breeding population of the remarkable Xantus' murrelet. When a chick is only two days old, it makes a bold foray into

Caliche "forest" on San Miguel Island

night, tumbling down to the sea where it joins its waiting parents. Except for the nesting season, the murrelet will spend the remainder of its life on the ocean. In spring and summer, you can usually see pelicans and sea lions, but don't expect to come across the rock-dwelling island night lizard. It is shy, secretive, and protected; visitors are strictly forbidden to turn over any rock.

Protected elephant seal

Information & Activities

Headquarters
1901 Spinnaker Drive, Ventura, Calif. 93001. Phone (805) 658-5730. www.nps.gov/chis

Accessibility & Boat Information
Park open year-round. Access to islands is subject to weather conditions, which are unpredictable; the channel can be rough. Call headquarters for information.
Anacapa, Santa Rosa, San Miguel, and Santa Barbara: Boat trips offered by Island Packers and Truth Aquatics, the park's authorized concessioners (see below). Visitors using private boats must obtain landing permits for Santa Rosa and San Miguel from the park. Air service available to Santa Rosa via Channel Island Aviation (see below).
Santa Cruz: Island Packers and Truth Aquatics offer day trips to east end. For day trips to west end and permits for private boats, contact well in advance the Nature Conservancy, Santa Cruz Island Project Office, 213 Stearns Wharf, Santa Barbara, Calif. 93101. Phone (805) 962-9111 (trips), (805) 964-7839 (permits).

For boat schedules from Ventura, contact headquarters or Island Packers, 1867 Spinnaker Drive, Ventura, Calif. 93001, (805) 642-1393 for info. and reservations or www.islandpackers.com. For weekend trips, reserve at least 2 weeks in advance. One- to multi-day trips to all islands. From Santa Barbara, contact Truth Aquatics, 301 W. Cabrillo Blvd., Santa Barbara, Calif. 93101, (805) 962-1127 or www.truthaquatics.com.

For plane information, contact Channel Island Adventures, 233 Durley Avenue, Camarillo, Calif. 93010. Phone (805) 987-1301.

Visitor & Information Centers
Visitor center on Spinnaker Drive in Ventura open daily year-round, except Thanksgiving and Christmas. Visitor centers on East Anacapa and Santa Barbara also open year-round. Ranger station on San Miguel.

Entrance Fee
None. For boat fares to islands; inquire at headquarters or Island Packers, and Travel Aquatics (see above).

Pets
Not permitted in park headquarters or on islands.

Facilities for Disabled
Visitor center at Ventura, rest rooms, theater, exhibits, and observation tower accessible. Boats and islands are not.

Things to Do
Santa Barbara Channel: whale watching from late December through March and June through September. **Anacapa**: free ranger-led walks and evening programs; also, wildlife watching, birdwatching, tide-pool walks, swimming and snorkeling, scuba and skin diving, fishing (license needed; certain areas closed). **Santa Barbara**: nature hikes, marine life observation, birdwatching, tide-pool walks. **Santa Rosa**: free ranger-led nature hike. **San Miguel**: free ranger-led hike to caliche "forest"; also, seal- and sea lion-watching, tide-pool walks. **Santa Cruz**: hikes, marine life observation, birdwatching.

Special Advisories
● When hiking on the islands, stay on trails and away from cliffs.
● All birds, animals, tide pools, shells, rocks, and plants are protected; do not take anything but photos.

Overnight Backpacking

All five islands have campgrounds; 14-day limit. Year-round. Reservations and permits required; contact headquarters. No fees. No showers. Tent sites only. No water or supplies on islands. Group camping available.

Hotels, Motels, & Inns

(unless otherwise noted, rates for 2 persons, double room, high season)
In Ventura, Calif.:
Bella Maggiore Inn 67 S. California St. 93001. (800) 523-8479 or (805) 652-0277. 28 units. $95, breakfast. **Country Inn by the Sea** 298 S. Chestnut St. 93001. (800) 456-4000 or (805) 653-

1434. 120 units. $89-$119, breakfast. AC, pool. **Four Point Sheraton** 1050 Schooner Dr. 93001. (800) 229-5732 or (805) 658-1212. 150 units. $89. Pool, rest. **Inn on the Beach** 1175 S. Seaward Ave. 93001. (805) 652-2000. 24 units. $100-$185. AC. **La Mer European Bed & Breakfast** (411 Poli St.) P.O. Box 23318. 93002. (805) 643-3600. 5 units. $115-$185, breakfast.

For additional lodgings, contact the Ventura Visitor & Convention Bureau, 89 S. California Street, Ventura, Calif. 93001. (805) 648-2075.

Excursions

Santa Monica Mountains National Recreation Area
Agoura Hills, California

Here southern California's rare Mediterranean climate offers habitats ranging from chaparral to oak woodlands to rocky canyons to marshes and sandy beaches. Government and private efforts preserve the area's natural and cultural resources including Paramount Ranch (a working Hollywood set), spectacular Mulholland Drive, Zuma Beach, Cold Creek Canyon Preserve, and the Will Rogers State Historic Park. 150,000 acre boundary. 100 campsites, hiking, mountain biking, horseback riding, water sports. Open all year, dawn to dusk (some areas 9 a.m.- 5 p.m. or by reservation). Info. at NPS headquarters in Agoura Hills, about 20 miles west of Los Angeles. (818) 597-9192.

Los Padres National Forest
Santa Barbara, California

This rugged forest preserves a vast area of central California coast and mountain ranges. Chaparral, high mountains, and desert ecosystems are all a short drive from Ventura. The Jacinto Reyes Scenic Byway (Calif. 33) threads through the park north of Ojai. 1,700,000 acres. Facilities: camping, backpacking, hiking, and picnic areas. Open year-round. Information at Ojai Ranger Station, approximately 30 miles from Channel Islands NP. (805) 646-4348.

Wind-rippled sand dunes

Death Valley

California

Established October 31, 1994

About 3.3 million acres

Our largest national park south of Alaska, Death Valley is known for extremes: It is North America's driest and hottest spot (with less than 2 inches of rainfall annually and a record high of 134°F), and has the lowest elevation in the Western Hemisphere—282 feet below sea level. Even with its extremes, the park still receives 1.3 million visitors each year.

In 1849 emigrants bound for California's gold fields strayed into the 120-mile-long basin, enduring a two-month ordeal of "hunger and thirst and an awful silence." One of the last to leave looked down from a mountain at the narrow valley and said, "Good-bye, Death Valley."

The forbidding moniker belies the beauty in this vast graben, the geological term for a sunken fragment of the earth's crust. Here are rocks sculptured by erosion, richly tinted mudstone hills and canyons, luminous sand dunes, lush oases, and a 200-square-mile salt pan surrounded by mountains, one of America's greatest vertical rises. In some years spring rains trigger wildflower blooms amid more than 900 varieties of plants.

From 1883 to 1889, wagon teams hauled powdery white borax from mines since fallen to ruin, an enterprise that spread word of Death Valley's striking landscapes, deep solitude, and crystalline air.

As night falls, Death Valley's elusive population of bobcats, kit foxes, and rodents ventures out. Far above on steep mountain slopes, desert bighorn sheep forage among

When to Go

All-year park. Temperatures from November through February average between 39°F and 75°F. From May through September, average highs range between 100°F and 116°F; overnight lows may top 100°F.

How to Visit

Death Valley's remote location and size make an automobile essential. An overnight stay allows time for the valley's vivid sunrises and sunsets, and a visit to the **Death Valley Museum** and **Furnace Creek Visitor Center.** Plan also to visit the **Harmony Borax Works** near the Furnace Creek Campground, to walk the 1-mile **Golden Canyon Interpretive Trail,** and to drive to **Zabriskie Point** for fine views of the valley. A second day permits exploration of the valley's northern reaches and **Scotty's Castle,** the retreat of an early-century millionaire, and nearby **Ubehebe Crater,** blasted out during the region's volcanic past. If you are a seasoned hiker, consider the strenuous all-day hike from **Wildrose Canyon** to sweeping views atop 11,049-foot **Telescope Peak,** Death Valley's highest point.

Joshua trees, scrubby junipers, and pines, while hawks soar on thermals rising into vivid blue, usually cloudless skies.

How to Get There

No airlines, public transit services, or railroads serve the park. Most visitors arrive by automobile from Los Angeles, Calif., or Las Vegas, Nev.

From L.A., the most scenic route crosses the eastern Mojave Desert via I-15 through Barstow. At Baker it turns north onto Calif. 127 to Shoshone, where Calif. 178 runs west and north along the valley floor to Furnace Creek.

From Las Vegas, take Nev. 160 west 42 miles to Old Spanish Trail (Tecopa Rd.), continuing through Tecopa to Calif. 127, turning north to Shoshone and picking up Calif. 178 to Furnace Creek. To include a visit to the early-century Nevada gold-mining ghost town of Rhyolite, take US 95 to Beatty, picking up Nev. 374, which becomes Calif. 190 and leads west to the park.

Entering from the East: Shoshone to Furnace Creek

130 miles (including side trips); one to two days

From the mining town of Shoshone, head west on Calif. 178 through the **Amargosa Range,** whose colorful dusky palette reflects the high mineral content in its sediments. Cresting 3,315-foot **Salsberry Pass,** you'll descend through the weathered **Black Mountains** to 1,290-foot **Jubilee Pass,** where wildflowers sometimes bloom in spring.

Approaching the ruins of gold-mining **Ashford Mill** and the **Death Valley Salt Pan**—the residue of a saline lake that existed over 20,000 years ago—you reach zero elevation. From here to Furnace Creek you travel *below* sea level, dipping to minus 282 feet at **Badwater** 27 miles north, the Western Hemisphere's lowest point. Park at Badwater, where sunrises ignite the Amargosa ridgeline. Continue north 4 miles to the turn-off onto a rough road

Kilns in Wildrose Canyon, a legacy of mining era

to **Natural Bridge,** a limestone arch spanning a richly tinted canyon. A ¼-mile trail to the bridge passes other striking formations.

About 1½ miles north, look left for the ½-mile spur road to **Devil's Golf Course,** a meringue of rock salt crystals that forms as water evaporates up through the salty crust.

Another 5 miles north brings you to the 9-mile one-way **Artists Drive** loop road through the **Artists Palette,** a rumpled terrain of volcanic ash whose yellows, red-oranges, greens, and muted purples challenge plein-air painters. About 4 miles north, the moderate 1-mile-long **Golden Canyon Interpretive Trail** winds through a canyon that near sunset gleams as if dusted with gold.

Continue on Calif. 178 north to the Calif. 190 junction. If you want to rest or refuel, stop at the **Furnace Creek Visitor Center.** If not, turn right onto Calif. 190 for the short drive to **Zabriskie Point,** a popular sunrise viewing spot, where rain and wind have shaped rock into dramatic contours. The promontory commands a broad view of mudstone badlands. To explore them, continue on for a mile to **Twenty Mule Team Canyon,** which is threaded by a gravel loop road.

Return to the highway, turn right and continue to the 13-mile spur road to 5,475-foot **Dantes View.** The mile-high panorama plunges to Badwater and sweeps across the salt pan to the forbidding **Panamint Range** and 11,049-foot **Telescope Peak.**

If you have not yet visited **Furnace Creek,** backtrack 24 miles to the

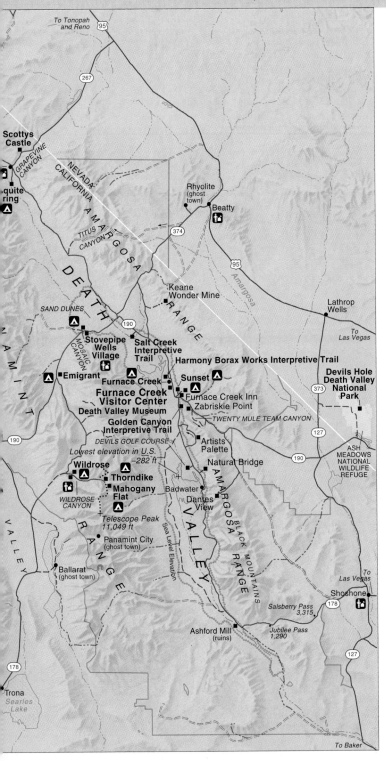

To Tonopah
and Reno
95

267

Scottys
Castle

GRAPEVINE CANYON

quite
ring

NEVADA
CALIFORNIA

AMARGOSA

Rhyolite
(ghost
town)

Beatty

TITUS CANYON

374

D
E
A
T
H

95

Amargosa

R
A
N
G
E

Keane
Wonder Mine

Lathrop
Wells

To
Las Vegas

SAND DUNES

190

MOSAIC CANYON

Stovepipe
Wells
Village

Salt Creek
Interpretive
Trail

Harmony Borax Works Interpretive Trail

Devils Hole
Death Valley
National
Park

373

Emigrant

Furnace Creek

Sunset

Furnace Creek
Visitor Center

Furnace Creek Inn

Death Valley Museum

Zabriskie Point

127

Golden Canyon
Interpretive Trail

TWENTY MULE TEAM CANYON

190

DEVILS GOLF COURSE

Artists
Palette

ASH
MEADOWS
NATIONAL
WILDLIFE
REFUGE

190

Lowest elevation in U.S.
−282 ft

Natural Bridge

Wildrose

Thorndike

Mahogany
Flat

Badwater

Dantes
View

WILDROSE
CANYON

A
M
A
R
G
O
S
A

Telescope Peak
11,049 ft

Panamint City
(ghost town)

Sea Level Elevation

V
A
L
L
E
Y

P
A
N
A
M
I
N
T

Ballarat
(ghost town)

R
A
N
G
E

B
L
A
C
K

To
Las Vegas

Shoshone

178

M
O
U
N
T
A
I
N
S

Salsberry Pass
3,315

R
A
N
G
E

V
A
L
L
E
Y

178

Ashford Mill
(ruins)

Jubilee Pass
1,290

127

Trona
Searles
Lake

To Baker

Creek Visitor Center, which has exhibits and a bookstore. Check for ranger-guided walks and evening programs (offered from Oct. to April) and visit the Death Valley Museum.

The springs at Furnace Creek oasis produce over 1 million gallons a day, watering oleanders, palms, mahogany, and tamarisk trees, and the incongruously verdant fairways of the golf course at the Furnace Creek Inn. Guests may explore the interior and gardens of this classic Spanish Mission-style structure, constructed in 1927 of adobe and native stone.

Furnace Creek to Scotty's Castle

90 miles (including excursions); a half day

One mile north of the Furnace Creek Visitor Center, leave your car and walk the 2¼-mile paved Harmony Borax Works Interpretive Trail to the ruins of Death Valley's first successful borax mining venture. Original equipment includes a borax wagon with 6-foot-high rear wheels.

Continue north on Calif. 190 past the Beatty Cutoff to the 1-mile spur road to the Salt Creek Interpretive Trail. Spring-fed marshy pools here are home to Death Valley's unusual desert pupfish, descendant of creatures that flourished in the basin's ancient lake at least 12,000 years ago. Like the oasis at Scotty's Castle, this is a prime birdwatching area, frequented by many of the 350 species found in Death Valley, including Canada geese, peregrine falcons, hawks, and eagles.

Nearby sand dunes ripple across 14 square miles. At sunrise and sunset the wind-sculptured waves of quartz-grain sand take on a luminous rosy glow. Accessible via paved road near Stovepipe Wells Village, these dunes have no established trails; park and walk where you please.

Continue on for about 30 miles to Grapevine Canyon and Scotty's Castle, a Mediterranean-style architectural gem dating from 1922. Once the retreat of a wealthy Chicago couple, the ranch is named for frequent house guest and "desert rat" Walter Scott. Daily on the hour, the Park Service conducts tours through the mansion, which holds original furnishings. In winter, be prepared to wait up to 2 hours for a tour. While waiting, consider a meal at the Castle's restaurant, a picnic outside, or an amble up Windy Point Trail.

Information & Activities

Headquarters
Death Valley, California 92328-0579. Phone (619) 786-2331. www.nps.gov/deva

Seasons & Accessibility
Open year-round.

Visitor & Information Centers
Furnace Creek Visitor Center in Furnace Creek, off Calif. 190.

Entrance Fee
$10 per vehicle, good for one week.

Pets
Must be leashed at all times. Not allowed on trails or in backcountry.

Facilities for Disabled
The visitor center Scotty's Castle, and Furnace Creek, Texas Spring, and Sunset Campgrounds are wheelchair accessible.

Things to Do
Free ranger- and naturalist-led activities available mid-Oct.–mid-April: nature walks and talks, evening programs, children's programs. Also, hiking, nature trails, living history tours, bicycling, birdwatching, horseback riding.

Special Advisories
● Death Valley's heat can make any emergency situation life-threatening. For advice on hot weather travel, consult the *Death Valley Guide*, available at roadside kiosks, ranger stations, and the visitor center.
● Drink plenty of water; one gallon per person per day is recommended, two gallons if hiking. Emergency radiator water is available from barrels located along main park roads.
● Hat and sunglasses are essential.
● Desert rains, though brief, cause flash floods. Never ford washouts, even

Salt crystals of Devil's Golf Course

in a 4-wheel-drive vehicle.

● Abandoned mineshafts and prospect holes pose dangers. *Never* enter an abandoned tunnel.

Overnight Backpacking

Backcountry camping permitted in areas at least 2 miles from main roads and ¼ mile from water sources. Permit not required, but hikers should register at visitor center and inquire about which areas prohibit camping.

Campgrounds

Nine campgrounds, 30-day limit. **Furnace Creek, Mesquite Spring, Wildrose Flat** open year-round; **Texas Spring, Sunset, Stovepipe Wells** open Oct. to April; **Emigrant, Thorndike, Mahogany Flat** open April to Oct. Reservations taken only at **Furnace Creek** (call National Parks Reservation Service; see page 11); all others first come, first served. Fees: $16 at Furnace Creek; $10 at Sunset, Stovepipe Wells, Mesquite Spring; $12 at Texas Spring; free at Thorndike, Emigrant, Mahogany Flat, Wildrose Flat.

Hotels, Motels, & Inns

(unless otherwise noted, rates are for 2 persons in a double room, high season)
INSIDE THE PARK:
Furnace Creek Inn Furnace Creek off Calif. 190. (619) 786-2361. 66 units. $270-$335, including all meals.
Furnace Creek Ranch Furnace Creek off Calif. 190. Box 1, Death Valley 92328. (800) 528-6367 or (619) 786-2345. 225 units. $154. Two restaurants.
Stovepipe Wells Village Motel Stovepipe Wells Village, Death Valley 92328. (619) 786-2387. 83 units. $63-$84. Rest. 14 RV hookups.

For other lodgings, contact the Death Valley Chamber of Commerce in Shoshone, Calif. (619) 852-4524.

Kaluu O Ka Oo cinder cone in the volcanic desert near Sliding Sands Trail

Haleakala

Maui, Hawaii

Established August 1, 1916

30,183 acres

Haleakala, a giant shield volcano, forms the eastern bulwark of the island of Maui. According to legend, it was here, in the awe-inspiring basin at the mountain's summit, that the demigod Maui snared the sun, releasing it only after it promised to move more slowly across the sky. Haleakala means "house of the sun"; the park encompasses the basin and portions of the volcano's flanks.

A United Nations International Biosphere Reserve, the park comprises starkly contrasting worlds of mountain and coast. The road to the summit of Haleakala rises from near sea level to 10,000 feet in 38 miles—possibly the steepest such gradient for autos in the world. Visitors ascend through several climate and vegetation zones, from humid tropical lowlands to subalpine desert. Striking plants and animals such as the Haleakala silversword and the nene may be seen in this mountain section. The summit-area depression, misnamed Haleakala Crater, formed as erosion ate away the mountain, joining two valleys. This 19-square-mile wilderness area, 2,720 feet deep, is the park's major draw.

From east of the rim, the great rain forest valley of Kipahulu drops thousands of feet down to the coast. The upper Kipahulu Valley is a protected wilderness, home to a vast profusion of flora and fauna, including some of the world's rarest birds, plants, and invertebrates. Some insects evolved in the Kipahulu Valley and live nowhere else.

Visitors reach the lower valley of Kipahulu via a sliver of parkland on

Maui's southeastern coast. Dominated by intense hues—azure sea, black rock, silver waterfalls, green forest and meadow—the coastal area was first farmed in early Polynesian times, more than 1,200 years ago. Mark Twain, who traveled to Hawaii in 1866, may well have had this part of Kipahulu in mind when he wrote: "For me its balmy airs are always blowing, its summer seas flashing in the sun; the pulsing of its surfbeat is in my ear; I can see its garlanded crags, its leaping cascades, its plumy palms drowsing by the shore."

How to Get There

Fly directly from the mainland, or from another Hawaiian island, to Kahului in central Maui. To reach the summit of Haleakala, follow, sequentially, Hawaii 36, 37, 377, and 378. The 37-mile route is well marked; last chance to buy food and gas is at Pukalani or Makawao. Continue on the switchback road through miles of lush mountain range-land to the park's northwest entrance. Allow up to 2 hours.

For the 62-mile drive to Kipahulu, allow up to 3½ hours. Take Hawaii 36 from Kahului around the northeastern side of the island to the town of Hana. The road to Hana, which becomes Hawaii 360, is famous for its narrow, tortuous course along 1,000-foot sea cliffs, into deep gorges. This drive affords many views of waterfalls and cascade pools, but few places to access them. Proceed past Hana on Hawaii 31 for about 7 miles. Just beyond the Pools of Oheo, signs will point to off-road parking.

When to Go

All-year park. Most rain comes in winter, although temperatures vary little month to month. To avoid crowds, visit the summit after 3 p.m.; sunsets can be as spectacular as the famous sunrises. At Kipahulu, avoid crowds by arriving early or camping overnight. Weather varies most at high elevations, and can change from very hot to rainy, cold, and windy in the same day. Temperatures can drop to freezing inside the wilderness area, although snow is rare. Coastal Kipahulu stays warm but receives considerable rain all year.

How to Visit

With an early start, it's possible to tour both the **Haleakala** summit and **Kipahulu** coastal regions of the park in 1 day, but you will spend much time in your car. To absorb more of the ambience of this unique sea-girt volcano, try to spend a day on the mountain, with a hike through the moonscape of the "crater," and a second day on the coast. Van and bus tours—some starting in predawn hours to take in a magical summit sunrise—can be arranged from most island hotels. Some companies will drive a group to the summit, then provide bicycles to ride down the mountain.

Consider taking a guided walk from **Hosmer Grove** into the Nature Conservancy's **Waikamoi Preserve,** home of living treasures including various species of honeycreepers, Hawaii's premier family of native birds. Call ahead for the schedule.

Air tours of Maui and the park are available from Kahului, but regulations limit them to high altitude.

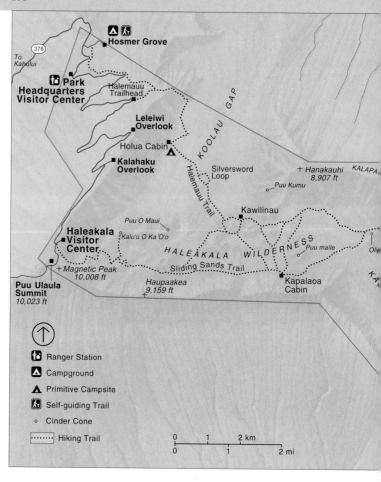

Hosmer Grove to Haleakala Summit

11 miles; at least a half day

A short distance above the park entrance lies **Hosmer Grove,** a cool, shady spot to picnic and camp. You may recognize some of the trees, which include Douglas-fir, California redwood, and eucalyptus. Around 1910, forester Ralph Hosmer planted trees from all over the world to test their potential for watershed protection and timber here. A ½-mile loop trail will refresh you after your drive. Guided nature walks are also available. Back on the road, you reach Park Headquarters Visitor Center 1³⁄₁₀ miles above the Hosmer turnoff. At this 7,000-foot elevation, you will see vegetation native to Hawaii. In front of

headquarters, plantings of Haleakala geranium and silversword offer photo opportunities and biology lessons in adaptation and evolution. These two plants are endemic—found only on Haleakala volcano.

Leaving headquarters, drive up the mountain through subalpine heath of soft earthy hues. In spring, mamane, a dominant shrub, brightens these slopes with sprays of yellow blossoms. The small birds here are mainly native. With luck you may see some of the famous honeycreepers—brightly feathered birds that may be descendants of the first land birds to reach Hawaii. From their original ancestors, the honeycreepers have evolved at least 47 species, some adapted to only one island, some spread more widely. More than half of these species have become extinct. Driven from the

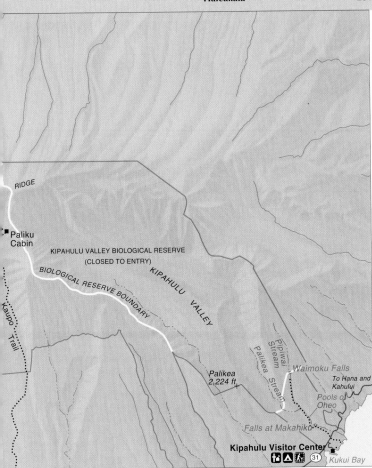

RIDGE

■ Paliku
Cabin

KIPAHULU VALLEY BIOLOGICAL RESERVE
(CLOSED TO ENTRY)

KIPAHULU VALLEY

BIOLOGICAL RESERVE BOUNDARY

Kaupo Trail

Palikea
2,224 ft

Pipiwai Stream

Palikea Stream

Waimoku Falls

To Hana and
Kahului

Pools of Oheo

Falls at Makahiku

Kipahulu Visitor Center

31

Kukui Bay

Nene, birds unique to Hawaii

Silky balls of the Ahinahina (Haleakala silversword)

Iiwi, a tiny, rare honeycreeper

lowlands by habitat change and disease, others are making their last stand high on the mountain.

Summit hikers often start at the **Halemauu Trailhead,** three miles above the headquarters visitor center. This trail takes you through rolling country to the rim, then switchbacks as it steeply drops 1,000 feet down the spectacular northwest wall of the wilderness area to **Holua Cabin** and the campground (four miles from the trailhead). The wall is broken here by **Koolau Gap,** a wide, wet canyon that descends to the sea. In this corner, vegetation thrives on moisture carried by waves of clouds that slowly ebb and flow in the gap, and you will find the-leathery fern, called amau, and other unusual plants.

Motorists can get first views of the crater at **Leleiwi Overlook.** Drive approximately 2 more miles to the Haleakala Visitor Center, where rangers lead hikes part-way into the center (call ahead for schedules).

An exhibit shelter crowns the highest point—**Puu Ulaula,** or "red hill"— where park naturalists give several interpretive talks daily.

At 10,023 feet, Puu Ulaula offers the ultimate view: Often you can see the giant volcanoes of the Big Island, as well as Maui's neighboring islands of **Lanai** and **Molokai** and sometimes, at night, far to the northwest, the lights of **Oahu.** Nearby, but outside the park, are the Haleakala Observatories, a cluster of buildings that are closed to the public.

The best way to experience the wilderness area is on a 2-day hike, spending the night at one of the three cabins or two campgrounds inside the crater. (Reserve well in advance for cabins—see **Information & Activities** p. 234.) One popular overnight trip involves hiking the **Sliding Sands Trail** to **Kapalaoa Cabin** (5⅘ miles from the visitor center). This strenuous 7 to 10 hour hike loses and gains 3,000 feet on its descent and ascent through loose cinder. Many choose to exit via **Halemauu Trail,** an easier 8-mile hike from the cabin back to the road. You'll need to arrange a ride between the two trailheads.

Another challenging hike is to take the Sliding Sands Trail down to **Kaluu O Ka Oo,** the first big cinder cone, 5 miles round-trip.

Pools of Oheo

Kipahulu: Pools of Oheo

a full day

In this strip of parkland along the gorge of **Pipiwai Stream,** visitors hike through lush rain forest and past breath-taking ocean overlooks. Perhaps the area's greatest draw, however, is Hawaii's cultural past. Archaeological evidence shows that large numbers of Hawaiians once lived in Kipahulu, from pre-contact inhabitants (before 1778) to those who worked as cattle ranchers at the turn of the 20th century and in the sugar cane industry from 1880-1925. Trails reveal traces of the past: stone-walled gardens, pictographs, evidence of taro and sweet potato patches, and temple and shelter sites. Please respect this legacy by staying on trails and reporting to park rangers anyone seen damaging cultural resources.

Camping is permitted on the oceanfront meadows south of the stream at the **Kipahulu Campground**. Bring your own drinking water, or boil stream water or treat it with halozone. No permit is required, but there is a 3-night limit per month.

If you have 2 or 3 hours, take **Pipiwai Trail,** one of the most memorable short hikes in the islands. This walk is easy for anyone in good health, but is usually slippery with mud in spots; wear sturdy footgear. Don't hike if the river is swollen.

Begin about 200 yards south of the Oheo bridge, near Kipahulu Visitor Center. Walk up through gently sloping pasture about ½ mile to overlook **Makahiku Falls,** 184 feet high. After another ½ mile, the trail enters the woods and crosses two bridges near a lovely double falls. Continue about a mile more through lush forest, including a stand of dense, 50-foot-high bamboo, which on a breezy day clacks and creaks with a mysterious percussive music. Aromatic ginger and ti form the understory. Your destination looms above the forest as you get close: **Waimoku Falls,** more than 300 feet high, fills its jungle clearing with cool mists. Much of the year, mango, guava, and mountain apple provide refreshment.

Swimming is a pleasant pastime in this part of the park. Those who fancy a dip congregate around the big, cool pools and waterfalls below the highway bridge in **Oheo Gulch,** but less crowded spots await upstream. Some pools are deep, but beware of slippery or hidden rocks. Also, flash floods can follow heavy rains in the watershed above. There is no ocean access.

Information & Activities

Headquarters
P.O. Box 369, Makawao, Hawaii 96768.
Phone (808) 572-4400.
www.nps.gov/hale

Seasons & Accessibility
All-year park. Call (808) 572-4400 for
information on weather and roads.

Visitor & Information Centers
Park Headquarters Visitor Center,
one mile from park entrance, and
Haleakala Visitor Center, near the
summit, 11 miles from the park
entrance, open daily all year. For park
information, call (808) 572-4400, or
ask the rangers at the Kipahulu Visitor
Center. (808) 248-7375.

Entrance Fees
$10 per car per week, multiple entries;
$20 for an annual pass.

Pets
Permitted on leashes in drive-in
campgrounds only; not allowed on
hiking trails.

Facilities for Disabled
All visitor centers, park headquarters,
and some campsites are wheelchair
accessible. A free brochure about visiting Maui is available from: Commission on the Handicapped, Old Federal
Building, 335 Merchant St., No. 215,
Honolulu, Hawaii 96813.

Things to Do
Free naturalist-led activities: nature
walks and hikes, interpretive talks,
cultural demonstrations. Also available, hiking, horseback riding, swimming in Pools of Oheo.

Special Advisory
● Wilderness area hikes are at high
altitudes, with lower oxygen levels; take
it easy. Be prepared for unpredictable
weather that can change quickly from
heat to cold and rain.

Overnighting in the Wilderness Area
Tent camping allowed only at Holua
and Paliku campsites; free permit
required; issued first come, first served
at park headquarters on the day of the
hike; 2-night limit at each campground;
limit of 3 nights total per month.

Three small, primitive cabins at
Holua, Kapalaoa, and Paliku contain
12 bunks, minimum equipment; can
be reached by trail only. Reservation
requests must be received by mail
before the first of the month, 3 months
prior to desired stay; give alternate
dates; assignments made by lottery;
limited to 3 nights per month (2 con-
secutive nights in one cabin); $40 per
night for 1 to 6 people; $80 per night
for 7 to 12 people. Send request to
headquarters. Call (808) 572-4400 for
recorded information on cabins and
campgrounds.

Campgrounds
Two drive-in campgrounds, both
with 3-day limit. **Hosmer Grove** and
Kipahulu open all year first come, first
served. No fees. No showers. Tent sites;
no hookups.

Hotels, Motels, & Inns
(unless otherwise noted, rates are for 2
persons in a double room, high season)
In Hana, Hawaii 96713:
Aloha Cottages (73 Keawa Pl.)
P.O. Box 205. (808) 248-8420. 5
small cottages, all with full kitchens,
in residential areas of Hana. $65-$85.
Hana AAA Bay Vacation Rentals
P.O. Box 318. (800) 959-7727 or
(808) 248-7727. Five cottages, all with
full kitchens, in various areas of Hana.
$75-$200. **Hana Kai Maui Resort
Condominiums** (1533 Uakea Rd.)
P.O. Box 38. (800) 346-2772 or
(808) 248-7506. 17 units, kitchenettes.
$125-$195. **Heavenly Hana Inn**
(4155 Hana Hwy.) P.O. Box 790.
(808) 248-8442. Three units. $185-
$250. **Hotel Hana Maui** P.O. Box 8.
(800) 321-4262 or (808) 248-8211. 93
units. $395. Restaurant.
In Kahului, Hawaii 96732:
Maui Beach Hotel (170 Kaahumanu
Ave.) Hawaii Reservation Center, 1150
S. King St., Honolulu, Hawaii 96814.
(888) 649-3222 or (808) 877-0051. 148
units. $90-$110. AC, pool, restaurant.
Maui Seaside Hotel 100 W. Kaahumanu Ave. (800) 367-7000 or (808)
877-3311. 190 units, 10 with kitchenettes. $125. AC, pool, restaurant.
In Kula, Hawaii 96790:
Kula Lodge (Rte. 377) RR l, Box 475.
(800) 233-1535 or (808) 878-1535. 5
units. $110-$165. Restaurant.

Excursions

Waianapanapa State Park
Hana, Maui, Hawaii

Low volcanic cliffs and native hala (pandanus) forest line the coast in this remote, rugged park. Here, visitors can fish in the surf, explore a cave, observe an immense seabird colony, and hike the ancient coastal trail leading to Hana. 120 acres. Facilities include a campground (permits required), 12 cabins, picnic areas. Activities include hiking, fishing, swimming. Open year-round. Off Hawaii 360 (Hana Highway) about 80 miles from Haleakala NP. (808) 984-8109.

Iao Valley State Park
Wailuku, Maui, Hawaii

Velvety moss-covered cliffs surround the verdant Iao Valley and its center-piece, the Iao Needle, a 2,250-foot basalt spire sacred to the people of Maui. Swirling waters fashioned the spire from a natural altar in an ancient volcanic caldera. Six acres. Facilities: observation pavilion, botanic gardens. Open year-round from 7 a.m. to 7 p.m. End of Iao Valley Road, off Hawaii 32, about 40 miles from Haleakala NP. (808) 984-8109.

Hawaiian ferns and ohia blossoms near Halemaumau crater, atop Kilauea

Hawaii Volcanoes

Hawaii

Established August 1, 1916

229,177 acres

Hawaii Volcanoes National Park, on the "Big Island" of Hawaii, offers the visitor a look at two of the world's most active volcanoes: Kilauea and Mauna Loa.

More than 4,000 feet high and still growing, Kilauea abuts the southeastern slope of the older and much larger Mauna Loa, or "long mountain." Mauna Loa towers some 13,677 feet above the sea: Measured from its base 18,000 feet below sea level, it exceeds Mount Everest in height. Mauna Loa's gently sloping bulk— some 10,000 cubic miles in volume— makes it the planet's most massive single mountain.

The park stretches from sea level to Mauna Loa's summit. Beyond the end of the road lies Mauna Loa's wilderness area, where backpackers encounter freezing nights and rough lava trails amid volcanic wonders: barren lava twisted into nightmarish shapes, cinder cones, gaping pits. Kilauea, however, provides easy access to a greater variety of scenery and cultural sites.

On the slopes of Kilauea, whose name means "spreading, much spewing," lush green rain forest borders stark, recent lava flows. This natural laboratory of ecological change displays all stages of forest regeneration— from early regrowth of lichens and ferns to dense forest. The rain forest on the windward side of Kilauea's summit gives way to the stark, windswept Kau Desert on the hot, dry southwestern slope. At the shore, waves create lines of jagged cliffs; periodic eruptions send fresh lava flows to meet the sea amid colossal clouds of steam.

Geological dynamism forms the park's primary natural theme, followed closely by evolutionary biology. Thousands of unique species have evolved on the isolated Hawaiian islands. Cultural sites abound as well, reminders of the Polynesian pioneers who steered their great double-hulled canoes to Hawaii beginning some 1,500 years ago.

The United Nations has named the park both an International Biosphere Reserve and a World Heritage site. Many of the park's intriguing native plants and animals, however, are in peril, defenseless against alien species including weedy invasive plants and feral pigs.

How to Get There

Fly to the island of Hawaii, also called the Big Island. Airlines serve the Kona airport from the mainland and from other Hawaiian islands; only interisland flights land in Hilo. From Kona, head south around the island on Hawaii 11 past Kealakekua Bay, where Captain Cook met his death, and Ka

Lae, or South Point, southernmost land in the 50 states. You'll reach the Kilauea summit after a 95-mile drive on a good road.

From Hilo, Hawaii 11 rises 4,000 feet in 30 miles on your way past small towns, macadamia orchards, and rain forest, to reach the park at Kilauea's summit.

When to Go

All-year park. The weather is often driest in September and October. The climate ranges from warm and breezy on the coast, to cool and frequently wet at the summit of Kilauea, to nightly freezing with occasional snowstorms above about 10,000 feet on Mauna Loa. To avoid most tour bus crowds, plan to visit the major sights before 11 a.m. or after 3 p.m.

How to Visit

An intensive 1-day visit can encompass highlights of the **Kilauea** summit via **Crater Rim Drive** and the coastal region via **Chain of Craters Road.** Regular tours by bus and small van operate daily from many Hilo and Kona hotels. Those with a botanical or ornithological bent will enjoy exploring **Mauna Loa Road** (accessible from Hawaii 11), which takes you through upland forest to the **Mauna Loa Trailhead** at 6,660 feet: At **Kipukapuaulu,** be sure to take the 1-mile loop trail wending through 100-acre Kipuka (an island of vegetation surrounded by a more recent lava flow) containing one of Hawaii's richest concentrations of native plants and birdlife.

Puu Oo spewing molten lava

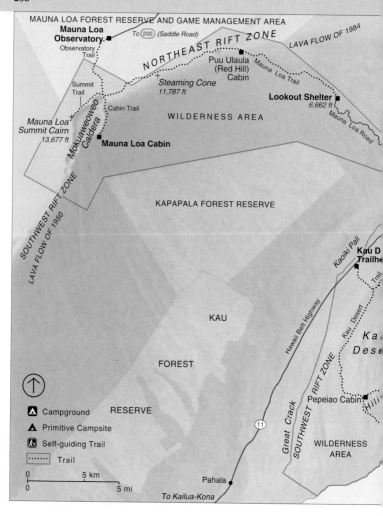

MAUNA LOA FOREST RESERVE AND GAME MANAGEMENT AREA
Mauna Loa
Observatory. ■   To (200) (Saddle Road)
Observatory
Trail

NORTHEAST RIFT ZONE

LAVA FLOW OF 1984

Puu Ulaula
(Red Hill)
Cabin

Mauna Loa Trail

Steaming Cone
11,787 ft

Summit
Trail

Cabin Trail

WILDERNESS AREA

Lookout Shelter ■
6,662 ft

Mauna Loa Road

Mauna Loa
Summit Cairn
13,677 ft

Mokuaweoweo Caldera

Mauna Loa Cabin

SOUTHWEST RIFT ZONE

LAVA FLOW OF 1950

KAPAPALA FOREST RESERVE

Kaolki Pali

Kau D
Trailhe

Trail

KAU

Hawaii Belt Highway

Kau Desert

Ka
Dese

FOREST

SOUTHWEST RIFT ZONE

Pepeiao Cabin

Hili

↑

Campground   RESERVE

Primitive Campsite

Self-guiding Trail

Great Crack

11

WILDERNESS
AREA

•••••   Trail

0   5 km
├────────┤
0   5 mi

Pahala •

To Kailua-Kona

Kilauea Summit: Crater Rim Drive

11-mile loop; about a half day

Since Kilauea's summit areas can be rainy and chilly at any time of the year, visitors should be prepared. Bring a windbreaker or jacket and wear long pants. Begin at the **Kilauea Visitor Center,** where you can get the latest information on park roads and safety precautions. Don't miss the stunning film of recent volcanic eruptions. The rustic **Volcano House** and the **Volcano Art Center** are just a short stroll away. Walk through the lobby of the Volcano House to the rear of the hotel for a first dramatic view across **Kilauea Caldera,** a 3-mile-wide, 400-foot-deep depression that marks the volcanic summit.

After leaving the visitor center, continue clockwise on **Crater Rim Drive.** For a time, the road traverses rain forest featuring Hawaiian tree ferns that lend the roadsides a prehistoric look. Scenic turnouts begin with a huge crater, **Kilauea Iki** ("little Kilauea") just east of the main caldera. In 1959 Kilauea Iki erupted in a lava fountain 1,900 feet high, a record for Hawaiian volcanism.

Visit the **Nahuku** (Thurston Lava Tube) by taking an easy 15-minute loop trail that starts in lush jungle. The lava tube formed when the surface of a lava stream cooled to a crust while the still molten interior lava flowed out.

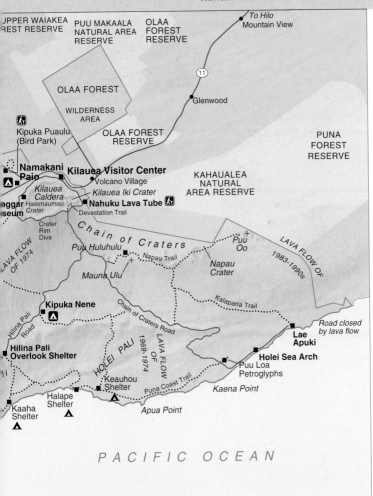

UPPER WAIAKEA
REST RESERVE

PUU MAKAALA
NATURAL AREA
RESERVE

OLAA
FOREST
RESERVE

To Hilo
Mountain View

OLAA FOREST

11

WILDERNESS
AREA

Glenwood

Kipuka Puaulu
(Bird Park)

OLAA FOREST
RESERVE

PUNA
FOREST
RESERVE

**Namakani
Paio**

Kilauea Visitor Center

Volcano Village

KAHAUALEA
NATURAL
AREA RESERVE

Kilauea
Caldera

Kilauea Iki Crater

aggar Halemaumau
seum Crater

Nahuku Lava Tube

Devastation Trail

Crater
Rim
Drive

C h a i n   o f   C r a t e r s

Puu
Oo

LAVA FLOW OF

LAVA FLOW
OF 1974

Puu Huluhulu

Napau Trail

Napau
Crater

1983-1990s

Mauna Ulu

Kipuka Nene

Chain of Craters Road

Kalapana Trail

Hilina Pali
Road

HOLEI PALI

LAVA FLOW OF 1969-1974

Lae
Apuki

Road closed
by lava flow

**Hilina Pali
Overlook Shelter**

*Keauhou
Shelter*

Puna Coast Trail

Holei Sea Arch
Puu Loa
Petroglyphs

Kaena Point

Halape
Shelter

Apua Point

Kaaha
Shelter

P A C I F I C   O C E A N

The Nahuku (Thurston Lava Tube), a natural tunnel

New growth among cinders at Devastation Trail

From the Nahuku parking area, trails lead down to the floor of Kilauea Iki Crater and along its rim. You can take a loop hike or walk back to Volcano House in 2 to 3 miles. Either way, you'll pass dramatic vistas of the Kilauea Caldera, vertical lava cliffs, and verdant rain forest.

Another option is to hike the popular 4-mile **Kilauea Iki Trail,** which winds around the rim and across the floor of a crater that last erupted in 1959. Taking about 2 hours to walk, the trail descends 400 feet, passing rain forest and steaming lava flows.

Now continuing back along Crater Rim Drive, look for Koa e Kea, white-tailed tropicbirds. These ethereal-looking creatures nest on cliffside ledges, often soaring above **Kilauea Caldera.** With luck, you may spot a nene, an endemic Hawaiian bird probably descended from lost Canada geese that landed here. The state bird of Hawaii, the nene are a federally protected endangered species. Do not feed or approach any nene and take care to avoid hitting them when driving (you'll spot "nene crossing" road signs).

Devastation Trail is a short (½-mile) but unforgettable walk through remains of a forest killed by falling cinder during the 1959 eruption. The forest is now beginning to recover.

As the road descends along the southwestern side of Kilauea Caldera, you will notice the landscape becoming more arid. In the rain shadow of the summit, the **Kau Desert** receives about half as much rain as the 100 inches which fall annually at the Kilauea Visitor Center. It also bears the brunt of trade winds blowing sulphuric volcanic fumes and natural acid rain—which stunt plants—down from above.

You reach the **Halemaumau Crater Overlook.** Walk the short path to look into the crater, a favorite abode of Pele, goddess of the volcano. Many native Hawaiians still revere her; throughout the year they privately chant and dance at the crater's edge.

The **Hawaiian Volcano Observatory** of the US Geological Survey, and the small, excellent **Jaggar Museum** of volcano lore and research are next on your route. Nearing the visitor center once more, you'll pass fumaroles, or steam vents. Some have produced the **Sulphur Banks** with crystalline deposits of pure sulphur. From here you can opt for a short hike back toward the visitor center. Alternatively, a 1- to 2-mile walk along the caldera rim provides fine views.

Chain of Craters Road

20 miles one way; about 3 hours

From the Kilauea Visitor center follow Crater Rim Drive clockwise to the well-marked turnoff for **Chain of Craters Road.** For about 4 miles as you head toward the coast, your route follows the upper part of the active **East Rift Zone** of Kilauea volcano. Scenic turnouts and short walks bring you to the rims of several impressive craters. If you have time, hike the

Lava sizzling into ocean near the park

Ripples of hardened pahoehoe lava on Kilauea

Napau Trail up **Puu Huluhulu** ("shaggy hill") to the overlook at the top, just over 1 mile. The overlook provides splendid views of the East Rift Zone and **Mauna Ulu**, the large, steaming domelike hill directly to the south. Look for steam from **Puu Oo,** a major vent of Kilauea's ongoing eruption, far to the east.

Back on Chain of Craters Road, you will drive over several miles of pahoehoe lava flows produced when Mauna Ulu formed in the 1970s. At the turnouts, you stand on some of the newest ground on earth. Pahoehoe (pa-hoy-hoy) lava flows at more than 2000 degrees F. It begins fluid then chills to a smooth, ropy surface. This rock contrasts with aa (ah-ah)— thicker, slow-moving lava that has hardened into a chaotic jumble of rough jagged cinders.

The climate becomes drier, and patches of forest in various stages of recovery appear, as you descend toward the sea. Sulphur fumes sweep down from active volcanic vents on the rift to

the east. Turnouts offer sweeping views of lava flows and white-capped waves pounding the black shoreline. About 21 miles off this coast, a huge undersea volcano is building a future Hawaiian island. Named Loihi, the volcano could breach the ocean's surface in some 100,000 years.

A steep descent of about 800 feet marks **Holei Pali,** a cliff formed by vertical faulting; the huge coastal shelf is breaking away from the uplands and sinking into the sea, albeit slowly on a human time scale. Reaching the lowlands, look for the **Puu Loa Petroglyphs** turnout; a modest hike will bring you to fine examples of ancient Hawaiian carvings, some 15,000 images and figures pecked into the lava. Visitors are asked to stay on the boardwalk to help preserve these carvings.

Hawaiians lived on this dry, rocky land for centuries. Your route along the coast takes you past several of their ancient settlements, though they are difficult to discern.

The road ends abruptly at a 1995 lava flow. Since 1986, an almost continuous flow of lava from Puu Oo has buried several miles of the road, as well as the Kamoamoa picnic site and campground, and the Wahaula Visitor Center. Park rangers mark a path to a viewpoint close to current flows. Lava flow viewing and access are unpredictable; obey all off limit signs and heed the instructions of any park rangers on duty here. Ask at the visitor center for current lava flow information.

Information & Activities

Headquarters
P.O. Box 52, Hawaii National Park, Hawaii 96718. Phone (808) 967-7311. www.nps.gov/havo

Seasons & Accessibility
Park open year-round. Chain of Craters Road is closed by lava flow at its eastern end. For eruption bulletins call (808) 985-6000.

Visitor & Information Centers
Kilauea Visitor Center, located just off Hawaii 11 on Crater Rim Drive, ¼ mile from park entrance gate, and the Thomas A. Jaggar Museum on Crater Rim Drive, 3 miles from park entrance gate, are both open all year.

Entrance Fee
$10 per car per week.

Pets
Not permitted on hiking trails or in backcountry; elsewhere must be leashed.

Facilities for Disabled
Visitor center and museum are accessible to wheelchairs, with assistance. One trail and many scenic overlooks along Crater Rim Drive also accessible. Free brochure about visiting the Big Island from: Commission on Persons with Disabilities, 919 Alamoana Blvd., Rm. 101, Honolulu, Hawaii 96814. (808) 586-8121.

Things to Do
Free ranger-led activities: nature walks and talks, slide shows, films, museum exhibits on volcanism. Also, hiking, backcountry fishing (check park headquarters for regulations), art center, workshops, seminars.

Special Advisories
• Be prepared for intensive sunlight.
• Persons with heart or respiratory problems must beware of noxious sulphur fumes.
• Stay on marked trails; vegetation may conceal deep cracks.
• Coastline collapse can occur fast; do not go beyond barriers.
• Strong winds and unpredictable surf along the coast make swimming dangerous; it is prohibited in places.
• Do not enter any closed areas.

Overnight Backpacking
Registration at the visitor center is required. No fee.

Campgrounds
Three campgrounds, **Kamoamoa, Kipuka Nene,** and **Namakani Paio,** all with a 7-day limit. Open all year first come, first served. No fees. No showers. Tent sites only. Two patrol cabins on **Mauna Loa Trail** and one at **Kipuka Pepeiao** may be used free first come, first served. Must register at headquarters. Food services in park.

Hotels, Motels, & Inns
(unless otherwise noted, rates are for 2 persons in a double room, high season)
INSIDE THE PARK:
Volcano House (Crater Rim Dr.) P.O. Box 53, Hawaii Volcanoes NP, Hawaii 96718. (808) 967-7321. 42 rooms. $85-$185. Restaurant.
Namakani Paio Cabins (off Hawaii Hwy. 11) P.O. Box 53, Hawaii Volcanoes NP, Hawaii 96718. (808) 967-7321. 10 cabins with central bath. $40.
OUTSIDE THE PARK:
In Hilo, Hawaii 96720:
Country Club Apartment Hotel 121 Banyan Dr. (808) 935-7171. 148 units, 24 with kitchenettes. $45-$95. AC, restaurant.
Dolphin Bay Hotel 333 Iliahi St. (808) 935-1466. 18 units with kitchenettes. $72-$107.
Hawaii Naniloa Resorts 93 Banyan Dr. (800) 367-5360 or (808) 969-3333. 325 units. $100-$140. AC, pool, restaurant.
In Kailua-Kona, Hawaii 96740:
King Kamehameha Kona Beach Hotel 75-5660 Palani Rd. (800) 367-2111 or (808) 329-2911. 456 units. $120-$195. AC, pool, restaurant.
In Pahala, Hawaii 96777:
SeaMountain at Punaluu (on Hawaii Hwy. 11) P.O. Box 70. (800) 488-8301 or (808) 928-8301. 28 condominiums. $95-$170. Pool, tennis, golf.

For additonal lodgings contact the Chambers of Commerce of Hilo, 180 Kinoole St., Suite 118, Hilo, Hawaii 96720. (808) 935-7178; and Kailua-Kona, 75-5737 Kuakini Hwy., Kailua-Kona 96740. (808) 329-1758.

Excursions

Mauna Kea Observatory

Hilo, Hawaii

Mauna Kea, the world's highest island mountain, is the world's premier astronomical site. Clear, dry skies and a 13,796-foot elevation provide ideal viewing conditions; ten countries have built state-of-the-art telescopes on the dormant volcano's summit. The visitor center at 9,300 feet has astronomical displays and, Thurs.-Sun. p.m., stargazing from an 11-inch telescope. Saturday and Sunday tours to summit available for persons 16 and older who are not pregnant and have no heart or respiratory problems. Summit goers must provide their own vehicles equipped with four-wheel-drive. Five-mile trail to summit from visitor center. Open year-round. Located off Hawaii 200 (Saddle Road), about 55 miles from Hilo. (808) 961-2180.

Akaka Falls State Park

Honomu, Hawaii

This park's ancient legend bears a decidedly modern ring: It says that the god Akaka, fleeing across the canyon after his wife returned home unexpectedly and discovered his infidelity, slipped and fell off 442-foot Akaka Falls. A self-guided paved path leads visitors through a lush jungle ablaze with colorful and fragrant blossoms to viewpoints over these falls and the 100-foot cascading Kahuna Falls. 65 acres. No facilities other than the hiking trails. Located at the end of Akaka Falls Road, off Hawaii 220, about 15 miles north of Hilo. (808) 974-6200.

At sunset, Joshua trees etching the sky

Joshua Tree

California

Established October 31, 1994

794,000 acres

Two desert systems, the Mojave and the Colorado, abut within Joshua Tree, dividing California's southernmost national park into two arid ecosystems of profoundly contrasting appearance. The key to their differences is elevation. The Colorado, the western reach of the vast Sonoran Desert, thrives below 3,000 feet on the park's gently declining eastern flank, where temperatures are usually higher. Considered "low desert," compared to the loftier, wetter, and more vegetated Mojave "high desert," the Colorado seems sparse and forbidding. It begins at the park's midsection, sweeping east across empty basins stubbled with creosote bush. Occasionally decorated by "gardens" of flowering ocotillo and cholla cactus, it runs across arid Pinto Basin into a parched wilderness of broken rock in the Eagle and Coxcomb Mountains.

Many newcomers among the 1.3 million visitors who pass through each year are surprised by the abrupt transition between the Colorado and Mojave ecosystems. Above 3,000 feet, the Mojave section claims the park's western half, where giant branching yuccas thrive on sandy plains studded by massive granite monoliths and rock piles. These are among the most intriguing and photogenic geological phenomena found in California's many desert regions.

Joshua Tree's human history commenced sometime after the last Ice Age with the arrival of the Pinto people, hunter-gatherers who may have been part of the Southwest's earliest

cultures. They lived in Pinto Basin, which though inhospitably arid today, had a wet climate and was crossed by a sluggish river some 5,000 to 7,000 years ago. Nomadic groups of Indians seasonally inhabited the region when harvests of pinyon nuts, mesquite beans, acorns, and cactus fruit offered sustenance. Bedrock mortars—holes ground into solid rock and used to pulverize seeds during food preparation—are scattered throughout the Wonderland of Rocks area south of the Indian Cove camping site.

A flurry of late 19th-century gold-mining ventures left ruins; some are accessible by hiking trails, or unmaintained roads suited only to four-wheel-drive vehicles and mountain bikes.

How to Get There

The west and north park entrances are at the towns of Joshua Tree and Twentynine Palms. From Los Angeles, take I-10 east to Calif. 62 (Twentynine Palms Highway) to Twentynine Palms (about 140 miles total). The south entrance is located at Cottonwood Spring, approximately 25 miles east of Indio off I-10.

When to Go

All-year park. Temperatures are most comfortable in the spring and fall, with an average high and low of 85°F and 50°F. Winter brings cooler days, around 60°F, and freezing nights. Summers are hot, with midday temperatures frequently above 100°F, and ground temperatures reaching 180°F. The Mojave Desert zone on the park's western half is on average 11° cooler than the Colorado. In winter, snow may blanket the Mojave's higher elevations.

Spring blooming periods vary according to winter precipitation and spring temperatures, usually beginning in February at lower elevations and peaking park-wide in March and April, although cactuses may bloom into June. (Check with park headquarters.) For up-to-date recorded wildflower information, call (760) 767-4684 or (760) 346-5694.

How to Visit

The park's premier attractions, forests of giant branching yuccas known as Joshua trees, massive rock formations, fan palm oases, and seasonal gardens of cholla and ocotillo, can be enjoyed on a leisurely half-day auto tour that includes both "high" and "low" desert zones—although most of your time will be spent in your car. Scenic paved roads lead to viewpoints, all campgrounds, and trailheads. Roadside interpretive exhibits have pull-outs and parking areas, and offer insights into the region's complex desert ecology, wildlife, and human history.

If you plan to explore the park by mountain bike, you would be wise to avoid the main paved roads, which are narrow and without shoulders. You'll find far greater solitude and safety cycling the park's backcountry dirt roads, many of which, like those in **Queen Valley,** date from the area's 19th-century homestead and gold-mining era. Be sure to acquire reliable information from headquarters about your route, however, as soft sand and occasional steep climbs can make for arduous pedaling.

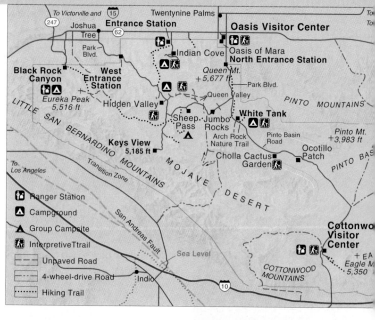

For a half-day visit starting from the park's northern boundary, take the **Park Boulevard loop** either from the town of Joshua Tree through the West Entrance Station, or from Twentynine Pines, by way of the North Entrance Station. If the air is clear (ask at the entrance about haze conditions), take the 20-minute side trip to 5,185-foot-high **Keys View,** which overlooks a vast panorama of arid desert basin and range stretching south into Mexico. If you are starting from Joshua Tree, return to Park Boulevard and continue east over **Sheep Pass** to **Jumbo Rocks,** turning right (south) onto Pinto Basin Road for the drive down into long vistas in the Colorado Desert zone. Be sure to stroll the self-guided nature trails through the **Cholla Cactus Garden** and the **Ocotillo Patch.**

Backtrack to Twentynine Palms and the **Oasis Visitor Center,** which features a small cactus garden and superb desert ecology interpretive displays. It adjoins the historic **Oasis of Mara** (one of five spring-fed oases within the park's boundaries), where Indians once found water, shade, food, and game. If you are starting from Twentynine Palms and the Oasis Visitor Center, proceed south as far as the Ocotillo Patch, then backtrack to Park Boulevard and follow it westward to Joshua Tree.

Park Boulevard

64 miles (including side trips); a half to full day

A scenic drive connecting the north and west entrances skirts the sparse Colorado low desert ecosystem, then climbs into the Joshua Tree forest and its surrounding plateau of mammoth rocks. Begin at the **Oasis Visitor Center** in Twentynine Palms. (Or, if entering from the south, begin at the **Cottonwood Visitor Center** and follow Pinto Basin Road north and east past the Ocotillo Patch and the Cholla Cactus Garden to the Oasis Visitor Center.) Both visitor centers provide insights into how plants and animals survive the region's withering heat and aridity, and how its unusual geology was formed, though the Oasis Visitor Center's interpretive displays are more extensive.

The Oasis Visitor Center adjoins the **Oasis of Mara,** a cluster of fan palms (the only palms native to the Southwest desert), Frémont cottonwood, arrow weed, and mesquite shrubs watered by a seeping spring. Take the ½-mile path to this scruffy bit of green, which once sustained Indian encampments and later slaked the thirst of prospectors and homesteaders. A minute's stroll leads to a shady respite amid the chatter of birds. (Birdwatchers

when rocks are aglow in warm pinks and yellows. On weekends, ask at a visitor center about ranger-led campfire talks, walks, and tours, or check campground bulletin boards.

Continue south from Twentynine Palms on Park Boulevard to the North Entrance Station. The road climbs, skirting the **Pinto Mountains** that rise to the east. Where the pavement forks (after about 5 miles), bear left onto Pinto Basin Road. You'll soon enter **Wilson Canyon** and the transition zone, where the Mojave and Colorado Desert ecosystems join. The sweep of **Pinto Basin** trending east is in fact an ancient dry lake bed, and a typical Sonoran Desert landscape dominated by the pale creosote bush.

Stroll through the **Cholla Cactus Garden,** a picturesque cluster about 6.5 miles south of the fork, and threaded by a short nature trail interestingly keyed to self-guided brochures provided there. Known as "jumping" cholla for the tendency of its spiny joints to break off and cling to hapless passersby, the crooked-arm cactus appears velvety but is actually covered by tiny, sharply piercing bristles.

Continue southeast about 2 miles to the **Ocotillo Patch,** where hundreds of the spindly Sonoran Desert plants seem to languish, their rigid gray spines wobbling skyward. After rains in March and April, their tips flame with dense bouquets of blood-red flowers, a life-saver for hummingbirds migrating north from Mexico (and a highlight of the flowering calendar).

may want to include a visit to **Cottonwood Springs,** an oasis sheltering many species and located about 1 mile from the Cottonwood Visitor Center at the south entrance.)

If your schedule allows a full day's visit, take time for short walks along nature trails that offer close-up looks at plant and animal life, or interesting terrain. (Park brochures describe trail highlights.) Consider starting early; sunlight playing across Joshua Tree's granite monoliths, peaks, and basins accentuates their contours and colors—especially at dawn and sunset—

Giant boulders at Jumbo Rocks campground

Backtrack northwest to the White Tank Campground and the **Arch Rock Nature Trail.** The easy ⅓-mile path to **Arch Rock** features interpretive information on how the surrounding geology and the natural arch were formed.

At the fork, turn left to rejoin Park Boulevard and enter the Mojave high desert. Westbound, you'll see mammoth granite formations rising from a sandy plateau. Some 800 million years in the making, worn by eons of weather into the contours of melting ice cream, the **Jumbo Rocks** are a product of this region's seismic restlessness—tectonic tumult evidenced by frequent small temblors that affect the flow of springs watering the park's oases.

Here visitors will likely see climbers scaling the monoliths, for Joshua Tree National Park contains one of America's most accessible, yet challenging, rock-climbing areas. Guidelines designed for safety and the protection of rock surfaces govern climbing within the park. Spectators gather in parking areas to watch the equipment-laden enthusiasts struggle hand-over-hand up seemingly impossible routes.

Keep an eye out for aptly named **Skull Rock,** which flanks the road as you continue west toward **Hidden Valley,** a scenic garden of huge piled-up boulders resembling animals, human faces, and abstract forms.

A popular picnic and camping area, this part of Joshua Tree is heavily populated by the park's trademark branching yucca. Named by early Mormon settlers who saw in their uplifted arms a symbol of the Biblical supplicant Joshua, *Yucca brevifolia* can reach 50 feet in height over a lifespan that may exceed 200 years. Some 25 bird species find protected nesting spots between its short, spiky leaves. The 1¼-mile **Hidden Valley Trail** follows a circuitous path through a stony maze to a "hidden" bowl where, according to local lore, rustlers once hid with their stolen cattle. The northern portion of this loop requires some boulder scrambling.

If you're not yet ready for a picnic, take the 6-mile scenic side trip up to **Keys View.** Just short of a mile high (5,185 feet), the mountain top is the park's premier vantage point for motorists. Smog and natural haze from the Los Angeles Basin sometimes obscure the horizon; however, clear days afford a splendid southerly panorama of Coachella Valley farmlands, the Salton Sea, and Sonoran Desert mountains in Mexico. Across the valley looms 10,804-foot Mount Jacinto, towering above Palm Springs.

Park Boulevard continues northwest through the Joshua tree forest, descending to the West Entrance Station and the town of Joshua Tree.

Information & Activities

Headquarters
74485 National Park Drive, Twentynine Palms, California 92277. Phone (619) 367-7511. www.nps.gov/jotr

Seasons & Accessibility
Open year-round.

Visitor & Information Centers
Park headquarters located at Oasis Visitor Center, off Calif. 62 near Twentynine Palms and the north entrance. Open daily except Christmas. Cottonwood Visitor Center, off I-10 at south entrance. Open daily except Christmas.

Entrance Fee
$10 per vehicle, good for seven consecutive days; $25 for annual pass.

Pets
Permitted on leashes. Not allowed on trails or in backcountry (more than 100 yards from the road). Must be attended at all times.

Facilities for Disabled
The Oasis Visitor Center's interpretive displays, garden, and bookstore are all wheelchair accessible, as are the ¼- and ½-mile loop trails to the adjoining Oasis of Mara. The Keys View wheelchair viewpoint is just below the summit. The Cap Rock Nature Trail (½-mile loop from parking area) and the Bajada Nature Trail (¼-mile loop) are also accessible. No campsites are officially wheelchair accessible, however the Belle or White Tank camping areas have accessible rest rooms.

Chuckwalla lizard

Things to Do
Free ranger-led activities held week-ends year-round, including tours to Keys Ranch homestead. Also, interpretive exhibits, self-guided cactus garden trails, auto touring, bicycling (on established roads only), hiking, rock climbing, horseback riding on approved trails, birdwatching. All-terrain vehicles and off-road motorized travel and bicycling prohibited.

Special Advisories
• Always carry water, even on short hikes. There are no potable water sources within the park. Potable water is available at the Oasis of Mara, at Black Rock and Cottonwood Camp-grounds, and at the Indian Cove Ranger Station. Recommended: One gallon per person per day, two gallons if hiking.
• Campfires are not allowed in the backcountry. Collecting vegetation, living or dead, is prohibited, so bring your own firewood.
• Rock climbers should regard all fixed protection (bolting, for example) found in place as unsafe. Motorized drilling is prohibited within park boundaries.
• Bolting not allowed in designated wilderness areas without permit. Use extreme caution around old mine workings. Never enter abandoned tunnels or shafts.
• Hikers should carry a compass and a topographic map. Established trails can be obscured by washes and animal routes. Park landscapes have few prominent features, disorienting even experienced backcountry hikers.
• Avoid camping in washes, which are subject to flash flooding, even from distant mountain cloudbursts.
• Archaeological sites and remains may not be disturbed in any way. This includes rock art, habitation sites, and cultural remains such as pottery vessels and sherds, projectile points, stone tools, and beads.

• Climbing within 50 feet of Native American rock art is prohibited.

Overnight Backpacking
Registration required at one of 12 backcountry boards. Check with rangers at entrance stations about current conditions and rules governing backcountry camping. A permit is required for horses. Call (619) 367-3523.

Campgrounds
Nine campgrounds, all with 14-day limit from September through May, and a 30-day limit from June through August. Open all year on a first-come, first-served basis. Fees for individuals and groups up to six: None to $10. Group camping (site maximums vary from 20 to 70) available at **Cottonwood, Indian Cove,** and **Sheep Pass** by reservation only. Call (800) 365-2267 or National Parks Reservation Service (see page 11). Fees from $10 to $30. Horses permitted at **Black Rock.**

Hotels, Motels, & Inns
(unless otherwise noted, rates are for 2 persons in a double room, high season)
In Twentynine Palms, Calif. 92277:
Best Western Gardens Motel 71487 Twentynine Palms Hwy. (619) 367-9141. 84 units, 12 with kitchenettes. $85. AC, pool.
Motel 6 72562 Twentynine Palms Hwy. (800) 466-8356. 67 units. $44. AC, pool, restaurant.
In Indio, Calif. 92201:
Quality Inn 43-505 Monroe Street. (760) 347-4044. 62 units. $99. AC, pool.
Royal Plaza Inn 82-347 Hwy. 111. (800) 228-9559 or (619) 347-0911. 99 units. $69-$110. AC, pool, restaurant.
In Yucca Valley, Calif. 92284:
Oasis of Eden Inn & Suites 56377 Twentynine Palms Hwy. (800) 606-6686. 40 units. $106-$199. AC, pool.
Yucca Inn 7500 Camino del Cielo. (619) 365-3311. 75 units. $49-$55. AC, pool.

For other lodgings contact Twentynine Palms Chamber of Commerce, 6455 Mesquite Ave., Unit A, Twentynine Palms, Calif 92384. (760) 367-3445.

Sequoia and Pacific dogwood in Giant Forest

Sequoia & Kings Canyon

California

*Established September 25, 1890;
March 4, 1940*

863,741 acres

Bigness—big trees and big canyons—
inspired the separate founding of each
of these parks. In 1943 Sequoia and
Kings Canyon National Parks began
to be jointly administered. The two
contiguous parks form one superpark
66 miles long and 36 miles at its
widest point.

Nearly every square mile of this vast
park is wilderness. A backpacker here
can hike to a spot that is farther from
a road than any other place in the 48
contiguous states. But visitors can easily reach Sequoia Park's famed attraction, the Giant Forest of sequoias.

Relatively few visitors hike any of the
parks' hundreds of miles of trails. Still,

there are enough backpackers to worry
officials, who protect the backcountry
by regulating the number of people
entering it.

Mount Whitney, at 14,494 feet
the highest peak in the United States
south of Alaska, rises at the border.
Backpackers coming in from the east
can get to Whitney in 1 or 2 days.
From the park's western trailheads,
backpackers reach it by a 70-mile, 8-
day trek across the park's snow-swept,
glacier-dotted heights.

Visitors are startled to learn that
the smoke they sometimes see rises
from "prescribed burning"—controlled fires deliberately set by
park employees to help the sequoias
by removing undergrowth. In the
past, when the park fought all fires,
brush and deadwood built up.
This fueled fires that imperiled
the sequoias, which resist flames

appreciate the rugged splendor, you must hike a trail. No east-west road crosses either park. But a drive-in visitor, in a day, can see sequoias in **Giant Forest,** along the **Generals Highway,** and in **Grant Grove.** A quiet walk in a grove of sequoias will give you more than a drive to named trees, which are constantly surrounded by shutterbugs.

Stay long enough to explore both vast parks. Drive to Kings Canyon's beautiful valley, **Cedar Grove.** On another day visit **Crystal Cave** and climb **Moro Rock.** Hike in Sequoia's spectacular **Mineral King** area.

Giant Forest & Grant Grove

48 miles; a full day

From **Ash Mountain Entrance, on Generals Highway,** drive 17 miles to **Giant Forest,** home of the **General Sherman Tree,** the world's largest tree. About 6 miles along the road from the Ash Mountain Entrance, stop to see the Indian exhibit at **Hospital Rock.** Indians lived here from prehistoric times until the 1870s, when the white man's diseases killed off the last of them. The Western Mono made flour from acorns—the most important staple food of California Indians. They crushed the acorns in small hollows gouged into streamside bedrock; you can see several such rock mortars at the exhibit.

The **Four Guardsmen,** a quartet of sequoias, stand as sentinels near the

at their bases but can die if fire attacks their crowns.

How to Get There

From Visalia (about 35 miles west), take Calif. 198 to Sequoia's Ash Mountain Entrance. From Fresno, take Calif. 180 to Kings Canyon's Big Stump Entrance. The only road entrance into the main part of Kings Canyon is a dead-end, summer-only extension of Calif. 180 into Cedar Grove. Airport: Fresno.

When to Go

Spring through fall is the best time for sequoia gazing. Generals Highway, which connects Sequoia and Kings Canyon, is open year-round except during heavy snows. From December to April, there are cross-country skiing and snowshoeing in the Giant Forest area and at Grant Grove.

How to Visit

The two immense parks challenge anyone planning a 1-day visit. To

Towering sequoia

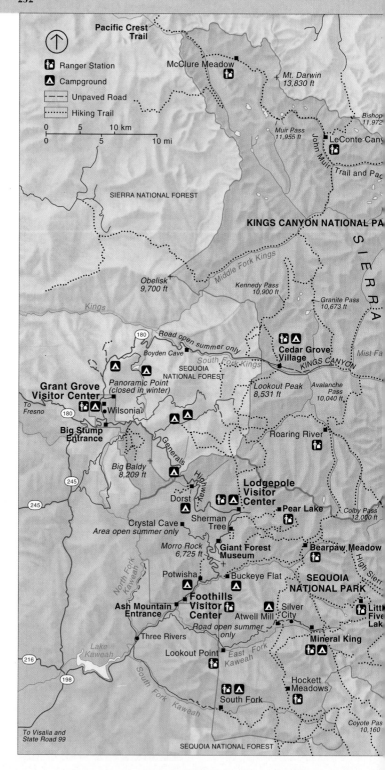

Pacific Crest Trail

⬆

🚹 Ranger Station

🔺 Campground

– – – Unpaved Road

· · · · · Hiking Trail

| 0 | 5 | 10 km |
| 0 | 5 | 10 mi |

McClure Meadow

Mt. Darwin
13,830 ft

Muir Pass
11,955 ft

Bishop
11,972

LeConte Canyon

John Muir Trail and Pac

SIERRA NATIONAL FOREST

KINGS CANYON NATIONAL PA

SIERRA

Obelisk
9,700 ft

Middle Fork Kings

Kennedy Pass
10,900 ft

Granite Pass
10,673 ft

Kings

Mist Fa

180
Road open summer only

Boyden Cave

South Fork Kings

SEQUOIA
NATIONAL FOREST

Cedar Grove
Village

KINGS CANYON

Grant Grove
Visitor Center

Panoramic Point
(closed in winter)

Lookout Peak
8,531 ft

Avalanche
Pass
10,040 ft

To
Fresno

180

Wilsonia

Big Stump
Entrance

Roaring River

Generals

Big Baldy
8,209 ft

245

Highway

Lodgepole
Visitor
Center

245

Dorst

Pear Lake

Colby Pass
12,000 ft

Crystal Cave
Area open summer only

Sherman
Tree

Morro Rock
6,725 ft

Giant Forest
Museum

Bearpaw Meadow

Potwisha

Buckeye Flat

SEQUOIA
NATIONAL PARK

High Sierr

Ash Mountain
Entrance

Foothills
Visitor
Center

Atwell Mill

Silver
City

Litt
Five
Lak

Three Rivers

Road open summer
only

East Fork Kaweah

Mineral King

North Fork Kaweah

216

Lake
Kaweah

Lookout Point

198

South Fork Kaweah

Hockett
Meadows

South Fork

Coyote Pas
10,160

To Visalia and
State Road 99

SEQUOIA NATIONAL FOREST

entrance to **Giant Forest.** Trails radiate from the star attraction, the General Sherman Tree, around 2,100 years old, $274\frac{9}{10}$ feet tall, and $102\frac{3}{5}$ feet in circumference, with a volume of 52,500 cubic feet. (In board feet, this is the equivalent of $119\frac{1}{3}$ miles of 1-by-12-inch planks.) A 13-story building would fit beneath its first large branch. The tree was named by a pioneer cattleman who had served in the Civil War under Gen. William Tecumseh Sherman.

The easy 2-mile **Congress Trail** (the name honors the institution that gave legal protection to the sequoias) takes 1 to 2 hours and begins at the base of the champion tree, where you can buy a self-guiding pamphlet. At stops along the way, you will see young sequoias (a mere 140 or so years old); sequoias scarred by fire but standing tall because their bark, thick and lacking resin, protects them; and fallen sequoias, not rotting because they contain tannin, which helps them resist decay.

Return to Generals Highway and begin the 30-mile drive to **Grant Grove** in Kings Canyon by heading northwest to Calif. 180. Turn east on Calif. 180. On your right a road loops in and out of Wilsonia, a private community.

Just beyond the **Grant Grove Visitor Center,** take the road on your left to **General Grant Tree Trail,** a $\frac{1}{2}$-mile loop leading to the **General Grant Tree** ($267\frac{2}{5}$ feet tall, $107\frac{3}{5}$ feet in circumference at ground). The name of the tree recalls the original 1890 name of the park, created to preserve General Grant Grove. To counteract lumbering, champions of the sequoias bought more and more land to expand the 4-square-mile grove. When **Kings Canyon** and its trees were added to the park system in 1940, sequoias within the boundaries were forever protected from logging.

On the trail are many giants saved by the park, along with a reminder of the years of casual havoc: **Centennial Stump,** a sequoia cut down for exhibition at the 1875 Centennial in Philadelphia. Near the park entrance is **Big Stump Trail** (1-mile loop), where stumps, logs, downed trees, and a pile of sawdust help you imagine the sequoia logging of the past and where regenerating trees grow into the giants of the future.

Woods Creek near Rae Lakes

Drive back to the visitor center and head east on the steep, narrow, 2½-mile road to **Panoramic Point** (no trailers or large vehicles allowed). From the parking lot, take the ¼-mile trail to the 7,520-foot ridge. Before you stretches the Sierra Nevada. A trailside diagram of the landscape names the mountains. You won't see Mount Whitney; the Great Western Divide blocks the view.

Cedar Grove

36 miles; a full day

Drive north and east on Generals Highway; from Grant Grove follow Calif. 180 for 30 miles through Sequoia NF. The road winds into the canyon of the **South Fork** of the **Kings River.** Stop at **Junction View** to gaze down on a wild river flanked by sheer canyon walls glistening in the sun. The road dead-ends at **Cedar Grove,** a mile-deep valley. Scouring streams began the carving of the valley, which got its U-shape from subsequent glaciers that

pushed into the canyon and widened the floor.

Incense-cedar, ponderosa pine, black oak, live oak, white fir, and sugar pine grow in the valley's flats. In the 1870s the area attracted stockmen as well as gold and silver prospectors. Even so, John Muir, who explored here in 1873, would still recognize this well-preserved high-country valley.

The **Cedar Grove Motor Nature Trail,** just beyond **Cedar Grove Village,** gives the drive-in visitor a tame tour on what had been a livestock trail. Better to park, get out, and walk, even for a short distance, to savor this beautiful hidden valley. The easy ½-mile **River Trail** takes you from the South Fork of the Kings River to **Roaring River Falls.** Back at the parking lot you can return to your car or continue on for a hike along the curves of the river. Cross a suspension bridge and climb a slight rise for a view of the valley. Retrace your steps to the bridge and take the **Zumwalt Meadow Trail,** a 1-mile loop.

Crystal Cave

18 miles; a half day

The cave temperature is a constant 48°F, so bring a jacket. Tickets must be purchased at either the Lodgepole or Foothills Visitor Centers. Take the Generals Highway south from Lodgepole Visitor Center. Turn right down the rough, summer-only road (no trailers or large vehicles) to **Crystal Cave.** The twisting 9-mile trip consumes about 45 dusty minutes. From the parking lot you walk a paved, steep path along a canyon wall, down to the entrance. Don't expect multicolored lights or tales of goblins; the 1-hour tours, conducted from 11 a.m. to 4 p.m., introduce you to a cave that got its name from an unusual geological phenomenon. The cave is formed of marble—instead of limestone—that underground water slowly dissolved and then redeposited as dazzling stalactites, stalagmites, and columns.

Moro Rock

4⅗ miles round-trip; a half day

Although you can drive to **Moro Rock,** a huge granite monolith, via the 2-mile **Moro Rock-Crescent Meadow Road** from Giant Forest Village, you get a better perception of its setting by hiking to it. Either way, try to be there at sunset when the view is spectacular. The 2-mile **Moro Rock Trail** begins near Giant Forest Museum and quickly leads you away from the throngs. About 1⅓ miles along the trail, a short path veers off to **Hanging Rock,** a high granite stage for viewing Sierra Nevada scenery.

Return to the trail and continue to the base of Moro Rock. Here you start climbing a stone stairway of nearly 400 steps (and several welcome spots for resting). Your 300-foot ascent takes you to an elevation of 6,725 feet, about 4,000 feet above the canyon floor. From here you can look down on the tops of the sequoias you craned at from the ground. On clear days you can see the Coast Ranges, more than 100 miles west.

When you return from the summit, you can retrace your steps on the Moro Rock Trail or return to the Generals Highway via the 2⅓-mile Soldiers Trail, named for the US Cavalry troopers who patrolled the sequoias before the Park Service's rangers took over the task.

Mineral King

50 miles round-trip; at least a full day

Three miles north of the town of Three Rivers, near the Ash Mountain Entrance, is the sign for **Mineral King,** in 1978 Sequoia's last major addition. It was named in the 1870s by gold prospectors who gained little more than unfulfilled dreams from it. In the 1960s dreams of a ski resort also failed to come true because of public opposition.

Turn off Calif. 198 onto a narrow, twisting, 25-mile road. (One driver counted 29 turns in a single mile.) To avoid driving it twice in one grueling day, plan your schedule so that you'll be able to stay at least a night. But, if you must do it in a single day, start early. Mineral King is a hiker's paradise. And the road is the secret to the paradise's solitude. "The road is terrible," one grinning hiker said. "And we hope it stays that way."

During the summer, stop at the **Mineral King Ranger Station** and check to see whether a ranger-guided walk is scheduled that day. Or take a hike on your own. Get a map at the station, find a legal parking place, and select a trail. Remember that all trails here begin at altitudes of at least 7,500 feet and climb steeply. If you are not acclimated to the high elevations here, you may suffer altitude sickness.

A good hike for beginners just getting their legs in shape is **Eagle Lake Trail,** which starts at the Eagle-Mosquito Parking Area. This trail starts gently, then begins to get steep near **Spring Creek,** which sprouts from the mountainside. Every switchback treats visitors to an overlook with a stunning view. If you keep your eyes open, you may catch sight of marmots, which sometimes stand up and watch back, and tiny pikas, which whistle and scurry around. After a 2-mile climb, you reach the **Eagle Sink Holes,** where water disappears just as suddenly as the creek appeared. Here you can turn around and start down or continue up another 1½ miles to **Eagle Lake,** a tarn.

Information & Activities

Headquarters
Ash Mountain, 47050 Generals Hwy, Three Rivers, California 93271. Phone (209) 565-3341. www.nps.gov/seki

Seasons & Accessibility
Park open year-round. Roads to Mineral King (Sequoia) and to Cedar Grove (Kings Canyon) closed in winter; Generals Highway from Lodgepole to Grant Grove may close after heavy snowstorms; also at night in winter. Call (209) 565-3341 for current weather and road information.

Visitor & Information Centers
Sequoia: Lodgepole Visitor Center and Giant Forest Museum, both in the Giant Forest area; Foothills Visitor Center in Ash Mountain, where Calif. 198 enters park; Mineral King Ranger Station in south of park. Foothills open daily all year; others open in winter, reduced hours. **Kings Canyon**: Grant Grove Visitor Center open daily all year; Cedar Grove open daily in summer; on Calif. 180. For visitor information call (209) 565-3341.

Entrance Fees
$10 per vehicle per week, good for multiple entries. $5 per person on bus, foot, bicycle, motorcycle.

Facilities for Disabled
Visitor centers are wheelchair accessible, as are some trails in Grant Grove and Giant Forest.

Things to Do
Free naturalist-led activities (many offered in summer only): nature walks and talks, night sky watches, children's programs, evening programs, snowshoe walks. Also available, Crystal Cave tours, nature center, fishing (license needed), horseback trail rides, pack trips, cross-country skiing.

Overnight Backpacking
Free permits required. Reservations for specific trails and dates must be made by mail. (Fee charged for reservations.) A few permits issued on departure day, first come, first served. Information (209) 565-3341.

Campgrounds
Sequoia: seven campgrounds, 14-day limit mid-June to mid-September. **Lodgepole, Potwisha,** and **South Fork** open all year. Others open spring to fall, depending on weather. First come, first served, except **Lodgepole** and Dorst which require reservations in advance through National Parks Reservation Service (see page 11) mid-May to mid-Oct. Fees $6-$12 per night. Showers near **Lodgepole,** closed in winter. RV sites at **Dorst, Lodgepole,** and **Potwisha;** no hookups. Food services available in park.

Kings Canyon: seven campgrounds, 14-day summer limit. **Azalea** open all year, others late April to mid-Sept. First come, first served. Fees $14 per night. Showers nearby. Tent and RV sites; no hookups. Reservations required for group campsites; write Sunset/Canyon View Group Sites, Box 926, Kings Canyon National Park, CA 93633. Food services available in park.

Hotels, Motels, & Inns
(unless otherwise noted, rates are for 2 persons in a double room, high season)
INSIDE THE PARKS:
For the following lodges In Sequoia, call (888) 252-5757:
Bearpaw Meadow Camp Six group tent cabins, central showers. $250, includes meals. Mid-June–mid-Sept. Wuksachi Village 102 units. $134. Restaurant, gift shop.
For the following lodges in Kings Canyon, call (559) 335-5500:
Cedar Grove Lodge 21 units. $92. AC, rest. May–Oct. **Grant Grove Lodge** 45 units. 33 cabins, $45-$75; 12 summer tent cabins, $35. Rest. **Stoney Creek Lodge** 11 units. $106. Restaurant. Mid-May–mid-October.
OUTSIDE THE PARKS:
In Three Rivers, Calif. 93271:
Best Western Holiday Lodge (40105 Sierra Dr./Calif. 198) P.O. Box 129. (209) 561-4119. 54 units. $85. AC, pool. **Lazy J Ranch Motel** 39625 Sierra Dr. (800) 341-8000 or (209) 561-4449. 18 units, 7 with kitchenettes. $55. AC, pool. **The River Inn** 45176 Sierra Dr. (209) 561-4367. 11 units. $63. AC.

Excursions

Sequoia National Forest
Porterville, California

Thirty-eight groves of giant sequoias, including the largest tree in any national forest, are only part of the attractions here. Four stretches of Wild and Scenic Rivers and six wilderness areas provide recreational challenges. 1,123,100 acres. Facilities include over 2,000 campsites, hiking, boating, white-water rafting, climbing, bicycling, fishing, horseback riding, hunting, picnic areas, scenic drives, winter sports, handicapped access. Open year-round. Adjoins Sequoia & Kings Canyon National Parks on south, west, and north. (209) 784-1500.

Pinnacles National Monument
Paicines, California

Rising abruptly from gentle hill country, the spires and crags of the Pinnacles formation are remains of a volcanic mountain formed some 200 miles to the south. Pulled north and west by the San Andreas Rift, the Pinnacles are still in migration. Hiking trails, ranging from easy to extremely strenuous, take visitors from chaparral-covered slopes, through caves, to the high peaks. 24,154 acres. Facilities include climbing, picnic areas, handicapped access. Visitor center near east entrance off Calif. 25, about 130 miles west of Sequoia & Kings Canyon NPs. (408) 389-4485.

Inyo National Forest
Bishop, California

Inyo boasts Mount Whitney, at 14,494 feet the highest peak in the lower 48 states; the spectacular saline Mono Lake; and bristlecone pines, earth's oldest living things. Also contains parts of seven wilderness areas, notably the John Muir and Ansel Adams areas. Two million acres. 73 campgrounds, hiking, boating, boat ramp, climbing, bicycling, fishing, horseback riding, hunting, picnic areas, scenic drives, winter sports, water sports. Open year-round; most campsites open May-October. Visitor center at Mammoth Lakes on Calif. 203. (619) 873-2400.

Wintry Yosemite Valley; at left, El Capitan

Yosemite

California

Established October 1, 1890

747,956 acres

In a high-country meadow two hikers crouch near the edge of a mirroring lake and watch a pika as it harvests blades of grass for a nest deep within a huge rock pile. When they resume walking, there is no other person in sight for as far as they can see. And on this sparkling summer's day, the view seems endless.

In the valley's crowded mall, families stroll by, eating ice cream, dodging bicycles. People pile in and out of buses. Shoppers hunt for souvenirs. Kids hang around a pizza place. Rock climbers, coils of rope slung over their shoulders, swap stories over beers on a patio. On this summer's day about 14,000 people are in Yosemite Village.

Both the solitude of the alpine ridge and the throngs of the valley are part of the experience when you visit Yosemite National Park. "No temple made with hands can compare with Yosemite," wrote naturalist John Muir, whose crusading led to the creation of the park. To this temple come four million visitors a year. And about 90 percent of them go to the valley, a mile-wide, 7-mile-long canyon cut by a river, then widened and deepened by glacial action. Walled by massive domes and soaring pinnacles, it covers about one percent of the park. In summer, the concentration of automobiles brings traffic jams and air pollution.

Beyond the valley some 800 miles of marked trails offer hikers easy jaunts or grueling tests of endurance in the High Sierra wilderness. Even the casual visitor can explore this solitude without getting outfitted for a backpack expedition.

When to Go

All-year park. Avoid holiday weekends. Expect filled campgrounds from June through August and some crowding in late spring and early fall. Be sure you have reserved accommodations before attempting an overnight visit. You will find skiing and other winter activities in the Badger Pass Ski Area from about Thanksgiving to mid-April.

How to Visit

When a visitor asked a Yosemite ranger what he would do if he had only a day to visit the park, the ranger answered, "I'd weep." If you must zip through this huge park in a day, begin with **Yosemite Valley.** But even a dawn-to-dusk, one-day visit hardly allows enough time for more than a tour of the valley plus a look at one or two of the park's other major areas, such as the vistas from **Glacier Point** (in winter, road closed beyond the ski area) and the sequoias of the **Mariposa Grove.** As an alternative or on another day between late May and early November, take the High Sierra **Tioga Road** to explore the park's alpine country. Better still, stay long enough to get beyond the crowds and discover the sense of seclusion this great park can give you.

The park, roughly the size of Rhode Island, is a United Nations World Heritage site. Here, in five of the seven continental life zones, live the mule deer and chipmunks of the valley and the marmots and pikas of the heights; the brush rabbit and chaparral of the near desert; the dogwood and warblers of mid-elevation forests; the red and Jeffrey pine of mile-high forests; the dwarf willow and matted flowers of Yosemite's majestic mountains.

How to Get There

From Merced (about 70 miles away): Follow Calif. 140 to the Arch Rock Entrance. Also from the west: Take Calif. 120 to the Big Oak Flat Entrance. From the south, via Fresno: Calif. 41 takes you to the South Entrance. From the northeast, via Lee Vining: Follow Calif. 120 to the Tioga Pass Entrance (closed early to mid-November to late May). Trains stop at Merced; check with Amtrak about connecting buses to Yosemite. Airports: Fresno and Merced.

Yosemite Valley

12 miles; at least a half to full day

Don't add to the traffic congestion by driving the heavily used one-way valley roads. Park at one of the lots along the shuttle bus route and take the free bus, which loops through the east end of the valley. (See inset map on pages 262-263.) You can also explore the valley on a rented bike or on foot. Or, buy a ticket for a 2-hour guided tram tour. (The open-air trams also venture out on moonlit nights and glide through the ghostly light that bathes the valley.)

If you're traveling by shuttle bus, get off at the **Valley Visitor Center** in **Yosemite Village,** where a short slide presentation introduces Yosemite's history, grandeur, and geology. For an easy stroll in an oasis of quiet, look for **Cook's Meadow** just south of the visitor center. The trail begins at the west end of the mall; pick up a self-guiding

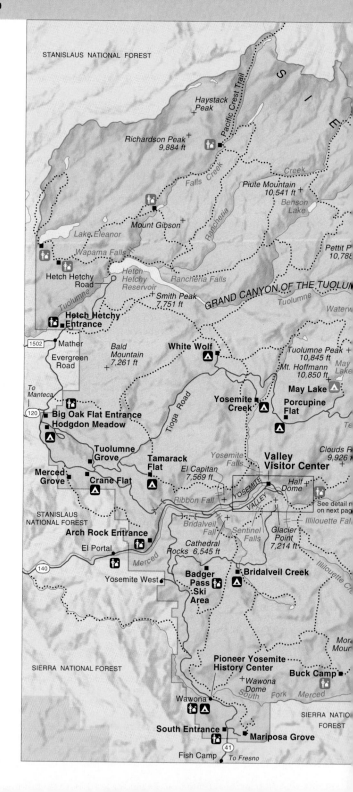

STANISLAUS NATIONAL FOREST

Haystack Peak

Richardson Peak
9,884 ft

Piute Mountain
10,541 ft

Benson Lake

Pacific Crest Trail

Falls

Creek

Creek

Rancheria

Mount Gibson

Lake Eleanor

Wapama Falls

Pettit P
10,788

Hetch Hetchy
Reservoir

Rancheria Falls

GRAND CANYON OF THE TUOLUM

Hetch Hetchy Road

Tuolumne

Tuolumne

Waterw

Hetch Hetchy Entrance

Smith Peak
7,751 ft

1502

Mather

Evergreen Road

Bald Mountain
7,261 ft

White Wolf

Tuolumne Peak
10,845 ft

Mt. Hoffmann
10,850 ft

May Lake

To Manteca

120

Big Oak Flat Entrance
Hodgdon Meadow

Tioga Road

Yosemite Creek

Porcupine Flat

May Lake

Te

Tuolumne Grove

Tamarack Flat

Yosemite Falls

Clouds R
9,926

Merced Grove

Crane Flat

El Capitan
7,569 ft

Valley Visitor Center

Half Dome

STANISLAUS NATIONAL FOREST

Ribbon Fall

YOSEMITE

See detail
on next pa

VALLEY

Arch Rock Entrance

Bridalveil Fall

Sentinel Falls

Glacier Point
7,214 ft

Illilouette Fal

El Portal

Cathedral Rocks 6,545 ft

Merced

Illilouette Cr

Yosemite West

Badger Pass Ski Area

Bridalveil Creek

Yosemite West

Mor
Mour

Pioneer Yosemite History Center

Buck Camp

SIERRA NATIONAL FOREST

Wawona Dome

South Fork

Merced

Wawona

SIERRA NATIO
FOREST

South Entrance

Mariposa Grove

Fish Camp

41

To Fresno

Yosemite Falls above meadows of cow parsnip

brochure. Deer and human sometimes encounter each other here. Keep your distance.

Walk around the nearby **Indian Village of Ahwahnee**, where exhibits and bark houses evoke the life of the valley's earlier dwellers. Visit the **Indian Cultural Exhibit** to see the baskets and other works of art produced by Yosemite area tribes.

At the bustling village shops you can find just about what you would find in any resort-town mall. But if you want to see the park, don't tarry here.

Get back on the bus and travel to the **Yosemite Falls** shuttle bus stop. The upper, middle, and lower falls form the highest waterfall in North America (2,425 feet) and the second highest in the world. A quarter-mile walk takes you to the base of **Lower Yosemite Fall.** If you have the stamina and another full day, take the strenuous 3 ½-mile hike to **Upper Yosemite Fall,** where you will be rewarded with spectacular valley views away from the crowds. (Look for the trailhead behind the Camp 4 parking lot.)

Reboard the bus, and crane your neck for other scenic wonders. And get off when you want to absorb them; you will not have to wait long for another bus. On the 3,593-foot vertical wall of **El Capitan** you may spot the tiny figures of climbers. During their ascent, which may take days, they sleep in slings hanging from the cliff. After looping east you'll pass **Sentinel Rock** and then **Glacier Point,**

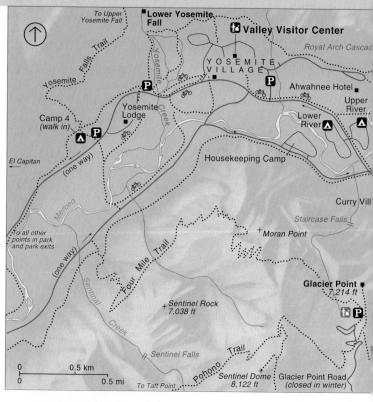

Cathedral Peak, near Tuolumne Meadows

Steller's jay

both giant granite blocks shaped by glaciers. (An arduous hike up **Four Mile Trail** takes you in three or four hours to Glacier Point's breathtaking vistas; for the trailhead, get off the bus at Yosemite Lodge and walk behind it to Southside Drive, then west a quarter mile to road marker V18.)

If you're still on the shuttle bus, alight at the stop near the **Happy Isles Nature Center.** After a walk around these two bridge-linked river islands, consider hiking the moderately strenuous 1½-mile trail to the top of 317-foot **Vernal Fall.** From higher up this trail, you can also see **Nevada Fall** with its 594-foot cascade. Massive **Half Dome,** a cracked block of gray granite gnawed by a glacier, soars 4,733 feet, its round face dominating this part of the valley.

A gentle hike from the next shuttle bus stop takes you to lovely **Mirror Lake** a mile away; a three-mile trail loops around it and above it. In spring and early summer, the lake's serene surface reflects stunning mountain scenery; during the summer, most of

Snow Creek
Trail

+Ahwiyah Point

Washington Column +

Mirror Lake/Meadow
4,094 ft

ROYAL
ARCHES

Half Dome ■
8,842 ft

Group
Camp

Tenaya   Creek

■Stables

Merced

▲
**Upper
Pines**

Mount Broderick +
6,706 ft

Happy Isles
Nature Center
4,035 ft ■

+Grizzly Peak

Liberty Cap
7,076 ft+

Emerald
Pool

To Half Dome and
Tuolumne Meadows

Vernal Fall ■

Mist Trail

Nevada Fall ■

John   Trail

Muir

Panorama
Trail

👤 Ranger Station
👤 Ranger Station (summer only)
▲ Campground
🅿 Parking
⬜ Shuttlebus and Bicycles only
🚲 Bikeway and Foot Trail

Eroded granite atop Sentinel Dome

its contents evaporate.

As you turn back toward Yosemite
Village, you'll pass the **Royal Arches,**
glacier-carved granite shells. You will
see the full spectrum of Yosemite
accommodations along the shuttle
bus route: from tents, trailers, and
clusters of concrete shelters to comfortable lodges, cabins, and a luxury
hotel—the Ahwahnee.

Glacier Point &
Mariposa Grove

52 miles one way; a half to full day

Leave the valley by taking Calif. 41
(the Wawona Road) to the **Wawona
Tunnel.** Park at the turnout at the tunnel's eastern end and walk over to the
Tunnel View Overlook to see what has

Staghorn lichens on conifer

Wildflowers at Tuolumne Meadows

been called the most photographed vista on earth. Spread before you is a granite panorama encompassing El Capitan, Half Dome, Sentinel Rock, **Cathedral Rocks,** and 620-foot **Bridalveil Fall,** in the late afternoon a scrim of shimmering rainbows. About 7 miles beyond the tunnel, turn left on the **Glacier Point Road** (in winter, closed beyond the ski area). The 16-mile road, flanked by fir-and-pine forests, ends in a parking lot. Walk about 300 yards to the first of several overlooks on Glacier Point, which thrusts 3,214 feet above the valley, providing an enormous stage for a scenic spectacular of lights and shadows. Mirror Lake lies below; Half Dome looms across; Vernal Fall and Nevada Fall hang like white tassels in the distance.

Return to the intersection of Calif. 41 and drive south 13 miles to **Wawona,** site of a hotel, golf course, and other facilities. Stop at the **Pioneer Yosemite History Center,** where, in summer, visitors enter restored buildings and chat about the past with costumed interpreters who portray such real people as a cavalry trooper, a 19th-century homesteader, and a mountaineer. From conversations with these players you learn Yosemite Valley's modern history, which began in 1851, when members of the Mariposa Battalion were tracking down Indians accused of raiding nearby trading posts. Foothill Miwok called Miwok living in the valley "*Yohemite,*" which means "some of them are killers." Thinking that this

was the Indians' name, the whites gave an approximation of it to the valley.

Word of the radiantly beautiful valley spread quickly, and the first tourists arrived in 1855. They were soon followed by homesteaders and hotelkeepers. Next came the nation's early conservationists, who campaigned to protect not only the valley but also a grove of giant sequoias.

Return to Calif. 41 and continue south. At the **South Entrance** continue straight to Yosemite's other long-cherished feature, the **Mariposa Grove.** From early May to late October you can take a guided tram tour of the grove's giant sequoias ($7 adult, $4 child). Or, you can walk among them at any time of year.

On June 30, 1864, President Lincoln took time out from the Civil War to sign a bill granting both the valley and this grove to the State of California. Never before had a nation set aside land as a wilderness preserve. Yosemite became a national park in 1890, although not until 1906 did California formally give the original grants back to the federal government. More land was added in 1913, the year automobiles were again allowed in the park after a ban.

The best known of the grove's more than 200 giant sequoias is the **Grizzly Giant,** whose estimated age, 2,700 years, makes it one of the oldest living sequoias. A trail takes you past the **Fallen Monarch;** its shallow roots help explain why winds sometimes topple these giants. Another fallen star, the **Wawona Tunnel Tree,** recalls another

Mule deer in Yosemite Valley

era. The living sequoia, gutted in 1881 to make a drive-through tree for horse-drawn wagons, became a photogenic attraction for generations of automobile travelers. The tree toppled in 1969. The decision not to cut a hole in another tree symbolized the dawning of an ecologically enlightened age.

Tioga Road & Tuolumne Meadows

124 miles round-trip; at least a full day

Take the **Big Oak Flat Road,** a modern version of an old mining town road, west out of the valley for 9 miles to 6,200-foot **Crane Flat** (a local term for "meadow") and turn right onto **Tioga Road,** which climbs into an alpine world of snowy peaks, crystal lakes, wind-tousled meadows, and relatively few people. The road (closed in winter) crosses the park. Even in July you may see snow alongside the road. Stop at the frequent turnouts for mag-

nificent views and interpretive signs that explain the geology behind the splendor. Gauge your time and gasoline. The nearest gas station on this winding, climbing mountain road is 1 mile east of the **Tuolumne Meadows Visitor Center,** 55 miles from **Yosemite Valley.**

At the visitor center are **Tuolumne Meadows,** which, millions of years ago, were under a sea of ice more than 2,000 feet deep. Wildflowers—among them Jeffrey shooting stars, Lewis paintbrushes, monkeyflowers, and marsh marigolds—carpet this High Sierra realm in spring and summer. Trails of varying difficulty branch out here and elsewhere along the road. Some trails link five commercially run High Sierra camps with showers and dining halls (reservations required). The camps are spaced 8 to 10 miles apart.

The road climbs to 9,945-foot **Tioga Pass,** highest automobile pass in California, at the park's eastern boundary. At a trailhead here you can take a ½-day alpine hike that rewards you with glimpses of both beauty and history. The 2½-mile trail climbs sharply from 9,945 feet to about 10,500, then descends to **Middle Gaylor Lake,** a gem set in a broad meadow prowled by marmots and ground squirrels. The trail again winds upward, first to **Upper Gaylor Lake,** then to a surprise: the ruins of a stone cabin, rusting bits of machinery, and half-filled shafts—relics of a failed 19th-century silver mine.

Information & Activities

Headquarters
P.O. Box 577, Yosemite National Park, CA 95389. Phone (209) 372-0200. www.nps.gov/yose

Seasons & Accessibility
Park open year-round. Tioga (Calif. 120 east) and Glacier Point Roads closed by snow from about mid-November to late May. Call (209) 372-0200 for recorded conditions. In winter, call (209) 372-8437 for Badger Pass ski information.

Free shuttle buses operate in the valley year-round and at Wawona and Tuolumne Meadows in summer.

Visitor & Information Centers
Valley Visitor Center open all year. Tuolumne Meadows Visitor Center near Tioga Pass Entrance open summer only. Information also available at Happy Isles Nature Center, in valley, and at Big Oak Flat Entrance on Calif. 120 at western edge of park, both open spring through fall; and at Wawona Information Station, open summer-fall. For information call (209) 372-0200.

Entrance Fee
$20 per car per week.

Pets
Not permitted in buildings, backcountry, on beaches, or trails.

Facilities for Disabled
Visitor centers, the nature and art centers, and some trails are wheelchair accessible. Free brochure.

Things to Do
Free naturalist-led activities: day and evening walks and talks, hikes, camera walks, children's and evening programs, living history; Indian cultural interpretation. Also, auto tape tours, bus and tram tours, films, plays, concerts, art and photography classes, museums, horseback riding—call (209) 372-8348—climbing, fishing, swimming, ice-skating, downhill and cross-country skiing.

Overnight Backpacking
Free permit required; issued first come, first served; apply up to 24 hours in advance of trip to a park wilderness permit station. Advance reservations available by mail; write wilderness office at park address. Call (209) 372-0740 for more information.

Campgrounds
Thirteen campgrounds; in summer, 7-day to 14-day limits; other times some have 30-day limit. Four open all year; others open mid-spring to mid-fall or summer only. Reservations through National Parks Reservation Service (see page 11) required year-round for all in the valley, except Camp 4, for **Hodgdon Meadow** spring through fall, and for Crane Flat and half of **Tuolumne Meadows** in summer. Fees $3-$15 per night. Most have RV sites, w/o hook-ups. Four group campgrounds; reserve through National Parks Reservation Service.

Hotels, Motels, & Inns
(unless otherwise noted, rates are for 2 persons in a double room, high season)
INSIDE THE PARK:
Yosemite Concession Services Corp., 5410 East Home Ave., Fresno, Calif. 93727, operates the following. Reservations: (209) 252-4848. **The Ahwahnee** (Yosemite Valley) 123 units. $279. AC, pool, rest. **Curry Village** (Yosemite Valley) 18 rooms; 80 cabins; 427 tent-cabins. $40-$100. Pool, rest. **High Sierra Camps** 5 camps with tent-cabins. Accessible by hiking trail only. Guided trips avail. $90 per person and up. Late June-Labor Day. Reserve by mail Sept.-Nov. **Tuolumne Meadows Lodge** (8,600 ft., at Tuolumne Meadows). 69 tent-cabins, central showers. $48-$53. Rest. Open summer. **Wawona Hotel** (Calif. 41, 27 miles south of valley) (209) 375-6556. 104 rooms, 50 private baths. $94-$129. Pool, rest. Open all year. **White Wolf Lodge** (Tioga Road) 4 cabins, private baths; 24 tent-cabins, central bath. $45-$71. Rest. Open summer. **Yosemite Lodge** (Yosemite Valley) 495 rooms/cabins, some with private baths. $100-$125. Pool, rest. Also, **Redwoods Guest Cottages** (Chilnualna Falls Rd.) P.O. Box 2085, Wawona Station, Calif. 95389. (209) 375-6666. 133 units with kitchens. $140-$552.

Excursions

Stanislaus National Forest
Sonora, California

This High Sierra forest offers an array of recreational activities—from white-water rafting on the Wild and Scenic Tuolumne River to trout fishing on timbered Alpine Lake. Contains parts of three wilderness areas. 898,322 acres. Facilities: 1,143 campsites, hiking, boating, boat ramp, fishing, horseback riding, hunting, off-road-vehicle routes, scenic drives, winter sports, water sports. Open all year; backcountry open June-October. Most campsites open May-October. Adjoins Yosemite NP on north and east. Information at office at 19777 Greenley Rd. (off Calif. 108) in Sonora. (209) 532-3671.

Devils Postpile National Monument
Mammoth Lakes, California

Surrounded by the Inyo National Forest, this monument boasts a spectacular formation of basalt columns 60 feet high, which were born of the fire of volcanic eruptions and carved by the ice of overriding glaciers. At Rainbow Falls, water plunges 101 feet over a rhyodacite cliff. 798 acres. Facilities include 21 campsites (open July-Oct.), hiking, fishing, shuttle bus. Open July-Oct. Off Calif. 203 about 40 miles from Yosemite NP. June-Oct. (760) 934-2289; Nov.–May (760) 872-4881.

Sierra National Forest
Mariposa, California

Like the Stanislaus NF to the north, Sierra offers both rugged backcountry and developed recreational facilities. Contains parts of five wilderness areas, a stretch of white water on the Kings River, groves of giant sequoias, and the mountain-ringed Mammoth Pool Reservoir. 1,303,037 acres. Facilities include 1,500 campsites, food services, hiking, boating, boat ramp, bicycling, fishing, horseback riding, hunting, picnic areas, water sports, winter sports, handicapped access. Open all year; some backcountry areas closed in winter. Most campsites open May–Oct. Adjoins Yosemite NP. Office at 1600 Toll House Rd. Clovis. (559) 297-0707.

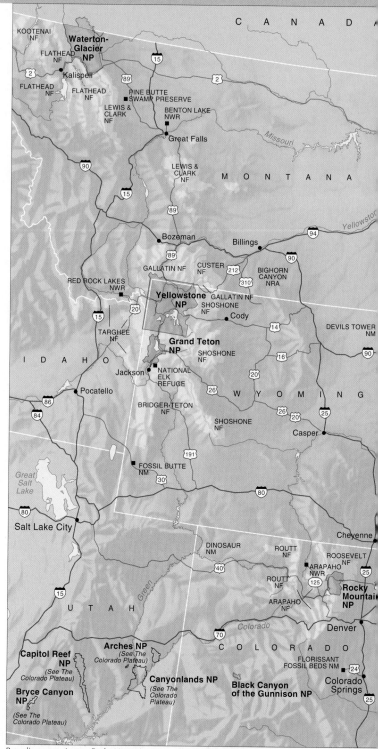

CANADA

KOOTENAI
NF

Waterton-
Glacier
NP

FLATHEAD
NF

Kalispell

FLATHEAD
NF

FLATHEAD
NF

LEWIS &
CLARK
NF

PINE BUTTE
SWAMP PRESERVE

BENTON LAKE
NWR

Great Falls

Missouri

LEWIS &
CLARK
NF

M O N T A N A

Yellowstone

Bozeman

Billings

GALLATIN NF

CUSTER
NF

212

BIGHORN
CANYON
NRA

94

90

RED ROCK LAKES
NWR

310

Yellowstone
NP

GALLATIN NF

SHOSHONE
NF

Cody

14

DEVILS TOWER
NM

TARGHEE
NF

Grand Teton
NP

SHOSHONE
NF

16

90

I D A H O

Jackson

NATIONAL
ELK
REFUGE

26

W Y O M I N G

20

Pocatello

BRIDGER-TETON
NF

SHOSHONE
NF

26
20

25

Casper

86

84

191

FOSSIL BUTTE
NM

30

80

Great
Salt
Lake

Cheyenne

80

Salt Lake City

DINOSAUR
NM

ROUTT
NF

ROOSEVELT
NF

ARAPAHO
NWR

25

40

ROUTT
NF

125

Rocky
Mountain
NP

15

Green

ARAPAHO
NF

U T A H

Colorado

70

Denver

Capitol Reef
NP
*(See The
Colorado Plateau)*

Arches NP
*(See The
Colorado Plateau)*

C O L O R A D O

FLORISSANT
FOSSIL BEDS NM

24

Canyonlands NP
*(See The
Colorado
Plateau)*

Black Canyon
of the Gunnison NP

Colorado
Springs

Bryce Canyon
NP

*(See The
Colorado Plateau)*

25

Preceding pages: Aspens, Rocky Mountains

0   50   100 km

0   50   100 mi

This map plots all the U.S. national parks, plus the Excursions sites featured in this book.

CROSBY WETLAND MANAGEMENT DISTRICT ■

LOSTWOOD NWR
8
2
Minot

N O R T H
D A K O T A

Theodore Roosevelt NP
200
LAKE ILO NWR

Glendive   Belfield

94

LITTLE MISSOURI NAT. GRASSLAND

Bismarck

85

S O U T H
D A K O T A

BLACK HILLS NF

MT. RUSHMORE NAT. MEMORIAL

Rapid City

JEWEL CAVE NM
79
Custer

BUFFALO GAP NAT. GRASSLAND

90

Kadoka

Wind Cave NP
Hot Springs
Badlands NP

BUFFALO GAP NAT. GRASSLAND

385

North Platte

N E B R A S K A

80

76

70

K A N S A S

The Rocky Mountains

Craggy peaks capped by glimmering glaciers, fields run riot with wild flowers, lakes as smooth and blue as a summer sky—these images from the Rocky Mountains epitomize for many just what a national park should look like. Not surprisingly, four of the Rockies' parks rank among the country's most visited.

Yet this region offers more than mountains, since the forces that created the peaks contoured neighboring landscapes as well. The Black Hills of South Dakota uplifted along with the Rocky Mountains some 70 million years ago, cracking as they buckled upward. Enlarged by acidic groundwater, the cracks eventually produced the numerous underground passageways of Wind Cave. Streams flowing from the young Rockies also laid down the colorful mud that rivers would later carve into the buttes and gorges of the Dakota badlands, showcased in Badlands and Theodore Roosevelt National Parks.

The Rockies' parks and forests preserve the spirit of America's western frontier not only in their rugged scenery, but also in historic ranches, ghost towns, and in their abundance of wildlife. Yellowstone and Waterton-Glacier—together with their surrounding public lands—remain two of the last strongholds of the grizzly bear. In some of the parks visitors can watch elk, bighorn sheep, mule deer, and remnants of the great bison herds that once thundered across the Great Plains.

Rockies parks provide case studies in how wilderness manages itself. In Yellowstone, for instance, the visitor can get excellent glimpses of natural recovery in the wake of the 1988 fires. Less encouraging are the real estate development and plans for oil and gas drilling on the fringes of some parks. Such activities can shrink the habitats of wide-roaming animals, endangering their future.

The Rocky Mountain region invites the visitor to experience peaks along the Continental Divide, plus geysers, prairies, caverns, badlands—and lots of driving. Count on a drive of 520 miles from Rocky Mountain National Park to Grand Teton and nearly 400 miles from Yellowstone to Waterton-Glacier.

Badlands, feared by early pioneers, dwarfing a car headed west through the North Unit

Badlands

South Dakota

Established November 10, 1978

244,300 acres

They call it The Wall. It extends for a hundred miles through the dry plains of South Dakota—a huge natural barrier ridging the landscape, sculptured into fantastic pinnacles and tortuous gullies by the forces of water. Those who pass through the upper prairie a few miles north might not even know it exists. Those who traverse the lower prairie to the south, however, can't miss it; it rises above them like a city skyline in ruins, petrified.

The Badlands Wall, much of which is preserved within the boundaries of Badlands National Park, may not conform to everyone's idea of beauty, but nobody can deny its theatricality. It's been compared to an enormous stage set—colorful, dramatic, and not quite real. Water, the main player on this stage, has been carving away at the cliffs for the past half million years or so, and it carves away an entire inch or more in some places each year. But there have been other players, too. Beasts with names like titanothere and archaeotherium once roamed here; their fossilized bones can be found by the hundreds. And today the Badlands Wall serves as a backdrop for bison, pronghorn, and bighorn sheep, as well as the million human visitors who pass through the park every year.

A national monument since 1939, Badlands acquired the South Unit in 1976, adding yet another dimension to the drama. This large stretch of land belongs to the Oglala, and one of their most sacred places is now preserved within it. It was here, on Stronghold Table, that the final Ghost

Dance took place in 1890, just a few days before more than 150 Lakota were massacred at Wounded Knee, 25 miles south.

How to Get There

The park is about 3 miles south of I-90 at S. Dak. 240, 75 miles east of Rapid City and 27 miles west of Kadoka. Airport: Rapid City Regional.

When to Go

All-year park. Summer is the most popular season, though daytime temperatures may top 100° F. Spring and fall are usually pleasant, with moderate temperatures and fewer crowds. Winters can be bitter cold, but snow accumulations are rarely a problem in this arid climate.

How to Visit

The 32-mile **Badlands Loop** provides a rich eyeful of classic badlands for a 1-day **North Unit** visit (a shorter loop can be devised as described below).

Make sure to take advantage of the informative nature trails. For those with a second day and a pioneering spirit, a trip to the park's undeveloped **South Unit** can be rewarding; don't fail to check with rangers about road conditions before going.

North Unit: Badlands Loop

32 or 89 miles; a half day or full day

Enter the park at the **Northeast Entrance** on S. Dak. 240 and stop at the **Big Badlands Overlook** for your first, but by no means best, view of **The Wall** from above. Before you are the characteristic tiered cliffs of the badlands, dropping precipitously to the lower prairie, where the **White River** meanders between a fringe of cottonwood trees.

Stop next at the **Windows Overlook,** which serves as the trailhead for three short nature trails—the **Door, Window,** and **Notch Trails.** Guide leaflets are available for the Door Trail. While these trails may sound like the components of an architectural tour, they are actually brief forays into the Badlands Wall. The Door Trail (¾-mile round-trip, partly paved) passes through a narrow opening in The Wall into a jumble of barren, eroded hills reminiscent of the lunar surface. The Window Trail (¼-mile round-trip, paved) leads to a natural window overlooking a deeply cut canyon. And the Notch Trail (1½ miles round-trip, very rough) leads up a ladder and along the side of a gully to a break in The Wall, where you can look out over prairie and badlands, the White River, and the Pine Ridge Reservation on the plain down below.

Back in the car, a short drive brings you to the head of the **Cliff Shelf Nature Trail.** This ½-mile, steep loop takes you through a fascinating microenvironment in the badlands. Many years ago, a giant block of stone fell from the surrounding cliffs, creating this relatively flat shelf. The impact of the fall compacted the stone, making it less porous and allowing water to collect here. The resulting vegetation makes this place a delightful oasis in the otherwise barren wall. You can see mule deer browsing at dawn or dusk, and

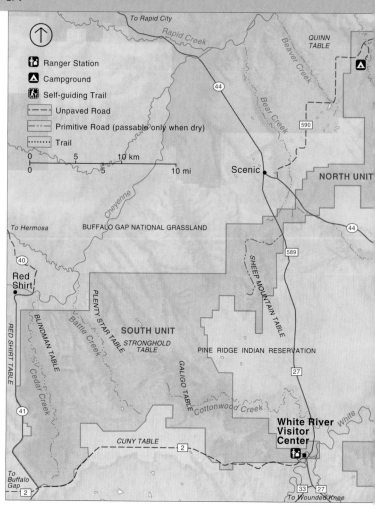

Ranger Station

Campground

Self-guiding Trail

Unpaved Road

Primitive Road (passable only when dry)

Trail

flamboyant magpies careening across the sky anytime.

Stop next at the **Ben Reifel Visitor Center,** where a video and various exhibits provide a good introduction to the park's history and geology. From this point, the road descends to the lower prairie for a brief stretch and then begins a gradual, stunning climb back up the Badlands Wall. The **Fossil Exhibit Trail** takes you on a ¼-mile paved walk through an area dense with fossils. Copies of some are displayed at trailside under clear plastic domes.

The road then continues level for 15 miles, punctuated by a dozen or so pullouts; each offers a slightly different perspective on the knife-sharp ridges, twisted canyons, and multicolored hills

that characterize this broken terrain. Particularly spectacular among these are the **Yellow Mounds** and **Pinnacles Overlooks.**

If you're short of time, exit the park at this point and rejoin the interstate at the town of Wall. Otherwise make a left turn onto Sage Creek Rim Road and continue along the **Sage Creek Wilderness Area.** This is excellent wildlife country; bison and pronghorn are numerous, and the road passes a town of those always entertaining prairie dogs. Longer hikes into the wilderness area start at the primitive campground about a mile off the road near the park's western boundary.

Beyond the campground turnoff, the road leaves the park. To complete the

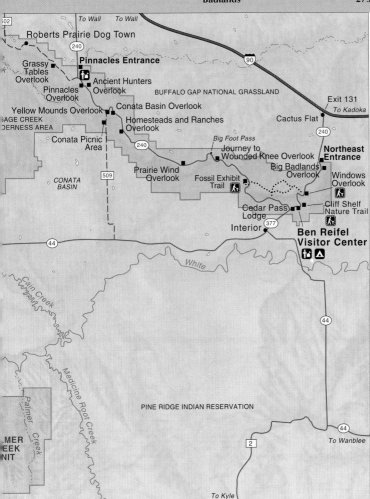

To Wall   To Wall

502

Roberts Prairie Dog Town

(240)

Pinnacles Entrance

Grassy
Tables
Overlook

Pinnacles
Overlook

Ancient Hunters
Overlook

BUFFALO GAP NATIONAL GRASSLAND

Yellow Mounds Overlook

Conata Basin Overlook

SAGE CREEK
DERNESS AREA

Homesteads and Ranches
Overlook

Exit 131
To Kadoka

Cactus Flat

Conata Picnic
Area

(240)

Big Foot Pass

(240)

Journey to
Wounded Knee Overlook

**Northeast
Entrance**

(240)

509

CONATA
BASIN

Prairie Wind
Overlook

Fossil Exhibit
Trail

Big Badlands
Overlook

Windows
Overlook

Cliff Shelf
Nature Trail

Cedar Pass
Lodge

Interior   (377)

**Ben Reifel
Visitor Center**

(44)

White

(44)

Cain Creek

Medicine Root Creek

Palmer
Creek

LMER
EEK
NIT

PINE RIDGE INDIAN RESERVATION

(44)

2

To Wanblee

To Kyle

Prairie beyond Big Foot Overlook, North Unit

Frosty sunrise on the Badlands

Pronghorn, Badlands denizen

loop, continue along unpaved County Road 590 and make a left (south) onto S. Dak. 44. If you're heading toward Rapid City, turn right; this stretch takes you through beautiful **Cheyenne River Valley** prairie and gives you views of the Black Hills. The highway goes through Scenic, the turnoff for the **South Unit,** if you want to continue directly there.

South Unit Drive

about 54 miles; at least a half day

The South Unit is almost entirely undeveloped, so exploring it by car will involve backtracking, driving on rough dirt roads, and generally putting a lot of wear and tear on your vehicle. For you safety, be sure to check with a ranger before setting out.

Begin at the town of Scenic, with its automobile graveyard and shanty-like saloon, and head south on County Road 589 for 4 miles. The turnoff for **Sheep Mountain Table** is marked.

Follow the road across the flats and up a seemingly impregnable cliff to a grass-topped table dotted with yuccas. If you go on to the juniper grove at the road's end, you can stand on a finger of high land and be almost surrounded by a stunning assortment of rock spires and pinnacles—perhaps the park's best view.

Return to the paved road and continue south for 16 miles until you arrive at the **White River Visitor Center** (open only in summer). It offers exhibits on Indian culture and a videotape on the Oglala. Here you can also get detailed directions to the many other sites worth visiting in the South Unit.

A visit to the **Stronghold Table** will either be a disappointment or the emotional culmination of your visit, depending on your perspective and imagination. Getting there involves driving some extremely rutted tracks through lonely grasslands, where you will probably get lost (bring along a topographical map). It also involves opening and closing many gates. The reward for this effort? An unspectacular view, but the chance to stand in the place where, in December 1890, a group of Sioux danced the Ghost Dance for the last time. In this impassioned ritual, converts fell into hypnotic trances, "died," and envisioned the paradise soon to come, sweeping the white man from the land and repopulating it with bison, elk, and antelope. If you go there, keep in mind that for Indians this is a sacred place.

Information & Activities

Headquarters
Interior, South Dakota 57750. Phone (605) 433-5361. www.nps.gov/badl

Seasons & Accessibility
Park open year-round. Snowstorms may block roads temporarily in winter. Call park headquarters to check on current road and weather conditions and accessibility to the undeveloped South Unit.

Visitor & Information Centers
Ben Reifel Visitor Center, in the North Unit, open daily all year except Thanksgiving, Christmas, and New Year's Day. White River Visitor Center, in the South Unit, open only in summer.

Entrance Fee
$10 per car; $20 annual.

Pets
Permitted on leashes except in Sage Creek Wilderness and on trails.

Facilities for Disabled
Visitor centers and some trails are wheelchair accessible. Free brochure available.

Things to Do
Free naturalist-led activities during summer: nature walks and hikes, evening programs, night walks, fossil demonstrations. Also available, interpretive exhibits and audiovisual programs, hiking, wildlife watching.

Special Advisories
● Prairie rattlesnakes and cactuses live here: Watch where you step when walking.
● Bison are unpredictable and can be dangerous: Keep your distance.
● Be prepared for sudden changes in weather and severe thunderstorms in summer. Check weather conditions by contacting headquarters or a visitor center before you hike.

Overnight Backpacking
No permit required; ask a ranger for advisories.

Campgrounds
Two campgrounds, both with a 14-day limit. **Cedar Pass** and **Sage Creek** rarely fill up and are open all year, first come, first served. (Heavy snows may close them in winter.) Cedar Pass is $10 in summer, with water; $8 in winter, without water; Sage Creek is free year-round, without water. No showers. Tent and RV sites; no hookups. **Cedar Pass Group Campground;** reservations accepted Memorial Day to Labor Day; campsites $2 per person, $20 minimum; contact park headquarters. Food service in park.

Hotels, Motels, & Inns
(unless otherwise noted, rates are for 2 persons in a double room, high season)
INSIDE THE PARK:
Cedar Pass Lodge (on S. Dak. 240 near visitor center) P.O. Box 5, Interior, S. Dak. 57750. (605) 433-5460. 24 cabins. $47.25. AC, restaurant. Open mid-April through October.
OUTSIDE THE PARK:
In Interior, South Dakota 57750:
Badlands Inn (½ mile from park entrance) P.O. Box 103. (605) 433-5401. 24 units. $48. AC, pool. Open mid-May through Labor Day.
In Wall, South Dakota 57790:
Best Western Plains Motel (1 block off I-90, 712 Glenn St.) P.O. Box 393. (800) 528-1234 or (605) 279-2145. 74 units. $75-$95. AC, pool. Open March through November.
Elk Motel (South Blvd.) P.O. Box 424. (800) 782-9402 or (605) 279-2127. 47 units. $56. AC, pool.
Hitching Post Motel (Tenth Ave.) P.O. Box 171. (800) 456-2018 or (605) 279-2133. 30 units. $28-$72. AC, pool. Open May through October.
Kings Inn Motel 608 Main St. (800) 782-2613 or (605) 279-2178. 26 units. $60. AC.
IMA Sands Motor Inn (804 Glenn St.) P.O. Box 426. (800) 341-8000 or (605) 279-2121. 49 units, 2 with kitchenettes. $70. ac, pool. Open mid-April to mid-November.

For additional accommodations contact the Wall Chamber of Commerce, P.O. Box 527, Wall, S. Dak. 57790. (605) 279-2665.

View from the South Rim at Cedar Point

Black Canyon of the Gunnison

Colorado

Established October 21, 1999

30,385 acres

Sheer walls of dark gray stone rise more than 2,600 feet above the swift and turbulent Gunnison River to create one of the most dramatic canyons in the country. Deeper than it is wide in some places, this great slit in the earth is so narrow that sunlight penetrates to the bottom only at midday. The park protects the deepest, most thrilling 14 miles of the gorge, about 75 miles upstream of the Gunnison's junction with the Colorado River.

Imagine chiseling two parallel walls of hard gneiss and schist running the length of Manhattan and standing as high as the two World Trade Centers stacked atop each other, with water as your only tool. At the inconceivable rate of one inch per century, it would take all of human history just to cut through five feet of rock. What you see from the rim is the product of two million years of patient work.

The metamorphic rocks exposed at the bottom of the canyon are nearly two billion years old, dating from the Precambrian or oldest era of the Earth. Here and there are swirling pink veins of igneous peg-

Today, three dams upstream have further tamed the Gunnison, but the canyon and its section of river remain wild.

Rim drives and hikes offer plenty of opportunities for peering into the magnificent canyon and marveling at its cliffs and towers of stone. Ravens, golden eagles, and peregrine falcons soar the great gulf of air out in front. On top grows a thick forest of Gambel oaks and serviceberry, which provide cover for mule deer and black bear, while farther down the canyon Douglas-firs thrive in the shade, and cottonwoods and box elders find footholds along the river.

How to Get There

The South Rim is located 15 miles northeast of Montrose, via US 50 and Colo. 347. The North Rim is 80 miles by car from the South Rim, via US 50 west and Colo. 92. Turn south off Colo. 92 onto the 15-mile North Rim Rd., the first half of which is paved. Airports: Montrose and Gunnison.

When to Go

Summer is the most popular time to visit. But be prepared to sweat if you hike at midday on exposed trails, and bring lots of water. Crisp days in late spring and early fall make for excellent walks. Winter affords

matite, shooting through the walls and livening up the canyon's somber appearance.

Indians and white explorers generally avoided the formidable canyon up through the 19th century. In 1900, five men attempted to run the river in wooden boats to survey it as a possible source of irrigation for the Uncompahgre Valley. After a month, with their boats in splinters and their supplies gone, they gave up. But the next year two men ran it in nine days on rubber air mattresses. A water diversion tunnel was soon in the works; the four-year project, completed in 1909, resulted in a 6-mile-long tunnel through rock, clay, and sand. The labor was so grueling and dangerous that the average period of employment was only two weeks.

Gnarled juniper trunks

opportunities for backcountry camping, cross-country skiing, and snowshoeing. With the rim at 8,000 feet above sea level, winter can set in as early as November and last until April. Snow closes vehicle access to the North Rim; the South Rim road stays open to the second overlook year-round.

How to Visit

You can spend most of a day driving the 7-mile (one-way) South Rim, exploring its 5 or so miles of trails. Reserve the afternoon, or a second day, for a walk down to the canyon floor. If you have more time, visit the North Rim and its 5-mile (unpaved) drive.

South Rim

Rim Drive, 7 miles one way;
2-3 hours

With a dozen scenic overlooks and several short trails, this dramatic drive offers plenty of topside angles on the canyon and river. The first overlook, **Tomichi Point,** allows access to the **Rim Rock Trail,** which runs north-south for about a mile between the campground and the visitor center. This trail gives you fine views of the vertiginous walls of the eastern part of the canyon and the glinting ribbon of water sluicing down its middle. You walk through a scrubby forest of Gambel oaks and sagebrush, studded with pinyons and junipers. The latter has dark purple berries and a cedary look and smell. Breathe in the refreshing air; look for tracks of elk, bobcat, mountain lion, and other rim dwellers; and listen for the scold of Steller's jays.

Make a 2-mile loop by following the **Uplands Trail** across the road. Continue up through scrub oak forest before walking past the **Visitor Center** and rejoining the Rim Rock Trail. At the Visitor Center, exhibits on the park's geology, history, flora, and fauna will help get you started. Just outside the Visitor Center you can take the invigorating **Oak Flat Trail,** which makes a loop of about 2 miles and gets you a little way below the rim. Head west, then turn right at the River Access sign and dip into a grove of aspens. At the next junction, turn left and wind through a thicket of scrub oak to an outcrop with a good view. Circle back through a forest of aspen and Douglas-fir.

Ranger Station
Campground
Unpaved Road
Hiking Trail

0   1   2 km
0   1   2 mi

One of the shortest ways to the canyon floor is the **Gunnison Route,** off the Oak Flat Trail. It's a mere mile to the river, but it's a tough one—even for those in good shape, the walk down takes at least an hour. Since most of the canyon is a designated wilderness, hikers end up following drainage gullies, which plunge 1,800 vertical feet over scree slopes littered with big rocks. To avoid ankle injuries in some places, crouch and slide; a mounted 80-foot-long chain helps out on one stretch, but the rest is a wild free-for-all. At the bottom, rest and massage your legs, staring up at the spectacular stonework all around. The walk back up—at times a hand-over-hand pull—is harder than the downhill.

Back on the road, continue driving northwest. The aptly named **Pulpit**

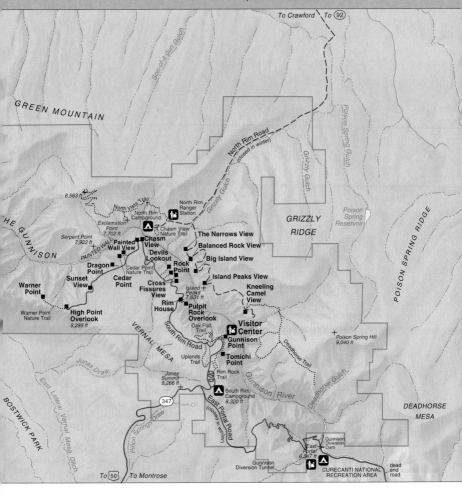

Rock offers a terrific long view of the river knifing its way through the canyon. A walk out to **Chasm View** takes you to within about 1,100 feet of the North Rim, on the opposite side of the canyon. At this point, the canyon's 1,800-foot depth exceeds its width, and it looks extremely narrow. But the narrowness is a result of the river's precipitous angle and its high volume. You're left with a sense of something newly created, which in geological terms is true.

The road now bends southwest. Several pulloffs provide views of the magnificent **Painted Wall**, a 2,250-foot sheer cliff decorated with stripes and flourishes of pink and white crystalline pegmatite, an extrusion of magma that seeped into cracks and hardened. Take the **Cedar Point Nature Trail**, an easy $\frac{2}{3}$-mile out-and-back, to views of the wall, the river, and islands of stone rising from the canyon depths.

Drive on to **High Point,** the end of the road and, at 8,289 feet, the highest point on the rim. From here it is a dizzying 2,689-foot drop to the river. You can take a 1.5-mile round-trip walk out to **Warner Point** for exquisite canyon views to the north. Turning to the south you can see the verdant farmlands of the Uncompahgre Valley irrigated by water diverted from the canyon's own Gunnison River. Beyond rise the San Juan Mountains. The trail meanders among pinyon pine, juniper, mountain mahogany, and white-flowering serviceberry. Other plants scattered about include Fendler bush, mule's ear, lupine, and scarlet gilia, the latter bearing lovely tubular flowers.

Gunnison Point

North Rim

*Rim Drive (unpaved) 5 miles
one way; 2-3 hours*

While it is only 1,100 feet from one side of the canyon to the other, you must endure an 80-mile drive to reach the North Rim from the South Rim—the last several miles of it unpaved along North Rim Road. You can also reach the North Rim from the east side—a 90-mile drive on US 50 and Colo. 92 thru the Curecanti National Recreation Area. On the North Rim, you'll find yourself in a remote and awesome wilderness where the canyon walls plunge nearly vertically.

Whichever way you come, leave Colo. 92 at North Rim Road and follow it to the end. Turn right and drive to the ranger station, where one of the finest hikes in the park begins. The **North Vista Trail** wanders in and out of scrub forest along the rim for 1.5 miles. Detour at **Exclamation Point** for a jaw-dropping look into the canyon's depths. Turn back around, or continue 2 more miles to trail's end on Green Mountain. This difficult section climbs from 7,702 feet to 8,563 feet. Here stirring panoramas take in Grand Mesa and the Uncompahgre Plateau to the west, the West Elk Mountains to the north, and, in the south, the San Juans.

Once back at the ranger station, drive about a mile south and get out for the short **Chasm View Nature Trail,** that meanders through a pinyon-juniper forest and comes out at two stunning overlooks. White-throated swifts and violet-green swallows dart from cliffside nests. The southern 4 miles of the drive zigzag along the canyon's rim. At **Balanced Rock View** and **Kneeling Camel View,** near the end of the drive, steep unmarked trails wind down side canyons to the river.

Practical Information

Headquarters
102 Elk Creek, Gunnison, CO 81230
Phone (970) 641-2337
www.nps.gov/blca

Seasons & Accessibility
South Rim open daily, limited access in winter; North Rim Road and Ranger Station closed in winter. Contact park for current information.

Visitor & Information Centers
Visitor Center open daily except holidays in winter. North Rim Ranger Station open in summer only.

Entrance Fees
$7 per vehicle per week; yearly fee $15.

Pets
Pets allowed in park on leash; not allowed on trails or in backcountry.

Facilities for Disabled

Aceessible on South Rim, Visitor Center, comfort stations, 2 camping sites; and Tomichi Point, Chasm View, and Sunset View overlooks. On North Rim, Balanced Rock overlook accessible.

Things to do

Free naturalist-led activities. Exhibits, scenic drives, hiking, fishing, kayaking, rock climbing, winter activities. Contact park headquarters for a list of concessioners.

Special Advisories

Permits required for all inner canyon routes; available at Visitor Center and North Rim Ranger Station.

Overnight Backpacking

Backcountry permits required. Wood fires prohibited; use camp stoves only.

Campgrounds

South Rim 102 sites; North Rim 13 sites. Auto campgrounds $10 per night. All sites first come, first served, usually available. Vault toilets, limited water, no hook-ups.

For accommodations contact the Montrose Visitors and Convention Bureau (970) 240-1429 and the Gunnison County Chamber of Commerce 970) 641-1501.

Walls of gneiss and schist flanking the Gunnison River below

Snake River meandering through Jackson Hole toward the Tetons

Grand Teton

Wyoming

Established February 26, 1929

309,993 acres

The peaks of the Teton Range, regal and imposing as they stand nearly 7,000 feet above the valley floor, make one of the boldest geologic statements in the Rockies. Unencumbered by foothills, they rise through steep coniferous forest into alpine meadows strewn with wildflowers, past blue and white glaciers to naked granite pinnacles. The Grand, Middle, and South Tetons form the heart of the range. But their neighbors, especially Mount Owen, Teewinot Mountain, and Mount Moran, are no less spectacular.

A string of jewel-like lakes, fed by mountain streams, are set tightly against the steep foot of the mountains. Beyond them extends the broad valley called Jackson Hole, covered with sagebrush and punctuated by occasional forested hills and groves of aspen trees—excellent habitats for pronghorn, deer, elk, and other animals. The Snake River, having begun its journey in southern Yellowstone National Park near the Teton Wilderness, winds leisurely past the Tetons on its way to Idaho. The braided sections of the river create wetlands that support moose, elk, deer, beavers, trumpeter swans, sandhill cranes, Canada geese, and all sorts of ducks.

The Tetons are normal fault-block mountains. About five to nine million years ago, two blocks of the Earth's crust began to shift along a fault line, one tilting down while the other lifted up. So far, movement has measured some 30,000 vertical feet, most of it from the subsidence of Jackson Hole.

trails in the valley lead around lakes and beside wetlands where visitors see moose, elk, deer, and all kinds of birds.

How to Get There

From Jackson, take US 26/89/191 north past the National Elk Refuge; Moose Visitor Center and Entrance Station are at Moose. From Dubois, follow US 26/287 to Moran Junction and turn west to the Moran Entrance Station. From Yellowstone NP, the South Entrance road leads directly into the park. The Jackson Hole Airport is inside the park—a concern for environmentalists.

When to Go

Any time of year is a joy in the Tetons. Most people visit during July and August, when it's sunny and warm, after the snow has melted in the high country. In September and October, the days are pleasant, nights are brisk, the park is less crowded, and the animals are still active. You have a better chance of seeing elk than in summer.

Winter, although spectacular, can be very demanding; snowshoeing and cross-country skiing are popular. The main park road, US 26/89/191, remains open all year, but snow closes Teton Park Road (the "inner road") north of Cottonwood Creek from November through April. The Moose-Wilson Road is also closed. At Teton Village, just south of the park, you'll find excellent downhill skiing.

Before Europeans arrived, the Teton area was an important plant-gathering and hunting ground for Indians of various tribes. In the early 1800s, mountain men spent time here; it was they who called this flat valley ringed by mountains Jackson's Hole after the trapper Davey Jackson. (In recent times the name has lost its apostrophe s.) The first settlers were ranchers and farmers. Some of their buildings are historic sites today, although ranching is still practiced in the vicinity. When the park was established, it included only the mountains and the glacial lakes at their feet. Portions of the valley were added in 1950.

Today the park's 485 square miles encompass both the Teton Range and much of Jackson Hole. Park roads, all in the valley, offer an ever changing panorama of the Tetons. Most visitors never go far from the road. But the Tetons are also popular with hikers; backcountry trails climb high into the mountains—and behind them. Easy

Arrowleaf balsam root, early summer

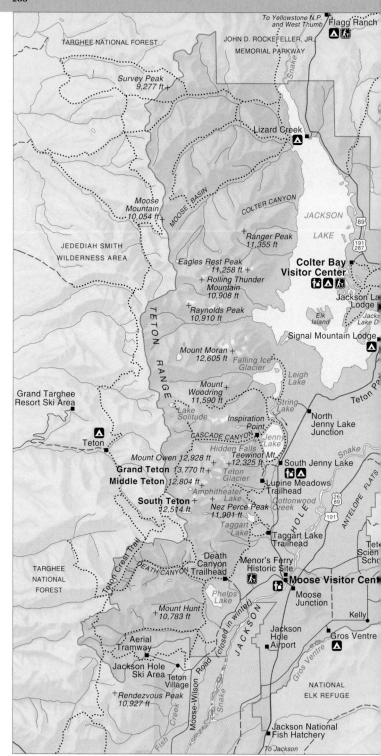

To Yellowstone N.P. and West Thumb

Flagg Ranch

TARGHEE NATIONAL FOREST

JOHN D. ROCKEFELLER, JR.
MEMORIAL PARKWAY

Survey Peak
9,277 ft +

Lizard Creek

JACKSON LAKE

Moose
Mountain
10,054 ft +

MOOSE BASIN

COLTER CANYON

JEDEDIAH SMITH
WILDERNESS AREA

+ Ranger Peak
11,355 ft

Colter Bay
Visitor Center

Eagles Rest Peak
11,258 ft +

Jackson Lake
Lodge

+ Rolling Thunder
Mountain
10,908 ft

Elk
Island

Jacks
Lake D

+ Raynolds Peak
10,910 ft

Signal Mountain Lodge

TETON RANGE

Mount Moran +
12,605 ft

Falling Ice
Glacier

Leigh
Lake

Grand Targhee
Resort Ski Area

Mount
Woodring
11,590 ft

Lake
Solitude

Inspiration
Point

String
Lake

Teton Pa

Teton

North
Jenny Lake
Junction

CASCADE CANYON

Hidden Falls

Jenny
Lake

Snake

Mount Owen 12,928 ft +

Teewinot Mt.
+12,325 ft

South Jenny Lake

Grand Teton 13,770 ft +

Teton
Glacier

Middle Teton 12,804 ft +

Lupine Meadows
Trailhead

26
89

+ Amphitheater
Lake

Cottonwood
Creek

191

South Teton +
12,514 ft

+ Nez Perce Peak
11,901 ft

ANTELOPE FLATS

Taggart
Lake

JACKSON

HOLE

Tet
Scien
Scho

TARGHEE
NATIONAL
FOREST

Teton Crest Trail

DEATH CANYON

Death
Canyon
Trailhead

Taggart Lake
Trailhead

Menor's Ferry
Historic Site

Moose Visitor Cent

Phelps
Lake

Moose
Junction

Kelly

+ Mount Hunt
10,783 ft

Moose-Wilson Road (closed in winter)

Jackson
Hole
Airport

Gros Ventre

+ Aerial
Tramway

Jackson Hole
Ski Area

Teton
Village

Snake

Gros Ventre

NATIONAL
ELK REFUGE

+ Rendezvous Peak
10,927 ft

Fish Creek

Jackson National
Fish Hatchery

To Jackson

Ranger Station

Campground

Self-guiding Nature Trail

- - - Unpaved Road

.... Hiking Trail

0   5 km
0   5 mi

BRIDGER-TETON
NATIONAL FOREST

Pacific Creek

Two Ocean
Lake

mma
atilda
Lake

ckson Lake
nction

Moran
Entrance Station

nal
untain
93 ft

Moran
Junction

To
Dubois

26
287

Hatchet

26
89

nake

191

Cunningham Cabin
Historic Site

BRIDGER-TETON
NATIONAL FOREST

Atherton
Creek

Lower
Slide
Lake

Red Hills

Crystal
Creek

Gros Ventre

How to Visit

On a 1-day visit take the **Teton Park Road** from **Moose Junction** to **Jenny Lake** for excellent views of the **Tetons** and short walks or longer hikes. On the second day, go farther north to **Signal Mountain** and **Jackson Lake.** For a longer stay, consider floating the **Snake River,** hiking, canoeing, climbing, or attending a ranger-guided activity.

Teton Park Road & Jenny Lake Loop

17 miles; at least a half day

From **Moose Junction,** cross the **Snake River** to the **Moose Visitor Center,** which includes a small exhibit area. The first right turn after the entrance station leads to **Menor-Noble Historic District,** a pioneer homestead. Save that for another day; there are mountains ahead. The **Teton Park Road** climbs up from the river onto a sage-covered flat with the whole Teton panorama in view. You will see the mountains clearly throughout this drive from various changing angles; each viewpoint reveals striking perspectives different from the last.

If you look toward the mountains at Taggart Parking Area, you can see the results of a 1985 forest fire. An easy trail offers a closeup view of forest regeneration—an especially interesting and encouraging sight if you plan to visit Yellowstone, where fires burned extensively in the summer of 1988.

Stop at **Teton Glacier Turnout** for a close-in view of the three **Tetons.** The **Grand Teton,** at 13,770 feet, is the highest point in the range. A major route used by climbers follows the left-hand, southern skyline; just as it appears, there is no easy way to the top.

Cottonwood Creek Turnout

Looking over a field of wildflowers into Targhee National Forest

Looking to the left of the Grand, you see the **Middle** and **South Tetons.** The sharp pinnacle jutting up over the shoulder of the South Teton (actually in front of it), is the peak called **Nez Perce.** To the right of the Grand are the sharp peak of **Mount Owen** and, in the foreground, the craggy battlements of **Teewinot Mountain.**

Notice the steep, glacier-carved gulch coming straight down from the Grand Teton. At the head of the gulch, beneath the mountain's near-vertical north face, lies **Teton Glacier.** During an ancient ice age, glaciers covered **Jackson Hole** to a depth of 3,000 feet and carved the canyons in the **Teton Range.** The glaciers that exist now only at high elevations established themselves more recently.

If you can take your eyes off the mountains, scan the sage flats on both sides of the road for pronghorn, elk, deer, and coyotes, especially in the fall. Across Jackson Hole to the southeast is the **Gros Ventre Range,** where herds of elk and mule deer roam the deeply forested gorges and bighorn sheep the highest peaks.

Heading north, the **Lupine Meadows** spur road leads to a major trailhead. From here you can take a very rewarding but strenuous hike, which climbs 3,000 feet to **Amphitheater Lake** near timberline. Lupine Meadows itself is a good place to look for wildlife in the evening.

Back on the main road, the **South Jenny Lake** area is next, but unless you're planning to hike around the lake, or to take the boat across to **Cascade Canyon** at this point in your tour, you should drive past it for now. Four miles ahead is the junction for **Jenny Lake Scenic Drive,** where a narrow one-way road provides the best approach to the area, which many consider to be the scenic heart of the Tetons. The one-way road angles back to the southwest, offering stunning views of the central peaks. Stop at **Cathedral Group Turnout** to take it all in.

The north face of the Grand is visible from here, flanked by Teewinot on the left, and Owen on the right. North of them, in order, are precipitous Cascade Canyon (one of the park's best hikes), **Mount Saint John, Mount Woodring,** and then the massive, flat-topped **Mount Moran.** Moran's **Falling Ice Glacier** is prominent. Notice also the obvious line of black rock rising above the glacier. Called the **Black Dike,** it was caused when molten rock intruded into a crack in the older granitelike rock called gneiss, before the Tetons rose. The dike, now exposed by

The Grand, highest peak in the Tetons, towering over skiers on Blacktail Butte

erosion of the gneiss, actually stands out from the mountain face near the summit. Similar dikes are on the Middle Teton (not visible from here) and Grand Teton.

Just ahead, a short road forks off the scenic drive and leads to tiny **String Lake.** An easy trail leaves from the end of the road to follow the shoreline through open forest to sparkling **Leigh Lake,** named after a 19th-century mountain man, Richard "Beaver Dick" Leigh, who, it was said, could "trap beaver where there warn't any." The lake has superb views of soaring Mount Moran, and, in summer, the water is sometimes warm enough for swimming.

Continuing on, the one-way road reaches **Jenny Lake.** For understandable reasons, this place is highly popular; the road in summer is crowded with vehicles. Even so, if you desire solitude amid the grandeur, you can generally find it. Leave your car in a parking area and walk down to the shore. Instantly you are isolated from the world of automobiles. If you have more time, catch the boat that usually leaves three times an hour from the south end of the lake. Near the parking area you will find the **Jenny Lake Visitor Center,** rest rooms, ranger station, a store, and a camp-

Hidden Falls

ground for tents only.

The passenger boat crosses Jenny Lake to join **Cascade Canyon Trail.** It is a ½-mile walk to **Hidden Falls,** one of the park's beauties. A ½-mile farther, aptly named **Inspiration Point** overlooks the lake. If you still have the energy, the trail is not steep after Inspiration Point, and the views keep getting better. You might consider walking back to the visitor center along the south shore; the easy trail is nearly 3 miles long.

Jackson Lake

about 30 miles; at least a half day

Start at North Jenny Lake Junction on the Teton Park Road. Drive north 2½ miles through sage land and lodge-pole pine to the **Mount Moran Turnout.** Mount Moran, at 12,605 feet, is more than a thousand feet lower than the Grand Teton, but you wouldn't know that looking up. On its summit there is a patch of sandstone which corresponds to a sandstone layer an estimated 24,000 feet below where you stand; five to nine million years of movement on the Teton fault has separated the layers by some 30,000 feet.

North of Mount Moran, **Bivouac Peak, Rolling Thunder Mountain,** and **Eagles Rest Peak** dominate the most remote section of the park, cut off from roads and easy trail access by **Jackson Lake,** just ahead. The natural lake was enlarged by a dam built before the park was established.

Before you get to the lake, take the right-hand turn to **Signal Mountain.** The road, on which trailers and RVs are not allowed, winds to the summit of a low mountain which, because it stands alone in Jackson Hole, provides a panoramic view of the region. There's no better place than here to appreciate the unusual geology of the Teton area: the abrupt meeting of valley floor and the Teton Range; the meandering course of the Snake River through deposits of gravel and clay brought down by ice age glaciers; and the ranges to the east. From Signal Mountain, it is easy to see why the early trappers thought of mountain-ringed valleys like this one as holes.

Back on the Teton Park Road, you pass Signal Mountain Campground and cross the Snake River over the rebuilt dam. A mile farther, the road joins US 89/191/287. If you're headed north toward Yellowstone, it's worthwhile to turn right and take a short side trip (about a mile) to **Oxbow Bend,** for a classic view of the Tetons dominated by Mount Moran. Wildlife frequent this area.

Going north once again, stop at **Willow Flats Overlook.** The willows are a likely place to see moose. Failing that, watch the meadows below the bridge just to the north as you cross **Christian Creek.**

Day breaking over Mt. Moran and Oxbow Bend

Bull moose in rut

Climbing Blacktail Butte, just east of Moose

A few minutes north, **Colter Bay Visitor Center** has an excellent **Indian Arts Museum.** Consider stretching your legs on the easy 3-mile **Colter Bay Nature Trail;** self-guiding booklets can be had at the trailhead or at the visitor center.

North of **Colter Bay,** the main road stays close to the lake. Just before Lizard Creek Campground, you catch one last glimpse of the Tetons and Jackson Lake, before entering dense lodgepole forest. Ten miles farther, along the John D. Rockefeller, Jr., Memorial Parkway, is the South Entrance to Yellowstone.

Other Hikes & Activities

The park has more than 200 miles of maintained trails; many lead up canyons separating the major peaks. All the trails have something to offer, but they vary in difficulty, and some are more scenic than others. Keep in mind that most trails begin at about 6,800 feet, so shortness of breath can come quickly.

Cascade Canyon is most popular. Begin at Jenny Lake, and either walk along the lakeshore or take the boat across to Hidden Falls and Inspiration Point. It is a long hike to **Lake Soli-**tude—7 miles if you take the boat, 9½ miles if you walk the lakeshore—but it's worthwhile to go at least partway up the canyon.

From Lupine Meadows parking area, the **Amphitheater Lake Trail** climbs to 9,700 feet and rewards those who make the strenuous 9-mile round-trip with a breathtaking view of Jackson Hole. The lake nestles beneath craggy peaks; allow 8 hours minimum.

Death Canyon Trailhead, off the **Moose-Wilson Road,** leads up to a nice view of **Phelps Lake;** from there, it climbs to join the **Teton Crest Trail,** a magnificent backcountry route that traverses the range and ends at **Paintbrush Canyon** near String Lake, a trip of about 40 miles and 3 days (backcountry permit required).

Consider taking a raft trip on the Snake River for fine Teton views and a chance to see beavers, otters, moose, eagles, ospreys, and waterfowl. Ask about outfitters at a visitor center or check the park newspaper.

You can also sign up for a mountain climbing lesson; rent a canoe and paddle on a lake; or take a summer course taught by the **Teton Science School.** The school offers 1- to 5-day seminars on ecology and the region's natural history for ages 8 and up.

Information & Activities

Headquarters
Post Office Drawer 170, Moose, Wyoming 83012. Phone (307) 739-3300. www.nps.gov/grte

Seasons & Accessibility
Main road into park (US 26/89/191) open year-round. Side roads closed due to snow from about November to May. Call headquarters number for winter road conditions.

Visitor & Information Centers
Moose Visitor Center at park's south end, open daily all year except Christmas. Colter Bay Visitor Center on Jackson Lake, open mid-May through Sept. Jenny Lake Visitor Center open June through Labor Day. Call (307) 739-3399.

Entrance Fee
$20 per car, good for one week at both Grand Teton and Yellowstone. $40 annual.

Pets
Permitted on leashes except on trails, ranger-led activities, in backcountry and visitor centers; not permitted on boats on the Snake River or on lakes other than Jackson Lake.

Facilities for Disabled
Visitor centers, Indian Arts Museum, some rest rooms, and some ranger-led activities are accessible.

Things to Do
Free ranger-led activities: wildlife walks and talks, day and twilight hikes, bicycle tours, slide talks, illustrated campfire programs, children's programs, skill development programs, tepee demonstration, wildlife watches, snowshoe walks. Also, boat cruise, Indian arts workshop, natural history seminars, wayside exhibits, boating (permit required), river rafting, climbing, bicycling, horseback riding (stables in park), fishing and ice fishing (license required), snowshoeing, cross-country skiing, dogsledding, snowmobiling. Ask park for list of concessioners offering variety of rental and guide services.

Overnight Backpacking
Permits required. Free, they can be obtained at visitor centers and Jenny Lake Ranger Station. One-third of permits can be reserved; the rest are first come, first served. Mail requests between Jan. and mid-May to Permits Office c/o park.

Campgrounds
Five campgrounds, **Jenny Lake** has 7-day limit, others 14-day limit. Generally late May to Oct., except **Lizard Creek,** mid-June to early Sept. Reservations required for **Colter Bay Trailer Village;** contact Grand Teton Lodge Co., Box 240, Moran, Wyo. 83013. (307) 543-2855. All other campgrounds first come, first served. $12 per night; **Trailer Village** $22 per night. Showers at **Colter Bay**. Tent sites only at **Jenny Lake;** RV sites only at **Colter Bay Trailer Village,** with hookups; all others have tent and trailer sites, no hookups. Two group campgrounds; reservations suggested; contact park headquarters. Food services in park.

Hotels, Motels, & Inns
(unless otherwise noted, rates for 2 persons, double room, high season)
INSIDE THE PARK:
The following 3 lodges and cabins are operated by Grand Teton Lodge Co., P.O. Box 250, Moran, Wyo. 83013. (800) 628-9988 or (307) 543-2811. **Colter Bay Village and Marina** 208 cabins. $68-$125. Rest. Mid-May to Oct. **Jackson Lake Lodge** (1 mi. N. of Jackson Lake Jct.) 385 units. $120-$210. Rest., pool. Mid-May–mid-Oct. **Jenny Lake Lodge** 37 cabins. $340-$590, includes 2 meals. Rest. Late May to early Oct.
Also, **Lost Creek Ranch** (8 mi. N. of Moose) P.O. Box 95, Moose, Wyo. 83012. (307) 733-3435. 13 cabins. $5,200-$12,000 per week, all inclusive. June–Nov. **Signal Mountain Lodge** P.O. Box 50, Moran, Wyo. 83013. (800) 672-6012 or (307) 543-2831. 79 units. Cabins $85-$120; rooms $105-$175. Rest. Mid-May to mid-Oct. **Triangle X Ranch** Moose, Wyo. 83012. (307) 733-2183. 19 cabins. $1,000-$1,400 per person, per week, all inclusive. May through Oct.

Contact the Jackson, Wyo., Chamber of Commerce for a full list of accommodations open year-round. (307) 733-3316.

Excursions

National Elk Refuge

Jackson, Wyoming

In winter, visitors can ride a horse-drawn sleigh into the protected winter range of a 10,000-head herd of elk. The refuge offers supplemental feeding to the animals, many of which migrate south from Yellowstone. 24,700 acres. Facilities include limited hiking, fishing, scenic drives, visitor center. Open year-round, dawn to dusk. Adjoins Grand Teton NP on south. (307) 733-9212.

Bridger-Teton National Forest

Jackson, Wyoming

This immense forest encompasses wildlife-rich Jackson Hole; the glaciers and lakes of the Wind River Range; and Two Ocean Creek along the Continental Divide. Contains three wilderness areas. 3.5 million acres. Includes 40 campgrounds, hiking, boating, boat ramp, fishing, horseback riding, hunting, water sports, winter sports. Open all year; campgrounds open spring to fall. Adjoins Grand Teton NP on east. (307) 739-5500.

Targhee National Forest

St. Anthony, Idaho

Here, on the Tetons' western flank, lies a forest of lodgepole pine and fir with many rivers, streams, and lakes. Contains two wilderness areas. 1,810,000 acres, part in Wyo. 32 campgrounds, food services, hiking, boating, boat ramp, fishing, horseback riding, hunting, picnic areas, winter sports, water sports. Open all year; campsites open late May-Sept. Adjoins Grand Teton & Yellowstone NPs. (208) 624-3151.

Fossil Butte National Monument

Kemmerer, Wyoming

Fifty million years ago, this semi-arid country was the site of Fossil Lake, a rich depository of the Eocene. Features exquisitely preserved freshwater fishes. 8,198 acres. Hiking, picnic area, scenic drive. Visitor center open year-round; site usually closed by snow Nov.-early May. Off US 30, about 180 miles south of Grand Teton NP. (307) 877-4455.

Tundra along Trail Ridge Road; Longs Peak in the distance

Rocky Mountain

Colorado

Established January 26, 1915

265,751 acres

Nowhere else in the United States can a visitor see so much alpine country with such ease. Only 2 hours' drive from Denver, Trail Ridge Road takes visitors into the heart of Rocky Mountain National Park, traversing a ridge above 11,000 feet for 10 miles. Along the way, tiny tundra flowers contrast with sweeping vistas of towering summits; 78 of them exceed 12,000 feet. Alpine lakes reflect the grandeur.

The summits form at least the third generation of mountains to rise in this region. The first probably protruded as islands above a shallow sea more than 135 million years ago, when dinosaurs reigned. Another range grew out of a later sea some 75 million years ago. Over the eons these summits eroded to rolling hills, which rose once again, although unevenly: Some portions sank along fault lines, helping create the striking texture of the current scenery.

Rock as old as that at the bottom of the Grand Canyon—nearly two billion years—caps the Rockies' summits. Within the last million years, glaciers, grinding boulders beneath them, carved deep canyons. Erosion later scoured the more jagged summits into their present profiles.

Rocky Mountain, though only about ⅛ the size of Yellowstone, accommodates nearly as many visitors—3.3 million or more a year. In 1917 a superintendent promoted the park by hiring a young woman to live off the land, clad in a leopard-skin; visitation soared. But today overcrowding worries park officials

to visit: Elk move to lower elevations, and you can hear their mating bugles. The tundra turns crimson early in the month; aspens turn golden later. In the winter there is skiing and snowshoeing.

How to Visit

On a 1-day blitz, drive **Trail Ridge Road** as far as **Farview Curve** for the classic overview of the park's mountains, valleys, and tundra, then double back and take **Bear Lake Road** to see a collection of scenic lakes (which can get very congested in summer). If you wish, make a loop of the first leg by driving one-way, unpaved **Old Fall River Road** west, then Trail Ridge Road east. Old Fall River Road gives you an intimate look at a wooded mountainside, but it's usually closed by snow until early July.

With more time, drive all the way to **Grand Lake** on the west side the first day, then take your trip to **Bear Lake** the second day. Spend extra time on the excellent nature trails and day hikes.

If you go in summer and plan to backpack and hike, be sure not to be caught above timberline between about 12 and 4 p.m., when lightning storms are frequent.

and conservationists, who cite distressed animals, trodden plants, and eroded trails. Condominium development is crowding the park's borders also, shrinking the habitats of elk and other wildlife and threatening to turn the park into an island of nature.

How to Get There

Take I-25 north from Denver (about 65 miles away) or south from Cheyenne, Wyo. (about 90 miles away), then US 34 west at Loveland. From the west, pick up US 34 at Granby. Airports: Denver and Cheyenne.

When to Go

If possible, avoid mid-June to mid-August, when the park receives about half its yearly visitors. Trail Ridge Road stays open from roughly late May to mid-October; trails thaw out by around July 4. In May, subalpine wildflowers bloom; in late June, the tundra flowers. September, the sunniest month, is a prime time

Trail Ridge Road to Grand Lake, via Farview Curve

50 miles; at least a full day

Trail Ridge Road roughly follows a 10,000-year-old trail; prehistoric people once hunted where you'll drive. The road climbs to a land like the vast arctic expanses of Siberia, Alaska, and northern Canada. Take warm clothing and sunscreen. From Estes Park, enter the park on US 36 and stop by the visitor center to pick up information—including a useful flyer about Trail Ridge Road—and a weather report. (If coming from the west on US 34, stop at the visitor center near **Grand Lake** and reverse this tour.) Continue straight on US 36 after the entrance station. The road ascends **Deer Mountain** through open ponderosa woodland.

At **Deer Ridge Junction,** either bear left onto Trail Ridge Road, or, if it's summer, detour to the right, circling

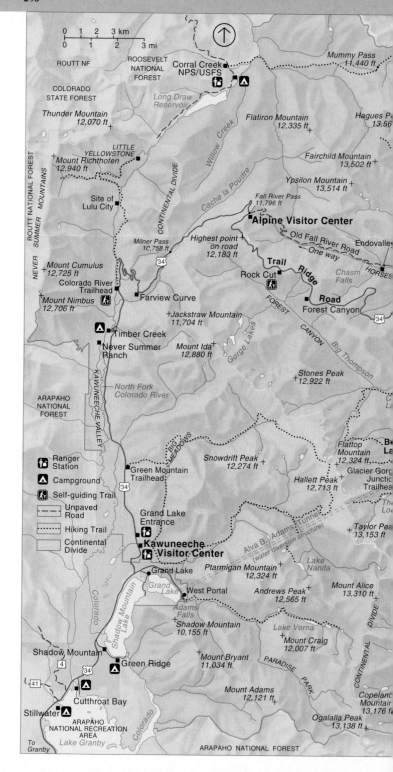

0 1 2 3 km
0 1 2 3 mi

ROUTT NF

ROOSEVELT
NATIONAL
FOREST

Corral Creek
NPS/USFS

Mummy Pass
11,440 ft

COLORADO
STATE FOREST

Long Draw
Reservoir

Thunder Mountain
12,070 ft

Flatiron Mountain
12,335 ft

Hagues P.
13,56

LITTLE
YELLOWSTONE

Mount Richthofen
12,940 ft

Fairchild Mountain
13,502 ft

Ypsilon Mountain
13,514 ft

Site of
Lulu City

Fall River Pass
11,796 ft

Alpine Visitor Center

Milner Pass
10,758 ft

Highest point
on road
12,183 ft

Old Fall River Road

Endovalle

One way

Mount Cumulus
12,725 ft

Colorado River
Trailhead

Trail

Rock Cut

Ridge

Chasm
Falls

HORSE

Mount Nimbus
12,706 ft

Farview Curve

Road

Forest Canyon

Jackstraw Mountain
11,704 ft

CANYON

Big Thompson

Timber Creek

Never Summer
Ranch

Mount Ida
12,880 ft

Gorge Lakes

North Fork
Colorado River

Stones Peak
12,922 ft

ARAPAHO
NATIONAL
FOREST

KAWUNEECHE VALLEY

BIG MEADOWS

Snowdrift Peak
12,274 ft

Flattop
Mountain
12,324 ft

B.
La

Glacier Gorg.
Junctic
Trailhea

Ranger
Station

Green Mountain
Trailhead

Hallett Peak
12,713 ft

Campground

Self-guiding Trail

Unpaved
Road

Hiking Trail

Continental
Divide

Grand Lake
Entrance

Alva B. Adams Tunnel
(water diversion structure)

Taylor Pea.
13,153 ft

Kawuneeche
Visitor Center

Grand Lake

Ptarmigan Mountain
12,324 ft

Lake
Nanita

West Portal

Andrews Peak
12,565 ft

Mount Alice
13,310 ft

Adams
Falls

Shadow Mountain
10,155 ft

Lake Verna

Mount Craig
12,007 ft

Shadow Mountain

Green Ridge

Mount Bryant
11,034 ft

PARADISE PARK

Cutthroat Bay

Stillwater

Mount Adams
12,121 ft

Copeland
Mountair
13,176 ft

ARAPAHO
NATIONAL RECREATION
AREA

Lake Granby

Ogalalla Peak
13,138 ft

To
Granby

ARAPAHO NATIONAL FOREST

ROUTT NATIONAL FOREST

NEVER SUMMER MOUNTAINS

CONTINENTAL DIVIDE

Cache la Poudre

Willow Creek

Colorado

Shadow Mountain Lake

Grand
Lake

CONTINENTAL DIVIDE

Indian paintbrush and death camas

through **Horseshoe Park** and past **Sheep Lakes** to look for bighorn sheep, which sometimes visit the natural mineral lick there. (In fall, take time to see Horseshoe Park at dawn or dusk to view elk; bugling mating calls start soon after sunset.) If you made the detour, either continue on **Old Fall River Road** to **Fall River Pass** (see next tour), or return to Deer Ridge Junction and turn west onto US 34, Trail Ridge Road.

Stop at an unmarked pullover on the right in just under 2 miles. Here, among the willows and alders, beavers have dammed **Hidden Valley Creek,** creating a series of ponds. Take a few minutes to stroll the boardwalk. Watch, too, for greenback cutthroat trout, a native fish being restored to park waters.

Continue along Trail Ridge Road, which soon enters the subalpine zone, dominated by forests of Engelmann spruce and subalpine fir. Stop again on the right just past **Many Parks Curve,** and walk back to the overlook. The "parks" in the Rockies are mountain meadows: When the glaciers of the last Ice Age melted, they often left lakes, dammed in by debris the glaciers had pushed along their edges. The lakes eventually silted up and drained, becoming flat meadows. In another 5⅘ miles, the road crosses timberline, where subzero winter temperatures and 100-mph winds blast trees into twisted shrubs. Higher still, the road enters tundra. Don't miss the 5-minute stroll to the overlooks of **Forest Canyon,** a glacier-carved, U-shaped valley 2,500 feet below. *Do stay on the trail*—damaged tundra plants take decades to recover.

Back in your car, drive on 2 miles, crossing smooth mountaintops that are part of a plain formed when an

Bighorn sheep on a winter slope near Fall River

ancestral mountain range eroded. The plain was uplifted largely intact and remained above the ice age glaciers. Stop at **Rock Cut** (12,110 feet) and hike the relatively easy 1-mile round-trip, paved nature trail. High altitude can cause dizziness and nausea, *so walk slowly and don't overdo.* (If you feel ill, you'll most likely recover as soon as the road descends.) The trail leads from a parking lot to the **Toll Memorial Mountain Index,** a peak-finder atop a rock pile. The 360-degree views of mountain, tundra, and weird rocks are splendid. Plaques introduce the geology, animals, and plants of this environment. About 4 miles farther along the road, exhibits on alpine life—and a chance to quench your thirst—await you at the **Alpine Visitor Center** and the Trail Ridge store and snack shop at Fall River Pass.

To continue the tour, exit the visitor center parking lot and turn right. Trail Ridge Road crosses the Continental Divide after about 4 miles, at **Milner Pass,** named for the surveyor of a never-built railway route through the Rockies. Water flowing east of the Divide will eventually find its way to the Atlantic, and water wending west will flow to the Pacific. The overlook at **Farview Curve,** about 2 miles farther, provides a riveting view of the **Never Summer Mountains** and glacier-carved **Kawuneeche Valley.** Through this valley winds the infant **Colorado River,** whose headwaters lie just 5 miles north. About halfway up on the western part of the Never Summer range,

you can see a horizontal scar. It is the 14-mile-long **Grand Ditch,** built between 1890 and 1932 to divert water from the wetter western side of the Continental Divide to the drier Great Plains to the east.

If short of time, turn back now. Otherwise continue the 14 miles remaining on Trail Ridge Road, descending to the beaver ponds, willows, and conifer forests of the valley floor. You might spot moose, reintroduced in 1978 after settlers eliminated them in this area. Hunters also killed off wolves, grizzly bears, and bison in the region.

In the late 19th century, smatterings of silver and gold lured miners by the hundreds to the valley. Resulting boomtowns vanished as quickly as they arose when mining claims proved unprofitable. From the **Colorado River Trailhead,** about 4 miles past Farview Curve, an easy 1⅘-mile hike brings you to the decaying 1870s cabins of miner Joe Shipler. About 2½ miles farther up the trail lies the site of Lulu City, once a bustling mining camp. Whether or not you hike, pick up an engaging leaflet on the human and natural history of this area at the trailhead or at a visitor center.

Stop again 2 miles down the road to stroll the easy ½ mile through the rippling grasses, and over the Colorado River, to **Never Summer Ranch,** a dude ranch dating from the 1920s. By that time it had become clear that the real gold was in tourists' pockets. Return to your car; the road exits the park near Grand Lake.

Sunrise over Sprague Lake

Old Fall River Road to Fall River Pass

9⅗ miles; a scant half day

Old Fall River Road provides an unpaved, leisurely (15 mph) drive through conifer forest and tundra. It is also a self-guided auto tour (no RVs or vehicles over 25 feet long), with leaflets for sale at the start, about 4 miles from the **Fall River Entrance Station.** En route you'll see traces of ancient glaciers and of recent rockslides and avalanches.

You can enter the park at the entrance station on US 34 or begin the tour off US 34 shortly before Sheep Lakes. (See **Trail Ridge Road** p. 295 for information on Sheep Lakes and Horseshoe Park.) Turn onto the **Endovalley** road. The huge assembly of boulders the road crosses is a reminder of the 1982 Lawn Lake flood. A dam, built prior to the creation of the park, burst one July morning, releasing a flood that turned the **Roaring River** into a tree-ripping torrent and deposited boulders, mud, and debris as far as the main street of Estes Park.

Pull over at the alluvial fan trailhead and take a few minutes to stroll the short paved pathway over the debris—up to 44 feet thick—and observe how

nature recovers: Young aspens and dozens of species of willows and grasses are claiming the area, as are a wide variety of birds and other animals. Walk back to your car along the trail, not the road.

As you drive on, note the scars on the aspens: Elk and other animals gnaw the bark, which then becomes infected with the black fungus you see; given enough damage, the aspens eventually die. Some observers cite the extent of aspen damage within the park as evidence that elk have reached or exceeded their population limit here. At Endovalley, continue on to the one-way Old Fall River Road with your self-guiding leaflet. Join Trail Ridge Road at Fall River Pass.

Bear Lake Road

10 miles; at least a half day

Popular especially for its trails, wildflowers, and fall foliage, **Bear Lake Road** starts off US 36 just past **Beaver Meadows Entrance Station.** Make your first stop the **Moraine Park Museum,** near the homestead of pioneer and resort owner Abner Sprague. Buy a pamphlet for the nature trail, an easy stroll that starts in front of the building. Along the trail, be sure

Beaver damming a river to make a pond and home

to smell the ponderosa pine bark; its vanilla scent is luscious.

Except in summer, drive on to the Bear Lake Road terminus. If the park is crowded, avoid the frustration of finding the parking lot full; park instead at the shuttle bus lot at **Glacier Basin.** The bus comes frequently; its schedule is in the park newspaper. Ride on through stands of lodgepole pine and aspen—dazzling in fall—to **Bear Lake.** Buy a pamphlet and stroll the ½-mile **Bear Lake Nature Walk,** enjoying this dramatic, oft-photographed scenery while you learn about forest ecology. The park's most popular hike climbs a mile from Bear to **Dream Lake,** over which tower the distinctive profiles of **Hallett Peak** and **Flattop Mountain.**

For a somewhat less crowded walk to another spectacular lake, start from **Glacier Gorge Junction Trailhead,** about ¾ mile back down the road. The **Loch Vale Trail** passes **Alberta Falls** in ½ mile, and reaches the rocky shoreline of **The Loch** in a moderately steep 2 7/10 miles.

Other Hikes

The park's excellent 355-mile trail system presents you with endless possibilities, just a few of which are listed below. See a ranger for details and ideas on less crowded walks.

Sprague Lake: Located off Bear Lake Road, Sprague Lake is a fishing pond created by Abner Sprague. Here's an easy, ½-mile self-guided nature walk, a loop dominated by views of Continental Divide peaks.

Wild Basin: This less congested corner of the park—14 miles south of Estes Park off Colo. 7—offers fine day hikes, including those to **Calypso Cascades** (1 4/5 miles) and **Ouzel Falls** (2 7/10 miles) through spruce-fir and mixed conifer forests along **North Saint Vrain Creek** and its tributaries. Pick up a nature booklet to learn how the forest has been making a comeback since a major fire in 1978.

Longs Peak, Chasm Lake: More than eight hundred people were counted climbing Longs on a summer's day. The predawn climb (8 miles one way) to the park's tallest peak requires planning—check with a ranger, especially about lightning. Some consider the challenging trail to Chasm Lake (4 1/5 miles one way) the park's most beautiful and rewarding hike. Both hikes begin at Longs Peak Ranger Station, 1 mile off Colo. 7, 10 miles south of Estes Park.

Cub Lake: The less traveled **Cub Lake Trail** (an easy 4 3/5-mile roundtrip) is known for birding and wildflowers, including the yellow water lilies afloat on Cub Lake in summer. The trail begins from a spur road off Bear Lake Road at **Moraine Park.**

Green Mountain Trail to **Big Meadows:** This easy trail (3 3/5 miles roundtrip) passes spruce-aspen woods, lodgepole forest, marshland, beaver ponds, and meadow. It starts from Trail Ridge Road, about 3 miles north of the **Grand Lake Entrance.**

Information & Activities

Headquarters
Estes Park, Colorado 80517. Phone
(970) 586-1206. www.nps.gov/romo

Seasons & Accessibility
Park open year-round. Trail Ridge
Road closes mid-Oct. to late May,
depending on snow. Old Fall River
Road closes Oct. to early July. In sum-
mer, free shuttle bus service on Bear
Lake Road.

Visitor & Information Centers
Beaver Meadows Visitor Center, on
US 36 at east entrance to park, and
Kawuneeche Visitor Center, on
US 34, all year. Alpine Visitor Center,
June–Sept. Fall River Visitor Center,
on US 34 west of Estes. Park at Fall
River entrance, May–Sept. Moraine
Park Museum and Visitor Center,
May to Oct. Call (970) 586-1206 for
information.

Entrance Fee
$15 per car; $30 annual.

Pets
Not permitted on trails or in backcountry. Must be on leashes at all times
in parking lots and campgrounds.

Facilities for Disabled
Visitor centers and museum are wheelchair accessible, as are amphitheaters
in campgrounds, but not all rest
rooms. Also accessible, the Lily Lake,
Bear Lake, and Sprague Lake nature
walks and the boardwalk at Hidden
Valley Creek beaver ponds. Hand-
icamp, at Sprague Lake, accommodates
wheelchair backcountry campers—call
(970) 586-1242.

Things to Do
Free naturalist-led activities: nature
and history walks, hikes, campfire
talks, slide shows, arts programs,
snowshoe walks. Also, hiking, horseback trail rides (stables in Grand Lake;
phone 303-627-3514), bicycling, fishing, and ice fishing, rock- and mountain climbing, cross-country skiing,
snowshoeing, limited snowmobiling.

Overnight Backpacking
Permits required, obtainable by mail
or in person from headquarters or the
Kawuneeche Visitor Center. Call (970)
586-1242. Fees charged for backcountry permits in summer.

Campgrounds
Five campgrounds. **Longs Peak,** 3-day
limit; others, 7-day limit June–Sept.
Add'l days permitted other times of
year. **Glacier Basin** and **Moraine Park**
open June–Sept.; reservations
required late May–Labor Day. Reserve
through National Parks Reservation
Service (see page 11). Other campgrounds open all year—first come,
first served. $16 per night in summer;
$10 per night in winter, when water is
not available. No showers. RV sites
except at **Longs Peak;** no hookups.
Reservations required at Glacier Basin
Group Campground; contact National
Parks Reservation Service. Cafeteria in
Trail Ridge store (summer only).

Hotels, Motels, & Inns
*(unless otherwise noted, rates are for 2
persons in a double room, high season)*
In Estes Park, Colorado 80517:
Aspen Lodge Ranch Resort 6120 Hwy.
7, Longs Peak Route. (800) 332-6867
or (970) 586-8133. 56 units. $300 per
person, all inclusive. 3-day min. June
through Aug. Pool. **RiverSong Bed &
Breakfast Inn** P.O. Box 1910. (970)
586-4666. 9 units. $150-$275, includes
breakfast. **The Stanley Hotel** (333
Wonderview Ave.). (800) 976-1377 or
(970) 586-3371. 135 units. $139-$290.
Pool, rest. **Winding River Ranch** 5770
Hwy 7. (970) 586-4212. 28 units.
$855-$1355 per person per week,
includes meals. Pool. Memorial
Day–Labor Day.
In Grand Lake, Colorado 80447:
Bighorn Lodge (613 Grand Ave.).
(800) 341-8000 or (970) 627-8101. 20
units. $90. **Driftwood Lodge** (12255
Hwy. 34). (970) 627-3654. 17 units,
9 with kitchenettes. $75-$95. Pool.
Western Riviera Motel (419 Garfield).
(970) 627-3580. 15 units. $90. Open
year round.

*For additional accommodations
contact the Chambers of Commerce
of Estes Park (800) 443-7837; and
Grand Lake (970) 627-3372.*

Excursions

Roosevelt National Forest
Fort Collins, Colorado

This high mountain forest in the Front Range offers craggy peaks with canyons and passes and clear alpine lakes. Contains five wilderness areas. 788,333 acres. More than 800 campsites, hiking, boating, boat ramp, fishing, horseback riding, hunting, picnic areas, scenic drives, water sports, winter sports. Four campgrounds open all year; others open May-September. Backcountry open July-October. Adjoins Rocky Mountain NP on east. Information at Fort Collins off I-25, about 45 miles from the park. (970) 498-2770.

Routt National Forest
Steamboat Springs, Colorado

Routt's three sections encompass high grasslands, forests, and jagged peaks along the Continental Divide. Alpine lakes brim with trout. Also contains waterfalls and parts of three wilderness areas. 1,124,774 acres. Facilities include 450 campsites, hiking, boating, boat ramp, fishing, horseback riding, hunting, picnic areas, winter sports, water sports, handicapped access. Open all year; most campsites open May-October. Information at Steamboat Springs, off US 40, about 75 miles from Rocky Mountain NP. (970) 879-1870.

Arapaho National Wildlife Refuge
Walden, Colorado

Set in a glacial basin ringed by mountains, Arapaho offers carefully maintained irrigated meadows that provide essential nesting habitat for waterfowl such as gadwall, lesser scaup, mallard, and wigeon. Black-crowned night herons breed along the Illinois River and sage grouse winter in upland hills. Features 6-mile-long self-guided auto tour (sometimes closed in winter due to snow). 23,267 acres. Facilities include fishing, hunting, scenic drives. Open year-round, dawn to dusk. Headquarters on Colo. Hwy. 125 south of Walden, about 50 miles from Rocky Mountain NP. (970) 723-8202.

Arapaho National Forest
Fort Collins, Colorado

The nation's highest paved highway traverses the steep mountains of this ski-country forest. Five wilderness areas feature stands of virgin timber, alpine lakes, and streams. 1,025,077 acres. Facilities include 633 campsites, hiking, boating, boat ramp, climbing, bicycling, fishing, horseback riding, hunting, picnic areas, scenic drives, winter sports, water sports. Open year-round, most campsites open June-September. Visitor center at Idaho Springs on I-70, about 50 miles from Rocky Mountain NP. (970) 498-2770.

Florissant Fossil Beds National Monument
Florissant, Colorado

Some 35 million years ago a nearby volcanic field erupted, trapping wildlife in the ash that fell on ancient Lake Florissant. More than 1,000 species of fossil insects, 140 plants, and numerous fish, bird, and small mammal species have been excavated from the Florissant shales—making this one of the world's most comprehensive fossil sites. 5,998 acres. Facilities include hiking, horseback riding, picnic areas, cross-country skiing, handicapped access. Open all year, dawn to dusk. Visitor center on County Road 1, off US 24, about 150 miles from Rocky Mountain NP. (719) 748-3253.

Dinosaur National Monument
Dinosaur, Colorado

Apatosaurus, Diplodocus, Stegosaurus—these Jurassic period giants once roamed here. Now their bones lie exposed in a fossil-filled cliff in the Dinosaur Quarry building. Each summer excavators add to the specimens. White-water rafting on Green and Yampa Rivers and Fremont pictographs and petroglyphs are also featured. 210,278 acres, part in Utah. Facilities include 134 campsites, boating, fishing, picnic areas, handicapped access. Open all year; most campsites open May-Oct. Dinosaur Quarry on Utah Hwy. 149, off US 40, about 220 miles from Rocky Mountain NP. (435) 789-2115.

Trail riders from the Peaceful Valley Ranch crossing the Little Missouri River

Theodore Roosevelt

North Dakota

Established November 10, 1978

70,447 acres

Theodore Roosevelt is unique among the scenic parks in that it preserves not only an extraordinary landscape but also the memory of an extraordinary man. It honors the president who probably did more for the National Park System than anyone before or since.

Theodore Roosevelt, who would later establish five national parks and help found the US Forest Service, first came to Dakota Territory as a young man in 1883 to "bag a buffalo." He tried cattle ranching with no luck, but returned many times over the next 13 years, developing into a confirmed conservationist. It was the rugged badlands that taught him a healthy respect for nature while toughening him phys-

ically and mentally. "I would not have been President," he would later say, "had it not been for my experience in North Dakota."

The history of the North Dakota badlands, however, goes back long before Roosevelt—65 million years, to be exact. It was then that streams flowing from the newly arisen Rockies began depositing sediments here that would later be carved by the Little Missouri River and its tributaries. The results of this ongoing process of deposition and erosion are spectacular: wildly corrugated cliffs; steep, convoluted gullies; and dome-shaped hills, their layers of rock and sediment forming multicolored horizontal stripes that run for miles.

This austere landscape is home to a surprisingly dense population of wildlife. Bison, pronghorn, elk,

When to Go

Although this is an all-year park, portions of the park road may close in winter, and services are quite limited from October to May. Summer is the most popular time to visit; the days are very long.

Late spring and early autumn are best for wildflower enthusiasts.

How to Visit

If you have only one day, take the **Scenic Loop Drive** in the **South Unit,** allowing yourself time for nature trails and longer hikes. A second day can be devoted to the **Scenic Drive** in the **North Unit,** 70 miles away. A visit to the undeveloped site of Roosevelt's **Elkhorn Ranch** or an overnight horse packing trip from the **Peaceful Valley Ranch** in the South Unit can fill out a longer stay.

South Unit: Scenic Loop Drive

36 miles; a half to full day

Start at the visitor center near **Medora,** where you can visit the relocated **Maltese Cross Cabin,** the rustic headquarters of Roosevelt's first ranch, which contains period furnishings, ranching equipment, and some of Roosevelt's personal belongings. Then follow the road up the side of the eroded cliff to the **Medora Overlook.** Here you get a good view of the rough little town that epitomized the Wild West back in Roosevelt's day.

white-tailed and mule deer, wild horses, and bighorn sheep inhabit the three units of the park, as do numerous smaller mammals, amphibians, and reptiles. After a rainy spring, a wealth of wildflowers colors the river bottomlands and prairie flats. And perhaps best of all is the shortage of one particular mammal—human beings. This relatively isolated park is hardly ever crowded, so you can experience the gorgeous loneliness of the badlands much the way Roosevelt did more than a hundred years ago.

How to Get There

South Unit: From Bismarck, 130 miles east, take I-94 west across the prairie to the entrance near Medora. From points south, take US 85 north to Belfield, then I-94 west 17 miles to Medora. **North Unit:** US 85 north from Belfield will bring you to the North Unit entrance.

Airports: Bismarck and, from the west, Billings, Mont. (280 miles).

Cabin from Roosevelt's Maltese Cross Ranch

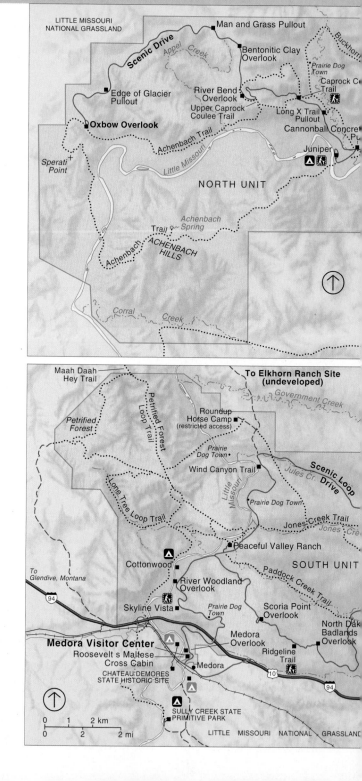

LITTLE MISSOURI
NATIONAL GRASSLAND

Scenic Drive

Appel Creek

Man and Grass Pullout

Bentonitic Clay
Overlook

Buckhorn

Prairie Dog
Town

Edge of Glacier
Pullout

River Bend
Overlook

Upper Caprock
Coulee Trail

Caprock C
Trail

Oxbow Overlook

Achenbach Trail

Long X Trail
Pullout

Cannonball Concre
Pu

Sperati
Point

Juniper

Little Missouri

NORTH UNIT

Achenbach
Spring

Trail

Achenbach

ACHENBACH
HILLS

↑

Corral Creek

Maah Daah
Hey Trail

To Elkhorn Ranch Site
(undeveloped)

Government Creek

Petrified Forest Loop Trail

Petrified
Forest

Roundup
Horse Camp
(restricted access)

Prairie
Dog Town

Wind Canyon Trail

Scenic Loop Drive

Jules Cr.

Little Missouri

Lone Tree Loop Trail

Prairie Dog Town

Jones Creek Trail

Jones Cre

To
Glendive, Montana

Peaceful Valley Ranch

SOUTH UNIT

Cottonwood

Paddock Creek Trail

River Woodland
Overlook

94

Skyline Vista

Prairie Dog
Town

Scoria Point
Overlook

North Dak
Badlands
Overlook

Medora Visitor Center

Medora
Overlook

Roosevelt s Maltese
Cross Cabin

Ridgeline
Trail

Medora

10

94

CHATEAU DEMORES
STATE HISTORIC SITE

↑

0   1   2 km
0   2   2 mi

SULLY CREEK STATE
PRIMITIVE PARK

LITTLE MISSOURI NATIONAL GRASSLAND

To Watford City

85

North Unit Visitor Center

Slump Block Pullout

Longhorn Pullout

CCC Campground, Forest Service

85

TLE MISSOURI NAL GRASSLAND

To Belfield

| 0 | 1 | 2 km |
| 0 | 1 | 2 mi |

LE MISSOURI NATIONAL RASSLAND

🏠 Ranger Station

🔺 Campground

🔺 Campground (private)

🧗 Self-guiding Trail

--- Unpaved Road

...... Trail

Prairie Dog Town

Talkington

Buck Hill 2,855 ft

Coal Vein Trail

Prairie Dog Town

Trail

ed Canyon itor Center

To Belfield and Bismarck

Continue on, making sure to stop at the roadside prairie dog town (they bark warnings to each other as you approach). A little farther along is the **Skyline Vista.** Here you are on a high plateau, looking over the broken badlands. Actually, you are not so much "up" as the badlands are "down." The plateau is just a remnant of the original prairie before erosion took its toll, scooping out the bewildering landscape below.

The road descends again to the **River Woodland Overlook.** Beyond the row of cottonwood trees on the left lies an agent of the visual feast around you— the **Little Missouri River.** Notice how, in this arid environment, the vegetation is rigidly stratified according to the availability of water. There are tall cottonwoods near the river, and dark green junipers on the relatively moist northern hillsides and in places where water-bearing layers are exposed. On the dry southern slopes, where the sun quickly evaporates rainwater, little grows except grasses.

Turn right at the T to begin the **Scenic Loop Drive.** When you reach **Scoria Point,** you are deep into classic badlands territory. The bricklike material around you, which provides the brightest color in the badlands pallette, was formed when a layer of black lignite ignited. It baked the gray clay above, turning it into the reddish material known locally (but inaccurately) as scoria.

Along the next 6 miles of road, you will encounter two self-guided nature trails that are well worth

Calf from the South Unit's herd of 400 bison

Little Missouri winding through rugged badlands of the North Unit

taking. The **Ridgeline Nature Trail,** while only ⅗ of a mile long, involves some strenuous climbing; a pamphlet at the trailhead introduces the complex interaction of wind, fire, water, and vegetation in this harsh environment. The **Coal Vein Trail,** at the end of the short unpaved road branching off at mile 15.6 (there's a sign), is a full mile but less difficult; look for the manifold effects of a lignite bed that burned here from 1951 until early 1977. Between these two trails, pull off at the **North Dakota Badlands Overlook** for an exceptional view of the surroundings.

One-and-a-half miles past the turnoff for Coal Vein is the short road to **Buck Hill.** Take the 100-yard path to the summit for a 360-degree panorama of the eastern end of the park and beyond. Those oil wells on the horizon remind you that, although the badlands stretch for hundreds of miles, the park does not.

Return to the main road and turn right. The backstretch of the loop, running from Buck Hill to **Wind Canyon,** offers several possibilities for longer hikes. The **Talkington Trail** can be followed to the east or to the west, but even better is the **Jones Creek Trail** at mile 21. This trail follows a deeply eroded creek bed for about 3½ miles, bisecting the loop road and offering good opportunities to see wildlife (including prairie rattlesnakes, *so be careful*). Since this trail is not a loop, you'll want to turn back at the halfway point or arrange to be picked up at the other end.

Back in the car, continue to the **Wind Canyon Trail.** This short but steep path offers a double treat: Not only do you get a magnificent vista of a long oxbow curve in the Little Missouri River, you also get a glimpse of how wind plays a part in shaping this unique landscape. The prevailing winds pick up sand from the riverbed and elsewhere and blow it into the northwest-facing canyon to your left, sandblasting the rock into smooth, bizarre shapes.

Back on the road, you pass another prairie dog town and then the **Peaceful Valley Ranch** on your right. These historic buildings have had a number of incarnations over the years, from working cattle ranch to park headquarters. These days the ranch is a private saddle horse concession, so you can stop for a ride (May to September) before rejoining the entrance road back to the visitor center.

North Unit: Scenic Drive

30 miles round-trip; a half to full day

Many people regard the **North Unit** as the more attractive of the two major portions of the park. Certainly the canyons seem steeper here, the river bottomlands lusher, and the blue, black, red, and beige stripes on every butte more pronounced. Located about 52 miles north of I-94, the North Unit is also more isolated, and consequently less visited. According to one ranger, there are times off-season when visitors can be almost alone in the North Unit.

Starting at the visitor center, take the **Scenic Drive** west into the park. Stop at the **Longhorn Pullout** to catch a glimpse of the park's demonstration herd of longhorn steers, kept here to commemorate the historic Long-X Trail, the major conduit for longhorns traveling from Texas to the Long-X Ranch just north of the park. If you hike the 11-mile **Buckhorn Trail Loop,** you'll travel along a part of this Old West "highway."

Stop at the **Slump Block Pullout** to see badlands erosion in action. The small hill to your right was once part of the higher cliff beyond— until unstable underlying sediments caused this piece to slump away. Try matching the diagonal layers of the slump block to the horizontal layers on the cliff to see how the block once fit in.

Pull off at the **Cannonball Concretions Pullout** to see how weathering agents have eroded out sandstone spheres formed by groundwater minerals cementing. Opposite the pullout, look for the **Little Mo Nature Trail.** This easy ½-mile loop takes you through typical river woodlands, and a guide leaflet (available at the trailhead) allows you to identify many native plants the Plains Indians used for medicine, food, and raw materials. Watch for beavers and white-tailed deer.

Returning to the car, follow the road to the **Caprock Coulee Pullout,** where you can pick up the nature trail of the same name. Take this easy trail ¾ of a mile up a dry canyon (a "coulee") to a grove of pedestal rocks ("caprocks"). The harder caprocks protect the sediments below while the surrounding sediments erode away, leaving the mushroom-shaped formations around you. At the end of the nature trail, you can either turn back or make a 5-mile loop by continuing to the **Upper Caprock Coulee Trail,** a choice which involves some steeper climbing but lots of opportunities to view wildlife.

Beyond the Caprock parking lot, the road climbs steeply to the level of the original prairie. At the top, the **River Bend Overlook** offers an absolutely stunning vista of the deep Little Missouri Valley and the extensive badlands on either side. The **Bentonitic Clay Overlook** a little farther on offers a less dramatic but perhaps more

Caprock formation

Prairie dog eyeing a rattler

instructive view. The blue-colored bentonite layer visible for miles is composed of an extremely absorbent volcanic ash that flows when wet. The plasticity of this layer accounts for much of the dynamism of the badlands landscape.

The road now traces the edge of a grassy plateau. This is prime bison territory; you may even have to wait while a herd crosses the road in front of you. At the **Man and Grass Pullout** you can get some idea of the extensive grasslands that made this part of Dakota worth the trip up the Long-X Trail. Finally, the road ends—spectacularly—at the **Oxbow Overlook.** After enjoying the visual banquet of badlands, return along the same road to the visitor center.

Information & Activities

Headquarters
P.O. Box 7, Medora, North Dakota
58645. Phone (701) 623-4466.
www.nps.gov/thro

Seasons & Accessibility
Park open all-year, but access may
be limited in winter due to snow. The
South Unit road from Medora Visitor
Center through Wind Canyon to the
north boundary is kept plowed, but
not the Scenic Loop Drive. The North
Unit road is plowed from the entrance
to the Caprock Coulee Trailhead. Call
headquarters for weather and road
information.

Visitor & Information Centers
Medora Visitor Center and the Maltese
Cross Cabin, at the entrance to the
South Unit, open daily all year, except
Thanksgiving, Christmas, and New
Year's Day. Painted Canyon Visitor
Center, in the southeastern part of
the South Unit off I-94, open from
April to mid–November. North
Unit Visitor Center, open daily April
through September, open weekends
in winter. Call headquarters for
visitor information.

Entrance Fee
$10 per vehicle per week; $20 annually.

Pets & Horses
Pets are permitted on leashes except
on backcountry trails and in buildings. Horses are prohibited in campgrounds, picnic areas, and on
self-guided trails.

Facilities for Disabled
Visitor centers, rest rooms, campground sites, and some trails are
wheelchair accessible.

Things to Do
Free naturalist-led activities: nature
walks and talks, tours of Roosevelt's
Maltese Cross Cabin (mid-June to
mid-September), evening campfire
programs. Also available, hiking,
horseback riding (contact the
Peaceful Valley Ranch in South
Unit; phone 701-623-4568),
interpretive exhibits, auto tours,
limited canoeing and float trips,
fishing (license needed), and cross-
country skiing.

Special Advisories
● View bison from a distance; they
are known to attack if provoked.
● Rattlesnakes and black widow
spiders often live in prairie dog burrows; be alert for them when hiking.
● Do not feed the prairie dogs; they
bite and may carry disease.
● Be prepared for extremes of
temperatures and sudden violent
thunderstorms.

Overnight Backpacking
Permits required. They are free and
can be obtained at visitor centers.

Campgrounds
Two campgrounds, both with 14-day
limit. **Cottonwood** and **North Unit**
open all year, first come, first served.
Fees $10 per night. No showers. Tent
and RV sites; no hookups. Two group
campgrounds, **Halliday Well** and
North Unit; reservations required;
contact park headquarters.

Hotels, Motels, & Inns
*(unless otherwise noted, rates are for 2
persons in a double room, high season)*
OUTSIDE THE PARK:
In Dickinson, N. Dak. 58601:
Comfort Inn 493 Elk Dr. (800) 228-
5150 or (701) 264-7300. 115 units.
$69. AC, pool. **Rodeway Inn** (1000 W.
Villerd St.). (701) 225-6703. 35 units.
$57. AC, pool. **Travelodge** 532 15th St.
W. (800) 422-0949 or (701) 227-1853.
149 units. $64. AC, pool, restaurant.
In Medora, N. Dak. 58645:
Badlands Motel 501 Pacific Ave. (800)
633-6721 or (701) 623-4444. 116
units. $83. AC, pool. Open May to
October. **Medora Motel** (1 Main St.)
400 E. River Rd. South. (800) 633-
6721 or (701) 623-4444. 208 units.
$64. AC, pool. Open June to Labor
Day. **Rough Riders Hotel** 301 3rd Ave.
(800) 633-6721 or (701) 623-4444. 10
units. $83. AC, rest. Open June to
Labor Day. **Sully Inn** (4th & Broadway). (701) 623-4444. 19 units. $55-
$70. AC.
In Watford City, N. Dak. 58854:
Roosevelt Inn (600 2nd Ave. S.W.)
P.O. Box 1466. (888) 206-0400 or
(701) 842-3686. 50 units. $40-$45.
AC, restaurant.

Excursions

Little Missouri National Grassland

Dickinson & Watford City, North Dakota

Bighorn sheep, elk, pronghorn, eagles, hawks, and grouse live in the prairie and badlands around Theodore Roosevelt NP. 1.1 million acres. 5 campgrounds, hiking, horseback riding, hunting. Open all year; campgrounds open late May-Labor Day. Info. in Dickinson, off I-94. (701) 225-5151 or (701) 842-2393.

Lake Ilo National Wildlife Refuge

Dunn Center, North Dakota

Waterfowl nest in the grasslands surrounding 1,240-acre Lake Ilo, offering recreation not found on all refuges. 3,903 acres. Boating, fishing, picnic areas, nature trail, archaeological exhibits, scenic drives. Open year-round. Located on N. Dak. 200, about 50 miles from Theodore Roosevelt NP's North Unit. (701) 548-8110.

Lostwood National Wildlife Refuge

Kenmare, North Dakota

Ducks, marsh birds, grouse, hawks, Baird's sparrows, and Sprague's pipits inhabit this stretch of prairie dotted with shallow glacial lakes, attracting birdwatchers from near and far. 26,900 acres. Facilities include hiking, hunting, scenic drives. Open all year, dawn to dusk. Located off N. Dak. 8, about 135 miles northeast of Theodore Roosevelt NP's North Unit. (701) 848-2722.

Crosby Wetland Management District

Crosby, North Dakota

This prairie region comprises 92 water-fowl areas as well as Lake Zahl NWR. Features whooping cranes in migration, grouse on spring dancing grounds. 85,819 acres. Facilities: hunting. Permission required to use privately owned easement areas. Open all year. Lake Zahl NWR is off US 85, north of Theodore Roosevelt NP's North Unit. (701) 965-6488.

Prince of Wales Hotel on Waterton Lakes

Waterton-Glacier

Alberta, Canada, and Montana

Established June 18, 1932

Waterton Lakes, 73,800 acres

Glacier, 1,013,572 acres

Waterton-Glacier International Peace Park World Heritage site contains 2,000 square miles of what naturalist John Muir called "the best care-killing scenery on the continent." Many-hued summits—whittled by ancient glaciers into walls and horns—rise abruptly from gently rolling plains. Some 650 lakes, dozens of glaciers, and uncounted waterfalls glisten in forested valleys. A scenic highway crosses the park, making much of its beauty accessible to the casual visitor. More than 700 miles of trails await hikers and horseback riders.

In 1932 Canada and the United States declared Waterton Lakes National Park (founded in 1895)

and neighboring Glacier National Park (founded in 1910) the world's first International Peace Park. While administered separately, the park's two sections cooperate in wildlife management, scientific research, and some visitor services.

The tremendous range of topography in Waterton-Glacier supports a rich variety of plants and wildlife. More than 1,800 plant species provide food and haven for 63 native species of mammals and more than 270 species of birds. In the 1980s the gray wolf settled into Glacier for the first time since the 1950s.

But now strip-mining and oil, gas, housing, and logging projects proposed or underway near the park's borders threaten the habitats of both water and land animals, including elk, bighorn sheep, and the threatened grizzly. Park officials and conservation

Browning, and East Glacier Park; by prior arrangement, buses take travelers into the park. Nearest airports: Kalispell, Great Falls, and Lethbridge, Alberta.

When to Go

Summer. All of Going-to-the-Sun Road open about mid-June to mid-October; Chief Mountain International Hwy., mid-May to late September. Trails at lower elevations usually clear of snow by mid-June; higher trails can remain snowed-in until mid-July. Cross-country skiing popular late December to April in many areas of the park.

How to Visit

Spend your first day on and around **Going-to-the-Sun Road,** considered by many one of the world's most spectacular highways. On a second day, travel the **Chief Mountain International Highway** north to Waterton Lakes, enjoying the contrast of peak and prairie. Drive Waterton's **Akamina Parkway** and **Red Rock Canyon Parkway.** Stay at least another day to visit **Many Glacier.** For a longer visit, drive to **Two Medicine** for a boat ride and walk to an exquisite lake, then continue on to the **Walton Goat Lick Overlook.** If you have the stamina and overnight reservations, hike or ride horseback to one of the two remaining chalets built early in this century by the Great Northern Railway.

groups are working with the US Forest Service, the Canadian government, the Blackfeet Indian Reservation, and private companies to try to protect critical habitats.

Sheltered valleys and bountiful food have lured people here for more than 8,000 years. Ancient cultures tracked bison across the plains, fished the lakes, and traversed the mountain passes. The Blackfeet controlled this land during the 18th and much of the 19th century.

How to Get There

Approach West Glacier (from Kalispell, Mont., about 35 miles) and East Glacier Park from US 2. US 89 leads to Many Glacier and St. Mary in the east; US 89 and Mont. 17 (Chief Mountain International Hwy.) form the shortest connection between Glacier and Waterton Lakes. Coming from Canada, follow Alberta 2, 5, or 6. Amtrak trains from Chicago and Seattle stop year-round just outside the park at West Glacier (Belton), Essex,

Going-to-the-Sun Road

50 miles; a full day

Begin early at **Apgar** on Glacier's west side. At the visitor center pick up details about trails and, since this is grizzly and black bear country, cautionary advice on avoiding encounters. Then take time to admire **Lake McDonald** from an excellent vantage point a little farther down the road. The park's largest lake, McDonald is 10 miles long and 472 feet deep; a glacier more than 2,000 feet thick gouged out its basin. Kootenai Indians, who performed lakeshore ceremonies, called the waters Sacred Dancing Lake.

Continue driving the Apgar loop and turn left at **Going-to-the-Sun Road.** Then pull over at **McDonald**

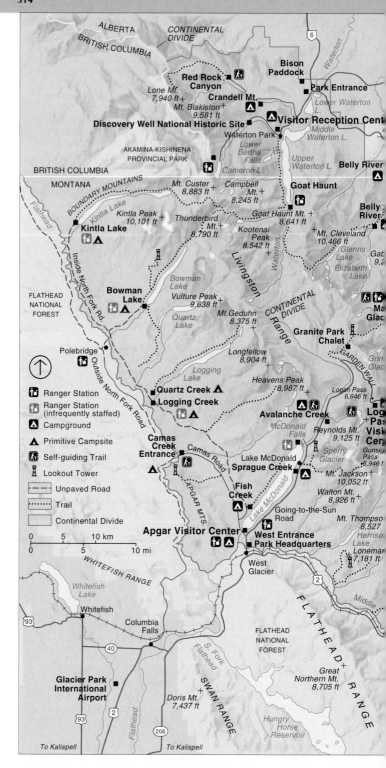

ALBERTA
BRITISH COLUMBIA
CONTINENTAL DIVIDE

Red Rock Canyon
Bison Paddock
Lone Mt. 7,940 ft +
Crandell Mt.
Mt. Blakiston + 9,581 ft
Park Entrance
Lower Waterton L.
Discovery Well National Historic Site
Waterton Park
Visitor Reception Cent
Middle Waterton L.

AKAMINA-KISHINENA PROVINCIAL PARK
Lower Bertha Falls
Cameron L.
Upper Waterton L.
Belly River

BRITISH COLUMBIA
MONTANA
BOUNDARY MOUNTAINS
Mt. Custer 8,883 ft +
Campbell Mt. + 8,245 ft
Goat Haunt
Belly River

Kintla Lake
Kintla Peak + 10,101 ft
Thunderbird Mt. + 8,790 ft
Goat Haunt Mt. + 8,641 ft
Kootenai Peak 8,542 ft +
Mt. Cleveland + 10,466 ft
Glenns Lake
Gat 9,2

Kintla Lake
Flathead
Inside North Fork Rd.

Bowman Lake
Bowman Lake
Vulture Peak 9,638 ft +
Mt. Geduhn 8,375 ft +
CONTINENTAL DIVIDE
Granite Park Chalet
GARDEN WAL
Grin
Gla
Ma
Glac

FLATHEAD NATIONAL FOREST
Quartz Lake
Livingston Range
Longfellow 8,904 ft +

Polebridge
Outside North Fork Road
Logging Lake
Heavens Peak 8,987 ft +
Logan Pass 6,646 ft
Grin
Gla

Quartz Creek
Logging Creek
Avalanche Creek
McDonald Falls
Reynolds Mt. 9,125 ft +
Sperry Glacier
Lo
Pas
Visi
Cer

Camas Creek Entrance
Camas Road
Lake McDonald
Sprague Creek
Mt. Jackson + 10,052 ft
Gunsig Pass 6,946 ft

APGAR MTS.
Fish Creek
Lake McDonald
Going-to-the-Sun Road
Walton Mt. 8,926 ft +
Mt. Thompso 8,527
Harriso Lake
Lonema 7,181 ft +

Apgar Visitor Center
West Entrance
Park Headquarters
West Glacier

Ranger Station
Ranger Station (infrequently staffed)
Campground
Primitive Campsite
Self-guiding Trail
Lookout Tower
Unpaved Road
Trail
Continental Divide

0   5   10 km
0   5   10 mi

WHITEFISH RANGE
FLATHEAD RANGE
Middle

Whitefish Lake
Whitefish
Columbia Falls
FLATHEAD NATIONAL FOREST
Great Northern Mt. 8,705 ft +

Glacier Park International Airport
Swan Range
Doris Mt. 7,437 ft +
Hungry Horse Reservoir

To Kalispell
To Kalispell

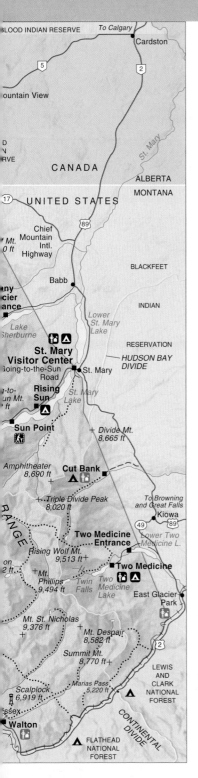

Falls, on your left after about 10 miles. Stroll down to the viewpoint and note the layered rock. Waterton-Glacier's mountains are built mainly of sedimentary rock formed from mud and sand at the bottom of a sea that existed here for nearly a billion years. Over the eons, pressures in the Earth uplifted, thrusted, and folded the seabed into mountains. The rock exposed at McDonald Falls is among the oldest in the park.

Pull over near the campground at **Avalanche Creek** and start the self-guided **Trail of the Cedars** from the right side of the road. This wheel-chair-accessible trail is on a board-walk. The easy ¾-mile nature stroll acquaints you with the cedar-hemlock forest through which you've been dri-ving. Along the trail, Avalanche Creek tumbles through contoured walls of surprisingly red stone, formed during a period when the sea here retreated. In contact with oxygen, iron-bearing minerals in the mud formed the bright red mineral hematite that colors the rock. Extend your walk, if you wish, by taking the **Avalanche Lake Trail** from near the gorge up to glacier-fed **Avalanche Lake.** The gently climbing trail, about 4 miles round-trip, offers fine views of creek, lake, and waterfalls.

Return to your car. Directly ahead about 2 miles, you'll see the **Garden Wall,** part of the Continental Divide. West of the Divide, waters flow to the Pacific; east of it, to the Arctic and Atlantic. Two glaciers ground down

On the Continental Divide

Massive Grinnell Glacier

opposite sides of a ridge to form the knife-edged Garden Wall. At the **Bird Woman Falls** viewpoint (some 10 miles from the campground at Avalanche Creek), an exhibit illustrates how glaciers also carved this spectacular U-shaped valley. Glacier National Park takes its name from the huge rivers of ice that sculptured the landscape during ice ages of the last two million years.

At **Logan Pass,** atop the Continental Divide, the peaks crowd around as if nearly close enough to touch. Park and walk up the hill past the visitor center to take the **Hidden Lake Nature Trail.** Be sure to buy or borrow a self-guiding pamphlet at the trailhead. The 3-mile round-trip begins on the boardwalk and offers vast displays of wildflowers framed by dramatic peaks. A breath-taking vista of **Hidden Lake** awaits you at the end. Watch for mountain goats grazing, marmots sunning, and golden eagles scanning for rodents. *Always stay on the trail:* Alpine plants, growing for short seasons in thin soil, are extremely fragile.

Return to your car and turn right onto the main road. Soon you'll be approaching **Going-to-the-Sun Mountain**—at 9,642 feet, the highest in this area of the park. The name comes, depending on which story you believe,

from a Blackfeet legend or an early explorer. The legend says that Napi, the creator, came to help the Blackfeet, then climbed this mountain to return to the sun.

Pull over again to view **Jackson Glacier,** one of the few glaciers visible from the road, about 4½ miles after Logan Pass. The turnoff for **Sun Point** leads to picnic tables, fine vistas of **St. Mary Lake,** and a nature trail that introduces the ecology of the drier eastern portion of the park. Stop at the **Wild Goose Island Overlook,** another 1½ miles down the road, and again at the display about **Triple Divide Peak,** less than 3 miles beyond. The road now crosses grasslands punctuated by groves of aspen and conifers. Going-to-the-Sun Road ends at **Divide Creek,** the border of the Blackfeet Indian Reservation.

Chief Mountain International Highway to Waterton Lakes

75 miles; at least a full day

Chief Mountain International Highway begins north of Babb off US 89. **Chief Mountain** (9,080 feet) dominates the horizon to your left, a soli-

Rainbows on Swiftcurrent Lake

Mountain goat and kid

tary peak that commands awe. Black-feet seeking spiritual guidance still tie a traditional offering of colored cloth to trees at its base.

Chief Mountain also represents the easternmost extension of the Lewis Overthrust, a major geological feature. About 8½ miles after the US-Canada customs station, an exhibit explains the overthrust. Pull over again in 1½ miles for a superb view of **Waterton Valley** and a display that identifies the summits.

Follow the signs for Waterton Lakes National Park. The park's main information center will be on your right, just before the town, about 4 miles past the entrance. On your left is the **Prince of Wales Hotel,** which commands a first-rate view of **Upper Waterton Lake** from its lobby. For a loftier panorama, climb the steep but gratifying **Bears Hump Trail,** 2 miles round-trip. The path starts from the information center.

Back in your car, turn right onto **Akamina Parkway,** which traces **Cameron Valley** 10 miles to **Cameron Lake.** At the lake, which lies in a large glacier-carved basin, rent a boat, fish for trout, or stroll the 2-mile round-trip **Cameron Lakeshore Trail** through the forest of Englemann spruce and

subalpine fir. *Do not continue past the end of the trail*—grizzlies are often sighted there.

Back in your car, return to Alberta 5; turn left, then left again onto 10-mile-long **Red Rock Canyon Parkway.** The prairie here brims with flowers in May, June, and early July. Indians hunted bison along **Blakiston Creek,** driving them over the cliff to your left. In about 3 miles, near Crandell Mountain Campground, stop at the exhibit on ancient Indian life. Drive on to the road's end at **Red Rock Canyon,** where archaeologists found a camp dating from 8,400 years ago. Don't miss the ½-mile **Red Rock Canyon Loop Trail.**

Waterton Park townsite, a village of about a hundred year-round residents, blossoms in summer with eateries and gift shops. From Red Rock Canyon Parkway head south on Mont. 5 and turn left onto Mount View Road, which leads to town. On the lakeshore, near the road's end, a pavilion reviews the park's history.

Many Glacier & Swiftcurrent Valley

13 miles from Babb; at least a half day

Many Glacier, named for the glaciers on surrounding mountains, is a hiker's Eden and a good place to see bighorn sheep and other wildlife. A dam a few miles outside the park created **Lake Sherburne,** on your left as you enter the park. The lake submerged much of Altyn, a boomtown built during the mining frenzy that started and fizzled out here at the turn of the century.

Just beyond the lake, to your left, is the **Many Glacier Hotel.** The Great Northern Railway built this hotel in 1915 to help promote tourism along its tracks. The company also built more than a dozen backcountry tent camps and chalets in Waterton-Glacier. Early tourists rode horses between the railway stations, hotels, and chalets. Park at the hotel and, for an easy walk and fine introduction to the area's plants, animals, peaks, and glaciers, take the **Swiftcurrent Nature Trail.** This 2⅖-mile loop around the lake starts at the shore south of the hotel. The trail traverses both 400-year-old spruce-fir forest and 60-year-old lodgepole pine forest, planted in the aftermath of a great fire in 1936.

For an easy 2½-mile stroll through old-growth forest, go on the **Swiftcurrent and Josephine Lakes** boat tour and hike. With more time and plenty of stamina, join a naturalist-led hike (11 miles round-trip) to the edge of **Grinnell Glacier,** one of the largest in the park. Check departure times in the park newspaper.

Other Sights & Trails

Before hiking, be sure to stop by a visitor center or ranger station to pick up maps and schedules—and check for trail closings due to bears.

Drive to **Two Medicine,** inside the park's southeastern border off Mont. Hwy. 49, and take the boat across **Two Medicine Lake.** Then walk past **Twin Falls** through huckleberry meadows to **Upper Two Medicine,** which is surrounded by brightly colored cliffs (4⅖ miles round-trip). Back in your car, head south on Mont. Hwy. 49 and west on US 2 to the **Walton Goat Lick Overlook.** A natural salt lick attracts mountain goats from miles

around, usually in spring and early summer.

From Logan Pass, the **Highline Trail** offers splendid panoramic views on the way to **Granite Park Chalet** (7⅗ miles), one of the Great Northern's two remaining chalets. A part of the trail is cut into the cliff face, so it is not for the faint-hearted. The other chalet, **Sperry,** was recently restored. Sperry can be reached by horseback or hiking from **Jackson Glacier Overlook** or Lake McDonald.

From Many Glacier, **Iceberg Lake Trail** leads you among wide panoramas to an iceberg-studded turquoise lake, a 10-mile round-trip. **Cracker Lake Trail,** 12¼ miles round-trip, parallels boulder-strewn **Canyon Creek** partway to this glacier-fed lake. Nearby lie remains of **Cracker Mine.**

From Waterton, **Rowe Meadow Lakes** (a moderately strenuous 6½-mile round-trip) offers a rainbow of wildflowers in early summer. Climb another ⁷⁄₁₀ mile to **Upper Rowe Lake** through an alpine larch forest. The **International Peace Park Hike,** held on Saturday mornings, leads from Waterton Townsite 8⅖ miles to **Goat Haunt** in the United States. Return by boat.

The Grizzly

Blackfeet Indians called it Real Bear, this huge, intelligent, unpredictable animal we call the grizzly. An adult male may weigh 400 to 600 pounds, twice as much as a black bear, yet it can sprint up to 35 mph.

Tens of thousands of grizzlies roamed western North America in 1850; by 1975, the guns of settlers, hunters, and livestock owners, coupled with loss of habitat, had driven the bears close to extinction in the lower 48 states. While some 50,000 grizzlies may remain in Alaska and Canada, fewer than 1,000 now inhabit the rest of the United States, perhaps 300 of them in Waterton-Glacier and nearby wilderness lands.

Though mythologized as a ruthless predator, the grizzly eats mostly grass, berries, and roots. It will also consume insects and rodents and even larger animals if easy prey. Unless accustomed to human scent and food, most grizzlies will move on when they hear a human coming.

Grizzly

In Glacier they say that 90 percent of grizzly management is people management. And people management has changed greatly since 1967, when two Glacier campers were killed by grizzlies accustomed to eating garbage. (Before then at least one park lodge fed bears garbage to entertain visitors.) Today rangers carefully instruct visitors on sharing the wilderness with bears.

Information & Activities

Headquarters

Waterton: Waterton Park, Alberta, TOK 2MO, Canada. (403) 859-2224. **Glacier:** West Glacier, Montana 59936. (406) 888-7800. www.nps.gov/glac

Seasons & Accessibility

Parks open year-round; winter snows limit access and services.

Visitor & Information Centers

Waterton: Waterton Information Centre in Waterton Townsite. (403) 859-2224. Usually open mid-May through Sept.; call ahead.
Glacier: Apgar Visitor Center, inside West Entrance, open daily late April–Oct., weekends in winter (406) 888-7800. Logan Pass Visitor Center, open mid-June to mid-Oct. St. Mary Visitor Center at east entrance open late May to mid–October.

Entrance Fees

Waterton: Canadian $4 per person. **Glacier:** $10 per car valid for 7 days; $20 annual.

Facilities for Disabled

Waterton: International Peace Park Pavilion, Heritage Centre, Cameron Lake exhibit building wheelchair accessible.
Glacier: Most visitor center facilities accessible; also, Trail of the Cedars, Running Eagle Falls Trail, Oberlin Bend Trail, and Apgar Bike Path.

Things to Do

Waterton: Free naturalist-led activities: walks and hikes, canoe tours, puppet shows, junior workshops, slide shows, campfire programs. Also, swimming, fishing (license needed), boating, launch tours, nature courses, horseback rides, golf, fishing, cross-country skiing.
Glacier: Free naturalist-led activities: walks and hikes, slide talks, campfire programs. Also, hiking, horseback rides, boating, fishing (no license required), bicycling, launch tours, nature courses, cross-country skiing.

Overnight Backpacking

Permits required. Call in advance about reservations and fees.

Backcountry Chalets

Granite Park Chalet, (800) 521-7238, $60 and Sperry Chalet (888) 345-2649, $50 per room plus $100 per person offer lodgings and food services.

Campgrounds

Waterton: Three campgrounds, 14-day limit. Open mid-May to early Sept. (**Townsite** open to mid-Oct.). First come, first served. Fees Can. $7.25-$19 per night. Tent and RV sites; hookups at **Townsite.** Must reserve at **Belly River Group Campgrounds;** contact park. Food services available in park.
Glacier: 13 campgrounds, limit 7 days July-Aug., otherwise 14 days. **Apgar** and **St. Mary** open all year, others late spring to mid-fall. Resevations for Fish Creek and St. Mary through National Parks Reservation Service (see p. 11). Others, first come, first served. Fees $12-$17 per night. Tent and RV sites; no hookups. **Apgar Group Campground** first come, first served. Food in park.

Hotels, Motels, & Inns

(unless otherwise noted, rates are for 2 persons in a double room, high season)
INSIDE WATERTON, Alberta TOK 2MO:
Windflower Motels P.O. Box 100. (403) 859-2255. 50 units. Can. $129. Open mid-May to mid-Oct. **Bayshore Inn** (111 Waterton Ave.) Summer (403) 859-2211; winter (403) 238-4847. 70 units. Can. $139. Rest. Open April to Oct. **Crandell Mt. Lodge** (1 Waterton Park) (403) 859-2288. 17 units. Can. $107. Open March to Oct. **Prince of Wales Hotel** (in Waterton Townsite) Glacier Park, Inc. 1850 North Central Ave., Phoenix, Ariz. 85077-0928. (406) 756-2444. 88 units. Can. $269-$309. Rest. Open mid-May to late Sept.
INSIDE GLACIER:
The following are open generally from June to mid-September. They are operated by Glacier Park, Inc. 1850 North Central Ave., Phoenix, Arizona 84077-0928. For reservations phone (406) 756-2444.
Glacier Park Lodge 161 units. $135-$500. Pool, restaurant. **Lake McDonald Lodge** 100 units. $86-$135. Restaurant. **Many Glacier Hotel** 211 units. $106-$205. Rest. **Rising Sun Motor Inn** 72 units. Rooms $81-$86; cabins $86. Rest. **Swiftcurrent Motor Inn** 86 units. Cabins $41-$79; rooms $88. **The Village Inn** 36 units. $91-$143.

Excursions

Flathead National Forest

Kalispell, Montana

Recreation opportunities abound here amid mountains, lakes, wild and scenic rivers, and more than 2,000 miles of trails. Contains parts of three wilderness areas, notably the Bob Marshall. 2,346,000 acres. Facilities include 400 campsites, hiking, boating, boat ramp, climbing, fishing, horseback riding, hunting, picnic areas, scenic drives, winter sports, water sports. Open all year; campsites open June to mid-September. Visitor center off US 2 at Hungry Horse Dam, about 7 miles from Waterton-Glacier NP. (406) 758-5200.

Lewis & Clark National Forest

Great Falls, Montana

This forest has two sections separated by plains: The Rockies section boasts steep terrain with parts of two wilderness areas; the Jefferson section contains gentler peaks and rolling hills with broad plateaus. Large bighorn herd. 1,843,000 acres. 24 campsites, 5 winter cabins (reservations required), hiking, boating, boat ramp, climbing, fishing, horseback riding, hunting, winter sports, water sports, handicapped access. Open all year; campsites open late spring to fall. Adjoins Waterton-Glacier NP on south; info. at 1101 15th St. North, Great Falls. (406) 791-7700.

Kootenai National Forest

Libby, Montana

With a climate closer to that of the Pacific coast than to the rest of Montana, Kootenai features virgin stands of western red cedar. Lake Koocanusa, 90 miles long, and many other streams and reservoirs offer abundant recreation. Contains Cabinet Mountains Wilderness. 2,250,000 acres, part in Idaho. Facilities include 703 campsites, hiking, boating, climbing, bicycling, fishing, hunting, picnic areas, scenic drives, winter sports. Open all year; most campsites open late spring to fall. Information at Libby on US 2, about 120 miles from Waterton-Glacier NP. (406) 293-6211.

Pine Butte Swamp Preserve
Choteau, Montana

Pine Butte, a 500-foot promontory, overlooks this Nature Conservancy refuge dedicated to maintaining the essential habitat of the grizzly. Also contains many other wildlife species, including lynx, cougar, sandhill crane, golden eagle, mink, and bighorn sheep. Features the Egg Mountain duckbill dinosaur nesting site; daily paleontological tours during summer. Permission required to explore. 18,000 acres, along the Teton River. Facilities: hiking, climbing, and the Pine Butte Guest Ranch offering horseback riding, natural history tours (open May-October). Preserve open all year. Off US 89, about 60 miles southeast of Waterton-Glacier NP. (406) 466-5526.

Benton Lake National Wildlife Refuge
Black Eagle, Montana

More than 200 species of birds find food, protection, and carefully maintained nesting areas on this large prairie marsh in the midst of Montana wheat fields and grasslands. Northern pintail, gadwall, Franklin's gull, white-faced ibis, mallard, and Canada goose are among the species that nest in the ancient glacial lake bed that holds the marsh. 12,383 acres. Facilities include hunting, self-guided auto tour. Open March to November, dawn to dusk. Headquarters off US 87, about 100 miles from Waterton-Glacier NP. (406) 727-7400.

Evening light bathing prairie at Wind Cave

Wind Cave

South Dakota

Established January 9, 1903

28,295 acres

Too many visitors leave Wind Cave National Park knowing only half of its charms. Ironically, the half they know is the half that's not visible from the surface.

Above the spectacular underground labyrinth for which the park is named lies an unusual ecosystem, one that marks the boundary between the mixed-grass prairie of the western Great Plains and the ponderosa pine forests of the Black Hills. Thus, the park plays host to plant and animal species from several distinct geographical areas—prairie falcons and meadowlarks from the grasslands coexist here with nuthatches and wild turkeys from the forests.

Wildlife should be a major draw here. Because of the park's small size and relatively large bison population, the chances of seeing bison—the so-called American buffalo—are probably better at this park than at almost any other; indeed it's often difficult to avoid the great beasts. Pronghorn, mule deer, and prairie dogs are present in large numbers—and highly visible since 75 percent of the park is open grassland. Elk live in the forest fringes; you probably won't see many of them, but if you have the good luck to come in the autumn you'll hear their eerie bugling.

Below ground lies Wind Cave, where over 92 miles of explored passages make it one of the longest caves in the world. Because the cave is relatively dry, it contains few of the stalactites and stalagmites you see in other caves. But it has many unusual mineral

formations, including perhaps the world's best collection of boxwork, a calcite formation resembling irregular honeycombs. The most distinctive feature of the cave may be the strong winds that alternately rush in and out of its mouth, equalizing air pressure between the passages inside and the atmosphere outside.

How to Get There

For the scenic route from Rapid City (74 miles away), take US 16 to US 16A south, detouring for a glimpse of Mount Rushmore, to S. Dak. 87 south. This route—not open to RVs and trailers—takes you along the Needles Highway and through Custer State Park to Wind Cave's north entrance. The faster route is to follow S. Dak. 79 south from Rapid City to Hot Springs and then turn north onto US 385 to the south entrance. From the west, take US 16 east to Custer and US 385 south from there. Airport: Rapid City Regional.

When to Go

All-year park. Although the cave and visitor center are open every day except Thanksgiving, Christmas, and New Year's Day, the park offers far fewer cave tours off-season (late September to June). Late spring to mid-summer are best for wildflowers. Mondays, Tuesdays, and Wednesdays in summer are the days least likely to be crowded. The campground is rarely, if ever, full.

How to Visit

A good plan of action for a single-day visit would be to spend the morning in **Wind Cave** on one of the shorter introductory tours and the afternoon exploring the park's prairies and forests on the Scenic Drive. A second day would be the time for one of the longer **Candlelight** or **Caving Tours.** If you arrive off-season, the longer tours will no longer be offered, and much of the territory covered in even the introductory tours will be closed.

People with physical limitations will want to stick to the shorter, less strenuous tours, although even the shortest involves climbing up and down about 150 steps. (If claustrophobia is a problem for you, you might think twice about entering the cave at all.) Wear good walking shoes, and, since the cave temperature is a constant 53°F, take a jacket even on hot summer days.

Wind Cave: Guided Tours

1 hour to a half day

All tours begin at the visitor center, where several exhibits provide important background information. A short slide show describes how the cave began forming 60 million years ago. The same forces that lifted the nearby Black Hills created cracks in the limestone layers beneath the present-day park. Water seeped into these cracks and, over millions of years, gradually dissolved the rock, creating the maze of passages and tunnels we see today.

Most first-timers will choose to take either the **Natural Entrance Tour,** which lasts about $1\frac{1}{4}$ hour, or else the **Fairgrounds Tour,** which is 15 minutes

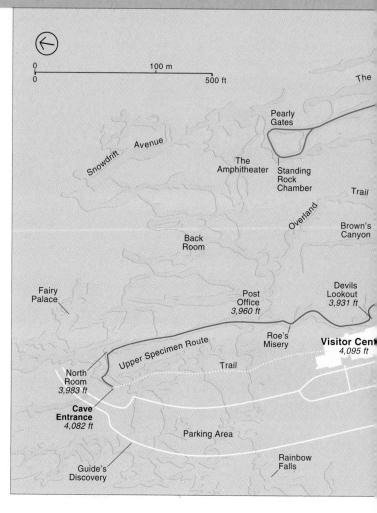

longer. These tours introduce you to the underground world, stressing basic information about caves and cave formations; they take you through such colorfully named places as the **Post Office** (named for the extensive boxwork on the walls), the **Devil's Lookout,** and the **Blue Grotto.**

The **Garden of Eden Tour** is a loop around from the elevator to the **Garden of Eden** lasting one hour; it is recommended for people with time or physical limitations.

If you're a history buff, by all means take the **Candlelight Tour** (summer only). Conducted by the light of candle lanterns, this 2-hour tour harkens back to the 1890s, when **Wind Cave** was owned by the Wonderful Wind Cave Improvement Company and tours were measured by the number of candles needed to complete them. The tour goes up past the **Fairgrounds** to the **Pearly Gates** and beyond; it stresses the cave's ambience and exploration. The tour involves some stooping and stairclimbing.

For those in good physical condition with a keen interest in caves, the park offers a 4-hour **Caving Tour,** designed to simulate a cave exploration trip. Rangers lead participants into the ghostly far reaches of the cave. You crawl through narrow openings, squeeze into tight passages, and make a glorious mess of yourself (take a change of clothes). The guide's commentary focuses on recreational caving and its impact on cave ecology.

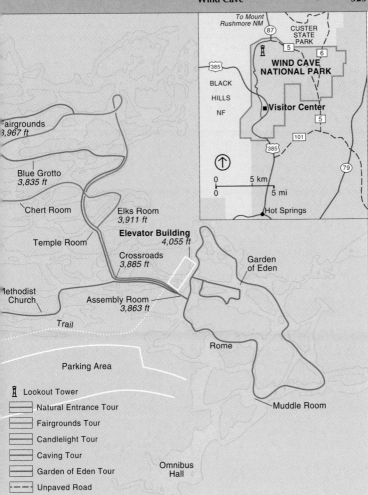

Fairgrounds
3,967 ft

Blue Grotto
3,835 ft

Chert Room

Temple Room

Elks Room
3,911 ft

Elevator Building
4,055 ft

Crossroads
3,885 ft

Methodist
Church

Assembly Room
3,863 ft

Trail

Garden
of Eden

Rome

Parking Area

Muddle Room

🗼 Lookout Tower

⬜ Natural Entrance Tour

⬜ Fairgrounds Tour

⬜ Candlelight Tour

⬜ Caving Tour

⬜ Garden of Eden Tour

- - - Unpaved Road

Omnibus
Hall

To Mount
Rushmore NM

87 CUSTER
STATE
PARK

5   6

385

WIND CAVE
NATIONAL PARK

BLACK

HILLS

NF

■ Visitor Center

5

101

385

79

0   5 km

0   5 mi

Hot Springs

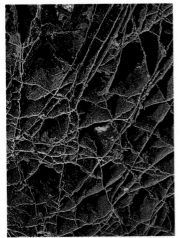

The cave's famous boxwork, a calcite formation

Scenic Drive

13 miles; at least a half day

Begin on US 385 at the southern boundary of the park, about 11 miles north of Hot Springs. At the **Bison Pullout** you get the first of many excellent views of the prairie, much as it existed before the plows of the white man drastically changed it. You may see bison and pronghorn grazing side by side on the grassy hillsides. The **Mineral Lick Pullout** a little farther on overlooks a site where bison lick salt from the soil.

From the visitor center, drive out to the campground for the self-guided **Elk Mountain Nature Trail.** This easy 1-mile hike takes you through a transitional prairie-and-pine-forest environment, where you'll see the grasses and trees encroaching on each other's domain. An accompanying trail guide points out some of the plant life around you, including prickly pear cactus and yucca.

Back on the road, continue to the junction with S. Dak. Hwy. 87 and turn right, stopping at the **Prairie Dog Pullout** just after the turn. This is a good place to observe these once abundant rodents, who survive the predation of many natural enemies by their system of scanning territory and warning their fellows of eminent danger. Your approach will probably set off a cacophony of barks. If you stay in the car, you'll have more to watch; cars don't spook the prairie dogs but people do. At dawn or dusk, watch the outskirts of the prairie dog town for patrolling coyotes.

The road now climbs from the prairie into the higher ponderosa pine forests that cover much of the Black Hills. Stop at the **Ancient Foundations Pullout** to learn about the granite core of the Black Hills. Other pullouts show how various kinds of plants and animals coexist in this dynamic prairie-forest border area.

Turn right at the **Rankin Ridge Pullout** and follow the $\frac{1}{2}$-mile road to the trailhead. The Rankin Ridge Trail, a 1-mile loop, climbs up among the pines to a fire tower. In summer, you can climb the tower for a great view.

Back at the car, return to the main road and continue to the north entrance of the park to complete the tour. Those with maneuverable vehicles may wish to make a loop by turning right on unpaved Park Road 5. This road connects with Park Road 6 and then County Road 101; it takes you through pronghorn and bison territory. Turn right on Cty. Road 101 to return to US 385 south of the park.

Information & Activities

Headquarters
Hot Springs, South Dakota 57747.
Phone (605) 745-4600.
www.nps.gov/wica

Seasons & Accessibility
Open year-round.

Visitor & Information Centers
Visitor center located 11 miles from Hot Springs on US 385; both it and the cave open all year, except Thanksgiving, Christmas, and New Year's Day. Several tours offered daily Memorial Day to Labor Day.

Entrance Fees
None. Fees for cave tours: $6-$20 adults; $3-4.50 children ages 6-16.

Facilities for Disabled
The visitor center and a cave tour are wheelchair accessible.

Things to Do
Naturalist-led activities: a variety of cave tours, nature walks, campfire talks. Also, interpretive exhibits, scenic drive, nature trails, hiking, bicycling, wildlife watching.

Overnight Backpacking
Permits req'd; free at visitor center.

Campgrounds
One campground; 14-day limit. Fees $10 per night mid-May to mid-Sept.; $5 per night April to mid-May and mid-Sept. to late Oct., with reduced services. Closed remainder of year. First come, first served. Tent and RV sites; no hookups or showers.

Hotels, Motels, & Inns
(unless otherwise noted, rates are for 2 persons in a double room, high season)
In Custer, S. Dak. 57730:
Bavarian Inn Motel P.O. Box 152. (800) 657-4312 or (605) 673-2802. 64 units. $86. AC, pool, restaurant.
Dakota Cowboy Inn 208 W. Mt. Rushmore Rd. (800) 279-5079 or (605) 673-4659. 48 units. $94. AC, pool, restaurant. Open May to early Oct.
In Hot Springs, S. Dak. 57747:
Best Western Inn by the River 602 W. River St. (888) 605-4292 or (605) 745-4292. 32 units. $104. AC, pool.
Historic Braun Hotel 902 N. River St. (605) 745-3187. 11 units. $125. AC, restaurant.

Also, write or phone adjacent Custer State Park for info. about its lodges: HCR 83 Box 74, Custer, S. Dak. 57730. Phone (800) 658-3530.

Excursions

Buffalo Gap National Grassland

Wall, South Dakota

This mixed grassland and badlands dotted with prairie dog towns offer superb rock hunting. 591,727 acres. Hiking, fishing, horseback riding, hunting, mountain biking, camping. Open year-round. National Grassland Visitor Center at Wall, off I-90, about 75 miles from Wind Cave NP. Surrounds Badlands NP. (605) 279-2125.

Mount Rushmore National Memorial

Keystone, South Dakota

Colossal visages of Washington, Jefferson, Theodore Roosevelt, and Lincoln gaze out over the Black Hills NF. From May through September the sculptor's studio is open; a year-round evening program ends in the dramatic lighting of the memorial. 1,240 acres. Food services, handicapped access. Located on S. Dak. 244, about 25 miles north of Wind Cave NP. (605) 574-2523.

Jewel Cave National Monument

Custer, South Dakota

Sparkling crystals of calcite are the "jewels" of this 107-mile-long cave. 1,275 acres. Spelunking, hiking, picnic areas, visitor center. Open all year (cave tours year-round). In Black Hills NF on US 16, about 35 miles NW of Wind Cave NP. (605) 673-2288.

Devils Tower National Monument

Devils Tower, Wyoming

Theodore Roosevelt established the first national monument in 1906 to preserve this 865-foot column of hardened magma—now a mecca for technical rock-climbers. 1,347 acres. Facilities also include 51 campsites, hiking, picnic areas, handicapped access. Open all year, roads plowed in winter; full facility open mid-April through Nov. Campground closes Oct. 31. On Wyo. 110, off Wyo. 24, about 130 miles from Wind Cave NP. (307) 467-5283.

Summer morning along the Yellowstone River at Lower Falls

Yellowstone

Wyoming, Idaho, and Montana

Established March 1, 1872

2,221,766 acres

Yellowstone is a geological smoking gun that reminds us of how violent the Earth can be. One event overshadows all others: Some 600,000 years ago, an area many miles square at what is now the center of the park suddenly exploded. In minutes the landscape was devastated. Fast-moving ash flows covered thousands of square miles. At the center there remained only a smoldering caldera, a collapsed crater 28 by 47 miles. At least two other cataclysmic events preceded this one. Boiling hot springs, fumaroles, and geysers serve as reminders that another could occur.

Yellowstone, however, is much more than hot ground and gushing steam. Located astride the Continental Divide, most of the park occupies a high plateau surrounded by mountains and drained by several rivers. Park boundaries enclose craggy peaks, alpine lakes, deep canyons, and vast forests. In 1872, Yellowstone became the world's first national park, the result of great foresight on the part of many people about our eventual need for the solace and beauty of wild places.

In early years, what made Yellowstone stand out was the extravaganza of geysers and hot springs. The wild landscape and the bison, elk, and bears were nice but, after all, America was still a pioneer country filled with scenic beauty and animals.

As the west was settled, however, Yellowstone's importance as a wildlife sanctuary grew. The list of park animals is a compendium of Rocky Mountain fauna: elk, bison, mule

oil and gas drilling. Cooperative management between the park and the seven forests that make up the greater Yellowstone ecosystem is essential if wildlife and thermal features are to survive.

How to Get There

There are five entrances: from the west, West Yellowstone (Montana); from the north and northeast, Gardiner and Cooke City (Montana); from the east, on US 14/16/20 from Cody (Wyoming); and from the south, at Flagg Ranch (Wyoming), which is north of Grand Teton National Park and Jackson (64 miles away). Airports are at West Yellowstone (summer only), Bozeman, and Billings in Montana; and at Cody and Jackson in Wyoming.

When to Go

More than half of the 3 million annual visitors come in July and August. In September and early October, the weather is good, the visitors few, and the wildlife abundant. In May and June, you can see newborn animals, but the weather may be cold, wet, and even snowy. Between about November 1 and May 1 most park roads are closed to vehicles.

deer, bighorn sheep, grizzly bear, black bear, moose, pronghorn, coyote, mountain lion, beaver, trumpeter swan, eagle, osprey, white pelican, and more.

During the summer of 1988, fire touched many sections of the park, in some areas dramatically changing the appearance of the landscape. Yet not one major feature was destroyed. The geysers, waterfalls, and herds of wildlife are still here. Many places show no impact at all, while those that are regenerating benefit both vegetation and animal life. Side by side, burned areas and nonburned areas provide an intriguing study in the causes and effects of fire in wild places. Yellowstone has witnessed bigger natural events than this and may well again.

Of far greater concern to environmentalists than the fires are the impact of increasing numbers of visitors, the dwindling grizzly bear population, and, on nearby lands, the planned geothermal development and

Bull moose wading in the Yellowstone River

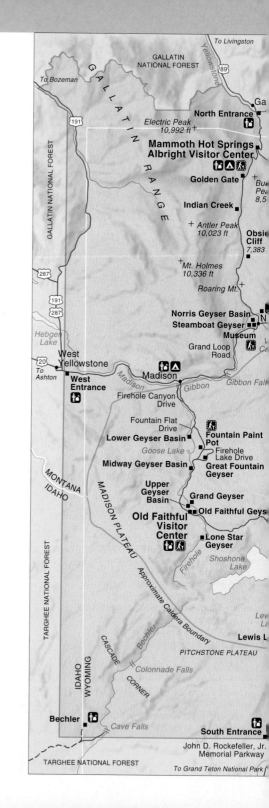

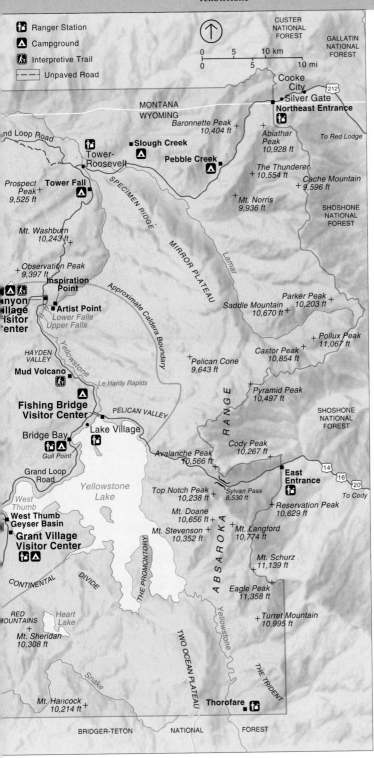

Legend:
- Ranger Station
- Campground
- Interpretive Trail
- - - - Unpaved Road

0 5 10 km
0 5 10 mi

CUSTER NATIONAL FOREST

GALLATIN NATIONAL FOREST

Cooke City
Silver Gate
212
Northeast Entrance

MONTANA
WYOMING

Baronnette Peak 10,404 ft

Abiathar Peak 10,928 ft

To Red Lodge

Slough Creek

Pebble Creek

The Thunderer 10,554 ft

Cache Mountain 9,596 ft

Tower-Roosevelt

SPECIMEN RIDGE

Mt. Norris 9,936 ft

SHOSHONE NATIONAL FOREST

Prospect Peak 9,525 ft

Tower Fall

nd Loop Road

Mt. Washburn 10,243 ft

MIRROR PLATEAU

Lamar

Observation Peak 9,397 ft

Inspiration Point

Approximate Caldera Boundary

Parker Peak 10,203 ft

Saddle Mountain 10,670 ft

nyon illage isitor enter

Artist Point

Lower Falls
Upper Falls

Pollux Peak 11,067 ft

HAYDEN VALLEY

Yellowstone

Castor Peak 10,854 ft

Mud Volcano

Le Hardy Rapids

Pelican Cone 9,643 ft

Pyramid Peak 10,497 ft

RANGE

SHOSHONE NATIONAL FOREST

Fishing Bridge Visitor Center

PELICAN VALLEY

Bridge Bay

Lake Village

Gull Point

Cody Peak 10,267 ft

14

East Entrance

16

Grand Loop Road

Yellowstone Lake

Avalanche Peak 10,566 ft

20

To Cody

West Thumb

Top Notch Peak 10,238 ft

Sylvan Pass 8,530 ft

Reservation Peak 10,629 ft

West Thumb Geyser Basin

Grant Village Visitor Center

Mt. Doane 10,656 ft

Mt. Stevenson 10,352 ft

Mt. Langford 10,774 ft

THE PROMONTORY

ABSAROKA

Mt. Schurz 11,139 ft

CONTINENTAL

DIVIDE

RED MOUNTAINS

Heart Lake

Eagle Peak 11,358 ft

Turret Mountain 10,995 ft

Mt. Sheridan 10,308 ft

Yellowstone

TWO OCEAN PLATEAU

THE TRIDENT

Snake

Mt. Hancock 10,214 ft

Thorofare

BRIDGER-TETON NATIONAL FOREST

Old Faithful blasting off at sunset

During the winter season, mid-December to mid-March, Yellowstone becomes a fantasy of steam and ice; facilities are limited but sufficient. Only the road between the North and Northeast Entrances stays open to cars, but snowmobiling is permitted on unplowed roads. Heated snow coaches offer tours and give cross-country skiers access to about 50 miles of groomed trails.

How to Visit

The 142-mile **Grand Loop Road** forms a figure eight, with connecting spurs to the five entrances. In early years, visitors took a week going around the loop—still a good idea. On any visit, start with the geyser basins and **Mammoth Hot Springs** to see wildlife and thermal features (*caution: both can be hazardous if approached too closely*). On the second day, travel to the **Grand Canyon of the Yellowstone, Hayden Valley,** and **Yellowstone Lake.**

On a longer stay, visit the **Northern Range,** or consider a boating or fishing trip on Yellowstone Lake; a backcountry excursion on foot or horse; or any of the numerous easy nature trails throughout the park.

Your best chance of seeing wildlife is in early morning or evening.

The Geyser Basins: Old Faithful to Mammoth Hot Springs

51 miles; a full day

Begin by leaving your car in the parking lot at **Old Faithful.** Check at the visitor center for predicted eruption times of the major geysers. While there, pick up an **Upper Geyser Basin** map (also available from area dispensers). Wait on benches near the visitor center for the eruption of Old Faithful (named and celebrated for its steadiness rather than a predictable schedule of eruptions) or walk the path that circles it. Almost any point along the path offers a good view of the eruption so don't worry if you're not at the benches when it happens. You can see from here that Old Faithful is not alone. The mile-long Upper

Morning Glory Pool, named for the flower

Mud pot near the Grand Canyon

Fumaroles in Norris Geyser Basin

Geyser Basin contains the world's greatest concentration of hot springs and geysers.

Try to allow a minimum of two hours to see more of it. This must be done on foot, but trails are easy and diversions many. The best choice is to start from the back side of Old Faithful, on the trail that crosses the **Firehole River** to **Geyser Hill,** and follow the map (or your nose; you can't get lost here). You can cross the river at several points and return on the other side, making the walk as long or short as you like. You'll pass dozens of colorful boiling springs and delicate formations of geyserite, a silicate mineral deposited by hot water. Chances are good to see one or more geysers erupt at short range. Keep an eye out for elk and bison. **Morning Glory Pool,** named for its resemblance to the flower, marks the far end of the basin.

Back in your car, drive north. **Black Sand Basin** is worth a quick stop, but bypass **Biscuit Basin.** The road follows the Firehole River several miles to **Midway Geyser Basin,** where a 20-minute stroll on the boardwalk takes you past the enormous crater of **Excelsior Geyser.** It erupted for two days in 1985. A huge boiling vat, it produces about 4,000 gallons of

Minerva Terrace at Mammoth Hot Springs

scalding water each minute. The boardwalk continues across the delicate terraces of **Grand Prismatic Spring,** 370 feet wide, the largest and most beautiful hot spring in the park. The bright colors are caused by algae and bacteria, different types of which thrive in different water temperatures.

Two miles farther, turn right on the one-way **Firehole Lake Drive** to **Great Fountain Geyser.** Check the prediction board for the estimated time of eruption. If you have time to wait—Great Fountain goes off every 11 hours or so—this eruption is one of the best. A bit farther along is **White Dome Geyser.** Its cone may be massive, but its eruption is a thin spray. Perhaps centuries ago it had more power. Yellowstone is always changing.

Rejoin the main road at **Fountain Paint Pot,** a cauldron of hot reddish-pinkish mud, blooping and spitting—always entertaining. Any hot spring could become a mud pot with the right balance of acidity, moisture, and clay; however, a constant flow of water keeps most springs clear.

For the next few miles, rest your eyes on meadows and forest. Look for bison on **Fountain Flat;** also for purple-colored western fringed

gentian, the park flower. **Fountain Flat Drive** is closed to vehicles 1 mile from the main road. But it's open to visitors walking to **Goose Lake,** a peaceful picnic site. The Firehole River, warmed by hot water from springs and geysers along its course, flows through the meadows and along the main road before dropping into a canyon with nice waterfalls; to see them, turn left on **Firehole Canyon Drive** just before **Madison Junction.**

At Madison Junction, a left turn follows the **Madison River** to the **West Entrance,** but stay on the road to Norris. In this area, the fires of 1988 burned extensively. Their effects—the jagged sweeps of charred lodgepole pine forest—will be visible for a long time. However, billions of new lodgepole pines have since grown back (the fires' heat released seedlings from cones on the forest floor). And because the fires moved erratically, the burned areas are not far from unburned areas, another source of seeds for regrowth.

The road climbs beside the **Gibbon River** to **Gibbon Falls,** and continues through the **Gibbon Canyon** and large meadows, where elk are commonly seen, to Norris.

Norris Geyser Basin contains the hottest ground in the park, as well as

Bison grazing near Firehole River

Male elk in fall mating season

Storm Creek fire, near Northeast Entrance, 1988

Rust-colored cones that release seeds after fire

the world's tallest geyser, **Steamboat.** The geyser's eruptions are infrequent and unpredictable; it may stay quiet for years at a time. Steamboat last erupted on May 2, 2000, the first time since October 2, 1991. Contrast its sleepy behavior with that of **Echinus,** which goes off about every 40 to 80 minutes, an easy show to witness.

Highlights of the drive north include the steamy fumaroles of **Roaring Mountain** that snore rather than roar and **Obsidian Cliff,** an outcrop containing black volcanic glass that was valued for arrowpoints by Indians throughout the area. The road crosses **Gardners Hole,** with nice views of the **Gallatin Range** to the west, and drops toward Mammoth through **Golden Gate,** cliffs gilded with the bright yellow lichen that grows on them.

At **Mammoth Hot Springs** you can drive or walk around the dozens of colorful steaming terraces. They are made of travertine—calcium carbonate—which the hot water brings to the surface from beds of limestone. The formations look quite different from the silica-based geyserite deposits seen elsewhere in the park. The park's headquarters and largest visitor center are at Mammoth. The **North Entrance** is located 5 miles down the **Gardner River Canyon.**

Landing a cutthroat trout on Slough Creek

Yellowstone Lake & River: Canyon to West Thumb

37 miles; at least a half day

From the **Canyon Village Visitor Center,** follow the one-way **Canyon Rim Drive** to lookout points for great views of the canyon and the **Yellowstone River**'s 308-foot **Lower Falls,** nearly twice as high as Niagara. The bright yellow, orange, and red of the canyon walls are caused by heat and chemical action on gray or brown rhyolite rock.

Walk the rim trail from **Inspiration Point** to **Grandview Point** for the best look at the canyon's natural grandeur. Also consider the paved but strenuous **Brink of the Lower Falls Trail,** which descends several hundred feet through steep forest. Standing beside the green river where it suddenly drops into space is one of the most exciting experiences in the park.

Continue south on the main road. The **Upper Falls** are, at 109 feet high, almost as impressive as the lower falls and easier to reach. A short trail leads to **Upper Falls View.** Half a mile far-ther south, a side road crosses the river to **Artist Point,** the best overall view of the canyon.

Upriver, the Yellowstone flows gently through the sage-covered hills of **Hayden Valley.** Go slowly and stop often in the roadside parking areas; this is prime wildlife country. American white pelicans and trumpeter swans share the river with Canada geese, gulls, and ducks. Bison are visible most of the year. *Keep your distance.* Use binoculars to check meadows across the river for grizzlies digging for roots or rodents. Grizzlies are often seen in the open; black bears, their smaller, shier relations, rarely. But be careful not to surprise one; both are dangerous.

Well-named **Mud Volcano** and **Black Dragon's Caldron** are not pretty to look at, but they are impressive. Springs in this area have been known to hurl football-sized blobs of mud tens of feet. From here to the lake, the Yellowstone River provides excellent catch-and-release fishing for cutthroat trout. At **Le Hardy Rapids** in June you can watch cutthroat jumping on their way to spawning grounds (no fishing).

Look for trout also at **Fishing Bridge** (no fishing allowed) where the river flows out of the lake. Two miles farther east is **Pelican Valley,** a lush lakeside meadow where you might find moose or white pelicans.

Return to the loop road, following the shore of **Yellowstone Lake** most of the next 21 miles. This is the largest lake in North America above 7,000

Petrified Forest on Specimen Ridge

feet. The **Absaroka Range,** visible across the blue waters, was named for the Absaroka, or Crow Indians. The volcanic peaks define the park's eastern boundary.

Bison frequent the meadows near **Bridge Bay,** while moose favor ponds along the **Gull Point Road. Gull Point** is a good picnic site.

West Thumb, almost a separate lake, is a water-filled caldera created by an eruption about 150,000 years ago, a smaller version of the great Yellowstone caldera. A boardwalk leads around the **West Thumb Geyser Basin,** a modest group of thermal features made charming by its location beside the lake.

Northern Range

Between Mammoth Hot Springs and Cooke City, Yellowstone is warmer and drier than the interior. Called the **Northern Range** for its importance as wintering ground for large animals, this area is characterized by sagebrush and grassy valleys. Open all year, the road from Mammoth stays high above the Yellowstone River, crosses it near **Tower-Roosevelt,** and follows the **Lamar River** and **Soda Butte Creek**

to the **Northeast Entrance,** a magnificent little-used gateway. A few miles past Tower, **Specimen Ridge** contains the world's largest fossil forest. Over 100 plant species, including redwoods, grow in 27 layers of volcanic ash from repeated eruptions 50 million years ago.

Hiking, Fishing, & Boating

More than a thousand miles of trails lead to wilderness valleys, mountaintops, lakes, and thermal basins. Take horses and a guide for a week-long trip, or go on foot for an hour or two. Even a short walk can put you in a wilderness setting beyond roads and crowds. Ask for recommended hikes at any visitor center.

Yellowstone offers fine trout fishing, especially for the fly-fisherman. A permit is required ($10 for 10 days; $20 for the season), available at visitor centers and ranger stations. Regulations are complicated, so read them carefully. Guide service is available at fishing shops in surrounding communities.

Motorboating is permitted on most of Yellowstone Lake and **Lewis Lake;** passenger boats operate from **Bridge Bay Marina** for sightseeing and fishing. Other lakes are limited to hand-propelled craft. Rivers and streams are closed to all boating to avoid disturbing wildlife; an exception is the channel between Lewis and **Shoshone Lakes,** where paddlers are permitted.

Information & Activities

Headquarters

P.O. Box 168, Yellowstone National Park, Wyoming 82190. Phone (307) 344-7381. www.nps.gov/yell

Seasons & Accessibility

Park open year-round. Road from North Entrance to Northeast Entrance open all year; most other park roads closed to cars November through April. Call headquarters for latest weather and road conditions.

Visitor & Information Centers

Mammoth Hot Springs/Albright Visitor Center open daily all year. Old Faithful Visitor Center open May through Oct. and mid-Dec. to mid-March, depending on weather. Canyon Village Visitor Center, near center of park, and Fishing Bridge and Grant Village Visitor Centers, on Yellowstone Lake, open May through Sept. (reduced hours in Sept.).

Entrance Fees

$20 per vehicle, good for one week at both Yellowstone and Grand Teton. $40 annual.

Facilities for Disabled

Visitor centers, Madison Canyon, Bridge Bay, Grant, Lewis Lake, and Fishing Bridge Campgrounds, most rest rooms, amphitheaters, numerous ranger-led activities, walks, and exhibits are wheelchair accessible. Free brochure available.

Things to Do

Free naturalist-led activities: nature walks, camera walks, evening programs. Also available, hiking, boating, fishing (permit required), horseback riding (stables at Roosevelt, Canyon, and Mammoth), bicycling, stagecoach rides, courses in natural history and photography, art exhibits, children's activities, bus and boat tours, snow-coach tours, cross-country skiing, ice-skating, snowshoeing, and snowmobiling.

Overnight Backpacking

Permits required. They are free and available at visitor centers and ranger stations; apply in person not more than 48 hours in advance of use. Advance reservations $15.

Campgrounds

Twelve campgrounds all with 14-day limit (except Fishing Bridge RV Park) from mid-June to mid-Sept.; other times 30-day limit. **Mammoth** open all year, others open late spring to mid-fall. Reservations accepted for **Fishing Bridge RV Park, Madison, Grant Village, Canyon Village,** and **Bridge Bay;** contact AmFac Parks & Resorts, P.O. Box 165, Yellowstone NP, Wyo. 82190. (307) 344-7311. All others first come, first served. Fees $10-$15 per night; Fishing Bridge RV Park $27. Pay showers near several campgrounds. Both tent and RV sites at most campgrounds; at Fishing Bridge RV Park hard-sided units only. Hookups at Fishing Bridge RV Park only. For group campgrounds, reserve through AmFac Parks & Resorts. Food services in park.

Hotels, Motels, & Inns

(unless otherwise noted, rates are for 2 persons in a double room, high season)
INSIDE THE PARK:
The following are operated by AmFac Parks & Resorts, Yellowstone NP, Wyo. 82190. For reservations call (307) 344-7311.
Canyon Lodge 619 cabins. $62-$136. Restaurant. **Grant Village** 300 units. $98-$111. Restaurant. Open May through Sept. **Lake Lodge & Cabins** 186 units. $55-$118. Restaurant. Open June to mid-Sept. **Lake Yellowstone Hotel & Cabins** 296 units. Hotel $93-$434. Restaurant. Open mid-May through Sept. **Mammoth Hot Springs Hotel & Cabins** 116 cabins; 97 rooms. $57-$299. Rest. Open May to Oct. **Old Faithful Inn** 327 units. $72-$369. Rest. Open early May to late Oct. **Old Faithful Lodge & Cabins** 97 units. $39-$69. Open mid-May to late Sept. **Old Faithful Snow Lodge & Cabins** 100 rooms; 24 cabins. $69-$140. Restaurant. Open mid-May to mid-Oct. and mid-Dec. to mid-March. **Roosevelt Lodge & Cabins** 82 cabins. $48-$95. Restaurant. Open mid-June to late August.

See also Grand Teton NP listings.

Excursions

Shoshone National Forest
Cody, Wyoming

Teddy Roosevelt dubbed this forest's Wapiti Valley "the most scenic 52 miles in the United States." Wapiti (elk) find a year-round home here in the lee of the Absaroka and Beartooth Ranges, as do bighorn sheep, grizzlies, moose, and deer. Contains parts or all of five wilderness areas. 2,433,000 acres. Facilities include 374 campsites, food services, hiking, boating, boat ramp, fishing, horseback riding, hunting, picnic areas, winter sports. Some parts open year-round; campsites open June-September. Adjoins Yellowstone NP on the east. (307) 527-6241.

Red Rock Lakes National Wildlife Refuge
Lakeview, Montana

In this Centennial Valley refuge, trumpeter swans and nesting sandhill cranes find shelter among grasslands, lakes, and marshes. Large mammals include moose, mule deer, pronghorn, and coyotes. 45,000 acres. Facilities: 10 campsites, hiking, canoeing, fishing, hunting, scenic drives. Open all year, though snow closes roads in winter. Off US 20/191, about 45 miles from Yellowstone NP. (406) 276-3536.

Bighorn Canyon National Recreation Area
Fort Smith, Montana

Water-based recreation is the focus of this 71-mile-long reservoir impounded from the Bighorn River by the Yellowtail Dam. Fossils exposed in steep canyon walls, wildlife from four life zones, and historic and archaeological sites also featured. Surrounded by Crow Indian Reservation. 120,284 acres, part in Wyoming. Facilities include 125 campsites, hiking, boating, boat ramps, bicycling, fishing (and ice fishing), hunting, picnic areas, scenic drives, water sports, handicapped access. Visitor center at Lovell on US 14A, about 100 miles from Yellowstone NP. (307) 548-2251.

Preceding pages: Sea stacks, Olympic Peninsula

The Pacific Northwest

In the late 19th and early 20th centuries, East Coast loggers pushed west, downing mile after mile of the continent's primeval forests. Today, almost all of the large ancient forests left in the lower 48 states grow in the Pacific Northwest, most of them in national forests and parks.

Visitors to Mount Rainier, Olympic, and North Cascades can hike cathedral-like glades of Douglar-fir, western red cedar, and other conifers. The redwoods in the park named for them include trees in their second millennium, some of the tallest on Earth. In Olympic, temperate rain forests soar near some of the nation's wildest coastline; in the US, only there and at Mount Rainier do such forests still exist. All these ancient forests knit together the lives of hundreds of species of plants, animals, and microbes in a web we don't fully understand. Yet the web is increasingly threatened as trees in private, state, and national forests are cut down.

The Northwest is also known for its volcanoes, many of which, including Mount Rainier and Mount St. Helens, lie in the Pacific Ring of Fire, the great belt of crustal instability responsible for three-quarters of the world's active volcanoes. Visitors to Lassen Volcanic can see evidence of the planet's violence in broken mountains and boiling mud pots. At Crater Lake, they can imagine the titanic forces that collapsed a mountaintop, turning it into a lake bed 6 miles wide and the deepest in the nation. They can marvel at the majesty of cloud-swathed Mount Rainier, which grew on a foundation of lava flows from extinct volcanoes, and now shoulders breathtaking wildflowers and more glaciers than any other US peak south of Alaska.

Each of the region's northernmost national parks is less than half a day's drive from Seattle. This group merits at least a week of touring, more if you want to visit other natural areas nearby. The more southern peaks can each be seen in a day, but allow plenty of time for travel between them. Beautiful but winding Calif. 299 that connects the Lassen Volcanic and Redwood areas can wash out in spring, so check conditions if that's when you plan to go.

Wizard Island rising out of Crater Lake

Crater Lake

Oregon

Established May 22, 1902

183,227 acres

Few forget their first glimpse of Crater Lake on a clear summer's day—21 square miles of water so intensely blue it looks like ink, ringed by cliffs towering up to 2,000 feet above its surface. The mountain bluebird, Indian legend says, was gray before dipping into Crater Lake's waters.

The tranquil Gem of the Cascades is set in a dormant volcano called Mount Mazama, one in the chain of volcanoes that includes Mount. St. Helens. Mount Mazama's final eruption occurred around 5700 BC. The explosion catapulted volcanic ash miles into the sky and expelled so much pumice and ash that soon Mount Mazama's summit collapsed, creating a huge, smoldering caldera.

Over the centuries, rain and snowmelt accumulated in this caldera, forming a lake more than 1,900 feet deep, the deepest lake in the United States. Wildflowers, along with hemlock, fir, and pine, recolonized the lava-covered surroundings. Black bears and bobcats, deer and marmots, eagles and hawks returned.

Scientists have yet to understand completely Crater Lake's ecology. In 1988 and 1989, using a manned submarine, they discovered evidence that proves hydrothermal venting exists on the lake's bottom and may play a role in the lake's character.

Crater Lake forms a superb setting for day hikes. Thanks to some of the cleanest air in the nation, you can see more than 100 miles from points along many of the park's 140 miles of trails. Forests of mountain hemlock and Shasta red fir predominate near the

caldera rim. At the rim twisted white-bark pine testify to the harshness of the long winter, during which, on average, 45 feet of snow fall. Ponderosa pine, the park's largest tree, and lodgepole pine are common farther down from the rim.

How to Get There

Enter the park from the west (Medford, about 75 miles away) or the south (Klamath Falls, about 55 miles away) on Oreg. 62, or from the north on Oreg. 138. Airports: Medford and Klamath Falls.

When to Go

The lake best displays its dazzling color in summer. Oreg. 62 and the access road leading to Rim Village remain open during daylight in winter, and cross-country skiing is becoming increasingly popular. The drive around the lake usually closes in October because of snow; in some years, the drive may not reopen completely until mid-July.

How to Visit

Spend at least a half day touring the 33-mile Rim Drive, enjoying its many overlooks and several hiking trails. On a second day, consider a hike down to the shore for the 1¾-hour, narrated boat tour of the lake. The boat stops at Wizard Island; if time and weather permit, climb to the top of it and catch a later boat back.

Rim Drive & Godfrey Glen Trail

33-38 miles; a half to full day

Rim Drive circles **Crater Lake,** providing more than 25 scenic overlooks and some good picnic areas. (Trailers and other oversize vehicles not recommended on east Rim Drive.) Begin your tour by parking in **Rim Village** and strolling to the **Sinnott Memorial Overlook,** a prime vantage point directly over the lake. Crater Lake's vivid color is a sign of purity and depth. The lake contains few minerals and impurities. Its only fish—rainbow trout and kokanee salmon—were introduced. As sunlight penetrates the deep, pure lake, water molecules absorb the colors of the spectrum except for blue, which is scattered back to the surface. Scientists have found green algae growing at a record 725 feet below the surface, indicating that sunlight may penetrate deeper here than in any other body of water in the world.

To begin your lake tour, set your car's odometer at zero (or note the setting) as you leave Rim Village parking lot. Head west or clockwise around the lake, and be careful: The road is narrow and has sharp curves. Watch out for bikers and pedestrians. Turn right at 0.1 mile for Rim Drive. The first stop (mile 1.3) brings you near **Discovery Point,** where, on June 12, 1853, a group of prospectors searching for a gold mine happened upon the lake, which they named Deep Blue Lake. Indians, believing the lake sacred, had told no outsiders about it. **Hillman Peak,** to the far left on the rim, is named for one of the prospectors. The peak is a 70,000-year-old volcano—one of the compact cluster of overlapping volcanic cones that formed Mount Mazama. It was cleaved in half when the summit collapsed. At 1,975 feet

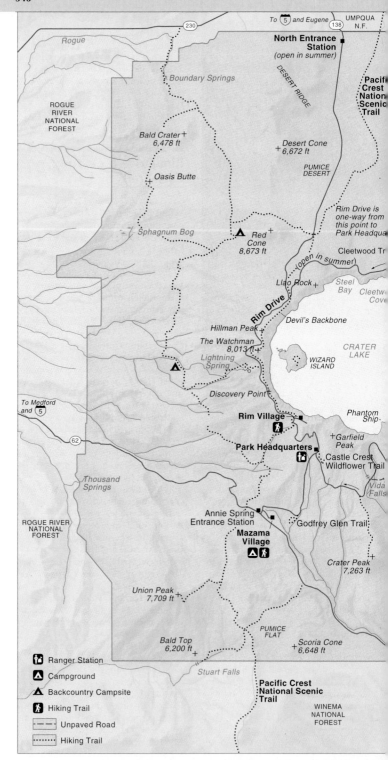

230

To **5** and Eugene
UMPQUA N.F.
138

North Entrance Station
(open in summer)

Rogue

Boundary Springs

DESERT RIDGE

Pacific Crest National Scenic Trail

ROGUE RIVER NATIONAL FOREST

Bald Crater +
6,478 ft

+ Desert Cone
6,672 ft

PUMICE DESERT

+ Oasis Butte

Rim Drive is one-way from this point to Park Headquar

Sphagnum Bog

Red +
Cone
8,673 ft

Cleetwood Tr

Rim Drive (open in summer)

Llao Rock +

Steel Bay

Cleetw Cove

Hillman Peak

Devil's Backbone

CRATER LAKE

The Watchman
8,013 ft +

Lightning Spring

WIZARD ISLAND

Discovery Point +

To Medford and **5**

62

Rim Village
🚶

Phantom Ship

Park Headquarters
🏚

+Garfield Peak

Castle Crest Wildflower Trail

Vida Falls

Thousand Springs

ROGUE RIVER NATIONAL FOREST

Annie Spring Entrance Station

Godfrey Glen Trail

Mazama Village
🏕 🚶

Crater Peak
7,263 ft

Union Peak +
7,709 ft

PUMICE FLAT

Bald Top
6,200 ft +

+ Scoria Cone
6,648 ft

Stuart Falls

Pacific Crest National Scenic Trail

WINEMA NATIONAL FOREST

🏚 Ranger Station

🏕 Campground

▲ Backcountry Campsite

🚶 Hiking Trail

– – – Unpaved Road

••••• Hiking Trail

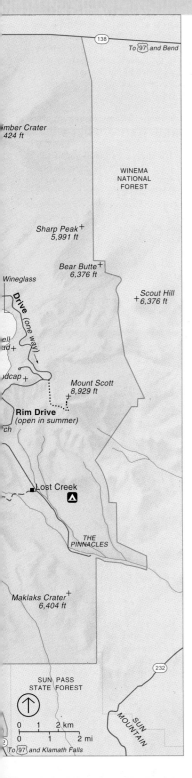

138
To 97 and Bend

WINEMA
NATIONAL
FOREST

imber Crater
424 ft

Sharp Peak +
5,991 ft

Bear Butte +
6,376 ft

Wineglass

Scout Hill
+ 6,376 ft

Drive (one way)

ell
ad +

dcap +

Mount Scott
8,929 ft

Rim Drive
(open in summer)

ch

Lost Creek
▲

THE
PINNACLES

Maklaks Crater +
6,404 ft

232

SUN PASS
STATE FOREST

↑

0   1   2 km
0   1   2 mi
To 97 and Klamath Falls

SUN MOUNTAIN

Rabbit brush at Cleetwood Cove

above the water, it forms the highest
point on the rim.

The overlook at mile 4 offers a good
view of **Wizard Island,** named for its
resemblance to a sorcerer's hat. Rising
764 feet above the surface of the lake,
Wizard Island is a classic cinder
cone—built of red-hot cinders ejected
from the caldera floor sometime after
Mount Mazama collapsed. An Indian
legend portrays the island as the head
of Llao, Chief of the Below World.
Skell, Chief of the Above World, killed
and dismembered Llao in the final, literally earth-shattering battle waged on
the mountaintop. Time and weather
permitting, you'll enjoy superb views
in every direction if you take the
moderately steep $\frac{4}{5}$-mile trail that
leads from here to the fire tower on
The Watchman (8,013 feet) south of
the overlook.

Back in your car, turn away from the
lake at the **Mount Thielsen Overview**
on the left. A plaque identifies the
major landmarks of the countryside.
When the road forks at North Junction
(mile 6.1), bear right to remain on Rim
Drive. Straight, the road leads to the
North Entrance.

Steel Bay (mile 8.8) commemorates
William Gladstone Steel, who dedicated his fortune and career to making Crater Lake a national park. Steel
became fascinated by the lake when
he read about it in a newspaper used
to wrap his school lunch. Seventeen
years of lobbying, culminating
in a personal appeal to President
Theodore Roosevelt, succeeded in
making it the country's sixth national
park in 1902. The tireless Steel
stocked the lake with fish and led
the efforts to build Rim Drive and the
Crater Lake Lodge.

Six miles farther on, pull off
the road at **Skell Head** for another

The Pinnacles, southeast of Kerr Notch

pumice and ash 250 feet thick. The fluted pinnacles on the walls of the gorges began as the same material, but hot gases seeped up from within the Earth and hardened these areas. They defied erosion as the creeks formed canyons.

Boat Tour & Hikes

The mile-long **Cleetwood Trail,** at mile 10.7 by car from the visitor center, leads steeply down to the water and the landing for the boat tour (fee charged). The hike back up is strenuous (and there's no other way), so only attempt the trail if you are in good physical condition, and take it slowly. Wear sturdy shoes and bring water, a snack, and a jacket. The boat tour shows you the lake from a different perspective. You will see waterfalls and geological features invisible from the rim, and a ranger-guide offers a detailed account of the lake and its environs.

The tour leaves every hour between 10 a.m. and noon, and every 45 minutes between noon and 4:30 p.m. (July to mid-September). Beginning 2002, the park will reduce the number of tours offered. The relatively steep **Wizard Island Summit Trail** ($\frac{9}{10}$ of a mile one way) begins at the island's dock and winds through mountain hemlock, Shasta red fir, and wildflowers to the crater at the top. Awaiting you are superb views of bleached, contorted whitebark pines against the blue water.

Another good park hike is on the **Annie Creek Trail,** a $1\frac{7}{10}$-mile self-guided loop that wends through beds of wildflowers to the bottom of a canyon and back. It begins behind the amphitheater at the Mazama Campground. The **Mount Scott Trail,** considered by many to be the most spectacular in the park, starts from the left side of Rim Drive just after mile 17. It ascends $2\frac{1}{2}$ miles to the park's highest point. On this trail you might see falcons, hawks, and eagles, particularly in spring and fall.

excellent view of the entire lake. **Mount Scott,** highest point in the park, looms ahead as you drive on toward **Cloudcap;** it may have been the oldest of Mount Mazama's volcanic cones. Bear right (mile 17.4) for the short spur road to Cloudcap, Rim Drive's highest overlook (7,960 feet). **Phantom Ship,** an island to the southwest, consists of 400,000-year-old lava flows from the extinct Phantom cone. Dwarfed by the surrounding cliffs, it nevertheless stands 160 feet above the water.

Circle back to Rim Drive and turn right. For a closer look at Phantom Ship, which in some lights seems to vanish and reappear, stop at **Kerr Notch** (mile 23.2), one of the U-shaped valleys carved by a glacier before Mount Mazama exploded. A road here leads to **The Pinnacles,** spires of hardened volcanic ash. Just after Kerr Notch, bear right to stay on Rim Drive.

At mile 31.2 you can stretch your legs on the **Castle Crest Wildflower Trail.** This fragrant $\frac{1}{2}$-mile loop begins in a forest of mountain hemlock and red fir, then enters a meadow run riot with flowers, many of them identified by plaques. Watch your step—the wet rocks can be slippery.

From here you can either proceed back to Rim Village or, if time permits, turn left toward Oreg. 62 and after $2\frac{1}{3}$ miles park on the left for a final stroll through **Godfrey Glen Trail,** an easy, 1-mile-loop accessible-nature trail. The path leads through forest that developed on a flow of

Information & Activities

Headquarters
P.O. Box 7, Crater Lake, Oregon 97604.
Phone (541) 594-2211.
www.nps.gov/crla

Seasons & Accessibility
South and west entrances open
year-round. North entrance open
mid-June to mid-October, snow permitting. East side of Rim Drive, from
Cleetwood Cove to park headquarters,
may remain closed by snow until
mid-July.

Visitor & Information Centers
Rim Village Visitor Center, on rim
overlooking the lake, 7 miles off
Oreg. 62, open daily from early June
to end of September. Closed rest of
year. Steel Center, located at park
headquarters, open daily all year
except Christmas.

Entrance Fee
$10 per car per week; $20 annual.

Pets
Pets must be leashed at all times and
are not permitted on the trails.

Facilities for Disabled
Most viewpoints are accessible
to wheelchairs, as are the visitor
centers, Mazama Campground, the
cafeteria/gift shop at Rim Village,
the Crater Lake Lodge, and the 1-mile
Godfrey Glen Trail.

Things to Do
Free naturalist-led activities: nature
walks, children's programs, campfire
programs, historical tours. Fees for the
1¾-hour ranger-narrated boat tours.
Also available, hiking, bicycling, fishing
(license required), snowshoeing, and
cross-country skiing.

Special Advisory
● Hiking inside the caldera rim permitted only on the Cleetwood Trail.
Volcanic rock and soil are unstable
and dangerous to climb on.

Overnight Backpacking
Permits required. They are free and can
be obtained at the Steel Information
Center, the Rim Village Visitor Center,
and on the Pacific Crest Trail where it
enters the park.

Campgrounds
Two campgrounds, both with 14-day
limit. **Lost Creek** open mid-July to late
September. **Mazama** open late-June
to mid-October. Both first come, first
served. Fees $10-$15 per night. Showers at Mazama Village. Both tent and
RV sites at **Mazama;** no hookups. Tent
sites only at **Lost Creek.** Food services
at Rim Village.

Hotels, Motels, & Inns
*(unless otherwise noted, rates are for 2
persons in a double room, high season)*
INSIDE THE PARK:
Rim Village/Crater Lake Lodge
1211 Avenue C, White City, Oregon
97503. (541) 830-8700. 71 units. $100-
$190. Restaurant. Open late May to
mid-October.
Mazama Village Motel (541) 830-
8700. 40 units. $96. Open early June
to mid-October.
OUTSIDE THE PARK:
In Chiloquin, Oregon 97624:
Melita's Motel 39500 Hwy. 97. (541)
783-2401. 13 units. $33-$42. AC,
restaurant.
Sportsman Motel 27627 Hwy. 97 N.
(541) 783-2867. 9 units, 6 with
kitchenettes. $42.
Spring Creek Ranch Motel 47600
Hwy. 97 N. (541) 783-2775. 10 units,
7 with kitchenettes. $42.
Rapid River Bend Motel 33551 Hwy.
97 N. (541) 783-2271. 10 units. $47-
$52. Restaurant.
In Diamond Lake, Oregon 97731:
Diamond Lake Resort (541) 793-3333.
92 units, 42 with kitchenettes. Rooms
$68; cabins $129; studios $79.
In Prospect, Oregon 97536:
Union Creek Resort (541) 560-3565.
14 cabins, 8 with kitchenettes; 9 rooms
with shared baths. Cabins $50-$100;
rooms $38-$48. Restaurant.

*Ask the park for a complete list
of accommodations within a
one-hour drive.*

Excursions

Rogue River National Forest

Medford, Oregon

Sugar pines and Douglas-firs here cloak the slopes of the western Cascades where the Rogue River emerges from underground lava tubes. Forest contains parts of three wilderness areas, numerous lakes, and a stretch of the Pacific Crest Trail. 628,750 acres, part in Calif. Facilities include 30 rooms, 400 campsites, food services, hiking, boating, boat ramp, fishing, horseback riding, hunting, picnic areas, scenic drives, winter sports, water sports. Open all year; most campsites open May-September. In two sections; one adjoins Crater Lake NP on west and south, with entrance at Prospect on Oreg. 62. Lower section reached by following I-5 south of Ashland, about 85 miles from the park. (541) 858-2200.

Oregon Caves National Monument

Cave Junction, Oregon

Guided tours take visitors through the "Marble Halls of Oregon," chambers and corridors formed by groundwater dissolving marble bedrock. 480 acres. Facilities include 22 rooms, food services, hiking, picnic areas, child care during tour. Open all year; lodge closed in winter. East on Oreg. 46 from Cave Junction, about 125 miles from Crater Lake NP. (541) 592-2100.

Siskiyou National Forest

Grants Pass, Oregon

This coniferous forest boasts five wilderness areas, notably the Kalmiopsis, named for a flowering plant unique to the area. A section of the Wild and Scenic Rogue River offers white-water boating, fishing, and hiking along the river's National Scenic Trail. 1,092,302 acres, part in California. Facilities include over 300 campsites, hiking, boating, boat ramp, fishing, horseback riding, hunting, picnic areas, scenic drives, water sports. Open year-round; most campsites open May-September. Headquarters at Grants Pass on I-5, about 100 miles southwest of Crater Lake NP. (541) 471-6500.

Oregon Dunes
National Recreation Area
Reedsport, Oregon

Forty-seven miles of towering dunes—
some as high as 400 feet—stretch along
the Pacific coast, inviting visitors to
explore. Half of area open to off-road
vehicles. The 426 wildlife species
include black bears, black-tailed deer,
and tundra swans. 32,000 acres. Facilities include 13 campgrounds, 13 hiking
trails, boating, fishing, horseback riding,
picnic areas, swimming, handicapped
access. Open all year. Headquarters at
Reedsport on US 101, about 200 miles
west of Crater Lake NP. (541) 271-3611.

Lava Beds
National Monument
Tulelake, California

Myriad lava-tube caves and cinder
cones mark this rugged terrain where
prehistoric Indians left glyphs on the
soft rock. Excellent spring and fall birdwatching. 46,560 acres. Facilities include
41 campsites, hiking, picnic areas. Open
year-round. Headquarters 30 miles
south of Tulelake (26 miles off Calif.
139), about 120 miles south of Crater
Lake NP. (530) 667-2282.

Klamath Basin
National Wildlife Refuges
Tulelake, California

These six refuges protect diverse habitats—marsh, open water, meadows,
croplands, coniferous forest, sagebrush
and juniper uplands, rocky slopes—and
numerous waterfowl. The basin also
provides a home for the largest wintering bald eagle population in the lower
48 states. Facilities include bicycling,
hiking, boating, fishing, hunting. Open
all year, dawn to dusk, except Bear Valley (closed Nov.-April to protect eagles)
and Clear Lake (closed in spring-
summer). In Oregon: Klamath Forest,
16,376 acres; Upper Klamath, 14,886
acres; Bear Valley, 4,120 acres; Lower
Klamath, 51,713 acres (part in Calif.).
In Calif.: Tule Lake, 38,908 acres; Clear
Lake, 33,440 acres. Visitor center near
Tulelake, off Calif. 139, about 100 miles
from Crater Lake NP. (530) 667-2231.

Lassen Peak looming over the remains of Mt. Tehama

Lassen Volcanic

California

Established August 9, 1916

106,372 acres

On June 14, 1914, three men climbed Lassen Peak to see why a seemingly dead volcano had started rumbling 16 days before. Now, peering into a newborn crater, they felt the ground tremble. As they turned and ran down the steep slope, the mountain erupted. Rocks hurtled through the ash-filled air. One struck a man, knocking him out. Ashes rained down on the men. They seemed doomed. But the eruption stopped as suddenly as it had begun, and the three men survived.

From 1914 to early 1915, Lassen spewed steam and ashes in more than 150 eruptions. Finally, on May 19, 1915, the mountaintop exploded. Lava crashed through the 1914 crater. A 20-foot-high wall of mud, ash, and melted snow roared down the mountain, snapping tree trunks. Three days later, a huge mass of ashes and gases shot out of the volcano, devastating a swath a mile wide and 3 miles long. Above the havoc a cloud of volcanic steam and ash rose 30,000 feet.

Since then, except for a small eruption in 1921, Lassen Peak has been quiet. But it is still a volcano, the centerpiece of a vast panorama, where volcanism displays its spectaculars—wrecked mountains, devastated land, bubbling cauldrons of mud. Until Mount St. Helens blew in 1980, Lassen's eruption was the most recent volcanic explosion in the lower 48 states. Ecologists now study Lassen's landscape to see what the future may bring to the barren terrain around St. Helens.

and Manzanita Lake Entrances, encompasses the major volcanic features. Explore Bumpass Hell and other sites along the way. If you can stay longer, climb Cinder Cone, an outstanding example of the results of volcanism, and, if you have the stamina for a more demanding trek, try Lassen Peak.

Lassen Park Road & Bumpass Hell Trail

30 miles; a half to full day

If you start at the Southwest Entrance, your first stop on this twisting, climbing road will be the Sulphur Works. At a roadside exhibit you walk through sulphur fumes and see hissing fumaroles, sputtering mud, and gurgling clay tinted in pastels by minerals. Here was the heart of Mount Tehama, the great volcano that spawned Lassen. The peaks around you once formed part of the rim of Tehama, created by lava oozing from the inner Earth 600,000 to 200,000 years ago. Layer by layer, the lava built a mountain 11,500 feet high and 11 miles across.

Tehama gave birth to small volcanoes that emerged on its flanks. Repeated eruptions weakened the structure of the volcano, which collapsed, leaving behind a bowl-like caldera. Glaciers later scoured the caldera, wiping out the last remains of Tehama. **Lassen Peak,** born at least 27,000 years ago, was one of Tehama's offspring.

How to Get There

From Redding (about 45 miles away), take Calif. 44 east to Manzanita Lake Entrance; from Red Bluff, follow Calif. 36 east to Mineral, turn north on Calif. 89 to the Southwest Entrance. The three other entrances—at Warner Valley, Butte Lake, and Juniper Lake—are reached via unpaved roads. Airports: Redding and Chico; Reno, Nevada.

When to Go

The volcanic areas can be visited from spring through fall. Heavy snows close most of the main road in winter. But small sections at the southern and northern ends remain open for snowshoe hikes and cross-country skiing.

How to Visit

On a one-day visit, drive the Lassen Park Road, linked to Calif. 89. The road, snaking across the western side of the park between the Southwest

Thermal steam at Bumpass Hell

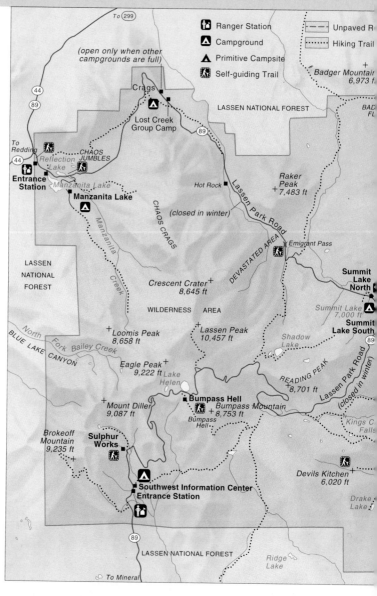

Ranger Station

Campground

Primitive Campsite

Self-guiding Trail

Unpaved R

Hiking Trail

To 299

(open only when other campgrounds are full)

Crags

Lost Creek Group Camp

LASSEN NATIONAL FOREST

Badger Mountain 6,973 f

BAD
FL

CHAOS JUMBLES

Reflection Lake

To Redding

Entrance Station

Manzanita Lake

Manzanita Lake

Hot Rock

Lassen Park Road

(closed in winter)

Raker Peak 7,483 ft

CHAOS CRAGS

Manzanita Creek

Emigrant Pass

DEVASTATED AREA

Summit Lake North

Crescent Crater 8,645 ft

LASSEN

NATIONAL

FOREST

WILDERNESS   AREA

Summit Lake 7,000 ft

Summit Lake South

Loomis Peak 8,658 ft

Lassen Peak 10,457 ft

Shadow Lake

North Fork Bailey Creek

BLUE LAKE CANYON

Eagle Peak 9,222 ft

Lake Helen

READING PEAK 8,701 ft

Lassen Park Road (closed in winter)

Mount Diller 9,087 ft

Bumpass Hell

Bumpass Mountain 8,753 ft

Bumpass Hell

Kings C
Falls

Brokeoff Mountain 9,235 ft

Sulphur Works

Devils Kitchen 6,020 ft

Southwest Information Center
Entrance Station

Drake Lake

89

LASSEN NATIONAL FOREST

Ridge Lake

To Mineral

At **Bumpass Hell**, the road's next major stop, note a large balanced rock at the edge of the parking lot; it's a glacial erratic—a polished, glacier-borne boulder. Nearby begins the **Bumpass Hell Trail**, a fairly easy 3-mile hike that takes about 3 hours. Go on it if you have time.

The place is named after K.V. Bumpass, a local guide and promoter, who in the 1860s plunged a leg through the thin crust covering a seething mud pot. Though badly burned, he wisecracked about his easy descent into hell.

Sulphurous vapors drift over parts of the trail, which leads down to a railed boardwalk that winds past boiling mud pots, rumbling fumaroles, and hissing hot springs. At the springs' steamy pools look for floating golden flakes. They are crystals of iron pyrite—fool's gold—carried along in the superheated steam. The trail returns you to the parking lot.

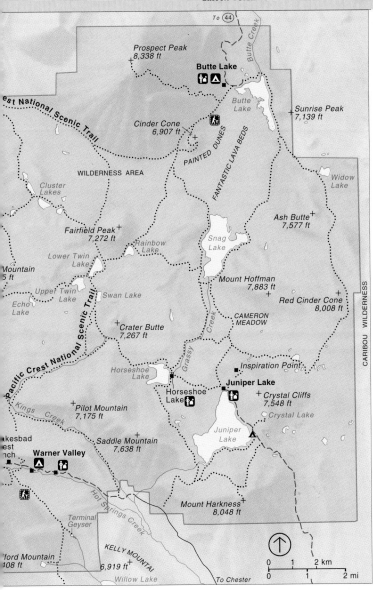

Resume driving on the road, which curves around Lassen Peak. Continue to the **Devastated Area,** wrecked by a massive May 1915 eruption. Amid the scarred and fallen trees notice the signs of renewal: Young trees and stubborn grasses are growing in a slow, natural comeback unaided by human hand. The road offers many turnoffs for viewing the crags and canyons that are Lassen's volcanic heritage.

You'll pass churned-up landscape dubbed **Chaos Crags** and **Chaos Jum-** **bles;** if space along the road permits, stop and walk around it. Here, about 300 years ago, a nearby volcanic dome suddenly collapsed, perhaps because of an earth tremor. Millions of tons of rock, riding a cushion of trapped air, sped across 2 miles of flat land. The horizontal avalanche smashed into a mountain and veered into a creek, damming it and forming **Man-zanita Lake.** Just beyond, the road ends its course through the park and enters Lassen National Forest.

Cinder Cone Nature Trail
31-mile drive, 5-mile hike; a full day

Leave the park via the Manzanita Lake Entrance. Head north on Calif. Hwy. 44 toward the Butte Lake Entrance. From Calif. 44 take the marked dirt road 6 miles to the Butte Lake Campground, where the trail begins. Cinder Cone, a nearly symmetrical, 755-foot-high mound of lava surrounded by multicolored cinders, stands black and solitary above a pine forest. Why all the cinders? This type of cone volcano ejects light lava that shatters in the air and falls back as cinders, which pile up around the volcanic vent. Don't expect to hurry on the cone trail, a round-trip of about 5 miles. Walking on loose cinders is like walking through sand, your feet sinking with every step. At the top (6,907 feet), you will see the craters of recent eruptions; the last was in the mid-1600s.

Lassen Peak Trail
5 miles round-trip; a half to full day

The Lassen Peak Trail is a steep, arduous climb. The zigzagging trail begins at 8,463 feet, near the park road, and takes you to the 10,457-foot summit. The going can get tough for people used to breathing at sea level. Before you try the climb be sure you are acclimatized to the park's high elevations. Carry water, wear a hat, and bring a jacket. Turn back if a storm threatens; the peak is a lightning attractor. Lassen has scant vegetation. "A desert standing on end," a parched climber called it. But you can almost always spot a ground squirrel. And sometimes thousands of tortoiseshell butterflies suddenly flit by, their shadows cascading along the grayish volcanic rocks. At the summit, you can see the hardened vestige of the 1915 lava flow. And visible on a clear day, 75 miles away, is Mount Shasta.

Information & Activities

Headquarters
P.O. Box 100, Mineral, California 96063. Phone (530) 595-4444. www.nps.gov/lavo

Seasons & Accessibility
Park and both its entrances open year-round. Lassen Park Road is usually closed by snow from November to May. For road conditions in the park phone (530) 595-4444.

Visitor & Information Centers
Both the visitor center on Calif. 89 at Manzanita Lake and the Southwest Information Center are open daily from mid-June to Labor Day. Contact the park headquarters for current information.

Entrance Fees
$10 per car; good for 7 days. Those entering on foot or by bicycle pay $5 for 7 days.

Facilities for Disabled
The visitor center, information center, most rest rooms, the Devastated Area Nature Trail, and some picnic areas are wheelchair accessible. Free brochures available.

Things to Do
Among the free ranger-led activities are nature walks and hikes, talks, nature and history demonstrations, children's programs, evening programs (including stargazing and a "prowl" in summer), snowshoe walks, cross-country ski tours. Other activities include hiking, swimming, fishing, boating (no motors), and cross-country skiing.

Overnight Backpacking
Permits required. They are free and can be obtained at headquarters, visitor centers, and ranger stations. No wood fires permitted.

Campgrounds
Six campgrounds, Summit Lake-North and Summit Lake-South have a 7-day limit; all others have a 14-day limit. Open late May through September, weather permitting. First come, first served. Fees: None to $14 per night. Showers are available at Manzanita Lake. RV sites except at Juniper Lake and Southwest; no hookups. Three group campgrounds; reservations required; contact headquarters. Food services in park.

Hotels, Motels, & Inns
(unless otherwise noted, rates are for 2 persons in a double room, high season)
INSIDE THE PARK:
Drakesbad Guest Ranch (47 miles SE of headquarters) Chester, Calif. 96020. Off season call (530) 529-1512; June to Oct. call long-distance operator and ask for the Susanville, Calif., operator; then ask for Drakesbad #2. 6 lodge rooms, 4 cabins, $128 single, $199 double; 6 bungalows, $125 double. All meals included. Pool. Open mid-June to early October.
OUTSIDE THE PARK:
In Mineral, Calif. 96063:
Lassen Mineral Lodge (on Calif. 36 East, 8 miles from park gate) P.O. Box 160. (530) 595-4422. 20 units, 2 with kitchenettes. $75. Restaurant.

In Redding, Calif. 96002:
Best Western Hilltop Inn 2300 Hilltop Drive. (800) 336-4880 or (530) 221-6100. 114 units. $99. AC, pool, restaurant.
Comfort Inn 2059 Hilltop Dr. (800) 228-5150 or (530) 221-6530. 90 units. $66. AC, pool.
Red Lion Inn 1830 Hilltop Drive. (800) 547-8010 or (530) 221-8700. 192 units. $78-$105. AC, pool, restaurant.
Vagabond Inn 536 E. Cypress Ave. (800) 522-1555 or (530) 223-1600. 71 units. $80-$85. AC, pool, restaurant.

For more information on area accommodations, contact the park or the Redding Chamber of Commerce, P.O. Box 1180, Redding, California 96099. (530) 225-4433.

Excursions

Lassen National Forest
Susanville, California

Volcanic features dot this mountain forest surrounding the Lassen Volcanic National Park. Also contains many lakes and streams. 1.5 million acres. Facilities include 66 campsites, hiking, boating, boat ramp, fishing, horseback riding, hunting, picnic areas, winter sports, water sports, handicapped access. Open year-round; most campsites open from May 15 to October 15. Information at Chester on Calif. 36, about 40 miles from the park. (530) 258-2141.

Whiskeytown-Shasta-Trinity National Recreation Area
Whiskeytown, California

Here in Gold Rush country, three impounded lakes provide unlimited opportunities for recreation on, in, and around water. Backcountry hiking and recreational gold panning also featured. 254,388 acres. Facilities include 1,156 campsites, cabins, food services, hiking, boat ramp, fishing, horseback riding, hunting, picnic areas, scenic drives, water sports, handicapped access. Open year-round. Whiskeytown headquarters on Calif. 299, off I-5, about 60 miles west of Lassen Volcanic NP. (916) 241-6584. For Shasta and Trinity units call (530) 246-5222.

Mount Rainier, known to Indians as Tahoma—"the great mountain"

Mount Rainier

Washington

Established March 2, 1899

235,625 acres

One of the world's most massive volcanoes, Mount Rainier can dominate the skyline for 100 miles before you reach the park named after it. At nearly 3 miles in height, Mount Rainier is the tallest peak in the Cascade Range; it dwarfs 6,000-foot surrounding summits, appearing to float alone among the clouds.

Mount Rainier may be the centerpiece of the park, but it is hardly the only attraction. Here, less than 3 hours' drive from Seattle, you can stroll through seemingly endless fields of wildflowers, listen to a glacier flow, wander among trees nearly a thousand years old. The park's convenient location, however, also leads to weekend traffic jams, both summer and winter, and guarantees you company on popular trails.

Mount Rainier is the offspring of fire and ice. Still active, it was probably born more than a half million years ago, on a base of lava spewed out by previous volcanoes. Lava and ash surged out of the young volcano's vent thousands of times, filling the neighboring canyons and building up a summit cone, layer by layer, to a height of some 16,000 feet.

Even while Mount Rainier was growing, glaciers carved valleys on and around the mountain. The 25 major glaciers here form the largest collection of permanent ice on a single US peak south of Alaska.

Mount Rainier's summit deteriorated over time, but eruptions in the last 2,000 years rebuilt it to its current height of 14,410 feet. The mountain last erupted about a century ago.

How to Get There

From Seattle (95 miles) or Tacoma (70 miles) to the Nisqually Entrance (open year-round) take I-5 to Wash. 7, then follow Wash. 706. From Yakima, take Wash. 12 west to Wash. 123 or Wash. 410, and enter from the park's east side (Stevens Canyon or White River Entrances closed in winter). For the northwest entrances (Carbon River and Mowich Lake), take Wash. 410 to Wash. 169 to Wash. 165, then follow the signs. Carbon River Road is subject to flooding in all seasons and may close at any time. Contact the park. Airports: Seattle and Portland, Oreg.

When to Go

All seasons. Wildflowers are at their best in July and August. High trails may remain snow covered until mid-July. Cross-country skiing and snowshoeing are popular in winter. Summer and winter, to miss the crowds, time your visit to midweek.

How to Visit (Summer)

If you have only a day, drive from **Nisqually Entrance** in the southwest to the flowered fields of **Paradise,** then on to **Sunrise,** the highest point accessible by car, open early July–early Oct. If you have 2 days, take the same route but do it more leisurely: Plan to explore as far as Paradise the first day, then tour **Stevens Canyon Road** and the route to Sunrise the next; arrive before 10 a.m. to catch the early light and wend your way back. For a longer stay, drive out and reenter the less known northwest corner at **Carbon River** for a look at a rain forest and a hike to a dark, shiny glacier. Because **Mount Rainier** creates its own clouds and can hide for days or weeks at a time, come prepared to focus on delights close at hand: waterfalls, woods, and wildflowers.

Nisqually to Paradise

18 miles; a half to full day

The pilgrimage to **Paradise** has been a classic for nearly a century. The first miles of your tour wind through a forest of giant Douglas-fir, western red cedar, and western hemlock. As you cross **Kautz Creek,** about 3 miles from the Nisqually entrance, look for flood debris and dead trees amidst the recovering forest. In 1947 the **Kautz Glacier** disgorged a flash flood of meltwater. The flood raged down the creek valley, carrying volcanic debris, trees, and boulders, and burying the road under 28 feet of mud. Similar, though mostly smaller, mudflows occur at least every few years at Mount Rainier.

Park at **Longmire Museum,** 6 miles from the entrance. Pioneer James Longmire discovered mineral springs here in 1883 and built Mount Rainier's first hotel; his ads for miraculous water cures helped generate early tourism and a constituency for the creation of the park. Take time for the easy ½-mile **Trail of the Shadows** that starts on the opposite side of the main road. While in Longmire, also visit the **Wilderness Information Center,** closed October to late-April, for trail and weather information and back-country permits.

Back in your car, continue east for about 6½ miles, then take the spur road to the right to **Ricksecker Point.** To the south loom the sawtoothed

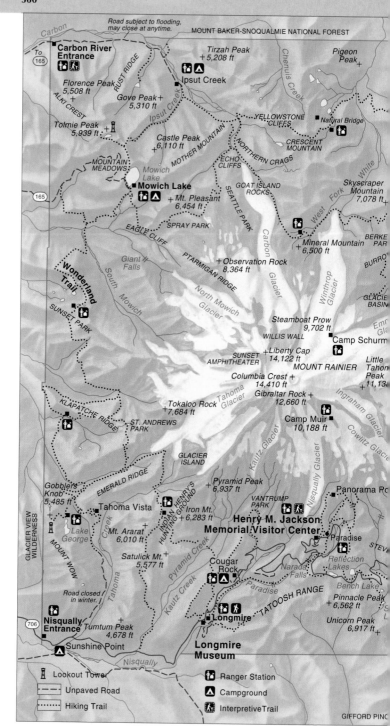

Road subject to flooding, may close at anytime.

MOUNT BAKER-SNOQUALMIE NATIONAL FOREST

To 165

Carbon River Entrance

Florence Peak 5,508 ft +

Gove Peak + 5,310 ft

Tolmie Peak 5,939 ft

RUST RIDGE

ALKI CREST

Carbon

Ipsut Creek

Tirzah Peak + 5,208 ft

Ipsut Creek

Chenuis Creek

Pigeon Peak +

YELLOWSTONE CLIFFS

Natural Bridge ■

CRESCENT MOUNTAIN

Castle Peak + 6,110 ft

MOTHER MOUNTAIN

NORTHERN CRAGS

ECHO CLIFFS

MOUNTAIN MEADOWS

Mowich Lake

Mowich Lake

+ Mt. Pleasant 6,454 ft

GOAT ISLAND ROCKS

SEATTLE PARK

White

West Fork

Skyscraper Mountain 7,078 ft +

165

EAGLE CLIFF

SPRAY PARK

Giant Falls

Wonderland Trail

SUNSET PARK

South Mowich

PTARMIGAN RIDGE

+ Observation Rock 8,364 ft

North Mowich Glacier

Mineral Mountain + 6,500 ft

BERKE PAR

BURRO

Carbon Glacier

Winthrop Glacier

GLACIE BASIN

Steamboat Prow 9,702 ft ■

WILLIS WALL

Camp Schurm

Emr Gla

KLAPATCHE RIDGE

ST. ANDREWS PARK

Tokaloo Rock + 7,684 ft

SUNSET AMPHITHEATER

+ Liberty Cap 14,122 ft

Columbia Crest + 14,410 ft

Tahoma Glacier

Gibraltar Rock + 12,660 ft

MOUNT RAINIER

Little Tahom Peak + 11,13

Ingraham Glacier

Camp Muir ■ 10,188 ft

GLACIER ISLAND

Kautz Glacier

Nisqually Glacier

Cowlitz Glacie

EMERALD RIDGE

Gobbler's Knob 5,485 ft +

Tahoma Vista

Lake George

Mt. Ararat 6,010 ft +

GLACIER VIEW WILDERNESS

MOUNT WOW

INDIAN HENRY'S HUNTING GROUND

Iron Mt. + 6,283 ft

Pyramid Peak + 6,937 ft

VANTRUMP PARK

Panorama Ro

Henry M. Jackson Memorial Visitor Center

Paradise

STEV

Satulick Mt. + 5,577 ft

Pyramid Creek

Cougar Rock

Narada Falls

Reflection Lakes

Bench Lake

Tahoma Creek

Road closed in winter.

706

Nisqually Entrance

Tumtum Peak + 4,678 ft

Kautz Creek

Paradise

Longmire

TATOOSH RANGE

Pinnacle Peak + 6,562 ft

Unicorn Peak 6,917 ft +

Sunshine Point

Longmire Museum

Nisqually

🔭 Lookout Tower

– – – Unpaved Road

········· Hiking Trail

🏠 Ranger Station

⛺ Campground

👣 Interpretive Trail

GIFFORD PINC

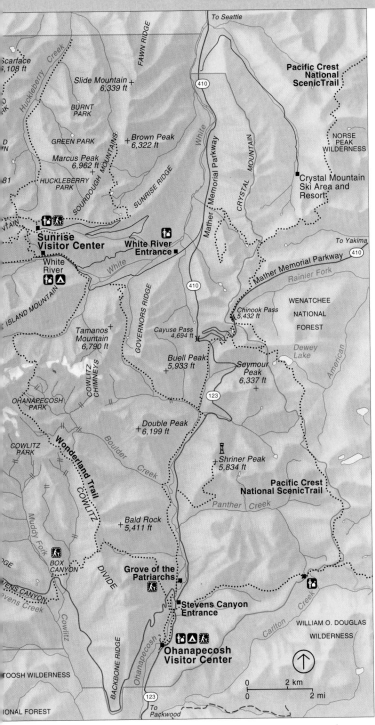

To Seattle

Scarface
3,108 ft

Huckleberry Creek

FAWN RIDGE

Slide Mountain
6,339 ft

BURNT
PARK

GREEN PARK

Brown Peak
6,322 ft

Marcus Peak
6,962 ft

HUCKLEBERRY
PARK

SOURDOUGH MOUNTAINS

SUNRISE RIDGE

White River

Mather Memorial Parkway

CRYSTAL MOUNTAIN

410

Pacific Crest
National
ScenicTrail

NORSE
PEAK
WILDERNESS

Crystal Mountain
Ski Area and
Resort

To Yakima

Sunrise
Visitor Center

White River
Entrance

White River

410

Mather Memorial Parkway

410

Rainier Fork

WENATCHEE

NATIONAL

FOREST

GOVERNORS RIDGE

ISLAND MOUNTAIN

Tamanos
Mountain
6,790 ft

Chinook Pass
5,432 ft

Cayuse Pass
4,694 ft

Buell Peak
5,933 ft

Seymour
Peak
6,337 ft

Dewey
Lake

American

COWLITZ
CHIMNEYS

OHANAPECOSH
PARK

123

COWLITZ
PARK

Wonderland Trail

COWLITZ

Boulder Creek

Double Peak
6,199 ft

Shriner Peak
5,834 ft

Pacific Crest
National ScenicTrail

Panther Creek

Muddy Fork

BOX
CANYON

DIVIDE

Bald Rock
5,411 ft

Grove of the
Patriarchs

Stevens Canyon
Entrance

Carlton Creek

WILLIAM O. DOUGLAS

WILDERNESS

STEVENS CANYON

Stevens Creek

Cowlitz

BACKBONE RIDGE

Ohanapecosh

Ohanapecosh
Visitor Center

0   2 km

0   2 mi

TOOSH WILDERNESS

IONAL FOREST

123

To
Packwood

Paradise Valley and visitor center

peaks of the **Tatoosh Range**, dramatic remains of lava flows that predated **Mount Rainier** by some 25 to 35 million years. Glaciers that developed and receded during the last million years carved the sharp pinnacles and the steep-sided mountainside hollows called cirques. Below meanders the **Nisqually River**, which originates at the snout of the **Nisqually Glacier** that faces you on Mount Rainier. This glacier is about 4 miles long and flows downhill a foot every summer's day.

Rejoin the highway. Another 1½ miles brings you to the **Narada Falls** pullover. The shimmering, 168-foot plunge of the **Paradise River** is well worth the steep but short walk down to the viewing area below the bridge. Climb back up to your car and proceed; in less than 3 miles you'll reach the most popular part of the park.

"It looks just like paradise!" exclaimed Martha Longmire in 1885 on first sighting the rolling hills swathed in wildflowers and framed by Mount Rainier's white dome. An average of 140 inches of precipitation falls here each year; as many as 40 species of flowers bloom on the thin, volcanic soil during July and August. Park near the **Henry M. Jackson Memorial Visitor Center**, or the **Paradise Inn**, built in 1917.

Begin your exploration of Paradise meadows on the **Nisqually Vista Trail** (1⅕ miles), especially if time is short. This easy, self-guided nature walk starts at the staircase to the west of the

Narada Falls in summer

visitor center. Its booklet acquaints you with the geology and meadow life of Mount Rainier.

Make sure you stay on the path, no matter how tempting a meadow stroll. Trampling by just a few people can kill these fragile plants. Park staffers are still at work replanting old trails and other damaged areas. Only recently have the meadows recovered from the Camp of the Clouds, a tent city in operation here from 1898 to 1915. Not only people damage meadows, though. Elk, introduced in the first part of the century and now numbering some 2,000 inside the park, trample and graze the meadows. Researchers are seeking a solution to the problem.

If you're up to tackling some steep hills, try the 5-mile **Skyline Trail**. Start from the staircase west of the visitor center. The trail will take you to **Panorama Point** for some spectacular views.

Paradise to Sunrise

50 miles; a half to full day

Leaving Paradise, turn left at the sign for **Sunrise** and Yakima. You'll soon pass the glacier-carved **Reflection Lakes** on your left; on a calm day, the reflection looks as solid as the mountain. Continue a mile past the lakes' pullover and park on the right for a 2½-mile, hilly, round-trip walk to **Snow** and **Bench Lakes,** gems surrounded by the steep headwalls of the Tatoosh Range.

Drive on and stop after about 3 miles at an overlook of **Stevens Canyon.** Huge glaciers grating through this river gorge deepened and widened it into a classic U-shaped valley. Tributaries of **Stevens Creek** spill from the canyon's rim as waterfalls. Drive on another 3 miles, to **Box Canyon** (just past the picnic area). Park and cross the street for the nearly level ½-mile **Canyon Stroll** and you'll see a 100-foot-deep gorge whose straight walls were carved by the **Muddy Fork** of the **Cowlitz River.**

Continue another 9½ miles, then park to walk the **Grove of the Patriarchs** nature trail. This easy 1⅓-mile loop leads to an island in the **Ohanapecosh River** dominated by grand Douglas-fir, western red cedar, and western hemlock, many of them 500 to 1,000 years old. After rejoining the road, turn left on Wash. 123 for Sunrise. If time allows, take a short detour south on Wash. 123 to visit Ohanapecosh Visitor Center.

At **Cayuse Pass,** continue north on Wash. 410, then make a sharp left toward the **White River Entrance.** The road ends at Sunrise. Spire-shaped subalpine fir and whitebark pine grow here. Near tree line, harsh temperatures and winds stunt the trees into twisted shrubs called krummholz, or elfin timber; trees only inches in diameter may be 250 years old. Fragile wildflowers bloom among grass and sedge in terrain inhospitable to trees.

At the visitor center ask about snow conditions on the higher trails. If time is short, take the self-guided

Grove of the Patriarchs

Marmot eating Indian paintbrush

Northern saw-whet owl

Four-mile-long Nisqually Glacier

Sourdough Ridge Nature Trail for 1½ miles, then the **Emmons Vista Trail** for ½ mile. The Sourdough Ridge trail, which starts with a climb, introduces plants and animals of the subalpine region. The former flourish in this fertile but fragile volcanic soil. The Emmons Vista Trail offers an easy way to view **Emmons Glacier,** Mount. Rainier's largest, covering more than 4 square miles.

But if you have more time and energy, and the snow has melted (snow on the slopes can be dangerous if you're not equipped with an ice ax and trained to use it), take the **Burroughs Mountain Trail** (5 miles to **First Burroughs,** or 7 miles to **Second Burroughs).** Begin as you did for the nature trail, but turn left about half way up the hill and follow the signs. The trail soon enters tundra. Compact little plants sport exquisite lilliputian blossoms and leaves that are a dull gray from the tiny hairs that protect them against drying winds. *It is most important that you stay on the trail:* If trod on, these delicate plants can take decades to heal. At Second Burroughs it feels as if you could almost touch Mt. Rainier's imposing peak. Return to your car by way of the **Sunrise Rim Trail.**

The Northwest Corner: Carbon River

5 miles inside park boundary; a half day

The Carbon River is subject to flooding. Call the park's visitor center for status before attempting this drive.

To visit a rare inland temperate rain forest and peer at a glacier, take the **Carbon River Road** (it forks left off Wash. 165 about 6 miles past Wilkeson). Unpaved inside the park, the road may be passable for ordinary cars. Stop at the entrance to take the self-guided **Carbon River Rain Forest Trail,** a ½-mile loop among colossal Sitka spruce, Douglas-fir, and western red cedar. If the road is passable, drive to the parking lot at Ipsut Creek Campground. If you're up to a 7-mile round-trip hike with a short, moderately steep climb, take the **Carbon Glacier Trail.** Bear right at first fork, left at second, then cross the swinging bridge over the river and continue on to the glistening glacier. *Don't get close:* Boulders continually tumble off the glacier's snout.

Mountain Wildflowers

Giant red paintbrush and daisies along Tatoosh Range

Glacier lilies

Pink mountain heather

Fireweed

Western pasque flowers

Phlox

Shooting star

Information & Activities

Headquarters
Tahoma Woods, Star Route, Ashford, Washington 98304. Phone (360) 569-2211. www.nps.gov/mora

Seasons & Accessibility
Park open year-round. Many roads closed by snow from late November through May or June. Check the website or call (360) 569-2211 for recorded weather, road, and trail information, or in the Nisqually area tune in to 1610 AM.

Visitor & Information Centers
Longmire Wilderness Information Center open daily mid-May–Sept. Longmire Museum open daily. Henry M. Jackson Memorial Visitor Center, at Paradise, open daily from early May to mid-October, weekends the rest of the year. Ohanapecosh Visitor Center, at park's southeast entrance, open daily Memorial Day through mid-Oct. Sunrise Visitor Center open daily, July to early October.

Entrance Fee
$10 per car per week; $20 annual.

Pets
Permitted leashed on roads. Pets not allowed on trails or in the backcountry.

Facilities for Disabled
Most public buildings and some rest rooms are wheelchair accessible. Portions of some trails may be accessible (assistance may be needed). Inquire at park for details.

Things to Do
Free naturalist-led activities: nature and history walks, hikes, campfire and children's programs, talks, films, slide shows. Also available, hiking, mountain climbing, fishing (license not needed), cross-country skiing, snowshoeing.

Special Advisories
• Mount Rainier is an active volcano. While eruptions are usually preceded by an increase in earthquake activity, other hazards, such as mudflows, glacial outburst floods, or rockfalls can occur without warning.
• Watch out for falling rocks, debris, and avalanches. Look up!

• Some areas may be subject to flash floods, especially in late summer and fall. Inquire about current conditions before hiking.
• Stop by a visitor center for additional safety information.

Overnight Backpacking
Permit required; available from visitor centers, ranger stations, and wilderness centers, where you can also get help with your trip planning. Contact the Wilderness Information Center c/o park headquarters or call (360) 569-2211. Make reservations through National Parks Reservation Service (see p. 11).

Campgrounds
Five campgrounds, all with 14-day limit. **Sunshine Point** open all year. Others open late spring to early fall. All campgrounds first come, first served. Fees $10-$14 per night. Showers available in the visitor center at Paradise. Both tent and RV sites; no hookups. Advance reservations required at Cougar Rock and Ohanapecosh from late June–Labor Day. Call National Parks Reservation Service (see p. 11). All others, first come, first served. Food services in park.

Hotels, Motels, & Inns
(unless otherwise noted, rates are for 2 persons in a double room, high season)
INSIDE THE PARK:
National Park Inn (at 2,700 ft. level of Mount Rainier) Mt. Rainier Guest Services, P.O. Box 108, Ashford, Wash. 98304. (360) 569-2275. 25 units, 18 with private baths. $71-$99. Restaurant.
Paradise Inn (at 5,400 ft. level of Mount Rainier) Mount Rainier Guest Services, see above. 126 units, 96 with private baths. $73-$103. Restaurant. Open late May to early October.

For more information on area accommodations, contact the park.

Excursions

Gifford Pinchot National Forest

Vancouver, Washington

Dense coniferous forest encompassing Mount St. Helens National Volcanic Monument offers superb views of the volcano. Contains glaciers and seven wilderness areas. 1,251,000 acres. 900 campsites, hiking, boating, climbing, fishing, horseback riding, hunting, picnic areas, winter sports, water sports, handicapped access. Open all year; most campsites open June-October. Adjoins Mount Rainier NP on the south. Information at Packwood on Wash. 12, about 10 miles from the park. (360) 494-0600.

Mount St. Helens National Volcanic Monument

Amboy, Washington

This monument owes its existence to the day in May 1980 when Mount St. Helens erupted, laying waste to the surrounding forest. Visitors witness the rebirth of a forest through interpretive programs and tours. 110,000 acres. Hiking, bicycling, climbing (reservations required), fishing, hunting, picnic areas, scenic drives, winter sports, handicapped access. Open year-round, but winter snows close many roads. Within Gifford Pinchot NF. Four visitor centers east of Castle Rock on Wash. 504. Many viewpoints and trails accessed from the north via Wash. 12 at Randle and from the south via Wash. 503 at Woodland. (360) 274-2100.

Ridgefield National Wildlife Refuge

Ridgefield, Washington

Established to protect the winter habitat of the dusky Canada goose, this site on the floodplain of the Columbia River provides a winter haven for many waterfowl species. It also serves as a year-round home for great blue herons and a resting spot for migrating sandhill cranes. 5,150 acres. Facilities include hiking, boating, hunting, scenic drives. Open all year, dawn to dusk (winter best time). Off I-5, about 90 miles from Mount Rainier NP. (360) 887-4106.

Glacier-carved peaks of the North Cascades

North Cascades

Washington

Established October 2, 1968

684,000 acres, includes two recreation areas

With glacier-clad peaks rising almost vertically from thickly forested valleys, the North Cascades are often called the American Alps. The national park forms two units, North and South, of the North Cascades National Park Service Complex. The two other units— Ross Lake National Recreation Area and Lake Chelan National Recreation Area—contain most visitor facilities and permit private land ownership and commercial activity.

The park complex preserves virgin forests, fragile subalpine meadows, and hundreds of glaciers. Mule deer and black-tailed deer graze the high meadows, where black bears gorge on berries and hoary marmots sunbathe.

Mountain goats clamber on rock faces. Mountain lions and bobcats, seldom seen, help keep other wildlife populations in balance.

The wildness and ruggedness of the park especially lure hikers, backpackers, and mountaineers. "A more difficult route to travel never fell to man's lot," complained trapper Alexander Ross, who came here in 1814. But today the main road (through Ross Lake NRA) and easy access into the park—on some of its 360 miles of trails—also allow more casual visitors to experience the peaceful forests and the drama of the mountains.

The region forms part of the Cascade Range, named for its innumerable waterfalls. The range extends from British Columbia to northern California. A geological theory proposes that the mountains

How to Get There

From Seattle (about 115 miles from the park), take I-5 to Wash. 20, also called the North Cascades Highway. From the east, get on Wash. 20 south of Mazama. To reach Stehekin Valley, either hike over Cascade Pass from the Cascade River Road or take a one-hour, high-speed catamaran or chartered floatplane from Chelan, at the southern tip of Lake Chelan. Chelan is on US 97. Airports: Seattle and Bellingham.

When to Go

Summer gives the best access, though snow can block high trails into July. The North Cascades Highway, from Ross Dam to beyond Washington Pass, closes in winter. Stehekin, a year-round community, offers winter cross-country skiing.

How to Visit

On a day trip, take the **North Cascades Highway** through the **Ross Lake National Recreation Area** for an over-view of the recreation area's lakes and dams, the park's mountains, and the glacier-fed **Skagit River**. If you have 2 days, drive up the unpaved **Cascade River Road** and picnic and hike among the park's peaks and alpine meadows. On a longer stay, drive south to **Chelan,** and take the ferry or fly to **Stehekin** to overnight in a serene, isolated community or in the backcountry.

North Cascades Highway: Marblemount to Washington Pass

60 miles; a half to full day

The ease of driving the **North Cascades Highway** belies the terrain's ruggedness, although names supplied by explorers and climbers attest to it: Mount Terror, Mount Despair, Damnation Peak, Mount Fury, Mount Challenger. This transmountain road was completed only in 1972.

Enter the **Ross Lake National Recreation Area** after crossing **Bacon Creek,** 6½ miles from the Wilderness Information Center at **Marblemount.** Parallel to the road, the **Skagit River** appears emerald in summer—evidence of the park's many glaciers. As they move, glaciers grind bedrock into a fine "flour." Water carrying a high

began as a micro-continent several hundred miles out in the Pacific Ocean. Over the eons the island floated on its plate towards North America. About a hundred million years ago, it smashed into the North American continent, folding and crumpling into a mountain range as it lodged against the landmass. Those mountains eroded; the Cascades you see today rose only five or six million years ago.

The western part of the park differs markedly from the east. Moisture blows in from Puget Sound and the Strait of Juan de Fuca. It hits the western slopes and rises, condensing to rain and snow. Western red cedar, hemlock, and Douglas-fir luxuriate on slopes that receive 110 inches of precipitation a year. When the winds reach the east, they are mostly wrung dry: Only 35 inches of precipitation fall in Stehekin at the head of Lake Chelan. Arid-dwelling sagebrush and ponderosa pine grow in the peaks' rain shadow.

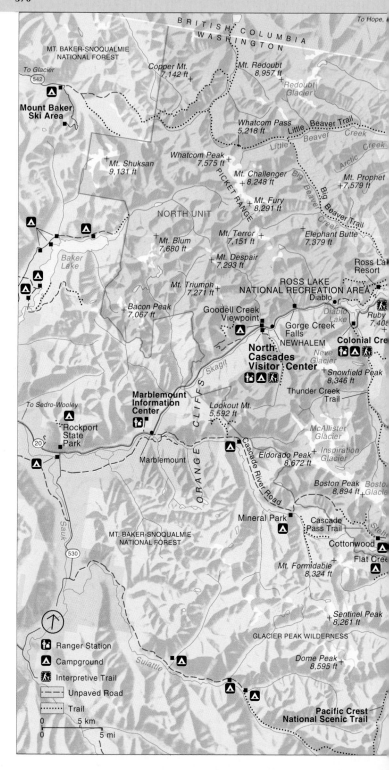

BRITISH COLUMBIA
WASHINGTON

To Hope,

MT. BAKER-SNOQUALMIE
NATIONAL FOREST

To Glacier

542

Copper Mt.
7,142 ft

Mt. Redoubt
8,957 ft

Redoubt
Glacier

Mount Baker
Ski Area

Whatcom Pass
5,218 ft

Little Beaver Trail

Little Beaver Creek

Arctic Creek

Mt. Shuksan
9,131 ft

Whatcom Peak
7,575 ft

Mt. Challenger
8,248 ft

Mt. Prophet
7,579 ft

PICKET RANGE

NORTH UNIT

Mt. Fury
8,291 ft

Big Beaver Trail

Big Beaver Creek

Mt. Blum
7,680 ft

Mt. Terror
7,151 ft

Elephant Butte
7,379 ft

Ross Lake
Resort

Baker Lake

Mt. Despair
7,293 ft

Mt. Triumph
7,271 ft

ROSS LAKE
NATIONAL RECREATION AREA

Diablo

Bacon Peak
7,067 ft

Goodell Creek
Viewpoint

Gorge Creek
Falls

NEWHALEM

Diablo
Lake

Ruby
7,408

Colonial Cre

To Sedro-Wooley

North
Cascades
Visitor Center

Neve
Glacier

Snowfield Peak
8,346 ft

Skagit

Marblemount
Information
Center

Thunder Creek
Trail

Rockport
State
Park

20

Lookout Mt.
5,592 ft

ORANGE CLIFFS

McAllister
Glacier

Cascade River Road

Eldorado Peak
8,672 ft

Inspiration
Glacier

Marblemount

Sauk

Boston Peak
8,894 ft

Bosto
Glacie

Mineral Park

Cascade
Pass Trail

Stehe

MT. BAKER-SNOQUALMIE
NATIONAL FOREST

530

Cottonwood

Flat Cree

Mt. Formidable
8,324 ft

Sentinel Peak
8,261 ft

GLACIER PEAK WILDERNESS

Ranger Station

Campground

Interpretive Trail

Unpaved Road

Trail

Suiattle

Dome Peak
8,595 ft

0   5 km

0   5 mi

Pacific Crest
National Scenic Trail

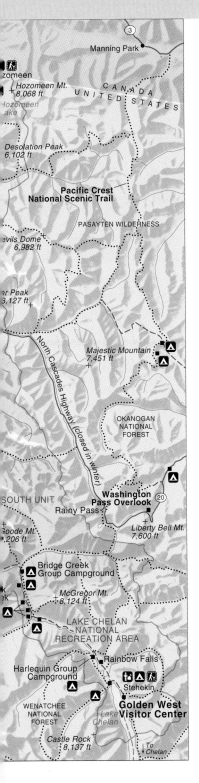

concentration of glacial flour reflects the green part of the light spectrum. In winter bald eagles feast on salmon running the Skagit.

At **Goodell Creek Bridge** (milepost 119), look left to catch a rare glimpse of the high, sawtoothed peaks of the **Picket Range.** Discover the natural and human history of these mountains along trails or at the **North Cascade Visitor Center.** The visitor center features slide and film programs about the North Cascade Wilderness. Near by is an accessible viewpoint trail.

Farther east on Wash. 20, turn right onto Main Street at **Newhalem,** a town of Seattle City Light (milepost 121). The company's dams—Gorge, Diablo, and Ross—generate about a quarter of Seattle's peak-time electricity. The dams created **Diablo, Ross,** and **Gorge Lakes.** To haul men and materials for construction, the company built a railway from Rockport to Diablo in the 1920s. Call the Seattle City Light information center to see if there is room on City Light's 4-hour Ross Dam Deluxe Meal Tour, which includes a cruise on Diablo Lake and a ride up Sourdough Mountain for a tour of the Ross Dam Generators, and dinner. (For reservations, see **Information & Activities.**) Or board a City Light ferry traveling between **Diablo** and **Ross Dams.** This enjoyable 1-hour roundtrip begins across Diablo Dam Road at **Ross Lake Resort.**

Drive on to **Diablo,** another City Light settlement, by turning left at milepost 126. Near here in 1901, pioneer Lucinda Davis and her three children cleared land and put up a roadhouse to feed and house the miners who still trudged the mountains in the wake of two abortive gold rushes. The Davis family built the first hydroelectric project on the Skagit—a waterwheel that generated enough electricity to light three light bulbs. A replica of the waterwheel stands next to the modern Diablo power-house; the **Davis Museum** preserves mementos of the era.

Drive back to the highway and, if you are looking for an invigorating climb, turn right after about 4 miles at Colonial Creek Campground. Behind the amphitheater the **Thunder Woods Nature Trail** begins. This moderately steep 1-mile loop rises among giant, fragrant cedar trees, some of them more than three centuries old. The

Backpackers on the trail above Cascade Pass

red cedar—characterized by ropy, cinnamon-colored bark and flat, fern-like foliage—provided Indians with wood for canoes and houses and fiber for mats, clothing, and baskets. To extend your walk, continue along the 19-mile **Thunder Creek Trail** for a while; the views are good and the hiking relatively easy at first. (Eventually it ascends 6,100 feet.)

When you're back in the car, don't miss the **Diablo Lake Overlook** (1,600 feet), milepost 132. Amid the splendid scenery are exhibits that honor Senator Henry M. Jackson, who helped create the park and to whom Congress dedicated it in 1987. The highest mountain visible here is **Colonial Peak** (7,771 feet) to the southwest; note the glacial cirque, or bowl-shaped depression, carved out of its side. North is **Sourdough Mountain,** site of a fire lookout.

Near milepost 134 you'll find an informative ⅓-mile boardwalk nature trail, the **Happy Creek Forest Walk.** A few miles farther on, the highway leaves the park complex and enters the Okanogan National Forest (milepost 139). For a superb overview of Cascade peaks, follow the road about 20 miles to **Washington Pass Overlook** (5,477 feet), the highest point on the North Cascades Hwy. Exit to the left at milepost 162, and walk to the overlook. Directly to the south is massive **Liberty Bell Mountain** (7,720 feet), south of that are **Early Winter Spires** (7,807 feet). With binoculars you might spot climbers and mountain goats on the solid granite faces.

Cascade River Road

45 miles round-trip; a half day

The **Cascade River Road,** the only road to enter the park proper from the west, passes through national forest for most of its length. The road starts in front of the Log House Inn in Marblemount. Before departing, pick up maps and check road conditions at the Marblemount Wilderness Information Center. The road becomes progressively narrower, steeper, and bumpier, though high-clearance cars can travel it in an hour without difficulty (trailers should not attempt the last few miles). The drive ends at a parking lot and picnic area (3,660 feet) between the glacier-studded summits of **Johannesburg Mountain** (8,200 feet) to the west and **Boston Peak** (8,894 feet) to the east.

Hikers will enjoy the 3¾-mile trail to **Cascade Pass** (5,384 feet). The Skagit and Chelan Indians used the pass to and from **Lake Chelan** for hunting and trading. The trail leaves the lowland forest to enter woods of silver fir, mountain hemlock, and Alaska yellow cedar, then flower-strewn subalpine meadows. Stay on the path; previous visitors have damaged the fragile meadow flora.

Park employees grow native plants in a greenhouse in Marblemount, then backpack or airlift them in for planting in summer to revegetate the pass. The greenhouse (near Wilderness Information Center) is open for visits.

Lake Chelan, a year-round resort

Stehekin Valley

An overnight or 2

Stehekin has been a tourist hideaway since hotels first opened here at the turn of the century and miners spread tales of magical scenery. On the northern shores of glacier-carved Lake Chelan and inaccessible by road, Stehekin is a community of hardy contemporary homesteaders, complete with a one-room schoolhouse in use from 1921 to 1988. The valley offers many lodging alternatives as well as backcountry camping without backpacking: Simply fill out a backcountry permit after you get there, take a shuttle bus to any of 12 backcountry camps, and stake your claim.

Even if you don't plan to camp, head for the **Golden West Visitor Center** when you arrive at Stehekin Landing to pick up hiking maps and schedules of tours and buses. Be sure to ask about trail conditions; high trails—and the last stretch of the shuttle bus route—can be closed by snow or flood damage.

After lunch, tour the **Buckner Homestead**. Home of the Buckner family from 1911 to 1970, it offers a look at the challenges of frontier life.

Next morning follow the nature trails near the landing. The informative ¾-mile **Imus Creek Nature Trail** starts near the visitor center, and the **McKellar Cabin Historical Trail** begins just past the post office. Or catch the early shuttle bus upvalley. The buses currently run 20 winding miles on the old mine-to-market road. Ask ranger for latest bus schedule; reservations may be required. The scenic round-trip to the terminus at Glory Mountain takes 4 hours and can be wearing. If you have the time, it may be better to get off at a trailhead, hike, and catch the later bus back. Another good bet is the **Horseshoe Basin Trail** (off the **Cascade Pass Trail**), a moderately steep 3¾-mile trail that passes more than 15 waterfalls among spectacular glacial and mountain views.

For an easier hike try the **Agnes Gorge Trail**, 5 miles round-trip and level. Get off the bus at **High Bridge** near the intersection with the Pacific Crest Trail and walk across the bridge, past the sign for **Agnes Creek,** to the trailhead for **Agnes Gorge**. The trail provides excellent views of the 210-foot gorge and **Agnes Mountain** (8,115 feet). Be sure to keep a bus schedule with you at all times to avoid being stranded.

Information & Activities

Headquarters
2105 Wash. 20, Sedro Woolley, Washington 98284. Phone (360) 856-5700. www.nps.gov/noca

Seasons & Accessibility
Park open year-round, but snow prevents access to much of it from mid-October to April.

Visitor & Information Centers
North Cascades Visitor Center (near Newhalem) open daily mid-April to mid-Nov., weekends only rest of year. To contact, call (206) 386-4495. Information center on Wash. 20 (North Cascades Highway), in Sedro Woolley open daily late May through mid–Oct., weekdays rest of year. Marblemount Information Center (just west of park boundary off North Cascades Hwy.) open daily summer only. **Lake Chelan NRA:** Golden West Visitor Center (Stehekin), access by ferry, floatplane, or foot, open mid–May to mid–Oct. Ranger station open weekdays all year. For information call (509) 682-2549.

Entrance Fee
No entrance fee, but $5 for one-day vehicle pass to park at overlooks or trailheads. $30 for annual pass.

Pets
Prohibited in national park except on Pacific Crest Trail, if leashed. Permitted on leashes in NRAs.

Facilities for Disabled
Most information facilities are wheelchair accessible.

Things to Do
Free naturalist-led activities: **Ross Lake NRA,** guided nature walks, evening campfire programs. **Lake Chelan NRA,** nature and Buckner Orchard walks, evening programs. Also available, hiking, boating, fishing, hunting (NRAs only, in season), horseback riding, rafting on upper Skagit, cross-country skiing.

In summer, Seattle City Light sponsors tours of Diablo Lake and Ross Dam. Reserve at least a month in advance through Seattle City Light's Skagit Tour Desk, 500 Newhalem St., Rockport, Wash. 98283. Phone (206) 684-3030.

Overnight Backpacking
Permits required; available free at ranger stations and the Golden West Visitor Center.

Campgrounds
Ross Lake NRA: Three campgrounds, 14-day limit. **Colonial Creek** open mid-spring to mid-fall. **Newhalem Creek** open mid-May to early Oct. **Goodell Creek** open all year. All first come, first served. Fees: None to $12 per night. No showers. Tent and RV sites; no hookups. **Goodell Creek and Newhalem Creek Group Campground,** reservations required; contact the park (206) 386-4495. **Lake Chelan NRA:** Three campgrounds, **Harlequin, Bullion,** and **Purple Point,** 14-day limit. Open mid-spring to mid-fall. First come, first served. No fees. Showers are located near **Purple Point.** Tent sites only. Reservations required at **Harlequin Group Campground** (see above); contact the park (see above). Limited food service is available in Lake Chelan NRA.

Hotels, Motels, & Inns
(unless otherwise noted, rates are for 2 persons in a double room, high season)
In Ross Lake NRA:
Ross Lake Resort Rockport, Wash. 98283. (206) 386-4437. (Access by boat or foot.) 15 units floating on lake, kitchens. $97. Open early June to late October.
In Lake Chelan NRA:
North Cascades Stehekin Lodge P.O. Box 457. (509) 682-4494. 28 units. $98. Rest. **Silver Bay Inn** P.O. Box 85, Stehekin, Wash. 98852. (509) 682-2212. 4 cabins, 3 kitchenettes, $125-$225. **Stehekin Valley Ranch** P.O. Box 36, Stehekin, Wash. 98852. (509) 682-4677. 12 tent-cabins, shared showers. $65-$75 per person, meals. Open June to Sept. 30.
In Concrete, Wash. 98237:
Cascade Mountain Inn 40418 Pioneer Lane, Birdsview. (360) 826-4333. 6 units. $120, includes breakfast.

For information on accommodations in Chelan, contact the Chamber of Commerce, P.O. Box 216, Chelan, Wash. 98816. (509) 682-3503; (800) 424-3526.

Excursions

Mt. Baker-Snoqualmie National Forest

Mountlake Terrace, Washington

The Cascades' evergreen-covered western slopes feature active and dormant volcanoes, glaciers, lakes, streams, and waterfalls. Contains eight wilderness areas. Long winter sports season. Over 1.7 million acres. More than 700 campsites, hiking, boating, boat ramp, climbing, fishing, horseback riding, hunting, picnic areas, scenic drives, winter sports, swimming. Open all year; campsites open May-September. Roads often impassable in winter. Adjoins North Cascades NP on west; also borders Mount Rainier NP. (425) 775-9702.

Skagit River Bald Eagle Natural Area

Rockport, Washington

This Nature Conservancy refuge is the favored wintering ground of several hundred bald eagles that feed on chum salmon carcasses on gravel bars along the upper Skagit River. Population peaks in mid-January. 6,000 acres. No visitor facilities. Marked viewing vistas with handicapped access located off Wash. 20 about 10 miles from North Cascades NP. (425) 775-1311.

Okanogan National Forest

Okanogan, Washington

In a remote, rugged mountain area, this national forest features high peaks, mountain lakes, meadows, evergreens, and open woodlands. Contains the Pasayten and Lake Chelan-Sawtooth Wilderness Areas. 1,706,000 acres. Facilities include 39 campgrounds, hiking, boating, boat ramp, climbing, fishing, horseback riding, hunting, picnic areas, scenic drives, winter sports. Open year-round; most campsites open May-October. Adjoins North Cascades NP on east. (509) 826-3275.

Club moss on vine maple and bigleaf maple in the Hoh Rain Forest

Olympic

Washington

Established June 29, 1938

922,000 acres

Encompassing 1,441 square miles of the Olympic Peninsula, Olympic National Park invites visitors to explore three distinct ecosystems: subalpine forest and wildflower meadow; temperate forest; and the rugged Pacific shore. Because of the park's relatively unspoiled condition and outstanding scenery, the United Nations has declared Olympic both an International Biosphere Reserve and a World Heritage site.

Inside the park, the Olympic mountain range is nearly circular, contoured by 13 rivers that radiate out like the spokes of a wheel. No road traverses the park, but a dozen spur roads lead into it from US 101, making it easily accessible from outside the park.

Residents of the Olympic Peninsula refer to it as a gift from the sea, and its features were indeed shaped by water and ice. The rock of the Olympics developed under the ocean—marine fossils are embedded in the mountain summits. Another component, basalt, originated from undersea lava vents. About 30 million years ago, the plate carrying the Pacific Ocean floor collided with the plate supporting the North American continent. As the heavy oceanic plate slid beneath the lighter continental plate, the upper layers of seabed jammed against the coastline, crumpling into what would become the Olympic Mountains. Glaciers and streams sculptured the mountains into their current profiles.

Glaciers nearly 1-mile thick also gouged out Puget Sound and Hood Canal to the east, and the Strait of Juan

How to Get There

Approach the park from US 101, which skirts three sides of the Olympic Peninsula. The main visitor center and entrance are in Port Angeles. From Seattle, take the Washington State Ferry to Bainbridge Island, then drive north to Wash. 104 to join US 101 west to Port Angeles, a drive of about 60 miles. Airports: Port Angeles, Seattle, Sequim, and Olympia.

When to Go

All-year park. Summer is the "dry" season, but be prepared for cool temperatures, fog, and rain at any time. Hurricane Ridge opens for skiing on winter weekends and holidays, weather permitting.

How to Visit

Plan to spend at least 2 days. On the first day, stroll subalpine meadows at **Hurricane Ridge** while admiring the peaks and glaciers in the distance. Savor the **Lake Crescent** area and, if you're feeling energetic, wind up with a dip at **Sol Duc Hot Springs**. On the second day, drive to the **Hoh Rain Forest** and sample its nature trails before heading west for the Pacific Ocean beaches and tide pools. If you have more time, consider a trip to Ozette in the northwest, or visit less known **Quinault**.

de Fuca to the north, isolating the peninsula from the mainland.

Ice Age isolation led to the 15 animals and 8 plants that evolved nowhere else on Earth, including the Olympic mountain milkvetch, Olympic marmot, Olympic Mazama pocket gopher, and Olympic mud minnow.

There are also the 11 mammals common in the nearby Cascades and Rockies that either died out in the Olympics or never found their way into the peninsula. The missing include the grizzly bear, lynx, and mountain sheep. Mountain goats, introduced in the 1920s, have so damaged alpine meadows in Olympic that in 1988 the park staff began efforts to manage the population.

Moist winds from the Pacific condense in the cool air of the Olympics and drop rain or snow, bestowing on the mountains' western slopes the wettest climate in the lower 48 states. Mount Olympus, which crowns the park at 7,965 feet, receives 200 inches of precipitation a year.

Port Angeles to Hurricane Ridge, Lake Crescent, & Sol Duc

76 miles; a very full day

Plan to spend the night in the area to get an early start. At the **Olympic National Park Visitor Center** in Port Angeles, inquire about the weather on **Hurricane Ridge** and pick up a tide table for the next day. On a clear day, the ridge offers spectacular views of the **Olympic Mountains** and northward as far as the Strait of Juan de Fuca and Canada's Vancouver Island. The 17-mile drive to Hurricane Ridge—so named for the force of its winter

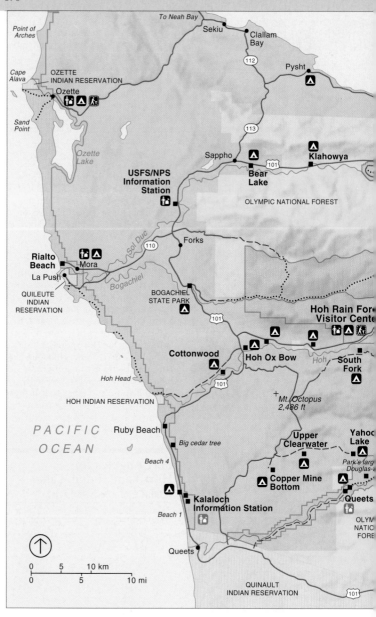

winds—takes you from lowland forest to tree line, nearly a mile above sea level, and reveals some of the remarkable geology of the peninsula.

After the tunnels, 9 miles in, stop at a pullover and look at the rock faces above the road. The bubbles of rock, called pillow basalt, are a clue that these mountains began under the ocean; when hot lava oozes into seawater, its surface cools and hardens quickly, often forming the globules you see here.

Drive on toward **Hurricane Ridge Visitor Center.** Plaques identify the peaks and glaciers of the inner Olympics. **Mount Olympus** carries 7 of Olympic's 60 major glaciers. Its **Blue Glacier** can receive up to 100 feet of snow a year and flows downhill as much as 5 inches a day.

You will probably see black-tailed

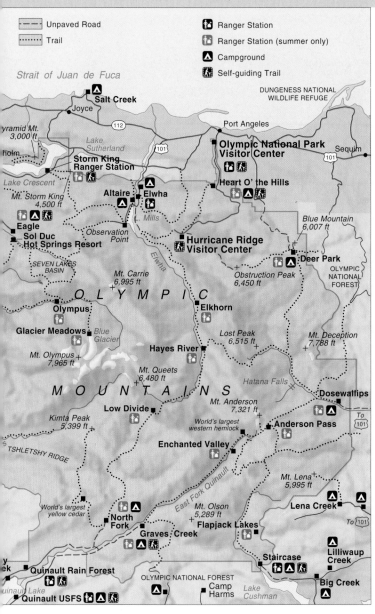

Unpaved Road

Trail

Ranger Station

Ranger Station (summer only)

Campground

Self-guiding Trail

Strait of Juan de Fuca

Salt Creek

Joyce

DUNGENESS NATIONAL WILDLIFE REFUGE

Pyramid Mt. 3,000 ft

Lake Sutherland

Port Angeles

Sequim

holm

Storm King Ranger Station

Olympic National Park Visitor Center

Lake Crescent

Mt. Storm King 4,500 ft

Altaire

Elwha

Heart O' the Hills

Blue Mountain 6,007 ft

Eagle

Sol Duc Hot Springs Resort

Mills

Observation Point

Hurricane Ridge Visitor Center

Deer Park

OLYMPIC NATIONAL FOREST

SEVEN LAKES BASIN

Mt. Carrie 6,995 ft

Elwha

Obstruction Peak 6,450 ft

O L Y M P I C

Olympus

Elkhorn

Glacier Meadows

Blue Glacier

Hayes River

Lost Peak 6,515 ft

Mt. Deception 7,788 ft

Mt. Olympus 7,965 ft

Mt. Queets 6,480 ft

Hatana Falls

Dosewallips

M O U N T A I N S

Low Divide

Mt. Anderson 7,321 ft

To 101

Kimta Peak 5,399 ft

World's largest western hemlock

Anderson Pass

TSHLETSHY RIDGE

Enchanted Valley

Mt. Lena 5,995 ft

World's largest yellow cedar

North Fork

East Fork Quinault

Mt. Olson 5,289 ft

Lena Creek

To 101

Graves Creek

Flapjack Lakes

Staircase

Lilliwaup Creek

Quinault Rain Forest

OLYMPIC NATIONAL FOREST

Camp Harms

Lake Cushman

Big Creek

Quinault Lake

Quinault USFS

deer here, and possibly Olympic marmots that whistle when approached. Most of the trees are subalpine fir. Their distinctive steeple shape helps shed snow. Near tree line, a 3-foot-tall tree may be 100 years old; summer wildflowers thrive where no tree can take hold.

Fine picnic sites lie toward the end of the road, about a mile beyond Hurricane Ridge. Try the **Hurricane Hill Trail,** starting where the road ends, for 3 miles (round-trip) of wildflowers and stunning mountain views. Layers of sedimentary rock along the trail stand folded and tilted on end from the continental collision.

If you prefer to continue driving—some of it is tricky—take the 8-mile, unpaved road to **Obstruction Peak** from the east end of the Hurricane Ridge parking lot for the park's best

Fog-filled Elwha Valley at sunset, from Hurricane Ridge

Glacier-carved Lake Crescent

windshield view of Mount Olympus and some of Olympic's most diverse wildflower displays. The road generally opens by July 4. **Grand Valley Trail** (3½ miles one way) starts at the parking lot at road's end. Take at least a stroll on it for grand ridgetop views. Then double back to Port Angeles and pick up US 101 west.

The highway passes **Lake Sutherland** before tracing the southern shore of **Lake Crescent.** Carved by a glacier, the two lakes began as one, but a great landslide created the dam that now divides them. Indian legend says that Mount Storm King, angered at the fighting between the Quileute and Clallam Indians, threw down a boulder, killing the combatants and splitting the lake in two. Lake Crescent, 600 feet deep, is known for its azure waters and trout.

Turn off at the **Storm King Information Station** to walk the **Marymere Falls Trail,** a 1¾-mile round-trip through lowland forest to a graceful, 90-foot waterfall. Fifty cents buys a booklet that identifies the trees—mostly Douglas-fir and western hemlock, with a few western red cedar. Back in the car, time permitting, turn left 1½ miles west of Fairholm to take the 14-mile road to Sol Duc. Indians, who named the springs Sol Duc, or "sparkling water," probably used the hot springs for medicinal treatments. Travelers have soothed tired muscles in pools here since a resort was first established in 1912. In case you want to stroll before you soak, the **Sol Duc Falls Trail,** starting at the end of the road, leads through ¾ of a mile of dense forest to a waterfall.

Marymere Falls

Hoh Rain Forest to the Pacific Beaches

45 miles; a full day

The **Hoh Rain Forest** is 2½ hours from Port Angeles. To see it and the coast, continue skirting the park as you drive west and south on US 101. Check the schedule of guided tide-pool walks in your park newspaper and then decide whether to go first to the rain forest or to the beaches.

For the rain forest, take the **Hoh Road** inland 19 miles to the visitor center. You'll pass large clear-cut areas on private, state, and national forest lands, but none in the park, where logging is prohibited. Still, environmentalists cite evidence of damage done to park wildlife—some of whose living area extends outside the park—by shrinking habitat.

Two nature trails start behind the visitor center and are well worth taking: the **Hall of Mosses Trail** (¾ mile) and the **Spruce Nature Trail** (1¼ miles). This is an enchanted land. Sitka spruce, western hemlock, and western red cedar, measuring up to 25 feet in circumference, tower 300 feet in the air. Club moss and licorice ferns drape the conifers and bigleaf maples, suffusing the air with green. Seedlings, unable to compete on the crowded forest floor, sprout luxuriantly on fallen trees, called nurse logs. Aged giants, lined up in colonnades, stand on huge roots called stilts where their nurse log rotted away. You may see Roosevelt elk—members of the largest herd in the nation—or hear their eerie bugle.

The Spruce Nature Trail shows how the forest develops. Where the **Hoh River** has shifted course in the last few decades, the first trees to move in needed full sunlight to grow—red alder, willow, and Douglas-fir. Later, shade-tolerant spruce and hemlock will succeed these pioneers to dominate the forest.

After your forest sojourn, rejoin US 101 south, stopping at Ruby Beach. Walk the trail down to the sand—and keep track of where you came out of the woods. It might be hard to find the trail again, and the tough, oval-leaved shrubs off the trail are virtually impenetrable.

Olympic preserves over 60 miles of coastal wilderness: To the north, the beaches tend to have more pebbles and rocks; to the south, the beaches are broader and sandier. Rock outcroppings called sea stacks, isolated from the shoreline by erosion, have caused many a shipwreck.

The driftwood you might have to climb over once grew where you just were: upriver in the forest. Toppled by a winter storm or undercut by a flooding creek, trees tumbled downstream to the sea. *Beware:* Picturesque at low tide, driftwood

Frost-clad ferns and grape leaves

can suddenly roll with lethal force at high.

You may see harbor seals, the most common marine mammal on this coast, swimming or lounging on the rocks. In the spring and fall, California gray whales dive and spout near land on their migration between Alaska and Baja California. Gulls and northwestern crows drop clams from 50 feet in the air to crack them open on the rocks. Bald eagles soar from their forest perches to nab fish. The possibility of offshore oil drilling worries conservationists concerned about the coast's delicate ecosystem. A government moratorium bans it at least until the year 2000.

Continue south on US 101 and turn left at the sign for the big cedar tree, one of the world's largest. Standing at the end of a short spur road, the tree looks like something conjured up from the land of Oz. Monstrous in scale, its girth exceeds 66 feet. Walk right inside and decide for yourself if it's one tree or several that grew together.

US 101 from here to the park's southwest border is dotted with overlooks and short access trails to the beaches. If it's low tide—and you missed the guided tide-pool walk—try the trail at **Beach 4,** just north of milepost 160. A short, steep hike brings you to the shoreline and the rocky tide pools. Alternately battered by waves and dried out by the sun, tide pools nevertheless teem with life. An area

1 foot square may support 4,000 individual creatures belonging to more than 20 species. Look closely to spot gooseneck and acorn barnacles, periwinkle snails, and rocks with holes drilled by piddock clams. Brightly colored sea stars, or starfish, prowl the rocky pools, preying on the mussels and other mollusks. Green sea anemones stun their tiny prey with stinging cells on their tentacles. Purple sea urchins dine on bits of kelp and other algae.

To view a third mood of Olympic beach, park near **Beach 1,** a stroller's delight, at milepost 155. Follow the sign to the **Spruce Burl Trail** for a brief detour before descending to the sand. Near the ocean, Sitka spruce commonly develop large, nobby growths that may be triggered by a virus, a bacterium, or some substance carried in the ocean spray.

Ozette & Quinault

A hiking experience in Olympic can range from a paved ¼-mile nature walk to the ascent of Mount Olympus. Of the more than 600 miles of trails, here are a few suggestions. Take US 101 to Sappho, head north to Wash. 112 and take it into Sekiu. Then go southwest to **Ozette.** There trails lead on wooden walkways through lush coastal forest to the beach. Register at the ranger station first.

For a level 9⅓-mile loop, take the **Cape Alava Trail,** walk south along the rocky beach, then return to your car along the **Sand Point Trail.** You'll pass **Cape Alava,** the westernmost point of the contiguous United States, stunning seacoast scenery, and rock etchings left by Indians who lived by whaling and fishing.

For a remote and peaceful visit to the rain forest, drive south to **Quinault** (32 miles from Kalaloch) and take the **North Fork** spur road. Walk the ½-mile **Quinault Rain Forest Nature Trail** from near the **Quinault Ranger Station** or the 2⅕-mile round-trip **Irely Lake Trail** from ¼ mile before the North Fork Campground. Look for beaver dams, herons, and ospreys, which often nest at the lake.

Information & Activities

Headquarters
600 E. Park Avenue, Port Angeles, WA 98362. Phone (360) 452-4501. www.nps.gov/olym

Seasons & Accessibility
Park open year-round. Some roads closed in winter.

Visitor & Information Centers
In Port Angeles, the Olympic National Park Visitor Center, 3002 Mt. Angeles Road; call (360) 452-0330. The Hoh Rain Forest Visitor Center off US 101 at western edge of park, (360) 374-6925. Both open daily all year. Hurricane Ridge Visitor Center also open all year, weather permitting.

In summer, information stations open at Storm King on Lake Crescent, Kalaloch, and other locations.

For park information, tune in to 530 AM in the Port Angeles and Lake Crescent areas.

Entrance Fee
$10 per vehicle for 7-day pass May to September. Some areas charge an entrance fee in winter.

Pets
Allowed on leashes except on trails and in backcountry.

Facilities for Disabled
Visitor centers are accessible to wheelchairs. Also accessible are Hurricane Ridge's paved trails; a short loop trail into the Hoh Rain Forest; the Madison Falls Trail in the Elwha Valley, and the "Moments in Time" trail at Lake Crescent.

Things to Do
Free naturalist-led activities: meadow, forest, beach, and tidepool walks; campfire programs. Also available, hiking, boating, fishing (no license needed), climbing, swimming, windsurfing, waterskiing, river rafting, cross-country and alpine skiing, snowshoeing.

Special Advisory
● Be careful when hiking along the coast; rocks and logs can be slippery and unstable. Be aware of incoming tides (current tables posted at trailheads). Surf logs can kill.

Overnight Backpacking
Call ahead for reservations. Permits required; obtain at Wilderness Information Center (directly behind Olympic National Park Visitor Center (360) 452-0330), visitor centers, ranger stations, or trailheads.

Campgrounds
Fifteen campgrounds, all with a 14-day limit. **Deer Park, Dosewallips, North Fork,** and **Queets** campgrounds do not allow RVs. All first come, first served. Fees: None to $12 per night. No showers. Three group campgrounds; reservations required; contact headquarters. Food services in park.

Hotels, Motels, & Inns
(unless otherwise noted, rates are for 2 persons in a double room, high season)
INSIDE THE PARK:
Kalaloch Lodge (on US 101, 36 miles south of Forks) 157151 Hwy. 101, Forks, Wash. 98331. (360) 962-2271. 20 rooms; 44 cabins, 38 with kitchenettes. Rooms $120-$225; cabins $135-$225. Rest. **Lake Crescent Lodge** (on US 101) 416 Lake Crescent Rd., Port Angeles, Wash. 98362. (360) 928-3211. 52 units, 47 with private bath. $118-$153. Rest. Open late April through Oct. **Log Cabin Resort** (on Lake Crescent) 3183 E. Beach Road, Port Angeles, Wash. 98363. (360) 928-3325 or 928-3245. 28 units, 3 with kitchenettes. $44-$156. Rest. Open April through Sept. **Sol Duc Hot Springs Resort** (12 miles off US 101) P.O. Box 2169, Port Angeles, Wash. 98362. (360) 327-3583. 32 cabins, 6 kitchens. $85-$95. Pool, rest. Open mid-May through Sept.

For other lodgings, contact the Chambers of Commerce in Port Angeles, 121 E. Railroad, 98362. (360) 452-2363; and Forks, P.O. Box 1249, 98331. (360) 374-2531 or (800) 443-6757.

Coast redwoods, a grove of giants

Redwood

California

Established October 2, 1968

108,400 acres including 3 state parks

Sometimes, when the morning fog caresses the great trees, you can imagine the past flowing through the long, misty shadows…Vast redwood forests flourishing across a lush and humid North America…After the final Ice Age, a last stand here in the sustaining climate along the Pacific coast…Tree after tree falling to the loggers. Then, in a windswept moment, the past vanishes and you stand beside other visitors, gazing up at the Earth's tallest living things. That is the essence of Redwood National and State Parks.

The park, near the northern limit of the coast redwood's narrow range, preserves the remnants of a forest that once covered two million acres and, at the turn of the century, was badly threatened by logging. The state of California and the Save-the-Redwoods League came to the rescue by acquiring hundreds of groves and protecting them within 26 state parks. Three redwood state parks—Jedediah Smith, Del Norte Coast, and Prairie Creek—were encompassed by the national park when it was created in 1968.

Logging on surrounding private land, however, threatened the parks' protected redwoods. Soil and sediments from the logged-over tracts washed into the rivers and creeks, settling to the bottom downstream. Silt deposits can smother redwoods—for the giants are amazingly vulnerable. And the waterlogged soil weakens the trees' resistance to wind. Their roots are shallow, often only 10 feet deep.

In 1978 Congress added 48,000 acres to the national park's 58,000 acres, including about 36,000 that had been logged. The raw, clear-cut land, a park official wrote, had "the look of an active war zone." Today, in an epic earthmoving project—a redwood renaissance—crews are beginning to reclaim vast stretches of logged-over lands. Hillsides, carved away for logging roads, are being restored. Most of the 400 miles of roads are being erased. It will take at least 50 years for the scars of logging to disappear and another 250 or so years for the replanted redwood seedlings to grow to modest size.

The renaissance has added a new dimension to the traditional rite of staring up at redwoods. Today's visitor can look at hillsides shorn of giants and know that generations from now the trees will grow there again.

How to Get There

Tree-lined US 101, the Redwood Highway, runs the length of the park.

From the south, take US 101 to the information center near Orick, about 40 miles north of Eureka. From the north, enter through Crescent City, also an information center site. From the east, take US 199, another redwood-flanked highway, to Hiouchi. Airport: Arcata and Crescent City.

When to Go

All-year park. Summer draws highway-clogging crowds, so think about a visit in spring or fall. In both seasons, bird migrations enhance the redwood groves. Rhododendrons burst forth in spring; deciduous trees add color in fall. Rains, welcome to the redwoods but not to visitors, drench the park in winter.

How to Visit

US 101, with its many redwood sentinels, gives you a windshield-framed panorama of the trees. But to appreciate the redwoods, you must walk among them. If you have only a day to visit this 50-mile-long park, stop and see the **Lady Bird Johnson Grove** and **Big Tree.** Hike or just stretch your legs (depending on your time) along the **Coastal Trail** and savor the Pacific prospect of the park. For a longer stay, visit the **Tall Trees Grove,** drive **Howland Hill Road,** and end your visit with a splash in a kayak on the **Klamath River** or a jouncy drive to **Fern Canyon** and **Gold Bluffs Beach.** If you are driving an RV or towing a trailer, some stretches of road may be closed to you; check at information centers.

Lady Bird Johnson Grove & Big Tree

13 miles; 2 hours

Just before Orick, stop at the **Redwood Information Center** (once the site of a redwood-slicing lumber mill) to see the exhibits, and then continue north on US 101 to the Bald Hills Road sign. Turn right and drive 2 miles to **Lady Bird Johnson Grove,** a jewel that gives you an understanding of the entire park treasure. On the grove's mile-long trail you feel the cool, moist air that redwoods need. You see a hollowed-out tree that still lives. Such redwoods—"goose-pen" trees—once sheltered settlers' fowl and livestock. You smell and touch

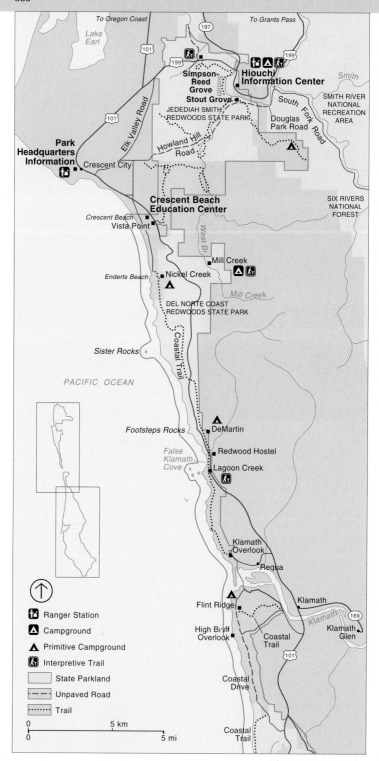

To Oregon Coast
To Grants Pass
197
Lake Earl
101
199
199
Simpson-Reed Grove
Hiouchi Information Center
Stout Grove
Smith
SMITH RIVER NATIONAL RECREATION AREA
101
JEDEDIAH SMITH REDWOODS STATE PARK
Douglas Park Road
South Fork Road
Elk Valley Road
Howland Hill Road
Park Headquarters Information
Crescent City
SIX RIVERS NATIONAL FOREST
Crescent Beach Education Center
Crescent Beach
Vista Point
West Br.
Mill Creek
Enderts Beach
Nickel Creek
Mill Creek
DEL NORTE COAST REDWOODS STATE PARK
Sister Rocks
Coastal Trail
PACIFIC OCEAN
DeMartin
Footsteps Rocks
Redwood Hostel
False Klamath Cove
Lagoon Creek
Klamath Overlook
Requa
Klamath
Flint Ridge
Klamath
High Bluff Overlook
Coastal Trail
101
Klamath Glen
169

Ranger Station
Campground
Primitive Campground
Interpretive Trail
State Parkland
Unpaved Road
Trail

0   5 km
0   5 mi

Coastal Drive

Coastal Trail

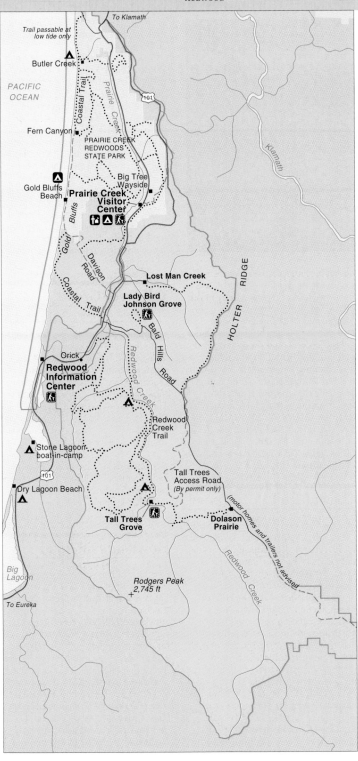

To Klamath

Trail passable at
low tide only

Butler Creek

PACIFIC
OCEAN

Coastal Trail

Prairie Creek

101

Fern Canyon

PRAIRIE CREEK
REDWOODS
STATE PARK

Big Tree
Wayside

Gold Bluffs
Beach

**Prairie Creek
Visitor
Center**

Gold Bluffs

Davison Road

Coastal Trail

HOLTER RIDGE

Lost Man Creek

**Lady Bird
Johnson Grove**

Bald Hills Road

Orick

**Redwood
Information
Center**

Redwood Creek

Redwood
Creek
Trail

Stone Lagoon
boat-in-camp

101

Dry Lagoon Beach

Tall Trees
Access Road
(By permit only)

(motor homes and trailers not advised)

**Tall Trees
Grove**

**Dolason
Prairie**

Big
Lagoon

Redwood Creek

*Rodgers Peak
2,745 ft*

To Eureka

Lady Bird Johnson Grove

the many plants that share the redwoods' domain. Most of all, you feel the peace; visitors speak quietly in this pillared place.

Return to US 101 and continue north about 4 miles. Near the entrance to **Prairie Creek Redwoods State Park,** pull into the turnout to watch the free-roaming Roosevelt elk that live in the park. A mile ahead on the right is a wayside sign for **Big Tree.** A short trail from the parking lot leads to the aptly named tree. It's 304 feet tall, 21⅕ feet in diameter, 66 feet in circumference, and about 1,500 years old. Here the experience is singular: you and one great tree.

Coastal Trail

4 miles one way; at least 2 hours

From Orick, drive north 20 miles on US 101, passing Klamath, and turn left onto Requa Road. Park and picnic at **Klamath Overlook,** a high hill. On a clear day you can see 65 miles down the bluff-guarded coast. **The Hidden Beach Section** of the **Coastal Trail** begins here, heads west, and then veers north along the wild, driftwood-decorated shore. Yurok Indians walked these shores, as did Jedediah Smith, the first white man to reach California's northern coast by land.

The trail, often bowered by branches of spruce and alder, sometimes seals you from the sight—though not the sounds—of the ocean. But there are many spots where you can sit and gaze out to sea. In spring and fall you may

see migrating gray whales. Almost any time you will see gulls, cormorants, and ospreys.

A short side path leads down to **Hidden Beach.** Even on a day when the park is crowded yours may be the only footprints on the sand. Look at the ocean but don't swim: The undertow is dangerous all along the park's coast. The beach walk ends at a wall of gnarled black rocks. Follow your footprints back to the path and return to the trail, which heads north along the wild shore, then veers inland.

The north trailhead is at **Lagoon Creek,** where fresh water and forest meet ocean and high bluff. If you don't want to trudge the 4 miles back, have someone drive up to meet you at the parking lot.

Tall Trees Grove

2⅔ miles; a half day

Obtain a permit to drive your vehicle to the Tall Trees Grove parking area, off Bald Hills Road. (Permits can be obtained at any of the information centers.) From the parking area, the trail is a very steep 2⅔-mile round-trip. The hike down to the grove, replete with ferns and rhododendrons, takes at least 30 minutes. Plan on another 30 to 45 minutes in the grove among the giant coast redwoods. The star is the **Nugget Tree,** which was measured at 365.5 feet in 1995. This is one of the world's tallest known trees. It's estimated to be between 900 and 1,500 years old.

Howland Hill Road

8 miles; about two hours

Just south of Crescent City, take Elk Valley Road northeast. Keep a sharp watch on your right for the turnoff to **Howland Hill Road,** once a miners' supply road partially redwood-planked for oxcarts and horse-drawn wagons. The 6-mile road winds between redwoods that loom much closer than the ones along highways. Mostly unpaved and often one lane, motor homes and trailers are not recommended. Stop at **Stout Grove,** where you can see one of many preserves set aside, this one donated by the wife of a logging company owner. Take time to enjoy the

Blueblossom, Enderts Beach

1-mile trail among the redwoods. (In summer you can also reach the grove from the **Hiouchi Information Center** via a footbridge across the crystal-clear **Smith River**.)

Continue past the grove to Douglas Park Road, which ends at South Fork Road. Turn left to US 199 and drive west about 2 ½ miles to the Hiouchi Information Center. Park here and sign up for an interpretive walk with a ranger. Or, continue west on US 199 to **Simpson-Reed Grove,** where you'll find a short pleasant self-guided trail.

Gold Bluffs Beach & Fern Canyon

20 miles; a half day

From the Redwood Information Center, head north for 4½ miles to Davison Road, on your left. Elk are often spotted on the first few hundred yards on this road. The rough dirt road bounces you for about 4 miles down to **Gold Bluffs,** named for the gold found here. The road continues for 4 miles along the beach, ending near **Fern Canyon,** where a ¾-mile loop trail climbs to a prairie—site of a vanished mining camp. Back down the canyon, walk through elk-roamed grass to a beautiful, desolate beach sprinkled with driftwood and often shrouded in fog. Return the way you came, pausing to admire the fern-covered 30-foot-high walls. The more adventurous can make a longer loop by climbing to **Prairie Creek** and walking along its banks before heading back toward the ocean. Return to the parking area at Fern Canyon via the windswept southern stretch of the **Coastal Trial.** Be on the lookout for a variety of birds, including pelicans, terns, gulls, and wading birds. In the fall or spring scan the horizon for the telltale spouts of migrating gray whales.

Information & Activities

Headquarters
1111 Second Street, Crescent City, CA 95531. Phone (707) 464-6101. www.nps.gov/redw

Seasons & Accessibility
Open year-round.

Visitor & Information Centers
Crescent City Information Center, at north end of park, open daily all year. For visitor information, phone (707) 464-6101. Redwood Information Center, at south end of park near Orick, also open all year. Hiouchi Information Center, at north end of park, open spring through summer.

Entrance Fee
No admission fee. $2 day-use fee for Jedediah Smith, Del Norte Coast, and Prairie Creek State Parks.

Pets
Permitted on leashes except on trails and in backcountry.

Facilities for Disabled
Information centers, Crescent Beach, Lagoon Creek picnic area, Klamath Overlook, and some trails are accessible to wheelchairs.

Things to Do
Free naturalist-led activities: tide pool and seashore walks, evening programs. Also available, hiking, canoeing, guided kayak trips, horseback riding, freshwater and ocean fishing (need license), swimming (inland only), whale-watching.

Special Advisories
● Be aware that ticks may transmit Lyme disease.
● Ocean swimming is not advised due to extremely cold water and treacherous undertow.

Overnight Backpacking
Permit required; can be obtained free at trailheads and at the National Park Information Centers and State Park Visitor Centers. The National Park lands offer three backcountry campsites—**DeMartin, Flint Ridge,** and **Nickel Creek;** 14-day limit. Open all year, first come, first served. No fees. Tent sites only. No showers.

Butler Creek campsite in Prairie Creek State Park is available to bikers and hikers only (for a fee). Reserve at Prairie Creek Visitor Center.

Campgrounds
There are four state-run campgrounds inside the park—**Gold Bluffs Beach, Jedediah Smith, Mill Creek,** and **Elk Prairie;** 15-day limit. **Mill Creek** open April to October; others open all year; Gold Bluffs Beach may close in bad weather. Showers available nearby. Tent and RV sites; no hookups; large RVs not recommended and trailers prohibited at **Gold Bluffs Beach.** Fees $12 per night. Reservations recommended from mid-May through August and are available through National Parks Reservation Service (see page 11) up to 5 months in advance. The reservations number for these state-run campgrounds is (800) 444-7275. No food services inside park.

Hotels, Motels, & Inns
(unless otherwise noted, rates are for 2 persons in a double room, high season)
In Crescent City, Calif. 95531:
Crescent City Quality Inn 725 Highway 101 North. (800) 228-5151 or (707) 464-6106. 52 units. $63-$73. AC. **Curly Redwood Lodge** 701 Redwood Hwy. South. (707) 464-2137. 36 units. $39-$65. **Best Value Inn** P.O. Box 595, 440 Highway 101 North. (707) 464-4141. 61 units. $62. **Royal Inn Motel** 102 L Street. (800) 752-9610 or (707) 464-4113. 35 units. $35-$55. Restaurant. Closed Mon.-Wed. in winter.
In Eureka, Calif. 95501:
Eureka Inn 7th and F Streets. (800) 862-4906 or (707) 442-6441. 181 units. $99. Pool, restaurant. **Hotel Carter** 301 L Street. (800) 404-1390 or (707) 444-8062. 31 units. $105-$275, includes continental breakfast. Restaurant.
In Klamath, Calif. 95548:
Motel Trees (on US 101) 15495 Hwy. 101. (800) 848-2982 or (707) 482-3152. 23 units. $55. Rest. **Requa Inn** 451 Requa Road. (707) 482-8205. 10 units. $60-$85, includes breakfast. Restaurant.

Excursions

Humboldt Bay National Wildlife Refuge

Loleta, California

The islands and wetlands of Humboldt Bay provide critical habitat for the brant, a small, stocky sea goose. From late winter to early spring, thousands of brant use the refuge as a staging area en route to northern nesting grounds. Other waterfowl and peregrine falcons are also present. 2,110 acres. Excellent birdwatching from the Hookton Slough Trail. Off US 101, about 40 miles from Redwood National Park. (707) 733-5406

Six Rivers National Forest

Eureka, California

Six major rivers cross this mountain forest of pine, fir, spruce, and cedar, providing nearly 10 percent of the state's runoff. Recreational opportunities include white-water rafting, kayaking, and excellent steelhead and salmon fishing. Contains parts of four wilderness areas. 957,590 acres. Facilities: 355 campsites, hiking, boating, boat ramp, fishing, horseback riding, hunting, picnic areas, scenic drives, winter sports, water sports, handicapped access. Open all year, though most off-highway routes close in winter. Campsites open May-November. Information at Gasquet on US 199, about 15 miles from Redwood NP. (707) 457-3131.

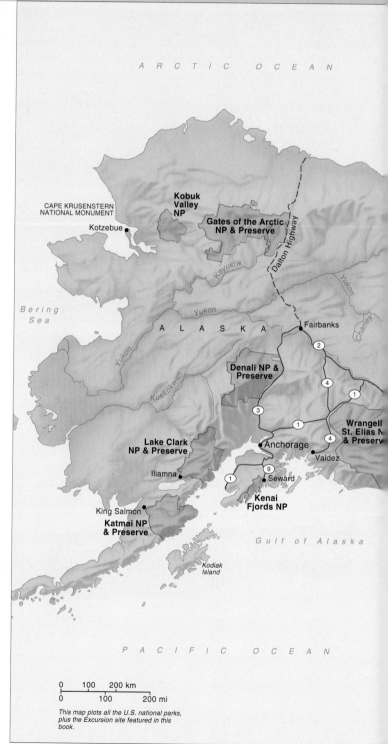

This map plots all the U.S. national parks, plus the Excursion site featured in this book.

Preceding pages: Lake Clark, Alaska

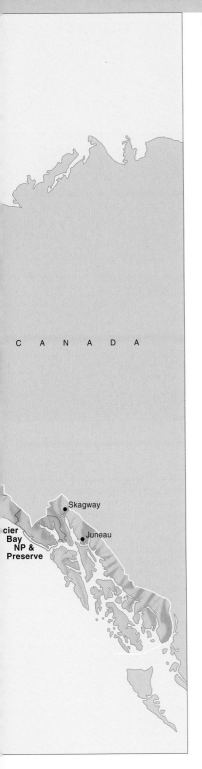

C A N A D A

Skagway

cier
Bay
NP &
Preserve

Juneau

Alaska

In 1867 Secretary of State William Seward bought Alaska from Russia for two cents an acre—and the public labeled the vast empty land Seward's Folly. Today, more than six billion barrels of oil have gushed through the Prudhoe Bay pipeline, and Alaska's wilderness and wildlife attract visitors by the thousands.

Eight national parks protect 41.5 million acres of these natural treasures. Katmai and Lake Clark lie along the Pacific Ring of Fire—a region of active volcanoes, earthquakes, giant brown bears, and salmon. Whales, sea lions, and flocks of seabirds seek out the cold, food-laden waters of Glacier Bay and Kenai Fjords. Wrangell-St. Elias is a jumble of mountains and glaciers so rugged that many remain unnamed and untrodden by humans. Above the Arctic Circle, Gates of the Arctic and Kobuk Valley protect the tundra and migrant herds of caribou. By comparison, Denali seems civilized with its nearby railroad and hotels; yet here the wildlife is so abundant and visible, the park is called a "subarctic Serengeti."

Alaska parks include national preserves that allow hunting, vast wilderness areas that prohibit buildings and roads, and native-owned lands still used for subsistence in a tradition thousands of years old.

In 1989 the Exxon Valdez ran aground in Prince William Sound, spilling nearly 11 million gallons of oil. The slick spread into the Gulf of Alaska and onto the beaches of Katmai and Kenai Fjords. It killed more than 3,500 sea otters and 350,000 seabirds, as well as unknown numbers of scavenging mammals. The visible oil slick is gone, but the damage to the area's ecological balance may well last forever.

Most of Alaska's national parks are accessible only by plane or boat, but you can drive to Denali and Wrangell-St. Elias and to the edges of Kenai Fjords and Gates of the Arctic. The loop connecting Anchorage to Denali to Fairbanks to Wrangell-St. Elias, with a side trip to Kenai Fjords, is 1,100 miles. It's a 600-mile round-trip from Fairbanks to Gates of the Arctic on the unpaved Dalton Highway. Alaska parks are rugged, yet fragile; tread lightly.

Moose on an autumn landscape beneath Mount McKinley

Denali

Alaska

Established February 26, 1917

6,028,091 acres

On any summer day in Denali, Alaska's most popular national park, hundreds of people see sights that will stay with them the rest of their lives. Perhaps a golden eagle will soar off the cliffs at Polychrome Pass, or 20 Dall's sheep will rest on a green shoulder of Primrose Ridge, or a grizzly will ramble over the tundra at Sable Pass. Maybe a caribou will pause on a ridgetop, silhouetted by the warm light of day's end, or a loon will call across Wonder Lake, or clouds will part to reveal the great massif of Mt. McKinley, 20,320 feet high, the roof of North America. The drama is always there. To see it, all you need to do is travel the 85-mile park road. The farther you go, the more

you'll see, for the subarctic landscape will open up as big as the sky and the animals will move through it with wild, ancient poetry.

Other North American parks have their wildlife, but none has animals so visible or diverse as Denali. And other parks have their mountains, but none with a stature so stunning, a summit so towering as McKinley.

Denali's visitors have increased 1,000 percent in 30 years. How to accommodate that many people without eroding the park's wilderness? A bus system has been designed that permits maximum wildlife viewing while holding down traffic. Campgrounds have been kept modest and unobtrusive. And the wilderness area has been divided into management units with strict visitation ceilings to prevent overcrowding and damage to the flora and fauna. Unless you plan ahead by using the

rich tones of red, orange, and yellow. In winter, visitors can take the road 3 miles to park headquarters and cross-country ski, snowshoe, or dogsled from there.

May and early June are the best times to climb Mount McKinley; after June, avalanches threaten. Most mountaineers fly by ski-plane from Talkeetna and land at 7,500 feet on the Kahiltna Glacier to begin a climb that will take 15 to 30 days.

How to Visit

The more time the better, but plan on at least two days. You can drive your car on the **park road** as far as the **Savage River Check Station** at mile 14 but no farther. Shuttle buses and tour buses operate on the road by day and into evening, late May to mid-September; schedules vary. **Mount McKinley** is often covered with clouds; you may be more likely to get a clear view of it early or late in the long day.

Park campgrounds and buses are usually full, so plan on the possibility of staying a night or two in a hotel or nearby private campground if you must wait for a campsite or bus ticket. The 85-mile shuttle bus trip along the park road to **Wonder Lake** takes 11 hours round-trip, including many stops to watch wildlife; other buses go part way. Take a jacket, binoculars, and a lunch (available near the **Visitor Access Center** or outside the park; no food along the way). In the park, consider getting off the bus for a hike; buses will stop almost anywhere. To get on another bus, just wave one down. In busy times, you may have to wait a while.

parks easy-to-use reservation system, you may have to wait a day or two to get your preferred campsite or bus reservation.

How to Get There

From Anchorage, take Alaska 1 (Glenn Hwy.) 35 miles north to Alaska 3 (George Parks Hwy.). Go north 205 miles. From Fairbanks, take Alaska 3 west and south 120 miles. In summer, the Alaska Railroad runs between Anchorage and Fairbanks and stops daily at the Denali railroad station. In winter, the train runs on weekends only. Air service available in summer to the nearby airstrips from Anchorage, Fairbanks, and Talkeetna.

When to Go

In summer, there are up to 24 hours of daylight. The park road is open from late May to mid-September. June is usually less crowded than July and August. In late August or early September, the tundra turns

Park Road

85 miles one way; 11 hours round-trip

Your bus journey begins at the **Visitor Center** (at mile 0.7), surrounded by the spruce forest, or taiga. Within minutes you'll see the railroad station used by the Alaska Railroad, and you'll pass park headquarters, where sled dogs are kept for winter patrols and summer demonstrations.

Soon the road begins climbing out of the taiga and into the treeless expanse of the tundra. Magnificent vistas open up; on clear days **Mount**

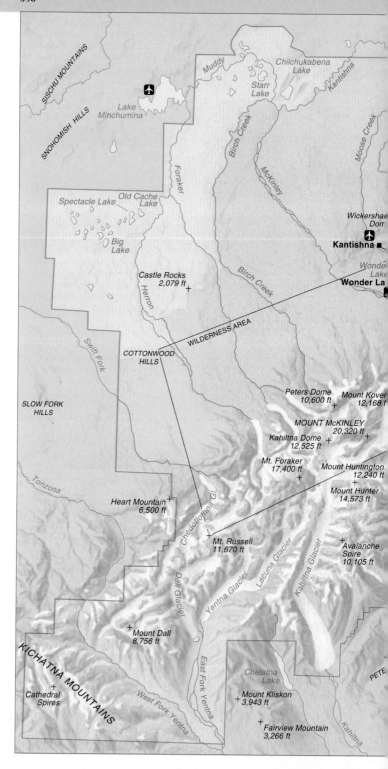

SISCHU MOUNTAINS

Muddy

Chilchukabena
Lake

Starr
Lake

Birch Creek

Kantishna

Moose Creek

SNOHOMISH HILLS

Lake
Minchumina

McKinley

Foraker

Old Cache
Lake

Spectacle Lake

Wickersham
Dome

Big
Lake

Kantishna ■

Wonder
Lake

Castle Rocks
2,079 ft

Herron

Birch Creek

Wonder La

WILDERNESS AREA

Swift Fork

COTTONWOOD
HILLS

Peters Dome
10,600 ft

Mount Kover
12,168 f

SLOW FORK
HILLS

MOUNT McKINLEY
20,320 ft

Kahiltna Dome
12,525 ft

Tonzona

Mt. Foraker
17,400 ft

Mount Huntington
12,240 ft

Heart Mountain
6,500 ft

Chedotlothna Gl.

Mount Hunter
14,573 ft

Avalanche
Spire
10,105 ft

Mt. Russell
11,670 ft

Yentna Glacier

Lacuna Glacier

Kahiltna Glacier

Dall Glacier

Mount Dall
8,756 ft

KICHATNA MOUNTAINS

Cathedral
Spires

West Fork Yentna

East Fork Yentna

Chelatna
Lake

PETE

Mount Kliskon
3,943 ft

Kahiltna

Fairview Mountain
3,266 ft

To Fairbanks

Nenana

Chitsia Mtn.
3,862 ft

Toklat

Teklanika

KANTISHNA HILLS

③ • Healy
✈

Mount Healy
5,716 ft
McKinley Park

PRIMROSE
RIDGE

**Visitor
Center**
🏕 △ ✈

Yanert Fork

Sanctuary River

Private vehicles
restricted
beyond this
point

**Savage
River**
△

**Riley
Creek**
△

Kankone
Peak
🏕

Teklanika River
△

Igloo Mountain
4,800 ft

Igloo Creek
△

Fang Mountain
6,736 ft

Polychrome Mountain
5,790 ft

Sable
Pass

Cathedral Mountain
4,905 ft

Toklat
🏕

Stony Hill

**Polychrome
Rest Area**

Thorofare Pass

Highway Pass

Stony Dome
4,700 ft

**Eielson
Visitor Center**

Mount Pendleton
7,840 ft

Foggy
Pass

✈ Cantwell

**Denali
Highway**
⑧

(closed in winter)

To
Paxson

Scott Peak
8,838 ft

Mudrow Glacier

Mount Brooks
11,880 ft

Mt. Mather
12,123 ft

Mount Deception
11,768 ft

Mt. Silverthrone
13,220 ft

Eldridge Glacier

eldon
phitheater

Mount Dickey
9,545 ft

The Great

Chulitna Pass

DEVILS CANYON

Susitna

Ruth Glacier

**DENALI
STATE PARK**

The Alaska Railroad

↑

🏕 Ranger Station

△ Campground

✈ Airstrip

- - - Unpaved Road

···· Primitive Road

☐ Park/Preserve

Petersville

③

Petersville Road

🏕 ✈
Talkeetna

0   10   20 km

0   10   20 mi

To Anchorage   To Alaska Highway 3

Backpackers above tree line

McKinley can be seen 70 miles to the southwest. As the bus crosses the **Savage River Bridge** (mile 14.8), note how the gentle, glacier-sculptured topography to the south meets the rugged river-cut canyon to the north; this spot marks the farthest advance of a glacier that flowed north out of the **Alaska Range** and across the valley thousands of years ago.

The road winds along **Primrose Ridge** before dropping into a marshy flat where spruce trees lean haphazardly in all directions. This "drunken forest" forms as permafrost thaws and the land slumps gradually downhill, tilting the trees. Watch for moose here and in other spruce forests, especially in areas with willow, their favorite browse.

Just beyond Teklanika River Campground (mile 29) is the **Teklanika River Bridge.** Like other rivers in Denali, the Teklanika is braided by channels. Its Athabaskan name means "middle water." The road passes Igloo Creek Campground and cuts between **Igloo** and **Cathedral Mountains,** favorite haunts of Dall's sheep, the world's only species of wild white sheep. Watch for them on the upper slopes.

If you want to see grizzly bears, a good place is just up the road at **Sable Pass** (3,895 feet). The grizzlies feed primarily on roots, berries, and other plant materials, and occasionally on arctic ground squirrels, moose calves, injured or infirm caribou, and carrion. To protect the bears' habitat, the Sable Pass area is closed to foot traffic, except on the road.

About 5 miles farther the road climbs a steep slope to **Polychrome Pass** and a spectacular view of the Alaska Range to the south. Below see the **Plains of Murie,** where fast running water has created alluvial terraces. At mile 53.1 the **Toklat River** has special significance, for it was here (5 miles north of where the bridge crosses the river today) that the naturalist Charles Sheldon built a cabin and wintered in 1907-08. The area so inspired him that he moved back East and spent 9 years lobbying for legislation to create Alaska's first national park. Originally called Mount McKinley, the park in 1980 was renamed Denali—a local name for the mountain meaning "the high one."

The road reaches its highest elevation at **Highway Pass** (3,980 feet) before descending to cross **Stony Creek** and climbing again to the **Stony Hill Overlook,** where, weather permitting, Mount McKinley looms into view 40 miles away. Watch for caribou as they funnel through the Stony Hill area. Although the total Denali herd numbers about 2,700, the caribou usually move in small groups. They can appear almost any time of day anywhere in the lowlands between the park road and the Alaska Range.

Eielson Visitor Center (mile 66) is a comfortable, scenic rest stop 33 miles from Mount McKinley. Arctic ground squirrels scamper about, begging for

Tussock grass

handouts they don't need and shouldn't have. Wildflowers splash the tundra with reds and yellows, and sometimes you'll see a grizzly on a distant ridge or on the road.

Continuing west, the road cuts along a steep cliff, then enters more gentle terrain as it comes within a mile of the dark, gravel-covered snout of the **Muldrow Glacier** to the south. Beginning just below the summit of Mount McKinley, the Muldrow flows 35 miles through a granite gorge and across the tundra to its terminus. Twice in the last 100 years (and for reasons not fully understood) the Muldrow has surged forward, most recently in the winter of 1956-57, when it advanced 5 miles.

The road passes several ponds where chances improve for sighting beavers, moose, and waterfowl, and finally arrives at Wonder Lake Campground. Here the shuttle bus will turn around for the 5½-hour trip back, after allowing you time to stroll and take pictures. Twenty-seven miles to the south looms Mount McKinley, its north face— the **Wickersham Wall**—rising more than 14,000 feet in a single precipice, one of the greatest mountain walls in the world. And just north of the campground lies **Wonder Lake,** 4 miles long, 280 feet deep, and home to lake trout, lingcod, burbot, and moose that occasionally wade in belly-deep to feed on aquatic vegetation near the shore. Loons, grebes, and mergansers also visit the lake.

Hikes

In a park larger than New Hampshire, the hiking opportunities are endless, but the only maintained trails are in the front country, beginning at the Visitor Center, where maps are available, and the park hotel and railroad station, near the park entrance.

The **Horseshoe Lake Trail** winds gently through a handsome forest of aspen and spruce 1¼ miles to **Horseshoe Lake,** an old oxbow of the **Nenana River.** It takes about one-hour round-trip. Branching off this trail just past the stream-crossing is a more strenuous one, the **Mount Healy Overlook Trail.** Climbing 1,700 feet in less than 3 miles (one way), it breaks above timberline and arrives at the overlook among wildflowers, rock outcrops, arctic ground squirrels, and pikas. And if the weather is clear, Mount McKinley is visible more than 80 miles to the southwest. A new accessible ¼-mile trail begins at the Savage Cabin Campground and leads to **Savage Cabin,** where demonstrations are held in summer.

For those seeking a moderate hike, the 3-mile **Triple Lakes Trail** is a good choice with its excellent views of **Mount Fellows, Pyramid Mountain,** and other peaks in the Alaska Range.

In the backcountry, hiking is a matter of taking whatever route you wish—down a drainage, up a ridge, across a valley. The object is to spread out and tread lightly, leaving no evidence of your visit.

Popular backcountry hiking areas (without trails) include Primrose Ridge, Mount Wright, Igloo Mountain, Cathedral Mountain, Calico Creek, Tattler Creek, the Polychrome Cliffs Loop, Stony Dome and Stony Hill, the Stony Creek Loop, the Sunrise Glacier Loop, Sunset Glacier, Eielson Visitor Center Ridge, and around Wonder Lake. Some of these hikes take an hour or more, some take several days.

Since a backcountry management unit might be closed or full, those wishing to camp are required to check at the Visitor Access Center before choosing an overnight hike. Some areas may be restricted in order to protect critical wildlife habitats, and animal activity may temporarily close backcountry sections.

Float Trips

If you enjoy rafting through a mix of calm water and white water, don't miss a trip down the Nenana River, along the George Parks Hwy. and the park's eastern border. Several companies offer guided trips lasting from 2 hours to 4 days. From McKinley Village, about 6 miles south of the park entrance, a 2-hour float takes you to the McKinley Chalet Resort, just outside the entrance. The next 2 hours, to Healy, offer a white-water experience. Allow an hour or 2 for travel and instruction.

Rafting along the Nenana River

Animals of Denali

Grizzly stretching in the sunshine

Dall's sheep

Willow ptarmigan

Caribou

Information & Activities

Headquarters
P.O. Box 9, Denali, Alaska 99755.
Phone (907) 683-2294.
www.nps.gov/dena

Seasons & Accessibility
Park open year-round. Park road open, weather permitting, Memorial Day through mid-Sept., but car travel is restricted beyond Savage River, 14 miles into the park. During snow season, park road is not plowed beyond headquarters (mile 3.5), which limits access to skiers and dogsledders.

Visitor & Information Centers
Visitor Center, at east border of park, open daily April to late Sept. (reduced hours after mid-Sept.). Eielson Visitor Center open early June to mid-September. Talkeetna Ranger Station open daily mid-April–Labor Day; Mon.-Fri., rest of year. Off-season information available at headquarters, open daily all year. Call (907) 683-2294 for information.

Entrance Fees
$5 fee per person per week; $10 per family; $20 annual.

Shuttle Bus Transportation
From the Visitor Center, buses operate regularly from 5:00 a.m. to 3:00 p.m. between late May and mid-September. Reserve in person. Fees range from $12 to $40, depending on destination. To make reservations, call (800) 622-7275 or (907) 272-7275. Trips not narrated, but buses stop for wildlife watching. Also, twice daily campers bus.

Facilities for Disabled
Most buildings accessible to wheelchairs, as are some tour and shuttle buses. Please advise staff of need when making reservations.

Things to Do
Free ranger-led activities: nature walks and hikes, children's programs, sled-dog demonstrations, talks, slide shows, and films. Also, narrated bus tours, hiking, limited fishing, mountain climbing, rafting, horseback riding, cross-country skiing, dogsledding.

Overnight Backpacking
Backcountry divided into units with limits (2-12) on the number of campers. Permits required; available free at Visitor Center, first come, first served. Must carry bear-proof containers. Backpacker shuttle fee $15.

Campgrounds
Seven campgrounds (291 sites), 14-day limit from mid-May to mid-Sept.; other times, 30-day limit. **Riley Creek** open all year. Others open late spring to early fall. In summer, reservations strongly recommended (800) 622-7275 or (907) 272-7275. Fees $6-$12 per night. RV sites except at **Sanctuary, Igloo Creek, Morino,** and **Wonder Lake;** no hook-ups. **Morino** inaccessible to vehicles. Buses transport campers to **Sanctuary, Igloo Creek, Wonder Lake,** and farther. Must reserve for **Savage River Group Campground;** contact headquarters.

Hotels, Motels, & Inns
(unless otherwise noted, rates are for 2 persons in a double room, high season)
INSIDE THE PARK:
Camp Denali and **North Face Lodge** P.O. Box 67, Denali NP, Alas. 99775. (907) 683-2290. Camp Denali: 17 cabins, central showers. North Face Lodge: 15 rooms. $345 per person, all inclusive. Early June–mid-Sept. **Denali Backcountry Lodge** Denali National Park, Alaska. (800) 841-0692. (Winter address: P.O. Box 810, Girdwood, Alaska 99587). 30 units. $330 per person per night, all inclusive. June to Sept. **Denali National Park Hotel** (1 mile inside park). (907) 683-2215. 100 units. $147. Rest. Mid-May to early Sept.
OUTSIDE THE PARK:
Denali Cabins (8 mi. S of entrance) P.O. Box 229, Denali NP, Alas. 99755. (907) 683-2643. 43 cabins. $139. Rest. Mid-May to mid-Sept. **Denali Princess Lodge** ($\frac{1}{2}$ mile from entrance) P.O. Box 110, Denali NP, Alas. 99755. (907) 683-2282. 350 units. $179-$249. Rest. Mid-May–mid-Sept. **McKinley Chalet Resort** (1 mile from entrance). (907) 276-7234. 350 units. $177. Pool, rest. Mid-May to mid-Sept. **McKinley Village Lodge** (6 mi. from entrance). (907) 276-7234. 50 units. $203. Rest. Late May–early Sept.

Autumn in August: Arrigetch Valley's poplar, spruce, and scrub

Gates of the Arctic

Alaska

Established December 2, 1980

8,500,000 acres

"The view from the top gave us an excellent idea of the jagged country toward which we were heading. The main Brooks Range divide was entirely covered with snow. Close at hand, only about ten miles to the north, was a precipitous pair of mountains, one on each side of the North Fork. I bestowed the name Gates of the Arctic on them...."

It was the early 1930s, and Robert Marshall had found his wilderness home, an unpeopled, uncluttered source of inspiration that would make him one of America's greatest conservationists. Gates of the Arctic was the ultimate North American wilderness. Congress created the park to keep it that way.

Climb practically any ridge in the heart of the park and you'll see a dozen glacial cirques side by side; serrated mountains that scythe the sky; and storms that snap out of dark, brooding clouds. Six National Wild and Scenic Rivers—Alatna, John, Kobuk, Noatak, North Fork Koyukuk, and Tinayguk—tumble out of high alpine valleys into forested lowlands. The park lies entirely above the Arctic Circle, straddling the Brooks Range, one of the world's northernmost mountain chains.

With Kobuk Valley National Park and Noatak National Preserve, Gates of the Arctic protects much of the habitat of the western arctic caribou. Grizzlies, wolves, wolverines, and foxes also roam over the severe land in search of food. Ptarmigan nibble on willow, and gyrfalcons dive for ptarmigan. Shafts of cinnabar sunlight

pour through the mountains at 2 a.m. in June, setting the wild land ablaze. "No sight or sound or smell or feeling even remotely hinted of men or their creations," wrote Marshall. "It seemed as if time had dropped away a million years and we were back in a primordial world."

How to Get There
Bush pilots say that where the road ends, the real Alaska begins. And so it is in Gates of the Arctic. You can fly or walk in; most people fly. From Fairbanks (about 250 miles away), scheduled flights serve Anaktuvuk Pass, an Eskimo village within the park borders; Bettles/Evansville; and Ambler, to the west. From those points or from Fairbanks, you can air taxi into the park. Allow time for bad weather and delayed flights. From Anaktuvuk Pass, you can also hike into the park along the John River.

Or, you can drive up from Fairbanks on the unpaved Dalton Highway (a pipeline haul road that's also open to the public) and hike to the park from Wiseman or other points. But it's a long, hard walk into the interior.

When to Go
Summer. It is short, but days are very long and for a while temperatures may be relatively mild. Weather is highly unpredictable. Expect snow or rain in any month. August can be very wet, with freezing temperatures by mid-month. Mosquitoes and gnats are bad in late June and July. Fall colors peak in mid-August at high elevations, late August to early September at low elevations.

How to Visit
Give yourself time to savor the subtle beauty of this vast wilderness. A combination river-hiking trip offers the best of both. Air taxis are equipped to land on lakes and gravel bars for drop-offs and pickups.

Plan carefully and bring everything you need; there are no visitor facilities in the park. This spare, harsh land is so fragile that a hiker's step can kill lichens that take 150 years to reach full growth. Certain areas were badly damaged by the increase in visitors after Gates of the Arctic became a park.

Write or call park headquarters in Fairbanks before planning a trip. There are no trails in the park, but you can ask for suggestions about areas to visit, along with names of air taxis, guides, and outfitters who operate in the park.

Black granite peaks of the Arrigetch

River Trips

Rivers are the main travel routes through Gates of the Arctic. Eskimos and caribou have followed them for centuries. Near some are lakes on which aircraft can land. Camping is good on the gravel bars, but be aware that summer rainstorms can quickly raise water levels. Most rivers are at their highest in May and June. Hiking is difficult but rewarding, especially in alpine areas. The following six rivers are only a sampling of what the park has to offer:

Alatna River is ideal for a first wilderness float trip. It takes 4 to 7 days, running gently down from the treeless Arctic Divide through beautiful tundra to the forested **Koyukuk River** lowlands. There are put-ins at **Takahula**

Castle Mt.
3,409 ft+
WILDERNESS
AREA

Chandler

Anaktuvuk

Nanushuk

Itkillik

Itkillik Lake

Shainin Lake

Chandler Lake

BROOKS RANGE

Anaktuvuk Pass

ENDICOTT MOUNTAINS

Summit Lake

Koyukuk

+ *Mount Doonerak 7,457 ft*

Frigid Crags 5,501 ft +   **Gates of the Arctic** +
+ *Boreal Mountain 6,654 ft*

Hunt Fork John

Hunt Fork Lake

WILDERNESS AREA

Thalyguk

North Fork

Dalton Highway (Haul Road)

MOUNTAINS

Wild Lake

North Fork Koyukuk

John

Wild

Middle Fork Koyukuk

•*Wiseman*

•*Coldfoot*

akuk ke

Ranger Station

Airport

Unpaved Road

Park/Preserve

0 10 20 30 40 km
0   10   20   30   40 mi

Bettles/ Evansville

Ice Road (winter use only)

S. Fork Koyukuk

Dalton Highway (Haul Road)

KANUTI
NATIONAL WILDLIFE
REFUGE

•*Prospect Creek*

↓*To Allakaket*

To Fairbanks

Lake, Circle Lake, or at a series of unnamed lakes farther upstream. Most boaters take-out at the village of Allakaket (75 and 85 miles from Takahula and Circle Lakes, respectively), where the Alatna meets the Koyukuk River.

John River is a mere stream at its headwater at Anaktuvuk Pass (the permanent settlement of the inland Nunamiut Eskimo), but it gains power

Tundra swan, a bird of summer

North Fork Koyukuk near the Gates of the Arctic

Purple saxifrage

and momentum as it flows south through the alpine heart of the park. **Hunt Fork Lake** is the best put-in; water levels above this point are usually too low. The John drops into lowland forest and joins the Koyukuk River just downstream of Bettles, a journey of a hundred miles.

Kobuk River begins at **Walker Lake** (a good put-in) and runs south and west through the mountains, canyons, foothills, and lowlands of Gates of the Arctic National Preserve. Kobuk

village, 140 river miles from Walker Lake, is a popular take-out. Or you can continue downriver to Ambler and on through Kobuk Valley National Park to Kiana.

North Fork Koyukuk begins at **Summit Lake** and cuts between **Boreal Mountain** and **Frigid Crags**— the **Gates of the Arctic**—then flows past **Redstar Creek Lakes** (a good put-in) and continues south a hundred miles to Bettles.

One of the largest wilderness river basins in North America, the **Noatak** flows west 450 miles from Gates of the Arctic through Noatak National Preserve into the Chukchi Sea. From a put-in at **Lake Matcharak** to Noatak village is a 350-mile trip. The river, a major thoroughfare in a trackless realm, demands minimal boating skills but maximal planning. Give yourself a month for the trip.

The seldom visited **Tinayguk** flows through a broad glacier-cut valley before joining the Koyukuk below Boreal Mountain and Frigid Crags. Put in after landing on a gravel bar along the Tinayguk 35 miles north of where it joins the Koyukuk. (Consult local maps and outfitters for the exact location.) Float down to the Koyukuk, then continue on for another 80 miles to Bettles.

Information & Activities

Headquarters
201 First Ave. Doyon Bldg., Fairbanks, Alaska 99701. Phone (907) 456-0281. For visitor information, write to P.O. Box 26030, Bettles, Alaska 99726. www.nps.gov/gaar

Seasons & Accessibility
Park open year-round. Access by air or foot; there are no roads to the park (except Dalton Highway, an unpaved pipeline haul road that's parallel to park's east boundary). There are no roads in park. Contact park headquarters before planning a visit.

Visitor & Information Centers
There are no visitor centers or facilities of any kind within the park. The only ranger stations are located in Bettles and Anaktuvuk Pass. An interagency visitor center is staffed in Coldfoot during the summer.

Gas & Supplies
Bring supplies with you (Fairbanks has a full selection); few available in communities of Bettles and Anaktuvuk Pass, which are not accessible by road. Gas stations on the Dalton Highway at milepost 56 (just north of the Yukon River) and at Coldfoot, milepost 173.6.

Pets
Only pack dogs allowed.

Facilities for Disabled
Bettles and Anaktuvuk Pass Ranger Stations and Coldfoot Visitor Center.

Things to Do
Hiking (no established trails), backpacking, canoeing, kayaking and rafting, fishing (license required), hunting (in preserve only, with license), rock and mountain climbing, wildlife watching. In winter: cross-country skiing, snowshoeing, dogmushing, skiing. Ask park for list of licensed guides and outfitters (www.nps.gov/gaar/commops.htm.).

Special Advisories
● All visitors should be well skilled in the outdoors; firearms may be carried for protection.

● Grizzly bears are unpredictable and dangerous. Visit ranger station in Bettles or Coldfoot for advice on preventing an encounter.

● Eskimos and other Native Alaskans use the park for subsistence fishing and hunting; respect them and their property.

● From mid-June through July, be prepared for plenty of mosquitoes and gnats; bring insect repellent, a head net, and an insect-proof tent.

● Swift currents and freezing water can make river crossings particularly hazardous.

Overnight Backpacking
No permit required, but get up-to-date bear information from ranger station. An orientation is available at ranger stations. Food, stoves, and all equipment must be carried. Camp on gravel bars to avoid damaging fragile tundra. Bear barrels recommended; purchase or rent beforehand.

Campgrounds
None; backcountry camping only.

Hotels, Motels, & Inns
INSIDE THE PARK:
Alatna Lodge (on the headwaters of the Alatna River) Alatna Guide Service, P.O. Box 80424, Fairbanks, Alas. 99708. (907) 479-6354. 6 rooms. $2,800 per person for 3 days, including airfare from Fairbanks and activities. Open June to early September.
Nahtuk Wilderness Cabins (on Alatna River near Arrigetch Peaks) P.O. Box 80424, Fairbanks, Alas. 99708. (907) 479-6354. 2 cabins. $195-$275 per day, per person, depending on activities. Open mid-June to early September.
OUTSIDE THE PARK:
Slate Creek Inn Mile 175, Dalton Hwy., Coldfoot, Alas. 99701. (907) 678-5224. 52 units. $145. Rest. Mid-May–mid-Sept. **Coldfoot Services Motel** Mile 175, Dalton Hwy., Coldfoot, Alas. 99701. (907) 678-5201. 50 units. $125. Rest. Open year-round.
Iniakuk Lake Wilderness Lodge (on Iniakuk Lake) P.O. Box 80424, Fairbanks, Alas. 99708. (907) 479-6354. 6 rooms, central bath. $450 per person, per day, all inclusive. Mid-June–mid-Sept.

Sunset view of Adams Inlet, from Muir Inlet

Glacier Bay

Alaska

Established December 2, 1980

3,280,198 acres

When Capt. George Vancouver sailed the Alaska coast in 1794, Glacier Bay did not exist. It lay beneath a sheet of glacial ice several miles wide and thousands of feet thick. Since then, in one of the fastest glacial retreats on record, the ice has shrunk back 65 miles to unveil new land and a new bay, now returning to life after a long winter's sleep.

Scientists call Glacier Bay a living laboratory for the grand processes of glacial retreat, plant succession, and animal dynamics. It is an open book on the last Ice Age. At the southern end of the bay, where the ice departed 200 years ago, a spruce-hemlock rain forest has taken root. Farther north, in areas more recently deglaciated, the land becomes rugged and thinly vegetated.

The bay branches into two major arms, the west arm and Muir Inlet, which themselves branch into smaller inlets. There, on slopes deglaciated 50 to 100 years ago, alder and willow grow, while mosses, mountain avens, and dwarf fireweed pioneer areas exposed within the last two or three decades.

The new vegetation creates habitats for wolves, moose, mountain goats, black bears, brown bears, ptarmigan, and other wildlife, and the sea supports a food chain that includes salmon, bald eagles, harbor seals, harbor porpoises, humpback whales, and killer whales—all in an environment less than 200 years old.

Roughly 13 tidewater glaciers still flow into the park. In part because of variations in snow accumulations,

When to Go

Late May to mid-September. Summer days are long and temperatures cool. May and June have the most sunshine, but the upper inlets can be thick with icebergs then and the tidewater glaciers less approachable. September is often rainy and windy.

How to Visit

Glacier Bay is a marine highway. Most visitors experience the park from the deck of a cruise ship, or a tour boat, or from the waterline of a sea kayak. Many of the large cruise ships that travel southeastern Alaska's Inside Passage go into Glacier Bay. Other tours offer accommodations at **Glacier Bay Lodge** (the park's center of activity) and a 1-day or overnight boat trip to the glaciers and back. Campers and kayakers can take the boat and be dropped off at one of three sites up the bay, either to be picked up at a later date or to paddle back to Bartlett Cove.

The Lower Bay

The lower bay reaches from **Bartlett Cove** north to **Tlingit Point,** where it separates into its two arms and continues north. Bartlett Cove has the only two maintained trails in the park. Beginning at the **Glacier Bay Lodge,** the **Forest Loop Trail** is a 1-mile, 1-hour round-trip through the young spruce-hemlock rain forest. A boardwalk covers the first part of the trail out to **Blackwater Pond.** For a $\frac{1}{2}$-day trip (and more rugged walking), the **Bartlett River Trail** begins at the roadside, a $\frac{1}{2}$ mile from the lodge, and winds another $1\frac{1}{2}$ miles through the rain forest to the **Bartlett River,** ending in a quiet meadow. It's not unusual to see red squirrels, blue grouse, and black bears along either of these trails.

If you want to kayak, the **Beardslee Islands** just north of Bartlett Cove offer a maze of shorelines and waterways—a quiet counterpoint to the buses and boats coming and going at Bartlett Cove.

Reaching across the lower bay, **Sitakaday Narrows** is a shoal that creates strong and dangerous whirlpools and currents as the tides (rising and falling an average of 15 feet in 6 hours) rush over it. Check the tide

most glaciers in the eastern and southwestern areas of the bay are receding, while several on its west side are advancing. The glaciers calve icebergs that hit the water with a sound like cannon-shot. "White thunder," the Tlingit Indians called it, the awesome voice of glacial ice. An iceberg's color often reveals its makeup; dense bergs are blue, while those filled with trapped air bubbles are white.

How to Get There

By boat or plane only. From Juneau, take a scheduled flight 53 miles to Gustavus. Catch the bus to Glacier Bay Lodge and Bartlett Cove Campground, 10 miles away at the park's southern end. Charter flights also service Gustavus from Juneau, Skagway, Haines, and Hoonah. The Auk Nu ferry departs daily from Juneau to Gustavus. Private boats can enter the bay with permits (required June to August) obtained by phone or mail from headquarters at Bartlett Cove.

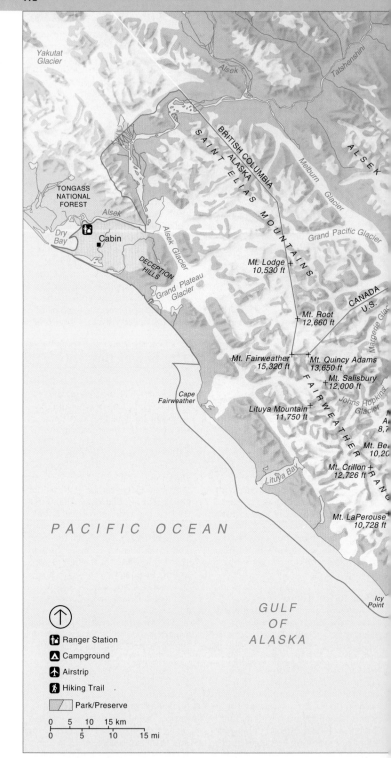

Yakutat
Glacier

Alsek

Tatshenshini

BRITISH COLUMBIA
ALASKA

S A I N T   E L I A S   M O U N T A I N S

Melburn Glacier

A L S E K

TONGASS
NATIONAL
FOREST

Alsek

Dry
Bay

Cabin

Alsek Glacier

DECEPTION
HILLS

Grand Plateau Glacier

Grand Pacific Glacier

Mt. Lodge
10,530 ft

CANADA
U.S.

Magerie Glac

Mt. Root
12,660 ft

Mt. Fairweather
15,320 ft

Mt. Quincy Adams
13,650 ft

Mt. Salisbury
12,000 ft

Johns Hopkins Glacier

F A I R W E A T H E R

Cape
Fairweather

Lituya Mountain
11,750 ft

N
A
8,7

Mt. Be
10,20

R A N G E

Mt. Crillon +
12,726 ft

Lituya Bay

Mt. LaPerouse
10,728 ft

PACIFIC   OCEAN

Icy
Point

GULF
OF
ALASKA

Ranger Station

Campground

Airstrip

Hiking Trail

Park/Preserve

0   5   10   15 km

0   5   10   15 mi

To Fairbanks, Alaska

3

BRITISH COLUMBIA
ALASKA

Chilkat

Klukwan

Skagway

White Pass and
Yukon Railroad

Taiya

7

Tsirku Glacier

Haines
Port
Chilkoot

T A K I N S H A   M O U N T A I N S

Muir Glacier

Riggs Glacier

MC CONNELL
RIDGE

McBride Glacier

Casement Glacier

Lynn Canal

Carroll Glacier

WHITE THUNDER RIDGE

Goose
Cove

Muir Inlet

Johns Hopkins Inlet

Reid Inlet

Adams Inlet

Mt. Wright
5,139 ft

TONGASS
NATIONAL
FOREST

C H I L K A T

Blue
Mouse
Cove

Tlingit
Point

G l a c i e r
B a y

Beartrack

Excursion

R A N G E

BRADY
ICEFIELD

North
Marble
Island

Drake
Island

South
Marble
Island

Willoughby
Island

Brady Glacier

Beardslee
Islands

Sitakaday Narrows

Bartlett

**Visitor Center and
Glacier Bay Lodge**

Bartlett
Cove

**Bartlett
Cove**

Gustavus

Taylor Bay

Pleasant
Island

Icy Strait

Cape Spencer

Lemesurier
Island

Inian
Islands

Elfin
Cove

Cross Sound

TONGASS NATIONAL FOREST

Chichagof   Island

Steller's sea lions

before venturing into the Narrows. Watch for phalaropes, gulls, terns, and other birds feeding here as the swirling water flushes small fish to the surface. To the north, the **Marble Islands** rise abruptly out of the middle of the bay. The islands, deglaciated around 1835, today support breeding colonies of gulls, cormorants, puffins, and murres (and are off-limits to visitors during the summer). Watch for Steller's sea lions on **South Marble Island.**

The West Arm

The bay's west arm contains the highest mountains and most active tidewater glaciers in the park. Clear days afford stunning views of the **Fairweather Range,** crowned by **Mount Fairweather** at 15,300 feet; cloudy days lend a moody, rich blue cast to the tidewater faces of the **Margerie, Grand Pacific, Lamplugh,** and **Reid Glaciers.**

In the wildest inlet, **Johns Hopkins,** seven glaciers tumble down mountains, whose surrounding peaks reach 8,000 feet. While glaciers are in retreat on the bay's east and southwest sides, here on the west side several of the glaciers are advancing. Each June thousands of harbor seals give birth to their pups on icebergs in Johns Hopkins Inlet (to protect the seals, the inlet is closed from May through June).

Blue Mouse Cove and the northwest corner of **Reid Inlet** are the best anchorages. Good camping sites can be found almost anywhere (except in Johns Hopkins Inlet where the terrain is generally too steep). Hiking is a matter of going where the spirit and the topography take you. Brown bears are common. This is their home, and you are the visitor. *Be careful.*

Muir Inlet

Reaching 25 miles into the northeast corner of the park, **Muir Inlet** is a mecca for kayakers. Tour boats, cruise ships, and fishing boats seldom come in here (and the waters north of McBride Glacier are closed to motor boats from June to mid-July). The camping is good, and so is the hiking, if you avoid thickets of alder. **Adams Inlet** branches east off lower Muir Inlet and is a favorite among kayakers; motorboats are not allowed in the inlet from May to mid-September. You can time your entry and exit by the strong tides that flow in and out through the narrow opening. To the north, **Sealers Island** was once a breeding site for arctic terns and black oystercatchers. Nearby is **Goose Cove,** an anchorage in Muir Inlet. In contrast to the tidewater glaciers that are advancing in the west arm, most in Muir Inlet continue to retreat. The **McBride** and **Riggs Glaciers** separated from the retreating **Muir Glacier** in 1941 and 1960 respectively; since then, all three have retreated long distances. A journey up **White Thunder Ridge** or **McConnell Ridge** rewards hikers with spectacular views of upper Muir Inlet. Both hikes are strenuous. Be prepared to struggle through alder—it takes a lot of time and energy. Each hike takes a full day and climbs about 1,500 feet. Also rewarding is a hike along **Wolf Creek** (beginning at the south end of White Thunder Ridge), where running water has exposed the remains of a forest buried by a glacier 4,000 to 7,000 years ago.

Information & Activities

Headquarters
P.O. Box 140, Gustavus, Alaska 99826.
Phone (907) 697-2232.
www.nps.gov/glba

Seasons & Accessibility
Park open year-round, but late May to
mid-September is visitor season; transportation and facilities limited rest of
year. Call the park before going in the
off-season.

There are no roads to or in the park;
access by airplane, boat, or ferry only.
Auk Nu Tours (phone 800-820-2628)
offers ferry service between Auke Bay
(north of Juneau) and Gustavus. Visitors with private boats need a permit
between June 1 and Aug. 30; phone
(907) 697-2627.

Visitor & Information Centers
Information centers on the dock
at Bartlett Cove and at Glacier Bay
Lodge. Call (907) 697-2627 for
visitor information.

Entrance Fee
None.

Pets
Permitted on leashes on Bartlett
Cove roads only. Prohibited in backcountry; boaters must keep pets
aboard vessels.

Facilities for Disabled
Glacier Bay Lodge is accessible to
wheelchairs. One trail, with a stretch
of boardwalk, is also accessible.

Things to Do
Free ranger-led activities (from
Glacier Bay Lodge): nature walks,
films, slide presentations, and evening
programs. Also available, kayaking,
fishing (license required), scheduled
boat tours, glacier viewing, whale-
watching and birdwatching, crabbing
(license required), hiking, berry picking, mountain and glacier climbing
(for the experienced only), aerial
sightseeing, cross-country skiing.

For information and reservations
for ranger-guided boat tours from
Bartlett Cove, contact Glacier Bay
Lodge, Inc., P.O. Box 199, Gustavus,
AK 99826 (907) 697-2225 or (800)
451-5952. Ask the park for a list of
other concessioners offering a variety
of rental and guide services.
www.nps.gov/glba/visit/services.htm

Special Advisories
● Do not get too close to icebergs
when boating, and do not climb on
the glaciers without a guide or plenty
of experience.
● Carry plenty of insect repellent.
● Be aware of bears. Obtain safety
guidelines from information centers
or rangers.

Overnight Backpacking
Permit required. Backcountry users
must receive orientation from rangers
before setting out. Use of Park Service
food storage canisters required.

Campgrounds
One campground only; **Bartlett Cove**
has 14-day limit. Open all year; first
come, first served. No fees. Showers
at lodge (within a mile) available only
seasonally. Warming hut provided.
Tent sites only. **Bartlett Cove Group
Campground;** open all year; first come,
first served.

Hotels, Motels, & Inns
*(unless otherwise noted, rates are for 2
persons in a double room, high season)*
INSIDE THE PARK:
Glacier Bay Lodge Gustavus, Alaska
99826. (800) 451-5952 or (907) 697-
2225. 55 units. $165. Packages that
include airfare available. Restaurant.
Open mid-May to mid-September.
OUTSIDE THE PARK:
In Gustavus, Alaska 99826
Glacier Bay Country Inn P.O. Box 5.
(800) 628-0912 or (907) 697-2288.
11 units. $322, includes all meals and
some activities. Open mid-May
through September.
Gustavus Inn P.O. Box 60. (907) 697-
2254. 13 units, 11 with private baths.
$140 per person, includes all meals
and some activities. Open May 1 to
September 15.
Salmon River Cabins P.O. Box 13.
(907) 697-2245. 10 rustic cabins with
kitchenettes, 4 private baths. $75. Open
mid-May through September.

Alaskan brown bears fishing for salmon at Brooks Falls

Katmai

Alaska

Established December 2, 1980

4,090,000 acres

Volcanoes and bears—powerful, unpredictable, and awe inspiring— embody the wild heart of Katmai. Within the borders of the national park and preserve are 15 volcanoes, some of them still steaming, and North America's largest population of protected brown bears—about 1,500 of them. You can hike, kayak, and canoe here. You can fish waist-deep in rivers as clear as glass. And you can watch the best fish catcher of all, the great Alaskan brown bear, sometimes diving completely under the water for its prey, sometimes catching fish in midair. At the end of the day you can relax in a rustic yet sumptuous lodge on the shore of a sapphire lake and recount the day's enchantments.

In 1912 a volcano here erupted with a force ten times that of Mount St. Helens in 1980. Suddenly Katmai, a place hardly anyone had heard of, was on front pages around the world. Ash filled the air, global temperatures cooled, acid rain burned clothing off lines in Vancouver, British Columbia, and on Kodiak Island, just across Shelikof Strait from Katmai, day became night.

Leading a 1916 expedition sponsored by the National Geographic Society, botanist Robert Griggs ascended Katmai Pass from Shelikof Strait. "The whole valley as far as the eye could reach was full of hundreds, no thousands—literally, tens of thousands—of smokes curling up from its fissured floor," he wrote. The smokes were fumaroles steaming 500 to 1,000 feet into the air. Griggs, who named the Valley of Ten Thousand

available between Brooks Camp and the Valley of Ten Thousand Smokes, are the lodges, cabins, and Brooks Camp Campground open. Bear watching, an increasingly popular pastime, is best in July when the sockeye salmon spawn. Fishing and hiking are good throughout summer, but come prepared for rain. Heavy snowpack may remain in the upper elevations into July. Summer daytime temperatures range from the mid-50s to mid-60s; the average low is 44°F.

How to Visit

If your time is short, get to **Brooks Camp.** People, fish, bears, boats, and planes concentrate here. Compared to the rest of the park, it's crowded. But the lodge and campground are comfortable (reservations required) and the bear viewing unforgettable. You'll find good hiking and fishing.

If at all possible, take the bus or van tour 23 miles out from Brooks Camp to the **Valley of Ten Thousand Smokes.** Return the same day or hike into the valley and camp. You can extend your stay by boating or flying to the many other lakes, streams, rivers, and lodges in the park. Pick your area, make a safe plan, and go.

Brooks Camp & Valley of Ten Thousand Smokes

Some very pleasant hikes begin near **Brooks Camp.** The trail you'll first want to take goes to the bear-viewing platform. The ½-mile boardwalk starts between Brooks Camp and **Brooks Lake** and winds gently through the forest to **Brooks Falls,** ending at the viewing platform. Wooden steps ascend a balcony overlooking the fascinating spectacle of jumping fish and feeding bears. Averaging a thousand pounds and measuring up to ten feet long, these Alaskan brown bears are the largest land carnivores on the continent of North America.

The hike up **Dumpling Mountain** is a good day trip. The trail begins at the campground and climbs to an 800-foot overlook in 1½ miles. From there you can continue another 2 miles over alpine tundra to the summit, elevation 2,440 feet. Both the overlook and summit afford tremendous views of **Naknek Lake** and the surrounding mountains.

Smokes, spearheaded the campaign to include Katmai in the National Park System.

The smokes are gone from the valley. But steam vents still appear elsewhere in the park.

How to Get There

From Anchorage, scheduled jets fly the 290 miles to King Salmon, park headquarters; from there, June to September 10, daily floatplanes fly the last 33 miles to Brooks Camp, site of a summer visitor center and the center of activity. Air charters can be arranged into other areas. You can drive the 9 miles from King Salmon to Lake Camp, at the western end of the park on the Naknek River, then go by boat to Brooks Camp, the Bay of Islands, and other areas of Naknek Lake.

When to Go

June to early September (Bear-watching suffers a brief lull in August). Only then, with transportation

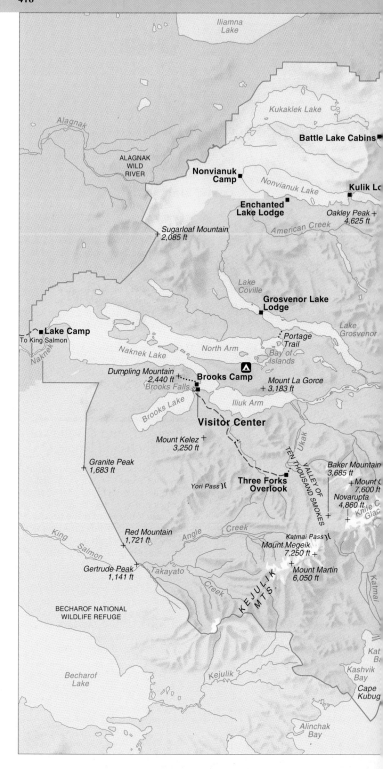

Iliamna Lake

Kukaklek Lake

Battle Lake Cabins

Alagnak

ALAGNAK WILD RIVER

Nonvianuk Camp

Nonvianuk Lake

Kulik Lo

Enchanted Lake Lodge

Oakley Peak + 4,625 ft

Sugarloaf Mountain + 2,085 ft

American Creek

Lake Coville

Grosvenor Lake Lodge

Lake Grosvenor

Lake Camp
To King Salmon

Naknek

Naknek Lake

North Arm

Portage Trail

Bay of Islands

Dumpling Mountain + 2,440 ft

Brooks Camp

Mount La Gorce + 3,183 ft

Brooks Falls

Iliuk Arm

Brooks Lake

Visitor Center

Mount Kelez + 3,250 ft

Ukak

Baker Mountain 3,685 ft

Granite Peak + 1,683 ft

Yori Pass)(

Three Forks Overlook

VALLEY OF TEN THOUSAND SMOKES

+ Mount G 7,600 ft

Novarupta 4,860 ft +

Knife C Glac

Red Mountain 1,721 ft

Angle *Creek*

Katmai Pass)(

Mount Megeik 7,250 ft +

Gertrude Peak 1,141 ft

Takayato

King *Salmon*

+ Mount Martin 6,050 ft

Katmai

BECHAROF NATIONAL WILDLIFE REFUGE

K E J U L I K M T S.

Kejulik *Creek*

Kat Ba

Kashvik Bay

Becharof Lake

Kejulik

Cape Kubug

Alinchak Bay

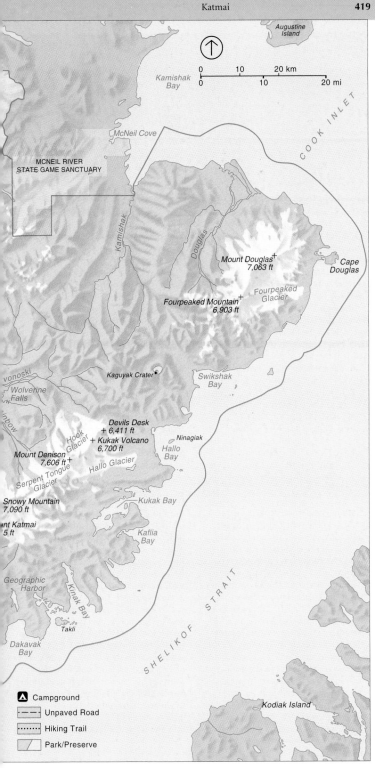

Augustine
Island

Kamishak
Bay

COOK INLET

McNeil Cove

MCNEIL RIVER
STATE GAME SANCTUARY

Kamishak

Douglas

Mount Douglas
7,063 ft

Cape
Douglas

Fourpeaked
Glacier

Fourpeaked Mountain
6,903 ft

Kaguyak Crater

Swikshak
Bay

vonoski
Wolverine
Falls

inbow

Hook Glacier

Devils Desk
6,411 ft
Kukak Volcano
6,700 ft

Ninagiak

Hallo
Bay

Mount Denison
7,606 ft

Serpent Tongue
Glacier

Hallo Glacier

Snowy Mountain
7,090 ft

Kukak Bay

nt Katmai
5 ft

Kaflia
Bay

Geographic
Harbor

Kinak Bay

SHELIKOF STRAIT

Takli

Dakavak
Bay

Kodiak Island

▲ Campground
--- Unpaved Road
····· Hiking Trail
Park/Preserve

Mount Katolinat bordering the Valley of Ten Thousand Smokes

The most popular and spectacular hiking in the park is in the **Valley of Ten Thousand Smokes.** There's no other landscape like it in the world. Daily tours connect Brooks Camp with the **Three Forks Overlook** and a cabin at the north end of the valley, where you can camp or picnic. A short trail descends 200 feet to where the **Ukak River** roars through a bedrock canyon crowned by cliffs of volcanic ash.

To hike into the valley, take the trail that begins ½ mile back from the end of the road and plan to camp overnight. The trail crosses **Windy Creek,** passes the north end of the **Buttress Range,** follows the **River Lethe,** and finally climbs 1,000 feet to the Baked Mountain Cabin, a shelter available for overnights. The challenging 12-mile trip takes a full day; drinking water is scarce.

Due south 5½ miles from the cabin is **Katmai Pass,** where Robert Griggs first beheld the valley in 1916. Strong winds often funnel through here.

A fascinating side trip between **Baked Mountain** and Katmai Pass is to **Novarupta,** a 200-foot-high dome of volcanic rock that was the extrusion plug of the great eruption. Scientists believe most of the 1912 lava and ash spewed out through a fissure here, drawing magma from nearby **Mount Katmai** and causing its summit to collapse into a caldera.

To reach the caldera (a strenuous 1- to 2-day trip), head east from Novarupta or Baked Mountain to the stagnant, ash-covered **Knife Creek Glaciers,** then climb 3,800 feet up ash and ice to the caldera rim, where, if you peer over the edge, you'll see what Robert Griggs saw: "a wonderful lake, of a weird vitriolic robin's-egg blue."

Water & Air Trips

Boaters, kayakers, and canoeists find no shortage of places to explore in Katmai. Guides and equipment are available for hire through Brooks Lodge or one of the other, smaller lodges catering mostly to fishermen. An especially popular and picturesque spot is the **Bay of Islands** in the **North Arm** of Naknek Lake, 22 miles from Brooks Camp.

For serious paddlers looking for the truly wild side of Katmai, the **Savonoski Loop** is an 85-mile round-trip from Brooks Camp that takes 4 to 8 days, depending on the weather. You paddle through the Bay of Islands, portage to **Lake Grosvenor,** and float the **Grosvenor** and **Savonoski Rivers** into the **Iliuk Arm** of Naknek Lake for the return to Brooks Camp. Follow the shorelines, for the wind can suddenly transform lakes from tranquil to tempestuous. If you'd like to take a river trip, inquire about the **Alagnak River,** a designated Wild and Scenic River, and the **Ukak River,** which, with class V rapids, is for the very experienced only.

Like the other national parks in Alaska, Katmai is spectacular from the air. Flight-seeing trips can be arranged in **King Salmon** or Brooks Camp. The grand tour might swing over the Valley of Ten Thousand Smokes, through Katmai Pass, up the coast from **Katmai Bay** to **Swikshak Bay,** over **Kaguyak Crater,** and down the Savonoski River back to Brooks Camp. Take plenty of film and a calm stomach.

Information & Activities

Headquarters
P.O. Box 7, King Salmon, Alaska 99613.
Phone (907) 246-3305.
www.nps.gov/katm

Seasons & Accessibility
Park open year-round, but scheduled
flights from Anchorage to King Salmon
(with connecting seaplane flights into
the park) available June to mid-Sept.
only. Reserve well in advance. Accessible by private or charter plane all year;
the park has a list of licensed air charter companies.

Visitor & Information Centers
Brooks Camp Visitor Center and
the concessions are open from June
to mid-Sept. All visitors to Brooks
Camp are required to attend the
15-min. orientation on bear etiquette.
For visitor information contact park
or Katmailand, Inc., the park's main
concessioner, at 4550
Aircraft Drive, Anchorage 99502,
or call (800) 544-0551 or (907) 243-
5448. King Salmon Visitor Center
is open year-round.

Entrance Fee
None, but there's a $10 per person
fee for day users of Brooks Camp. Call
National Parks Reservation Service (see
page 11) for advanced permits. Limited
day-use permits and advanced reservations are required.

Facilities for Disabled
Brooks Lodge is accessible, but
with assistance.

Things to Do
Free ranger-led activities: daily interpretive programs, evening programs,
nature walks. Also, bus trips to the
Valley of Ten Thousand Smokes, bear
watching, hiking, kayaking, canoeing,
boating, mountain climbing, aerial
sightseeing, fishing (license required;
available in park), float trips.

Katmailand, Inc., has guides, boating, and fishing equipment available
at Brooks Lodge. Reserve ahead. Ask
the park for a list of other outfitters
and guides within its borders.

Special Advisories
● Alaskan brown bears are unpredictable and dangerous; stay far away
from them unless at the bear-viewing
platforms.
● Be very careful when crossing glacial
streams.

Overnight Backpacking
Camping allowed anywhere in park
without reservations, except at Brook's
Camp (see below). Backcountry permits not required, but registration
strongly suggested. Information pamphlet available. Free bear-resistant food
canisters are available.

Campgrounds
One backcountry campground,
Brooks Camp (with 7-day limit
in July and September). Open year-
round; reservations required June 1
to Sept. 17. Call National Parks
Reservation Service (see page 11)
for reservations. Campground fee
$10 per night for groups up to six
people. Showers at Brooks Lodge.
Tent sites only. Three-sided shelters
for cooking. Limited food services
in park.

Hotels, Motels, & Inns
*Katmailand, Inc., offers multiday
package tours from Anchorage that
can include airfare, lodging at Brooks
Lodge, Grosvenor Lake Lodge, or
Kulik Lodge, meals, guides, fishing
tackle, rafts, licenses, and boats or
planes to fishing spots. For information, write Katmailand, Inc., 4550
Aircraft Drive, Anchorage 99502;
or call (800) 544-0551 or (907)
243-5448.*
INSIDE THE PARK:
Brooks Lodge 16 cabins. Packages
starting from $294 per person. Open
June to mid-September.
Grosvenor Lake Lodge 3 cabins.
Packages starting from $1,625 per
person. Open June to late September.
Kulik Lodge 12 cabins. Packages starting from $1,700 per person. Open
mid-June to late September.

Also, **Alaska's Enchanted Lake
Lodge** P.O. Box 97, King Salmon,
Alas. 99613. (907) 246-6878 (May to
September); (206) 643-2172 (winter).
7 cabins. Fly-in sportfishing only.
$5,200 per person per week, includes
meals, lodging, tackle, fishing license,
airfare from Anchorage. Open June
to October.

Granite Passage at the tip of Harris Peninsula

Kenai Fjords

Alaska

Established December 2, 1980

573,000 acres

Distill the essence of coastal Alaska into one place—wild, dynamic, and scenic, rich with the signatures of glaciers, light with the marks of people, unforgiving in stormy seas, unforgettable in warm sunshine—and you have Kenai Fjords, the smallest national park in Alaska. Here the south-central part of the state tumbles into the Gulf of Alaska; here the land challenges the sea with talon-like peninsulas and rocky headlands, while the sea itself reaches inland with long fjords and hundreds of quiet bays and coves.

Crowning the park is the Harding Icefield, almost 700 square miles of ice up to a mile thick. It feeds over 30 glaciers flowing out of the mountains, 8 of them to tidewater. The Harding Icefield is a vestige of the massive ice sheet that covered much of Alaska in the Pleistocene era.

The ancient ice gouged out Kenai's fjords, creating habitats for throngs of sea animals. About 20 species of seabirds nest along the rocky coastline; most of the birds are clown-faced puffins. Bald eagles swoop along the towering cliffs, and peregrine falcons hunt over the outer islands. Seabirds, by the tens of thousands, migrate or congregate here.

Twenty-three species of mammals, including harbor seals, northern sea lions, and sea otters, live here. Moose, black bears, wolverines, lynx, and marten roam narrow bands of forest between the coast and icefield. And just above them, on the treeless slopes, climb sure-footed mountain goats.

How to Visit

The most popular and accessible area in the park is **Exit Glacier,** 13 miles northwest of Seward. You can drive to it or take a tour bus. Trails offer ½-hour hikes to the glacier and a half-day hike to the **Harding Icefield.**

Otherwise, hiking is a matter of exploring wilderness shores and ridges accessible only by boat and plane. From mid-May to late September, daily tour boats from Seward offer round-trip ½-day and full-day excursions to the fjords and outlying islands. Charter boats take kayakers and campers to any fjord they wish (most often **Aialik Bay**) and pick them up the same day or days later. Kayaking, fishing, and backpacking guides are available. Ask the park for a list.

From Seward or Homer you can book a breathtaking one-hour flight over the Harding Icefield and Kenai coast. For extended adventures, ski-planes drop off and pick up skiers on the icefield, and floatplanes do the same for kayakers in the fjords, weather permitting.

Exit Glacier & Harding Icefield

Exit Glacier is one of many rivers of ice that flow off the **Harding Icefield.** From Seward, follow the highway north to mile 3.7 where a paved road leads 9 miles to a parking lot. There are three trails: The **Main Trail**

How to Get There

Seward is the gateway to Kenai Fjords. To get to Seward, take the Seward Highway (Alaska Hwy. 9) south from Anchorage. The 130-mile drive is spectacular. Buses and small commuter planes also connect Anchorage and Seward, and the Alaska Marine Highway (ferry) links Seward with Homer, Seldovia, Kodiak, Valdez, and Cordova. You can also charter a flight from Seward or Homer directly to the park. In summer, the Alaska Railroad serves Seward from Anchorage (with connections to Fairbanks and Whittier).

When to Go

Usually summer. The days lengthen, the seas calm down. The road to Exit Glacier generally opens in May and closes with the first snowfall, usually in October. Many winter visitors ski the road into Exit Glacier, or snowmobile in. Flight-seeing trips can be arranged in Seward any time of the year, subject to weather.

Climber on Bear Glacier

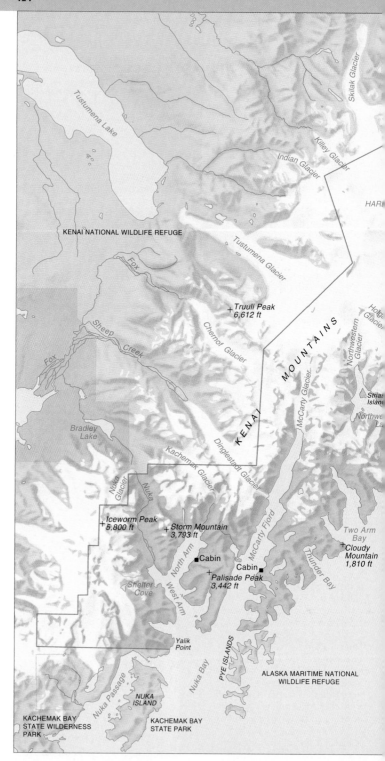

Skilak Glacier

Killey Glacier

Indian Glacier

Tustumena Lake

HARI

KENAI NATIONAL WILDLIFE REFUGE

Tustumena Glacier

Fox

Truuli Peak
6,612 ft

Hol
Glacier

Chernof Glacier

Sheep

Creek

K E N A I

M O U N T A I N S

Northwestern Glacier

Striar
Island

Fox

McCarty Glacier

Northwe
La

Bradley
Lake

Kachemak Glacier

Dinglestadt Glacier

Iceworm Peak
5,800 ft

Storm Mountain
3,793 ft

Nuka Glacier

Nuka

McCarty Fiord

Two Arm
Bay

Cloudy
Mountain
1,810 ft

Cabin

North Arm

Cabin

Palisade Peak
3,442 ft

Thunder Bay

Shelter
Cove

West Arm

Yalik
Point

PYE ISLANDS

ALASKA MARITIME NATIONAL
WILDLIFE REFUGE

Nuka Bay

Nuka Passage

NUKA
ISLAND

KACHEMAK BAY
STATE WILDERNESS
PARK

KACHEMAK BAY
STATE PARK

Resurrection River Trail
To Anchorage
Cabin
CHUGACH NATIONAL FOREST
Lost Lake Trail
Lowell Glacier
Exit Glacier Road
Exit Glacier
Ranger Station
Seward
Phoenix Peak 5,155 ft
Visitor Center
Resurrection Bay
FIELD
Bear Glacier
CAINES HEAD STATE RECREATION AREA
ialik Glacier
AIALIK PENINSULA
Cabin
Bulldog Cove
Callisto Head
Fox Island
Cabin
Holgate Arm
Aialik Bay
Rugged Island
RIS PENINSULA
Aialik Cape
ALASKA MARITIME NATIONAL WILDLIFE REFUGE
Granite Passage
Aligo Point
Granite Cape
CHISWELL ISLANDS
Gulf of Alaska

🥾 Hiking Trail
--- Unpaved Road
······ Hiking Trail
0   5   10 km
0   5   10 mi

is paved for ⅓ of a mile to a viewing area. The trail then separates into two loops. The lower loop continues to the outwash plain for a close view of the glacier terminus; the upper loop climbs ⅓ of a mile for a view of deep crevasses and towering seracs along the glacier's flank.

A ½-mile **nature trail** begins at the glacier and winds over old moraines and through cottonwood, alder, and willow before following **Exit Creek** to connect with the Main Trail. The **Harding Icefield Trail** branches off the Main Trail and climbs 3,000 feet in 3½ miles, ending on the icefield. The upper section of the trail is usually snow covered; the lower portion is slippery and muddy after rain. Ask a ranger about current conditions and sign in at the trail register. On the slopes you may see mountain goats and black bears.

The Fjords

Daily tour boats travel down **Resurrection Bay,** pass picturesque **Caines Head** and **Callisto Head,** then round rugged **Aialik Cape** and enter **Aialik Bay,** the most visited fjord in the park. The **Holgate** and **Aialik Glaciers** flow into this fjord. Tour boats usually visit the Holgate, then return to Seward via the **Chiswell Islands** (part of the Alaska Maritime NWR), an excellent place to see sea lions hauled out on rocks and nesting seabirds.

Endless exploring awaits boaters and hikers on the shores of Kenai Fjords. If you are without a guide, be sure to inquire at the visitor center about weather, landing sites, tides, and hazards. The farther down the coast to the southwest, the fewer the people. Narrow **Granite Passage** is an exciting entrance into **Harris Bay.** From 1910 to 1960, **Northwestern Glacier** retreated 9½ miles and opened up **Northwestern Lagoon** at the head of Harris Bay. The lagoon should be entered on calm water (preferably in a kayak) and at high tide only. Once you are inside and on the shore, you will find excellent hiking, especially to **Northeastern, Southwestern,** and **Sunlight Glaciers.**

Down the coast, **Thunder Bay** is a welcome anchorage during inclement weather. A narrow waterway cuts between the mainland and the **Pye Islands.** From here, **McCarty Fjord** slices 23 miles into the coast, its steep walls rising more than 4,000 feet overhead on either side of **McCarty Glacier.** The **West** and **North Arms** of **Nuka Bay** offer a variety of terrain and wildlife. Watch for the craggy profile of **Palisade Peak,** a 900-foot waterfall, historic gold mine sites, and for black bears, moose, and river otters near the **Nuka River,** for shorebirds along the mud flats at **Shelter Cove,** and for black sand beaches around **Yalik Point,** at the park's southern end. Few people come here; travel to Nuka Bay and you might have it all to yourself.

Horned puffins

Red fox and pup

Northern sea lions

Humpback whale in Aialik Bay

Information & Activities

Headquarters
P.O. Box 1727, Seward, Alaska 99664.
Phone (907) 224-3175.
www.nps.gov/kefj

Seasons & Accessibility
Park open year-round, but from about
mid-October to May, the road to Exit
Glacier may be closed by snow. Access
then is by ski, snowmobile, dog team,
or snowshoe only. Call headquarters
for information about weather and
road conditions.

Visitor & Information Centers
Visitor center in Seward, on Alaska 9
just outside the eastern border of the
park, open daily from Memorial Day
to Labor Day; weekdays only the rest
of the year. Ranger Station at Exit
Glacier open intermittently in summer
only. Phone headquarters number for
visitor information.

Entrance Fee
$5 per vehicle, per day; $15 annually.

Pets
Permitted leashed on the Exit Glacier
Road and in parking areas. Prohibited
on all trails.

Facilities for Disabled
Exit Glacier is the most accessible area.
From the Ranger Station, wheelchairs
can maneuver the glacier trail for the
first $\frac{1}{3}$ mile, to an interpretive shelter
offering exhibits and views of the
glacier. Visitor center is also wheelchair accessible.

Things to Do
Free ranger-led activities: In
summer (from the Exit Glacier
Ranger Station), walks to the glacier's
base, all-day hikes to the icefield, and
evening programs. Also available,
advanced mountain climbing,
sailing, fishing (license required),
wildlife watching, cross-country
skiing, dogsledding, snowshoeing.
   Authorized commercial guides
offer camping, fishing, kayaking,
flight-seeing, and boat trips for
exploring the fjords and watching
seabirds, whales, porpoises, and other
wildlife. Write or call park headquarters for a list of companies that do
business in the park.

Special Advisories
● If planning a backcountry trip without a guide, first check conditions with
park staff.
● Hypothermia is a danger on the icefield, even in summer.
● Do not venture out in a boat unless
well experienced in rough water.

Overnight Backpacking
Permit not required, but registration
requested for Harding Icefield.

Campgrounds
One walk-in campground at **Exit
Glacier.** Four cabins in the fjords available May through Sept. for overnight
use by permit. Access by boat or plane
only. In winter, a public-use cabin is
available at Exit Glacier. Write or
phone the visitor center.

Hotels, Motels & Inns
*(unless otherwise noted, rates are for 2
persons in a double room, high season)
In Seward, Alaska 99664:*
Best Western (on 5th Ave.) P.O. Box
330. (800) 528-1234 or (907) 224-
2378. 36 units. $192-$212. AC.
Breeze Inn (1311 4th Ave.) P.O. Box
2147. (907) 224-5237. 86 units, 1 with
a kitchenette. $119-$170. Restaurant.
Marina Motel (on Alaska Hwy. 9) P.O.
Box 1134. (800) 223-0888. (907) 224-
5518. 18 units, 1 with a kitchenette.
$105-$130.
Murphy's Motel (911 4th Ave.) P.O.
Box 736. (907) 224-8090. 24 units.
$99-$140.
Van Gilder Hotel (308 Adams St.)
P.O. Box 609. (800) 204-6835, (907)
224-3525 or (907) 224-3079. 24 units,
20 with private baths. $95. Suites $165.

Great Kobuk Sand Dunes, encroaching on a spruce forest

Kobuk Valley

Alaska

Established December 2, 1980

1,750,000 acres

"Now we were alone between fringes of spruce by a clear stream where tundra went up the sides of mountains," wrote John McPhee in *Coming into the Country.* The Kobuk Valley, said McPhee, "was, in all likelihood, the most isolated wilderness I would ever see." Located entirely above the Arctic Circle, Kobuk Valley has fewer tourist visits than any other national park. Float a river here in late August and the only other humans you're likely to encounter are Inupiaq Eskimos hunting the caribou that migrate through each year.

Twelve thousand years ago, when continental glaciers covered much of North America and a land bridge connected Alaska and Asia, Kobuk Valley was an ice-free refuge with grassy tundra similar to that found in Siberia today. Bison, mastodons, and mammoths roamed the valley, along with the humans who hunted them. Since then, the climate has shifted, and sea level has risen to flood the land bridge; many of the early mammals have disappeared. But today's shrubby flora harbors relics of the preglacial steppe, and in the cold, hard ground lie the legacies of ancient animals and peoples.

Here in Kobuk Valley the boreal forest reaches its northern limit, and the North American and Asiatic flyways cross. Pockets of tundra blend into birch and spruce, dwarfed by blasts of freezing air. And along the Kobuk River stretch 25 square miles of active sand dunes, where summer temperatures can climb to 100°F.

villages you can charter a boat or plane into the park.

When to Go

Summer. Days are long (from about June 6 to July 3 the sun doesn't set at all), and temperatures in many places can reach into the 80s or more. Ice breaks up on the Kobuk River in May, and begins to form again by mid-October. Ranger station at Onion Portage is staffed from June to September. Middle to late June is best for wildflowers. August can bring rain and September snow. In late August, the aspens begin to turn yellow and the tundra red, and the caribou migration begins.

How to Visit

Take a combination river-hiking trip that alternates between days out on the open water with days exploring the surrounding land. That way you can paddle to different landing points, leave your gear in the canoe, and hike unencumbered. Bring everything you need; no visitor facilities exist within the park. The **Kobuk River,** wide and placid, is a pleasant river to travel by canoe, kayak, or motorboat. Most people put in at Ambler and take out at Kiana, both outside the park. You can charter a boat in Kiana. You can also float or paddle the **Salmon,** a Wild and Scenic River, but it has rougher water and is harder to reach. Hiking in most places is excellent, but the park maintains no trails or river crossings. So be sure to plan your trip carefully.

While in the park, be respectful of Eskimo lands, most of which are along the Kobuk River.

How to Get There

Commercial planes fly daily from Anchorage to Kotzebue, where the park's information center is located. Connecting flights serve the Eskimo villages of Kiana and Ambler, both of which are situated along the Kobuk River, on the park's western and eastern sides respectively. From these two

Caribou migrating across the Kobuk River

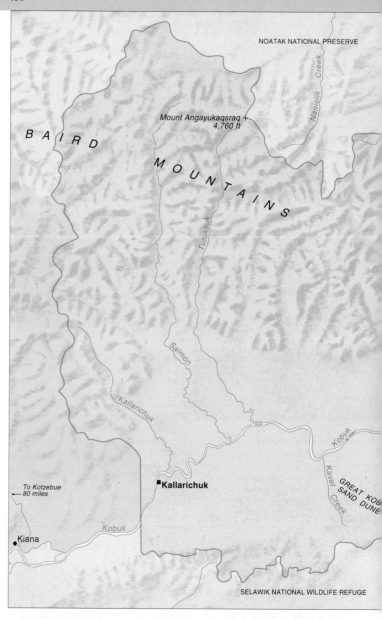

NOATAK NATIONAL PRESERVE

Nanielik Creek

Mount Angayukaqsraq +
4,760 ft

B A I R D

M O U N T A I N S

Tutuksuk

Salmon

Kallarichuk

Kobuk

Kavet Creek

GREAT KOB
SAND DUNE

■ **Kallarichuk**

To Kotzebue
← 80 miles

Kobuk

● Kiana

SELAWIK NATIONAL WILDLIFE REFUGE

Cranberries, club moss, and sphagnum in the tundra

Grizzly in a meadow

a lake than a river, with a current that's hardly detectable.

Although steep bluffs sometimes rise above the riverbanks, hiking opportunities from the Kobuk are limitless. Both shores have forest, lakes, and tundra; the south shore has sand dunes also. Hike high ground to avoid swamps. In late August and early September you can sit on a bluff and watch caribou in striking autumn pelage as they swim across the river. Huge antlers and white ruffs mark the bulls.

A river trip through the park from Ambler to Kiana, with plenty of time for hiking, takes about a week. Or, if you want a more ambitious trip (requiring 2 to 3 weeks, depending on weather and river conditions), begin at **Walker Lake,** in Gates of the Arctic National Park, and paddle or motor all the way to Kiana.

On either trip you'll pass **Onion Portage,** a river bend, where for thousands of years migrating caribou have crossed the Kobuk. Here, in 1961, archaeologist J. Louis Giddings dug into the earth and could hardly believe his eyes. He had discovered what a Smithsonian Institution ethnologist would later call "the most important archaeological site ever found in the Arctic." Giddings' two-acre plot yielded 30 artifact-bearing layers, reflecting seven stages of flint-working technology, the oldest dating back at least 10,000 years.

Today, the archaeological site is inactive and largely overgrown. But in late summer and fall, Eskimos hunt caribou

Kobuk River

Beginning in the central Brooks Range, the **Kobuk** flows west 200 miles, winds slowly through the park for 50 miles, dropping only 2 to 3 inches per mile, and then continues west to drain into **Hotham Inlet,** off **Kotzebue Sound.** At times its placid aspect makes it seem more like

Easily stowed inflatable craft for river runners

Hardy dune grass

here as they've done for millennia. During the summer, a backcountry ranger is stationed at Giddings' old cabin. Hiking is good at Onion Portage. The name comes from the wild chives that grow here.

Great Kobuk Sand Dunes

Farther downstream sprawl the **Great Kobuk Sand Dunes**, a 25-square-mile mini-Sahara. Visitors arrive by the river and leave their boats on shore for the short hike to the adventure of scaling the dunes. An Ice Age relic, the dunes formed from the windblown outwash of melting glaciers. A special combination of topography and eastern and northern winds keeps the dunes moving and inhospitable to vegetation. Some dunes measure 100 feet high. Older, thinly vegetated dunes surround this ever changing landscape located 35 miles above the Arctic Circle.

Information & Activities

Headquarters
P.O. Box 1029, Kotzebue, Alaska 99752. Phone (907) 442-3890. www.nps.gov/kova

Seasons & Accessibility
Open year-round but access—by boat or charter aircraft from Kotzebue—generally June through September. (The Kobuk River usually thaws by June 1 and freezes by mid-October.) There are no roads to or in the park. Be prepared for severe arctic weather at any time. Contact park headquarters before visiting. If you plan to charter in by air, ask the park for a list of licensed companies.

Information Centers
Located 80 miles from the park, the Kotzebue Headquarters and Information Center is open daily year-round, as is the ranger station at Onion Portage.

Entrance Fee
None.

Pets
Strongly discouraged.

Facilities for Disabled
Kotzebue information center accessible to wheelchairs; otherwise none.

Things to Do
Films at Kotzebue information center. The park organizes no activities, but rafting, kayaking, canoeing, hiking, sportfishing (license required), and aerial sightseeing are available. Commercial outfitters offer a variety of private guide services for floating, fishing, trekking trips. Call or write headquarters for a list of those licensed to work in the park.

Special Advisories
● Take a guide along unless you are well experienced in the wilderness.
● Mosquitoes and gnats can be brutal; bring plenty of repellent, a head net, and an insect-proof tent.
● Eskimos own much of the land along the river and engage in subsistence hunting and fishing. Respect them and their property.

Overnight Backpacking
No permit required, but call park for current information on weather, river conditions, bears, and Eskimo subsistence activities before venturing out.

Campgrounds
None; backcountry camping only.

Hotels, Motels, & Inns
(unless otherwise noted, rates are for 2 persons in a double room, high season)
In Ambler, Alaska 99786:
Kobuk River Lodge (on the Kobuk River) P.O. Box 30. (907) 445-2150 or 445-2166. 3 rooms with a central bath, $150; 2 cabins with private baths and kitchenettes, $100. Rest.
In Kotzebue, Alaska 99752:
Nullagvik Hotel (308 Front Street) P.O. Box 336. (907) 442-3331. 74 units. $144. Rest.

Excursion

Cape Krusenstern National Monument
Kotzebue, Alaska

For more than 6,000 years, Eskimos have forged a living on this stretch of gravel projecting into the Chukchi Sea; its 114 beach ridges, rich in artifacts, reveal their archaeological benchmarks. Today, the cape's large land and sea mammals are still crucial to local subsistence. 560,000 acres. Facilities: primitive camping, boating, fishing. Open year-round. Access by charter boat or plane from Kotzebue. (907) 442-3890.

Turquoise Lake, tinted by glacial silt

Lake Clark

Alaska

Established December 2, 1980

4,045,000 acres

"Think of all the splendors that bespeak Alaska," conservationist John Kauffmann has written, "glaciers, volcanoes, alpine spires, wild rivers, lakes with grayling on the rise. Picture coasts feathered with countless seabirds. Imagine dense forests and far-sweeping tundra, herds of caribou, great roving bears. Now concentrate all these and more into less than one percent of the state—and behold the Lake Clark region, Alaska's epitome."

Diversity is Lake Clark's hallmark. The Turquoise-Telaquana Plateau has tundra similar to Alaska's North Slope, while the coast has forests similar to the southeast panhandle. Black bears and Dall's sheep reach their southern limits here, and Sitka spruce, Alaska's state tree, reaches its northern limit. Three rivers— the Mulchatna, Chilikadrotna, and Tlikakila—have been officially designated Wild and Scenic.

The Chigmit Mountains, spine of the park, are as rugged as mountains get. They lie on the edge of the North American plate where the oceanic plate slides under it, and their jumbled contours reflect centuries of geological violence. Two volcanoes here, Iliamna and Redoubt, are still active and vent gases regularly. Redoubt erupted in 1966, spewing clouds of ash 40,000 feet into the air—and it erupted dramatically again in late 1989 and early 1990. The area averages one to two earthquakes per year that register at least a 5 on the Richter scale.

Archaeological finds show that humans, most recently Dena'ina Indians,

have lived in the area for centuries. The abundant salmon and game made their settled existence possible.

How to Get There

Take a plane into the heart of the park, or travel by boat or plane to the coast. Bush pilots in Anchorage say, "Lake Clark is just out the back-door"—a 1-hour flight. From Anchorage you can charter a plane to Port Alsworth, a small community on the southeast shore of Lake Clark. The flight through Lake Clark Pass takes you over immense blue glaciers, winding rivers, and snowcapped mountains. Planes also land on the coast for salmon fishing.

Another alternative is to take a scheduled flight from Anchorage to Iliamna, 30 miles outside the park, and an air taxi from there into the park. Air taxis fly in from Homer and Kenai, too. To reach the park by boat, you must travel down Cook Inlet from Anchorage or across the inlet from the Kenai Peninsula.

When to Go

Summer. Wildflowers are best in late June. Autumn colors peak in early September in upper elevations, in mid-September lower down. June through August daytime temperatures usually hover in the 50s and low 60s in the eastern part of the park and are somewhat higher in the western part and the interior.

How to Visit

Most visitors fly into the interior lake region of the park. Air taxis can make drop-offs and pickups at prearranged places. The smaller lakes offer excellent kayaking, and several rivers give kayakers and rafters great white-water experiences. Hiking is good around the lakes and from lake to lake. Fishing is usually first class. Write to park headquarters in Anchorage for information about guide services and lodges. Remember to make your reservations early. If you don't plan to be completely self-sufficient, be sure to make thorough arrangements before going.

On the Lakes & Rivers

Fishing is superb on the lakes and rivers of this fly-in park. Rainbow trout, Arctic grayling, northern pike, and five kinds of salmon—king, chum, coho, humpback, and sockeye—lure fishermen, many of whom take off from Port Alsworth, site of the park's field headquarters.

As in many Alaska parks, a kayak in Lake Clark is an invitation to freedom. You can explore large areas, carry a lot of gear, and take intermittent hikes as the mood strikes you. Keep in mind that sudden winds can stir up large waves in a matter of minutes. Good lakes for paddling are **Telaquana, Turquoise, Twin, Lake Clark, Kontrashibuna,** and **Tazimina.**

Another way to see the country is to let a river take you through it. Your options are long trips (averaging three to four days) on the Wild and Scenic **Mulchatna, Chilikadrotna,** and **Tlikakila,** or short trips (averaging one to two days) on the **Tanalian** and the **Tazimina.** Hire a guide or check with rangers on water conditions, places to put in and take out, and what to look out for along the way.

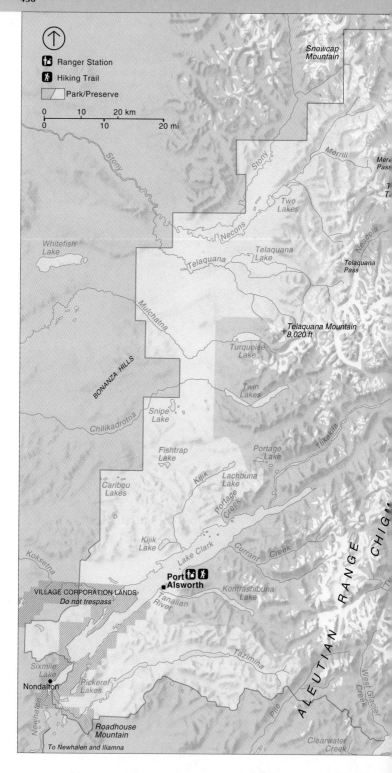

Ranger Station

Hiking Trail

Park/Preserve

0   10   20 km

0   10   20 mi

Snowcap Mountain

Stony

Stony

Merrill

Mer
Pass

T
T

Two
Lakes

Necons

Neacola

Whitefish
Lake

Telaquana

Telaquana
Lake

Telaquana
Pass

Mulchatna

Telaquana Mountain
+ 8,020 ft

BONANZA HILLS

Turquoise
Lake

Twin
Lakes

Snipe
Lake

Chilikadrotna

Tlikakila

Fishtrap
Lake

Portage
Lake

Caribou
Lakes

Kijik

Lachbuna
Lake

Portage
Creek

Kijik
Lake

Lake Clark

Currant   Creek

RANGE

CHIG

Port
Alsworth

Koksetna

Kontrashibuna
Lake

VILLAGE CORPORATION LANDS
Do not trespass

Tanalian
River

ALEUTIAN

Tazimina

Sixmile
Lake

Nondalton

Pickerel
Lakes

Pile

West Glacier
Creek

Newhalen

Roadhouse
Mountain

Clearwater
Creek

To Newhalen and Iliamna

Autumn rainbow over Stony River

Hiking

In a park with no trail system and only one maintained hiking trail, route selection is critical. So is being prepared: wind and rain gear for swift changes in the weather and repellent for mosquitoes. If you intend to hike without a guide, consult with a park ranger before starting out and take a good map with you. Some general rules for hikers are: Stay as long as possible on dry tundra where footing is good, avoid heavy brush, and choose your river crossings carefully. Hiking is generally best above 2,000 feet in the interior (where the dry tundra begins), or along the coast on the numerous gravel river bars. Below tree line the vegetation can be thick and nearly impenetrable, especially the alder.

The 2-mile **Tanalian Falls Trail** is the only developed trail in the park. Beginning in Port Alsworth, this easy hike takes you through a forest of black spruce and birch, past bogs and ponds, and up along the tumbling Tanalian River. Watch for moose in the ponds, Arctic grayling in the river, Dall's sheep on **Tanalian Mountain,** and bears everywhere.

Another hike from Port Alsworth is the strenuous 3,600-foot climb up Tanalian Mountain. You can begin the climb off the Tanalian Falls Trail, or by hiking the shore of Lake Clark and heading up a ridge where the

Tanalian Mountain rising from Lake Clark shores

Alpine bearberry and lichens

Arctic ground squirrel

walking is easier, a round-trip of about 7 miles.

North of Lake Clark are several lakes that offer excellent hiking. You can take an air taxi to one and hike to another, or stay at one lake—a world in itself—and go on day hikes along the shore and up the ridges. If a lake-to-lake trek appeals to you, try the 16 miles from Telaquana Lake south to Turquoise Lake, or from Turquoise Lake 13 miles south to Twin Lakes. From Twin Lakes you can hike 17 miles to **Portage Lake,** a beautiful tarn in an alpine valley, and from there 11 miles to **Lachbuna** Lake, over a ridge and down the **Portage Creek** drainage to Lake Clark.

For a longer, wilder, and more demanding hike through truly spectacular country, try taking the 50-mile trek from **Telaquana Lake** east over **Telaquana Pass,** along the **Neacola River** to **Kenibuna Lake.** From there, continue your hike to the huge rock spire called **The Tusk.**

Information & Activities

Headquarters
4230 University Dr. #311, Anchorage, Alaska 99508. (907) 271-3751. www.nps.gov/lacl

Seasons & Accessibility
Park open and accessible by small aircraft from Anchorage, Kenai, Homer, and Iliamna year-round. There are no roads to or in the park.

Weather changes rapidly. Call Port Alsworth at (907) 781-2218 for up-to-date conditions.

Visitor & Information Centers
Field headquarters and a visitor center are located in Port Alsworth, on the south shore of Lake Clark (1 Park Place, Port Alsworth, Alaska 99653). Call Anchorage headquarters at (907) 271-3751, or Port Alsworth field headquarters at (907) 781-2218 for visitor information.

Gas & Supplies
Bring everything you will need.

Entrance Fee
None.

Pets
Park recommends that you leave your pets at home because they can attract bears.

Facilities for Disabled
All park buildings and lodges are accessible.

Things to Do
Minimal interpretive programs (June through September). Also, hiking, backpacking, climbing, rafting, kayaking, fishing (license required), boating, birdwatching and wildlife watching, aerial sightseeing, hunting (in preserve).

Call or write headquarters for a list of concessioners offering a variety of guide services in the park, or visit the website at www.nps.gov/lacl/visiting_the_park.htm

Special Advisories
● You must possess good wilderness skills if you intend to hike, camp, or fish without a guide.

● Do not trespass onto or in any way disturb the property of local residents.

● Don't fail to bring insect repellent. A head net and insect-proof tent are also desirable.

Overnight Backpacking
No permit required, but campers are encouraged to contact field station before setting out. (907) 781-2218.

Campgrounds
None. Backcountry camping only. No showers or other visitor amenities except in lodges. Restrooms at the field headquarters at Port Alsworth.

Hotels, Motels, & Inns
INSIDE THE PARK:
Alaska's Wilderness Lodge (on southern shore of Lake Clark), P.O. Box 90748, Anchorage, Alaska 99519. (907) 781-2223 (from mid-May through Sept.), (800) 835-8032 (year-round). 7 cabins. $5,400 per person, per week. 7-day sportfishing packages available. All inclusive as well as airfare. Open mid-June to early October.
Lakeside Lodge (on southern shore of Lake Clark) Port Alsworth, Alaska 99653. (907) 781-2202. 3 cabins, 2 with kitchenettes. Sportfishing packages. Open June to mid-September.
Silver Salmon Creek Lodge (10 miles south of Tuxedni Bay on Silver Salmon Creek) P.O. Box 3234, Soldotna, Alaska 99669. (907) 398-1889. 3 lodge rooms; 3 cabins, shared baths. $305 rooms; $150 cabins. 3-, 5-, and 7-day packages available. Open mid-May through September.
OUTSIDE THE PARK:
Newhalen Lodge (near Nondalton). (907) 294-2233 (lodge) or (907) 522-3355 (all year). 9 rooms. Sportfishing packages. $4,700 per person, per week all inclusive. Open June to October.

Contact park headquarters for additional lodgings in and near the park.

Flowing Kennicott Glacier; Mount Blackburn at left

Wrangell-St. Elias

Alaska

Established December 2, 1980

13,188,000 acres

Even in a state famous for its size, Wrangell-St. Elias stands out. It is by far the largest national park in the United States—almost six times the size of Yellowstone. You fly over it and see mountains beyond mountains, glaciers after glaciers, rivers upon rivers. You float a river and watch the moods and mountains change by the minute. As you walk the tundra slopes, you find Dall's sheep and mountain goats grazing.

Three major mountain ranges converge here: the volcanic Wrangells, the St. Elias—tallest coastal mountains in the world—and the Chugach. Together they contain 9 of the 16 highest peaks in the United States, four of them above 16,000 feet. There are more than 150 glaciers; one, the Malaspina, is larger than Rhode Island. In 1980 Wrangell-St. Elias and adjoining Kluane National Park Reserve in Canada were designated a United Nations World Heritage site.

Vast and rugged as it is, the park is not a fortress. Two roads lead into small communities, remnants of the gold- and copper-mining towns that thrived in the early days of this century. Today not mining but the nearly limitless hiking, rafting, kayaking, and climbing opportunities beckon.

How to Get There

Drive or charter a plane. By car from Anchorage, take Alaska 1 (Glenn Hwy.) 189 miles northeast to Glennallen. Continue northeast 74 miles along the Copper River and the park's western boundary to Slana, where an unpaved road branches into the

When to Go

Summer. Lodges and guide services operate in the park from about mid-May to the end of September. June is best for wildflowers; July has the warmest days; berries ripen in August. Be prepared for cloudy skies, but September can be beautiful with clear skies, autumn colors, no mosquitoes, and a dusting of new snow on the mountain peaks. March and April offer excellent cross-country skiing for those of stout heart and strong will.

How to Visit

Take one of the two unpaved roads into the park. The **McCarthy Road** is maintained and usually passable in summer, though a four-wheel drive may be required. Stop at park headquarters in Copper Center for latest road conditions. The **Slana-Nabesna Road** is also maintained. Both roads bring you to trailheads for many hikes into the backcountry.

Or, charter a plane into a remote part of the park and hike or run a river. Several commercial companies offer guided rafting or kayaking trips on the rivers and in the spectacular coastal bays. You can get a full listing of them from the park.

park for 46 miles, ending at the town of Nabesna.

Or, head toward the town of McCarthy by taking Alaska 4 (Richardson Hwy.) from Glennallen 32 miles southeast to the Edgerton cutoff (Alaska 10), then turning left and continuing 33 miles to Chitina. There the pavement ends and a road follows an old railroad bed about 60 miles into the park. These same roads can be reached from Fairbanks via Delta Junction, and from Haines, Skagway, and Whitehorse (along the Alaska-Canada Hwy.) via Haines Junction and Tok. Buses run regularly in summer from Anchorage to Valdez with stops in Glennallen.

Air charters into the park operate out of Anchorage, Fairbanks, Yakutat, Cordova, Glennallen, Gulkana, Tok, and Northway. Commercial jets service Yakutat and Cordova year-round. In summer, the Alaska State Ferry serves Valdez from Whittier (reachable by train from Anchorage).

McCarthy Road to Kennicott

62 miles one way; a half day

From the town of Chitina and the confluence of the **Chitina** and **Copper Rivers,** the road follows the abandoned Copper River and Northwest Railroad bed. At mile 17 the road crosses the **Kuskulana River Bridge.** It spans 525 feet, crossing 260 feet above the river. Another abandoned railroad trestle spans the **Gilahina River** at mile 28.5. At the end of the road is a parking lot and the **Kennicott River.** To reach the old mining town of **McCarthy** on the other side of the river you pull yourself across on one of two cable trams—moderately hard work, but a great adventure. Today a tiny community of hardy individualists, McCarthy had a population near 2,000 in mining days.

From McCarthy, a dirt road climbs 500 feet in 5 miles to the former town and millsite of **Kennicott.** You can take a taxi or rent a bike in

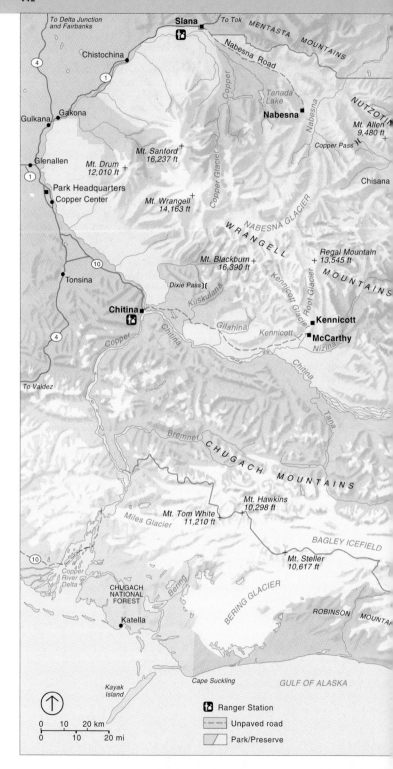

To Delta Junction
and Fairbanks

Slana

To Tok

MENTASTA MOUNTAINS

Nabesna Road

Chistochina

4

1

Copper

Tanada
Lake

Nabesna

NUTZOTIN

Nabesna

Mt. Allen
9,480 ft

Gulkana

Gakona

Copper Pass

Copper Glacier

Chisana

Glenallen

1

Mt. Drum
12,010 ft

Mt. Sanford
16,237 ft

Park Headquarters
Copper Center

Mt. Wrangell
14,163 ft

NABESNA GLACIER

W R A N G E L L

Regal Mountain
13,545 ft

10

Tonsina

Mt. Blackburn
16,390 ft

M O U N T A I N S

Dixie Pass

Kuskulana

Kennicott Glacier

Root Glacier

Chitina

Gilahina

Kennicott

Kennicott

Chitina

Kennicott

McCarthy

Copper

Chitina

Nizina

4

Chitina

Tana

To Valdez

Bremner

C H U G A C H   M O U N T A I N S

Mt. Hawkins
10,298 ft

Mt. Tom White
11,210 ft

Miles Glacier

BAGLEY ICEFIELD

10

Copper
River
Delta

Bering

Mt. Steller
10,617 ft

CHUGACH
NATIONAL
FOREST

BERING GLACIER

ROBINSON

MOUNTA

Katella

Kayak
Island

Cape Suckling

GULF OF ALASKA

↑

0   10   20 km

0   10   20 mi

🚶 Ranger Station

— — — Unpaved road

Park/Preserve

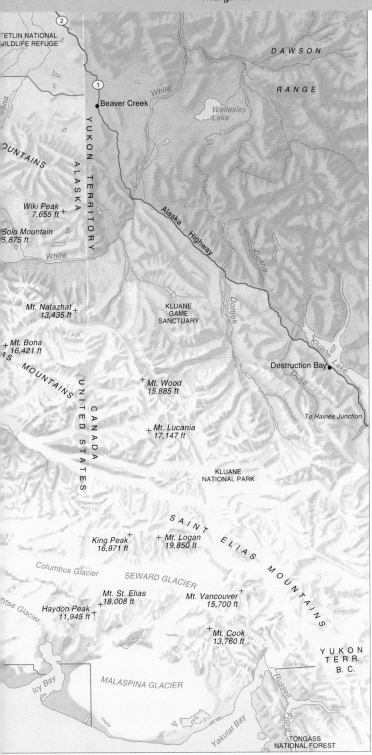

ETLIN NATIONAL
WILDLIFE REFUGE

② ①

D A W S O N

White

Beaver Creek

R A N G E

Wellesley
Lake

Y U K O N   T E R R I T O R Y

A L A S K A

Wiki Peak
7,655 ft +

Alaska Highway

Solo Mountain
5,875 ft

White

Kluane

Mt. Natazhat +
13,435 ft

KLUANE
GAME
SANCTUARY

Donjek

+ Mt. Bona
16,421 ft

Kluane Lake

M O U N T A I N S

U N I T E D   S T A T E S

+ Mt. Wood
15,885 ft

Destruction Bay

Duke

C A N A D A

+ Mt. Lucania
17,147 ft

To Haines Junction

KLUANE
NATIONAL PARK

S A I N T

King Peak +
16,971 ft

+ Mt. Logan
19,850 ft

E L I A S

Columbus Glacier

SEWARD GLACIER

M O U N T A I N S

Mt. St. Elias +
18,008 ft

Mt. Vancouver +
15,700 ft

htse Glacier

Haydon Peak +
11,945 ft

+ Mt. Cook
13,760 ft

Y U K O N
T E R R.
B. C.

Icy Bay

MALASPINA GLACIER

Russell

Yakutat Bay

Fiord

TONGASS
NATIONAL FOREST

Kennicott's copper mill, silent since 1938

McCarthy if you prefer not to walk. Kennicott was once the site of the world's richest copper mine. From 1906 to 1938, when the mine closed, yielded 591,000 tons of copper and 900,000 ounces of silver. Today, the silent 13-story mill and other Kennicott buildings are still dressed in mineral oxide red with white trim. Though deteriorating, they form one of Alaska's most photogenic collections of historic structures and are, since 1986, on the National Register of Historic Places.

After exploring Kennicott, you can hike the trail north of town for spectacular views of the Kennicott and Root Glaciers and Mount Blackburn.

Nabesna Road

46 miles one way; a half day

Since parts of this road into the **Wrangell Mountains** are subject to washouts, be sure to check conditions with the Park Service before you set out. The road passes homesteads and fishing camps on privately owned land and then climbs over the watershed divide (mile 25) between the Copper River, which drains into the Gulf of Alaska, and the **Nabesna River,** which drains into the **Tanana River,** the Yukon River, and finally the Bering Sea. There are excellent views of **Mount Sanford** and the **Copper Glacier** to the southwest. The final 4 miles, from **Devil's Mountain Lodge** to **Nabesna,** are the most rugged.

Other Hikes & Water Trips

At mile 13.5 on the **McCarthy Road,** the **Nugget Creek-Kotsina Road** branches northeast 2 ½ miles to the **Nugget Creek Trail.** Sixteen miles later and 1,000 feet higher, the trail arrives at a public-use cabin beneath Mount Blackburn, where you can picnic and camp. A dozen good day hikes can be taken from here. Watch for Dall's sheep. A little more than a mile past the Nugget Creek trailhead begins the **Dixie Pass Trail.** Climbing 3,600 feet in 10 miles, it's a strenuous hike, but worth it if the weather is clear.

Off the **Nabesna Road, Trail Creek** at mile 29.4 and **Lost Creek** at mile 31.2 offer good hiking routes. There are no defined trails, simply follow the creek bed northward as far as you like. Though the hiking is not generally difficult, you will run into rocky patches and may have to hop or wade the creek. But you will be rewarded with excellent views of the upper Copper River basin. Talk to a ranger and fill out a backcountry itinerary before any overnight stays.

Commercial outfitters offer rafting trips down the Nabesna, Kennicott, Copper, Chitina, and **Nizina Rivers.** Short trips last three hours, extended ones two weeks; there are all classes of water. It's an adventuresome way to see Wrangell-St. Elias. Contact the park for a full listing of the outfitters that operate there.

Information & Activities

Headquarters
P.O. Box 439, Copper Center, Alaska 99573. Phone (907) 822-5234. www.nps.gov/wrst

Seasons & Accessibility
Park open year-round, but best time is mid-May through September. Snow limits winter access.

Call headquarters for road conditions before attempting to drive to the park.

Visitor & Information Centers
Park headquarters at mile 105.5 on Old Richardson Hwy. (just off Alaska 4) at western edge of park. Open daily Memorial Day through Labor Day, weekdays the rest of year. Information also available at Yakutat, Slana, and Chitina Ranger Stations, all outside park boundaries. Chitina closed October through May. Call headquarters for information. A new headquarters will open in summer of 2002 on the Old Richardson Hwy., 8 miles south of Glennallen.

Entrance Fee
None.

Pets
Permitted on leashes except in public buildings; permitted off leashes in the backcountry.

Facilities for Disabled
None.

Things to Do
No park-organized activities, but the following are available: hiking, horseback riding (rentals in McCarthy), pack trips, river running, kayaking, jet-boat rentals, lake fishing, mountain climbing, air tours, cross-country skiing. Ask park for list of companies that offer guide and outfitting services, or visit the park website at www.nps.gov/wrst/wrstcommercialservices.htm

Special Advisories
• This is a wilderness park; hikers and backpackers must be wholly self-sufficient; do not attempt the backcountry without a guide unless you're experienced and equipped.
• Choose your river crossings carefully; many rivers are impassable.
• Be respectful of native camps, fishnets, and other private property.
• Mosquitoes can be brutal in July and August; bring repellent, a head net, and an insect-proof tent.

Overnight Backpacking
Permit not required, but best to register before going into backcountry. Let the park help plan your trip.

Campgrounds and Cabins
Two private campgrounds within park: **Silver Lake Campground** (milepost 9.3 on McCarthy Road) camping and limited services. **Nelson's Lakeside Campground** (milepost 10.9 on McCarthy Road) camping, boat rentals, and limited services. Camping is available at several roadside pullouts along Nabesna Road. First come, first served. No fee. The park also maintains 12 public-use cabins. First come, first served. No fee. Contact headquarters for information.

Hotels, Motels, & Inns
(unless otherwise noted, rates are for 2 persons in a double room, high season)
INSIDE THE PARK:
Kennicott Glacier Lodge (in Kennicott) P.O. Box 103940, Anchorage, Alaska 99510. (800) 582-5128 or (907) 258-2350. 20 rooms, shared baths. $179 per person, includes meals.
OUTSIDE THE PARK:
Copper Center Lodge (mile 101.5 on Old Richardson Hwy.) Drawer J, Copper Center, Alaska 99573. (907) 822-3245. 21 rooms, 11 with private baths. $89-$99. Open from mid-May through September. Restaurant.
Gakona Lodge (on Alas. 1, north of Glennallen) P.O. Box 285, Gakona, Alaska 99586. (907) 822-3482. 3 cabins, private baths $100; 8 rooms, shared baths $80. Open May through September. Restaurant.

Contact headquarters for additional accommodations in and near the park.

Acknowledgments

We are indebted to the many individuals and the federal, state, and private agencies that helped prepare this guide, especially to the National Park Service and the superintendents and chiefs of interpretation and their staffs at each park. Our thanks go also to the National Parks and Conservation Association for its cooperation and to Frances Kennedy, who offered wise counsel.

Illustrations Credits

Abbreviations for terms appearing below: (t)-top; (b)-bottom; (l)-left; (r)-right; (c)-center; BPS-Biological Photo Service; DRK-DRK Photo; NGP-National Geographic Photographer; P/A-Photographers/Aspen.

Cover, William Manning/The Stock Market; 2-3, Gary Moon; 6-7, Pat O'Hara; 8, Frank S. Balthis; 9 (t), Lowell Georgia; (b), Tom Bean.

The East

12-13, James Valentine; 18-19, Glenn Van Nimwegen; 19, John Netherton; 20, Sonja Bullaty; 23 (t), Raymond Gehman/NGS Image Collection; (b), John Netherton; 24, Glenn Van Nimwegen; 25 (t), Alan Nyiri; (b), Clyde Smith; 27 (t), Bates Littlehales; (c), John Netherton; (b), Stephen J. Krasemann/DRK; 28-29, Stephen Frink/WaterHouse; 29, Robert Holland; 31 (t), James Valentine; (b), Doug Perrine/DRK; 32, Bruce Mounier; 33 (t), Doug Perrine/DRK; (cl), Larry Lipsky/DRK; (cr), (bl) & (br), Stephen Frink/ WaterHouse; 35 (t), James Valentine; (tc), C.C. Lockwood; (bc), Caulion Singletary; (b), R.J. Erwin/DRK; 36-37, Matt Bradley; 37, Stephen Frink/WaterHouse; 39, Matt Bradley; 40-41, Stephen J. Krasemann/DRK; 44 (t), Stephen J. Krasemann/Peter Arnold, Inc. (c), James A. Kern; (b), Ron Sanford; 45, David Hiser, P/A; 46 (t), Otis Imboden; (b), Bianca Lavies; 47 (t), Glenn Van Nimwegen; (b), Fred Hirschmann; 49 (t), James Valentine; (c), Farrell Grehan; (b), Glenn Van Nimwegen; 50-51, John Netherton; 53 & 54, James P. Blair; 55 (both), Tim Black; 56 (t), Tim Thompson; (b), Tim Black; (br), John Netherton; 58 (t), Larry Ulrich; (c), Bill Peane; (b), Dick Durrance II; 59 (t), Pat O'Hara; (c), Larry Ulrich; (b), James Valentine; 60-61, Declan Haun; 61, Matt Bradley; 63, Declan Haun; 65 (t), (bc) & (b), Matt Bradley; (tc), Stephen J. Krasemann; 66-67, Daniel J. Cox; 67 & 69, John & Ann Mahan; 70, Jim Brandenburg; 72 (t) & (b), John & Ann Mahan; (c), Tom Bean; 73 (t), John & Ann Mahan; (c), Carl R. Sams II; (b), Stephen J. Krasemann/DRK; 74-79 (photos), Chip Clark; (artwork), Richard Schlecht; 81 (t), Dan Dry; (b), David Muench; 82-83, Jeff Gnass; 86, David Muench; 87 (both), Stephen J. Krasemann; 89 (t) & (c), Carr Clifton; (b), Stephen J. Krasemann/DRK; 90-91, Tom Bean/DRK; 93-95 (all), Jodi Cobb, NGP; 97, Stephen Frink/WaterHouse; 98-99, John & Ann Mahan; 99, Erwin & Peggy Bauer; 101, Jeff Gnass; 102 (t), Erwin & Peggy Bauer; (b), R. Stottlemyer, Michigan Technological University/BPS; 103, Stephen J, Krasemann/DRK; 105 (t), John & Ann Mahan; (c), Stephen J. Krasemann/DRK; (b), David Hiser.

The Southwest

106-107, David Muench; 110-111, Tom Bean; 111 & 114, Matt Bradley; 115 (t), Tom Bean; (b), Larry Ulrich; 116, George Mobley; 117 (t), Larry Ulrich; (b), Tom Bean; 118 (t), Bruce Dale; (b), Stephen J. Krasemann; 119, David Muench; 120-121, Danny Lehman; 122-123, Tibor Toth; 124, David S. Boyer; 125 (both), Stephen J. Krasemann; 127 (t), (b), Shattil/Rozinski; (c), Lewis Kemper; 128-129 & 132, Matt Bradley.

The Colorado Plateau

134-135, W.M. Edwards; 138-139, Tom & Pat Leeson; 141, Ron Sanford; 143 (t), Farrell Grehan; (b), Larry Ulrich; 144-145, Larry Ulrich; 146, Fred Hirschmann; 147, Grant Haist; 149 (t), Fred Hirschmann; (c), Larry Ulrich; (b), Pat O'Hara; 150-151, George Mobley; 151, David Muench; 153, Becky & Gary Vestal; 154 (t), W.M. Edwards; (b), Becky & Gary Vestal; 155 (t), Pat O'Hara; (b), David Hiser, P/A; 156, Becky & Gary Vestal; 158 (t), Tom Till; (c), Farrell Grehan; (b), John Gerlach/DRK; 159 (both), David Hiser, P/A; 160-161, Gordon Anderson; 161, Larry Ulrich; 163 (t), Charlie Borland; (b), Galen Rowell/Mountain Light; 164 (t), Kerrick James; (b), Joel Grimes; 166-167, Larry Ulrich; 169, Ron Sanford; 170, Tom & Pat Leeson; 171, Jack Dykinga; 172, W.E. Garrett; 173, Ned Seidler; 175 (t) & (b), Jeff Gnass; (c), Larry Ulrich; 176-177, Jeff Gnass; 177, David Muench; 179 (all), Larry Ulrich; 180 (all), Richard Olsenius; 181, Phil Schofield/Aperture; 183 (t), Jack Olson; (c), Gary Brettnacher; (b), Jan Nachlinger; 184-185, David Muench; 188 (l), Dewitt Jones; (r), Richard Alexander Cooke III; 189, William Belknap, Jr.; 191 (t), Larry Ulrich; (c) & (b), Tom Till; 192-193, Tom Algire; 195, Larry Ulrich; 197 (t) & (c), Fred Hirschmann; (b), George H.H. Huey; 198-199, Pat O'Hara; 201, Art Wolfe/stone; 202-203, Tom Algire; 203, James Randklev; 205, Fred Hirschmann; 206 (t), John Telford; (c), Fred Hirschmann; (b), George Mobley; 207 (t), Larry Ulrich; (b), David Muench; 208 (t), Pat O'Hara; (b), Stephen J. Krasemann/DRK.

The Pacific Southwest

210-211, Galen Rowell/Mountain Light; 214-215, Thomas Nebbia; 216-217, Jeff Gnass; 219, James P. Blair; 220, Nicholas DeVore III, P/A; 221 (t), Caroline Sheen; (b), David Muench; 222-223, Carr Clifton; 224, Marc Muench; 227, David Muench; 228-229, B.F. Molnia, Terraphotographics/BPS; 231, Stephen J. Krasemann; 232 (t), David Muench; (b), Robert J. Western; 233, David Muench; 235 (t), Jeff Gnass; (b), Steve Raymer; 236-237, David Muench; 237, James A. Sugar; 239, David Muench; 240, C.F. Miesche, Foto 64/BPS; 241 (t), Scott Rutherford; (b), Jeff Gnass; 243 (t), Roger Ressmeyer; (b), Jeff Gnass; 244-245, Harald Sund; 247 & 249, Peter Essick; 250-251, Larry Ulrich; 251, Angelo Lomeo; 254, David Muench; 257 (t) & (c), Pat O'Hara; (b) Richard Frear, National Park Service; 258-259, Dewitt Jones; 261, David Muench; 262 (t), Pat O'Hara; (b), Jim Brandenburg; 263, Gordon Wiltsie; 264, Farrell Grehan; 264-265, Glenn Van Nimwegen; 265, Steve Raymer; 267 (t), Pat O'Hara; (c), Lewis Kemper; (b), Larry Ulrich.

The Rocky Mountains

268-269, Paul Chesley; 272-273, Jim Brandenburg; 275, Tom Bean/DRK; 276 (t), Fred Hirschmann; (b), Don & Pat Valenti/DRK; 278-282 (all), David Muench; 283, George H.H. Huey; 284-285, Tom Danielsen; 285, Erwin & Peggy Bauer; 287, James P.

Blair; 288, Pat O'Hara; 289 (t), David Hiser; (b),
Virginia Karrels; 290 (t), Ken McGraw; (b), Scott
Rutherford; 290-291, Erwin & Peggy Bauer; 293 (t),
Jeff Foott/DRK; (tc), Pat O'Hara; (bc), Charles
Gurche; (b), James Amos; 294-295, David Hiser,
P/A; 297, Linde Waidhofer; 298 & 299,
Shattil/Rozinski; 300, Leonard Lee Rue IV; 302 (t),
Jeff Gnass; (c), John Ward; (b), Shattil/Rozinski;
303 (t), John Fielder; (c), Shattil/Rozinski; (b),
David Hiser; 304-307 (all), Steve Kaufman; 308,
Tom Bean/DRK; 309 (t), Tom Till/DRK; (b), Jim
Brandenburg; 311 (t), David Muench; (tc) & (b),
Stephen J. Krasemann; (bc), Wayne Lankinen/DRK;
312-313, Lowell Georgia; 315, Paul Chesley, P/A;
316, Steve Kaufman; 317 (both), Janis Miglavs; 318,
Erwin A. Bauer; 320 (t), Lowell Georgia; (c), Pat
O'Hara; (b), James P. Blair; 321 (t), Stephen J.
Krasemann; (b), Wayne Lankineh/ DRK; 322-323,
Gary Moon; 325, Tom Bean/DRK; 327 (t), Gary R.
Zahm/DRK; (tc), Jeff Gnass; (bc), Joel Strasser,
South Dakota Division of Tourism; (b), R. Stottle-
myer, Michigan Technological University/BPS; 328-
329, Larry Ulrich; 329, Dean Krakel II; 332, Jeff
Henry; 333 (t), Jim Brandenburg; (c), Steven Fuller;
(b), Tom Danielsen; 334-335, Jim Brandenburg;
335 (t), Pat O'Hara; (tc), Farrell Grehan; (bc), Craig
Fujii/The Seattle Times; (b), Jeff Vanuga, OVIS;
336, Larry Aiuppy; 337, Larry Ulrich; 339 (t), Pat
O'Hara; (c), Wanye Lankinen; (b), Randy Ury.

The Pacific Northwest

340-341, Pat O'Hara; 344-345, James A. Sugar,
Black Star; 347 & 348, Steve Terrill; 350 (t) & (b),
Steve Terrill; (c), Larry Ulrich; 351 (t), Steve Terrill;
(c), Jeff Gnass; (b), Farrell Grehan; 352-353, Jeff
Gnass; 353, Frank S. Balthis; 357 (t), Pat O'Hara;
(b), Jeff Gnass; 358-359, Art Wolfe; 362 (t), Charles
A. Mauzy; (b), Steve Terrill; 363 (t), David M. Seager; (c), Stephen J. Krasemann; (b), Art Wolfe; 364,
David Muench; 365 (t), (tcl) & (tcr), Pat O'Hara;
(cl), George Mobley; (cr) & (br), Farrell Grehan;
(bl), Charles A. Mauzy; 367 (t) & (c), Pat O'Hara;
(b), Stephen J. Krasemann; 368-369, Pat O'Hara;
372, David Hiser; 373, Bruce Dale; 375 (t) & (b),
Pat O'Hara; (c), Art Wolfe; 376-377, Pat O'Hara;
380, David M. Seager; 380-381, Charles A. Mauzy;
381, Steve Terrill; 382, Pat O'Hara; 384-385, David
Muench; 388, Bob Clemenz; 389, Larry Ulrich; 391
(t), Waye Lankinen/DRK; (b), Lewis Kemper/DRK.

Alaska

392-393, Jim Brandenburg; 396-397, Michio
Hoshino; 400, Bruce Dale; 401, Kennan Ward/DRK;
402 (t), Clark Mishler; (tc), Helen Rhode; (cl), Tom
Bean; (bl), Erwin & Peggy Bauer; (br), Becky &
Gary Vestal; 404-405, J.& M. Ibbotson/Alaska
Photo; 405, John Milton; 407, Stephen J. Krase-
mann/DRK; 408 (t), Bob Waldrop; (b), Fred
Hirschmann; 410-411, Tom Bean; 414, Steve Kauf-
man; 416-417, Fred Hirschmann; 420, Win Parks;
422-423, Boyd Norton; 423, George Wuerthner;
426 (tl), Johnny Johnson/ DRK; (cl); Stephen J.
Krasemann/DRK; (r), Boyd Norton; (b), George
Herben; 428-429, John Milton; 429, Michio
Hoshino; 430, Larry Ulrich; 431, Stephen J. Krase-
mann/DRK; 432 (t), Tim Thompson; 432 (b),
Stephen J. Krasemann/DRK; 433, M. Woodbridge
Williams; 434-435, Will Troyer/Alaska Photo; 437,
Fred Hirschmann; 438 (t) & (bl), Fred
Hirschmann; (br), Stephen J. Krasemann/DRK;
440-441, Kim Heacox; 444, Tom Bean/ DRK.

Back Cover (t), Glenn Van Nimwegen; (b), Pat
O'Hara.

Index of Parks & Excursions

Composition for this book by the National Geographic
Society Book Division. Printed and bound by R.R.
Donnelley & Sons, Willard, Ohio. Color separations
by The Lanman Companies, Washington D.C., North
American Color, Portage, MI., Phototype Color
Graphics, Pennsauken, N.J. Cover printed by Miken
Inc. Cheektowaga, New York.